ELEMENTS OF
Literature

SECOND COURSE

HOLT, RINEHART AND WINSTON

Harcourt Brace & Company

Austin • New York • Orlando • Atlanta • San Francisco • Boston • Dallas • Toronto • London

CREDITS

EDITORIAL
Project Director: Kathleen Daniel
Managing Editor: Richard Sime
Executive Editor: Laura Mongello
Editorial Staff: Patricia McCambridge, Robert Schirmer, John Haffner Layden, Robert R. Hoyt, Kathryn Rogers, Christopher LeCluyse
Editorial Support: Laurie Muir, Dan Hunter, Leila Jamal, David Smith
Editorial Permissions: Tamara Blanken, Sacha Frey, Mark Hughs

Research and Development: Joan Burditt

Index: Bob Zolnerzak

PRODUCTION, DESIGN, AND PHOTO RESEARCH
Director: Athena Blackorby
Design Coordinator: Betty Mintz
Program Design: Kirchoff/Wohlberg, Inc.
Design: Jeffrey Rutzky
Electronic Files: TSI Graphics, Inc.
Photo Research: Kirchoff/Wohlberg, Inc.
Photo Research Coordinator: Mary Monaco
Manufacturing: RR Donnelley & Sons Company, Willard, Ohio

COVER
Cover Artist: Greg Geisler
Photo Credits: *Coyotes Howling at the Moon* by Alonzo Jimenez. Courtesy Davis Mather Folk Art Gallery, Santa Fe, NM; rock formations, J. Eastcott/ Y. Mamatiuk/Earth Scenes; sky, David Makris/SuperStock; moon, Chad Ehlers/ Tony Stone Images; (back cover) Acoma Pueblo ceramic owl, Michal Heron/ Woodfin Camp and Associates.
Quotation on Cover: from "The First Americans" (page 631), courtesy of Jeannette Henry Costo.

Copyright © 2000 by Holt, Rinehart and Winston

Acknowledgments appear on pages 827–829, which are an extension of the copyright page.

Printed in the United States of America
ISBN 0-03-052059-2

2 3 4 048 02 01 00 99

PROGRAM AUTHORS

Robert E. Probst established the pedagogical framework for the 1997 and 2000 editions of *Elements of Literature*. Dr. Probst is Professor of English Education at Georgia State University. For several years he was an English teacher in Maryland and Supervisor of English for the Norfolk, Virginia, Public Schools. He is the author of *Response and Analysis: Teaching Literature in Junior and Senior High School*. He has also contributed chapters to such books as *Literature Instruction: A Focus on Student Response; Reader Response in the Classroom: Evoking and Interpreting Meaning in Literature; Handbook of Research on Teaching the English Language Arts; Transactions with Literature: A Fifty-Year Perspective;* and *For Louise M. Rosenblatt.* Dr. Probst is a member of the National Council of Teachers of English and has worked on the council's Committee on Research, the Commission on Reading, and the Commission on Curriculum. Dr. Probst has also served on the board of directors of the Adolescent Literature Assembly and is a member of the National Conference on Research in Language and Literacy.

Robert Anderson wrote the Elements of Literature essay on drama and contributed to the instructional materials for *The Diary of Anne Frank.* Mr. Anderson is a playwright, novelist, screenwriter, and teacher. His plays include *Tea and Sympathy; Silent Night, Lonely Night; You Know I Can't Hear You When the Water's Running;* and *I Never Sang for My Father.* His screenplays include *The Nun's Story* and *The Sand Pebbles.* Mr. Anderson has taught at the Writer's Workshop at the University of Iowa, the American Theater Wing Professional Training Program, and the Salzburg Seminar in American Studies. He is a past president of the Dramatists' Guild, past vice president of the Authors' League of America, and a member of the Theater Hall of Fame.

John Malcolm Brinnin wrote the Elements of Literature essays on poetry and contributed to the instructional materials on poetry. Mr. Brinnin is the author of six volumes of poetry, which received many prizes and awards. He was a member of the American Academy and Institute of Arts and Letters. He was also a critic of poetry and a biographer of poets and was for a number of years director of New York's famous Poetry Center. His teaching career, begun at Vassar College, included long terms at the University of Connecticut and Boston University, where he succeeded Robert Lowell as Professor of Creative Writing and Contemporary Letters. Mr. Brinnin's books include *Dylan Thomas in America: An Intimate Journal* and *Sextet: T. S. Eliot & Truman Capote & Others.*

John Leggett wrote the Elements of Literature essays on the short story and contributed to the instructional materials on short stories. Mr. Leggett is a novelist, biographer, and former teacher. He went to the Writer's Workshop at the University of Iowa in the spring of 1969, expecting to work there for a single semester. In 1970, he assumed temporary charge of the program, and for the next seventeen years he was its director. Mr. Leggett's novels include *Wilder Stone; The Gloucester Branch; Who Took the Gold Away?; Gulliver House;* and *Making Believe.* He also wrote the highly acclaimed biography *Ross and Tom: Two American Tragedies.*

Judith L. Irvin established the conceptual basis for the vocabulary and reading strands and developed the Reading Skills and Strategies exercises for grades 6–8. Dr. Irvin teaches courses in curriculum, middle school education, and educational leadership at Florida State University. She was chair of the Research Committee of the National Middle School Association and was the editor of *Research in Middle Level Education* for five years. She taught middle school for eight years before seeking her doctorate in Reading–Language Arts. Dr. Irvin writes a column, "What Research Says to the Middle Level Practitioner," for the *Middle School Journal.* Her many books include *Reading and the Middle School Student: Strategies to Enhance Literacy* and *What Current Research Says to the Middle Level Practitioner.*

SPECIAL CONTRIBUTOR

David Adams Leeming wrote the Elements of Literature essay on folk tales. Dr. Leeming was a Professor of English and Comparative Literature at the University of Connecticut for many years. He is the author of several books on mythology, including *Mythology: The Voyage of the Hero; The World of Myth;* and *Encyclopedia of Creation Myths.* For several years he taught English at Robert College in Istanbul, Turkey. He also served as secretary and assistant to the writer James Baldwin in New York and Istanbul. He is the author of the biographies *James Baldwin* and *Amazing Grace: A Biography of Beauford Delaney.*

WRITERS

The writers prepared instructional materials for the text under the supervision of Dr. Probst and the editorial staff.

Rusty Clark
Hallsville Independent School
  District
Hallsville, Texas

Phyllis Goldenberg
Educational Writer and Editor
Miami, Florida

Lynn Hovland
Former Teacher
Educational Writer and Editor
Berkeley, California

Erin Hurley
Former Faculty Member
Brown University
Providence, Rhode Island

Jan Meeks
Fairmont Junior High School
Boise, Idaho

Peter Mitchell
Wellesley Middle School
Wellesley, Massachusetts

Pam Ozaroff
Educational Writer and Editor
Newton Center, Massachusetts

Margaret Pickett
Wellesley Middle School
Wellesley, Massachusetts

Keylan Qazzaz
Educational Multimedia Content
  Designer
Rockville, Maryland

Mara Rockliff
Educational Writer and Editor
Louisa, Virginia

David Snyder
Wellesley Middle School
Wellesley, Massachusetts

Diane Tasca
Educational Writer and Editor
Palo Alto, California

Sara Tutek
Washington Elementary School
Montebello, California

REVIEWERS AND CONSULTANTS

The reviewers evaluated selections for use in the text and all instructional materials. Consultants assisted the editorial staff in securing student active-reading models and provided advice on current pedagogy.

Virginia Ruth Anderson
West Ridge Middle School
Austin, Texas

Kay Atteberry
Holmes Middle School
Colorado Springs, Colorado

Phyllis Ayers
Hanover County Public Schools
Hanover County, Virginia

Sheila Berman
Audubon Middle School
Culver City, California

Terry Bigelow
Middleton Middle School of
  Technology
Tampa, Florida

Elisabeth Blandford
McKinley Middle School
Racine, Wisconsin

Kathleen Bouska
Kealing Junior High School
Austin, Texas

Susan Braun
Milford Junior High School
Milford, Ohio

Sara Brennan
Murchison Middle School
Austin, Texas

Cathy Buchholz
Silas Deane Middle School
Wethersfield, Connecticut

Gail Craig
LaSalle Springs Middle School
Glencoe, Missouri

Mary D'Amour
Sanford Middle School
Minneapolis, Minnesota

Jan Dickson
Crockett Junior High School
Irving, Texas

Susan Gage
Fulmore Middle School
Austin, Texas

Linda Garza
Faye Ross Junior High School
Artesia, California

Angelia Grey
Bret Harte Preparatory Middle
  School
Los Angeles, California

Nancy Harper
Forest Hills Schools
Grand Rapids, Michigan

Linda Hermann
Wilmington Area Middle School
Wilmington, Pennsylvania

Judith Hernandez
Foshay Middle School
Los Angeles, California

Yvette Irizarry
Norland Middle School
Miami, Florida

Judy LeBoeuf
Pinellas Park Middle School
Pinellas Park, Florida

Jane Lee
Safety Harbor Middle School
Safety Harbor, Florida

Sarah Logan
Formerly of Bronte High School
Bronte, Texas

Ramona Lowe
Tomlinson Junior High School
Lawton, Oklahoma

Elise Martens
West Ridge Middle School
Austin, Texas

Lynn Langer Meeks, Ph.D.
English Department
Utah State University
Logan, Utah

Guadalupe Neidigh
Dobie Middle School
Round Rock, Texas

Joan Patriarch
St. Paul's Catholic School
Leesburg, Florida

Evelyn Pittman
Paterson School District
Paterson, New Jersey

Kay Price-Hawkins
Region 14 Education Service
  Center
Abilene, Texas

Mary Schultz
Our Lady of the Greenwood
Indianapolis, Indiana

Emma P. Spears
Israel Augustine Middle School
New Orleans, Louisiana

Lois Thompson
Dunbar Magnet Junior High School
Little Rock, Arkansas

Judith Underhill
Oak Grove Middle School
Clearwater, Florida

Raffy Vizcaino
Web Junior High School
Austin, Texas

Lena Williams
Churchland Junior High School
Portsmouth, Virginia

Karen Wiseman
Dade County Public Schools
Homestead, Florida

Frances Witherington
Formerly of Solomon Schechter
    Day School
West Orange, New Jersey

Clarinda Wright
Goliad Middle School
Big Spring, Texas

Maureen Young
Troy School District
Troy, Michigan

FIELD-TEST PARTICIPANTS

The following teachers participated in field-testing of prepublication materials for the series.

Janet Blackburn-Lewis
Western Guilford High School
Greensboro, North Carolina

Dana E. Bull
F. J. Turner High School
Beloit, Wisconsin

Maura Casey
Skyline High School
Oakland, California

Deborah N. Dean
Warner Robins Middle School
Warner Robins, Georgia

Gloria J. Dolesh
Friendly High School
Fort Washington, Maryland

Christina Donnelly
Parkdale High School
Riverdale, Maryland

Kay T. Dunlap
Norview High School
Norfolk, Virginia

Joseph Fitzgibbon
West Linn High School
West Linn, Oregon

Paul Garro
Taft High School
San Antonio, Texas

Suzanne Haffamier
Agoura High School
Agoura, California

Robert K. Jordan
Land O' Lakes High School
Land O' Lakes, Florida

Terry Juhl
Bella Vista High School
Fair Oaks, California

Elizabeth Keister
Blair Middle School
Norfolk, Virginia

Jane S. Kilgore
Warner Robins High School
Warner Robins, Georgia

Janet S. King
Reading High School
Reading, Pennsylvania

Cheryl L. Lambert
Milford Mill Academy
Baltimore, Maryland

Sarah A. Long
Robert Goddard Middle School
Seabrook, Maryland

Margaret E. McKinnon
Roger L. Putnam Vocational-
    Technical High School
Springfield, Massachusetts

Donna J. Magrum
Rogers High School
Toledo, Ohio

Nancy Maheras
Western High School
Las Vegas, Nevada

Mara Malone
Central High School
Baton Rouge, Louisiana

Lourdes J. Medina
Pat Neff Middle School
San Antonio, Texas

Joan Mohon
Todd County Central High
    School
Elkton, Kentucky

Terrence R. Moore
John Muir High School
Pasadena, California

Gayle C. Morey
Countryside High School
Clearwater, Florida

Beverly Mudd
Western High School
Las Vegas, Nevada

Jan Nichols
Apollo High School
Glendale, Arizona

Jeffrey S. Norton
Lewis and Clark High School
Spokane, Washington

Barbara Powell
Todd County Central High
    School
Elkton, Kentucky

Gloria S. Pridmore
Morrow High School
Morrow, Georgia

Dee Richardson
Moore High School
Moore, Oklahoma

Carole A. Scala
Southwest Middle School
Orlando, Florida

Barbara A. Slaughter
Lewis and Clark High School
Spokane, Washington

Barbara B. Smith
Dr. Phillips Ninth-Grade Center
Orlando, Florida

Sister Eileen Stephens, CSJ
Cathedral Preparatory Seminary
Elmhurst, New York

Sally Thompson
Andrew Jackson Middle School
Suitland, Maryland

Blanca M. Valledor
G. Holmes Braddock Senior
    High School
Miami, Florida

Charla J. Walton
John C. Fremont Junior High
    School
Las Vegas, Nevada

William Ward
Roger L. Putnam Vocational-
    Technical High School
Springfield, Massachusetts

Lynn White
Tascosa High School
Amarillo, Texas

Noretta M. Willig
Baldwin High School
Pittsburgh, Pennsylvania

Deborah K. Woelflein
Merrimack High School
Merrimack, New Hampshire

STUDENT CONTRIBUTORS

The following students wrote annotations for the active reading models (Dialogue with the Text).

Candace Ayers
Stonewall Jackson Middle School
Mechanicsville, Virginia

Sabrina Braswell
Mansfield Middle School
Storrs, Connecticut

Alesha Irvin
Alfred B. Maclay Day School
Tallahassee, Florida

Marina Pecson
Traner Middle School
Reno, Nevada

Joshua Roberts
Discovery Middle School
Orlando, Florida

Cory Rockliff
Solomon Schechter Day School
West Orange, New Jersey

Ricardo Romero
Foshay Middle School
Los Angeles, California

Enefiok Udi
Audubon Middle School
Los Angeles, California

CONTENTS

Collection One

We All Need Somebody to Lean On

COMMUNICATIONS WORKSHOPS

Collection Two

From Generation to Generation

COMMUNICATIONS WORKSHOPS

Language/Grammar Links

Collection Three

Tales of the Strange and Mysterious

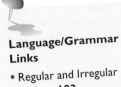

COMMUNICATIONS WORKSHOPS

Collection Four

Talk to the Animals

COMMUNICATIONS WORKSHOPS

Collection Five

I Still Believe

Language/Grammar Links

- Dangling and Misplaced Modifiers **415**
- Avoiding Double Comparisons **438**

COMMUNICATIONS WORKSHOPS

Collection Six

Sneaky Tricks and Whopping Lies

**Language/Grammar
Links**

• Personal Pronouns
459

• Two Pronoun
Problems **471**

• Pronoun Reference
479

• Pronoun-Antecedent
Agreement **495**

• Don't Double Your
Subject with a
Pronoun **511**

COMMUNICATIONS WORKSHOPS

Collection Seven

The American Hero: Myth and Reality

Language/Grammar Links

- Using Colons Before Lists **554**
- Joining Independent Clauses **572**
- Joining Independent Clauses **579**
- Capitalizing and Punctuating Titles **600**

COMMUNICATIONS WORKSHOPS

Collection Eight

We Shall Overcome: American Struggles and Dreams

Language/Grammar Links

- *Good or Well? Bad or Badly?* **635**
- Avoiding Double Negatives **655**
- Style: Using Words from Other Languages **668**
- Style: Avoiding Clichés **675**
- Style: Avoiding Wordiness **685**

COMMUNICATIONS WORKSHOPS

Resource Center

Elements of Literature on the Internet

TO THE STUDENT

Discover more about the stories, poems, and essays in *Elements of Literature* by logging on to the Internet. At **go.hrw.com** we help you complete your homework assignments, learn more about your favorite writers, and find facts that support your ideas and inspire you with new ones. Here's how to log on:

1. Start your Web browser and enter **go.hrw.com** in the location field.

2. Note the keyword in your textbook.

go.hrw.com
LEO 8-1

3. In your Web browser, enter the keyword and click on GO.

LEO 8-1   go!

Enter keyword

Now that you've arrived, you can peek into the palaces and museums of the world, listen to stories of exploration and discovery, or view fires burning on the ocean floor. As you move through *Elements of Literature,* use the best on-line resources at **go.hrw.com.**

Elements of Literature   Second Course

The Diary of
Anne Frank

Frances Goodrich and Albert Hackett

Choices: Building Your Portfolio, pages 413–414

Choices 2: Setting the Stage
While you ponder ways to set the stage for the Anne Frank play, take a virtual walk through the actual Anne Frank House in Amsterdam. Begin with a view from the street. Walk through the office, and swing open the bookcase that leads to the Secret Annex. You can even see how Anne decorated the walls in her bedroom.

Choices 6: Points of View
Meet the other occupants of the Secret Annex. Read the histories of those who hid with Anne Frank, and find out what happened to each of them after they left the Annex. How would they describe their experiences in hiding? Choose one person, and use the information you find here to help you write a diary entry from his or her point of view.

Choices 8: The Real Anne?
Gather more knowledge about the real Anne Frank before you write your evaluation of Goodrich and Hackett's play. Look at the online scrapbook, or read entries from Anne's diary. How well do you think the play captures the essence of Anne's personality?

Enjoy the Internet, but be critical of the information you find there. Always evaluate your sources for credibility, accuracy, timeliness, and possible bias.

Web sites accessed through **go.hrw.com** are reviewed regularly. However, on-line materials change continually and without notice. Holt, Rinehart and Winston cannot ensure the accuracy or appropriateness of materials other than our own. Students, teachers, and guardians should assume responsibility for checking all on-line materials. A full description of Terms of Use can be found at **go.hrw.com.**

We All Need Somebody to Lean On

Finger Snapping in the Car (1992) by Loris Few Tails, age 13,
Pine Ridge Reservation, South Dakota.

ELEMENTS OF
Literature

SECOND COURSE

We sang songs that carried
in their melodies all the sounds of nature—
the running of waters, the sighing of winds,
and the calls of the animals.

—The Grand Council Fire of American Indians

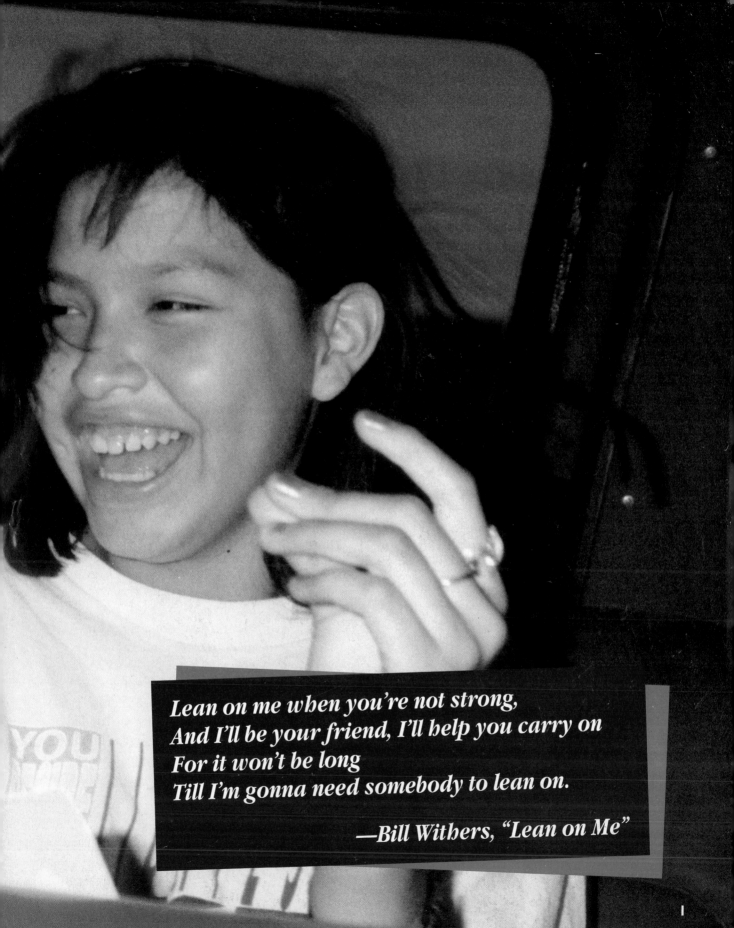

Lean on me when you're not strong,
And I'll be your friend, I'll help you carry on
For it won't be long
Till I'm gonna need somebody to lean on.

—Bill Withers, "Lean on Me"

Before You Read

RAYMOND'S RUN

Make the Connection

You Can't Judge a Book by Its Cover

The story you're about to read takes place in Harlem, a section of New York City. Its main character is a tough, smart, funny, streetwise girl called Squeaky.

Squeaky is a girl with strong opinions. She thinks she can tell what other people are like just from the way they look and talk. She doesn't take into account the fact that there is much more to people than what appears on the surface.

Think-pair-share. What are your hidden qualities and talents? Take five minutes to list some things you're good at or enjoy doing. Tell a classmate about *one* of the items on your list. (Try to pick something your partner doesn't already know about you.) Afterward,

tell the class what you learned about your partner.

Save your list—you'll refer to it when you get to page 13.

Elements of Literature

Conflict

As you read "Raymond's Run," you'll notice that Squeaky has a number of **conflicts**—struggles or disagreements—to resolve. Some of these conflicts are with other girls, some are with her family, and some are with herself. Think about how you would resolve these conflicts. What does Squeaky's way of dealing with them tell you about her?

> **C**onflict is a struggle between opposing forces.
>
> *For more on Conflict, see page 15 and the Handbook of Literary Terms.*

Reading Skills and Strategies

Dialogue with the Text: Monitoring Your Comprehension

When you read, a great deal goes on in your head:

- You connect what you read with your own experience.
- You picture what is happening in the text.
- You ask yourself questions and make predictions.
- You challenge the text.
- You reflect on the meaning of the text.

You can **monitor your reading comprehension** by having a dialogue with a text you're reading. Keep a sheet of paper next to each page so that you can write down your thoughts and questions. For example, as you read "Raymond's Run," you might comment on how some of the characters remind you of yourself or people you know. You might make predictions about how Squeaky will handle her **conflicts.** If you run into problems understanding a passage, try reading it aloud.

One reader's comments appear at the beginning of "Raymond's Run."

 go.hrw.com
LEO 8-1

RAYMOND'S RUN

Toni Cade Bambara

I don't have much work to do around the house like some girls. My mother does that. And I don't have to earn my pocket money by hustling; George runs errands for the big boys and sells Christmas cards. And anything else that's got to get done, my father does. All I have to do in life is mind my brother Raymond, which is enough.

Sometimes I slip and say my little brother Raymond. But as any fool can see he's much bigger and he's older too. But a lot of people call him my little brother cause he needs looking after cause he's not quite right. And a lot of smart mouths got lots to say about that too, especially when George was minding him. But now, if anybody has anything to say to Raymond, anything to say about his big head, they have to come by me. And I don't play the dozens[1] or believe in standing around with somebody in my face doing a lot of talking. I much rather just knock you down and take my chances even if I am a little girl with skinny arms and a squeaky voice, which is how I got the name Squeaky. And if things get too rough, I run. And as anybody can tell you, I'm the fastest thing on two feet.

There is no track meet that I don't win the first-place medal. I used to win the twenty-yard dash when I was a little kid in kindergarten. Nowadays, it's the fifty-yard dash. And tomorrow I'm subject to run the quarter-meter relay all by myself and come in first, second, and third.

1. **play the dozens:** trade insults (slang).

I'm the fastest and that goes for Gretchen, too, who says she's going to win this year. Ridiculous.

she's got freckles. In the first place, no one can beat me and that's all there is to it.

I'm standing on the corner admiring the weather and about to take a stroll down Broadway so I can practice my breathing exercises, and I've got Raymond walking on the inside close to the buildings, cause he's subject to fits of fantasy and starts thinking he's a circus performer and that the curb is a tightrope strung high in the air. And sometimes after a rain he likes to step down off his tightrope right into the gutter and slosh around getting his shoes and cuffs wet. Then I get hit when I get home. Or sometimes if you don't watch him he'll dash across traffic to the island[4] in the middle of Broadway and give the pigeons a fit. Then I have to go behind him apologizing to all the old people sitting around trying to get some sun and getting all upset with the pigeons fluttering around them, scattering their newspapers and upsetting the waxpaper lunches in their laps. So I keep Raymond on the inside of me, and he plays like he's driving a stage coach which is OK by me so long as he doesn't run me over or interrupt my breathing exercises, which I have to do on account of I'm serious about my running, and I don't care who knows it.

Now some people like to act like things come easy to them, won't let on that they practice. Not me. I'll high-prance down 34th Street like a rodeo pony to keep my knees strong even if it does get my mother uptight so that she walks ahead like she's not with me, don't know me, is all by herself on a shopping trip, and I am somebody else's crazy child. Now you take Cynthia Procter for instance. She's just the opposite. If there's a test tomorrow, she'll say something like, "Oh, I guess I'll play handball this afternoon and watch television tonight," just to let you know she ain't thinking about the test. Or like last week when she won the spelling bee for the millionth time, "A good thing you got 'receive,'

The big kids call me Mercury[2] cause I'm the swiftest thing in the neighborhood. Everybody knows that—except two people who know better, my father and me. He can beat me to Amsterdam Avenue with me having a two-fire-hydrant headstart and him running with his hands in his pockets and whistling. But that's private information. Cause can you imagine some thirty-five-year-old man stuffing himself into PAL[3] shorts to race little kids? So as far as everyone's concerned, I'm the fastest and that goes for Gretchen, too, who has put out the tale that she is going to win the first-place medal this year. Ridiculous. In the second place, she's got short legs. In the third place,

2. **Mercury:** in Roman mythology, messenger of the gods, known for his speediness.
3. **PAL:** Police Athletic League.

4. **island:** traffic island, a car-free area in the middle of a road.

Squeaky, cause I would have got it wrong. I completely forgot about the spelling bee." And she'll clutch the lace on her blouse like it was a narrow escape. Oh, brother. But of course when I pass her house on my early morning trots around the block, she is practicing the scales on the piano over and over and over and over. Then in music class she always lets herself get bumped around so she falls accidentally on purpose onto the piano stool and is so surprised to find herself sitting there that she decides just for fun to try out the ole keys. And what do you know—Chopin's[5] waltzes just spring out of her fingertips and she's the most surprised thing in the world. A regular prodigy. I could kill people like that. I stay up all night studying the words for the spelling bee. And you can see me any time of day practicing running. I never walk if I can trot, and shame on Raymond if he can't keep up. But of course he does, cause if he hangs back someone's liable to walk up to him and get smart, or take his allowance from him, or ask him where he got that great big pumpkin head. People are so stupid sometimes.

So I'm strolling down Broadway breathing out and breathing in on counts of seven, which is my lucky number, and here comes Gretchen and her sidekicks: Mary Louise, who used to be

5. **Chopin's:** Frédéric François Chopin (shō·pan′) (1810–1849), Polish composer and pianist.

a friend of mine when she first moved to Harlem from Baltimore and got beat up by everybody till I took up for her on account of her mother and my mother used to sing in the same choir when they were young girls, but people ain't grateful, so now she hangs out with the new girl Gretchen and talks about me like a dog; and Rosie, who is as fat as I am skinny and has a big mouth where Raymond is concerned and is too stupid to know that there is not a big deal of difference between herself and Raymond and that she can't afford to throw stones. So they are steady coming up Broadway and I see right away that it's going to be one of those Dodge City scenes[6] cause the street ain't that big and they're close to the buildings just as we are. First I think I'll step into the candy store and look over the new comics and let them

6. **Dodge City scenes:** showdowns like those in the television western *Gunsmoke,* which was set in Dodge City, Kansas. In a typical scene, a marshal and an outlaw face off with pistols on an empty street.

pass. But that's chicken and I've got a reputation to consider. So then I think I'll just walk straight on through them or even over them if necessary. But as they get to me, they slow down. I'm ready to fight, cause like I said I don't feature a whole lot of chit-chat, I much prefer to just knock you down right from the jump and save everybody a lotta precious time.

"You signing up for the May Day races?" smiles Mary Louise, only it's not a smile at all. A dumb question like that doesn't deserve an answer. Besides, there's just me and Gretchen standing there really, so no use wasting my breath talking to shadows.

"I don't think you're going to win this time," says Rosie, trying to signify[7] with her hands on her hips all salty, completely forgetting that I have whupped her behind many times for less salt than that.

"I always win cause I'm the best," I say straight at Gretchen who is, as far as I'm concerned, the only one talking in this ventriloquist-dummy routine. Gretchen smiles, but it's not a smile, and I'm thinking that girls never really smile at each other because they don't know how and don't want to know how and there's probably no one to teach us how, cause grown-up girls don't know either. Then they all look at Raymond who has just brought his mule team to a standstill. And they're about to see what trouble they can get into through him.

"What grade you in now, Raymond?"

7. **signify:** act boastful or insult someone (slang).

"You got anything to say to my brother, you say it to me, Mary Louise Williams of Raggedy Town, Baltimore."

"What are you, his mother?" sasses Rosie.

"That's right, Fatso. And the next word out of anybody and I'll be *their* mother too." So they just stand there and Gretchen shifts from one leg to the other and so do they. Then Gretchen puts her hands on her hips and is about to say something with her freckle-face self but doesn't. Then she walks around me looking me up and down but keeps walking up Broadway, and her sidekicks follow her. So me and Raymond smile at each other and he says, "Gidyap" to his team and I continue with my breathing exercises, strolling down Broadway toward the ice man on 145th with not a care in the world cause I am Miss Quicksilver[8] herself.

I take my time getting to the park on May Day because the track meet is the last thing on the program. The biggest thing on the program is the May Pole dancing, which I can do without, thank you, even if my mother thinks it's a shame I don't take part and act like a girl for a change. You'd think my mother'd be grateful not to have to make me a white organdy dress with a big satin sash and buy me new white baby-doll shoes that can't be taken out of the box till the big day. You'd think she'd be glad her daughter ain't out there prancing around a May Pole getting the new clothes all dirty and sweaty and trying to act like a fairy or a flower or whatever you're supposed to be when you should be trying to be yourself, whatever that is, which is, as far as I am concerned, a poor black girl who really can't afford to buy shoes and a new dress you only wear once a lifetime cause it won't fit next year.

I was once a strawberry in a Hansel and Gretel pageant when I was in nursery school and didn't have no better sense than to dance on tiptoe with my arms in a circle over my

8. **Quicksilver:** another name for mercury, a silver-colored liquid metal that flows rapidly.

head doing umbrella steps and being a perfect fool just so my mother and father could come dressed up and clap. You'd think they'd know better than to encourage that kind of non-sense. I am not a strawberry. I do not dance on my toes. I run. That is what I am all about. So I always come late to the May Day program, just in time to get my number pinned on and lay in the grass till they announce the fifty-yard dash.

I put Raymond in the little swings, which is a tight squeeze this year and will be impossible next year. Then I look around for Mr. Pearson, who pins the numbers on. I'm really looking for Gretchen if you want to know the truth, but she's not around. The park is jam-packed. Parents in hats and corsages and breast-pocket handkerchiefs peeking up. Kids in white dresses and light-blue suits. The parkees unfolding chairs and chasing the rowdy kids from Lenox[9] as if they had no right to be there. The big guys with their caps on backwards, leaning against the fence swirling the basketballs on the tips of their fingers, waiting for all these crazy people to clear out the park so they can play. Most of the kids in my class are carrying bass drums and glocken-spiels[10] and flutes. You'd think they'd put in a few bongos or something for real like that.

Then here comes Mr. Pearson with his clip-board and his cards and pencils and whistles and safety pins and fifty million other things he's always dropping all over the place with his clumsy self. He sticks out in a crowd because he's on stilts. We used to call him Jack and the Beanstalk to get him mad. But I'm the only one that can outrun him and get away, and I'm too grown for that silliness now.

"Well, Squeaky," he says, checking my name off the list and handing me number seven and two pins. And I'm thinking he's got no right to

9. **Lenox:** Lenox Avenue, a major street in Harlem (now called Malcolm X Boulevard).
10. **glockenspiels** (gläk′ən·spēlz′): musical instruments with flat metal bars that are struck with small hammers and produce bell-like sounds. Glockenspiels are often used in marching bands.

call me Squeaky, if I can't call him Beanstalk.

"Hazel Elizabeth Deborah Parker," I correct him and tell him to write it down on his board.

"Well, Hazel Elizabeth Deborah Parker, going to give someone else a break this year?" I squint at him real hard to see if he is seriously thinking I should lose the race on purpose just to give someone else a break. "Only six girls running this time," he continues, shaking his head sadly like it's my fault all of New York didn't turn out in sneakers. "That new girl should give you a run for your money." He looks around the park for Gretchen like a periscope in a submarine movie. "Wouldn't it be a nice gesture if you were . . . to ahhh . . ."

I give him such a look he couldn't finish putting that idea into words. Grown-ups got a lot of nerve sometimes. I pin number seven to myself and stomp away, I'm so burnt. And I go straight for the track and stretch out on the grass while the band winds up with "Oh, the Monkey Wrapped His Tail Around the Flag Pole," which my teacher calls by some other name. The man on the loudspeaker is calling everyone over to the track and I'm on my back looking at the sky, trying to pretend I'm in the country, but I can't, because even grass in the city feels hard as sidewalk, and there's just no pretending you are anywhere but in a "con-crete jungle" as my grandfather says.

The twenty-yard dash takes all of two minutes cause most of the little kids don't know no better than to run off the track or run the wrong way or run smack into the fence and fall down and cry. One little kid, though, has got the good sense to run straight for the white ribbon up ahead so he wins. Then the second-graders line up for the thirty-yard dash and I don't even bother to turn my head to watch cause Raphael Perez always wins. He wins before he even begins by psyching the runners, telling them they're going to trip on their shoelaces and fall on their faces or lose their shorts or something, which he doesn't really have to do since he is very fast, almost as fast as I am. After that is the forty-yard dash which I used to run when I was in first grade. Raymond is hollering from the swings cause he knows I'm about to do my thing cause the man on the loudspeaker has just announced the fifty-yard dash, although he might just as well be giving a recipe for angel food cake cause you can hardly make out what he's sayin for the static. I get up and slip off my sweat pants and then I see Gretchen standing at the starting line, kicking her legs out like a pro. Then as I get into place I see that ole Raymond is on line on the other side of the fence, bending down with his fingers on the ground just like he knew what he was doing. I was going to yell at him but then I didn't. It burns up your energy to holler.

Every time, just before I take off in a race, I always feel like I'm in a dream, the kind of dream you have when you're sick with fever and feel all hot and weightless. I dream I'm flying over a sandy beach in the early morning sun, kissing the leaves of the trees as I fly by. And there's always the smell of apples, just like in the country when I was little and used to think I was a choo-choo train, running through the fields of corn and chugging up the hill to the orchard. And all the time I'm dreaming this, I get lighter and lighter until I'm flying over the beach again, getting blown through the sky like a feather that weighs nothing at all. But once I spread my fingers in the dirt and crouch over the Get on Your Mark, the dream goes and I am solid again and am telling myself, Squeaky you must win, you must win, you are the fastest thing in the world, you can even beat your father up Amsterdam if you really try. And then I feel my weight coming back just behind my knees then down to my feet then into the earth and the pistol shot explodes in my blood and I am off and weightless again, flying past the other runners, my arms pumping up and down and the whole world is quiet except for the crunch as I zoom over the gravel in the track. I glance to my left and there is no one. To the right, a blurred Gretchen, who's got her chin jutting out as if it would win the race all by itself. And on the other side of the fence is Raymond with his arms down to his side and the palms tucked up behind him, running in his very own style, and it's the first time I ever saw that and I almost stop to watch my brother Raymond on his first run. But the white ribbon is bouncing toward me and I tear past it, racing into the distance till my feet with a mind of their own start digging up footfuls of dirt and brake me short. Then all the kids standing on the side pile on me, banging me on the back and slapping my head with their May Day programs, for I have won again and everybody on 151st Street can walk tall for another year.

"In first place . . ." the man on the loudspeaker is clear as a bell now. But then he pauses and the loudspeaker starts to whine. Then static. And I lean down to catch my breath and here comes Gretchen walking back, for she's overshot the finish line too, huffing and puffing with her hands on her hips taking it slow, breathing in steady time like a real pro and I sort of like her a little for the first time. "In first place . . ." and then three or four voices get all mixed up on the loudspeaker and I dig my sneaker into the grass and stare at Gretchen who's staring back, we both wondering just who did win. I can hear old Beanstalk arguing with the man on the loudspeaker and then a few others running their mouths about what the stopwatches say. Then I hear Raymond yanking at the fence to call me and I wave to shush him, but he keeps rattling the fence like a gorilla in a cage like in them gorilla movies, but then like a dancer or something he starts climbing up nice and easy but very fast. And it occurs to me, watching how smoothly he climbs hand over hand and remembering how he looked running with his arms down to his side and with the wind pulling his mouth back and his teeth showing and all, it occurred to me that Raymond would make a very fine runner. Doesn't he always keep up with me on my trots? And he surely knows how to breathe in counts of seven cause he's always doing it at the dinner table, which drives my brother George up the wall. And I'm smiling to beat the band cause if I've lost this race, or if me and Gretchen tied, or even if I've won, I can always retire as a runner and begin a whole new career as a coach with Raymond as my champion. After all, with a little more study I can beat Cynthia and her phony self at the spelling bee. And if I bugged my mother, I could get piano lessons and become a star. And I have a big rep[11] as the baddest thing around. And I've got

a roomful of ribbons and medals and awards. But what has Raymond got to call his own?

So I stand there with my new plans, laughing out loud by this time as Raymond jumps down from the fence and runs over with his teeth showing and his arms down to the side, which no one before him has quite mastered as a running style. And by the time he comes over I'm jumping up and down so glad to see him—my brother Raymond, a great runner in the family tradition. But of course everyone thinks I'm jumping up and down because the men on the loudspeaker have finally gotten themselves together and compared notes and are announcing "In first place—Miss Hazel Elizabeth Deborah Parker." (Dig that.) "In second place—Miss Gretchen P. Lewis." And I look over at Gretchen wondering what the "P" stands for. And I smile. Cause she's good, no doubt about it. Maybe she'd like to help me coach Raymond; she obviously is serious about running, as any fool can see. And she nods to congratulate me and then she smiles. And I smile. We stand there with this big smile of respect between us. It's about as real a smile as girls can do for each other, considering we don't practice real smiling every day, you know, cause maybe we too busy being flowers or fairies or strawberries instead of something honest and worthy of respect . . . you know . . . like being people.

11. **rep:** reputation (slang). People often create slang by clipping off parts of words.

MEET THE WRITER

"I Deal in Straight-Up Fiction Myself"

Toni Cade Bambara (1939–1995) grew up in New York City, where "Raymond's Run" takes place. She began writing very early:

Photograph © 1994 by Jill Krementz.

66 It's been a long apprenticeship. I began scribbling tales on strips from my daddy's *Daily News.* Then I'd wait by the bedroom door, chewing on a number two pencil, for those sturdy white squares my mama's stockings came wrapped around. . . . In junior high, I overwhelmed English teachers with three-for-one assignments. In high school, I hogged the lit journal. 99

Bambara's writing drew on the voices of her childhood: street-corner speechmakers, barbershop storytellers, performers at Harlem's legendary Apollo Theater. She said her stories came from her imagination, though:

66 It does no good to write autobiographical fiction, cause the minute the book hits the stand here comes your mama screamin how could you. . . . And it's no use using bits and snatches even of real events and real people, even if you do cover, guise, switch-around, and change-up, cause next thing you know your best friend's laundry cart is squeaking past but your bell ain't ringing so you trot down the block after her and there's this drafty cold pressure front the weatherman surely did not predict and your friend says in this chilly way that it's really something when your own friend stabs you in the back with a pen. . . . So I deal in straight-up fiction myself, cause I value my family and friends, and mostly cause I lie a lot anyway. 99

Toni Cade adopted the name Bambara from a signature on a sketchbook she found in her great-grandmother's trunk. The Bambara are a people of northwestern Africa known for their skill in woodcarving.

More by Toni Cade Bambara

"Raymond's Run" comes from a collection of short stories called *Gorilla, My Love* (Random House). Other stories in the collection with characters like Squeaky are "Blues Ain't No Mockin Bird" and the title story, "Gorilla, My Love."

Reward They Get Is Just

OMAR KELLY

Bob Johnson is sure he has the world's highest-paid staff of volunteers. Mainly, it's because everyone involved with the Special Olympics goes home feeling like a million bucks.

Many who will donate their time and effort for this weekend's 28th annual Special Olympics Massachusetts Summer Games come expecting to give only of themselves, but they walk away having taken much more than they've donated to the Games, which begin today and wrap up Sunday.

"Athletes are the focal point, but everyone goes home touched by the experience," said Johnson, president of Special Olympics Massachusetts, who has orchestrated the eight events of the competition taking place on the campuses of MIT and Boston University. "These events teach our athletes that they can do much more than they can't."

This summer's event has an added bonus. The athletes competing this weekend will be vying for a chance to qualify for the 1999 World Summer Games in Raleigh-Durham, N.C.

Phil Glendie, supervisor for the Lawrence Public Schools Special Olympics, will be coaching a team he calls "my little family," a group of 30 who compete in volleyball and track and field.

According to Glendie, participating in the Summer Games is an experience his students anticipate all year round because it's socially rewarding.

He gave as an example the story of a student who despised attending school until he reached high school age, which made him eligible for the Olympics. Now, because of training involved for the Special Olympics, that student is one of the first on the bus to school.

"They are so happy to be able to get out of the house two nights a week for training," said Glendie. "The excitement is like going to Disney World for them. They see the regular high school athletes— the football and basketball players—and it makes them feel worthwhile because they know that they are athletes, too."

The experience is just as rewarding for the volunteers, no matter what the job. Tony Carnevale, volunteer spokesman for the Summer Games, told a story about a first-year volunteer who thought he had an unrewarding job on the track.

"His assignment was to hold the ropes," Carnevale said. "When you tell them their responsibility, they kind of look at you funny. They say, 'I can't believe I gave up my time to hold a rope.' Then a blind runner uses that rope as their eyes—as a guide—flying along the rope during the competition. The person that's holding the rope watches the runner go by them, and instantly, they realize what a great deed they've just done. It's a great feeling."

Johnson's staff has estimated that it takes 42,400 hours just to train the 17,025 athletes for the Summer Games. But to the volunteers, it's considered a priceless experience, considering the feedback they receive.

"The Games give our athletes hope for the future, and they will carry that experience throughout other challenges that they will meet in their lives," Johnson said. "The athletes come back more outgoing, more confident, and they become willing to take chances."

Individuals wishing to volunteer should arrive at the Special Olympics event site on MIT's campus early in the morning and report to the volunteer desk. There they'll be put right to work, Johnson said.

If they're lucky, they might get to do something as rewarding as holding a rope.

—from *The Boston Globe*,
June 19, 1998

Getting ready for Special Olympics long jump event, San Marcos, Texas, January 1993.

MAKING MEANINGS

First Thoughts

1. Use your reading notes to help you complete one of the following statements:

   • If I were Squeaky, I would/would not have . . .

   • I was surprised when . . .

   • I didn't understand . . .

Shaping Interpretations

2. What do you think is the most important **conflict** in this story? Why? Try answering in this form: *The conflict between . . . and . . . about . . . is important because . . .*

3. How do Squeaky's opinions of people change in the course of the story? Use a chart like this one to organize your thoughts.

What Squeaky thinks of

	Gretchen	Raymond	Herself
Beginning			
End			

4. Squeaky and Gretchen almost get into a fight before the race. Why, then, do they smile at each other after the race?

5. Who "leans on" whom in this story? (More than one answer is possible.) Support your response with evidence from the text.

Connecting with the Text

6. Explain why you would or wouldn't want to be friends with Squeaky. (Consider: Did you like her better at the beginning or at the end of the story?)

Extending the Text

7. Is it ever necessary to fight or use threats to defend someone? Explain.

Challenging the Text

8. Would you have called this story "Raymond's Run"? Defend Bambara's choice, or invent a new title and explain why you think it's better.

CHOICES: Building Your Portfolio

Writer's Notebook

1. Collecting Ideas for an Autobiographical Incident

WORK IN PROGRESS

Write briefly about an incident (something that happened) in your life in which a first impression turned out to be wrong or someone you thought you knew well did something that surprised you.

- What happened during this incident?
- Why was this incident important to you? What did you learn from it?
- What details of the incident (sights, feelings, things people said) do you remember?

When I first met my best friend, I thought she was boring because she was so quiet — but then I found out that she liked the same music I did.

Creative Writing

2. Life Stories

If the writing prompt above doesn't spark your interest, freewrite in your Writer's Notebook about one of these topics:

- a time when you made a sacrifice or stood up for a friend, a brother, or a sister, or when someone stood up for you
- how participating in a sport or being good at something gave you a sense of self-confidence
- a conflict you had with a friend or an acquaintance and how it was resolved

Speaking

3. Get Loud and Proud

Go back to the list you made before you read the story. Pick one item from the list, and prepare a three-minute **oral presentation** on it for the class. Use visual aids or props if possible. For example, you could bring in bread to share if you're good at baking or pass around snapshots of your summer canoe trip.

Writing a Report/ Health

4. Meeting the Challenge

Find out what people who are physically or mentally challenged have accomplished in your community or in the country. For example, you might want to do research about athletes in the Special Olympics (see *Connections* on page 11).

Start your search in the library, on the Internet, or in local newspapers. You could also ask your teacher or librarian to help you locate published sources or people to contact.

Write a brief **report** on your findings, and display it in the classroom for other students to read.

GRAMMAR LINK

Three Common Usage Errors

Language Handbook HELP

See Glossary of Usage, pages 817 and 818.

Technology HELP

See Language Workshop CD-ROM. Key word entry: usage.

Can you spot three errors somewhere in this dialogue?

> "Congratulations!" Gretchen said, smiling.
> "Thanks alot," Squeaky replied. "I wish you could of won, too."
> "That's alright. You deserved it."

Many beginning writers have trouble with the phrases *a lot, all right,* and *could have*—and *should have, would have, might have,* and *must have*—because they've heard them more often than they've seen them in print. (When speaking, people often shorten *could have* to *could've,* which sounds as though it might be spelled *could of.*)

Note to computer users. If you write using a computer, your word processing program's spelling checker will catch misspellings of *a lot* and *all right.* Run the spelling checker just before printing out a final draft. It won't catch *could of* (can you figure out why?), so if that's your trouble spot, ask a classmate to check your writing.

Try It Out

Write three sentences of your own in response to "Raymond's Run." Use the phrases *a lot, all right,* and *could have* (or *should have, would have, might have,* or *must have*) at least once each. Exchange papers with another student, and check your partner's spelling while he or she checks yours.

SPELLING HOW TO OWN A WORD

Language Handbook HELP

See Spelling Rules, pages 812-816.

Spelling Strategies

A lot, all right, and *could have* are very commonly misspelled, but we all have our own set of words that give us trouble. Below are some strategies to help you with your spelling; you may develop others to fit your learning style.

- Don't worry about spelling while you're writing a first draft. If you're not sure how to spell a word, take a guess, circle the word, and look it up later.

- Keep a spelling log—a list of the correct spellings of words that often give you trouble. (You might set aside a page or two of your Writer's Notebook for your spelling log.) Refer to this list whenever you proofread a piece of writing.

Note to computer users. Remember that most computer spelling checkers do not correct errors automatically. Instead, they stop at a word and highlight it. The word may not be misspelled, however; it may be that the program's dictionary simply does not include the word. (This is often the case with proper nouns.) If any of the words from your spelling log are missing from your software dictionary, customize your dictionary by adding them.

Elements of Literature

CONFLICT: The Energy of a Story *by* John Leggett

"Little Red Riding Hood," Revised

Once upon a time, a girl named Little Red Riding Hood set off into the forest with a basket of goodies for her grandmother. She went merrily on her way and arrived safely at Grandma's house. The wolf who usually prowled the forest pathways was in New York that week, giving a lecture about endangered species.

No Problem, No Story

Imagine that your favorite novel or movie was written, like this revised tale of Little Red Riding Hood, with its main problem or struggle left out. Would you still find it interesting? Most readers would probably say no.

What quality attracts us to some stories, whether they are true stories or fiction? What keeps us reading some stories, even when we should be attending to other business or turning out the lights and going to sleep?

Conflict: The Energy of a Story

It is **conflict,** or struggle, that gives any story its energy and makes it interesting.

Here are some common types of conflicts:

1. a conflict between two characters

2. a conflict between a character and a group or a whole society

3. a conflict between two groups or cultures

4. a conflict between a character and a natural force or event, such as a flood or the law of gravity

5. a conflict between a character and something in himself or herself: perhaps fear, shyness, homesickness, or an inability to make a decision

Conflict Inside and Out

The first four items are examples of **external conflict.** In an external conflict a character struggles with an outside force. A conflict that takes place within a character's mind, on the other hand, is called an **internal conflict.**

A story may contain several conflicts. For example, in the story "Raymond's Run" (page 3), the main character, Squeaky, has a major external conflict with a rival named Gretchen. Yet Squeaky is also in conflict with others, such as people who "get smart" with her brother Raymond.

Squeaky struggles with herself, too. For example, she experiences an internal conflict when she tries to decide whether to face Gretchen and her friends or to duck into a store until they pass (pages 5–6). In literature, as in life, this kind of conflict, between opposing desires or emotions, can be the most interesting of all.

> ### *A Writer on Conflict*
>
> "I work to tell the truth about people's lives; I work to celebrate struggle."
>
> —Toni Cade Bambara, author of "Raymond's Run" (page 3)

Before You Read

Make the Connection

What Makes a Friend?

If you had to choose one word to describe the most important thing a friend is or does, what would it be? (Consider: What makes a friend different from an acquaintance?)

Quickwrite

Before discussing it with anyone, write down your word and a brief explanation of why you picked it. Then, share your response with a classmate if you wish.

Elements of Literature

Rhyme

Every line in this poem has a "friend"—another line that rhymes with it. Be sure to read the poem aloud at least once, listening for these **end rhymes,** or rhymes at the ends of lines. Can you hear the one rhyme that echoes across the space of five lines?

> **W**hen words **rhyme,** the accented vowel sounds and all sounds following them are repeated.
>
> *For more on Rhyme, see pages 544–545 and the Handbook of Literary Terms.*

A Time to Talk

Robert Frost

When a friend calls to me from the road
And slows his horse to a meaning walk,
I don't stand still and look around
On all the hills I haven't hoed,
5   And shout from where I am, "What is it?"
No, not as there is a time to talk.
I thrust my hoe in the mellow ground,
Blade-end up and five feet tall,
And plod: I go up to the stone wall
10 For a friendly visit.

MEET THE WRITER

The New England Poet

Although **Robert Frost** (1874–1963) was born in San Francisco, he lived in New England most of his life and was known as "the New England poet." Frost found his subjects in the landscapes and people of New England. He once wrote that a subject for poetry

66 . . . should be common in experience and uncommon in books. . . . It should have happened to everyone but it should have occurred to no one before as material. 99

In 1961, Frost read one of his poems at John F. Kennedy's inauguration. He was the first poet to be invited to participate in a presidential inauguration ceremony. (Maya Angelou, whose work appears on page 20, has also been honored in this way.)

go.hrw.com
LEO 8-1

The Stone Fence (1946) by Andrew Wyeth. Tempera on panel.

MAKING MEANINGS

First Thoughts

1. In your opinion, what is the most important word or phrase in this poem? Why? (If you prefer, state in your own words what the poem says to you.)

Shaping Interpretations

2. Frost describes two ways to act toward a friend. What are they? Which one does he seem to think is better?

3. Which **rhyme** echoes across five lines? How does this rhyme help to emphasize the **main idea** in the poem?

4. What might the stone wall in line 9 represent? What kinds of "walls" do people build that keep them apart?

Challenging the Text

5. What, if anything, would be a good reason *not* to take time to talk with someone you care about? *Or:* Do you feel that you always need to talk when you're with friends? Why or why not?

CHOICES: Building Your Portfolio

Writer's Notebook

1. Collecting Ideas for an Autobiographical Incident

Think of an occasion when you took time or didn't take time to talk with someone *or* when someone took time or didn't take time to talk with you. Jot down your memories of and feelings about the incident. Why was it important to you?

Creative Writing

2. A Time for Poetry

Write a **poem** about what you think being a friend means. If you like, use the word you chose for your Quickwrite in the title: for example, "A Time to Listen" or "A Time to Be Loyal." You may want to use this format, which is like Frost's poem:

When a friend _____
I don't _____.
No, not as there is a time
    to _____.
I _____.

Creative Writing

3. This Is Just to Say

Is there someone you *wish* would listen to you? Write a **letter** telling that person what you'd like to say.

Art

4. "Collage" Education

Using words and pictures cut out of magazines and newspapers, make a collage about friendship or about talk. Present your collage to the class, and explain why you chose the images you used.

Before You Read

MRS. FLOWERS

Make the Connection

A Matter of Opinion

Rate each of the statements that follow with a number from 0 to 4.

disagree 0 1 2 3 4 agree

1. Young people need older role models.

2. Friends should be the same age.

3. Adults can't understand how young people feel.

4. Everyone deserves to feel special.

Record your ratings on a piece of paper. Then, with your class, tally all the responses to each statement on the board. Don't discuss your responses yet; wait until you've done the Quickwrite.

Quickwrite

Respond to one of the four statements. You could explain your position or describe a related experience.

go.hrw.com
LEO 8-1

Elements of Literature

Imagery

In "Mrs. Flowers," Angelou describes a summer afternoon as "sweet-milk fresh in my memory" (page 20). She has created an **image**—a description that appeals to one or more of our senses: sight, smell, taste, hearing, and touch.

As you read, notice how Angelou uses other images to bring an important experience to life.

> **I**magery is writing that uses descriptive language to appeal to the senses.
>
> *For more on Imagery, see the Handbook of Literary Terms.*

Reading Skills and Strategies

Determining the Main Idea: What's It All About?

The **main idea** is the message, opinion, or insight that is the focus or key concept in a piece of writing. It's the most important idea that the writer wants you to remember. This important idea is developed by **supporting details**.

To find the main idea, you can do the following:

- Look for direct statements made by the writer.

- Look closely at the details that the writer gives. (*Who, what, when, where,* and *why* questions will help you identify the important details.)

- Think about what the details add up to.

- Try to put the main idea into your own words.

Background

Literature and Real Life

"Mrs. Flowers" is from Maya Angelou's autobiography. When Angelou (born Marguerite Johnson) was a little girl, her parents separated. She and her brother, Bailey, were sent to Stamps, Arkansas, to live with their grandmother (called Momma), who owned a general store. A year before meeting Mrs. Flowers, Marguerite was the victim of a violent act. She reacted by retreating behind a wall of silence.

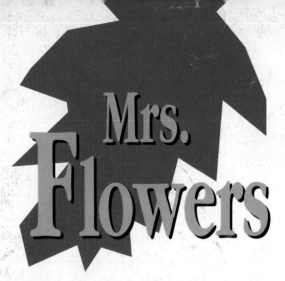

Mrs. Flowers

from **I Know Why the Caged Bird Sings**

Maya Angelou

For nearly a year, I sopped around the house, the Store, the school, and the church, like an old biscuit, dirty and inedible. Then I met, or rather got to know, the lady who threw me my first lifeline.

Mrs. Bertha Flowers was the aristocrat of Black Stamps. She had the grace of control to appear warm in the coldest weather, and on the Arkansas summer days it seemed she had a private breeze which swirled around, cooling her. She was thin without the taut look of wiry people, and her printed voile[1] dresses and flowered hats were as right for her as denim overalls for a farmer. She was our side's answer to the richest white woman in town.

Her skin was a rich black that would have peeled like a plum if snagged, but then no one would have thought of getting close enough to Mrs. Flowers to ruffle her dress, let alone snag her skin. She didn't encourage familiarity. She wore gloves too.

I don't think I ever saw Mrs. Flowers laugh, but she smiled often. A slow widening of her thin black lips to show even, small white teeth, then the slow effortless closing. When she chose to smile on me, I always wanted to thank her. The action was so graceful and inclusively benign.

She was one of the few gentlewomen I have ever known, and has remained throughout my life the measure of what a human being can be.

One summer afternoon, sweet-milk fresh in my memory, she stopped at the Store to buy provisions. Another Negro woman of her health and age would have been expected to carry the paper sacks home in one hand, but Momma said, "Sister Flowers, I'll send Bailey up to your house with these things."

She smiled that slow dragging smile, "Thank you, Mrs. Henderson. I'd prefer Marguerite, though." My name was beautiful when she said it. "I've been meaning to talk to her, anyway." They gave each other age-group looks.

There was a little path beside the rocky road, and Mrs. Flowers walked in front swinging her arms and picking her way over the stones.

She said, without turning her head, to me, "I hear you're doing very good schoolwork, Marguerite, but that it's all written. The teachers report that they have trouble getting you to talk in class." We passed the triangular farm on our left and the path widened to allow us to walk together. I hung back in the separate unasked and unanswerable questions.

"Come and walk along with me, Marguerite." I couldn't have refused even if I wanted to. She pronounced my name so nicely. Or more correctly, she spoke each word with such clarity that I was certain a foreigner who didn't understand English could have understood her.

---

1. **voile** (voil): thin, sheer fabric.

WORDS TO OWN

taut (tôt) *adj.*: tightly stretched.
benign (bi·nīn′) *adj.*: kind.

National Museum of American Art, Washington, D.C./Art Resource, New York.

Woman in Calico (1944) by William H. Johnson. Oil.

"Now no one is going to make you talk—possibly no one can. But bear in mind, language is man's way of communicating with his fellow man and it is language alone which separates him from the lower animals." That was a totally new idea to me, and I would need time to think about it.

"Your grandmother says you read a lot. Every chance you get. That's good, but not good enough. Words mean more than what is set down on paper. It takes the human voice to infuse them with the shades of deeper meaning."

I memorized the part about the human voice infusing words. It seemed so valid and poetic.

She said she was going to give me some books and that I not only must read them, I must read them aloud. She suggested that I try to make a sentence sound in as many different ways as possible.

"I'll accept no excuse if you return a book to me that has been badly handled." My imagination boggled at the punishment I would deserve if in fact I did abuse a book of Mrs. Flowers's. Death would be too kind and brief.

The odors in the house surprised me. Somehow I had never connected Mrs. Flowers with food or eating or any other common experience of common people. There must have been an outhouse, too, but my mind never recorded it.

The sweet scent of vanilla had met us as she opened the door.

"I made tea cookies this morning. You see, I had planned to invite you for cookies and lemonade so we could have this little chat. The lemonade is in the icebox."

It followed that Mrs. Flowers would have ice on an ordinary day, when most families in our town bought ice late on Saturdays only a few times during the summer to be used in the wooden ice cream freezers.

She took the bags from me and disappeared through the kitchen door. I looked around the room that I had never in my wildest fantasies

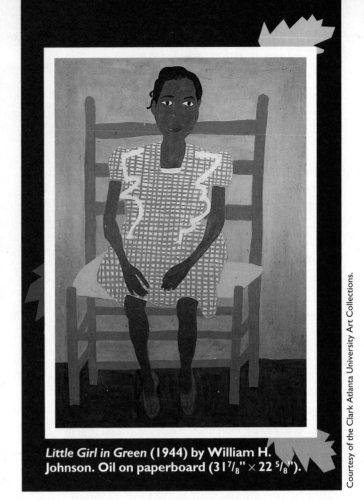

Little Girl in Green (1944) by William H. Johnson. Oil on paperboard (31 $^7/_8$" × 22 $^5/_8$").

Courtesy of the Clark Atlanta University Art Collections.

imagined I would see. Browned photographs leered or threatened from the walls and the white, freshly done curtains pushed against themselves and against the wind. I wanted to gobble up the room entire and take it to Bailey, who would help me analyze and enjoy it.

"Have a seat, Marguerite. Over there by the table." She carried a platter covered with a tea towel. Although she warned that she hadn't tried her hand at baking sweets for some time, I was certain that like everything else about her the cookies would be perfect.

They were flat round wafers, slightly browned on the edges and butter-yellow in the center. With the cold lemonade they were suffi-

---

WORDS TO OWN

infuse (in·fyōōz′) v.: fill.

---

cient for childhood's lifelong diet. Remembering my manners, I took nice little ladylike bites off the edges. She said she had made them expressly for me and that she had a few in the kitchen that I could take home to my brother. So I jammed one whole cake in my mouth and the rough crumbs scratched the insides of my jaws, and if I hadn't had to swallow, it would have been a dream come true.

As I ate she began the first of what we later called "my lessons in living." She said that I must always be intolerant of ignorance but understanding of illiteracy. That some people, unable to go to school, were more educated and even more intelligent than college professors. She encouraged me to listen carefully to what country people called mother wit. That in those homely sayings was couched the collective wisdom of generations.

When I finished the cookies she brushed off the table and brought a thick, small book from the bookcase. I had read *A Tale of Two Cities* and found it up to my standards as a romantic novel. She opened the first page and I heard poetry for the first time in my life.

"It was the best of times, it was the worst of times. . . ." Her voice slid in and curved down through and over the words. She was nearly singing. I wanted to look at the pages. Were they the same that I had read? Or were there notes, music, lined on the pages, as in a hymn book? Her sounds began cascading gently. I knew from listening to a thousand preachers that she was nearing the end of her reading, and I hadn't really heard, heard to understand, a single word.

"How do you like that?"

It occurred to me that she expected a response. The sweet vanilla flavor was still on my tongue and her reading was a wonder in my ears. I had to speak.

I said, "Yes, ma'am." It was the least I could do, but it was the most also.

"There's one more thing. Take this book of poems and memorize one for me. Next time you pay me a visit, I want you to recite."

I have tried often to search behind the sophistication of years for the enchantment I so easily found in those gifts. The essence escapes but its aura[2] remains. To be allowed, no, invited, into the private lives of strangers, and to share their joys and fears, was a chance to exchange the Southern bitter wormwood[3] for a cup of mead with Beowulf[4] or a hot cup of tea and milk with Oliver Twist. When I said aloud, "It is a far, far better thing that I do, than I have ever done . . ."[5] tears of love filled my eyes at my selflessness.

On that first day, I ran down the hill and into the road (few cars ever came along it) and had the good sense to stop running before I reached the Store.

I was liked, and what a difference it made. I was respected not as Mrs. Henderson's grandchild or Bailey's sister but for just being Marguerite Johnson.

Childhood's logic never asks to be proved (all conclusions are absolute). I didn't question why Mrs. Flowers had singled me out for attention, nor did it occur to me that Momma might have asked her to give me a little talking-to. All I cared about was that she had made tea cookies for *me* and read to *me* from her favorite book. It was enough to prove that she liked me.

---

2. **aura:** feeling or mood that seems to surround something like a glow.
3. **wormwood:** bitter-tasting plant. Angelou is referring to the harshness of life for African Americans in the South at that time.
4. **Beowulf** (bā′ə·woolf′): hero of an Old English epic. During the period portrayed in the epic, people drank **mead,** a drink made with honey.
5. **"It is . . . ever done":** another quotation from Charles Dickens's *A Tale of Two Cities.* One of the characters says these words as he goes to die in place of another man.

- -

WORDS TO OWN

intolerant (in·täl′ər·ənt) *adj.:* unwilling to put up with something.
illiteracy (il·lit′ər·ə·sē) *n.:* inability to read or write.

- -

MEET THE WRITER

"When You Get, Give"

On January 20, 1993, **Maya Angelou** (1928–   ) stood at a podium on Capitol Hill and recited her poem "On the Pulse of Morning" in honor of Bill Clinton's presidential inauguration. She may have thought at that moment that she had come a long way from her childhood in Stamps, Arkansas. Angelou has been an actor, a teacher, a speaker, a civil rights worker, and, above all, a writer—of poems, plays, songs, screenplays, and newspaper and magazine articles, as well as four autobiographies.

Angelou says that the two writers who have had the greatest influence on her work are William Shakespeare and the African American poet Paul Laurence Dunbar. (The title *I Know Why the Caged Bird Sings* is taken from a poem by Dunbar called "Sympathy.")

Angelou has in turn influenced the lives of many young people, both in person and through her writing. Six feet tall, gracious and commanding, Angelou is as much a gentlewoman as her childhood friend Mrs. Flowers. In an interview with *Essence* magazine, Angelou tells about a time when she was able to "throw a lifeline" to a young man she found cursing and fighting on a movie set in California:

66 I went over and I said, 'Baby, may I speak to you for a minute?' He dropped his head, and I said, 'Come on, let's walk.'

And I started talking to him and started crying. I said, 'Do you know how much at risk you are? Do you know how valuable

Maya Angelou reads her poem "On the Pulse of Morning" at Bill Clinton's inauguration.

you are to us? You're all we've got, baby.'

He started crying and said to me, 'Don't cry.' I don't know who has cried for him. And let him see how much he means . . .

Black people say, when you get, give; when you learn, teach. As soon as that healing takes place, then we have to go out and heal somebody, and pass on the idea of a healing day—so that somebody else gets it and passes it on. 99

More by Maya Angelou

I Know Why the Caged Bird Sings covers the first sixteen years of Angelou's life. Her autobiography continues in *Gather Together in My Name* (Bantam) and *Singin' and Swingin' and Gettin' Merry Like Christmas* (Bantam). You may also enjoy her *Poems* (Bantam).

MAKING MEANINGS

First Thoughts

1. Go back to your Quickwrite. Did reading "Mrs. Flowers" change your opinion or strengthen it? *Or:* Did the story remind you of the experience you described?

Shaping Interpretations

2. Think about the stone wall in "A Time to Talk" (page 17). How did Marguerite build a wall around herself? How did Mrs. Flowers help her knock it down?

3. Go back to the text and find the only two words spoken by Marguerite. What do you think Angelou means when she writes "It was the least I could do, but it was the most also"(page 23)?

4. At the beginning of "Mrs. Flowers," Maya Angelou says that she "sopped around" until Mrs. Flowers threw her a "lifeline." What **main idea** does Angelou suggest here? What **supporting details** throughout the memoir develop this main idea?

5. In your opinion, would Maya Angelou have become a famous writer if Mrs. Flowers hadn't singled her out for attention when she was young? Support your answer with evidence from the text.

Connecting with the Text

6. Who is "the measure of what a human being can be" for you? Why? (It doesn't have to be someone you know personally.)

7. What do you think Mrs. Flowers means when she tells Marguerite that she "must always be intolerant of ignorance but understanding of illiteracy" (page 23)? Is that good advice for today? Draw on your own experience to support your answer.

Extending the Text

8. Like Marguerite and the young man in California (see Meet the Writer), many young people today are at risk. How could a friendship with an older person like Mrs. Flowers help someone who is in trouble?

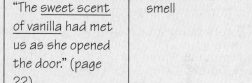

Reading Check

Draw a line down the middle of a blank page in your notebook. On the left, copy one or two of your favorite descriptive sentences from "Mrs. Flowers," and underline the key words that create **images** in your mind. On the right, identify the sense or senses the words appeal to: sight, smell, taste, hearing, or touch.

Double-Entry Journal

"The sweet scent of vanilla had met us as she opened the door." (page 22)	smell

CHOICES: Building Your Portfolio

Writer's Notebook

1. Collecting Ideas for an Autobiographical Incident

Write briefly about a time when somebody threw you a lifeline, singled you out for attention, or made you feel that you were liked and respected for yourself. Be sure to include details and **images.** What sights, sounds, tastes, smells, or feelings do you associate with this experience? (You may want to include sketches in your notes.)

> the day Coach took me along to pick up pizza—the smell of the cheese and the tomato sauce

Expressing an Opinion

2. Pass It On

Reread Meet the Writer on page 24, and pay special attention to what Maya Angelou says about the young man in California. (See the passage in large quotation marks.) What words in this passage connect with the story of Mrs. Flowers? Write a paragraph in which you tell how Mrs. Flowers's talk with Maya is similar to what Angelou says here. In your paragraph tell what you think of the idea of "going out" and helping other people. Be sure to quote passages from both stories that you think are especially important.

Oral Interpretation

3. Literature in Motion

With a partner, role-play the meeting between Marguerite and Mrs. Flowers from the time they leave the store together to the moment when Marguerite finally speaks.

The person playing Mrs. Flowers should read her dialogue from the text, focusing on speaking expressively. The person representing Marguerite should try to convey her feelings through gestures and facial expressions.

Write a brief reflection for your portfolio. Starters:

- What I liked best about this activity was . . . because . . .
- The hardest part was . . . because . . .

Critical Thinking/Art

4. Picture Perfect

Draw a sketch of Mrs. Flowers, using details from Angelou's description. Label each part with a quotation from the autobiography: for example, "Her skin was a rich black that would have peeled like a plum if snagged" (page 20). You will need to review the text carefully to find details. You can also use your imagination to add details.

GRAMMAR LINK

Its or It's?

Language Handbook HELP

See Apostrophes, pages 808-809.

Technology HELP

See Language Workshop CD-ROM. *Key word entry: homonyms.*

Confusing *its* and *it's* is one of the most common errors writers make.

1. *It's* is a **contraction** of *it is* or *it has*. Contractions shorten words by replacing one letter or more with an apostrophe.

> EXAMPLES It's [It is] wonderful to be liked for yourself.
>
> Although it's [it has] been years, Angelou still remembers the taste of those cookies.

The apostrophe in *it's* shows where a letter or letters were taken out.

2. *Its* is the **possessive** form of *it*. A possessive shows ownership: *Its* indicates something belonging to *it*.

> EXAMPLE Marguerite loved the novel for its [the novel's] exciting plot.

The possessive form of a noun—such as *novel's*—has an apostrophe. The possessive form of a personal pronoun—such as *its*—does not.

If you're unsure whether *its* or *it's* is correct, try using *it is* in the sentence. For example, which is correct: *It's author is Maya Angelou* or *Its author is Maya Angelou?* Since *It is author* doesn't make sense, *Its* is correct.

Try It Out

Copy the following paragraph, choosing the correct form from each underlined pair.

(1) Mrs. Flowers told Marguerite that its/it's not enough just to read and write. (2) Spoken language has its/it's importance, too. (3) Reading a sentence aloud helps bring out its/it's deeper meaning. (4) Marguerite found out that its/it's possible to read a sentence many different ways.

VOCABULARY HOW TO OWN A WORD

WORD BANK

taut
benign
infuse
intolerant
illiteracy

Getting Help with Words: The Glossary and the Dictionary

When you are learning new words, you can find help in your textbook and in outside **reference aids,** such as dictionaries.

1. Go to the **Glossary,** on pages 821–826, and find the entries for the five words in the Word Bank (You'll also find these words defined on pages 20, 22, and 23.) What kind of information does each Glossary entry provide?

2. Now, look up the words from the Word Bank in a **dictionary** to see what additional information you can discover. Take notes on other pronunciations, additional meanings, different parts of speech, and **synonyms** (words with similar meanings).

3. Show that you own each word by using it correctly in a sentence.

Before You Read

BROKEN CHAIN

Make the Connection

Dying of Embarrassment

In this story, Gary Soto writes about a boy's first date. Alfonso's problems are like those many of us face—he worries about how he looks and what to say, and *everything* seems to go wrong.

Role-play. With a classmate or two, prepare a skit about one of these situations:

- talking on the phone with a member of the opposite sex
- asking someone to dance
- being introduced to a friend's family

Try to make your skit as humorous or realistic (or both) as you can.

Quickwrite

Freewrite a response to the cartoon on this page or to the situation your skit was about. (If you prefer to draw, respond with a cartoon of your own.)

Elements of Literature

Figures of Speech

Have you ever thought that teeth could look like wrecked cars or be herded like sheep? Such comparisons of very different things are called **figures of speech.**

As you read "Broken Chain" and the poem that follows it, "Oranges," jot down two or three of Gary Soto's surprising figures of speech in your reading notes.

A **figure of speech** compares something to another, very different thing. A figure of speech is not meant to be understood literally.

For more on Figures of Speech, see pages 41–42 and the Handbook of Literary Terms.

Reading Skills and Strategies

Summarizing: Just the Essentials, Please

When you **summarize** a story, you tell "what happens" in your own words. A summary of a story tells who the characters are, what the sequence of events is, and how the main problem is finally resolved. When you write a summary, you avoid including minor details. You'll find that summarizing will help you understand "Broken Chain" and other stories you read.

For Better or For Worse © Lynn Johnston Productions, Inc./Dist. by United Features Syndicate, Inc.

go.hrw.com
LEO 8-1

Broken Chain

Gary Soto

"You got a girlfriend?"

Alfonso sat on the porch trying to push his crooked teeth to where he thought they belonged. He hated the way he looked. Last week he did fifty sit-ups a day, thinking that he would burn those already apparent ripples on his stomach to even deeper ripples, dark ones, so when he went swimming at the canal next summer, girls in cut-offs would notice. And the guys would think he was tough, someone who could take a punch and give it back. He wanted "cuts" like those he had seen on a calendar of an Aztec[1] warrior standing on a pyramid with a woman in his arms. (Even she had cuts he could see beneath her thin dress.) The calendar hung above the cash register at La Plaza. Orsua, the owner, said Alfonso could have the calendar at the end of the year if the waitress, Yolanda, didn't take it first.

1. **Aztec:** member of an American Indian people of what is now Mexico.

Alfonso studied the magazine pictures of rock stars for a hairstyle. He liked the way Prince looked—and the bass player from Los Lobos. Alfonso thought he would look cool with his hair razored into a V in the back and streaked purple. But he knew his mother wouldn't go for it. And his father, who was puro Mexicano, would sit in his chair after work, sullen as a toad, and call him "sissy."

Alfonso didn't dare color his hair. But one day he had had it butched on the top, like in the magazines. His father had come home that evening from a softball game, happy that his team had drilled four homers in a thirteen-to-five bashing of Color Tile. He'd swaggered into the living room but had stopped cold when he saw Alfonso and asked, not joking but with real concern, "Did you hurt your head at school? ¿Qué pasó?"[2]

Alfonso had pretended not to hear his father and had gone to his room, where he studied his hair from all angles in the mirror. He liked what he saw until he smiled and realized for the first time that his teeth were crooked, like a pile of wrecked cars. He grew depressed and turned away from the mirror. He sat on his bed and leafed through the rock magazine until he came to the rock star with the butched top. His mouth was closed, but Alfonso was sure his teeth weren't crooked.

Alfonso didn't want to be the handsomest kid at school, but he was determined to be better looking than average. The next day he spent his lawn-mowing money on a new shirt and, with a pocketknife, scooped the moons of dirt from under his fingernails.

He spent hours in front of the mirror trying to herd his teeth into place with his thumb. He asked his mother if he could have braces, like Frankie Molina, her godson, but he asked at the wrong time. She was at the kitchen table licking the envelope to the house payment. She glared up at him. "Do you think money grows on trees?"

His mother clipped coupons from magazines and newspapers, kept a vegetable garden in the summer, and shopped at Penney's and K-Mart. Their family ate a lot of frijoles,[3] which was OK because nothing else tasted so good, though one time Alfonso had had Chinese pot stickers[4] and thought they were the next best food in the world.

He didn't ask his mother for braces again, even when she was in a better mood. He decided to fix his teeth by pushing on them with his thumbs. After breakfast that Saturday he went to his room, closed the door quietly, turned the radio on, and pushed for three hours straight.

He pushed for ten minutes, rested for five, and every half hour, during a radio commercial, checked to see if his smile had improved. It hadn't.

Eventually he grew bored and went outside with an old gym sock to wipe down his bike, a ten-speed from Montgomery Ward. His thumbs were tired and wrinkled and pink, the way they got when he stayed in the bathtub too long.

Alfonso's older brother, Ernie, rode up on *his* Montgomery Ward bicycle looking depressed. He parked his bike against the peach tree and sat on the back steps, keeping his head down and stepping on ants that came too close.

Alfonso knew better than to say anything when Ernie looked mad. He turned his bike over, balancing it on the handlebars and seat, and flossed the spokes with the sock. When he was finished, he pressed a knuckle to his teeth until they tingled.

Ernie groaned and said, "Ah, man."

---

3. **frijoles** (frē·hôl′ās): Spanish for "beans."
4. **pot stickers:** dumplings.

WORDS TO OWN

sullen (sul′ən) *adj.:* sulky; resentful.

---

2. **¿Qué pasó?** (kā′ pä·sô′): Spanish for "What happened?"

Alfonso waited a few minutes before asking, "What's the matter?" He pretended not to be too interested. He picked up a wad of steel wool and continued cleaning the spokes.

Ernie hesitated, not sure if Alfonso would laugh. But it came out. "Those girls didn't show up. And you better not laugh."

"What girls?"

Then Alfonso remembered his brother bragging about how he and Frostie met two girls from Kings Canyon Junior High last week on Halloween night. They were dressed as Gypsies, the costume for all poor Chicanas[5]—they just had to borrow scarves and gaudy red lipstick from their abuelitas.[6]

Alfonso walked over to his brother. He compared their two bikes: His gleamed like a handful of dimes, while Ernie's looked dirty.

"They said we were supposed to wait at the corner. But they didn't show up. Me and Frostie waited and waited. . . . They were playing games with us."

Alfonso thought that was a pretty dirty trick but sort of funny too. He would have to try that someday.

"Were they cute?" Alfonso asked.

"I guess so."

"Do you think you could recognize them?"

"If they were wearing red lipstick, maybe."

Alfonso sat with his brother in silence, both of them smearing ants with their floppy high tops. Girls could sure act weird, especially the ones you meet on Halloween.

Later that day, Alfonso sat on the porch pressing on his teeth. Press, relax; press, relax. His portable radio was on, but not loud enough to make Mr. Rojas come down the steps and wave his cane at him.

Alfonso's father drove up. Alfonso could tell by the way he sat in his truck, a Datsun with a different-colored front fender, that his team had lost their softball game. Alfonso got off the porch in a hurry because he knew his father would be in a bad mood. He went to the back yard, where he unlocked his bike, sat on it with the kickstand down, and pressed on his teeth. He punched himself in the stomach, and growled, "Cuts." Then he patted his butch and whispered, "Fresh."

After a while Alfonso pedaled up the street, hands in his pockets, toward Foster's Freeze, where he was chased by a ratlike Chihuahua.[7] At his old school, John Burroughs Elementary, he found a kid hanging upside down on the top of a barbed-wire fence with a girl looking up at him. Alfonso skidded to a stop and helped the kid untangle his pants from the barbed wire. The kid was grateful. He had been afraid he would have to stay up there all night. His sister, who was Alfonso's age, was also grateful. If she had to go home and tell her mother that Frankie was stuck on a fence and couldn't get down, she would get scolded.

"Thanks," she said. "What's your name?"

Alfonso remembered her from his school and noticed that she was kind of cute, with ponytails and straight teeth. "Alfonso. You go to my school, huh?"

"Yeah. I've seen you around. You live nearby?"

"Over on Madison."

"My uncle used to live on that street, but he moved to Stockton."

"Stockton's near Sacramento, isn't it?"

"You been there?"

"No." Alfonso looked down at his shoes. He wanted to say something clever the way people do on TV. But the only thing he could think to say was that the governor lived in Sacramento. As soon as he shared this observation, he winced inside.

Alfonso walked with the girl and the boy as they started for home. They didn't talk much.

---

5. Chicanas (chi·käʹnəz): Mexican American girls and women.

6. abuelitas (ä′bwä·lēʹtäs): in Spanish, an affectionate term for "grandmothers," like *grandmas* in English.

7. Chihuahua (chi·wäʹwä): small dog with large pointed ears.

Every few steps, the girl, whose name was Sandra, would look at him out of the corner of her eye, and Alfonso would look away. He learned that she was in seventh grade, just like him, and that she had a pet terrier named Queenie. Her father was a mechanic at Rudy's Speedy Repair, and her mother was a teacher's aide at Jefferson Elementary.

When they came to the street, Alfonso and Sandra stopped at her corner, but her brother ran home. Alfonso watched him stop in the front yard to talk to a lady he guessed was their mother. She was raking leaves into a pile.

"I live over there," she said, pointing.

Alfonso looked over her shoulder for a long time, trying to <u>muster</u> enough nerve to ask her if she'd like to go bike riding tomorrow.

Shyly, he asked, "You wanna go bike riding?"

"Maybe." She played with a ponytail and crossed one leg in front of the other. "But my bike has a flat."

"I can get my brother's bike. He won't mind."

She thought a moment before she said, "OK. But not tomorrow. I have to go to my aunt's."

"How about after school on Monday?"

"I have to take care of my brother until my mom comes home from work. How 'bout four-thirty?"

"OK," he said. "Four-thirty." Instead of parting immediately, they talked for a while, asking questions like "Who's your favorite group?" "Have you ever been on the Big Dipper at Santa Cruz?" and "Have you ever tasted pot stickers?" But the question-and-answer period ended when Sandra's mother called her home.

Alfonso took off as fast as he could on his bike, jumped the curb, and, cool as he could be, raced away with his hands stuffed in his pockets. But when he looked back over his shoulder, the wind raking through his butch, Sandra wasn't even looking. She was already on her lawn, heading for the porch.

That night he took a bath, pampered his hair into place, and did more than his usual set of exercises. In bed, in between the push-and-rest on his teeth, he pestered his brother to let him borrow his bike.

"Come on, Ernie," he whined. "Just for an hour."

"Chale,[8] I might want to use it."

"Come on, man, I'll let you have my trick-or-treat candy."

"What you got?"

"Three baby Milky Ways and some Skittles."

"Who's going to use it?"

Alfonso hesitated, then risked the truth. "I met this girl. She doesn't live too far."

Ernie rolled over on his stomach and stared at the outline of his brother, whose head was resting on his elbow. "*You* got a girlfriend?"

"She ain't my girlfriend, just a girl."

"What does she look like?"

"Like a girl."

"Come on, what does she look like?"

"She's got ponytails and a little brother."

"Ponytails! Those girls who messed with Frostie and me had ponytails. Is she cool?"

"I think so."

Ernie sat up in bed. "I bet you that's her."

Alfonso felt his stomach knot up. "She's going to be my girlfriend, not yours!"

"I'm going to get even with her!"

"You better not touch her," Alfonso snarled, throwing a wadded Kleenex at him. "I'll run you over with my bike."

For the next hour, until their mother threatened them from the living room to be quiet or else, they argued whether it was the same girl who had stood Ernie up. Alfonso said over and over that she was too nice to pull a stunt like that. But Ernie argued that she lived only two blocks from where those girls had told them to wait, that she was in the same grade, and, the clincher, that she had ponytails. Secretly, however, Ernie was jealous that his brother, two years younger than himself, might have found a girlfriend.

Sunday morning, Ernie and Alfonso stayed away from each other, though over breakfast they fought over the last tortilla. Their mother, sewing at the kitchen table, warned them to knock it off. At church they made faces at one another when the priest, Father Jerry, wasn't looking. Ernie punched Alfonso in the arm, and Alfonso, his eyes wide with anger, punched back.

Monday morning they hurried to school on their bikes, neither saying a word, though they rode side by side. In first period, Alfonso worried himself sick. How would he borrow a bike for her? He considered asking his best friend, Raul, for his bike. But Alfonso knew Raul, a paperboy with dollar signs in his eyes, would charge him, and he had less than sixty cents, counting the soda bottles he could cash.

Between history and math, Alfonso saw Sandra and her girlfriend huddling at their lockers. He hurried by without being seen.

During lunch Alfonso hid in metal shop so he wouldn't run into Sandra. What would he say to her? If he weren't mad at his brother, he

---

8. **chale** (chä′lä): Spanish slang expression roughly meaning "it's not possible."

could ask Ernie what girls and guys talk about. But he *was* mad, and anyway, Ernie was pitching nickels with his friends.

Alfonso hurried home after school. He did the morning dishes as his mother had asked and raked the leaves. After finishing his chores, he did a hundred sit-ups, pushed on his teeth until they hurt, showered, and combed his hair into a perfect butch. He then stepped out to the patio to clean his bike. On an impulse, he removed the chain to wipe off the gritty oil. But while he was unhooking it from the back sprocket, it snapped. The chain lay in his hand like a dead snake.

Alfonso couldn't believe his luck. Now, not only did he not have an extra bike for Sandra, he had no bike for himself. Frustrated and on the verge of tears, he flung the chain as far as he could. It landed with a hard slap against the back fence and spooked his sleeping cat, Benny. Benny looked around, blinking his soft gray eyes, and went back to sleep.

Alfonso retrieved the chain, which was hopelessly broken. He cursed himself for being stupid, yelled at his bike for being cheap, and slammed the chain onto the cement. The chain snapped in another place and hit him when it popped up, slicing his hand like a snake's fang.

"Ow!" he cried, his mouth immediately going to his hand to suck on the wound.

After a dab of iodine, which only made his cut hurt more, and a lot of thought, he went to the bedroom to plead with Ernie, who was changing to his after-school clothes.

"Come on, man, let me use it," Alfonso pleaded. "Please, Ernie, I'll do anything."

Although Ernie could see Alfonso's desperation, he had plans with his friend Raymundo. They were going to catch frogs at the Mayfair canal. He felt sorry for his brother and gave him a stick of gum to make him feel better, but there was nothing he could do. The canal was three miles away, and the frogs were waiting.

Alfonso took the stick of gum, placed it in his shirt pocket, and left the bedroom with his head down. He went outside, slamming the screen door behind him, and sat in the alley behind his house. A sparrow landed in the weeds, and when it tried to come close, Alfonso screamed for it to scram. The sparrow responded with a squeaky chirp and flew away.

At four he decided to get it over with and started walking to Sandra's house, trudging slowly, as if he were waist-deep in water. Shame colored his face. How could he disappoint his first date? She would probably laugh. She might even call him menso.[9]

He stopped at the corner where they were supposed to meet and watched her house. But there was no one outside, only a rake leaning against the steps.

Why did he have to take the chain off? he scolded himself. He always messed things up when he tried to take them apart, like the time he tried to repad his baseball mitt. He had unlaced the mitt and filled the pocket with cotton balls. But when he tried to put it back together, he had forgotten how it laced up. Everything became tangled like kite string. When he showed the mess to his mother, who was at the stove cooking dinner, she scolded him but put it back together and didn't tell his father what a dumb thing he had done.

Now he had to face Sandra and say, "I broke my bike, and my stingy brother took off on his."

He waited at the corner a few minutes, hiding behind a hedge for what seemed like forever. Just as he was starting to think about going home, he heard footsteps and knew it was too late. His hands, moist from worry, hung at his sides and a thread of sweat raced down his armpit.

9. **menso** (men′sô): Spanish for "stupid."

- -

WORDS TO OWN
gritty (grit′ē) *adj.*: containing sand or dirt.

- -

He peeked through the hedge. She was wearing a sweater with a checkerboard pattern. A red purse was slung over her shoulder. He could see her looking for him, standing on tiptoe to see if he was coming around the corner.

What have I done? Alfonso thought. He bit his lip, called himself menso, and pounded his palm against his forehead. Someone slapped the back of his head. He turned around and saw Ernie.

"We got the frogs, Alfonso," he said, holding up a wiggling plastic bag. "I'll show you later."

Ernie looked through the hedge, with one eye closed, at the girl. "She's not the one who messed with Frostie and me," he said finally. "You still wanna borrow my bike?"

Alfonso couldn't believe his luck. What a brother! What a pal! He promised to take Ernie's turn next time it was his turn to do the dishes. Ernie hopped on Raymundo's handlebars and said he would remember that promise. Then he was gone as they took off without looking back.

Free of worry now that his brother had come through, Alfonso emerged from behind the hedge with Ernie's bike, which was mudsplashed but better than nothing. Sandra waved.

"Hi," she said.

"Hi," he said back.

She looked cheerful. Alfonso told her his bike was broken and asked if she wanted to ride with him.

WORDS TO OWN
emerged (ē·mʉrjd′) v.: came into view.

"Sounds good," she said, and jumped on the crossbar.

It took all of Alfonso's strength to steady the bike. He started off slowly, gritting his teeth, because she was heavier than he thought. But once he got going, it got easier. He pedaled smoothly, sometimes with only one hand on the handlebars, as they sped up one street and down another. Whenever he ran over a pothole, which was often, she screamed with delight, and once, when it looked like they were going to crash, she placed her hand over his, and it felt like love.

MEET THE WRITER

"Your Lives Are at Work, Too"

Gary Soto (1952–   ) was born and raised in Fresno, California, the setting of many of his stories, poems, and autobiographical pieces. In his writing, Soto tries to re-create the sights and sounds of the Mexican American neighborhood in which he grew up. He advises young writers to "look to your own lives," which is exactly what he does:

66 What are your life stories? Can you remember incidents from your childhood? Some of you will say that your lives are boring, that nothing has happened, that everything interesting happens far away. Not so. Your lives are at work, too. 99

Soto based "Oranges" on an actual incident in his life (see his comment on page 37), but "Broken Chain" is more loosely drawn from his experience:

66 No, I'm not Alfonso in the story 'Broken Chain.' It's pure fiction, with the wild purpose of stirring in you—the reader—the feeling of one day latching onto a girlfriend or boyfriend. When I was Alfonso's age, I would have loved to have a girlfriend on my handlebars. Instead, I had my little brother, better known as chipped-tooth Jimmy, who often hopped onto my bike and cruised the streets of my hometown, Fresno, California. He was no 'Sandra.' Instead, Jimmy was a heavy problem, because it was my job to take care of him while my parents went off to work. 99

More by Gary Soto

- "Broken Chain" comes from a book of short stories about growing up called *Baseball in April* (Harcourt Brace).

- You'll find "Oranges," along with other poems and some suggestions for young poets, in *A Fire in My Hands* (Scholastic).

Oranges

Gary Soto

Soto writes, "I don't know if you can call it a 'date' or not, but the first girl who allowed me to walk with her was named Margie. I couldn't think of anything to do but walk around the block three or four times."

The first time I walked
With a girl, I was twelve,
Cold, and weighted down
With two oranges in my jacket.
5 December. Frost cracking
Beneath my steps, my breath
Before me, then gone,
As I walked toward
Her house, the one whose
10 Porch light burned yellow
Night and day, in any weather.
A dog barked at me, until
She came out pulling
At her gloves, face bright
15 With rouge. I smiled,
Touched her shoulder, and led
Her down the street, across
A used car lot and a line
Of newly planted trees,
20 Until we were breathing
Before a drugstore. We
Entered, the tiny bell
Bringing a saleslady
Down a narrow aisle of goods.
25 I turned to the candies
Tiered° like bleachers,
And asked what she wanted—
Light in her eyes, a smile
Starting at the corners

30 Of her mouth. I fingered
A nickel in my pocket,
And when she lifted a chocolate
That cost a dime,
I didn't say anything.
35 I took the nickel from
My pocket, then an orange,
And set them quietly on
The counter. When I looked up,
The lady's eyes met mine,
40 And held them, knowing
Very well what it was all
About.

Outside,
A few cars hissing past,
Fog hanging like old
45 Coats between the trees.
I took my girl's hand
In mine for two blocks,
Then released it to let
Her unwrap the chocolate.
50 I peeled my orange
That was so bright against
The gray of December
That, from some distance,
Someone might have thought
55 I was making a fire in my hands.

26. **tiered:** arranged in tiers, or rows,
like the seats in a ballpark.

MAKING MEANINGS

First Thoughts

1. Finish one or more of these sentences:
   - "Broken Chain" is realistic/unrealistic because . . .
   - I know how it feels to . . . because . . .
   - Alfonso reminds me of . . .

Reading Check

Summarize (restate) the main events of "Broken Chain" by completing this sentence:

Alfonso wanted . . . but . . . so . . .

Shaping Interpretations

2. **Compare** Ernie in "Broken Chain" with the saleswoman in "Oranges" (see *Connections* on page 37). Consider the theme of the collection: How does each of them become "somebody to lean on"?

3. Choose one of the **figures of speech** you wrote down in your reading notes, and identify the two things it is comparing. Do you think it works? (That is, can you see how the two things being compared are alike, or is the comparison a stretch? Does the figure of speech help you form a picture in your mind?)

Connecting with the Text

4. In what ways is Alfonso's situation similar to or different from the situation you discussed in your Quickwrite? Do Alfonso's feelings and behavior seem realistic to you? Explain.

Extending the Text

5. This story is told from a boy's viewpoint. In your experience, which of Alfonso's feelings are shared by girls?

6. Alfonso doesn't have any trouble talking to his brother, but he worries about what to say to Sandra. Why might boys and girls have trouble talking with one another?

Challenging the Text

7. Soto says that he wrote this story to help his readers feel what it is like to find a girlfriend or boyfriend. If Soto asked you whether he had succeeded, what would you say to him?

8. "Broken Chain" has also been published under the title "First Love." Which **title** do you think is better? Why?

CHOICES: Building Your Portfolio

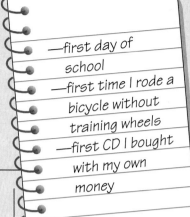

Writer's Notebook

1. Collecting Ideas for an Autobiographical Incident

Gary Soto got the idea for "Oranges" by remembering the first time he went for a walk with a girl. Make a list of important "firsts" in your life. Pick one that you might like to write about, and jot down anything that you remember of the incident.

—first day of school
—first time I rode a bicycle without training wheels
—first CD I bought with my own money

Explaining a Problem

2. Helpful Hints

Identify a problem that Alfonso has in the story (for example, worrying about his appearance or not knowing what to say to Sandra). Pretending you are Alfonso, write a **letter** to an advice column explaining your problem. Switch papers with a classmate, and take the role of the columnist, responding with practical, encouraging advice.

Performance

3. Try to See It My Way

We hear only the boy's side of the story in "Broken Chain." To present a different viewpoint, perform a **skit** showing Sandra speaking on the telephone with her best friend after she meets Alfonso at the school and walks home with him. What does Sandra think of Alfonso? Is she looking forward to going bicycle riding with him on Monday? You could perform your skit as a dialogue, with you and a classmate taking the roles of Sandra and her friend. Another option is to perform it as a monologue, showing only Sandra's end of the conversation.

Art

4. Worth a Thousand Words?

Go back to the story and the poem, and find a **figure of speech** that particularly appeals to you. Draw this comparison as you picture it. (For example, in "Oranges," Soto describes the fog as "hanging like old / Coats between the trees." A drawing of this image might show misty forms in the shape of coats hanging from the branches of trees.) If you have access to drawing or paint software, you may want to create your picture on a computer.

GRAMMAR LINK   MINI-LESSON

When to Use Apostrophes

Language Handbook
H E L P

See Apostrophes, pages 808-809.

Contractions	Possessive Pronouns
it's (It's broken.)	its (Its chain is on the ground.)
you're (You're kidding!)	your (Your girlfriend is here.)
they're (They're not the same girls.)	their (Their lipstick was too bright.)
who's (Who's going to borrow it?)	whose (Whose bike are you riding?)

1. Use an apostrophe
   - to show where letters are missing in a contraction (shortened form):

     Alfonso <u>didn't</u> [did not] like the way he looked.

   - to form the possessive case of a noun (showing ownership):

     <u>Sandra's</u> hair [hair belonging to Sandra] was in ponytails.

     The <u>boys'</u> bicycles [bicycles belonging to the boys] are parked in the back.

2. Don't use an apostrophe
   - to form the plural of a noun:

     The <u>girls</u> never showed up.

   - with the possessive form of a personal pronoun (*yours, hers, his, its, ours, theirs*):

     <u>His</u> bicycle is broken; can he borrow <u>yours</u>?

Technology
H E L P

See Language Workshop CD-ROM. *Key word entry: apostrophe.*

Try It Out

Take out a piece of your writing. Circle all the contractions, and underline all the possessive pronouns, correcting any errors you find in the use of apostrophes.

VOCABULARY   HOW TO OWN A WORD

WORD BANK

sullen
muster
clincher
gritty
emerged

Back to the Story

1. Alfonso's father is described as being as "sullen as a toad." Do you think toads look <u>sullen</u>? Why or why not?
2. Why was it hard for Alfonso to <u>muster</u> enough nerve to ask Sandra out?
3. Why would Sandra's ponytails be the <u>clincher</u> in Ernie's argument (page 33)? Does his reasoning make sense to you?
4. What do you think the <u>gritty</u> oil on the bicycle chain looked and felt like?
5. How do you think Sandra felt when Alfonso finally <u>emerged</u> from behind the hedge?

Elements of Literature

FIGURES OF SPEECH: Making Connections

Orioles Fly Away with World Series

Unexpected Connections

If you read the headline above in the paper, you wouldn't rush outside to catch a last glimpse of the baseball players as they soared beyond the horizon, trailing a stadium full of fans behind them. You'd understand that to "fly away" with the World Series meant to win it with ease.

Our everyday language includes thousands of **figures of speech** like this one—expressions that suggest unexpected similarities between unrelated things. Many figures of speech are used so commonly that we don't even notice that they are based on unusual comparisons and are not meant to be understood literally.

Writers try to create fresh, new figures of speech to make unexpected connections. They want us to see everyday things in new ways.

The figures of speech used most frequently by writers are similes, metaphors, personification, and symbols.

Similes

A **simile** is a comparison of two unlike things that links them with the words *like, as, than,* or *resembles:* fingers *as* cold *as* ice cubes, hair blacker *than* midnight, a voice *like* the sound of fingernails scraping a blackboard.

In "Broken Chain" the broken bicycle chain lies in Alfonso's hand "like a dead snake" (page 34). Then it pops up and cuts Alfonso "like a snake's fang." The similes help us see the chain in a new light, as if it were an evil creature bent on ruining Alfonso's plans.

Metaphors

A **metaphor** is a direct identification of two unlike things. In contrast to similes, metaphors make their connections without the use of the words *like, as, than,* or *resembles:* "He *is* a sullen toad," not "He is *as* sullen *as* a toad."

Like similes, metaphors extend the range of our imagination. When they are fresh and are based on a writer's first-hand observation, we often feel that a strong hidden relationship has been discovered by the writer. After reading this short poem, for example, you may suddenly see how fame is like a bee:

> Fame is a bee.
> It has song—
> It has a sting—
> Ah, too, it has a wing.
>
> —Emily Dickinson

Dickinson uses an **extended metaphor,** a metaphor in which the comparison is developed in a number of ways. In what ways is fame like a bee, according to Dickinson?

(continued on next page)

by John Malcolm Brinnin (continued from previous page)

Personification

We use **personification** when we speak of a non-human thing as if it had human qualities. In "Mrs. Flowers" we read that "browned photographs leered or threatened from the walls" (page 22). Photographs can't *really* leer or threaten, but to the main character they seem to, just as if they were people.

Cartoonists often use personification to tell their stories: Automobiles have eyes that blink and jaws that open wide; rabbits lean against lampposts and talk like philosophers. The same technique is used in writing, except that personification is not necessarily used for humor; it can be used to make serious points about the human experience.

We hear many examples of personification in everyday speech. An engine "coughs"; the wind "sighs"; fortune "smiles" on us. We are speaking about something nonhuman as if it were human.

Symbols

A **symbol** is a person, place, thing, or event that has meaning in itself and also stands for something beyond itself. Many symbols are traditional. We easily understand them because people have agreed on their meaning. Uncle Sam is a symbol of the United States. A dove with an olive branch represents peace.

Many writers create their own symbols. In "A Time to Talk" (page 17), the speaker goes "up to the stone wall / For a friendly visit." The stone wall is a real wall in the poem, but to Frost it may also represent the barriers that keep people apart.

Symbols in poetry can acquire deeper meanings from the experiences a reader brings to the text. For example, the wall in Frost's poem might have special meaning for someone living in East Germany when the Berlin Wall came down.

A Writer on Symbols

"Poetry is a concentrated form of writing; so much meaning is packed into such a little space. Therefore, each word in a poem is very important and is chosen very carefully to convey just the right meaning. For example, the word *tree* might stand for more than a tree in an orchard. It might symbolize life itself, or it might symbolize the strength of your grandfather or your father. *Rain* may symbolize tears; *dusk* may symbolize approaching death."

— Gary Soto, author of "Broken Chain" (page 29) and "Oranges" (page 37)

"HELP! I DON'T KNOW THIS WORD!"

No matter how impressive your vocabulary is, you'll probably come across an unfamiliar word in your reading every now and then. (Did you know that there are over five hundred thousand words in the largest dictionaries of the English language?) If you see a word you don't know, don't panic; follow these steps instead.

1. Decide if you can skip the word and still grasp the general meaning of the text. For example, you don't need to know that mauve is a bluish purple color to understand this sentence: *Her mauve skirt fluttered as she fell over the precipice.* Knowing that a precipice is a steep cliff, on the other hand, *is* essential

to understanding the sentence's meaning.

2. If you think you need to know the meaning of the word, use one or more of the following strategies:

- **Sound it out.** Apply what you know of phonics, and try sounding out the word; it may be one that you've heard but haven't seen in print before.

- **Look for family resemblances.** Ask yourself: Does any part of the word look familiar? It may be related to a word you know and have a similar meaning. For example, *educable* looks like *educate* and *able.* Even if you've never seen the word before, you could guess that it means "capable of being educated."

- **Use context clues.** Consider the general meaning of what you're reading, and check the surrounding words and sentences for context clues. If you read *Philip carefully knotted his silk cravat around his throat,* you'd

probably guess that a cravat is a kind of necktie.

- **Look it up.** Use various **reference aids** to help learn new words. First, guess what the word means; then, look it up in a dictionary (in book form, on a software program, or on the Internet) to see if you were correct. You might also look up the word in a thesaurus or a synonym finder to discover the word's **synonyms**—words that have the same or similar meanings.

You'll learn more about strategies like these in the Reading Skills and Strategies features throughout this book.

Apply the strategy on the next page.

Before You Read

Make the Connection

If You Had to Choose

Take a class poll: Would it be better to be the most popular person in your school or the smartest person in your school?

On a small piece of paper, write either *S* for "smartest" or *P* for "most popular." (Even if you'd like to be both, choose one for now.) Tally the class's votes on the board. How close was the vote?

• Discuss what you think people's reasons were for answering as they did.

• Would it be possible to be the smartest *and* the most popular? Why or why not?

Quickwrite

Respond briefly to one of these questions.

1. What are the advantages and disadvantages of popularity? of intelligence?

2. What sacrifices do people make to fit in?

3. What is good or bad about being unusual?

go.hrw.com
LEO 8–1

Reading Skills and Strategies

"Help! I Don't Know This Word!": Using Context Clues

Right at the start of "Flowers for Algernon," you'll notice that Charlie has trouble with spelling. To figure out what his misspelled words are meant to be, try sounding out each word. (Charlie usually spells words the way they sound.)

If you're still stuck, check the word's **context.** The context will often give you enough hints, or **context clues,** to help you figure out the word's meaning.

For example, on page 45, Charlie uses the word *faled.* You could figure out that this is his spelling of *failed* by sounding out the word. (It sounds just like the word spelled *f-a-i-l-e-d.*) You could even find a context clue in the sentence just before it: "I had a test today."

Accompanying the story are scenes from the movie *Charly,* starring Cliff Robertson.

Flowers for Algernon

Daniel Keyes

> **All my life I wanted to be smart . . .**

1

progris riport 1—martch 5 1965

Dr. Strauss says I shud rite down what I think and evrey thing that happins to me from now on. I dont know why but he says its importint so they will see if they will use me. I hope they use me. Miss Kinnian says maybe they can make me smart. I want to be smart. My name is Charlie Gordon. I am 37 years old and 2 weeks ago was my brithday. I have nuthing more to rite now so I will close for today.

progris riport 2—martch 6

I had a test today. I think I faled it. and I think that maybe now they wont use me. What happind is a nice young man was in the room and he had some white cards with ink spillled all over them. He sed Charlie what do you see on this card. I was very skared even tho I had my rabits foot[1] in my pockit because when I was a kid I always faled tests in school and I spilled ink to.

I told him I saw a inkblot. He said yes and it made me feel good. I thot that was all but when I got up to go he stopped me. He said now sit down Charlie we are not thru yet. Then I dont remember so good but he wantid me to say what was in the ink. I dint see nuthing in the ink but he said there was picturs there other pepul saw some picturs. I coudnt see any picturs. I reely tryed to see. I held the card close up and then far away. Then I said if I had my glases I coud see better I usally only ware my glases in the movies or TV but I said they are in the closit in the hall. I got them. Then I said let me see that card agen I bet Ill find it now.

1. **rabits foot:** The hind foot of a rabbit is sometimes used as a good-luck charm.

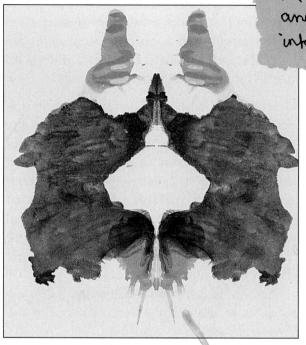

I tryed hard but I still coudnt find the picturs I only saw the ink. I told him maybe I need new glases. He rote somthing down on a paper and I got skared of faling the test. I told him it was a very nice inkblot with littel points all around the eges. He looked very sad so that wasnt it. I said please let me try agen. Ill get it in a few minits becaus Im not so fast somtimes. Im a slow reeder too in Miss Kinnians class for slow adults but I'm trying very hard.

He gave me a chance with another card that had 2 kinds of ink spillled on it red and blue.

He was very nice and talked slow like Miss Kinnian does and he explaned it to me that it was a *raw shok.*[2] He said pepul see things in the ink. I said show me where. He said think. I told him I think a inkblot but that wasnt rite eather. He said what does it remind you—pretend something. I closd my eyes for a long time to pretend. I told him I pretned a fowntan pen

with ink leeking all over a table cloth. Then he got up and went out.

I dont think I passd the *raw shok* test.

progris report 3—martch 7

Dr Strauss and Dr Nemur say it dont matter about the inkblots. I told them I dint spill the ink on the cards and I coudn't see anything in the ink. They said that maybe they will still use me. I said Miss Kinnian never gave me tests like that one only spelling and reading. They said Miss Kinnian told that I was her bestist pupil in the adult nite scool becaus I tryed the hardist and I reely wantid to lern. They said how come you went to the adult nite scool all by yourself Charlie. How did you find it. I said I askd pepul and sumbody told me where I shud go to lern to read and spell good. They said why did you want to. I told them becaus all my life I wantid to be smart and not dumb. But its very hard to be smart. They said you know it will probly be tempirery. I said yes. Miss Kinnian told me. I dont care if it herts.

Later I had more crazy tests today. The nice lady who gave it me told me the name and I asked her how do you spellit so I can rite it in my progris riport. THEMATIC APPERCEPTION TEST. I dont know the frist 2 words but I know what *test* means. You got to pass it or you get bad marks. This test lookd easy becaus I coud see the picturs. Only this time she dint want me to tell her the picturs. That mixd me up. I said the man yesterday said I shoud tell him what I saw in the ink she said that dont make no difrence. She said make up storys about the pepul in the picturs.

2. *raw shok:* Rorschach (rôr′shäk′) test, a psychological test in which people describe the images suggested to them by a series of inkblots.

I told her how can you tell storys about pepul you never met. I said why shud I make up lies. I never tell lies any more becaus I always get caut.

She told me this test and the other one the raw-shok was for getting personalty. I laffed so hard. I said how can you get that thing from inkblots and fotos. She got sore and put her picturs away. I dont care. It was silly. I gess I faled that test too.

Later some men in white coats took me to a difernt part of the hospitil and gave me a game to play. It was like a race with a white mouse. They called the mouse Algernon. Algernon was in a box with a lot of twists and turns like all kinds of walls and they gave me a pencil and a paper with lines and lots of boxes. On one side it said START and on the other end it said FINISH. They said it was *amazed* and that Algernon and me had the same *amazed* to do. I dint see how we could have the same *amazed* if Algernon had a box and I had a paper but I dint say nothing. Anyway there wasnt time because the race started.

One of the men had a watch he was trying to hide so I wouldnt see it so I tryed not to look and that made me nervus.

Anyway that test made me feel worser than all the others because they did it over 10 times with difernt *amazeds* and Algernon won every time. I dint know that mice were so smart. Maybe thats because Algernon is a white mouse. Maybe white mice are smarter then other mice.

progis riport 4—Mar 8

Their going to use me! Im so exited I can hardly write. Dr Nemur and Dr Strauss had a argament about it first. Dr Nemur was in the office when Dr Strauss brot me in. Dr Nemur was worryed about using me but Dr Strauss told him Miss Kinnian rekemmended me the best from all the people who she was teaching. I like Miss Kinnian becaus shes a very smart teacher. And she said Charlie your going to have a second chance. If you volenteer for this experament you mite get smart. They dont know if it will be perminint but theirs a chance. Thats why I said ok even when I was scared because she said it was an operashun. She said dont be scared Charlie you done so much with so little I think you deserv it most of all.

So I got scaird when Dr Nemur and Dr Strauss argud about it. Dr Strauss said I had something that was very good. He said I had a good *motorvation.*[3] I never even knew I had that. I felt proud when he said that not every body with an eye-q of 68 had that thing. I dont know what it is or where I got it but he said Algernon had it too. Algernons *motor-vation* is the cheese they put in his box. But it cant be that because I didnt eat any cheese this week.

Then he told Dr Nemur something I dint understand so while they were talking I wrote down some of the words.

He said Dr Nemur I know Charlie is not what you had in mind as the first of your new brede of intelek** (coudnt get the word) superman. But most people of his low ment** are host** and uncoop** they are usualy dull apath** and hard to reach. He has a good natcher hes intristed and eager to please.

Dr Nemur said remember he will be the first human beeng ever to have his intelijence trippled by surgicle meens.

Dr Strauss said exakly. Look at how well hes lerned to read and write for his low mentel age its as grate an acheve** as you and I lerning einstines therey of **vity[4] without help. That shows the intenss motor-vation. Its comparat** a tremen** achev** I say we use Charlie.

I dint get all the words and they were talking to fast but it sounded like Dr Strauss was on my side and like the other one wasnt.

---

3. **motor-vation:** motivation, the force or inner drive that makes someone want to do or accomplish something; here, Charlie's desire to learn.
4. **einstines therey of **vity:** Einstein's theory of relativity, which was developed by the German-born American physicist Albert Einstein (1879–1955) and deals with matter, time, space, and energy.

Then Dr Nemur nodded he said all right maybe your right. We will use Charlie. When he said that I got so exited I jumped up and shook his hand for being so good to me. I told him thank you doc you wont be sorry for giving me a second chance. And I mean it like I told him. After the operashun Im gonna try to be smart. Im gonna try awful hard.

progris ript 5—Mar 10

Im skared. Lots of people who work here and the nurses and the people who gave me the tests came to bring me candy and wish me luck. I hope I have luck. I got my rabits foot and my lucky penny and my horse shoe. Only a black cat crossed me when I was comming to the hospitil. Dr Strauss says dont be supersitis Charlie this is sience. Anyway Im keeping my rabits foot with me.

I asked Dr Strauss if Ill beat Algernon in the race after the operashun and he said maybe. If the operashun works Ill show that mouse I can be as smart as he is. Maybe smarter. Then Ill be abel to read better and spell the words good and know lots of things and be like other people. I want to be smart like other people. If it works perminint they will make everybody smart all over the wurld.

They dint give me anything to eat this morning. I dont know what that eating has to do with getting smart. Im very hungry and Dr Nemur took away my box of candy. That Dr Nemur is a grouch. Dr Strauss says I can have it back after the operashun. You cant eat befor a operashun . . .

Progress Report 6—Mar 15

The operashun dint hurt. He did it while I was sleeping. They took off the bandijis from my eyes and my head today so I can make a PROGRESS REPORT. Dr Nemur who looked at some of my other ones says I spell PROGRESS wrong and he told me how to spell it and REPORT too. I got to try and remember that.

I have a very bad memary for spelling. Dr Strauss says its ok to tell about all the things that happin to me but he says I shoud tell more about what I feel and what I think. When I told him I dont know how to think he said try. All the time when the bandijis were on my eyes I tryed to think. Nothing happened. I dont know what to think about. Maybe if I ask him he will tell me how I can think now that Im suppose to get smart. What do smart people think about. Fancy things I suppose. I wish I knew some fancy things alredy.

Progress Report 7—mar 19

Nothing is happining. I had lots of tests and different kinds of races with Algernon. I hate that mouse. He always beats me. Dr Strauss said I

Their really my friends and they like me.

WEEKLY TIME CARD

DAY	IN	OUT	IN	OUT	IN	OUT	Total
M							
T							
W							
T							
F							
S							
S							
					REG.		
					O.T.		

Foreman Signature

got to play those games. And he said some time I got to take those tests over again. Thse inkblots are stupid. And those pictures are stupid too. I like to draw a picture of a man and a woman but I wont make up lies about people.

I got a headache from trying to think so much. I thot Dr Strauss was my frend but he dont help me. He dont tell me what to think or when Ill get smart. Miss Kinnian dint come to see me. I think writing these progress reports are stupid too.

Progress Report 8—Mar 23

Im going back to work at the factery. They said it was better I shud go back to work but I cant tell anyone what the operashun was for and I have to come to the hospitil for an hour evry night after work. They are gonna pay me mony every month for lerning to be smart.

Im glad Im going back to work because I miss my job and all my frends and all the fun we have there.

Dr Strauss says I shud keep writing things down but I dont have to do it every day just when I think of something or something speshul happins. He says dont get discoridged because it takes time and it happins slow. He says it took a long time with Algernon before he got 3 times smarter then he was before. Thats why Algernon beats me all the time because he had that operashun too. That makes me feel better. I coud probly do that *amazed* faster than a reglar mouse. Maybe some day Ill beat Algernon. Boy that would be something. So far Algernon looks like he mite be smart perminent.

Mar 25 (I dont have to write PROGRESS REPORT on top any more just when I hand it in once a week for Dr Nemur to read. I just have to put the date on. That saves time)

We had a lot of fun at the factery today. Joe Carp said hey look where Charlie had his operashun what did they do Charlie put some brains in. I was going to tell him but I remembered Dr Strauss said no. Then Frank Reilly said what did you do Charlie forget your key and open your door the hard way. That made me laff. Their really my friends and they like me.

Sometimes somebody will say hey look at Joe or Frank or George he really pulled a Charlie Gordon. I don't know why they say that but they always laff. This morning Amos Borg who is the 4 man at Donnegans used my name when he shouted at Ernie the office boy. Ernie lost a packige. He said Ernie for godsake what

are you trying to be a Charlie Gordon. I dont understand why he said that. I never lost any packiges.

Mar 28 Dr Strauss came to my room tonight to see why I dint come in like I was suppose to. I told him I dont like to race with Algernon any more. He said I dont have to for a while but I shud come in. He had a present for me only it wasnt a present but just for lend. I thot it was a little television but it wasnt. He said I got to turn it on when I go to sleep. I said your kidding why shud I turn it on when Im going to sleep. Who ever herd of a thing like that. But he said if I want to get smart I got to do what he says. I told him I dint think I was going to get smart and he put his hand on my sholder and said Charlie you dont know it yet but your getting smarter all the time. You wont notice for a while. I think he was just being nice to make me feel good because I dont look any smarter.

Oh yes I almost forgot. I asked him when I can go back to the class at Miss Kinnians school. He said I wont go their. He said that soon Miss Kinnian will come to the hospitil to start and teach me speshul. I was mad at her for not comming to see me when I got the operashun but I like her so maybe we will be frends again.

Mar 29 That crazy TV kept me up all night. How can I sleep with something yelling crazy things all night in my ears. And the nutty pictures. Wow. I dont know what it says when Im up so how am I going to know when Im sleeping.

Dr Strauss says its ok. He says my brains are lerning when I sleep and that will help me when Miss Kinnian starts my lessons in the hospitl (only I found out it isnt a hospitil its a labatory). I think its all crazy. If you can get smart when your sleeping why do people go to school. That thing I dont think will work. I use to watch the late show and the late late show on TV all the time and it never made me smart. Maybe you have to sleep while you watch it.

PROGRESS REPORT 9—April 3

Dr Strauss showed me how to keep the TV turned low so now I can sleep. I dont hear a thing. And I still dont understand what it says. A few times I play it over in the morning to find out what I lerned when I was sleeping and I dont think so. Miss Kinnian says Maybe its another langwidge or something. But most times it sounds american. It talks so fast faster then even Miss Gold who was my teacher in 6 grade and I remember she talked so fast I coudnt understand her.

I told Dr Strauss what good is it to get smart in my sleep. I want to be smart when Im awake. He says its the same thing and I have two minds. Theres the *subconscious* and the *conscious*[5] (thats how you spell it). And one dont tell the other one what its doing. They don't even talk to each other. Thats why I dream. And boy have I been having crazy dreams. Wow. Ever since that night TV. The late late late late late show.

I forgot to ask him if it was only me or if everybody had those two minds.

(I just looked up the word in the dictionary Dr Strauss gave me. The word is *subconscious. adj. Of the nature of mental operations yet not present in consciousness; as, subconscious conflict of desires.*) Theres more but I still dont know what it means. This isnt a very good dictionary for dumb people like me.

Anyway the headache is from the party. My frends from the factery Joe Carp and Frank Reilly invited me to go with them to Muggsys Saloon for some drinks. I dont like to drink but they said we will have lots of fun. I had a good time.

Joe Carp said I shoud show the girls how I

mop out the toilet in the factory and he got me a mop. I showed them and everyone laffed when I told that Mr Donnegan said I was the best janiter he ever had because I like my job and do it good and never come late or miss a day except for my operashun.

I said Miss Kinnian always said Charlie be proud of your job because you do it good.

Everybody laffed and we had a good time and they gave me lots of drinks and Joe said

5. The **subconscious** (sub·kän′shəs) is mental activity that takes place below the level of the **conscious** (kän′shəs), or full awareness.

LITERATURE AND PSYCHOLOGY

More to IQ Than Meets the "I"

Howard Gardner, professor of education at Harvard University, thinks the whole question of IQ is—well, the wrong question. According to Gardner's theory of "multiple intelligences," intelligence is just too complicated to be boiled down to the results of an IQ test.

Everyone has a number of different intelligences. Let's say you have a friend who loves to write poetry (linguistic intelligence), play soccer (kinesthetic intelligence), and draw pictures of superheroes (spatial intelligence). You, on the other hand, do well in science (logical-mathematical intelligence), play first trumpet in the school band (musical intelligence), and are always called on to resolve conflicts (interpersonal intelligence).

So far, Howard Gardner has identified eight intelligences. Now, doesn't that make you feel smarter already?

Charlie is a card when hes potted. I dont know what that means but everybody likes me and we have fun. I cant wait to be smart like my best frends Joe Carp and Frank Reilly.

I dont remember how the party was over but I think I went out to buy a newspaper and coffe for Joe and Frank and when I came back there was no one their. I looked for them all over till late. Then I dont remember so good but I think I got sleepy or sick. A nice cop brot me back home. Thats what my landlady Mrs Flynn says.

But I got a headache and a big lump on my head and black and blue all over. I think maybe I fell but Joe Carp says it was the cop they beat up drunks some times. I don't think so. Miss Kinnian says cops are to help people. Anyway I got a bad headache and Im sick and hurt all over. I dont think Ill drink anymore.

April 6 I beat Algernon! I dint even know I beat him until Burt the tester told me. Then the second time I lost because I got so exited I fell off the chair before I finished. But after that I beat him 8 more times. I must be getting smart to beat a smart mouse like Algernon. But I dont *feel* smarter.

I wanted to race Algernon some more but Burt said thats enough for one day. They let me hold him for a minit. Hes not so bad. Hes soft like a ball of cotton. He blinks and when he opens his eyes their black and pink on the eges.

I said can I feed him because I felt bad to beat him and I wanted to be nice and make frends. Burt said no Algernon is a very specshul mouse with an operashun like mine, and he was the first of all the animals to stay smart so long. He told me Algernon is so smart that every day he has to solve a test to get his food. Its a thing like a lock on a door that changes every time Algernon goes in to eat so he has to lern something new to get his food. That made me sad because if he couldnt lern he would be hungry.

I dont think its right to make you pass a test to eat. How woud Dr Nemur like it to have to pass a test every time he wants to eat. I think Ill be frends with Algernon.

April 9 Tonight after work Miss Kinnian was at the laboratory. She looked like she was glad to see me but scared. I told her dont worry Miss Kinnian Im not smart yet and she laffed. She said I have confidence in you Charlie the way you struggled so hard to read and right better than all the others. At werst you will have it for a littel wile and your doing somthing for sience.

We are reading a very hard book. I never read such a hard book before. Its called *Robinson Crusoe* about a man who gets merooned on a dessert Iland. Hes smart and figers out all kinds of things so he can have a house and food and hes a good swimmer. Only I feel sorry because hes all alone and has no frends. But I think their must be somebody else on the iland because theres a picture with his funny umbrella looking at footprints. I hope he gets a frend and not be lonely.

April 10 Miss Kinnian teaches me to spell better. She says look at a word and close your eyes and say it over and over until you remember. I have lots of truble with *through* that you say *threw* and *enough* and *tough* that you dont say *enew* and *tew.* You got to say *enuff* and *tuff.* Thats how I use to write it before I started to get smart. Im confused but Miss Kinnian says theres no reason in spelling.

Apr 14 Finished *Robinson Crusoe.* I want to find out more about what happens to him but Miss Kinnian says thats all there is. *Why*

Apr 15 Miss Kinnian says Im lerning fast. She read some of the Progress Reports and she looked at me kind of funny. She says Im a fine person and Ill show them all. I asked her why. She said never mind but I shoudnt feel bad if I find out that everybody isnt nice like I think. She said for a person who god gave so little to you done more then a lot of people with brains they never even used. I said all my frends are smart people but there good. They like me and they never did anything that wasnt nice. Then she got something in her eye and she had to run out to the ladys room.

Apr 16 Today, I lerned, the *comma,* this is a comma (,) a period, with a tail, Miss Kinnian, says its importent, because, it makes writing better, she said, sombeody, coud lose, a lot of money, if a comma, isnt, in the, right place, I dont have, any money, and I dont see, how a comma, keeps you from losing it,

But she says, everybody, uses commas, so Ill use, them too,

Apr 17 I used the comma wrong. Its punctuation. Miss Kinnian told me to look up long words in the dictionary to lern to spell them. I said whats the difference if you can read it anyway. She said its part of your education so now on Ill look up all the words Im not sure how to spell. It takes a long time to write that way but I think Im remembering. I only have to look up once and after that I get it right. Anyway thats how come I got the word *punctuation* right. (Its that way in the dictionary). Miss Kinnian says a period is punctuation too, and there are lots of other marks to lern. I told her I thot all the periods had to have tails but she said no.

You got to mix them up, she showed? me" how. to mix! them(up,. and now; I can! mix up all kinds" of punctuation, in! my writing? There, are lots! of rules? to lern; but Im gettin'g them in my head.

One thing I? like about, Dear Miss Kinnian: (thats the way it goes in a business letter if I ever go into business) is she, always gives me' a

Last night Joe Carp and Frank Reilly invited me to a party.

reason" when—I ask. She's a gen'ius! I wish! I cou'd be smart" like, her;

(Punctuation, is; fun!)

April 18 What a dope I am! I didn't even understand what she was talking about. I read the grammar book last night and it explanes the whole thing. Then I saw it was the same way as Miss Kinnian was trying to tell me, but I didn't get it. I got up in the middle of the night, and the whole thing straightened out in my mind.

Miss Kinnian said that the TV working in my sleep helped out. She said I reached a plateau. Thats like the flat top of a hill.

After I figgered out how punctuation worked, I read over all my old Progress Reports from the beginning. Boy, did I have crazy spelling and punctuation! I told Miss Kinnian I ought to go over the pages and fix all the mistakes but she said, "No, Charlie, Dr. Nemur wants them just as they are. That's why he let you keep them after they were photostated, to see your own progress. You're coming along fast, Charlie."

That made me feel good. After the lesson I went down and played with Algernon. We don't race anymore.

April 20 I feel sick inside. Not sick like for a doctor, but inside my chest it feels empty like getting punched and a heartburn at the same time.

I wasn't going to write about it, but I guess I got to, because it's important. Today was the first time I ever stayed home from work.

Last night Joe Carp and Frank Reilly invited me to a party. There were lots of girls and some men from the factory. I remembered how sick I got last time I drank too much, so I told Joe I didn't want anything to drink. He gave me a plain Coke instead. It tasted funny, but I thought it was just a bad taste in my mouth.

We had a lot of fun for a while. Joe said I should dance with Ellen and she would teach me the steps. I fell a few times and I couldn't

understand why because no one else was dancing besides Ellen and me. And all the time I was tripping because somebody's foot was always sticking out.

Then when I got up I saw the look on Joe's face and it gave me a funny feeling in my stomack. "He's a scream," one of the girls said. Everybody was laughing.

Frank said, "I ain't laughed so much since we sent him off for the newspaper that night at Muggsy's and ditched him."

"Look at him. His face is red."

"He's blushing. Charlie is blushing."

"Hey, Ellen, what'd you do to Charlie? I never saw him act like that before."

I didn't know what to do or where to turn. Everyone was looking at me and laughing and I felt naked. I wanted to hide myself. I ran out into the street and I threw up. Then I walked home. It's a funny thing I never knew that Joe and Frank and the others liked to have me around all the time to make fun of me.

Now I know what it means when they say "to pull a Charlie Gordon."

I'm ashamed.

PROGRESS REPORT 11

April 21 Still didn't go into the factory. I told Mrs. Flynn my landlady to call and tell Mr. Donnegan I was sick. Mrs. Flynn looks at me very funny lately like she's scared of me.

I think it's a good thing about finding out how everybody laughs at me. I thought about it a lot. It's because I'm so dumb and I don't even know when I'm doing something dumb. People think it's funny when a dumb person can't do things the same way they can.

Anyway, now I know I'm getting smarter every day. I know punctuation and I can spell good. I like to look up all the hard words in the dictionary and I remember them. I'm reading a lot now, and Miss Kinnian says I read very fast. Sometimes I even understand what I'm reading about, and it stays in my mind. There are times when I can close my eyes and think of a page and it all comes back like a picture.

Besides history, geography, and arithmetic, Miss Kinnian said I should start to learn a few foreign languages. Dr. Strauss gave me some more tapes to play while I sleep. I still don't understand how that conscious and unconscious mind works, but Dr. Strauss says not to worry yet. He asked me to promise that when I start learning college subjects next week I wouldn't read any books on psychology—that is, until he gives me permission.

I feel a lot better today, but I guess I'm still a little angry that all the time people were laughing and making fun of me because I wasn't so smart. When I become intelligent like Dr. Strauss says, with three times my I.Q. of 68, then maybe I'll be like everyone else and people will like me and be friendly.

I'm not sure what an I.Q. is. Dr. Nemur said it was something that measured how intelligent you were—like a scale in the drugstore weighs pounds. But Dr. Strauss had a big argument with him and said an I.Q. didn't weigh intelligence at all. He said an I.Q. showed how much intelligence you could get, like the numbers on the outside of a measuring cup. You still had to fill the cup up with stuff.

Then when I asked Burt, who gives me my intelligence tests and works with Algernon, he said that both of them were wrong (only I had to promise not to tell them he said so). Burt says that the I.Q. measures a lot of different things including some of the things you learned already, and it really isn't any good at all.

So I still don't know what I.Q. is except that mine is going to be over 200 soon. I didn't want to say anything, but I don't see how if they don't know *what* it is, or *where* it is—I don't see how they know *how much* of it you've got.

Dr. Nemur says I have to take a *Rorschach Test* tomorrow. I wonder what *that* is.

Introduction to Cantonese

B

April 22 I found out what a *Rorschach* is. It's the test I took before the operation—the one with the inkblots on the pieces of cardboard. The man who gave me the test was the same one.

I was scared to death of those inkblots. I knew he was going to ask me to find the pictures and I knew I wouldn't be able to. I was thinking to myself, if only there was some way of knowing what kind of pictures were hidden there. Maybe there weren't any pictures at all. Maybe it was just a trick to see if I was dumb enough to look for something that wasn't there. Just thinking about that made me sore at him.

"All right, Charlie," he said, "you've seen these cards before, remember?"

"Of course I remember."

The way I said it, he knew I was angry, and he looked surprised. "Yes, of course. Now I want you to look at this one. What might this be? What do you see on this card? People see all sorts of things in these inkblots. Tell me what it might be for you—what it makes you think of."

I was shocked. That wasn't what I had expected him to say at all. "You mean there are no pictures hidden in those inkblots?"

He frowned and took off his glasses. "What?"

"Pictures. Hidden in the inkblots. Last time you told me that everyone could see them and you wanted me to find them too."

He explained to me that the last time he had used almost the exact same words he was using now. I didn't believe it, and I still have the suspicion that he <u>misled</u> me at the time just for the fun of it. Unless—I don't know any more—could I have been *that* feebleminded?

We went through the cards slowly. One of them looked like a pair of bats tugging at something. Another one looked like two men fencing with swords. I imagined all sorts of things. I guess I got carried away. But I didn't trust him any more, and I kept turning them around and even looking on the back to see if there was anything there I was supposed to catch. While he was making his notes, I peeked out of the corner of my eye to read it. But it was all in code that looked like this:

WF + A DdF-Ad orig. WF-A SF + obj

The test still doesn't make sense to me. It seems to me that anyone could make up lies about things that they didn't really see. How could he know I wasn't making a fool of him by mentioning things that I didn't really imagine? Maybe I'll understand it when Dr. Strauss lets me read up on psychology.

April 25 I figured out a new way to line up the machines in the factory, and Mr. Donnegan says it will save him ten thousand dollars a year in labor and increased production. He gave me a twenty-five-dollar bonus.

I wanted to take Joe Carp and Frank Reilly out to lunch to celebrate, but Joe said he had to buy some things for his wife, and Frank said he was meeting his cousin for lunch. I guess it'll take a little time for them to get used to the changes in me. Everybody seems to be frightened of me. When I went over to Amos Borg and tapped him on the shoulder, he jumped up in the air.

People don't talk to me much anymore or kid around the way they used to. It makes the job kind of lonely.

April 27 I got up the nerve today to ask Miss Kinnian to have dinner with me tomorrow night to celebrate my bonus.

At first she wasn't sure it was right, but I asked Dr. Strauss and he said it was okay. Dr. Strauss and Dr. Nemur don't seem to be getting along so well. They're arguing all the time. This evening when I came in to ask Dr. Strauss about having dinner with Miss Kinnian, I heard them shouting. Dr. Nemur was saying that it was *his* experiment and *his* research, and Dr. Strauss was shouting back that he contributed just as much, because he found me through Miss Kinnian and he performed the operation.

WORDS TO OWN
misled (mis'led') v.: led to believe something wrong.

I don't understand why I never noticed how beautiful Miss Kinnian really is.

Dr. Strauss said that someday thousands of neurosurgeons might be using his technique all over the world.

Dr. Nemur wanted to publish the results of the experiment at the end of this month. Dr. Strauss wanted to wait a while longer to be sure. Dr. Strauss said that Dr. Nemur was more interested in the Chair of Psychology at Princeton than he was in the experiment. Dr. Nemur said that Dr. Strauss was nothing but an opportunist who was trying to ride to glory on *his* coattails.

When I left afterwards, I found myself trembling. I don't know why for sure, but it was as if I'd seen both men clearly for the first time. I remember hearing Burt say that Dr. Nemur had

a shrew of a wife who was pushing him all the time to get things published so that he could become famous. Burt said that the dream of her life was to have a big shot husband.

Was Dr. Strauss really trying to ride on his coattails?

April 28 I don't understand why I never noticed how beautiful Miss Kinnian really is. She has brown eyes and feathery brown hair that comes to the top of her neck. She's only thirty-four! I think from the beginning I had the feeling that she was an unreachable genius—and very, very old. Now, every time I see her she grows younger and more lovely.

We had dinner and a long talk. When she

said that I was coming along so fast that soon I'd be leaving her behind, I laughed.

"It's true, Charlie. You're already a better reader than I am. You can read a whole page at a glance while I can take in only a few lines at a time. And you remember every single thing you read. I'm lucky if I can recall the main thoughts and the general meaning."

"I don't feel intelligent. There are so many things I don't understand."

She took out a cigarette and I lit it for her. "You've got to be a *little* patient. You're accomplishing in days and weeks what it takes normal people to do in half a lifetime. That's what makes it so amazing. You're like a giant sponge now, soaking things in. Facts, figures, general knowledge. And soon you'll begin to connect them, too. You'll see how the different branches of learning are related. There are many levels, Charlie, like steps on a giant ladder that take you up higher and higher to see more and more of the world around you.

"I can see only a little bit of that, Charlie, and I won't go much higher than I am now, but you'll keep climbing up and up, and see more and more, and each step will open new worlds that you never even knew existed."
She frowned. "I hope . . . I just hope to God——"

"What?"

"Never mind, Charles. I just hope I wasn't wrong to advise you to go into this in the first place."

I laughed. "How could that be? It worked, didn't it? Even Algernon is still smart."

We sat there silently for a while and I knew what she was thinking about as she watched me toying with the chain of my rabbit's foot and my keys. I didn't want to think of that possibility any more than

elderly people want to think of death. I *knew* that this was only the beginning. I knew what she meant about levels because I'd seen some of them already. The thought of leaving her behind made me sad.

I'm in love with Miss Kinnian.

April 30 I've quit my job with Donnegan's Plastic Box Company. Mr. Donnegan insisted that it would be better for all concerned if I left. What did I do to make them hate me so?

The first I knew of it was when Mr. Donnegan showed me the petition. Eight hundred and forty names, everyone connected with the factory, except Fanny Girden. Scanning the list quickly, I saw at once that hers was the only missing name. All the rest demanded that I be fired.

Joe Carp and Frank Reilly wouldn't talk to me about it. No one else would either, except Fanny. She was one of the few people I'd known who set her mind to something and believed it no matter what the rest of the world proved, said, or did—and Fanny did not believe that I should have been fired. She had been against the petition on principle and despite the pressure and threats she'd held out.

"Which don't mean to say," she remarked, "that I don't think there's something mighty strange about you, Charlie. Them changes. I don't know. You used to be a good, dependable, ordinary man—not too bright maybe, but honest. Who knows what you done to yourself to get so smart all of a sudden. Like everybody around here's been saying, Charlie, it's not right."

"But how can you say that, Fanny? What's wrong with a man becoming intelligent and wanting to acquire knowledge and understanding of the world around him?"

She stared down at her work and I turned to leave. Without looking at me, she said: "It was evil when Eve listened to the snake and ate from the tree of knowledge. It was evil when she saw that she was naked. If not for that none of us would ever have to grow old and sick, and die."

Once again now I have the feeling of shame burning inside me. This intelligence has driven a wedge between me and all the people I once knew and loved. Before, they laughed at me and despised me for my ignorance and dullness; now, they hate me for my knowledge and understanding. What in God's name do they want of me?

They've driven me out of the factory. Now I'm more alone than ever before . . .

Mr. Donnegan showed me the petition.

April 30, 1965

Dear Mr. Donnegan:

We, the undersigned employees of Donnegan's ~~~~~~ request that Charlie Gordon

MAKING MEANINGS (PART 1)

First Thoughts

1. Reread your Quickwrite; then, add two or three sentences connecting what you wrote earlier with your thoughts about the story.

Shaping Interpretations

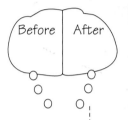

2. Draw a thought bubble and divide it in half, so that it looks like the one on the left. Fill the left side with words and symbols that describe or suggest what Charlie is like before the operation. On the right, fill in words and symbols that describe or suggest what Charlie is like as he becomes more intelligent.

3. Go back to Charlie's March 7 entry (pages 47–48). What **context clues** did you use to figure out what "crazy tests" Charlie is taking (such as the "*amazed*" with Algernon the rat)? Give some other examples of how you used context clues to figure out what Charlie is reporting.

4. Reread Fanny's comments about the changes in Charlie (page 60). How are Charlie's experiences similar to those of Adam and Eve? (Look especially at Charlie's entry for April 20. You may want to compare his description with the Biblical account, in Genesis 2:25–3:24.)

5. Charlie writes, "I think it's a good thing about finding out how everybody laughs at me" (page 55). Do you agree? Why or why not?

6. Early in the story, Dr. Strauss tells Dr. Nemur that Charlie's learning to read and write is as much of an achievement as their learning a difficult scientific theory without help would be (page 48). What does he mean? Challenge or defend his statement.

7. Does Charlie have "somebody to lean on"? Explain.

Extending the Text

8. Think about the last few lines in Part 1. Why do people often dislike anyone who is different from them? What do you think of such attitudes?

Challenging the Text

9. Why do almost all the workers in the factory sign the petition to have Charlie fired? Is their behavior believable? Explain.

Reading Check

a. What is the operation meant to do for Charlie?

b. Why does Dr. Strauss think Charlie would be a good subject for the experiment?

c. Who is Algernon? What happens when Charlie first races Algernon?

d. What are some signs that Charlie is changing after the operation?

Algernon and I were presented to the American Psychological Association...

2

May 15 Dr. Strauss is very angry at me for not having written any progress reports in two weeks. He's justified because the lab is now paying me a regular salary. I told him I was too busy thinking and reading. When I pointed out that writing was such a slow process that it made me impatient with my poor handwriting, he suggested that I learn to type. It's much easier to write now because I can type nearly seventy-five words a minute. Dr. Strauss continually reminds me of the need to speak and write simply so that people will be able to understand me.

I'll try to review all the things that happened to me during the last two weeks. Algernon and I were presented to the American Psychological Association sitting in convention with the World Psychological Association last Tuesday. We created quite a sensation. Dr. Nemur and Dr. Strauss were proud of us.

I suspect that Dr. Nemur, who is sixty—ten years older than Dr. Strauss—finds it necessary to see tangible results of his work. Undoubtedly the results of pressure by Mrs. Nemur.

Contrary to my earlier impressions of him, I realize that Dr. Nemur is not at all a genius. He has a very good mind, but it struggles under the specter of self-doubt. He wants people to take him for a genius. Therefore, it is important for him to feel that his work is accepted by the world. I believe that Dr. Nemur was afraid of further delay because he worried that someone else might make a discovery along these lines and take the credit from him.

Dr. Strauss on the other hand might be called a genius, although I feel that his areas of knowledge are too limited. He was educated in the tradition of narrow specialization; the broader aspects of background were neglected far more than necessary—even for a neurosurgeon.

I was shocked to learn that the only ancient languages he could read were Latin, Greek, and Hebrew, and that he knows almost nothing of mathematics beyond the elementary levels of the calculus of variations. When he admitted this to me, I found myself almost annoyed. It was as if he'd hidden this part of himself in order to deceive me, pretending—as do many people, I've discovered—to be what he is not. No one I've ever known is what he appears to be on the surface.

Dr. Nemur appears to be uncomfortable around me. Sometimes when I try to talk to him, he just looks at me strangely and turns away. I was angry at first when Dr. Strauss told me I was giving Dr. Nemur an inferiority complex. I thought he was mocking me and I'm oversensitive at being made fun of.

How was I to know that a highly respected psychoexperimentalist like Nemur was unacquainted with Hindustani and Chinese? It's absurd when you consider the work that is being done in India and China today in the very field of his study.

I asked Dr. Strauss how Nemur could refute Rahajamati's attack on his method and results if Nemur couldn't even read them in the first place. That strange look on Dr. Strauss's face can mean only one of two things. Either he doesn't want to tell Nemur what they're saying in India, or else—and this worries me—Dr. Strauss doesn't know either. I must be careful to speak and write clearly and simply so that people won't laugh.

May 18 I am very disturbed. I saw Miss Kinnian last night for the first time in over a week. I tried to avoid all discussions of intellectual concepts and to keep the conversation on a simple, everyday level, but she just stared at me blankly and asked me what I meant about

---

WORDS TO OWN

tangible (tan′jə·bəl) *adj.*: capable of being felt, observed, or understood.

refute (ri·fyo͞ot′) *v.*: prove wrong with evidence.

---

the mathematical variance equivalent in Dorbermann's Fifth Concerto.

When I tried to explain she stopped me and laughed. I guess I got angry, but I suspect I'm approaching her on the wrong level. No matter what I try to discuss with her, I am unable to communicate. I must review Vrostadt's equations on *Levels of Semantic Progression.* I find that I don't communicate with people much anymore. Thank God for books and music and things I can think about. I am alone in my apartment at Mrs. Flynn's boardinghouse most of the time and seldom speak to anyone.

May 20 I would not have noticed the new dishwasher, a boy of about sixteen, at the corner diner where I take my evening meals if not for the incident of the broken dishes.

They crashed to the floor, shattering and sending bits of white china under the tables. The boy stood there, dazed and frightened, holding the empty tray in his hand. The whistles and catcalls[1] from the customers (the cries of "Hey, there go the profits!" . . . "Mazel tov!"[2] . . . and "Well, *he* didn't work here very long . . ." which <u>invariably</u> seem to follow the breaking of glass or dishware in a public restaurant) all seemed to confuse him.

When the owner came to see what the excitement was about, the boy cowered as if he

1. **catcalls:** shouts and whistles made to express disapproval or ridicule, so called because people used to make noises like a cat's cry to show disapproval.
2. **Mazel tov** (mä′zəl tōv′): Yiddish expression meaning "Congratulations!"

WORDS TO OWN
invariably (in·ver′ē·ə·blē) *adv.:* always.

----

expected to be struck and threw up his arms as if to ward off the blow.

"All right! All right, you dope," shouted the owner, "don't just stand there! Get the broom and sweep that mess up. A broom . . . a broom, you idiot! It's in the kitchen. Sweep up all the pieces."

The boy saw that he was not going to be punished. His frightened expression disappeared and he smiled and hummed as he came back with the broom to sweep the floor. A few of the rowdier customers kept up the remarks, amusing themselves at his expense.

"Here, sonny, over here there's a nice piece behind you . . ."

"C'mon, do it again . . ."

"He's not so dumb. It's easier to break 'em than to wash 'em . . ."

As his vacant eyes moved across the crowd of amused onlookers, he slowly mirrored their smiles and finally broke into an uncertain grin at the joke which he obviously did not understand.

I felt sick inside as I looked at his dull, vacuous smile, the wide, bright eyes of a child, uncertain but eager to please. They were laughing at him because he was mentally retarded.

And I had been laughing at him too.

Suddenly, I was furious at myself and all those who were smirking at him. I jumped up and shouted, "Shut up! Leave him alone! It's not his fault he can't understand! He can't help what he is! But for God's sake . . . he's still a human being!"

The room grew silent. I cursed myself for losing control and creating a scene. I tried not to look at the boy as I paid my check and walked out without touching my food. I felt ashamed for both of us.

How strange it is that people of honest feelings and sensibility, who would not take advantage of a man born without arms or legs or eyes—how such people think nothing of abusing a man born with low intelligence. It infuri-

ated me to think that not too long ago I, like this boy, had foolishly played the clown.

And I had almost forgotten.

I'd hidden the picture of the old Charlie Gordon from myself because now that I was intelligent it was something that had to be pushed out of my mind. But today in looking at that boy, for the first time I saw what I had been. *I was just like him!*

Only a short time ago, I learned that people laughed at me. Now I can see that unknowingly I joined with them in laughing at myself. That hurts most of all.

I have often reread my progress reports and seen the illiteracy, the childish naiveté,[3] the mind of low intelligence peering from a dark room, through the keyhole, at the dazzling light outside. I see that even in my dullness I knew that I was inferior, and that other people had something I lacked—something denied me. In my mental blindness, I thought that it was somehow connected with the ability to read and write, and I was sure that if I could get those skills I would automatically have intelligence too.

Even a feeble-minded man wants to be like other men.

A child may not know how to feed itself, or what to eat, yet it knows of hunger.

This then is what I was like. I never knew. Even with my gift of intellectual awareness, I never really knew.

This day was good for me. Seeing the past more clearly, I have decided to use my knowledge and skills to work in the field of increasing human intelligence levels. Who is better equipped for this work? Who else has lived in both worlds? These are my people. Let me use my gift to do something for them.

Tomorrow, I will discuss with Dr. Strauss the manner in which I can work in this area. I may be able to help him work out the problems of

3. **naiveté** (nä·ēv·tā′): simplicity; foolish innocence.

widespread use of the technique which was used on me. I have several good ideas of my own.

There is so much that might be done with this technique. If I could be made into a genius, what about thousands of others like myself? What fantastic levels might be achieved by using this technique on normal people? On *geniuses*?

There are so many doors to open. I am impatient to begin.

PROGRESS REPORT 13

May 23 It happened today. Algernon bit me. I visited the lab to see him as I do occasionally, and when I took him out of his cage, he snapped at my hand. I put him back and watched him for a while. He was unusually disturbed and vicious.

May 24 Burt, who is in charge of the experimental animals, tells me that Algernon is changing. He is less cooperative, he refuses to run the maze any more; general motivation has decreased. And he hasn't been eating. Everyone is upset about what this may mean.

May 25 They've been feeding Algernon, who now refuses to work the shifting-lock problem. Everyone identifies me with Algernon. In a way we're both the first of our kind. They're all pretending that Algernon's behavior is not necessarily significant for me. But it's hard to hide the fact that some of the other animals who were used in this experiment are showing strange behavior.

Dr. Strauss and Dr. Nemur have asked me not to come to the lab anymore. I know what they're thinking but I can't accept it. I am going ahead with my plans to carry their research forward. With all due respect to both of these fine scientists, I am well aware of their limitations. If there is an answer, I'll have to find it out for myself. Suddenly, time has become very important to me.

May 29 I have been given a lab of my own and permission to go ahead with the research. I'm on to something. Working day and night. I've had a cot moved into the lab. Most of my writing time is spent on the notes which I keep in a separate folder, but from time to time I feel it necessary to put down my moods and my thoughts out of sheer habit.

I find the *calculus of intelligence* to be a fascinating study. Here is the place for the application of all the knowledge I have acquired. In a sense it's the problem I've been concerned with all my life.

May 31 Dr. Strauss thinks I'm working too hard. Dr. Nemur says I'm trying to cram a lifetime of research and thought into a few weeks. I know I should rest, but I'm driven on by something inside that won't let me stop. I've got to find the reason for the sharp regression in Algernon. I've got to know *if* and *when* it will happen to me.

June 4

> LETTER TO DR. STRAUSS *(copy)*
> Dear Dr. Strauss:
>
> Under separate cover I am sending you a copy of my report entitled, "The Algernon-Gordon Effect: A Study of Structure and Function of Increased Intelligence," which I would like to have you read and have published.
>
> As you see, my experiments are completed. I have included in my report all of my formulae, as well as mathematical analy-

---

WORDS TO OWN

regression (ri·gresh′ən) *n.:* return to an earlier or less advanced condition.

---

sis in the appendix. Of course, these should be <u>verified</u>.

Because of its importance to both you and Dr. Nemur (and need I say to myself, too?) I have checked and rechecked my results a dozen times in the hope of finding an error. I am sorry to say the results must stand. Yet for the sake of science, I am grateful for the little bit that I here add to the knowledge of the function of the human mind and of the laws governing the artificial increase of human intelligence.

I recall your once saying to me that an experimental *failure* or the *disproving* of a theory was as important to the advancement of learning as a success would be. I know now that this is true. I am sorry, however, that my own contribution to the field must rest upon the ashes of the work of two men I regard so highly.

Yours truly,
Charles Gordon

encl.: rept

WORDS TO OWN
verified (ver′ə·fīd′) v.: checked or tested for correctness; confirmed.

The Algernon-Gordon Effect: A Study of Structure and Function of Increased Intelligence

I have been given a lab of my own and permission to go ahead with the research.

June 5 I must not become emotional. The facts and the results of my experiments are clear, and the more sensational aspects of my own rapid climb cannot <u>obscure</u> the fact that the tripling of intelligence by the surgical technique developed by Drs. Strauss and Nemur must be viewed as having little or no practical applicability (at the present time) to the increase of human intelligence.

As I review the records and data on Algernon, I see that although he is still in his physical infancy, he has regressed mentally. Motor activity is impaired; there is a general reduction of glandular activity; there is an accelerated loss of coordination.

There are also strong indications of progressive amnesia.

As will be seen by my report, these and other physical and mental <u>deterioration</u> syndromes can be predicted with statistically significant results by the application of my formula.

The surgical stimulus to which we were both subjected has resulted in an intensification and acceleration of all mental processes. The unforeseen development, which I have taken the liberty of calling the *Algernon-Gordon Effect,* is the logical extension of the entire intelligence speed-up. The <u>hypothesis</u> here proven may be described simply in the

following terms: Artificially increased intelligence deteriorates at a rate of time directly proportional to the quantity of the increase.

I feel that this, in itself, is an important discovery.

As long as I am able to write, I will continue to record my thoughts in these progress reports. It is one of my few pleasures. However, by all indications, my own mental deterioration will be very rapid.

I have already begun to notice signs of emotional instability and forgetfulness, the first symptoms of the burnout.

June 10 Deterioration progressing. I have become absent-minded. Algernon died two days ago. Dissection shows my predictions were right. His brain had decreased in weight and there was a general smoothing out of cerebral convolutions as well as a deepening and broadening of brain fissures.[4]

I guess the same thing is or will soon be happening to me. Now that it's definite, I don't want it to happen.

I put Algernon's body in a cheese box and buried him in the back yard. I cried.

June 15 Dr. Strauss came to see me again. I wouldn't open the door and I told him to go away. I want to be left to myself. I have become touchy and irritable. I feel the darkness closing in. It's hard to throw off thoughts of suicide. I keep telling myself how important this <u>intro-spective</u> journal will be.

---

4. **brain fissures** (fish'ərz): grooves in the surface of the brain.

- -

WORDS TO OWN

obscure (əb·skyoor′) *v.:* hide.
deterioration (dē·tir′ē·ə·rā′shən) *n.* used as *adj.:* worsening; decline.
hypothesis (hī·päth′ə·sis) *n.:* explanation or theory to be proved.
introspective (in′trō·spek′tiv) *adj.:* looking inward; observing one's own thoughts and feelings.

- -

It's a strange sensation to pick up a book that you've read and enjoyed just a few months ago and discover that you don't remember it. I remembered how great I thought John Milton was, but when I picked up *Paradise Lost* I couldn't understand it at all. I got so angry I threw the book across the room.

I've got to try to hold on to some of it. Some of the things I've learned. Oh, God, please don't take it all away.

June 19 Sometimes, at night, I go out for a walk. Last night I couldn't remember where I lived. A policeman took me home. I have the strange feeling that this has all happened to me before—a long time ago. I keep telling myself I'm the only person in the world who can describe what's happening to me.

June 21 Why can't I remember? I've got to fight. I lie in bed for days and I don't know who or where I am. Then it all comes back to me in a flash. Fugues of amnesia.[5] Symptoms of senility—second childhood. I can watch them coming on. It's so cruelly logical. I learned so much and so fast. Now my mind is deteriorating rapidly. I won't let it happen. I'll fight it. I can't help thinking of the boy in the restaurant, the blank expression, the silly smile, the people laughing at him. No—please—not that again . . .

June 22 I'm forgetting things that I learned recently. It seems to be following the classic pattern—the last things learned are the first things forgotten. Or is that the pattern? I'd better look it up again. . . .

I re-read my paper on the *Algernon-Gordon Effect* and I get the strange feeling that it was written by someone else. There are parts I don't even understand.

---

5. **fugues** (fyo͞ogz) **of amnesia** (am·nē′zhə): temporary states of disturbed consciousness. A person who experiences fugues has no memory of them afterward.

Motor activity impaired. I keep tripping over things, and it becomes increasingly difficult to type.

June 23 I've given up using the typewriter completely. My coordination is bad. I feel that I'm moving slower and slower. Had a terrible shock today. I picked up a copy of an article I used in my research, Krueger's *Uber psychische Ganzheit,* to see if it would help me understand what I had done. First I thought there was something wrong with my eyes. Then I realized I could no longer read German. I tested myself in other languages. All gone.

June 30 A week since I dared to write again. It's slipping away like sand through my fingers. Most of the books I have are too hard for me now. I get angry with them because I know that I read and understood them just a few weeks ago.

I keep telling myself I must keep writing these reports so that somebody will know what is happening to me. But it gets harder to form the words and remember spellings. I have to look up even simple words in the dictionary now and it makes me impatient with myself.

Dr. Strauss comes around almost every day, but I told him I wouldn't see or speak to anybody. He feels guilty. They all do. But I don't blame anyone. I knew what might happen. But how it hurts.

July 7 I don't know where the week went. Todays Sunday I know becuase I can see through my window people going to church. I think I stayed in bed all week but I remember Mrs. Flynn bringing food to me a few times. I keep saying over and over Ive got to do something but then I forget or maybe its just easier not to do what I say Im going to do.

I think of my mother and father a lot these days. I found a picture of them with me taken at a beach. My father has a big ball under his arm and my mother is holding me by the hand.

I dont remember them the way they are in the picture. All I remember is my father drunk most of the time and arguing with mom about money.

He never shaved much and he used to scratch my face when he hugged me. My mother said he died but Cousin Miltie said he heard his mom and dad say that my father ran away with another woman. When I asked my mother she slapped my face and said my father was dead. I dont think I ever found out which was true but I don't care much. (He said he was going to take me to see cows on a farm once but he never did. He never kept his promises . . .)

July 10 My landlady Mrs Flynn is very worried about me. She says the way I lay around all day and dont do anything I remind her of her son before she threw him out of the house. She said she doesn't like loafers. If Im sick its one thing, but if Im a loafer thats another thing and she wont have it. I told her I think Im sick.

I try to read a little bit every day, mostly stories, but sometimes I have to read the same thing over and over again because I dont know what it means. And its hard to write. I know I should look up all the words in the dictionary but its so hard and Im so tired all the time.

Then I got the idea that I would only use the easy words instead of the long hard ones. That saves time. I put flowers on Algernons grave about once a week. Mrs Flynn thinks Im crazy to put flowers on a mouses grave but I told her that Algernon was special.

July 14 Its sunday again. I dont have anything to do to keep me busy now because my television set is broke and I dont have any money to get it fixed. (I think I lost this months check from the lab. I dont remember)

I get awful headaches and asperin doesnt help me much. Mrs Flynn knows Im really sick and she feels very sorry for me. Shes a wonderful woman whenever someone is sick.

July 22 Mrs Flynn called a strange doctor to see me. She was afraid I was going to die. I told the doctor I wasnt too sick and that I only forget sometimes. He asked me did I have any friends or relatives and I said no I dont have any. I told him I had a friend called Algernon once but he was a mouse and we used to run races together. He looked at me kind of funny like he thought I was crazy.

He smiled when I told him I used to be a genius. He talked to me like I was a baby and he winked at Mrs Flynn. I got mad and chased him out because he was making fun of me the way they all used to.

July 24 I have no more money and Mrs Flynn says I got to go to work somewhere and pay the rent because I havent paid for over two months. I dont know any work but the job I used to have at Donnegans Plastic Box Company. I dont want to go back there because they all knew me when I was smart and maybe theyll laugh at me. But I don't know what else to do to get money.

July 25 I was looking at some of my old progress reports and its very funny but I cant read what I wrote. I can make out some of the words but they dont make sense.

Miss Kinnian came to the door but I said go away I dont want to see you. She cried and I cried too but I wouldnt let her in because I didn't want her to laugh at me. I told her I didn't like her any more. I told her I didnt want to be smart any more. Thats not true. I still love her and I still want to be smart but I had to say that so shed go away. She gave Mrs Flynn money to pay the rent. I dont want that. I got to get a job.

Please . . . please let me not forget how to read and write . . .

July 27 Mr Donnegan was very nice when I came back and asked him for my old job of janitor. First he was very suspicious but I told him

Mr. Donnegan was very nice when I came back and asked him for my old job of janitor.

what happened to me then he looked very sad and put his hand on my shoulder and said Charlie Gordon you got guts.

Everybody looked at me when I came downstairs and started working in the toilet sweeping it out like I used to. I told myself Charlie if they make fun of you dont get sore because you remember their not so smart as you once thot they were. And besides they were once your friends and if they laughed at you that doesnt mean anything because they liked you too.

One of the new men who came to work there after I went away made a nasty crack he said hey Charlie I hear your a very smart fella a real quiz kid. Say something intelligent. I felt bad but Joe Carp came over and grabbed him by the shirt and said leave him alone you lousy cracker or Ill break your neck. I didn't expect Joe to take my part so I guess hes really my friend.

Later Frank Reilly came over and said Charlie if anybody bothers you or trys to take advantage you call me or Joe and we will set em straight. I said thanks Frank and I got choked up so I had to turn around and go into the supply room so he wouldnt see me cry. Its good to have friends.

July 28 I did a dumb thing today I forgot I wasnt in Miss Kinnians class at the adult center any more like I use to be. I went in and sat down in my old seat in the back of the room and she looked at me funny and she said Charles. I dint remember she ever called me that before only Charlie so I said hello Miss Kinnian Im redy for my lesin today only I lost my reader that we was using. She startid to cry and run out of the room and everybody looked at me and I saw they wasnt the same pepul who used to be in my class.

Then all of a suddin I rememberd some things about the operashun and me getting smart and I said holy smoke I reely pulled a Charlie Gordon that time. I went away before she come back to the room.

Thats why Im going away from New York for good. I dont want to do nothing like that agen. I dont want Miss Kinnian to feel sorry for me. Evry body feels sorry at the factery and I dont want that eather so Im going someplace where nobody knows that Charlie Gordon was once a genus and now he cant even reed a book or rite good.

Im taking a cuple of books along and even if I cant reed them Ill practise hard and maybe I wont forget every thing I lerned. If I try reel hard maybe Ill be a littel bit smarter then I was before the operashun. I got my rabits foot and my luky penny and maybe they will help me.

If you ever reed this Miss Kinnian dont be sorry for me Im glad I got a second chanse to be smart becaus I lerned a lot of things that I never even new were in this world and Im grateful that I saw it all for a littel bit. I dont know why Im dumb agen or what I did wrong maybe its becaus I dint try hard enuff. But if I try and practis very hard maybe Ill get a littl smarter and know what all the words are. I remember a littel bit how nice I had a feeling with the blue book that has the torn cover when I red it. Thats why Im gonna keep trying to get smart so I can have that feeling agen. Its a good feeling to know things and be smart. I wish I had it rite now if I did I would sit down and reed all the time. Anyway I bet Im the first dumb person in the world who ever found out somthing importent for sience. I remember I did somthing but I dont remember what. So I gess its like I did it for all the dumb pepul like me.

Good-by Miss Kinnian and Dr Strauss and evreybody. And P.S. please tell Dr Nemur not to be such a grouch when pepul laff at him and he woud have more frends. Its easy to make frends if you let pepul laff at you. Im going to have lots of frends where I go.

P.P.S. Please if you get a chanse put some flowrs on Algernons grave in the bak yard . . .

MEET THE WRITER

Fascinated by the Human Mind

Daniel Keyes (1927–   ) says that he is "fascinated by the complexities of the human mind." Many people share his interest, as the enormous popularity of "Flowers for Algernon" shows. The story won the 1959 Hugo Award, given by the Science Fiction Writers of America, and it has been widely translated. Keyes expanded it into a novel, which won another science fiction prize, the Nebula Award, in 1966. The story was also made into a movie, *Charly*, a television play, *The Two Worlds of Charlie Gordon*, and even a Broadway musical, *Charlie and Algernon*.

Daniel Keyes was born in Brooklyn, New York. He has worked as an English teacher, a merchant seaman, an editor, and a fashion photographer.

MAKING MEANINGS (PART 2)

First Thoughts

1. What do you think becomes of Charlie after the story ends? Why?

Shaping Interpretations

2. Why is Algernon important to Charlie?

3. What does Charlie want most
   - when we first meet him?
   - after he becomes intelligent?
   - after his intelligence declines?

   Fill in a chart like the one below to show how Charlie's goals change.

	March 5– April 18	April 20– June 15	June 19– July 28
What Charlie wants			

Reading Check

a. At the beginning of Part 2, what **conflicts** is Charlie having with the doctors? with himself?

b. How does Charlie react when the boy in the diner drops the dishes?

c. What does Charlie's research reveal about the results of the experiment?

d. List several signs of Charlie's mental decline.

e. At the end of the story, why does Charlie decide to leave New York?

4. In the April 9 entry in Part 1 (page 53), Charlie's comments while reading *Robinson Crusoe* **foreshadow,** or hint at, how he will later find himself abandoned and alone. (For more about foreshadowing, see page 170 and the Handbook of Literary Terms.) What other examples of foreshadowing do you find in "Flowers for Algernon"? How did that foreshadowing make you feel?

5. Would Charlie's situation be better or worse if he had not had the operation? Support your opinion with evidence from the story.

Connecting with the Text

6. At the end of the story, Charlie writes, "Its easy to make frends if you let pepul laff at you." Do you agree or disagree with this statement? Explain.

7. Describe your feelings about "human engineering"—for example, using science to change a person's intelligence or personality.

Challenging the Text

8. Comment on whether you find the story believable. (Do you think it shows how people really behave toward those who are mentally challenged? Do you think people will be able to increase intelligence through scientific means someday?)

CHOICES: Building Your Portfolio

Writer's Notebook

1. Collecting Ideas for an Autobiographical Incident

Freewrite about a time when you

- suddenly understood something that had been too hard for you (as Charlie does on page 55)
- were rejected by or excluded from a group
- made fun of someone, or defended someone whom other people were making fun of
- outgrew a friend or felt that you couldn't communicate with him or her anymore

the time I stuck up for the kid nobody liked—felt proud of myself, but scared—what if everyone started picking on me, too?

Creative Writing

2. Dear Diary . . .

This story is made up of Charlie's progress reports, which are like a diary. Pick another character from the story, and write a diary entry for him or her corresponding to one of Charlie's reports. For example, what might Miss Kinnian have written the night she and Charlie had dinner? What might Frank have written the day Charlie returned to work at the factory?

Use the first-person pronoun *I* to write from your character's **point of view.**

Research/Science

3. What Is Intelligence?

Make a list of questions about intelligence and intelligence tests. Conduct research to find the answers, using printed materials, databases, the Internet, and other sources. Then, if possible, arrange to interview an expert—such as a psychiatrist or a guidance counselor—in person, by phone, or by electronic mail. Prepare a list of questions you couldn't answer using other resources, and add any new questions that your research has raised.

Present your findings to the class in a creative format (for example, as a TV news report or a poster).

Learning for Life

4. Position Wanted

With a potential employer as your audience, write one of these items to help Charlie get a new job:

- a character reference from Mrs. Flynn
- a recommendation letter from Mr. Donnegan or Miss Kinnian
- a medical report from Dr. Strauss explaining Charlie's condition and capabilities

GRAMMAR LINK

Dialogue in Your Writing

Language Handbook HELP

See Quotation Marks, pages 805–807.

Technology HELP

See Language Workshop CD-ROM. *Key word entry: quotation marks.*

1. Put quotation marks around *direct* quotations of words spoken aloud.

   EXAMPLES   The man explained, "People see all sorts of things in these inkblots." [Sentence contains a direct quotation.]

   The man explained that people see all sorts of things in these inkblots. [Sentence does not contain a direct quotation.]

2. Begin a quoted remark with a capital letter.

   EXAMPLE   Charlie said, "**W**hy didn't I realize how beautiful Miss Kinnian was?"

3. Use a comma, a question mark, or an exclamation point (but not a period) to set off a quotation from the rest of the sentence.

   EXAMPLE   "What is the matter with Algernon?" Charlie asked.
   "He won't run the maze anymore," Burt responded sadly.

4. Begin a new paragraph whenever the speaker changes. (See the example just above.)

> **Try It Out**
>
> Find examples from the story to illustrate each of the four rules. Then, applying the rules, write four lines of dialogue that you could use in a piece of writing you are working on.

VOCABULARY   HOW TO OWN A WORD

WORD BANK

misled
tangible
refute
invariably
regression
verified
obscure
deterioration
hypothesis
introspective

Word Analogies: Perfect Pairs

An **analogy** is a word puzzle with two pairs of words that have the same relationship. They might have the same meaning or an opposite meaning, or they might share some other relationship, such as cause and effect or whole to part. For example, in the analogy "*Start* is to *stop* as *hate* is to _____," *start* and *stop* are opposites, so the word that will show the same relationship in the second pair is *love,* the opposite of *hate.* Complete each analogy below with a word from the Word Bank.

1. *Open* is to *close* as *reveal* is to _____.
2. *Defend* is to *protect* as *disprove* is to _____.
3. *Asked* is to *inquired* as *confirmed* is to _____.
4. *Forward* is to *progression* as *backward* is to _____.
5. *Sometimes* is to *occasionally* as *always* is to _____.
6. *Likeness* is to *similarity* as *theory* is to _____.
7. *Noisy* is to *quiet* as *outgoing* is to _____.
8. *See* is to *visible* as *touch* is to _____.
9. *Pretended* is to *imagined* as *deceived* is to _____.
10. *Ugly* is to *beautiful* as _____ is to *improvement.*

If I Can Stop One Heart from Breaking

Emily Dickinson

If I can stop one heart from breaking
I shall not live in vain
If I can ease one life the aching
Or cool one pain

Or help one fainting robin
Unto his nest again
I shall not live in vain.

MEET THE WRITER

A Hidden Talent

Although **Emily Dickinson** (1830–1886) is one of the most respected American poets today, she was almost completely unknown during her lifetime. Dickinson led an extremely private, quiet life in her family home in Amherst, Massachusetts. After she died, her sister, Lavinia, discovered the almost seventeen hundred poems Dickinson had written on envelopes and bits of newspaper and gathered into handmade booklets.

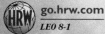

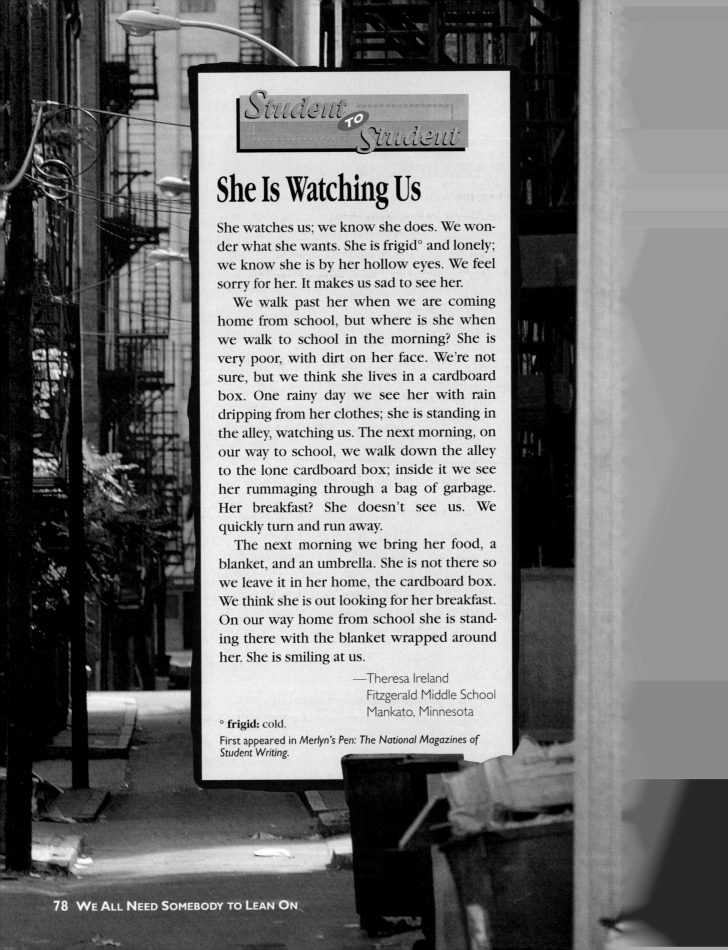

She Is Watching Us

She watches us; we know she does. We wonder what she wants. She is frigid° and lonely; we know she is by her hollow eyes. We feel sorry for her. It makes us sad to see her.

We walk past her when we are coming home from school, but where is she when we walk to school in the morning? She is very poor, with dirt on her face. We're not sure, but we think she lives in a cardboard box. One rainy day we see her with rain dripping from her clothes; she is standing in the alley, watching us. The next morning, on our way to school, we walk down the alley to the lone cardboard box; inside it we see her rummaging through a bag of garbage. Her breakfast? She doesn't see us. We quickly turn and run away.

The next morning we bring her food, a blanket, and an umbrella. She is not there so we leave it in her home, the cardboard box. We think she is out looking for her breakfast. On our way home from school she is standing there with the blanket wrapped around her. She is smiling at us.

—Theresa Ireland
Fitzgerald Middle School
Mankato, Minnesota

° **frigid:** cold.

First appeared in *Merlyn's Pen: The National Magazines of Student Writing.*

READ ON

Unlikely Acquaintances

You know her: the new kid in class no one wants for a friend. In *The Friends* by Rosa Guy (Bantam), the new girl is Phyllisia Cathy, from the West Indies. The only person who will befriend her is Edith, a Harlem-born girl trying to keep her family together despite the hardships of poverty.

Forbidden Friendship

It's World War II and everyone knows Nazis are the enemy—so why does Patty Bergen, a Jewish girl in Arkansas, take a risk by hiding a young German prisoner of war from the FBI? In *Summer of My German Soldier* by Bette Greene (Dell), Patty learns compassion from a stranger.

With a Little Help from Our Friends

It's important to have friends to lean on—especially if you don't have a family. This is painfully true for Buddy, street kid by day, mentor to other inner-city orphans by night, in Virginia Hamilton's *The Planet of Junior Brown* (Aladdin Books).

Other Picks

- Elizabeth Borton de Treviño, *I, Juan de Pareja* (Farrar, Straus & Giroux). A historical novel about the friendship between an enslaved artist and the great seventeenth-century Spanish painter Diego Velázquez

- Katherine Paterson, *Bridge to Terabithia* (Harper Trophy). A classic novel of friendship. Published in Spanish as *Un puente hasta Terabithia* (Alfaguara)

Speaking and Listening Workshop

INTERPERSONAL COMMUNICATION

It's Not Just What You Say, It's How You Say It

Think back to when you first met your best friend. What do you remember most clearly? What usually makes the strongest impression at first is **body language**—looks, clothing, posture, gestures, and facial expressions.

Being Clear: Avoiding Mixed Signals

"Pleased to meet you," Duane mumbles, jamming his fists into his pockets and staring at his feet.

Are you convinced that he means what he says? Probably not. We interpret both the **verbal** and **nonverbal** parts of a speaker's message. If our words send one message but our body language sends another, people will be less likely to believe what we say.

Being Confident: Assertive Communication

People who communicate clearly and confidently show that they like other people and expect other people to like them, too. Frowning and looking away may just mean you're shy—but your listener may think it means you don't like him or her.

Confident speakers *look* like this:

- They stand or sit up straight, with their shoulders back and their heads up.
- They look at their listeners frequently. (If you're not comfortable making eye contact, try looking at the bridge of your listener's nose—the person won't be able to tell the difference.)

Confident speakers *sound* like this:

- They make statements that sound like statements, not questions. When you ask a question, your voice rises at the end of the sentence. When you make a statement, your voice falls. A

<table><tr><td>

Try It Out

Form a group with two or three classmates. Using *only* **body language** (movements, gestures, facial expressions, and posture), convey a feeling to your group. Make your movements and expressions obvious and exaggerated—try to help the group identify the emotion as quickly as possible. Some ideas:

- anger
- boredom
- joy
- surprise
- shyness
- confusion
- embarrassment
- fear
- exhaustion

</td></tr></table>

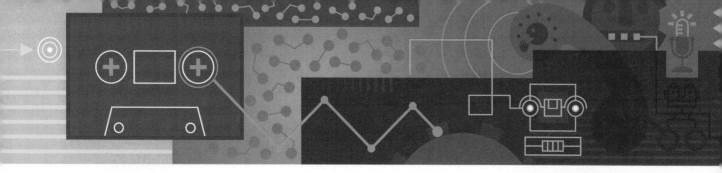

statement that sounds like a question is unclear and shows a lack of confidence.

- They avoid "filler" words and sounds. Listen to any conversation, and you'll probably hear these common fillers:

like	kind of	maybe	uh
you know	sort of	just	um

Instead of using your favorite filler, try pausing. You'll sound more thoughtful and sure of yourself.

Active Listening

Try this with a classmate: Take a few minutes to describe your favorite activity or something that happened to you. Your listener should give *no feedback:* no nodding, shaking the head, changes in facial expression, or speaking. Then, switch roles, and repeat. When you and your partner have finished, discuss how it felt not to give or receive any feedback.

Most people find it difficult to talk to an unresponsive listener. They assume that someone who is not giving feedback is not interested in listening to them. As an active listener, you can give positive feedback by looking and sounding interested.

- Look frequently at the person who is speaking.

- Smile and nod when appropriate.

- Lean slightly toward the speaker.

- Let the speaker know that you're following by using such expressions as "Yes," "I know," "Right," and "I see."

- Ask questions or share similar experiences of your own.

Try the listening exercise with your partner again. This time, give positive feedback as you listen. Discuss the difference between the feedback and no-feedback rounds. How did your partner's active listening make you feel as a speaker? Did active listening help you "hear" more of your partner's message?

Peanuts reprinted by permission of UFS, Inc.

Technology HELP

See Writer's Workshop 1 CD-ROM. *Assignment: Autobiographical Incident.*

ASSIGNMENT

Write a narrative describing an experience you have had.

AIM

To express yourself; to inform.

AUDIENCE

Your teacher, classmates, family, and friends; other people who were involved in the incident.

A play by Paul Zindel, Let Me Hear You Whisper, *appears on page 297.*

NARRATIVE WRITING

AUTOBIOGRAPHICAL INCIDENT

Most of us love to tell about ourselves—our experiences, our feelings and memories, the details of our lives. When you write an **autobiographical incident** (also called a personal narrative), you'll recount an important experience you've had and describe how you felt about it.

Professional Model

Nonno Frankie and Nonno Mamie had made the best meal I had ever seen or eaten on earth. Mom, Betty, me, and the twins sat around the big kitchen table while Connie and her mother and father put a breathtaking Sicilian gourmet feast before us. After the eel appetizer came large hot plates of spaghetti with shimmering lakes of tomato sauce ladled out from a ten-gallon pot bubbling on top of the stove. Nonno Frankie ran around with a big slab of Parmesan cheese, rubbing it like crazy against a metal-toothed rack. I had never seen fresh-grated cheese before.

"Ho! Ho! Ho! What's a ghost's favorite food?" he quizzed.

None of us knew.

"Spookghetti!" he howled. *"Spookghetti!"*

—Paul Zindel, from *The Pigman and Me*

First line grabs our attention.

Background information—setting and people—is provided.

Detailed description of the food appeals to our senses of taste and smell and makes us feel as if we were there.

Writer tells us what he was thinking.

Dialogue brings the experience to life and reveals character.

Prewriting

1. Writer's Notebook

Go back to your Writer's Notebook entries for this collection. Would you like to write further about an incident you described in one of these entries? If not, freewrite from one or more of the prompts that follow or on another topic of your choice.

2. Freewriting

a. Write freely for two minutes about one or two of the topics listed below. Write without stopping.

chores • standing up for yourself • confidence • loss • showing off • surprises • competition • peer pressure • waiting • tense moments • making new friends • friendly visits • a time to talk • first love

b. Finish one of these starters in as many ways as you can:

- I get upset just thinking about the time . . .
- I really learned something when . . .
- The best thing that ever happened to me was . . .

3. Choosing a Topic

Your next step is to choose one of these incidents as your topic. See the box on the right for some help in choosing.

4. What Does This Incident Mean to Me?

You chose your incident because it had a special meaning for you. If your writing doesn't make the significance of the incident clear, your reader will say, "So what?"

Explain what the incident means to you in a sentence or two—for example, *I disappointed myself by not being a hero when my cousin was in trouble.* As you draft, keep looking back at this statement to see whether what you've written is in line with it. If not, either rewrite your draft or rethink your statement.

Choosing a Topic

Ask yourself these questions as you think about which incident you want to write about:

- Does my mind keep going back to one particular incident?
- Does one of my freewrites suggest a conflict or a surprise?
- Do any of the incidents reveal something special about my personality?
- Am I willing to share any of these incidents with an audience?

The Good and the Bad

Few experiences are either all good or all bad; we often have mixed feelings. Your readers will get a more complete picture of what really happened to you if you **compare and contrast** both the good and the bad—the positive and the negative things—about your incident.

Drafting

A first draft is a discovery piece, an experiment to find out what you have to say about your topic.

Take a blank sheet of paper, and begin to tell your story. What happened? Where were you? Who was involved? Get your thoughts down as quickly as you can.

Evaluating and Revising

1. Elaborating with Description

Look over your first draft. You have your basic narrative—the people, places, and events that made up the incident—on paper. Now you're ready to fill in the details that will make your narrative come alive.

a. Reconstruct the event in your imagination. What were you thinking at the time? Do you recall what people said or movements, gestures, postures, or expressions (your own or others')? Ask a friend to record your thoughts in *your* Writer's Notebook as you think aloud, or take a break every few minutes to jot down your recollections yourself.

If possible, also use these strategies:

b. Return to the spot where the incident took place. Bring along your Writer's Notebook to record details. If just being there doesn't bring details to mind, try jogging your memory by acting out the scene.

c. Talk to people who were directly involved in the incident or whom you told about it. Record *their* memories. You may even be able to capture bits of remembered dialogue.

d. Gather objects that remind you of the incident—souvenirs, photographs, letters, diaries. What memories or feelings do they trigger? Write down anything you remember.

Sift through the material you have gathered, and decide what you can use in your second draft. Remember, it is easier to write out of abundance than out of poverty. You can always weed out unnecessary details.

2. Writing Your Second Draft

The excerpts on pages 85–86 are from the first and second drafts of an autobiographical incident.

Original title: Round and Round

Redraft title: Horsing Around

Original introduction:

As usual, every summer I take a trip to New Jersey to visit my cousins and grandmother. These trips are usually restful and not particularly exciting, but one summer it took a startling turn.

I was horseback riding with my cousin Alaina when it all began. We were to take the horses out and ride.

Redraft introduction:

"Help! Help!" Her cries pulled at my already flustered heart. I knew she was in danger, and I had to help!

Attention-grabbing opener.

I was at my grandmother's house in New Jersey, where I go almost every summer to visit my cousins and grandmother. These trips are usually restful and not particularly exciting, but this summer my rest and relaxation took a startling turn.

Background information.

Original conclusion:

Finally, after what seemed like ages, the horse slowed, probably from pure exhaustion. Slowly, shakily, Alaina climbed down off the back of the horse.

"W-why didn't you help me?" she weakly inquired as she checked her body for any visible damage. Finding none, she looked at me for an answer.

My reply was more regret than I had realized. "I couldn't," I stuttered.

(continued on next page)

Framework for an Autobiographical Incident

What the incident means to me: _____

Introduction (in the words you'll actually use):

_____

Order of events:

1. _____
2. _____
3. _____
4. _____

Conclusion (in the words you'll actually use, if possible):

_____

■ *Evaluation Criteria*

A good autobiographical incident

1. *focuses on a single incident*

2. *is usually narrated in chronological order*

3. *includes enough background information to let the reader understand the story*

4. *includes sensory details that make the people, places, and events described seem real*

5. *uses dialogue to reveal character*

6. *conveys what the incident means to the writer*

Sentence Workshop
H E L P

Sentence fragments: page 87.

Language/Grammar Link
H E L P

Common proofreading problems: pages 14, 27, 40, and 76.

Proofreading Tip

If you're working on a computer, use the spelling checker to catch spelling mistakes. It won't catch any words that are spelled correctly but used in the wrong way, however (see the Language / Grammar Links in this collection). Reread your final draft carefully.

Communications Handbook
H E L P

See Proofreaders' Marks.

Student Model (continued)

Redraft conclusion:

That night I sat in bed wide awake, even though I had long since been sent to bed. I replayed in my mind the day's course. I slowly played a scene where I was the hero. Then I replayed the scene that had actually happened. I was so angry with myself for not doing anything to help my cousin.

Slowly, a little unsurely, I began to realize that I would have to accept what had happened. I let myself fall asleep with that thought.

Description of feelings and insights the writer had at the time of the incident.

—Alison Conway
Wellesley Middle School
Wellesley, Massachusetts

Now you're ready to redraft your narrative, adding many of the *significant* details you've gathered. Filling in a writing framework like the one on page 85 will help you organize your second draft. You can make changes to this framework later, but at this stage it will give force and direction to your narrative.

3. Peer Editing

Read your draft to a small group of classmates. Ask the members of your group to tell you what they liked best about your paper. Then, ask them to complete one or more of these starters:

- I wanted to know more about . . .
- I didn't understand . . .
- How did you feel when . . .
- What happened after . . .

4. Self-Evaluation

Remember that revision is re-vision: seeing again. Ask yourself whether your narrative has the characteristics of a good autobiographical incident. (See the Evaluation Criteria on page 85.) Add, delete, or rearrange details, and make other necessary changes in wording or organization.

Sentence Workshop

SENTENCE FRAGMENTS

A **complete sentence** is a group of words that has a subject and a verb and expresses a complete thought. A **sentence fragment** is a group of words that has been punctuated as if it were a complete sentence but is really only part of a sentence.

FRAGMENT   Always wanted to be smarter. [The sentence's subject is missing. *Who* always wanted to be smarter?]

SENTENCE   Charlie always wanted to be smarter.

FRAGMENT   Alfonso's brother on his bicycle. [The sentence's verb is missing. What did Alfonso's brother *do* on the bicycle?]

SENTENCE   Alfonso's brother arrived on his bicycle.

FRAGMENT   After Squeaky won the race. [This group of words has a subject and a verb, but it does not express a complete thought. *What happened* after Squeaky won the race?]

SENTENCE   After Squeaky won the race, she smiled at Gretchen.

Sometimes writers chop off part of a sentence by putting in a period and a capital letter at the wrong point:

> Marguerite was thrilled. **When Mrs. Flowers invited her over for cookies.**

The fragment in heavy type should actually be a part of the sentence that comes before it:

> Marguerite was thrilled when Mrs. Flowers invited her over for cookies.

Writer's Workshop Follow-up: Proofreading

Take out your autobiographical incident, and exchange papers with a classmate. Circle any sentence fragments (except in dialogue), and suggest a correction for each. Exchange papers again, and revise any fragments your partner found in your paper.

Language Handbook
H E L P

See The Sentence, page 779.

Technology
H E L P

See Language Workshop CD-ROM. *Key word entry: sentence fragment.*

Try It Out

Copy the following paragraph onto a separate sheet of paper, correcting any sentence fragments.

Emily Dickinson saw friends and went on outings. When she was a child. She had changed. By her late twenties. She hardly spoke with her family. Instead sent them letters and packages of cookies. She would talk from behind a door. When visitors came. Dressed in white and rarely left her house. Now we know she spent her time writing poetry.

Reading for Life

Making Outlines and Graphic Organizers

Situation

Suppose you want to teach a group of fourth-graders how to write poems. To make sure you can explain figures of speech clearly, you reread pages 41–42. You want to put the ideas in a form you can review quickly.

Strategies

Find a form that fits.

- **Graphic organizers** show information visually. For example, a **time line** (see pages 344–345) shows events in the order in which they take place. A **Venn diagram** (see page 92) shows similarities and differences. A **cluster map** shows connected ideas and can help you brainstorm and organize your ideas (see page 676). For more on the use of visual aids, check page 137.

- A **topic outline** lists the main ideas in the order in which the writer presents them. A topic outline works especially well with nonfiction writing that divides a broad topic into subtopics. The essay on pages 41–42 divides figures of speech into subtopics, so you could put these ideas in the form of a topic outline.

> **Sample Outline for Page 41**
>
> Figures of Speech
> I. Uses
>   A. In everyday language
>   B. In writing
> II. Types
>   A. Simile
>   1. Compares two unlike things
>   2. Uses *like, as, than,* or *resembles*
>   B. Metaphor
>   1. Compares two unlike things directly
>   2. Does not use *like, as, than,* or *resembles*
>   3. Can be extended to develop the comparison further

Speak for yourself.

- Don't just copy the writer's words. Instead, **paraphrase** them—that is, put the ideas into your own words.

- When you write a topic outline, use only as many entries, and only as many words for each entry, as you need to make the outline clear.

Focus on the outline's framework.

- In a topic outline, use **Roman numerals** (I, II, III, etc.) for the main ideas. Indicate subtopics with **capital letters** (A, B, C, etc.), then with **Arabic numerals** (1, 2, 3, etc.), and then with **lowercase letters** (a, b, c, etc.)—in that order. Use a period after all numerals and letters.

- Never use just one subtopic. Use two (or more) or none.

Using the Strategies

1. Continue the outline above by rereading and outlining page 42.

2. Compare your outline with a classmate's. How similar are they?

3. Suggest at least one other way you could use your outline.

Extending the Strategies

Review and outline a section of your science textbook.

Learning for Life
Conflict Resolution

Problem

Conflict is a natural part of life as well as of literature. Conflict can help bring about positive changes, but it often leads to anger and violence instead. How can people resolve disagreements constructively?

Project

Discuss effective ways to handle disagreement, and creatively share what you have learned.

Preparation

Problem-Solving Plan

1. The people involved in the conflict decide together what the problem is.

2. Each person presents his or her view of the problem, using "I" statements ("*I* feel bad when you make fun of me") rather than "you" statements criticizing the other person ("*You* are always picking on me").

3. Each person summarizes what the other person said to show that it was understood.

4. Both people brainstorm and discuss possible solutions until they can agree about one.

A **mediator**—someone who is not involved in a conflict and who listens to both sides—can often help people arrive at a fair solution.

Procedure

1. List examples of conflicts in the news, in movies, or from your own experience (for instance, a time when your partner on a class assignment left most of the work to you).

   Discuss with your classmates how these disagreements were handled and how they could have been handled better.

2. With a classmate, role-play a solution to one of these conflicts for the class, using the problem-solving plan. Afterward, ask the class to comment on how successful you and your partner were in resolving the conflict.

3. Adapt the problem-solving plan, making changes suggested by the discussion and the role-play.

Presentation

Complete one of the following activities (or another that your teacher approves).

1. Role-Play

With a group of classmates, act out several conflicts for a group of younger students. Ask them what they would do in each situation. Then, act out a solution, using the problem-solving plan you and your class developed. After you and your group present a solution, discuss what makes it effective.

2. Poster

Design a poster illustrating one or more steps of the problem-solving plan. You may want to include a slogan of your own or a quotation by a famous person promoting peaceful conflict-resolution. Display your poster in your classroom or school hallway.

3. Song

Write and perform a song that explains the steps of the problem-solving plan, to convince your audience to try it.

Processing

Discuss these questions with a group of classmates: What did you like best about this project? What did you like least? Tell the group about one thing you learned.

Barbacoa para cumpleaños (*Birthday Barbecue*) by Carmen Lomas Garza. Alkyds on canvas (36" × 48").

From Generation to Generation

A traveler met an old man planting a tree.

"How foolish!" the traveler scoffed. "Surely you don't expect to live long enough to eat the fruit of that tree."

"Just as I found fruit trees when I came into the world," the old man replied, "so I am now planting trees for my children and grandchildren to enjoy."

—*Jewish folk tale*

Before You Read

THE TREASURE OF LEMON BROWN

Make the Connection

Generation Gap

Like many adults and teenagers, the father and son in the story you are about to read have some differences of opinion on what is important.

Make a Venn diagram like the one on the right, showing what is important to you, what is important to the adults in your family, and what is important to both you and them.

Elements of Literature

Character

Myers creates detailed pictures of the **characters** in this story—how they look, how they act, what they say, and how others react to them. As you read, think about your responses to these characters.

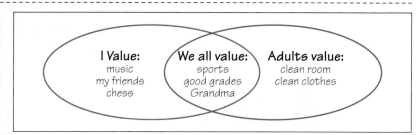

I Value:
music
my friends
chess

We all value:
sports
good grades
Grandma

Adults value:
clean room
clean clothes

Reading Skills and Strategies

Dialogue with the Text: Monitoring Your Comprehension

Monitoring your comprehension means being aware of your reading process and of how well you are understanding a text. Here are some strategies that can help you:

- **Respond to the text.** Write down your responses to what you are reading. "I like this." "I don't get that."

- **Reread.** If you get stuck, go back over the text to see if you missed some important information.
- **Question.** As you read, ask yourself questions about what you don't understand.

As you read this story, keep a notebook or sheet of paper next to the page you're on. Jot down your questions and thoughts. Pay special attention to your responses to the characters. One student's comments appear on the first page as an example.

> **A** **character** is a person or an animal who takes part in the action of a story.
>
> *For more on Character, see pages 106–107 and the Handbook of Literary Terms.*

go.hrw.com
LEO 8-2

Background

Literature and Geography

"The Treasure of Lemon Brown" takes place in Harlem, a famous section of New York City. Walter Dean Myers, who grew up in Harlem during the 1940s, describes it this way:

❝Thinking back to my boyhood days, I remember the bright sun on Harlem streets, the easy rhythms of black and brown bodies moving along the tar-and-asphalt pavement, the sounds of hundreds of children streaming in and out of red-brick tenements . . . I remember playing basketball in Morningside Park until it was too dark to see the basket and then climbing over the fence to go home.

"Harlem was a place of affirmation. The excitement of city living exploded in the teeming streets.❞

The figure shuffled forward again, and Greg took a small step backward.

Street Person (1982) by
Tom McKinney.
Watercolor (16" × 20").

The Treasure of
Lemon Brown

Walter
Dean
Myers

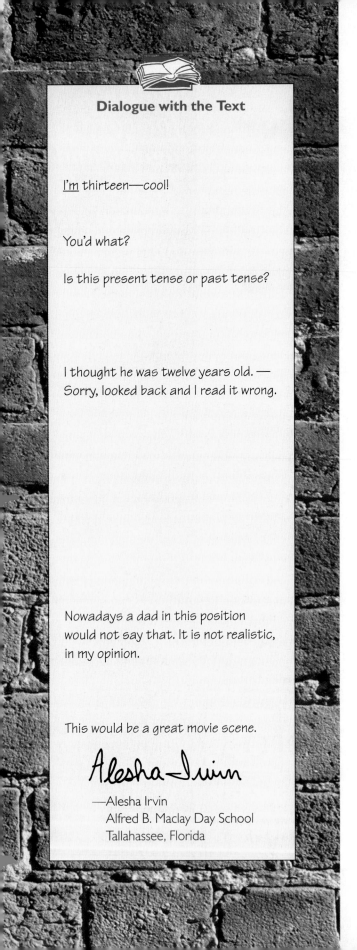
The dark sky, filled with angry, swirling clouds, reflected Greg Ridley's mood as he sat on the stoop of his building. His father's voice came to him again, first reading the letter the principal had sent to the house, then lecturing endlessly about his poor efforts in math.

"I had to leave school when I was thirteen," his father had said; "that's a year younger than you are now. If I'd had half the chances that you have, I'd . . ."

Greg had sat in the small, pale-green kitchen listening, knowing the lecture would end with his father saying he couldn't play ball with the Scorpions. He had asked his father the week before, and his father had said it depended on his next report card. It wasn't often the Scorpions took on new players, especially fourteen-year-olds, and this was a chance of a lifetime for Greg. He hadn't been allowed to play high school ball, which he had really wanted to do, but playing for the Community Center team was the next best thing. Report cards were due in a week, and Greg had been hoping for the best. But the principal had ended the suspense early when she sent that letter saying Greg would probably fail math if he didn't spend more time studying.

"And you want to play *basketball*?" His father's brows knitted over deep-brown eyes. "That must be some kind of a joke. Now you just get into your room and hit those books."

That had been two nights before. His father's words, like the distant thunder that now echoed through the streets of Harlem, still rumbled softly in his ears.

It was beginning to cool. Gusts of wind made bits of paper dance between the parked cars. There was a flash of nearby lightning, and soon large drops of rain splashed onto his jeans. He stood to go upstairs, thought of the lecture that probably awaited him if he did anything except shut himself in his room with his math book, and started walking down the

Children and Their Moments Alone Dare (1978) by Gilbert Fletcher.

street instead. Down the block there was an old tenement that had been abandoned for some months. Some of the guys had held an <u>impromptu</u> checkers tournament there the week before, and Greg had noticed that the door, once boarded over, had been slightly ajar.

Pulling his collar up as high as he could, he checked for traffic and made a dash across the street. He reached the house just as another flash of lightning changed the night to day for an instant, then returned the graffiti-scarred building to the grim shadows. He vaulted over the outer stairs and pushed <u>tentatively</u> on the door. It was open, and he let himself in.

The inside of the building was dark except for the dim light that filtered through the dirty windows from the street lamps. There was a room a few feet from the door, and from where he stood at the entrance, Greg could see a squarish patch of light on the floor. He entered the room, frowning at the musty smell. It was a large room that might have been someone's parlor at one time. Squinting, Greg could see an old table on its side against one wall, what

"You told me your name was orange or lemon or something like that."

looked like a pile of rags or a torn mattress in the corner, and a couch, with one side broken, in front of the window.

He went to the couch. The side that wasn't broken was comfortable enough, though a little creaky. From this spot he could see the blinking neon sign over the bodega[1] on the corner. He sat awhile, watching the sign blink first green, then red, allowing his mind to drift to the Scorpions, then to his father. His father had been a postal worker for all Greg's life and was proud of it, often telling Greg how hard he had worked to pass the test. Greg had heard the story too many times to be interested now.

For a moment Greg thought he heard something that sounded like a scraping against the wall. He listened carefully, but it was gone.

Outside, the wind had picked up, sending the rain against the window with a force that shook the glass in its frame. A car passed, its tires hissing over the wet street and its red taillights glowing in the darkness.

Greg thought he heard the noise again. His stomach tightened as he held himself still and listened intently. There weren't any more scraping noises, but he was sure he had heard something in the darkness—something breathing!

He tried to figure out just where the breathing was coming from; he knew it was in the room with him. Slowly he stood, tensing. As he turned, a flash of lightning lit up the room, frightening him with its sudden brilliance. He saw nothing, just the overturned table, the pile of rags, and an old newspaper on the floor.

Could he have been imagining the sounds? He continued listening, but heard nothing and thought that it might have just been rats. Still, he thought, as soon as the rain let up he would leave. He went to the window and was about to look out when he heard a voice behind him.

"Don't try nothin', 'cause I got a razor here sharp enough to cut a week into nine days!"

Greg, except for an involuntary tremor in his knees, stood stock-still. The voice was high and brittle, like dry twigs being broken, surely not one he had ever heard before. There was a shuffling sound as the person who had been speaking moved a step closer. Greg turned, holding his breath, his eyes straining to see in the dark room.

The upper part of the figure before him was still in darkness. The lower half was in the dim rectangle of light that fell unevenly from the window. There were two feet, in cracked, dirty shoes from which rose legs that were wrapped in rags.

"Who are you?" Greg hardly recognized his own voice.

"I'm Lemon Brown," came the answer. "Who're you?"

"Greg Ridley."

"What you doing here?" The figure shuffled forward again, and Greg took a small step backward.

1. **bodega** (bō·dā′gə): small grocery store.

WORDS TO OWN

intently (in·tent′lē) *adv.*: with close attention.
brittle (brit′'l) *adj.*: sharp and hard. *Brittle* also means "touchy or difficult to deal with."

"It's raining," Greg said.

"I can see that," the figure said.

The person who called himself Lemon Brown peered forward, and Greg could see him clearly. He was an old man. His black, heavily wrinkled face was surrounded by a halo of crinkly white hair and whiskers that seemed to separate his head from the layers of dirty coats piled on his smallish frame. His pants were bagged to the knee, where they were met with rags that went down to the old shoes. The rags were held on with strings, and there was a rope around his middle. Greg relaxed. He had seen the man before, picking through the trash on the corner and pulling clothes out of a Salvation Army box. There was no sign of the razor that could "cut a week into nine days."

"What are you doing here?" Greg asked.

"This is where I'm staying," Lemon Brown said. "What you here for?"

"Told you it was raining out," Greg said, leaning against the back of the couch until he felt it give slightly.

"Ain't you got no home?"

"I got a home," Greg answered.

"You ain't one of them bad boys looking for my treasure, is you?" Lemon Brown cocked his head to one side and squinted one eye. "Because I told you I got me a razor."

"I'm not looking for your treasure," Greg answered, smiling. "*If* you have one."

"What you mean, *if* I have one," Lemon Brown said. "Every man got a treasure. You don't know that, you must be a fool!"

"Sure," Greg said as he sat on the sofa and put one leg over the back. "What do you have, gold coins?"

"Don't worry none about what I got," Lemon Brown said. "You know who I am?"

"You told me your name was orange or lemon or something like that."

"Lemon Brown," the old man said, pulling back his shoulders as he did so, "they used to call me Sweet Lemon Brown."

"Sweet Lemon?" Greg asked.

"Yessir. Sweet Lemon Brown. They used to say I sung the blues so sweet that if I sang at a funeral, the dead would commence to rocking with the beat. Used to travel all over Mississippi and as far as Monroe, Louisiana, and east on over to Macon, Georgia. You mean you ain't never heard of Sweet Lemon Brown?"

"Afraid not," Greg said. "What . . . what happened to you?"

"Hard times, boy. Hard times always after a poor man. One day I got tired, sat down to rest a spell and felt a tap on my shoulder. Hard times caught up with me."

"Sorry about that."

"What you doing here? How come you didn't go on home when the rain come? Rain don't bother you young folks none."

"Just didn't." Greg looked away.

"I used to have a knotty-headed boy just like

"I sung the blues so sweet that if I sang at a funeral, the dead would commence to rocking with the beat."

Studio View (1977) by Gilbert Fletcher (24" × 20").

you." Lemon Brown had half walked, half shuffled back to the corner and sat down against the wall. "Had them big eyes like you got. I used to call them moon eyes. Look into them moon eyes and see anything you want."

"How come you gave up singing the blues?" Greg asked.

"Didn't give it up," Lemon Brown said. "You don't give up the blues; they give you up. After a while you do good for yourself, and it ain't nothing but foolishness singing about how hard you got it. Ain't that right?"

"I guess so."

"What's that noise?" Lemon Brown asked, suddenly sitting upright.

Greg listened, and he heard a noise outside. He looked at Lemon Brown and saw the old man was pointing toward the window.

Greg went to the window and saw three men, neighborhood thugs, on the stoop. One was carrying a length of pipe. Greg looked back toward Lemon Brown, who moved quietly across the room to the window. The old man looked out, then beckoned frantically for Greg to follow him. For a moment Greg couldn't move. Then he found himself following Lemon Brown into the hallway and up darkened stairs. Greg followed as closely as he could. They reached the top of the stairs, and Greg felt Lemon Brown's hand first lying on his shoulder, then probing down his arm until he finally took Greg's hand into his own as they crouched in the darkness.

"They's bad men," Lemon Brown whispered. His breath was warm against Greg's skin.

"Hey! Ragman!" a voice called. "We know you in here. What you got up under them rags? You got any money?"

Silence.

"We don't want to have to come in and hurt you, old man, but we don't mind if we have to."

Lemon Brown squeezed Greg's hand in his own hard, gnarled fist.

There was a banging downstairs and a light as the men entered. They banged around noisily, calling for the ragman.

"We heard you talking about your treasure." The voice was slurred. "We just want to see it, that's all."

"You sure he's here?" One voice seemed to come from the room with the sofa.

"Yeah, he stays here every night."

"There's another room over there; I'm going to take a look. You got that flashlight?"

"Yeah, here, take the pipe too."

Greg opened his mouth to quiet the sound of his breath as he sucked it in uneasily. A beam of light hit the wall a few feet opposite him, then went out.

"Ain't nobody in that room," a voice said. "You think he gone or something?"

"I don't know," came the answer. "All I know is that I heard him talking about some kind of treasure. You know they found that shopping-bag lady with that money in her bags."

"Yeah. You think he's upstairs?"

"HEY, OLD MAN, ARE YOU UP THERE?"

Silence.

"Watch my back, I'm going up."

There was a footstep on the stairs, and the beam from the flashlight danced crazily along the peeling wallpaper. Greg held his breath. There was another step and a loud crashing noise as the man banged the pipe against the wooden banister. Greg could feel his temples throb as the man slowly neared them. Greg thought about the pipe, wondering what he would do when the man reached them—what he *could* do.

Then Lemon Brown released his hand and moved toward the top of the stairs. Greg looked around and saw stairs going up to the next floor. He tried waving to Lemon Brown, hoping the old man would see him in the dim light and follow him to the next floor. Maybe, Greg thought, the man wouldn't follow them up there. Suddenly, though, Lemon Brown stood at the top of the stairs, both arms raised high above his head.

"There he is!" a voice cried from below.

"Throw down your money, old man, so I won't have to bash your head in!"

Lemon Brown didn't move. Greg felt himself near panic. The steps came closer, and still Lemon Brown didn't move. He was an eerie sight, a bundle of rags standing at the top of the stairs, his shadow on the wall looming over him. Maybe, the thought came to Greg, the scene could be even eerier.

Greg wet his lips, put his hands to his

> He was an eerie sight, a bundle of rags standing at the top of the stairs.

> # "If you know your pappy did something, you know you can do something too."

mouth, and tried to make a sound. Nothing came out. He swallowed hard, wet his lips once more, and howled as evenly as he could.

"What's that?"

As Greg howled, the light moved away from Lemon Brown, but not before Greg saw him hurl his body down the stairs at the men who had come to take his treasure. There was a crashing noise, and then footsteps. A rush of warm air came in as the downstairs door opened; then there was only an ominous silence.

Greg stood on the landing. He listened, and after a while there was another sound on the staircase.

"Mr. Brown?" he called.

"Yeah, it's me," came the answer. "I got their flashlight."

Greg exhaled in relief as Lemon Brown made his way slowly back up the stairs.

"You OK?"

"Few bumps and bruises," Lemon Brown said.

"I think I'd better be going," Greg said, his breath returning to normal. "You'd better leave, too, before they come back."

"They may hang around outside for a while," Lemon Brown said, "but they ain't getting their nerve up to come in here again. Not with crazy old ragmen and howling spooks. Best you stay awhile till the coast is clear. I'm heading out west tomorrow, out to East St. Louis."

"They were talking about treasures," Greg said. "You *really* have a treasure?"

"What I tell you? Didn't I tell you every man got a treasure?" Lemon Brown said. "You want to see mine?"

"If you want to show it to me," Greg shrugged.

"Let's look out the window first, see what them scoundrels be doing," Lemon Brown said.

They followed the oval beam of the flashlight into one of the rooms and looked out the window. They saw the men who had tried to take the treasure sitting on the curb near the corner. One of them had his pants leg up, looking at his knee.

"You sure you're not hurt?" Greg asked Lemon Brown.

"Nothing that ain't been hurt before," Lemon Brown said. "When you get as old as me, all you say when something hurts is, 'Howdy, Mr. Pain, sees you back again.' Then when Mr. Pain see he can't worry you none, he go on mess with somebody else."

Greg smiled.

"Here, you hold this." Lemon Brown gave Greg the flashlight.

He sat on the floor near Greg and carefully untied the strings that held the rags on his right leg. When he took the rags away, Greg saw a piece of plastic. The old man carefully took off the plastic and unfolded it. He revealed some yellowed newspaper clippings and a battered harmonica.

"There it be," he said, nodding his head. "There it be."

Greg looked at the old man, saw the distant

WORDS TO OWN

ominous (äm′ə·nəs) *adj.*: threatening; seeming to indicate that something bad will happen.
----

look in his eye, then turned to the clippings. They told of Sweet Lemon Brown, a blues singer and harmonica player who was appearing at different theaters in the South. One of the clippings said he had been the hit of the show, although not the headliner. All of the clippings were reviews of shows Lemon Brown had been in more than fifty years ago. Greg looked at the harmonica. It was dented badly on one side, with the reed holes on one end nearly closed.

"I used to travel around and make money for to feed my wife and Jesse—that's my boy's name. Used to feed them good, too. Then his mama died, and he stayed with his mama's sister. He growed up to be a man, and when the war come, he saw fit to go off and fight in it. I didn't have nothing to give him except these things that told him who I was, and what he come from. If you know your pappy did something, you know you can do something too.

"Anyway, he went off to war, and I went off still playing and singing. 'Course by then I wasn't as much as I used to be, not without somebody to make it worth the while. You know what I mean?"

"Yeah," Greg nodded, not quite really knowing.

"I traveled around, and one time I come home, and there was this letter saying Jesse got killed in the war. Broke my heart, it truly did.

"They sent back what he had with him over there, and what it was is this old mouth fiddle and these clippings. Him carrying it around with him like that told me it meant something to him. That was my treasure, and when I give it to him, he treated it just like that, a treasure. Ain't that something?"

"Yeah, I guess so," Greg said.

"You *guess* so?" Lemon Brown's voice rose an octave[2] as he started to put his treasure back

into the plastic. "Well, you got to guess, 'cause you sure don't know nothing. Don't know enough to get home when it's raining."

"I guess . . . I mean, you're right."

"You OK for a youngster," the old man said as he tied the strings around his leg, "better than those scalawags what come here looking for my treasure. That's for sure."

"You really think that treasure of yours was worth fighting for?" Greg asked. "Against a pipe?"

"What else a man got 'cepting what he can pass on to his son, or his daughter, if she be his oldest?" Lemon Brown said. "For a big-headed boy, you sure do ask the foolishest questions."

Lemon Brown got up after patting his rags in place and looked out the window again.

"Looks like they're gone. You get on out of here and get yourself home. I'll be watching from the window, so you'll be all right."

Lemon Brown went down the stairs behind Greg. When they reached the front door, the old man looked out first, saw the street was clear, and told Greg to scoot on home.

"You sure you'll be OK?" Greg asked.

"Now, didn't I tell you I was going to East St. Louis in the morning?" Lemon Brown asked. "Don't that sound OK to you?"

"Sure it does," Greg said. "Sure it does. And you take care of that treasure of yours."

"That I'll do," Lemon said, the wrinkles about his eyes suggesting a smile. "That I'll do."

The night had warmed and the rain had stopped, leaving puddles at the curbs. Greg didn't even want to think how late it was. He thought ahead of what his father would say and wondered if he should tell him about Lemon Brown. He thought about it until he reached his stoop, and decided against it. Lemon Brown would be OK, Greg thought, with his memories and his treasure.

Greg pushed the button over the bell marked "Ridley," thought of the lecture he knew his father would give him, and smiled.

2. **octave** (äk′tiv): eight whole notes.

MEET THE WRITER

"He Gave Me the Most Precious Gift"

Walter Dean Myers (1937–   ) was born in Martinsburg, West Virginia; he was one of eight children. Myers's mother died when he was three, and his father sent him and two of his sisters to New York City to be raised by foster parents, the Deans. When he became a published writer, Myers added their name to his to show how important they were to him.

66 My foster father was a wonderful man. He gave me the most precious gift any father could give to a son: He loved me. . . . My foster mother understood the value of education, even though neither she nor my father had more than a rudimentary education. She also understood the value of story, how it could serve as a refuge for people, like us, who couldn't afford the finer things in life or even all of what came to be the everyday things. 99

Myers has been an editor and a teacher as well as a writer of books for children and young adults. He says:

66 Every time I sit down to write, I think of television as a value setter. I may write about a moral kid. Good. But TV says being tough is better. The TV people know that a certain kind of value system—'cool' masculine—is what sells beer and bluejeans. I have to counter that. 99

More by Walter Dean Myers

- *Fallen Angels* (Scholastic), a novel about a seventeen-year-old named Richie who leaves New York City to fight in Vietnam
- *Hoops* (Dell), a novel about a Harlem teenager contending for a citywide basketball title against powerful opposition—both on and off the court

MAKING MEANINGS

First Thoughts

1. Why does Greg smile at the thought of the lecture he will get from his father?

Shaping Interpretations

2. In your opinion, why does Greg decide not to tell his father about Lemon Brown?

3. What has Greg learned from Lemon Brown?

4. What does Lemon Brown mean when he says that everyone's got a treasure (page 97)?

5. What do you think is Greg's treasure? What is Greg's father's treasure?

Connecting with the Text

6. What do *you* treasure? What does your family treasure? For ideas, look at the Venn diagram you made before you read the story.

7. Lemon Brown says, "If you know your pappy did something, you know you can do something too" (page 101). What does he mean? Do you agree? Explain.

Challenging the Text

8. Myers says (page 102) that in his writing he has to "counter" the values conveyed by TV. Do you think that is a worthwhile goal? If Myers asked you if his story presents a strong challenge to the values communicated by TV, what would you tell him?

9. Do you find these **characters** convincing? That is, do you think they act the way people do in real life? Go back to the text and your reading notes for examples to support your opinion.

Reading Check

a. Why are Greg and his father upset with each other?

b. How did Lemon Brown once make a living?

c. What do the men who enter the building want?

d. How do Lemon Brown and Greg scare them away?

e. What is Lemon Brown's treasure?

CHOICES: Building Your Portfolio

Writer's Notebook

1. Collecting Ideas for a Persuasive Essay

Lemon Brown convinces Greg that his treasure is worth fighting for and passing on.

When you convince other people that something you believe is true, you **persuade** them. You can only persuade people when you feel strongly about some issue and can back up your position with supporting evidence.

What do you believe in strongly? In your Writer's Notebook, jot down some issues or positions you could support. If you're stuck for ideas, look back over the story. Perhaps the story makes you think about the homeless. Maybe details in Walter Dean Myers's biography (page 102) make you think about the values we get from TV.

> Issues I feel strongly about:
> Values we get from TV (all those ads make you want stuff you can't afford)
> Problems with poor homeless guys like Lemon

Writing a Description

2. Family Keepsakes

A keepsake is an item that may not be worth a lot of money but is valued as a reminder of someone or something. Do you or your family have any keepsakes?

Write a description of a keepsake of yours. Imagine that it is found a hundred years from now. What would you want the finder to know about it? What stories in your life does it represent?

You may want to attach a photograph or a drawing of the keepsake.

Role-Play

3. Conflict Resolution

With a classmate, write a **dialogue** between Greg and his father for the scene after Greg returns from his visit with Lemon Brown.

- What does Greg's father say in his lecture?

- How does Greg respond?

- How can they constructively work out their disagreement?

- Is there a solution that will make both of them happy?

Perform the dialogue with your partner for your class.

Research/Music/Oral Presentation

4. Those Sweet Blues

Research some aspect of blues music that interests you. You might find out about the lives of classic blues musicians like "Sonny Boy" Williamson and Junior Wells, who, like Lemon Brown, were known for their "harp" (harmonica) playing.

Write up your findings, and present them to the class in an **oral report**. Try to get some classic blues recordings by blues greats, and play them for the class as part of your presentation.

LANGUAGE LINK MINI-LESSON

Style: Don't Dread *Said*

Some inexperienced writers try to avoid using *said* frequently because they don't want their writing to seem boring or repetitive. The result can be clumsy, as this dialogue (*not* written by Myers) shows:

> "Did you say your name was Grapefruit?" Greg quizzed.
> "Lemon," the old man exclaimed. "I told you my name is Lemon!"
> "It was just a mistake," Greg retorted. "You don't have to exclaim."

The use of too many substitutes for *said* can distract the reader. *Said* is an invisible word—it is simple and clear, so we read right past it without noticing how often it's used. If you look at published stories, you'll find that writers use *said* much more often than its synonyms. (Sometimes a writer will simply leave out the phrase identifying the speaker if it's clear who's speaking.)

When you do use replacements for *said*, keep them simple; words like *asked, replied, told, called,* and *shouted* are usually best. Save *bellowed* and *sighed* for occasions when you want to draw attention to the sound of the speaker's voice.

Try It Out

Go back to the text, and count the number of times Myers uses the word *said*. Then, find all the substitutes for *said*. How often does Myers use these substitutes? Would you make the same choices he does?

VOCABULARY HOW TO OWN A WORD

WORD BANK

impromptu
tentatively
intently
brittle
ominous

Vocabulary for the Workplace: The Job Interview

1. Imagine that you have an appointment tomorrow to be interviewed for a job. Will you rehearse what you want to say, or will your remarks to your potential employer be completely impromptu? Explain your decision.
2. Do you think speaking tentatively is likely to make a good impression on an interviewer? Why or why not?
3. As an employer, what would you think of a job candidate who listened intently, took notes, and asked questions?
4. Would you rather hire someone with a brittle personality or an easygoing type? Explain.
5. Which words would sound ominous to a hopeful job seeker: "Don't call us, we'll call you" or "When can you start?" Why?

Elements of Literature

CHARACTER: Living Many Lives *by* John Leggett

The Human Experience

Most people are fascinated by human nature. They like to know how other people respond to problems, disappointments, and temptations. A good story, whether it's true, made up, or somewhere in between, reveals some truth about the human experience. It does this through the people who live in its pages—its **characters.**

A well-drawn character comes alive in the reader's mind. When you read a story, you may find yourself thinking that the main character is very much like you or someone you know—or you may wish you could be more like the character. As you read, the characters in the story become your friends or your enemies. You may even lose yourself in a story and begin to think and feel as if you were in a character's shoes.

Some characters become the acquaintances of generations of readers. You may have met famous characters in books that your parents or even your grandparents also loved.

Creating Characters

Creating characters is an important but difficult part of writing. Writers create brand-new people to populate the world portrayed in a story.

How does a writer bring a character to life? First, the writer must be able to imagine the character. He or she may start by picturing the character's appearance, picking colors for the hair and the eyes, and adding a voice and a style of dress. The writer must also invent a whole personality. The character may be snobbish or heroic or happy-go-lucky, or have a mixture of personality traits. The writer must choose from an enormous number of possibilities while trying to put together a believable character.

Sometimes writers are surprised by the way their characters turn out. Some writers say that their characters just seem to create themselves as a story is being written.

A Writer on Character

"Sitting at my typewriter, I have lived many lives—I have been Jerry Renault refusing to sell those chocolates and Kate Forrester trying to start that hostaged bus and Adam Farmer pedaling his bicycle toward an unknown destination. I have both laughed and wept while sitting there."

—Robert Cormier, author of "The Moustache" (page 139)

Characterization: The Breath of Life

The way a writer reveals character is called **characterization.** Poor characterization can make a description of even a real person seem flat and unconvincing. Good characterization can make readers feel that the most unlikely characters—an enormous talking egg, a bumbling teddy bear—live and breathe.

Show, Don't Tell

"Don't say the old lady screamed. Bring her on and let her scream."

—Mark Twain

A writer may simply *tell* us directly that a character is mean-tempered or thrifty or brave or honest. This kind of characterization, called **direct characterization,** was often used by writers before the twentieth century. Present-day writers generally prefer to *show* their characters in action and let readers decide for themselves what kinds of people they are meeting. This method is called **indirect characterization.**

Methods of Characterization

Writers use several methods to reveal what a character is like.

Telling

1. Stating directly what the character is like:

   Sergeant Randolph was the cruelest drillmaster in the regiment.

Showing

2. Describing the appearance of the character:

   The woman's coat was gathered about her thin body and fastened with a safety pin.

3. Showing the character in action:

   Toni glanced around, then tossed her gum wrapper on the grass and kept walking.

4. Allowing the reader to hear the character speak:

   "I don't have to do what you say," declared Darlene, glaring at the new baby sitter.

5. Revealing the character's thoughts and feelings:

   Tyler didn't like the looks of the squash pudding but decided to eat some to please the cook.

6. Showing how others react to the character:

   "Team up with Erica?" said Jorge. "Well, OK, if you can't get anyone else. But when she was my partner before, I did all the work while she socialized."

Characters Who Change

The main character in a story almost always undergoes a significant change in the course of the story. A character who changes in this way is known as a **dynamic character.** (A character who doesn't change much is called a **static character.**) A dynamic character may grow in some way, gain in understanding, make an important decision, or take a crucial action.

Peanuts reprinted by permission of UFS, Inc.

Before You Read

THE COURAGE THAT MY MOTHER HAD
LEGACY II

Make the Connection

Legacies

What do you know about the word *legacy*? Using a dictionary if necessary, brainstorm with two or three classmates in response to the questions below.

Quickwrite

- Who might leave a legacy?
- How might someone feel about receiving a legacy?
- What are examples of legacies? (Does a legacy have to be something you can see?)

Elements of Literature

Rhythm

Read aloud "The Courage That My Mother Had," and you'll hear a regular rhythm that sounds like poetry. Read aloud "Legacy II," in contrast, and you'll hear the natural rhythms of ordinary speech. How do you know, in each poem, when to pause when you read aloud?

> **R**hythm is a rise and fall of the voice produced by repeated sound patterns.
>
> *For more on Rhythm, see pages 544–545 and the Handbook of Literary Terms.*

The Courage That My Mother Had

Edna St. Vincent Millay

The courage that my mother had
Went with her, and is with her still:
Rock from New England quarried;°
Now granite in a granite hill.

5   The golden brooch° my mother wore
She left behind for me to wear;
I have no thing I treasure more:
Yet, it is something I could spare.

Oh, if instead she'd left to me
10 The thing she took into the grave!—
That courage like a rock, which she
Has no more need of, and I have.

3. quarried: dug from a quarry, a pit from which building stone or marble is taken.
5. brooch (brōch): large decorative pin, usually worn at the neck.

go.hrw.com
LE0 8-2

El Norte

Poniente

Oriente

El Sur

Spanish Octogenarian by E. Martin Hennings.
Oil on canvas.

Stark Museum of Art, Orange, Texas.

Legacy II

Leroy V. Quintana

Grandfather never went to school
spoke only a few words of English

a quiet man; when he talked
talked about simple things
5   planting corn or about the weather
sometimes about herding sheep as a child

One day pointed to the four directions
taught me their names
        El Norte
10 Poniente   Oriente
        El Sur

He spoke their names as if they were
one of only a handful of things
a man needed to know

15 Now I look back
only two generations removed
realize I am nothing but a poor fool
who went to college

trying to find my way back
20 to the center of the world
where Grandfather stood
that day

MEET THE WRITERS

Family Ties

Edna St. Vincent Millay (1892–1950) was born and grew up in Rockland, Maine. She started writing poetry as a child. Millay wrote "Renascence" (ri·nas'əns), one of her most famous poems, when she was only nineteen, and published her first book of poetry the year she graduated from Vassar College.

As you might have guessed from "The Courage That My Mother Had," the strength of women is an important theme in Millay's writing. Millay worshiped her mother, a strong New Englander who worked as a practical nurse to support her three daughters after their father deserted the family.

Leroy V. Quintana (1944–   ) was born in Albuquerque, New Mexico, and raised by his grandparents. Many of his poems contrast his Mexican ancestors' traditional way of life with the way people live in big cities today. "In many ways I'm still basically a small-town New Mexico boy carrying on the oral tradition," he says.

66 I heard Grandmother tell me the old stories hundreds of times, over and over. To me it was like turning on the TV. She had the nuances of language, though she had no education; she knew the inflections, how to tell the story, how to keep you in suspense. You know, that seems to be lost, and I would hope that I could at least put a little bit of that on paper. 99

"Legacy II" builds on the theme of another poem by Quintana, "A Legacy," about an educated man who longs to return to the time when his grandfather told him *cuentos* (kwen'tôs), Mexican American folk tales.

MAKING MEANINGS

First Thoughts

1. Which poem do you like better? Why? Consider the feelings and ideas expressed by the speakers and the **rhythm** you feel in each poem.

Shaping Interpretations

2. What legacy did the speaker of each poem receive? What legacy does each speaker want instead?

3. What does Millay compare her mother's courage to? What does her comparison suggest to you about the nature of courage?

4. What do you think the speaker of "Legacy II" means when he says that his grandfather stood at the center of the world that day (lines 20–22)?

Extending the Text

5. Review what you wrote about legacies in your Quickwrite. Do you think it's possible for qualities like courage and wisdom to be handed down as legacies? Why or why not?

CHOICES: Building Your Portfolio

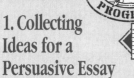

Writer's Notebook

1. Collecting Ideas for a Persuasive Essay

Refer to your Quickwrite notes, and respond to one of these statements:
- The most important legacies are those that can't be seen.
- Anyone—young or old, rich or poor—can leave a legacy.

Write down supporting evidence for your position. Be sure to think about the two poems you've just read.

Creative Writing

2. Thanks a Million

Think of a gift someone gave you that was *not* an object— perhaps knowledge, love, or just attention when you needed someone to listen. Write a **thank-you note** explaining what the gift meant to you.

World Languages

3. Make It Concrete

In a **concrete poem** the arrangement of the words on the page reflects their meaning, the way the placement of the Spanish words for the four directions in "Legacy II" indicates what the words mean.

Write a concrete poem designed to teach a word or a group of words in a language you know (it can be English) to speakers of other languages.

Make the Connection

Little Things Mean a Lot

Sometimes it's surprising what people remember from their childhood. When the poet Robert P. Tristram Coffin was a little boy, his father came to check on him one night as he lay sick in bed. This simple expression of love meant so much to Coffin that many years later he wrote a poem about it—"The Secret Heart."

Quickwrite

Describe a happy memory from your childhood. Who was there? What happened? Why was it important to you?

Elements of Literature

Symbol

As you read this poem, ask yourself: What does the "secret heart" **symbolize** (represent) for the son?

> **A symbol** is a person, a place, or a thing that has meaning in itself but that stands for something else as well.
>
> *For more on Symbol, see page 42 and the Handbook of Literary Terms.*

The Secret Heart

Robert P. Tristram Coffin

Across the years he could recall
His father one way best of all.

In the stillest hour of night
The boy awakened to a light.

5 Half in dreams, he saw his sire°
With his great hands full of fire.

The man had struck a match to see
If his son slept peacefully.

He held his palms each side the spark
10 His love had kindled in the dark.

His two hands were curved apart
In the semblance° of a heart.

He wore, it seemed to his small son,
A bare heart on his hidden one,

15 A heart that gave out such a glow
No son awake could bear to know.

It showed a look upon a face
Too tender for the day to trace.

One instant, it lit all about,
20 And then the secret heart went out.

But it shone long enough for one
To know that hands held up the sun.

5. **sire:** father.
12. **semblance:** form.

The Fire in Time (1993) by Jim Dine. Charcoal, enamel, and water-color on paper (31½" x 23").

Courtesy of PaceWildenstein. Photographer: Bill Jacobson.

MEET THE WRITER

"Saying the Best"

Robert P. Tristram Coffin (1892–1955) was born in Brunswick, Maine, and called himself "a New Englander by birth, by bringing up, by spirit." Coffin enjoyed growing up in rural Maine so much that as an adult he bought the red-brick schoolhouse he'd attended, to preserve it in honor of his child-hood. (Can you imagine buying your school in thirty years?)

Coffin was an artist as well as a writer and often drew the jacket designs and illustrations for his books. He won a Pulitzer Prize for a book of poetry called *Strange Holiness* (1935). He once said:

66 Poetry is saying the best one can about life. 99

MAKING MEANINGS

First Thoughts

1. In your opinion, what is the most important word or phrase in the poem? Explain your choice.

Shaping Interpretations

2. What does the boy realize about his father? How does he come to this realization?

3. What do the father's hands holding the match **symbolize** for the son?

4. What do you think is the meaning of the last two lines, in which the son realizes that "hands held up the sun"? Whose hands are they?

5. How does the expression "Little things mean a lot" relate to this poem? Does the expression also relate to the memory you described in your Quickwrite? Explain.

Connecting with the Text

6. The speaker says that the father's love was "too tender for the day to trace." Why do people sometimes hide their feelings from those they love?

CHOICES: Building Your Portfolio

Writer's Notebook

1. Collecting Ideas for a Persuasive Essay

The event described in "The Secret Heart" helps a boy know how much his father loves him. What "little things" can people do for one another to show that they care? What do children need most from their families? Freewrite your responses to these issues.

WORK IN PROGRESS

Creative Writing

2. Memory Lane

Write a poem about a memory of a special person. If you would like to write a poem with a regular pattern of **rhyme** and **rhythm,** like "The Secret Heart," you might start:

Across the years I can recall

_____ best of all.

Performance

3. Sound and Sense

With two or three classmates, prepare a **choral reading** of "The Secret Heart." Practice reading it aloud so that it doesn't sound singsong. Pay attention to the punctuation at the ends of lines. If there's no punctuation mark, read on without pausing; come to a full stop only when you get to a period. You may want to try reciting the poem from memory.

Before You Read

A Smart Cookie
Bien Águila

Make the Connection

Hopes and Dreams

"I want my children to have everything I missed." Have you ever heard an adult say something like this?

In "A Smart Cookie" a mother talks about her missed opportunities in hopes that her daughter, Esperanza, will have a better future. (*Esperanza,* in fact, means "hope" in Spanish.)

Quickwrite

Write briefly about someone's hopes for you or your own hopes for your future.

Background/ Elements of Literature

Literature and World Languages

"A Smart Cookie" appears here both in English, the language in which Sandra Cisneros writes, and in Spanish, her parents' language.

When Elena Poniatowska translated the story into Span-

ish, the title posed a special problem because it is an **idiom,** an expression that has a nonliteral meaning unique to a particular language. Do you know what the expression *smart cookie* means?

Poniatowska could have simply used the Spanish words for *smart* and *cookie,* but in Spanish the phrase would just mean "intelligent pastry." To a Spanish speaker it would make no sense. She chose instead to change the title to "Bien águila" ("good eagle"), a Spanish idiom whose meaning is similar to that of *smart cookie* in English.

> **A**n **idiom** is an expression peculiar to a particular language. An idiom means something different from the literal meaning of each word.
>
> *For more on Idiom, see the Handbook of Literary Terms.*

go.hrw.com
LE0 8-2

A Smart Cookie

Sandra Cisneros

Mercy (detail) (1992) by Nick Quijano.

I could've been somebody, you know? my mother says and sighs. She has lived in this city her whole life. She can speak two languages. She can sing an opera. She knows how to fix a TV. But she doesn't know which subway train to take to get downtown. I hold her hand very tight while we wait for the right train to arrive.

She used to draw when she had time. Now she draws with a needle and thread, little knotted rosebuds, tulips made of silk thread. Someday she would like to go to the ballet. Someday she would like to see a play. She borrows opera records from the public library and sings with velvety lungs powerful as morning glories.

Today while cooking oatmeal she is Madame Butterfly[1] until she sighs and points the wooden spoon at me. I could've been somebody, you know? Esperanza, you go to school. Study hard. That Madame Butterfly was a fool. She stirs the oatmeal. Look at my comadres.[2] She means Izaura whose husband left and Yolanda whose husband is dead. Got to take care all your own, she says shaking her head.

Then out of nowhere:

Shame is a bad thing, you know. It keeps you down. You want to know why I quit school? Because I didn't have nice clothes. No clothes, but I had brains.

Yup, she says disgusted, stirring again. I was a smart cookie then.

1. **Madame Butterfly:** tragic heroine of an opera of the same name by Giacomo Puccini. In the opera a U.S. naval officer stationed in Japan marries a young Japanese woman, Butterfly, then returns to the United States. She waits faithfully for him, with their child, for years. After he returns to Japan with an American wife, Butterfly commits suicide.
2. **comadres** (kô·mä′dräs): Spanish for "close female friends" (literally, a child's mother and godmother).

Bien águila

Sandra Cisneros,
translated by Elena Poniatowska

Yo pude haber sido alguien, ¿sabes? dice mi madre y suspira. Toda su vida ha vivido en esta ciudad. Sabe dos idiomas. Puede cantar una ópera. Sabe reparar la tele. Pero no sabe qué metro tomar para ir al centro. La tomo muy fuerte de la mano mientras esperamos a que llegue el tren.

Cuando tenía tiempo dibujaba. Ahora dibuja con hilo y aguja, pequeños botones de rosa, tulipanes de hilo de seda. Algún día le gustaría ir al ballet. Algún día también, a ver una obra de teatro. Pide discos de ópera en la biblioteca pública y canta con pulmones aterciopelados y poderosos como glorias azules.

Hoy, mientras cuece la avena, es Madame Butterfly hasta que suspira y me señala con la cuchara de palo. Yo pude haber sido alguien, ¿sabes? Ve a la escuela, Esperanza. Estudia macizo. Esa Madame Butterfly era una tonta. Menea la avena. Fíjate en mis comadres. Se refiere a Izaura, cuyo marido se largó, y a Yolanda, cuyo marido está muerto. Tienes que cuidarte solita, dice moviendo la cabeza.

Y luego, nada más porque sí:

La vergüenza es mala cosa, ¿sabes? No te deja levantarte. ¿Sabes por qué dejé la escuela? Porque no tenía ropa bonita. Ropa no, pero cerebro sí.

¡Ufa! dice disgustada, meneando de nuevo. Yo entonces era bien águila.

MEET THE WRITER
Crossing the Threshold

Like Esperanza, **Sandra Cisneros** (1954–) grew up in a Mexican American family in Chicago. She writes:

66 I've managed to do a lot of things in my life I didn't think I was capable of and which many others didn't think me capable of either. Especially because I am a woman, a Latina, an only daughter in a family of six men. My father would've liked to have seen me married long ago. In our culture, men and women don't leave their father's house except by way of marriage. I crossed my father's threshold with nothing carrying me but my own two feet. 99

More by Sandra Cisneros

"A Smart Cookie" comes from *The House on Mango Street* (Vintage), a collection of **vignettes,** or short sketches, about Esperanza. It was published in Spanish as *La Casa en Mango Street* (Vintage).

MAKING MEANINGS

First Thoughts

1. Look back at your Quickwrite. What connections, if any, do you see between what you wrote there and "A Smart Cookie"?

Shaping Interpretations

2. When Esperanza's mother uses the **idiom** "smart cookie" to describe herself, what does she mean?

3. What does Esperanza's mother mean when she says "Got to take care all your own"? How does this statement relate to her comments about education?

4. What advice is Esperanza's mother giving her daughter? From your experience, do you think Esperanza is likely to follow her mother's advice?

Extending the Text

5. Describe Esperanza's mother's attitude toward education. What do you think she would say about education to the speaker of "Legacy II" (page 109)? How would he reply?

CHOICES: Building Your Portfolio

Writer's Notebook

1. Collecting Ideas for a Persuasive Essay

Think about Cisneros's short story and your own experience, and jot down your responses to one of these opinions:

- Parents can put too much pressure on children by wanting their children to have better lives than they had.
- Children need to know the mistakes their parents made so they can avoid making the same mistakes.
- Education is the key to independence.

Art

2. Hearts and Cookies

Respond to "A Smart Cookie" or "The Secret Heart" (page 112) with a drawing or a sculpture (perhaps of clay, wire, or papier-mâché). Illustrate one of the scenes as you envision it, or creatively interpret feelings and memories that came to mind as you read.

Speaking and Listening

3. Life Before Me?

Interview an older family member about his or her life before you were born. You may want to concentrate on one or two of these areas: education; career plans; or talents, interests, and hobbies.

Write up the interview either in a question-and-answer format or in paragraph form, using a combination of your words and the words of the person you're interviewing.

Before You Read

THE MEDICINE BAG

Make the Connection

Coming of Age

"Today I am an adult." When will *you* say those words? In some families and cultures the passage into adulthood is marked by a ceremony, such as the Jewish bar mitzvah or bat mitzvah ritual. In others you're recognized as an adult when you get a driver's license, finish high school or college, or get your first job.

Quickwrite

Write for a few minutes about your own coming of age. Did it or will it include any special rituals? Who was or will be involved? Does more than one event mark adulthood for you?

Elements of Literature

Dynamic and Static Characters

A **dynamic character** is one who changes because of what happens in a story. Usually, the main character in a story changes, while less important characters are **static**—they stay basically the same.

As you read "The Medicine Bag," look for clues that Martin's character is changing in important ways. Ask yourself: What signs show that Martin is coming of age?

A **dynamic character** changes as a result of a story's events. A **static character** does not change much.

For more on Character, see pages 106–107 and the Handbook of Literary Terms.

Reading Skills and Strategies

Comparing and Contrasting: Before and After

When you **compare** people or things, you show their similarities—how they are alike. When you **contrast** people or things, you show how they are different. As you read "The Medicine Bag," pay attention to how Martin, the main character, changes. Compare the person Martin is at the beginning of the story to the person Martin is at its end.

Background

Literature and Culture

In "The Medicine Bag" a boy named Martin learns about the coming of age of his Teton Sioux (tē′tän′ sōō) great-great-grandfather, Iron Shell. In the Sioux tradition a teenage boy becomes a man by making a *vision quest,* going off alone to find spiritual power and guidance through a dream. Sometimes he also finds *medicine,* an object believed to provide protection or power.

*"When he was old and I was
a man, he gave it to me . . ."*

The
Medicine
Bag

Virginia Driving Hawk Sneve

My kid sister Cheryl and I always bragged about our Sioux grandpa, Joe Iron Shell. Our friends, who had always lived in the city and only knew about Indians from movies and TV, were impressed by our stories. Maybe we exaggerated and made Grandpa and the reservation sound glamorous, but when we'd return home to Iowa after our yearly summer visit to Grandpa, we always had some exciting tale to tell.

We always had some authentic Sioux article to show our listeners. One year Cheryl had new moccasins that Grandpa had made. On another visit he gave me a small, round, flat rawhide drum which was decorated with a painting of a warrior riding a horse. He taught me a real Sioux chant to sing while I beat the drum with a leather-covered stick that had a feather on the end. Man, that really made an impression.

We never showed our friends Grandpa's picture. Not that we were ashamed of him, but because we knew that the glamorous tales we told didn't go with the real thing. Our friends would have laughed at the picture, because Grandpa wasn't tall and

When the Eagle Spoke to Me (1979) by Jerry Ingram.

stately like TV Indians. His hair wasn't in braids but hung in stringy gray strands on his neck, and he was old. He was our great-grandfather, and he didn't live in a tepee, but all by himself in a part log, part tar-paper shack on the Rosebud Reservation in South Dakota. So when Grandpa came to visit us, I was so ashamed and embarrassed I could've died.

There are a lot of yippy poodles and other fancy little dogs in our neighborhood, but they usually barked singly at the mailman from the safety of their own yards. Now it sounded as if a whole pack of mutts were barking together in one place.

I got up and walked to the curb to see what the commotion was. About a block away I saw a crowd of little kids yelling, with the dogs yipping and growling around someone who was walking down the middle of the street.

I watched the group as it slowly came closer and saw that in the center of the strange procession was a man wearing a tall black hat. He'd pause now and then to peer at something in his hand and then at the houses on either side of the street. I felt cold and hot at the same time as I recognized the man. "Oh, no!" I whispered. "It's Grandpa!"

I stood on the curb, unable to move even though I wanted to run and hide. Then I got mad when I saw how the yippy dogs were growling and nipping at the old man's baggy pant legs and how wearily he poked them away with his cane. "Stupid mutts," I said as I ran to rescue Grandpa.

When I kicked and hollered at the dogs to get away, they put their tails between their legs and scattered. The kids ran to the curb, where they watched me and the old man.

"Grandpa," I said, and felt pretty dumb when my voice cracked. I reached for his beat-up old tin suitcase, which was tied shut with a rope. But he set it down right in the street and shook my hand.

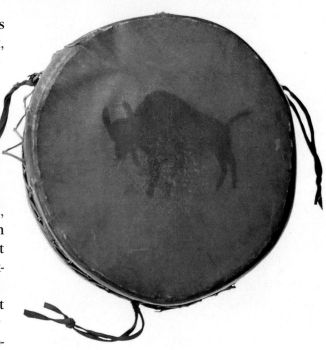

Dakota Sioux drum (c. 1910).

"Hau, Takoza, Grandchild," he greeted me formally in Sioux.

All I could do was stand there with the whole neighborhood watching and shake the hand of the leather-brown old man. I saw how his gray hair straggled from under his big black hat, which had a drooping feather in its crown. His rumpled black suit hung like a sack over his stooped frame. As he shook my hand, his coat fell open to expose a bright-red satin shirt with a beaded bolo tie[1] under the collar. His get-up wasn't out of place on the reservation, but it sure was here, and I wanted to sink right through the pavement.

"Hi," I muttered with my head down. I tried

---

1. **bolo tie:** cord with a decorated fastening, worn as a necktie.

- -

WORDS TO OWN
stately (stāt′lē) *adj.:* majestic; dignified; grand.
stooped (stoopt) *v.* used as *adj.:* bent forward from habit.

- -

to pull my hand away when I felt his bony hand trembling, and looked up to see fatigue in his face. I felt like crying. I couldn't think of anything to say, so I picked up Grandpa's suitcase, took his arm, and guided him up the driveway to our house.

Mom was standing on the steps. I don't know how long she'd been watching, but her hand was over her mouth and she looked as if she couldn't believe what she saw. Then she ran to us.

"Grandpa," she gasped. "How in the world did you get here?"

She checked her move to embrace Grandpa, and I remembered that such a display of affection is unseemly to the Sioux and would embarrass him.

"Hau, Marie," he said as he shook Mom's hand. She smiled and took his other arm.

As we supported him up the steps, the door banged open and Cheryl came bursting out of the house. She was all smiles and was so obviously glad to see Grandpa that I was ashamed of how I felt.

"Grandpa!" she yelled happily. "You came to see us!"

Grandpa smiled and Mom and I let go of him as he stretched out his arms to my ten-year-old sister, who was still young enough to be hugged.

"Wicincala, little girl," he greeted her, and then collapsed.

He had fainted. Mom and I carried him into her sewing room, where we had a spare bed.

After we had Grandpa on the bed, Mom stood there helplessly patting his shoulder.

"Shouldn't we call the doctor, Mom?" I suggested, since she didn't seem to know what to do.

"Yes," she agreed, with a sigh. "You make Grandpa comfortable, Martin."

I reluctantly moved to the bed. I knew Grandpa wouldn't want to have Mom undress him, but I didn't want to, either. He was so skinny and frail that his coat slipped off easily. When I loosened his tie and opened his shirt collar, I felt a small leather pouch that hung from a thong[2] around his neck. I left it alone and moved to remove his boots. The scuffed old cowboy boots were tight and he moaned as I put pressure on his legs to jerk them off.

I put the boots on the floor and saw why they fit so tight. Each one was stuffed with money. I looked at the bills that lined the boots and started to ask about them, but Grandpa's eyes were closed again.

Mom came back with a basin of water. "The doctor thinks Grandpa is suffering from heat exhaustion," she explained as she bathed Grandpa's face. Mom gave a big sigh, "Oh hinh, Martin. How do you suppose he got here?"

We found out after the doctor's visit. Grandpa was angrily sitting up in bed while Mom tried to feed him some soup.

"Tonight you let Marie feed you, Grandpa," spoke my dad, who had gotten home from work just as the doctor was leaving. "You're not really sick," he said as he gently pushed Grandpa back against the pillows. "The doctor said you just got too tired and hot after your long trip."

Grandpa relaxed, and between sips of soup he told us of his journey. Soon after our visit to him Grandpa decided that he would like to see where his only living descendants lived and what our home was like. Besides, he admitted sheepishly, he was lonesome after we left.

I knew everybody felt as guilty as I did—especially Mom. Mom was all Grandpa had left. So even after she married my dad, who's a white man and teaches in the college in our city, and after Cheryl and I were born, Mom

2. **thong:** narrow strip of leather.

- -

WORDS TO OWN

fatigue (fə·tēg') *n.*: exhaustion; tiredness.
reluctantly (ri·luk'tənt·lē) *adv.*: unwillingly.

- -

made sure that every summer we spent a week with Grandpa.

I never thought that Grandpa would be lonely after our visits, and none of us noticed how old and weak he had become. But Grandpa knew and so he came to us. He had ridden on buses for two and a half days. When he arrived in the city, tired and stiff from sitting for so long, he set out, walking, to find us.

He had stopped to rest on the steps of some building downtown and a policeman found him. The cop, according to Grandpa, was a good man who took him to the bus stop and waited until the bus came and told the driver to let Grandpa out at Bell View Drive. After Grandpa got off the bus, he started walking again. But he couldn't see the house numbers on the other side when he walked on the sidewalk, so he walked in the middle of the street. That's when all the little kids and dogs followed him.

I knew everybody felt as bad as I did. Yet I was proud of this eighty-six-year-old man, who had never been away from the reservation, having the courage to travel so far alone.

"You found the money in my boots?" he asked Mom.

"Martin did," she answered, and roused herself to scold. "Grandpa, you shouldn't have carried so much money. What if someone had stolen it from you?"

Grandpa laughed. "I would've known if anyone tried to take the boots off my feet. The money is what I've saved for a long time—a hundred dollars—for my funeral. But you take it now to buy groceries so that I won't be a burden to you while I am here."

"That won't be necessary, Grandpa," Dad said. "We are honored to have you with us and you will never be a burden. I am only sorry that we never thought to bring you home with us this summer and spare you the discomfort of a long trip."

Grandpa was pleased. "Thank you," he answered. "But do not feel bad that you didn't bring me with you, for I would not have come then. It was not time." He said this in such a way that no one could argue with him. To Grandpa and the Sioux, he once told me, a thing would be done when it was the right time to do it and that's the way it was.

"Also," Grandpa went on, looking at me, "I have come because it is soon time for Martin to have the medicine bag."

We all knew what that meant. Grandpa thought he was going to die and he had to follow the tradition of his family to pass the medicine bag, along with its history, to the oldest male child.

"Even though the boy," he said, still looking at me, "bears a white man's name, the medicine bag will be his."

I didn't know what to say. I had the same hot and cold feeling that I had when I first saw Grandpa in the street. The medicine bag was the dirty leather pouch I had found around his neck. "I could never wear such a thing," I almost said aloud. I thought of having my friends see it in gym class, at the swimming pool, and could imagine the smart things they would say. But I just swallowed hard and took a step toward the bed. I knew I would have to take it.

But Grandpa was tired. "Not now, Martin," he said, waving his hand in dismissal, "it is not time. Now I will sleep."

So that's how Grandpa came to be with us for two months. My friends kept asking to come see the old man, but I put them off. I told myself that I didn't want them laughing at Grandpa. But even as I made excuses, I knew it wasn't Grandpa that I was afraid they'd laugh at.

Nothing bothered Cheryl about bringing her friends to see Grandpa. Every day after school started, there'd be a crew of giggling little girls or round-eyed little boys crowded around the old man on the patio, where he'd gotten in the habit of sitting every afternoon.

Grandpa would smile in his gentle way and patiently answer their questions, or he'd tell them stories of brave warriors, ghosts, animals, and the kids listened in awed silence. Those little guys thought Grandpa was great.

Finally, one day after school, my friends came home with me because nothing I said stopped them. "We're going to see the great Indian of Bell View Drive," said Hank, who was supposed to be my best friend. "My brother has seen him three times, so he oughta be well enough to see us."

When we got to my house, Grandpa was sitting on the patio. He had on his red shirt, but today he also wore a fringed leather vest that was decorated with beads. Instead of his usual cowboy boots he had solidly beaded moccasins on his feet that stuck out of his black trousers. Of course, he had his old black hat on—he was seldom without it. But it had been brushed and the feather in the beaded headband was proudly erect, its tip a brighter

Dakota Sioux vest (c. 1880–1900).

white. His hair lay in silver strands over the red shirt collar.

I started just as my friends did and I heard one of them murmur, "Wow!"

Grandpa looked up and when his eyes met mine, they twinkled as if he were laughing inside. He nodded to me and my face got all hot. I could tell that he had known all along I was afraid he'd embarrass me in front of my friends.

"Hau, hoksilas, boys," he greeted, and held out his hand.

My buddies passed in a single file and shook his hand as I introduced them. They were so polite I almost laughed. "How, there, Grandpa," and even a "How do you do, sir."

"You look fine, Grandpa," I said as the guys sat on the lawn chairs or on the patio floor.

"Hanh, yes," he agreed. "When I woke up this morning, it seemed the right time to dress in the good clothes. I knew that my grandson would be bringing his friends."

"You guys want some lemonade or something?" I offered. No one answered. They were listening to Grandpa as he started telling how he'd killed the deer from which his vest was made.

Grandpa did most of the talking while my friends were there. I was so proud of him and amazed at how respectfully quiet my buddies were. Mom had to chase them home at suppertime. As they left, they shook Grandpa's hand again and said to me:

"Martin, he's really great!"

"Yeah, man! Don't blame you for keeping him to yourself."

"Can we come back?"

But after they left, Mom said, "No more visitors for a while, Martin. Grandpa won't admit it, but his strength hasn't returned. He likes having company, but it tires him."

That evening Grandpa called me to his room before he went to sleep. "Tomorrow," he said, "when you come home, it will be time to give you the medicine bag."

Sioux pipe bag.

I felt a hard squeeze from where my heart is supposed to be and was scared, but I answered, "OK, Grandpa."

All night I had weird dreams about thunder and lightning on a high hill. From a distance I heard the slow beat of a drum. When I woke up in the morning, I felt as if I hadn't slept at all. At school it seemed as if the day would never end and when it finally did, I ran home.

Grandpa was in his room, sitting on the bed. The shades were down and the place was dim and cool. I sat on the floor in front of Grandpa, but he didn't even look at me. After what seemed a long time, he spoke.

"I sent your mother and sister away. What you will hear today is only for a man's ears. What you will receive is only for a man's hands." He fell silent and I felt shivers down my back.

"My father in his early manhood," Grandpa began, "made a vision quest to find a spirit guide for his life. You cannot understand how it was in that time, when the great Teton Sioux were first made to stay on the reservation. There was a strong need for guidance from Wakantanka, the Great Spirit. But too many of the young men were filled with despair and hatred. They thought it was hopeless to search for a vision when the glorious life was gone and only the hated <u>confines</u> of a reservation lay ahead. But my father held to the old ways.

"He carefully prepared for his quest with a purifying sweat bath and then he went alone to a high butte[3] top to fast and pray. After three days he received his sacred dream—in which he found, after long searching, the white man's iron. He did not understand his vision of find-

---

3. butte (byo͞ot): steep, flat-topped hill standing alone on a plain.

WORDS TO OWN
confines (kän′fīnz′) *n.*: borders; boundaries.

ing something belonging to the white people, for in that time they were the enemy. When he came down from the butte to cleanse himself at the stream below, he found the remains of a campfire and the broken shell of an iron kettle. This was a sign which reinforced his dream. He took a piece of the iron for his medicine bag, which he had made of elk skin years before, to prepare for his quest.

"He returned to his village, where he told his dream to the wise old men of the tribe. They gave him the name Iron Shell, but neither did they understand the meaning of the dream. This first Iron Shell kept the piece of iron with him at all times and believed it gave him protection from the evils of those unhappy days.

"Then a terrible thing happened to Iron Shell. He and several other young men were taken from their homes by the soldiers and sent far away to a white man's boarding school. He was angry and lonesome for his parents and the young girl he had wed before he was taken away. At first Iron Shell resisted the teachers' attempts to change him and he did not try to learn. One day it was his turn to work in the school's blacksmith shop. As he walked into the place, he knew that his medicine had brought him there to learn and work with the white man's iron.

"Iron Shell became a blacksmith and worked at the trade when he returned to the reservation. All of his life he treasured the medicine bag. When he was old and I was a man, he gave it to me, for no one made the vision quest anymore."

Grandpa quit talking and I stared in disbelief as he covered his face with his hands. His shoulders were shaking with quiet sobs and I looked away until he began to speak again.

"I kept the bag until my son, your mother's father, was a man and had to leave us to fight in the war across the ocean. I gave him the bag, for I believed it would protect him in battle, but he did not take it with him. He was afraid

that he would lose it. He died in a faraway place."

Again Grandpa was still and I felt his grief around me.

"My son," he went on after clearing his throat, "had only a daughter and it is not proper for her to know of these things."

He unbuttoned his shirt, pulled out the leather pouch, and lifted it over his head. He held it in his hand, turning it over and over as if memorizing how it looked.

"In the bag," he said as he opened it and removed two objects, "is the broken shell of the iron kettle, a pebble from the butte, and a piece of the sacred sage."[4] He held the pouch upside down and dust drifted down.

"After the bag is yours, you must put a piece of prairie sage within and never open it again until you pass it on to your son." He replaced the pebble and the piece of iron and tied the bag.

I stood up, somehow knowing I should. Grandpa slowly rose from the bed and stood upright in front of me, holding the bag before my face. I closed my eyes and waited for him to slip it over my head. But he spoke.

"No, you need not wear it." He placed the soft leather bag in my right hand and closed my other hand over it. "It would not be right to wear it in this time and place, where no one will understand. Put it safely away until you are again on the reservation. Wear it then, when you replace the sacred sage."

Grandpa turned and sat again on the bed. Wearily he leaned his head against the pillow. "Go," he said, "I will sleep now."

"Thank you, Grandpa," I said softly, and left with the bag in my hands.

That night Mom and Dad took Grandpa to the hospital. Two weeks later I stood alone on the lonely prairie of the reservation and put the sacred sage in my medicine bag.

4. **sage:** plant with fragrant leaves.

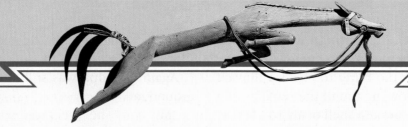

MEET THE WRITER

Passing on the Heritage

Like Grandpa in "The Medicine Bag," **Virginia Driving Hawk Sneve** (1933–   ) was born on the Rosebud Reservation in South Dakota and is a member of the Rosebud Sioux. Sneve (snā′vē) and her husband lived in Iowa for many years. Their children, like Martin and Cheryl, grew up knowing Rosebud only from summer visits. "The Medicine Bag" was inspired by Sneve's oldest son and his excitement over a great-uncle's visit, as she explains:

❝ The day of my uncle's arrival, there were about a dozen little boys sitting on each side of our driveway waiting for this Indian uncle to show up. I didn't think too much about it—I thought it was kind of neat that this welcoming committee was there. My uncle came driving up in a great big blue air-conditioned Oldsmobile, and when he got out, he was wearing a pair of slacks and a sports shirt. My aunt, too, had on slacks and a blouse. We welcomed them, and in the bustle of the visit we didn't pay too much attention to the kids.

Later I found out from my neighbor, who was non-Indian, that my son had primed all the little boys to expect this uncle to come riding up on a horse, in a breechcloth. Those little boys were disgusted and upset because this uncle looked like anybody else.

Until then, I hadn't thought about what my children thought about Indians.

When my daughter was in the third grade, she read the Laura Ingalls Wilder books, the 'Little House on the Prairie' books, which are about South Dakota pioneers, the white settlement period. She was fascinated with that period in history and wanted to know more. There wasn't much in the books about Indians, and she wanted to know why. So when I started writing for children, I did so with the specific purpose of informing my own children about their heritage and trying to correct some misconceptions about how they saw Indian people and how others thought about Indians. **❞**

Sioux war
shield
(c. 1850).

I Am Kwakkoli

A few months after my tenth birthday, my dad began to talk to me about receiving my Indian name. He said this had to be done in a ceremony by a medicine person or an elder in our tribe. My older sister, Megan, had received her Indian name, Maquegquay (Woman of the Woods), when she was only three. At that time my family lived on the Oneida Reservation just outside of Green Bay, Wisconsin. My grandfather was alive then, and he asked a medicine-man friend of his to name her and made the arrangements. I always thought my sister's Indian name was so perfect for her. I was told the medicine man meditated for three days before the name came to him.

My family moved from Wisconsin to Colorado three years before I was born. My grandfather died when I was only two and a half, and both of these major events delayed my Naming Ceremony. My dad talked about naming me for several years, but it was hard to pull it together long-distance. Because of the sacred and traditional aspects of this, it is not as if anyone can just call and order a Naming Ceremony, like ordering a pizza! As it happened, my uncle Rick became the chairman of the tribe when I was ten, and he was able to talk to the right people and select the time. The right time was the summer solstice, near June 20, and it was also the time of the annual Strawberry Ceremony.

There are many traditions connected to the Naming Ceremony. For one thing, there are a limited number of names among the Oneida people. When a person dies, that name returns to the pool of available names and can be given to someone else. The medicine person decides whose energy fits which available name, or a person may ask for a certain name. In my case, I was named after my grandfather through my Anglo name, but I also wanted to take his Indian name, which was available and had been waiting for me for seven years. I felt that if I had both of his names, it made a full circle and I was wholly connected to him and to my family. The name that was his is Kwakkoli, or "Whippoorwill" in English.

A few days before the ceremony, in June of 1990, my parents and I flew to the Oneida Reservation. A friend of my dad made me a beautiful "ribbon shirt." It was a shade of deep turquoise, stitched with pink, purple, and green ribbons. My family and I thought it was very special and that I looked good in it.

Two days before I was given my Indian name, my uncle Rick, my dad, and I drove around and looked at certain landmarks on the Oneida Reservation. I saw where my dad had grown up. There is a statue in the middle of the reservation of my great-grandmother, Dr. Rosa Minoka Hill. She was the first female Indian physician in the United States.

Oneida is very small and different from any other city I have known. It has only one school, several baseball fields, a small convent, a store, a post office, two churches, three cemeteries, a tribal building, and about twenty houses. My dad and his brother knew the names of everyone. They knew who was married to whom and who everyone's grandparents and parents were. They remembered all kinds of funny stories and laughed a lot. I thought it must be nice to live in a small town where everyone knows everyone for all those years. It is also a place where everyone is connected by common heritage, customs, and beliefs.

The night before the ceremony, I got very nervous. My stomach hurt as if I had the flu, but I think it was just butterflies. I finally fell asleep at about 3:30 in the morning. I don't know what I was afraid of—maybe just not knowing what was going to happen or what I would have to do. My mother could not come to the ceremony, because only tribal members were allowed. We had just learned about this and I was upset that she couldn't come. She was disappointed, but told me to remember the details and tell her about it later.

After getting about four hours of sleep, I woke up to the sound of a shower running. I quickly put on my ribbon shirt, a pair of black pants, and moccasins. The ceremony was set for 9:30 that morning, so we had to hurry.

On our short drive to the reservation, my stomach felt as if it were going to explode! I had to at least get those butterflies flying in formation! I was pretty anxious, but really excited about getting my Indian name. We arrived at the long house a little early, and I sat with my dad and one of his friends while other people finished setting up tables and chairs.

The ceremony finally began. The Faithkeeper called up the three clans of the Oneida Tribe: the Bear, the Turtle, and the Wolf. I am in the Turtle Clan, so I would be named in the second group. The Faithkeeper named all the children in the Bear Clan, then moved on to the Turtles. He named two people, then stepped in front of me. He spoke to me in Oneida. It is a language with unusual sounds like no other language I have ever heard. Most of the words were not understandable to me. He later translated them as, "You must try to learn the Oneida language and our ways. I would like you to come to some of the other ceremonies and events. You now have an Oneida name, Kwakkoli, and the Creator will know you by that name." I was proud to have both my grandfather's names, because he was an important man in our tribe.

The Faithkeeper named the others and we all sat down as the Chief said a few more prayers. After about an hour, we all danced to Indian songs and drum music. It was fun but became tiring after a while.

Next, we ate and drank. One of the drinks was a kind of strawberry juice. It is sacred and part of the ceremony because the Creator gave this gift of the strawberry to the Oneida people. The drink was very good.

When it was time to go, we thanked the Faithkeeper and the Chief and gave them gifts. The gift that I received, and will be mine for life, is a very special name that runs through my family and connects me to my grandfather, whom I barely knew. My name also reminds me of the many traditions and beliefs that are part of my heritage and about which I have a lot to learn and understand. I look forward to visiting my reservation as I grow up.

—Bisco Hill
Southern Hills Middle School
Boulder, Colorado

First appeared in *Merlyn's Pen: The National Magazines of Student Writing.*

MAKING MEANINGS

First Thoughts

1. What thoughts and memories did "The Medicine Bag" and "I Am Kwakkoli" call to mind—of people, events, feelings? Do you see any connection between either piece and your Quickwrite? Explain.

Shaping Interpretations

2. How is Martin's life different from Grandpa's? What problems do these differences cause for Martin?

3. Why is Martin ashamed of Grandpa at the beginning of the story?

4. Why does Martin feel like crying after he greets Grandpa? (Can you think of more than one reason?)

5. **Dynamic character.** Draw a thought bubble like the one on the right. Fill it with words, sketches, and symbols that **contrast** what Martin is like at the beginning of the story to the way he is at the end, after he receives the medicine bag. You might focus on his changed feelings about Grandpa.

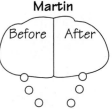

6. Martin's friends are impressed by Grandpa. Describe how Martin might feel about Grandpa if his friends laughed at him instead. Do you think his friends' opinion should make any difference? Explain.

Connecting with the Text

7. Describe what goes through Martin's mind as he is about to receive the medicine bag. How would you feel if you were in his place?

Extending the Text

8. What do you think Grandpa would do with the medicine bag if Martin were a girl? Why?

9. **Compare** the experiences of two of the following people:
   - Martin
   - Sneve's son
   - Bisco Hill
   - Cheryl
   - Sneve's daughter

CHOICES: Building Your Portfolio

Writer's Notebook

1. Collecting Ideas for a Persuasive Essay

Some people think that our society doesn't have ways of helping young people cross the threshold into adulthood. We need traditions and meaningful rituals for this important rite of passage, they say. In what ways do people today mark the passage into adulthood? Do you think there should be other ways of helping children to accept the duties and responsibilities of adult life? Do you think, instead, that things are all right the way they are? Write down some ideas supporting your point of view.

> Kids don't like to admit it, but they're insecure about becoming adults. Rituals help define what "being an adult" means.

Creative Writing

2. A Tough Decision

Grandpa's father's medicine bag contains several items of special importance to him (the iron and the pebble) or to his people (the sacred sage). Imagine that, like Martin, you have a pouch that you can open just once, to add one item to pass on to your own child. **Describe** the item, and explain why you chose it. You may want to make a drawing of the item to accompany your explanation.

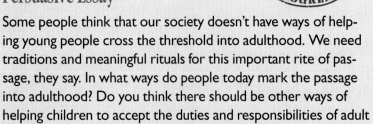

North Cheyenne ceremonial gourd rattle (c. 1850).

Research/Social Studies

3. Researching a Culture

With a small group of classmates, list everything you learned about Sioux customs and history from the story. Then, brainstorm questions you still have about the Sioux—perhaps about how they live today or their traditional religious beliefs.

Each member of the group should choose one question to explore. Use resources such as history books and computer databases; if possible, consult knowledgeable members of your community. Share with your group what you have learned; then, work together to create a presentation for the class.

Art/Critical Thinking

4. What's in a Name?

In some cultures, people are given one name when they are born and take another name when they come of age. Like the name Iron Shell in the story, the "earned" name reflects something about the person's character or life.

Invent a name that says something important about who you are. The name could reflect your personality, cultural background, interests, or talents.

On unlined paper, design a T-shirt or jacket with your new name, decorating it with an appropriate picture or symbol. Attach a note explaining what the name means to you.

Style: Choosing Precise Words

Language Handbook H E L P

See Using Specific Nouns, page 738.

Which creates a clearer, more vivid picture in your mind:

• *house* or *mansion*?

• *walk* or *shuffle*?

Choosing precise words when you write will help your reader "get the picture," too.

When you revise, make sure you haven't used modifiers (adjectives and adverbs) to do the job of precise nouns and verbs. Sneve could have begun her story, "My kid sister Cheryl and I always <u>talked boastfully</u> about our Sioux grandpa," but <u>bragged</u> says the same thing more efficiently. Add modifiers only when your nouns and verbs are already doing everything they can: "part log, part tar-paper shack," for example, or "beat-up old tin suitcase."

Try It Out

Take out a piece of your writing, and circle four or five general words. Substitute precise words (or add well-chosen modifiers) to create a clearer picture.

VOCABULARY   HOW TO OWN A WORD

WORD BANK

stately
stooped
fatigue
reluctantly
confines

Tracing Word Histories: Word Origins and Roots

You can track down a **word's origin** by looking up its **etymology**—its history—in a dictionary. The etymology appears in brackets after the word's pronunciation. The *oldest* known root is given last. (The **root** of a word carries its core meaning.) In the front of a dictionary, you'll find an explanation of abbreviations and symbols that will help you to read the etymologies. Sometimes you have to look at other forms of the word to find an etymology.

Below is a word web showing the etymology of *stately*. Use a word web to analyze each of the other words in the Word Bank.

Root: Latin *stare*, "to stand" — **stately** — **Word's meaning:** "majestic; dignified; grand"

Sample use: Grandpa was <u>stately</u> because he stood tall and proud.

Before You Read

GRANDMA LING

Make the Connection

A Magic Mirror

Has anyone ever told you that you have your great-grandfather's nose or that you're going to be as tall as your aunt? The special connection of a resemblance can cause mixed feelings. You may be proud of looking so much like your sister that people sometimes mistake you for her. On the other hand, you probably also want everyone to realize that you're a unique person with your own identity.

Quickwrite

Do people say you look like someone else? If so, who? (The person doesn't have to be a family member; you may be told you resemble a friend or someone famous.) How do you feel about the resemblance?

Elements of Literature

Imagery

As you read the poem, notice how the writer uses **images**— words that help you see the grandmother and her home. Which words create pictures

in your mind? What details come from your imagination?

Read the poem a second time, and write down the three or four images that you like best.

> **I**magery is language that appeals to the senses.
>
> *For more on Imagery, see the Handbook of Literary Terms.*

Background

Literature and Geography

In the poem you're about to read, a young Chinese American woman meets her grandmother for the first time. "Grandma Ling" lives halfway around the world, in Taiwan, an island off the southeastern coast of China.

go.hrw.com
LEO 8-2

Grandma Ling 祖母

Amy Ling

If you dig that hole deep enough,
you'll reach China, they used to tell me,
a child in a back yard in Pennsylvania.
Not strong enough to dig that hole,
5   I waited twenty years,
then sailed back, half way around the world.

In Taiwan I first met Grandma.
Before she came to view, I heard
her slippered feet softly measure
10   the tatami° floor with even step;
the aqua paper-covered door slid open
and there I faced
my five foot height, sturdy legs and feet,
square forehead, high cheeks and wide-set eyes;
15   my image stood before me,
acted on by fifty years.

She smiled, stretched her arms
to take to heart the eldest daughter
of her youngest son a quarter century away.
20   She spoke a tongue I knew no word of,
and I was sad I could not understand,
but I could hug her.

10. tatami (tə·tä′mē): floor mat woven of rice straw.

MEET THE WRITER

Between Worlds

As a child, **Amy Ling** (1939–   ) had a special reason for wanting to reach China: She'd be going home. Amy Ling, whose name was originally Ling Ying Ming, was born in Beijing, China, and moved to the United States with her family at the age of six.

"Grandma Ling" was inspired by a trip to Taiwan the poet made in the early 1960s. The photo shown here was taken during that visit.

BB This is a photo of my grandmother, my cousin May Li Ling (in the yellow dress, on the right), and me (in pale blue, on the left). We are celebrating our twenty-fourth birthday—my cousin is five days older than I—in my aunt's home in Da Ling Sugar Factory in Taiwan. See the tatami mats on the floor and the sliding paper doors. I thought this photo would be particularly appropriate, since this is the paternal grandmother I was writing about meeting in my poem. ""

Today Ling studies and writes about other American writers who are "between worlds," especially Asian American women writers.

MAKING MEANINGS

First Thoughts

1. Briefly describe or draw an **image** that this poem calls to mind.

Shaping Interpretations

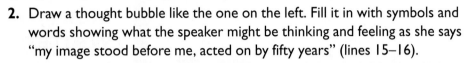

2. Draw a thought bubble like the one on the left. Fill it in with symbols and words showing what the speaker might be thinking and feeling as she says "my image stood before me, acted on by fifty years" (lines 15–16).

3. The speaker in the poem cannot understand her grandmother's words. Write what you think the grandmother is saying to her granddaughter.

Connecting with the Text

4. Look back at your Quickwrite. How do your feelings about looking like someone else compare with the feelings expressed in this poem?

5. Look at the adults around you. Do you see in them any clues about what you might be like when you're older? Which traits do you hope to share? Which would you like to change?

CHOICES: Building Your Portfolio

Writer's Notebook

1. Collecting Ideas for a Persuasive Essay

One of your friends says that it's important to know something about your heritage and culture. Someone else says it doesn't matter if you don't know anything about your ancestors—it's what *you* do that counts. How do you feel about this issue? Freewrite about whether or not it is important to know where you came from.

Oral Interpretation

2. Grandma Ling Alive

Work with a group to present an oral interpretation of "Grandma Ling." First, decide if you will read individually or as a group. Then, note places where you want to read slowly or softly or swiftly. Watch for punctuation marks. Ask your audience to evaluate your performance.

Art

3. Traveling in Time

What will you look like in fifty years? Draw yourself as sixty-something.

Performance

4. Getting to Know You

Suppose you meet someone who speaks a language different from yours. With a partner, show how you would communicate that

- you are happy to meet the person
- you want to learn the person's name
- you want to offer the person a drink

What **gestures, facial expressions,** and **props** would you use?

Reading Skills and Strategies

"HELP! I'M STUCK!"

Earlier you learned strategies for getting past an unknown word in a text (page 43)—but what if you don't understand a sentence, a passage, or even the whole point of a text you're reading? All readers get stuck sometimes. Being a successful reader means recognizing when you're stuck and using the best strategies, such as those below, to get unstuck.

1. Ask yourself: What is it that I don't understand here? Is it a single sentence or an entire paragraph? Is it the text's vocabulary, topic, or organization?

2. You may want to jot down notes or make an outline, a sketch, or a map. Various kinds of **graphic organizers,** like those at right, can help you check your understanding of a text.

3. Go back to the last point at which you understood the text. Reread the troublesome passage more slowly.

4. Maybe you haven't "read between the lines." Not everything will be spelled out in a text; the successful reader always has to make **inferences**—educated guesses. You make inferences when you put together information in the text with what you already know and then make a leap—you guess what it means. Do I understand *why* something just happened? Do I understand the result of some action or decision? (For more about drawing inferences, see page 416.)

Story Map
(to show sequence)

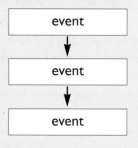

Venn Diagram
(to compare and contrast)

Word Web
(to connect ideas)

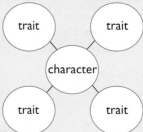

CALVIN AND HOBBES © Watterson. Dist. by UNIVERSAL PRESS SYNDICATE.
Reprinted with permission. All rights reserved.

Apply the strategy on the next page.

Before You Read

THE MOUSTACHE

Make the Connection

A Trip into the Unknown

In the story you're about to read, seventeen-year-old Mike visits his grandmother for the first time since she became ill and moved into the Lawnrest Nursing Home. Have you ever visited a nursing home? What ideas do you have about nursing homes?

Making a map is a good way to organize your ideas. Create a cluster map like the one that follows, filling it in with all the words and phrases that come to mind when you think about visiting someone in a nursing home.

Visiting a Nursing Home

Discuss your map with your classmates. What made you think of these words and phrases? Which of your associations are like those of other students? Which are yours alone?

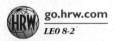
go.hrw.com
LEO 8-2

Quickwrite

Complete three of these sentences:

- Most elderly people are . . .
- They like . . .
- They don't really . . .
- Older people feel . . .
- They worry about . . .

Reading Skills and Strategies

Drawing Inferences: Understanding Character

An **inference** is a kind of guess you make based on clues in the story combined with your own experience. When you make inferences about characters, you try to find out what kind of people they are.

- Take note of information the writer tells you directly— for example, that a character is kind or mean or fussy.

- Pay attention to what the character thinks, says, and does.

- Watch how other people react to the character.

- Think about people you know in real life who resemble the character.

As you read "The Moustache," look for evidence that helps you understand Mike, the main character.

The Moustache

Robert Cormier

Frankly, I wasn't too crazy about visiting a nursing home.

At the last minute Annie couldn't go. She was invaded by one of those twenty-four-hour flu bugs that sent her to bed with a fever, moaning about the fact that she'd also have to break her date with Handsome Harry Arnold that night. We call him Handsome Harry because he's actually handsome, but he's also a nice guy, cool, and he doesn't treat me like Annie's kid brother, which I am, but like a regular person. Anyway, I had to go to Lawnrest alone that afternoon. But first of all I had to stand inspection. My mother lined me up against the wall. She stood there like a one-man firing squad, which is kind of funny because she's not like a man at all, she's very feminine, and we have this great relationship—I mean, I feel as if she really likes me. I realize that sounds strange, but I know guys whose mothers love them and cook special stuff for them and worry about them and all but there's something missing in their relationship.

Anyway. She frowned and started the routine.

"That hair," she said. Then admitted: "Well, at least you combed it."

I sighed. I have discovered that it's better to sigh than argue.

"And that moustache." She shook her head. "I still say a seventeen-year-old has no business wearing a moustache."

"It's an experiment," I said. "I just wanted to see if I could grow one." To tell the truth, I had proved my point about being able to grow a decent moustache, but I also had learned to like it.

"It's costing you money, Mike," she said.

"I know, I know."

The money was a reference to the movies. The Downtown Cinema has a special Friday night offer—half-price admission for high school couples seventeen or younger. But the woman in the box office took one look at my moustache and charged me full price. Even when I showed her my driver's license. She charged full admission for Cindy's ticket, too, which left me practically broke and unable to take Cindy out for a hamburger with the crowd afterward. That didn't help matters, because Cindy has been getting impatient recently about things like the fact that I don't own my own car and have to concentrate on my studies if I want to win that college scholarship, for instance. Cindy wasn't exactly crazy about the moustache, either.

Now it was my mother's turn to sigh.

"Look," I said, to cheer her up. "I'm thinking about shaving it off." Even though I wasn't. Another discovery: You can build a way of life on postponement.

"Your grandmother probably won't even recognize you," she said. And I saw the shadow fall across her face.

Let me tell you what the visit to Lawnrest was all about. My grandmother is seventy-three years old. She is a resident—which is supposed to be a better word than *patient*—at the Lawnrest Nursing Home. She used to make the greatest turkey dressing in the world and was a nut about baseball and could even quote batting averages, for crying out loud. She always rooted for the losers. She was in love with the Mets until they started to win. Now she has arteriosclerosis, which the dictionary says is "a chronic disease characterized by abnormal thickening and hardening of the arterial[1] walls." Which really means that she can't live at home anymore or even with us, and her memory has betrayed her, as well as her body. She used to wander off and sometimes didn't recognize people. My mother visits her all the time, driving the thirty miles to Lawnrest almost every day. Because Annie was home for a semester break from college, we had decided to make a special Saturday visit. Now Annie was in bed, groaning theatrically—she's a drama major—but I told my mother I'd go anyway. I hadn't seen my grandmother since she'd been admitted to Lawnrest. Besides, the place is located on the Southwest Turnpike, which meant I could barrel along in my father's new Le Mans. My ambition was to see the speedometer hit seventy-five. Ordinarily, I used the old station wagon, which can barely stagger up to fifty.

Frankly, I wasn't too crazy about visiting a nursing home. They reminded me of hospitals, and hospitals turn me off. I mean, the smell of ether[2] makes me nauseous, and I feel faint at the sight of blood. And as I approached Lawnrest—which is a terrible, cemetery kind of name, to begin with—I was sorry I hadn't avoided the trip. Then I felt guilty about it. I'm loaded with guilt complexes. Like driving like a madman after promising my father to be careful. Like sitting in the parking lot, looking at the nursing home with dread and thinking how I'd rather be with Cindy. Then I thought of all the Christmas and birthday gifts my grand-

mother had given me and I got out of the car, guilty as usual.

Inside, I was surprised by the lack of hospital smell, although there was another odor or maybe the absence of an odor. The air was antiseptic, sterile. As if there was no atmosphere at all or I'd caught a cold suddenly and couldn't taste or smell.

A nurse at the reception desk gave me directions—my grandmother was in East Three. I made my way down the tiled corridor and was glad to see that the walls were painted with cheerful colors like yellow and pink. A wheelchair suddenly shot around a corner, self-propelled by an old man, white-haired and toothless, who cackled merrily as he barely missed me. I jumped aside—here I was, almost getting wiped out by a two-mile-an-hour wheelchair after doing seventy-five on the pike. As I walked through the corridor seeking East

---

1. **arterial:** of the arteries, the tubes that carry blood away from the heart.
2. **ether** (ē′thər): strong-smelling anesthetic (substance used to deaden pain or cause unconsciousness).

WORDS TO OWN

chronic (krän′ik) *adj.:* lasting a long time; constant.
sterile (ster′əl) *adj.:* free from germs. *Sterile* also means "unproductive."

Three, I couldn't help glancing into the rooms, and it was like some kind of wax museum—all these figures in various stances and attitudes,[3] sitting in beds or chairs, standing at windows, as if they were frozen forever in these postures. To tell the truth, I began to hurry because I was getting depressed. Finally, I saw a beautiful girl approaching, dressed in white, a nurse or an attendant, and I was so happy to see someone young, someone walking and acting normally, that I gave her a wide smile and a big hello and I must have looked like a kind of nut. Anyway, she looked right through me as if I were a window, which is about par for the course whenever I meet beautiful girls.

I finally found the room and saw my grandmother in bed. My grandmother looks like Ethel Barrymore. I never knew who Ethel Barrymore was until I saw a terrific movie, *None but the Lonely Heart,* on TV, starring Ethel Barrymore and Cary Grant. Both my grandmother and Ethel Barrymore have these great craggy faces like the side of a mountain and wonderful voices like syrup being poured. Slowly. She was propped up in bed, pillows puffed behind her. Her hair had been combed out and fell upon her shoulders. For some reason, this flowing hair gave her an almost girlish appearance, despite its whiteness.

She saw me and smiled. Her eyes lit up and her eyebrows arched and she reached out her hands to me in greeting. "Mike, Mike," she said. And I breathed a sigh of relief. This was one of her good days. My mother had warned me that she might not know who I was at first.

I took her hands in mine. They were fragile. I could actually feel her bones, and it seemed as if they would break if I pressed too hard. Her skin was smooth, almost slippery, as if the years had worn away all the roughness the way the wind wears away the surfaces of stones.

"Mike, Mike, I didn't think you'd come," she said, so happy, and she was still Ethel Barrymore, that voice like a caress. "I've been waiting all this time." Before I could reply, she looked away, out the window. "See the birds? I've been watching them at the feeder. I love to see them come. Even the blue jays. The blue jays are like hawks—they take the food that the small birds should have. But the small birds, the chickadees, watch the blue jays and at least learn where the feeder is."

She lapsed into silence, and I looked out the window. There was no feeder. No birds. There was only the parking lot and the sun glinting on car windshields.

She turned to me again, eyes bright. Radiant, really. Or was it a medicine brightness? "Ah, Mike. You look so grand, so grand. Is that a new coat?"

"Not really," I said. I'd been wearing my Uncle Jerry's old army-fatigue jacket for months, practically living in it, my mother said. But she insisted that I wear my raincoat for the visit. It was about a year old but looked new because I didn't wear it much. Nobody was wearing raincoats lately.

3. **stances and attitudes:** poses and positions.

"You always loved clothes, didn't you, Mike?" she said.

I was beginning to feel uneasy because she regarded me with such intensity. Those bright eyes. I wondered—are old people in places like this so lonesome, so abandoned that they go wild when someone visits? Or was she so happy because she was suddenly <u>lucid</u> and everything was sharp and clear? My mother had described those moments when my grandmother suddenly emerged from the fog that so often obscured her mind. I didn't know the answers, but it felt kind of spooky, getting such an emotional welcome from her.

"I remember the time you bought the new coat—the Chesterfield," she said, looking away again, as if watching the birds that weren't there. "That lovely coat with the velvet collar. Black, it was. Stylish. Remember that, Mike? It was hard times, but you could never resist the glitter."

I was about to protest—I had never heard of a Chesterfield, for crying out loud. But I stopped. Be patient with her, my mother had said. Humor her. Be gentle.

We were interrupted by an attendant who pushed a wheeled cart into the room. "Time for juices, dear," the woman said. She was the standard forty- or fifty-year-old woman: glasses, nothing hair, plump cheeks. Her manner was cheerful but a businesslike kind of cheerfulness. I'd hate to be called "dear" by someone getting paid to do it. "Orange or grape or cranberry, dear? Cranberry is good for the bones, you know."

My grandmother ignored the interruption. She didn't even bother to answer, having turned away at the woman's arrival, as if angry about her appearance.

The woman looked at me and winked. A <u>conspiratorial</u> kind of wink. It was kind of horrible. I didn't think people winked like that anymore. In fact, I hadn't seen a wink in years.

"She doesn't care much for juices," the woman said, talking to me as if my grandmother weren't even there. "But she loves her coffee. With lots of cream and two lumps of sugar. But this is juice time, not coffee time." Addressing my grandmother again, she said, "Orange or grape or cranberry, dear?"

"Tell her I want no juices, Mike," my grandmother commanded <u>regally</u>, her eyes still watching invisible birds.

The woman smiled, patience like a label on her face. "That's all right, dear. I'll just leave some cranberry for you. Drink it at your leisure. It's good for the bones."

She wheeled herself out of the room. My grandmother was still absorbed in the view.

WORDS TO OWN

lucid (lōō′sid) *adj.*: clearheaded. *Lucid* also means "easily understood."

conspiratorial (kən·spir′ə·tôr′ē·əl) *adj.*: suggesting a secret plot.

regally (rē′gəl·ē) *adv.*: majestically; in the manner of a queen or king.

Somewhere a toilet flushed. A wheelchair passed the doorway—probably that same old driver fleeing a hit-run accident. A television set exploded with sound somewhere, soap-opera voices filling the air. You can always tell soap-opera voices.

I turned back to find my grandmother staring at me. Her hands cupped her face, her index fingers curled around her cheeks like parenthesis marks.

"But you know, Mike, looking back, I think you were right," she said, continuing our conversation as if there had been no interruption. "You always said, 'It's the things of the spirit that count, Meg.' The spirit! And so you bought the baby-grand piano—a baby grand in the middle of the Depression. A knock came on the door and it was the deliveryman. It took five of them to get it into the house." She leaned back, closing her eyes. "How I loved that piano, Mike. I was never that fine a player, but you loved to sit there in the parlor, on Sunday evenings, Ellie on your lap, listening to me play and sing." She hummed a bit, a fragment of

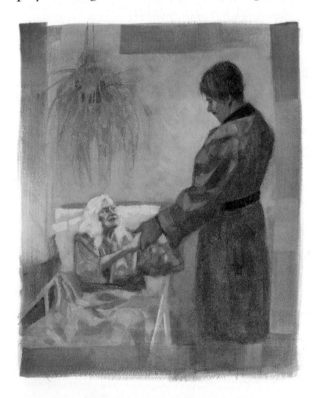

melody I didn't recognize. Then she drifted into silence. Maybe she'd fallen asleep. My mother's name is Ellen, but everyone always calls her Ellie. "Take my hand, Mike," my grandmother said suddenly. Then I remembered— my grandfather's name was Michael. I had been named for him.

"Ah, Mike," she said, pressing my hands with all her feeble strength. "I thought I'd lost you forever. And here you are, back with me again. . . ."

Her expression scared me. I don't mean scared as if I were in danger but scared because of what could happen to her when she realized the mistake she had made. My mother always said I favored her side of the family. Thinking back to the pictures in the old family albums, I recalled my grandfather as tall and thin. Like me. But the resemblance ended there. He was thirty-five when he died, almost forty years ago. And he wore a moustache. I brought my hand to my face. I also wore a moustache now, of course.

"I sit here these days, Mike," she said, her voice a lullaby, her hand still holding mine, "and I drift and dream. The days are fuzzy sometimes, merging together. Sometimes it's like I'm not here at all but somewhere else altogether. And I always think of you. Those years we had. Not enough years, Mike, not enough . . ."

Her voice was so sad, so mournful, that I made sounds of sympathy, not words exactly but the kind of soothings that mothers murmur to their children when they awaken from bad dreams.

"And I think of that terrible night, Mike, that terrible night. Have you ever really forgiven me for that night?"

"Listen . . ." I began. I wanted to say: "Nana, this is Mike your grandson, not Mike your husband."

"Sh . . . sh . . ." she whispered, placing a finger as long and cold as a candle against my lips. "Don't say anything. I've waited so long for this moment. To be here. With you. I wondered what I would say if suddenly you walked in that door like other people have done. I've thought and thought about it. And I finally made up my mind—I'd ask you to forgive me. I was too proud to ask before." Her fingers tried to mask her face. "But I'm not proud anymore, Mike." That great voice quivered and then grew strong again. "I hate you to see me this way— you always said I was beautiful. I didn't believe it. The Charity Ball when we led the grand march and you said I was the most beautiful girl there . . ."

"Nana," I said. I couldn't keep up the pretense any longer, adding one more burden to my load of guilt, leading her on this way, playing a pathetic game of make-believe with an old woman clinging to memories. She didn't seem to hear me.

"But that other night, Mike. The terrible one. The terrible accusations I made. Even Ellie woke up and began to cry. I went to her and rocked her in my arms and you came into the room and said I was wrong. You were whispering, an awful whisper, not wanting to upset little Ellie but wanting to make me see the truth. And I didn't answer you, Mike. I was too proud. I've even forgotten the name of the girl. I sit here, wondering now—was it Laura or Evelyn? I can't remember. Later, I learned that you were telling the truth all the time, Mike. That I'd been wrong . . ." Her eyes were brighter than ever as she looked at me now, but tear-bright, the tears gathering. "It was never the same after that night, was it, Mike? The glitter was gone. From you. From us. And then the accident . . . and I never had the chance to ask you to forgive me. . . ."

My grandmother. My poor, poor grandmother. Old people aren't supposed to have those kinds of memories. You see their pictures in the family albums and that's what they are: pictures. They're not supposed to come to

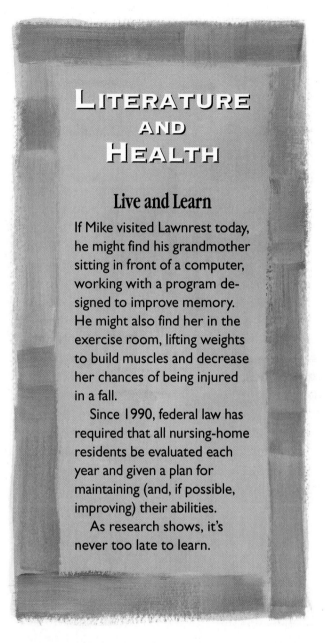

LITERATURE AND HEALTH

Live and Learn

If Mike visited Lawnrest today, he might find his grandmother sitting in front of a computer, working with a program designed to improve memory. He might also find her in the exercise room, lifting weights to build muscles and decrease her chances of being injured in a fall.

Since 1990, federal law has required that all nursing-home residents be evaluated each year and given a plan for maintaining (and, if possible, improving) their abilities.

As research shows, it's never too late to learn.

life. You drive out in your father's Le Mans doing seventy-five on the pike and all you're doing is visiting an old lady in a nursing home. A duty call. And then you find out that she's a person. She's *somebody*. She's my grandmother, all right, but she's also herself. Like my own mother and father. They exist outside of their relationship to me. I was scared again. I wanted to get out of there.

"Mike, Mike," my grandmother said. "Say it, Mike."

I felt as if my cheeks would crack if I uttered a word.

"Say you forgive me, Mike. I've waited all these years. . . ."

I was surprised at how strong her fingers were.

"Say *'I forgive you, Meg.'*"

I said it. My voice sounded funny, as if I were talking in a huge tunnel. "I forgive you, Meg."

Her eyes studied me. Her hands pressed mine. For the first time in my life, I saw love at work. Not movie love. Not Cindy's sparkling eyes when I tell her that we're going to the beach on a Sunday afternoon. But love like something alive and tender, asking nothing in return. She raised her face, and I knew what she wanted me to do. I bent and brushed my lips against her cheek. Her flesh was like a leaf in autumn, crisp and dry.

She closed her eyes and I stood up. The sun wasn't glinting on the cars any longer. Somebody had turned on another television set, and the voices were the show-off voices of the panel shows. At the same time you could still hear the soap-opera dialogue on the other television set.

I waited awhile. She seemed to be sleeping, her breathing serene and regular. I buttoned my raincoat. Suddenly she opened her eyes again and looked at me. Her eyes were still bright, but they merely stared at me. Without recognition or curiosity. Empty eyes. I smiled at her, but she didn't smile back. She made a kind of moaning sound and turned away on the bed, pulling the blankets around her.

I counted to twenty-five and then to fifty and did it all over again. I cleared my throat and coughed tentatively. She didn't move; she didn't respond. I wanted to say, "Nana, it's me." But I didn't. I thought of saying, "Meg, it's me." But I couldn't.

Finally I left. Just like that. I didn't say good-bye or anything. I stalked through the corridors, looking neither to the right nor the left, not caring whether that wild old man with the wheelchair ran me down or not.

On the Southwest Turnpike I did seventy-five—no, eighty—most of the way. I turned the radio up as loud as it could go. Rock music—anything to fill the air. When I got home, my mother was vacuuming the living-room rug. She shut off the cleaner, and the silence was deafening. "Well, how was your grandmother?" she asked.

I told her she was fine. I told her a lot of things. How great Nana looked and how she seemed happy and had called me Mike. I wanted to ask her—hey, Mom, you and Dad really love each other, don't you? I mean—there's nothing to forgive between you, is there? But I didn't.

Instead I went upstairs and took out the electric razor Annie had given me for Christmas and shaved off my moustache.

MEET THE WRITER

"The Stuff of Fiction"

Robert Cormier (1925–   ) lives in Leominster, Massachusetts, just three miles away from the house in which he was born. Although he has traveled all over the world, he says he gets the ideas for his stories from "watching and listening, pondering the comings and goings of my hometown."

"The Moustache" was inspired by events very close to home:

Photograph © 1994 by Jill Krementz.

66 When my son, Peter, was a teenager, his maternal grandmother became a resident in a local nursing home. The victim of an accident from which she never really recovered—she was struck by a car as she crossed a street—she had more recently suffered the terrible onslaught of arteriosclerosis. Those were shatter-ing days for us all, particularly my wife, who visited her daily but found little comfort because her mother often did not recognize her. . . .

One Saturday, Peter visited her in the nursing home. He returned visibly moved, shaken. Her condition had af-fected him greatly. His grandmother had been uncommunicative, ravaged by the disease, only a dim echo of the Mémère he had known and loved throughout his boyhood. . . .

Thus the stuff of actuality is trans-formed into the stuff of fiction.

The underlying problem, of course, is to have the characters appear as distinct personalities of their own and not carbon copies of the actual people. In effect, I have used real emotions but the people are real only on the printed page—the boy in the story is not Peter and the woman is not his grandmother. 99

More by Robert Cormier

"The Moustache" is the first story in a collection called *8 Plus 1* (Bantam). Cormier introduces each story in the collection with a comment like the one you've just read.
The Chocolate War (Dell) is an award-winning classic novel about a teenager named Jerry and his lonely fight against peer pressure and violence.

Grandpa

His eyes glow like pearls in the water
sitting like a majestic eagle
staring into nothing—
dusty old hat
5 that's seen many years.

Knobby old cane shines in the sun;
he walks through the small
sand canyon which once was flat.
The lizard bows to the aging man
10 for soon he will be gone
like the lady he loves.

Cars zooming by like a trail of ants—
the sound of kids playing
like the sound of a storm
15 he only can hear—
the thought of the years.

—Shandin Pete
Arlee Junior High School
Arlee, Montana

Na Na

If I had magic powers I could
Get my Na Na an elevator chair
for her stairway.
She would eat all the cooked
5 cabbage she wanted to eat.
I would give her another
set of teeth;
they would be strong
enough so she could
10 eat hard things like carrots.
I would give her some more
hair because her hair-
line is receding.
She would be free of pills,
15 Very healthy.
She would be able to drink
other things, like
KOOL-AID
Instead of drinking orange
20 juice all the time.
School would end on
Thursday
So I could visit my Na Na
more often.
25 And when I'd go over to my Na Na's house,
I'd be so strong I'd pick up the
REFRIGERATOR
And clean behind it.

—Jaqueta Oliver
Weston Middle School
Weston, Massachusetts

First appeared in *Merlyn's Pen: The National Magazines of Student Writing.*

MAKING MEANINGS

First Thoughts

1. Draw a line down the middle of a blank page. On the left, copy two or three short passages from the text that made a strong impression on you. On the right, jot down your thoughts about each passage. An example follows.

Double-Entry Journal

Passage	Response
"I'd hate to be called 'dear' by someone getting paid to do it." (page 143)	It makes me think of how I'd feel if I lived in a nursing home.

Reading Check

a. What clues tell Mike that it is *not* one of his grand-mother's "good days"?

b. Who does his grand-mother think he is? Why?

c. What event in the past is she sorry about?

d. Why does Mike's visit give his grandmother her only chance to be forgiven?

Shaping Interpretations

2. Complete the following sentence in at least two ways: *Mike expected . . . but . . . so . . .*

3. What **inference** can you make about the fact that when Mike returns from the nursing home he does not tell his mother about what happened there?

4. Mike directly reveals a lot about himself in this story, but he doesn't tell us why he shaves off his moustache. What did you **infer** about his reasons for the shave?

5. What do Mike and his grandmother give each other? (What is passed from generation to generation?)

Connecting with the Text

6. Go back to page 145, and reread the paragraph starting "My grandmother." Have you ever come to a similar realization about an adult in your life? If so, what event brought you that awareness?

Extending the Text

7. Look back at your Quickwrite. Now that you've read "The Moustache," what changes, if any, would you make to what you wrote?

Challenging the Text

8. Does Mike do the right thing by saying "I forgive you, Meg"? What would you do if you were Mike?

CHOICES: Building Your Portfolio

Writer's Notebook

1. Collecting Ideas for a Persuasive Essay

A **position statement** is a brief, direct statement of where you stand on an issue. The following are position statements on three issues raised by "The Moustache." Where do you stand on these issues? Write your own position statement about one of them. Jot down several details you could use to support your position.

- It is better to let older people stay at home.
- Health care for all elderly people should be free.
- We should forgive others instead of judging them.

Position Statement:
Nursing homes should help old people be as independent as possible.

—with good care, some people will get better—good care makes them happy
—relatives will feel better if a nursing home is like a real home

Creative Writing

2. Found: A Poem

A **found poem** is made up of words, phrases, or sentences from a piece of writing that are chosen and arranged to communicate the essence of the piece. Go back to "The Moustache," and choose the ten words, phrases, and sentences that you feel best communicate what the story means to you. Copy each onto a separate strip of paper. Try out different arrangements of the strips until you find one you like. (You don't have to use all your strips.) Glue your arrangement onto a sheet of paper, and give your found poem a title.

Performance

3. Freeze! It's a Tableau

With two or three classmates, choose a scene from the story to perform as a **tableau** (tab′lō′). In a tableau the actors create a frozen scene, silently holding the positions and wearing the expressions of the characters they are representing. The director brings the tableau to life by tapping the actors one at a time. After being tapped, each actor moves and speaks in character, telling what the character is thinking and feeling at that moment, while the other actors remain frozen. The actor who was tapped freezes when tapped again.

Character Sketch

4. What to Make of Mike

Write a brief **character sketch** of Mike. Skim back over the story for evidence of the following:

- what Mike looks like
- how Mike acts
- what Mike says about himself
- what he says to others
- what others say about Mike and how they respond to him

You might want to gather details about Mike in a word web before you begin writing.

LANGUAGE LINK MINI-LESSON

Style: Connotations

Handbook of Literary Terms HELP

See Connotation.

Connotations are the feelings or ideas associated with words in addition to their **denotations,** or literal (dictionary) meanings. *Petite* and *runty* are both words used to describe small people, but one word has positive connotations and the other has negative connotations. As a result, their meanings are very different.

Words' connotations can also convey finer shades of difference. *Cute, attractive,* and *gorgeous* are all positive words, but they create very different images in a reader's mind.

One way to find a word with just the right connotations is to look up the word you're using in a **thesaurus** (book of synonyms and antonyms) and see whether any of the word's synonyms express your meaning even more precisely. If you're not sure what the connotations of some of the synonyms are, look up the words in a dictionary.

Use thesaurus words in moderation. If you use too many, you'll drown out your natural voice.

Try It Out

Go back to the story, and look for the sentences in which Mike discusses the connotations of the following expressions:

1. "one-man firing squad" (page 140)
2. "resident" (page 140)
3. "Lawnrest" (page 141)

Do the words have the same connotations for you as they do for Mike? Explain your responses.

VOCABULARY HOW TO OWN A WORD

WORD BANK

chronic
sterile
lucid
conspiratorial
regally

Digging into the Past: Greek and Latin Roots

The **root** of every word carries the word's core meaning. Many English words are based on root words that have their origin in the ancient classical languages of Greek and Latin. Here are six Greek and Latin roots that are found in many English words.

Greek Roots	Latin Roots
chron, chrono, "time"	*luc, lum,* "light"
dem, demos, "the people"	*rex, regis,* "king"
steria, "barren"	*spirare,* "to breathe"

- Match each Word Bank word with its root listed in the chart. (Look up each word's **etymology,** or history, in a dictionary to make sure.)
- Work with a partner to list other English words that come from the root words in the chart. Include definitions of these words. How many words did you come up with?

NO **Questions** ASKED

"I have no use for old people in my village."

The Wise Old Woman

traditional Japanese, retold by
Yoshiko Uchida

go.hrw.com
LEO 8-2

Many long years ago, there lived an arrogant and cruel young lord who ruled over a small village in the western hills of Japan.

"I have no use for old people in my village," he said haughtily. "They are neither useful nor able to work for a living. I therefore decree that anyone over seventy-one

must be banished from the village and left in the mountains to die."

"What a dreadful decree! What a cruel and unreasonable lord we have," the people of the village murmured. But the lord fearfully punished anyone who disobeyed him, and so villagers who turned seventy-one were tearfully carried into the mountains, never to return.

Gradually there were fewer and fewer old people in the village and soon they disappeared altogether. Then the young lord was pleased.

"What a fine village of young, healthy, and hard-working people I have," he bragged. "Soon it will be the finest village in all of Japan."

Now, there lived in this village a kind young farmer and his aged mother. They were poor, but the farmer was good to his mother, and the two of them lived happily together. However, as the years went by, the mother grew older, and before long she reached the terrible age of seventy-one.

"If only I could somehow deceive the cruel lord," the farmer thought. But there were records in the village books and everyone knew that his mother had turned seventy-one.

Each day the son put off telling his mother that he must take her into the mountains to die, but the people of the village began to talk. The farmer knew that if he did not take his mother away soon, the lord would send his soldiers and throw them both into a dark dungeon to die a terrible death.

"Mother——" he would begin, as he tried to tell her what he must do, but he could not go on.

Then one day the mother herself spoke of the lord's dread decree. "Well, my son,"

Peach Blossom Spring (detail) (1780s) by Tani Bunchō. Handscroll; ink, color, and gold on silk, after the Chinese artist Qiu Ying.

she said, "the time has come for you to take me to the mountains. We must hurry before the lord sends his soldiers for you." And she did not seem worried at all that she must go to the mountains to die.

"Forgive me, dear mother, for what I must do," the farmer said sadly, and the next morning he lifted his mother to his shoulders and set off on the steep path toward the mountains. Up and up he climbed, until the trees clustered close and the path was gone. There was no longer even the sound of birds, and they heard only the soft wail of the wind in the trees. The son walked slowly, for he could not bear to think of leaving his old mother in the mountains. On and on he climbed, not wanting to stop and leave her behind. Soon, he heard his mother breaking off small twigs from the trees that they passed.

"Mother, what are you doing?" he asked.

"Do not worry, my son," she answered gently. "I am just marking the way so you will not get lost returning to the village."

The son stopped. "Even now you are thinking of me?" he asked, wonderingly.

The mother nodded. "Of course, my son," she replied. "You will always be in my thoughts. How could it be otherwise?"

At that, the young farmer could bear it no longer. "Mother, I cannot leave you in the mountains to die all alone," he said. "We are going home and no matter what the lord does to punish me, I will never desert you again."

So they waited until the sun had set and a lone star crept into the silent sky. Then, in the dark shadows of night, the farmer carried his mother down the hill and they returned quietly to their little house. The farmer dug a deep hole in the floor of his kitchen and made a small room where he could hide his mother. From that day, she spent all her time in the secret room and

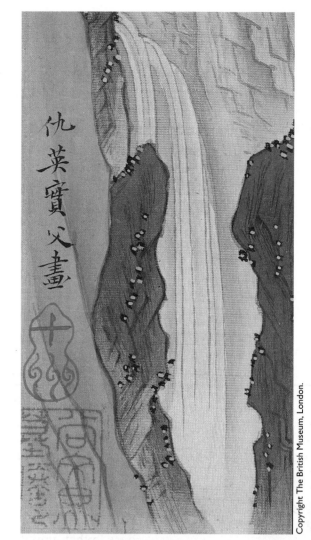

Peach Blossom Spring (detail) (1780s) by Tani Bunchō. Handscroll; ink, color, and gold on silk, after the Chinese artist Qiu Ying.

the farmer carried meals to her there. The rest of the time, he was careful to work in the fields and act as though he lived alone. In this way, for almost two years he kept his mother safely hidden and no one in the village knew that she was there.

Then one day there was a terrible commotion among the villagers, for Lord Higa of the town beyond the hills threatened to conquer their village and make it his own.

"Only one thing can spare you," Lord Higa announced. "Bring me a box containing one thousand ropes of ash and I will spare your village."

The cruel young lord quickly gathered together all the wise men of his village. "You are men of wisdom," he said. "Surely you can tell me how to meet Lord Higa's demands so our village can be spared."

But the wise men shook their heads. "It is impossible to make even one rope of ash, sire," they answered. "How can we ever make one thousand?"

"Fools!" the lord cried angrily. "What good is your wisdom if you cannot help me now?"

And he posted a notice in the village square offering a great reward of gold to any villager who could help him save their village.

But all the people in the village whispered, "Surely, it is an impossible thing, for ash crumbles at the touch of the finger. How could anyone ever make a rope of ash?" They shook their heads and sighed, "Alas, alas, we must be conquered by yet another cruel lord."

The young farmer, too, supposed that this must be, and he wondered what would happen to his mother if a new lord even more terrible than their own came to rule over them.

When his mother saw the troubled look on his face, she asked, "Why are you so worried, my son?"

So the farmer told her of the impossible demand made by Lord Higa if the village was to be spared, but his mother did not seem troubled at all. Instead she laughed softly and said, "Why, that is not such an impossible task. All one has to do is soak ordinary rope in salt water and dry it well. When it is burned, it will hold its shape and there is your rope of ash! Tell the villagers to hurry and find one thousand pieces of rope."

The farmer shook his head in amazement. "Mother, you are wonderfully wise," he said, and he rushed to tell the young lord what he must do.

"You are wiser than all the wise men of the village," the lord said when he heard the farmer's solution, and he rewarded him with many pieces of gold. The thousand ropes of ash were quickly made and the village was spared.

In a few days, however, there was another great commotion in the village as Lord Higa sent another threat. This time he sent a log with a small hole that curved and bent seven times through its length, and he demanded that a single piece of silk thread be threaded through the hole. "If you cannot perform this task," the lord threatened, "I shall come to conquer your village."

The young lord hurried once more to his wise men, but they all shook their heads in bewilderment. "A needle cannot bend its way through such curves," they moaned. "Again we are faced with an impossible demand."

"And again you are stupid fools!" the lord said, stamping his foot impatiently. He then posted a second notice in the village square asking the villagers for their help.

Once more the young farmer hurried with the problem to his mother in her secret room.

"Why, that is not so difficult," his mother said with a quick smile. "Put some sugar at one end of the hole. Then tie an ant to a piece of silk thread and put it in at the other end. He will weave his way in and out of the curves to get to the sugar and he will take the silk thread with him."

"Mother, you are remarkable!" the son cried, and he hurried off to the lord with the solution to the second problem.

Once more the lord commended the young farmer and rewarded him with many pieces of gold. "You are a brilliant man and you have saved our village again," he said gratefully.

But the lord's troubles were not over even then, for a few days later Lord Higa sent still another demand. "This time you will undoubtedly fail and then I shall conquer your village," he threatened. "Bring me a drum that sounds without being beaten."

"But that is not possible," sighed the people of the village. "How can anyone make a drum sound without beating it?"

This time the wise men held their heads in their hands and moaned, "It is hopeless. It is hopeless. This time Lord Higa will conquer us all."

The young farmer hurried home breathlessly. "Mother, Mother, we must solve another terrible problem or Lord Higa will conquer our village!" And he quickly told his mother about the impossible drum.

His mother, however, smiled and answered, "Why, this is the easiest of them all. Make a drum with sides of paper and put a bumblebee inside. As it tries to escape, it will buzz and beat itself against the paper and you will have a drum that sounds without being beaten."

The young farmer was amazed at his mother's wisdom. "You are far wiser than any of the wise men of the village," he said, and he hurried to tell the young lord how to meet Lord Higa's third demand.

When the lord heard the answer, he was greatly impressed. "Surely a young man like you cannot be wiser than all my wise men," he said. "Tell me honestly, who has helped you solve all these difficult problems?"

The young farmer could not lie. "My lord," he began slowly, "for the past two years I have broken the law of the land. I have kept my aged mother hidden beneath the floor of my house, and it is she who solved each of your problems and saved the village from Lord Higa."

He trembled as he spoke, for he feared the lord's displeasure and rage. Surely now the soldiers would be summoned to throw him into the dark dungeon. But when he glanced fearfully at the lord, he saw that the young ruler was not angry at all. Instead, he was silent and thoughtful, for at last he realized how much wisdom and knowledge old people possess.

"I have been very wrong," he said finally. "And I must ask the forgiveness of your mother and of all my people. Never again will I demand that the old people of our village be sent to the mountains to die. Rather, they will be treated with the respect and honor they deserve and share with us the wisdom of their years."

And so it was. From that day, the villagers were no longer forced to abandon their parents in the mountains, and the village became once more a happy, cheerful place in which to live. The terrible Lord Higa stopped sending his impossible demands and no longer threatened to conquer them, for he too was impressed. "Even in such a small village there is much wisdom," he declared, "and its people should be allowed to live in peace."

And that is exactly what the farmer and his mother and all the people of the village did for all the years thereafter.

Bamboo (1835) by Tani Bunchō.
Folding fan; ink on paper.

MEET THE WRITER

Preserving the Magic

Yoshiko Uchida
(1921–1992) was born in
Alameda, California, and grew
up in Berkeley. During World
War II, Uchida and her family
were imprisoned in one of the
camps set up for the 110,000
Japanese Americans living on
the West Coast. She later
wrote about this experience
in *The Invisible Thread* (1991).

After the war, Uchida traveled to Japan to rediscover
her roots and to collect
Japanese folk tales to add to
the ones she had heard as a child from
her mother. "The Wise Old Woman" is
one of these tales.

Late in her life, Uchida reflected on
her lifelong love for the written word:

❝ It seems to me I've been interested
in books and writing for as long as I can
remember. I was writing stories when I
was ten, and being the child of frugal immigrant parents, I wrote them on brown
wrapping paper which I cut up and
bound into booklets, and because I am
such a saver, I still have them. The first is
titled 'Jimmy Chipmunk and His Friends:
A Short Story for Small Children.'

I not only wrote stories, I also kept a
journal of important events which I
began the day I graduated from elementary school. Of course my saver self kept
the journal as well, and even today I can
read of the special events of my young
life, such as the times my parents took us
to an opera or concert in San Francisco,
or the day I got my first dog, or the sad
day he died, when I drew a tombstone
for him in my journal and decorated it
with floral wreaths.

By putting these special happenings
into words and writing them down, I was
trying to hold on to and somehow preserve the magic, as well as the joy and
sadness, of certain moments in my life,
and I guess that's really what books and
writing are all about. ❞

More by Yoshiko Uchida

"The Wise Old Woman" comes from
The Sea of Gold and Other Tales from Japan
(Creative Arts). *The Magic Listening Cap:
More Folk Tales from Japan* (Creative
Arts) is a book Uchida both wrote and
illustrated.

The Old Grandfather and His Little Grandson

traditional European, retold by **Leo Tolstoy**

Count Leo Nikolayevich Tolstoy (1828–1910) was a Russian writer and philosopher whose ideas greatly influenced Russian society and literature. He is best known for his novels War and Peace *and* Anna Karenina.

Tolstoy with his grandson.

The grandfather had become very old. His legs would not carry him, his eyes could not see, his ears could not hear, and he was toothless. When he ate, bits of food sometimes dropped out of his mouth. His son and his son's wife no longer allowed him to eat with them at the table. He had to eat his meals in the corner near the stove.

One day they gave him his food in a bowl. He tried to move the bowl closer; it fell to the floor and broke. His daughter-in-law scolded him. She told him that he spoiled everything in the house and broke their dishes, and she said that from now on he would get his food in a wooden dish. The old man sighed and said nothing.

A few days later, the old man's son and his wife were sitting in their hut, resting and watching their little boy playing on the floor. They saw him putting together something out of small pieces of wood. His father asked him, "What are you making, Misha?"

The little grandson said, "I'm making a wooden bucket. When you and Mama get old, I'll feed you out of this wooden dish."

The young peasant and his wife looked at each other and tears filled their eyes. They were ashamed because they had treated the old grandfather so meanly, and from that day they again let the old man eat with them at the table and took better care of him.

Gapless Generations

In Paul Zindel's novel *The Pigman* (Bantam), John and Lorraine befriend Mr. Pignati, a widower with a passion for bad jokes and miniature pigs. (*The Pigman* is available in the HRW Library.) Then tragedy tears the Pigman away. John and Lorraine's story continues in *The Pigman's Legacy* (Bantam).

   The Pigman and Me (HarperCollins) tells the true story of the year the teenage Zindel met his own "pigman." You'll find an excerpt on page 82.

Together in a Strange Land

The year is 1903. Eight-year-old Moon Shadow leaves his mother in China and journeys across the ocean to join his father, in Laurence Yep's *Dragonwings* (HarperCollins). In the land of the golden mountain—America—Moon Shadow comes to love his father and understand his dream of flying.

Parent Past Perfect

Do you ever think that your parents can't possibly understand what it's like to be young? Victoria does, in this book by Francine Pascal, until a freak accident sends her spinning back in time and she finds herself *Hangin' Out with Cici* (Puffin), a girl her own age who seems strangely familiar.

Other Picks

- Pat Derby, *Visiting Miss Pierce* (Farrar, Straus & Giroux). A boy visits an elderly woman in a nursing home and gradually uncovers the truth about her past.
- Will Hobbs, *Bearstone* (HRW Library). In this coming-of-age story an American Indian youth is helped by an elderly farmer.
- *Strings: A Gathering of Family Poems* (Bradbury Press), selected by Paul B. Janeczko. Poems by such poets as Gary Soto, Anne Sexton, and George Ella Lyon tell about the ups and downs of family life.

Writer's Workshop

PERSUASIVE WRITING

SUPPORTING A POSITION

In your everyday conversations, you probably spend a lot of time supporting your positions—maybe about school rules, homework, or people and events in the news. In this workshop, you'll write an essay in which you support your position on an important issue and try to convince an audience to agree with you.

ASSIGNMENT

Write an essay supporting your position, or opinion, on an important issue.

AIM

To persuade.

AUDIENCE

Your classmates, teachers, parents, school board, readers of a school or local newspaper, etc. (You choose.)

Professional Model

We don't look up in wonder nearly enough these days. We look down instead, absorbed in the minutiae of our own demanding lives. Our focus is in, not out.

Thesis statement and elaboration.

As a result we miss things. Amazing things. Such as the fact that several times a year, a group of brave women and men will climb aboard a spaceship and ride a pillar of fire into the dark unknown.

Topic sentence.
Specific example.

It happens all the time, after all, so we forget to be awed. . . . Except that, there went John Glenn rocketing into space again the other day, and we all watched, didn't we? School kids and grown folks. Maybe we felt something stirring in us, something quiet and proud and strangely familiar. Something that felt good.

Topic sentence.

Anecdote.

If thirty-six years ago, he bolstered our flagging confidence, perhaps by this return engagement, Senator Glenn does

Emotional appeal— uses loaded words.

The history
of the written
word is rich and
Page

> something equally important—
> reminds us what a glorious thing
> it is to venture and dream. What a
> life-affirming gift it is to look
> up in wonder.
>
> —Leonard Pitts, Jr.,
> *Miami Herald,* Nov. 7, 1998

*Conclusion—
repeats thesis.*

Prewriting

1. Choose a Topic

Check your Writer's Notebook entries from this collection for topic ideas. If you aren't satisfied with those topics, brainstorm more issues with a partner or small group. The topic you choose should meet these criteria:

- You must have strong feelings about the topic.
- There must be reasonable "pro" and "con" arguments on the topic.
- You must be able to find out more about the topic by researching.

2. Take a Stand

Once you've chosen your topic (and done research if necessary), draft a **thesis statement** that (a) clearly identifies the issue and (b) states your position on the issue.

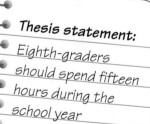

Thesis statement:
Eighth-graders should spend fifteen hours during the school year volunteering to help the elderly.

CALVIN AND HOBBES © 1993 Watterson.
Reprinted with permission of UNIVERSAL PRESS SYNDICATE. All rights reserved.

Language/Grammar Link
H E L P

Connotations: page 151.

3. Create An Argument to Fit Your Audience

Choose a specific audience, and think about the following:

- What are their main concerns about the issue?
- What reasons are most likely to persuade this audience?

4. Elaborate: Appeal to Reason

The key to successful persuasion is developing a strong argument. Once you have stated your thesis, your task is to find two or three strong **reasons** to support your position.

The Framework at the top right on page 163 outlines the bare bones of a logical argument. Each paragraph begins with a **topic sentence** that clearly states the reason being presented in that paragraph. The rest of the paragraph contains the **supporting evidence** (facts, statistics, examples, quotations, and anecdotes) that backs up and elaborates the reason.

5. Elaborate: Appeal to Emotions

It's okay to appeal to your audience's emotions as well as to their reason. **Loaded words**—words that have strong positive or negative connotations—can be powerful persuasive tools when used thoughtfully and in moderation. Note the loaded words in the Professional Model, including *brave, proud, glorious*.

6. Organize Your Argument

Organize your argument in a logical way that works best for the topic. One effective way to present an argument is **order of importance**, in which you present the most important reason first and follow it with less important reasons *or* begin with the least important reason and build up to the most important.

7. End with a Punch

You can end your paper forcefully with a **call to action.** Ask your audience to take a specific action on the issue: to vote in a certain way, for instance, or to write a letter. You'll find a call to action in the Student Model on pages 163–164.

Drafting

Whenever you're trying to persuade an audience, use a confident **tone**—as if you're very sure that you're right. Avoid hesitant words such as *probably, maybe,* and *perhaps*—they will weaken your argument.

Distinguished Members of the
School Board:

I am in favor of the proposed
requirement that eighth-graders
spend fifteen hours during the
school year volunteering to help
the elderly.

*Thesis
statement.*

One reason this would be a good
idea is that I feel it would be an
awesome learning experience.
Students could learn how to work
with and relate to older people. My
mother works at a nursing home, so
I have had the opportunity to help
her in the summer. I have learned
to help with the residents there, and
I also learned interesting things
from the people themselves and
things about their lives.

*Reason #1—
topic
sentence.*

*Personal
experience.*

*What writer
learned.*

Another reason I think this rule
would be magnificent is that it is a
good way to help others. Eighth-
graders can help people who cannot
do things for themselves. Students
could do yardwork, housework, run
errands, or just spend time with the
elderly so they would not be alone.

*Reason #2—
topic
sentence.*

*Specific
examples.*

Finally, I think just spending at
least fifteen hours a school year
with the elderly would improve students' people skills. Students would
learn to talk to and relate to others.
They would learn how to be less
shy, too. In a recent *Time* magazine
poll, sixty percent of people becoming nurses in care homes said they
learned how to be able to talk to
residents and their families more
confidently. A woman who works
with my mother did volunteer work

*Reason #3—
topic
sentence.*

*Supporting
survey,
statistic.*

Anecdote.

(continued on next page)

Framework for an Essay Supporting a Position

Introduction

State issue and position in a **thesis statement.**

Body

Paragraph 1: Reason #1
- Topic sentence
- Supporting evidence (facts, examples, statistics, anecdotes, quotations)

Paragraph 2: Reason #2
- Topic sentence
- Supporting evidence

Paragraph 3: Reason #3
- Topic sentence
- Supporting evidence

Conclusion

Restate position; may end with a **call to action.**

**Sentence Workshop
H E L P**

*Run-on sentences:
page 165.*

**Language/Grammar Link
H E L P**

Alternatives to said: *page
105. Choosing precise
words: page 133.*

A good persuasive essay

1. *has a thesis statement that clearly states a position on an issue*

2. *develops at least two strong reasons to support the position*

3. *supports each reason with evidence (facts, statistics, examples, anecdotes, quotations, etc.)*

4. *may contain emotional as well as logical appeals*

5. *is clearly organized*

6. *ends with a conclusion that restates the writer's position*

7. *may also end with a call to action*

Proofreading Tip

If you're writing on a computer, look for errors caused by cutting and moving material.

Communications Handbook
H E L P

See Proofreaders' Marks.

Publishing Tip

Present your essay as a persuasive speech to an appropriate audience.

Student Model (continued)

when she was in high school and has told me she is grateful for that experience.

For all these reasons, I believe the proposed requirement for volunteering would make a good rule. I hope that you will consider my reasons and vote to accept the proposed requirement.

Conclusion.

Call to action.

—Teresa Lacey
Franklin Middle School
Abilene, Texas

Evaluating and Revising

1. Peer Response

Make copies of your draft for your writing group, or read it aloud to them. If you're not sure about certain issues or parts of your paper, ask specifically for feedback about them. For example, you might ask if the group thinks you have enough strong supporting evidence. You might ask how the order in which you've presented your argument might be improved.

2. Self-Evaluation

Check your ideas. Read your essay, looking for places to strengthen it. Does your opening paragraph clearly state your position and grab the readers' attention? Have you used strong supporting evidence? Are the ideas in each paragraph clearly presented? (For example, have you used transition words such as *first, next, another, finally,* and *therefore?*)

Check your correctness. Be sure to check your paper carefully for correct grammar and punctuation. For example, fragments are not usually considered correct in formal compositions. Yet you may have noticed that the Professional Model on pages 160–161 (a newspaper article) includes some fragments. Fragments are often used for effect by professional writers, especially in news magazines and newspapers. However, if your teacher does not accept fragments, you will have to check your paper carefully to be sure you have used full sentences. As an exercise in editing, you might go back to the Professional Model and correct the fragments. Does the tone of the article change?

Sentence Workshop

RUN-ON SENTENCES

A **run-on sentence** is made up of two complete sentences run together as if they were one sentence. In some run-on sentences, no punctuation is used to connect the two sentences. In others, called **comma splices,** the sentences are joined with only a comma. Run-ons are confusing because the reader can't tell where one idea ends and another one begins.

There are several ways you can revise run-on sentences. Here are two of them.

1. You can divide the run-on sentence into two sentences.

   RUN-ON   Lemon Brown had a treasure, it was a harmonica and some old newspaper clippings.

   CORRECT   Lemon Brown had a treasure. **It** was a harmonica and some old newspaper clippings.

2. You can connect the ideas with a comma and a coordinating conjunction such as *and, but,* or *or.*

   RUN-ON   Mike thought his grandmother recognized him she'd actually mistaken him for her husband.

   CORRECT   Mike thought his grandmother recognized him**, but** she'd actually mistaken him for her husband.

Writer's Workshop Follow-up: Proofreading

The easiest way to catch run-ons is to read your writing aloud. When you hear a clear pause in your voice, you've probably reached the end of a thought. If you don't see end punctuation at that point, you may have found a run-on sentence.

Language Handbook
HELP

See Run-on Sentences, page 789.

Technology
HELP

See Language Workshop CD-ROM. *Key word entry: run-on sentences.*

Try It Out

Revise the following run-on sentences, using either of the methods you've learned.

1. Count Leo Tolstoy's parents died when he was young, he was raised by relatives.

2. He fought in the Russian Army, later he became a farmer and opened a school for peasant children.

3. He had nine children of his own they all lived on his family estate in the province of Tula.

4. Tolstoy wrote books opposing violence, he said we can improve society only by improving ourselves.

5. Tolstoy was a successful writer he gave up all his property to work in the fields with the peasants.

Reading for Life

Reading to Take Action

Situation

Suppose you want to recommend that your school set up a special program that will bring kids into the community and involve the community in your school. Here are some strategies you can use to gather information that you need for a project like this and to make your recommendation.

Strategies

Focus your research.

- In a group, brainstorm to develop a list of specific topics you want to research.
- Next, list at least three questions you would like to answer about each topic.

Search for information.

- If you are doing your research on the computer, conduct an on-line search.
- First, decide what key words you will use. Then, once you have a list of possible sources, check those sources that will probably offer the information you need.
- For more details, write or e-mail the contact person listed.
- You might also talk directly to people involved in your

> **Memo**
> **To:** Mr. Thaddeus Conklin, Principal
> **From:** Grade Eight
> **Date:** October 15
> **Subject:** Getting Kids and Seniors Together
>
> We have been researching ways our school can contribute to our community. We agree that it would be good to get kids and seniors together so that kids can help seniors and seniors can help kids. We would like to recommend that our school set up a volunteer program. We would contact senior-citizen groups in our community and ask for volunteers to work at school. The seniors would help teachers tutor kids that need help. They would also help us do an oral history of our community. The kids would go to the senior centers and do things there, such as put on plays and sing holiday songs and share our pets. We think this program will work because it is working right now in twelve schools that we have located on the Internet.

project. What are their feelings about your ideas?

Gather information together.

- You may want to put your data in a chart form for easy access.

Take a stand.

- As a group, decide what specific action you will recommend.
- Present your recommendations in written form.

Using the Strategies

1. What specific recommendation for action have the stu-

dents made in the memo above?

2. What details support their recommendation?

3. What key words do you guess these students used to conduct their on-line search for information?

Extending the Strategies

Research a community problem that interests you, and make a recommendation on what action your city council should take.

Problem

In this collection, and probably in your own life, you've seen generations working together and generations in conflict. What are some ways our communities can strengthen relationships between the generations?

Project

Interview an older person about his or her experiences, feelings about the role of older people in the community, and ideas on what can be done to bring the generations together.

Preparation

1. Think of a person you would like to interview, and arrange a meeting.

2. Prepare a list of questions that cannot be answered just yes or no.

3. If you plan to use a tape recorder, make sure you have permission to record.

Procedure

1. When you begin the interview, introduce yourself, if necessary, and begin with friendly conversation to help you and your interviewee relax.

2. Think of the questions you've prepared as just a general guide. If the person says something interesting, follow it up before you move to another topic.

3. Don't interrupt the flow of the interview by writing down every word. Instead, just take notes.

4. After the interview, be sure to send a thank-you note. If possible, include a copy of your presentation.

Presentation

Present your interview in one of the following formats (or another that your teacher approves).

1. Tape Recording

Create a cover for your tape recording of the interview. A title and a photograph or drawing of your subject should appear on the front. Inside the cover, include liner notes identifying the voices heard on the tape and the place, date, and occasion of the interview. Provide any other information or comments that you think would be helpful to someone listening to your taped interview.

2. Q-and-A Article

Write a report of your interview in question-and-answer format:

HOLLY: What's the hardest decision you ever made?

JONAS: I guess I'd say it was . . .

If you edit, use an ellipsis (. . .) in each place where you cut words.

Introduce the interview with a paragraph in your own words. Give any necessary background information, and describe your impressions of the person and of the interview.

3. Monologue

Write and perform a monologue from the point of view of the person you interviewed. You can either use your interviewee's actual words or interpret the information you collected in the interview to write lines for the monologue. On your script, note what you made up. You may even want to use a costume and props.

Processing

What did you learn from this project? Write a reflection on the experience for your portfolio.

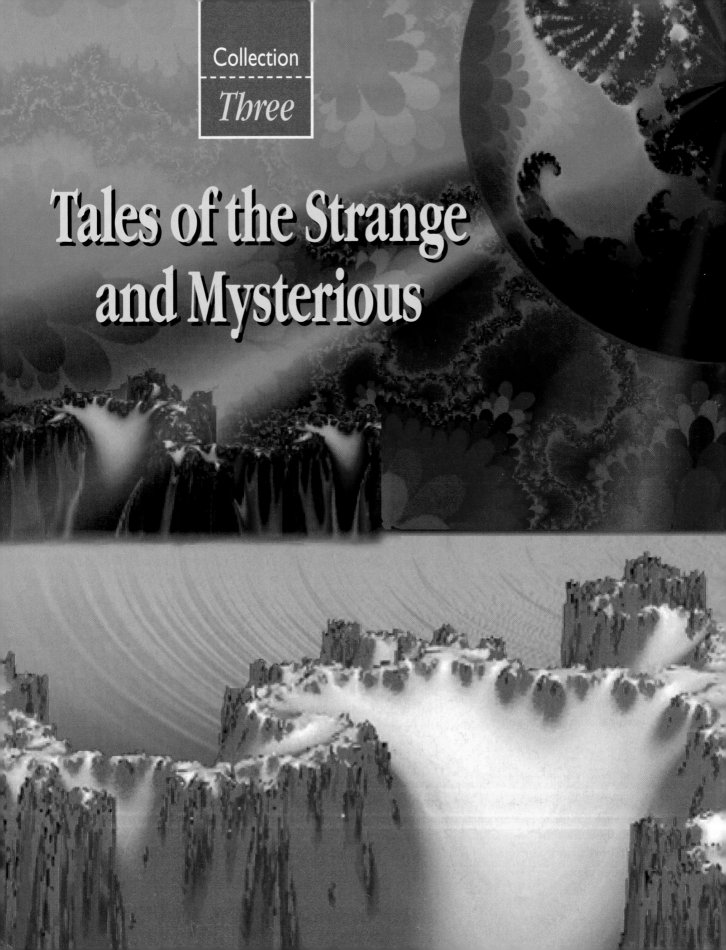

Tales of the Strange
and Mysterious

The most beautiful thing we can experience is the mysterious. It is the source of all true art and science.

—Albert Einstein

Before You Read

THE LANDLADY

Make the Connection

Open House

Picture this: You've just arrived in a new town by train and you're looking for a place to stay. As you walk down the street, you see this sign in a boardinghouse window:

> BED AND BREAKFAST

There are yellow flowers in a vase in the window and green curtains. You walk up to the window and look in. What do you see inside? What sort of a place is this boardinghouse?

Draw an outline of a house like the one below. Fill it with words and symbols showing what—and whom—you imagine you would find in the boardinghouse.

Elements of Literature

Foreshadowing

Foreshadowing, the use of clues to suggest what will happen later in a plot, is a tool used by writers to build suspense or anxiety in their readers. As you read "The Landlady," put your-self in the place of Billy, the main character. Pay close attention to what Billy sees and senses. Be on your toes—you may find yourself tripping over the many cleverly disguised clues.

> **F**oreshadowing is the use of clues or hints suggesting events that will occur later in the plot.
>
> *For more on Foreshadowing, see pages 212–213 and the Handbook of Literary Terms.*

Reading Skills and Strategies

Dialogue with the Text: Monitoring Your Comprehension

"The Landlady" is filled with clues that you'll want to pay close attention to as you read. In order to **monitor your comprehension** of the unfolding events, keep a piece of paper handy. Jot down your **questions,** your **predictions** about what might happen, and any other **comments** or **responses.** At the end, write down any questions you still have.

One student's notes appear on the first page of the story as an example.

"Please *come in,*" she said pleasantly.

The Landlady

Roald Dahl

Dialogue with the Text

Billy Weaver had traveled down from London on the slow afternoon train, with a change at Reading on the way, and by the time he got to Bath, it was about nine o'clock in the evening, and the moon was coming up out of a clear starry sky over the houses opposite the station entrance. But the air was deadly cold and the wind was like a flat blade of ice on his cheeks.

"Excuse me," he said, "but is there a fairly cheap hotel not too far away from here?"

"Try The Bell and Dragon," the porter[1] answered, pointing down the road. "They might take you in. It's about a quarter of a mile along on the other side."

Billy thanked him and picked up his suitcase and set out to walk the quarter-mile to The Bell and Dragon. He had never been to Bath before. He didn't know anyone who lived there. But Mr. Greenslade at the head office in London had told him it was a splendid town. "Find your own lodgings," he had said, "and then go along and report to the branch manager as soon as you've got yourself settled."

Billy was seventeen years old. He was wearing a new navy-blue overcoat, a new brown trilby hat,[2] and a new brown suit, and he was feeling fine. He walked briskly down the street. He was trying to do everything briskly these days. Briskness, he had decided, was *the* one common characteristic of all successful businessmen. The big shots up at the head office were absolutely fantastically brisk all the time. They were amazing.

There were no shops on this wide street that he was walking along, only a line of tall houses on each side, all of them identical. They had porches and pillars and four or

I like the description; it makes me picture the scene in my mind.

It sounds as if this would hurt.

He doesn't have much money.

"The Bell and Dragon" sounds like the Middle Ages.

He must not have a lot of things to have only one suitcase.

I would be lonely if I were Billy.

Billy must be in Bath for a job.

I thought Billy was much older.

The word briskly reminds me of the wind.

—Candace Ayers
Stonewall Jackson Middle School
Mechanicsville, Virginia

1. **porter:** person employed to carry luggage.
2. **trilby hat:** soft hat with the top deeply indented.

five steps going up to their front doors, and it was obvious that once upon a time they had been very swanky residences. But now, even in the darkness, he could see that the paint was peeling from the woodwork on their doors and windows and that the handsome white facades were cracked and blotchy from neglect.

Suddenly, in a downstairs window that was brilliantly illuminated by a street lamp not six yards away, Billy caught sight of a printed notice propped up against the glass in one of the upper panes. It said BED AND BREAKFAST. There was a vase of yellow chrysanthemums, tall and beautiful, standing just underneath the notice.

He stopped walking. He moved a bit closer. Green curtains (some sort of velvety material) were hanging down on either side of the window. The chrysanthemums looked wonderful beside them. He went right up and peered through the glass into the room, and the first thing he saw was a bright fire burning in the hearth. On the carpet in front of the fire, a pretty little dachshund was curled up asleep with its nose tucked into its belly. The room itself, so far as he could see in the half darkness, was filled with pleasant furniture. There was a baby grand piano and a big sofa and several plump armchairs, and in one corner he spotted a large parrot in a cage. Animals were usually a good sign in a place like this, Billy told himself; and all in all, it looked to him as though it would be a pretty decent house to stay in. Certainly it would be more comfortable than The Bell and Dragon.

On the other hand, a pub would be more congenial than a boardinghouse. There would be beer and darts in the evenings, and lots of people to talk to, and it would probably be a good bit cheaper, too. He had stayed a couple of nights in a pub once before and he had liked it. He had never stayed in any boardinghouses, and, to be perfectly honest, he was a tiny bit frightened of them. The name itself conjured up[3] images of watery cabbage, rapacious landladies, and a powerful smell of kippers[4] in the living room.

After dithering about[5] like this in the cold for two or three minutes, Billy decided that he would walk on and take a look at The Bell and Dragon before making up his mind. He turned to go.

And now a queer thing happened to him. He was in the act of stepping back and turning away from the window when all at once his eye was caught and held in the most peculiar manner by the small notice that was there. BED AND BREAKFAST, it said. BED AND BREAKFAST, BED AND BREAKFAST, BED AND BREAKFAST. Each word was like a large black eye staring at him through the glass, holding him, compelling him, forcing him to stay where he was and not to walk away from that house, and the next thing he knew, he was actually moving across from the window to the front door of the house, climbing the steps that led up to it, and reaching for the bell.

He pressed the bell. Far away in a back room he heard it ringing, and then *at once*—it must have been at once because he hadn't even had time to take his finger from the bell button— the door swung open and a woman was standing there.

3. **conjured up:** called to mind.
4. **kippers:** fish that have been salted and dried or smoked. Kippers are commonly eaten for breakfast in Great Britain.
5. **dithering about:** acting nervous and confused.

WORDS TO OWN

facades (fə·sädz′) *n.*: fronts of buildings. *Facades* also means "false fronts or appearances."
congenial (kən·jēn′yəl) *adj.*: agreeable; pleasant.
rapacious (rə·pā′shəs) *adj.*: greedy.

Normally you ring the bell and you have at least a half-minute's wait before the door opens. But this dame was like a jack-in-the-box. He pressed the bell—and out she popped! It made him jump.

She was about forty-five or fifty years old, and the moment she saw him, she gave him a warm, welcoming smile.

"*Please* come in," she said pleasantly. She stepped aside, holding the door wide open, and Billy found himself automatically starting forward. The compulsion or, more accurately, the desire to follow after her into that house was extraordinarily strong.

"I saw the notice in the window," he said, holding himself back.

"Yes, I know."

"I was wondering about a room."

"It's *all* ready for you, my dear," she said. She had a round pink face and very gentle blue eyes.

"I was on my way to The Bell and Dragon," Billy told her. "But the notice in your window just happened to catch my eye."

"My dear boy," she said, "why don't you come in out of the cold?"

"How much do you charge?"

"Five and sixpence a night, including breakfast."

It was fantastically cheap. It was less than half of what he had been willing to pay.

"If that is too much," she added, "then perhaps I can reduce it just a tiny bit. Do you desire an egg for breakfast? Eggs are expensive at the moment. It would be sixpence less without the egg."

"Five and sixpence is fine," he answered. "I should like very much to stay here."

"I knew you would. Do come in."

She seemed terribly nice. She looked exactly like the mother of one's best school friend welcoming one into the house to stay for the Christmas holidays. Billy took off his hat and stepped over the threshold.

"Just hang it there," she said, "and let me help you with your coat."

There were no other hats or coats in the hall. There were no umbrellas, no walking sticks—nothing.

"We have it *all* to ourselves," she said, smiling at him over her shoulder as she led the way upstairs. "You see, it isn't very often I have the pleasure of taking a visitor into my little nest."

The old girl is slightly dotty,[6] Billy told himself. But at five and sixpence a night, who cares about that? "I should've thought you'd be simply swamped with applicants," he said politely.

"Oh, I am, my dear, I am, of course I am. But the trouble is that I'm inclined to be just a teeny-weeny bit choosy and particular—if you see what I mean."

"Ah, yes."

"But I'm always ready. Everything is always ready day and night in this house just on the off chance that an acceptable young gentleman will come along. And it is such a pleasure, my dear, such a very great pleasure when now and again I open the door and I see someone standing there who is just *exactly* right." She was halfway up the stairs, and she paused with one hand on the stair rail, turning her head and smiling down at him with pale lips. "Like you," she added, and her blue eyes traveled slowly all the way down the length of Billy's body, to his feet, and then up again.

On the second-floor landing she said to him, "This floor is mine."

They climbed up another flight. "And this one is *all* yours," she said. "Here's your room. I do hope you'll like it." She took him into a small but charming front bedroom, switching on the light as she went in.

"The morning sun comes right in the window, Mr. Perkins. It *is* Mr. Perkins, isn't it?"

"No," he said. "It's Weaver."

6. **dotty:** crazy.

"Mr. Weaver. How nice. I've put a water bottle between the sheets to air them out, Mr. Weaver. It's such a comfort to have a hot-water bottle in a strange bed with clean sheets, don't you agree? And you may light the gas fire at any time if you feel chilly."

"Thank you," Billy said. "Thank you ever so much." He noticed that the bedspread had been taken off the bed and that the bedclothes had been neatly turned back on one side, all ready for someone to get in.

"I'm so glad you appeared," she said, looking earnestly into his face. "I was beginning to get worried."

"That's all right," Billy answered brightly. "You mustn't worry about me." He put his suitcase on the chair and started to open it.

"And what about supper, my dear? Did you manage to get anything to eat before you came here?"

"I'm not a bit hungry, thank you," he said. "I think I'll just go to bed as soon as possible because tomorrow I've got to get up rather early and report to the office."

"Very well, then. I'll leave you now so that you can unpack. But before you go to bed, would you be kind enough to pop into the sitting room on the ground floor and sign the book? Everyone has to do that because it's the law of the land, and we don't want to go breaking any laws at *this* stage in the proceedings, do we?" She gave him a little wave of the hand and went quickly out of the room and closed the door.

Now, the fact that his landlady appeared to be slightly off her rocker didn't worry Billy in the least. After all, she not only was harmless—there was no question about that—but she was also quite obviously a kind and generous soul. He guessed that she had probably lost a son in the war, or something like that, and had never gotten over it.

So a few minutes later, after unpacking his suitcase and washing his hands, he trotted downstairs to the ground floor and entered the living room. His landlady wasn't there, but the fire was glowing in the hearth, and the little dachshund was still sleeping soundly in front of it. The room was wonderfully warm and cozy. I'm a lucky fellow, he thought, rubbing his hands. This is a bit of all right.

He found the guest book lying open on the piano, so he took out his pen and wrote down his name and address. There were only two other entries above his on the page, and as one always does with guest books, he started to read them. One was a Christopher Mulholland from Cardiff. The other was Gregory W. Temple from Bristol.

That's funny, he thought suddenly. Christopher Mulholland. It rings a bell.

Now where on earth had he heard that rather unusual name before?

Was it a boy at school? No. Was it one of his sister's numerous young men, perhaps, or a friend of his father's? No, no, it wasn't any of those. He glanced down again at the book.

Christopher Mulholland
231 Cathedral Road, Cardiff

Gregory W. Temple
27 Sycamore Drive, Bristol

As a matter of fact, now he came to think of it, he wasn't at all sure that the second name didn't have almost as much of a familiar ring about it as the first.

"Gregory Temple?" he said aloud, searching his memory. "Christopher Mulholland? . . ."

"Such charming boys," a voice behind him answered, and he turned and saw his landlady sailing into the room with a large silver tea tray in her hands. She was holding it well out in front of her, and rather high up, as though the tray were a pair of reins on a frisky horse.

"They sound somehow familiar," he said.

"They do? How interesting."

"I'm almost positive I've heard those names before somewhere. Isn't that odd? Maybe it was in the newspapers. They weren't famous in any way, were they? I mean famous cricketers[7] or footballers or something like that?"

"Famous," she said, setting the tea tray down on the low table in front of the sofa. "Oh no, I don't think they were famous. But they were incredibly handsome, both of them, I can promise you that. They were tall and young and handsome, my dear, just exactly like you."

Once more, Billy glanced down at the book. "Look here," he said, noticing the dates. "This last entry is over two years old."

"It is?"

"Yes, indeed. And Christopher Mulholland's is nearly a year before that—more than *three years* ago."

"Dear me," she said, shaking her head and heaving a dainty little sigh. "I would never have thought it. How time does fly away from us all, doesn't it, Mr. Wilkins?"

"It's Weaver," Billy said. "W-e-a-v-e-r."

"Oh, of course it is!" she cried, sitting down on the sofa. "How silly of me. I do apologize. In one ear and out the other, that's me, Mr. Weaver."

"You know something?" Billy said. "Something that's really quite extraordinary about all this?"

"No, dear, I don't."

"Well, you see, both of these names—Mulholland and Temple—I not only seem to remember each one of them separately, so to speak, but somehow or other, in some peculiar way, they both appear to be sort of connected

---

7. **cricketers:** people who play cricket, a game that is popular in Great Britain.

together as well. As though they were both famous for the same sort of thing, if you see what I mean—like . . . well . . . like Dempsey and Tunney, for example, or Churchill and Roosevelt."[8]

"How amusing," she said. "But come over here now, dear, and sit down beside me on the sofa and I'll give you a nice cup of tea and a ginger biscuit[9] before you go to bed."

"You really shouldn't bother," Billy said. "I didn't mean you to do anything like that." He stood by the piano, watching her as she fussed about with the cups and saucers. He noticed that she had small, white, quickly moving hands and red fingernails.

"I'm almost positive it was in the newspapers I saw them," Billy said. "I'll think of it in a second. I'm sure I will."

There is nothing more <u>tantalizing</u> than a thing like this that lingers just outside the borders of one's memory. He hated to give up.

"Now wait a minute," he said. "Wait just a minute. Mulholland . . . Christopher Mulholland . . . wasn't *that* the name of the Eton[10] schoolboy who was on a walking tour through the West Country, and then all of a sudden . . ."

"Milk?" she said. "And sugar?"

"Yes, please. And then all of a sudden . . ."

"Eton schoolboy?" she said. "Oh no, my dear, that can't possibly be right, because *my* Mr. Mulholland was certainly not an Eton schoolboy when he came to me. He was a Cambridge[11] undergraduate. Come over here now and sit next to me and warm yourself in front of this lovely fire. Come on. Your tea's all ready for you." She patted the empty place beside her on the sofa, and she sat there smiling at Billy and waiting for him to come over.

He crossed the room slowly and sat down on the edge of the sofa. She placed his teacup on the table in front of him.

"*There* we are," she said. "How nice and cozy this is, isn't it?"

Billy started sipping his tea. She did the same. For half a minute or so, neither of them spoke. But Billy knew that she was looking at him. Her body was half turned toward him, and he could feel her eyes resting on his face, watching him over the rim of her teacup. Now and again, he caught a whiff of a peculiar smell that seemed to <u>emanate</u> directly from her person. It was not in the least unpleasant, and it reminded him—well, he wasn't quite sure what it reminded him of. Pickled walnuts? New leather? Or was it the corridors of a hospital?

At length, she said, "Mr. Mulholland was a great one for his tea. Never in my life have I seen anyone drink as much tea as dear, sweet Mr. Mulholland."

"I suppose he left fairly recently," Billy said. He was still puzzling his head about the two names. He was positive now that he had seen them in the newspapers—in the headlines.

"Left?" she said, arching her brows. "But my dear boy, he never left. He's still here. Mr. Temple is also here. They're on the fourth floor, both of them together."

Billy set his cup down slowly on the table and stared at his landlady. She smiled back at

---

8. **Dempsey and Tunney . . . Churchill and Roosevelt:** Jack Dempsey and Gene Tunney were American boxers who competed for the world heavyweight championship in 1926. Winston Churchill was prime minister of Britain and Franklin Delano Roosevelt was president of the United States during World War II.
9. **biscuit:** British term meaning "cookie."
10. **Eton:** boys' prep school near London.
11. **Cambridge:** famous university in England.

WORDS TO OWN

tantalizing (tan′tə·līz′iŋ) *adj.:* teasing by remaining unavailable or by withholding something desired by someone; tempting. (In Greek mythology, Tantalus was a king condemned after death to stand in water that moved away whenever he tried to drink it and to remain under branches of fruit that were just out of reach.)

emanate (em′ə·nāt′) *v.:* come forth.

---

him, and then she put out one of her white hands and patted him comfortingly on the knee. "How old are you, my dear?" she asked.

"Seventeen."

"Seventeen!" she cried. "Oh, it's the perfect age! Mr. Mulholland was also seventeen. But I think he was a trifle shorter than you are; in fact I'm sure he was, and his teeth weren't *quite* so white. You have the most beautiful teeth, Mr. Weaver, did you know that?"

"They're not as good as they look," Billy said. "They've got simply masses of fillings in them at the back."

"Mr. Temple, of course, was a little older," she said, ignoring his remark. "He was actually twenty-eight. And yet I never would have guessed it if he hadn't told me, never in my whole life. There wasn't a *blemish* on his body."

"A what?" Billy said.

"His skin was *just* like a baby's."

There was a pause. Billy picked up his teacup and took another sip of his tea; then he set it down again gently in its saucer. He waited for her to say something else, but she seemed to have lapsed into another of her silences. He sat there staring straight ahead of him into the far corner of the room, biting his lower lip.

"That parrot," he said at last. "You know something? It had me completely fooled when I first saw it through the window. I could have sworn it was alive."

"Alas, no longer."

"It's most terribly clever the way it's been done," he said. "It doesn't look in the least bit dead. Who did it?"

"I did."

"*You* did?"

"Of course," she said. "And have you met my little Basil as well?" She nodded toward the dachshund curled up so comfortably in front of the fire. Billy looked at it. And suddenly, he realized that this animal had all the time been just as silent and motionless as the parrot. He put out a hand and touched it gently on the top of its back. The back was hard and cold, and when he pushed the hair to one side with his fingers, he could see the skin underneath, grayish black and dry and perfectly preserved.

"Good gracious me," he said. "How absolutely fascinating." He turned away from the dog and stared with deep admiration at the little woman beside him on the sofa. "It must be most awfully difficult to do a thing like that."

MEET THE WRITER

Advice to Young Writers

Roald (roo′ôl) **Dahl** (1916–1990) was born in Wales, in Great Britain, to Norwegian parents. When he was nine years old, Dahl was sent to boarding school. Many people believe that Dahl's dark humor had its source in his unpleasant experiences at the two boarding schools he attended. The strict and often brutal discipline practiced at these schools apparently didn't help his writing at the time, however. When Dahl

"Not in the least," she said. "I stuff *all* my little pets myself when they pass away. Will you have another cup of tea?"

"No, thank you," Billy said. The tea tasted faintly of bitter almonds, and he didn't much care for it.

"You did sign the book, didn't you?"

"Oh, yes."

"That's good. Because later on, if I happen to forget what you were called, then I could always come down here and look it up. I still do that almost every day with Mr. Mulholland and Mr. . . . Mr. . . ."

"Temple," Billy said, "Gregory Temple. Excuse my asking, but haven't there been *any* other guests here except them in the last two or three years?"

Holding her teacup high in one hand, inclining her head slightly to the left, she looked up at him out of the corners of her eyes and gave him another gentle little smile.

"No, my dear," she said. "Only you."

was fourteen, his English teacher wrote on his report card, "I have never met a boy who so persistently writes the exact opposite of what he means." Another teacher commented, "A persistent muddler. Vocabulary negligible, sentences malconstructed. He reminds me of a camel."

In "Lucky Break," the true story of how the "persistent muddler" became a professional writer, Dahl offers advice to young writers:

❝ Here are some of the qualities you should possess or should try to acquire if you wish to become a fiction writer:

1. You should have a lively imagination.

2. You should be able to write well. By that I mean you should be able to make a scene come alive in the reader's mind. Not everybody has this ability. It is a gift, and you either have it or you don't.

3. You must have stamina. In other words, you must be able to stick to what you are doing and never give up, for hour after hour, day after day, week after week, and month after month.

4. You must be a perfectionist. That means you must never be satisfied with what you have written until you have rewritten it again and again, making it as good as you possibly can.

5. You must have strong self-discipline. You are working alone. No one is employing you. No one is around to fire you if you don't turn up for work, or to tick you off if you start slacking.

6. It helps a lot if you have a keen sense of humor. This is not essential when writing for grown-ups, but for children, it's vital.

7. You must have a degree of humility. The writer who thinks that his work is marvelous is heading for trouble. ❞

More by Roald Dahl

- Dahl wrote about attending boarding school and other childhood experiences in his autobiography *Boy* (Viking Penguin).

- *The Wonderful Story of Henry Sugar and Six More* (Bantam) includes "Lucky Break" and six short stories.

The Listeners

Walter de la Mare

"Is there anybody there?" said the Traveler,
　Knocking on the moonlit door;
And his horse in the silence champed the grasses
　Of the forest's ferny floor:
5　And a bird flew up out of the turret,°
　Above the Traveler's head:
And he smote° upon the door again a second time;
　"Is there anybody there?" he said.
But no one descended to the Traveler;
10　No head from the leaf-fringed sill
Leaned over and looked into his gray eyes,
　Where he stood perplexed and still.
But only a host of phantom° listeners
　That dwelt in the lone house then
15　Stood listening in the quiet of the moonlight
　To that voice from the world of men:
Stood thronging° the faint moonbeams on the dark stair,
　That goes down to the empty hall,
Hearkening° in an air stirred and shaken
20　By the lonely Traveler's call.
And he felt in his heart their strangeness,
　Their stillness answering his cry,
While his horse moved, cropping the dark turf,
　'Neath the starred and leafy sky;
25　For he suddenly smote on the door, even
　Louder, and lifted his head—
"Tell them I came, and no one answered,
　That I kept my word," he said.
Never the least stir made the listeners,
30　Though every word he spake
Fell echoing through the shadowiness of the still house
　From the one man left awake:
Ay, they heard his foot upon the stirrup,
　And the sound of iron on stone,
35　And how the silence surged softly backward,
　When the plunging hoofs were gone.

5. turret: small tower.
7. smote: struck; here, knocked loudly.
13. phantom: imaginary.
17. thronging: crowding; filling.
19. hearkening (härk′ən·iŋ): listening.

MAKING MEANINGS

First Thoughts

1. Review your reading notes.

   - At what point in the story did you first become suspicious that things in the boardinghouse were not quite normal?

   - What **predictions** did you make? Did events turn out as you predicted?

   - Were any questions left unanswered at the end of the story?

Shaping Interpretations

2. What seems to be the landlady's idea of a perfect guest? What happens to her guests, and how do you know?

3. One relevant fact you may not know is that potassium cyanide, a favorite poison in mystery and suspense stories, has a faint bitter-almond taste. Go back to the text, and find other clues throughout the story that **foreshadow** Billy's fate. (Can you find a hint in the very first paragraph?)

4. What do you think happens just after the story ends? (Does Billy realize the danger he faces? If he does, is it too late, or does he escape?) Explain.

5. Skim back through the story to find the points at which Billy makes fateful decisions. Choose one of these moments, and describe what Billy does and why he does it. How might a different decision have changed the outcome of the story?

Connecting with the Text

6. How does the Open House you drew before you read the story compare with the boardinghouse in "The Landlady"? What do you think Dahl's reasons were for not making the house seem frightening from the beginning?

Extending the Text

7. Both "The Landlady" and "The Listeners" (see *Connections* on page 180) present a lone traveler arriving at a house that hides a secret. What descriptions of the "phantom listeners" and the "lone house" in the poem could also be applied to the landlady and her "bed and breakfast"?

> ### Reading Check
>
> a. What are Billy's first impressions when he peers through the window of the boardinghouse?
>
> b. Why does Billy enter the boardinghouse, even though he likes staying in pubs?
>
> c. Describe the landlady's house. What in the house is not what it appears to be?
>
> d. Billy keeps thinking he knows something about Mulholland and Temple. What is it that he knows but can't recall?

Choices: Building Your Portfolio

Writer's Notebook

1. Collecting Ideas for a Character Analysis

Roald Dahl often writes about very ordinary people who do very extraordinary things. In "The Landlady" he introduces us to two very ordinary people, Billy and his landlady. Suppose you want to analyze the character of the landlady. First, you might review the story and take notes on what she looks like. Then, note exactly what her house is like, inside and outside. Finally, note what she does to her guests. After you gather these details, make some generalizations: What do these details tell you about the landlady's **traits,** or personal characteristics? The notebook at the right shows one reader's notes on a very different character in this book.

Mrs. Flowers, page 20

Looks: pretty, nice dresses, rich black skin like a plum

House: neat, books, sweet odor of cookies baking

Actions: helps Maya, reads to her, lets her know she likes her

Traits: elegance, kindness, generosity, understanding

Creative Writing

2. Write All About It

Choose two newspapers or two magazines or two TV news shows with very different styles—for example, your local paper and *The National Enquirer* or *60 Minutes* and *Hard Copy*. Write an account of Billy's disappearance for each audience. Remember to include answers to the *5W-How?* questions: *who, what, where, when, why,* and *how.*

Role-Play

3. Just the Facts, Ma'am

Since the branch manager is expecting Billy, chances are good that a police detective will eventually knock on the landlady's door to investigate Billy's disappearance. With a partner, prepare a dialogue between the landlady and the investigator. Perform the dialogue for your class.

Supporting a Position

4. Television Terror

Would "The Landlady" make a good episode in a television suspense series? Write a letter that you might send to a television producer, supporting a pro or con position on adapting "The Landlady" for an hour-long TV episode. Be sure to address such issues as target audience, sponsors, and any changes that might have to be made in the story. Support your position with convincing reasons and with specific examples from the story.

GRAMMAR LINK MINI-LESSON

Regular and Irregular Verbs

Language Handbook HELP

See Irregular Verbs, pages 755-757.

Technology HELP

See Language Workshop CD-ROM. *Key word entry: verb forms.*

A **regular verb** forms its past tense and past participle by simply adding *–d* or *–ed* to its base form.

Base Form	Past	Past Participle
preserve	preserved	(have) preserved
disappear	disappeared	(have) disappeared

Irregular verbs are more complicated.

Base Form	Past	Past Participle
leave	left	(have) left
eat	ate	(have) eaten
know	knew	(have) known

There are hundreds of irregular verbs, each with its own special forms. You can increase your knowledge of the forms of irregular verbs by reading widely and listening to skilled speakers of English as often as possible.

Try It Out

Proofread the following paragraph, and correct the incorrect verb forms. (For help, see pages 755–757.)

I once seen one of Dahl's stories on TV, and some people leaved the room because they thinked Dahl had went too far. In this story a husband was missing. The detectives who had went to his home to talk to his wife actually ate the weapon. It turned out that the wife had murdered her husband with a leg of lamb that was frozed, which she then cooked and served to the police.

VOCABULARY   HOW TO OWN A WORD

WORD BANK

facades
congenial
rapacious
tantalizing
emanate

Word Origins: The Story Behind the Word

At the bottom of page 177, you learned that the origin, or **etymology** (et'ə·mäl'ə·jē) of the word *tantalizing* can be traced to an ancient Greek myth. You can find a word's etymology in a dictionary. It usually is given in brackets after the word's pronunciation. Use a dictionary to find the etymology of each word in the Word Bank. Copy the etymology; then "translate" the "story behind the word," as in this example for *cozy*:

> **Etymology of *cozy*:** [Scot; prob. < Scand, as in Norw *kose sig*, to make oneself comfortable, *koselig*, snug]
> **Translation:** *Cozy* is a Scottish word. It probably comes from Scandinavian, as in Norwegian *kose sig*, meaning "to make oneself comfortable." This expression comes from *koselig*, meaning "snug."

READING ACTIVELY: ESTABLISHING A PURPOSE AND MAKING PREDICTIONS

Imagine an airplane pilot taking off with no flight plan, ignoring air traffic, and not steering the plane. "I just want to sit back and enjoy the ride," the pilot says. Would you expect a smooth, safe flight?

Your own flights into the world of reading will go more smoothly if you take control by reading actively: set your purpose, make and confirm predictions, and think about your thinking.

1. Establishing and Adjusting Your Purpose

We read for many reasons: to get information, to understand something better, to solve problems—and, of course, to simply enjoy a good story. Being aware of *why* you are reading helps you to **establish a purpose for reading,** which helps you to decide your reading rate.

If you are reading a science fiction novel just for fun, you might read quickly and eagerly to find out what happens next.

If you decide to read that same novel to write a book report, however, you would read more slowly and carefully. You might even reread to evaluate its scientific accuracy.

Sometimes you read to find an answer to a particular question, such as "Where do penguins live?" To find the answer, you may need to use an index or table of contents first and then skim (read quickly) to locate the information you want.

2. Previewing and Making Predictions

When you **preview** a book, you read the title and covers, you flip through the pages, you glance at the pictures and headings—and you use all this information to **predict** what you will find in the text. You ask yourself "What do I know about this topic?" Then, you make some predictions: I think this story will be scary.

3. Thinking About Your Thinking: Metacognition

As an active reader, you continually watch for problems in your understanding. What you're doing is thinking about your thinking—a process called **metacognition** (met′ə·käg·nish′ən). When you have problems understanding the text, **reread** sections of it, ask for **someone else's help,** and use **reference aids,** such as a dictionary and an encyclopedia.

4. Adjusting and Confirming Your Predictions

Keep your predictions in mind as you read a text. Are events turning out as you expected? If not, did you miss some major clues? Can you make new predictions now that you have more information? You should make, adjust, and confirm your predictions throughout your reading of any text. That process makes reading fun— you match your wits with the writer's.

Apply the strategy on the next page.

Before You Read

THE MONKEY'S PAW

Make the Connection

Three Wishes

Suppose you received an object that had the power to grant its owner three wishes. What would you do?

Quickwrite

Take a moment to imagine the possibilities. Then, without discussing it with anyone, write down what you would do with your three wishes. (Also consider: What might go wrong if your wishes were granted?)

Round robin. Now, share your wishes with a group of three or four classmates. Are any of their wishes similar to yours?

Elements of Literature

Suspense: That Glued-to-Your-Seat Feeling

That "what's going to happen next?" feeling—the curiosity, or even anxiety, that a good story makes us feel—is called **suspense.** It's suspense that keeps us glued to our seats in a theater. It's suspense that keep us turning the pages of a book long into the night. As you read this play, notice how the suspense builds as the powers of the ugly paw are slowly revealed.

> **S**uspense is the uncertainty or anxiety that a reader feels about what will happen next in a story.
>
> *For more on Suspense, see pages 212–213 and the Handbook of Literary Terms.*

Reading Skills and Strategies

Making Predictions: What Next?

The Monkey's Paw is a masterpiece of **suspense** that keeps the reader guessing—and dreading—what will happen next. Try playing a guessing game with the play as you read. Look at the symbols next to the questions on the right. When you come across a symbol in the play, turn back to this page, and find the question appearing next to the same symbol. (Note, for example, that the symbol next to the title on page 186, a dot, is the same as the one next to the first question below.) Respond briefly to the question in your notebook. Then, continue reading to see if events turn out as you predicted.

● Look at the title and the illustration on page 186. What do you think this story will be about? What role will the monkey's paw play?

■ What do you think the consequences of Mr. White's wish will be?

▲ Before you start reading Scene 3, jot down your thoughts on what the Whites will do next. What would you do?

◆ What do you think will be the result of the second wish?

✱ What was the third wish? Did you predict it?

go.hrw.com
LEO 8-3

The Monkey's Paw

W. W. Jacobs
dramatized by **Mara Rockliff**

*If you keep it,
don't blame me
for what happens.*

Characters

Mr. White
Mrs. White
Herbert, their son, about
nineteen years old.
Sergeant Major Morris, a tall, heavy
man with a ruddy complexion
who served with the British
Army in India for 21 years.
Stranger

Setting: The White family's home,
in a newly developed English
suburb, around 1920.

Scene 1

A dark and stormy winter night.

The sound of heavy rain can be heard and an occasional thunderclap. The Whites' living room is cozy and bright. MR. WHITE *and* HERBERT *play chess, while* MRS. WHITE *knits by the fire.* HERBERT *is winning.*

Herbert. Not looking too good for you, is it, Dad?

Mr. White. Could you please be quiet? I'm trying to concentrate. (*He pauses another moment, then makes a move.*) Listen to that wind howling out there.

Herbert (*keeping his attention on the chessboard*). I hear it.

Mr. White. He won't show up in a storm like this, I bet.

Herbert. Maybe, maybe not. (*He moves.*) Check . . .

[MR. WHITE *reaches for a chess piece.*]

Herbert (*triumphant*). . . . Mate![1]

[MR. WHITE *pulls his hand back.*]

Mr. White (*angrily*). That's what I can't stand about living out in the middle of nowhere like this! Every time it rains, the road gets flooded and no one can get out here. And what do those politicians in town do about it? Nothing! I suppose our three votes just don't count.

Mrs. White (*soothingly*). Never mind, dear. Maybe you'll win the next game.

[MR. WHITE *looks up sharply and sees* MRS. WHITE *and* HERBERT *smiling at him in amusement. His annoyance fades, and he smiles*

---

1. **mate:** short for "checkmate," the winning move in a chess game.

guiltily. A gate bangs, and heavy footsteps are heard approaching the door.]

Herbert. Sounds like he made it after all!

[MR. WHITE *goes to the door and greets* SERGEANT MAJOR MORRIS, *who comes in and begins wiping his feet, shaking out his umbrella, etc.*]

Mr. White (*introducing them*). Sergeant Major Morris, my wife, and this is our son, Herbert.

[*They shake hands, and the three older people sit down while* HERBERT *goes to fix tea.*]

Mr. White. Glad you made it. We didn't know if you'd come out in this storm.

Morris. Storm? This little shower? (*Chuckles*) You wouldn't think much of this if you'd ever been holed up in Bombay during the monsoon season. Now *there* are some storms, let me tell you.

Mrs. White. Did you live in India a long time, Sergeant Major?

Mr. White. Twenty-one years he's been gone. When he joined up with the army, he wasn't a day older than Herbert there—and neither was I, for that matter. We started out in the warehouse together.

Morris. Well, time flies, time flies.

Herbert (*bringing the tea*). I'd like to go to India. See the old temples, maybe catch one of those holy men performing miracles.

Morris (*shaking his head and sighing*). You're better off here.

Herbert. But you must have all kinds of great stories to tell—the places you saw, the people you met. . . .

Mr. White. Does he ever! What was that story you started telling me the other day, Morris? About a monkey's paw or something?

Morris (*quickly*). Nothing, really. Nothing worth hearing.

Mrs. White. A monkey's paw?
Morris. Well, it's just a bit of what you might call magic, I guess.
Herbert. Magic!

[*The* WHITES *look at* MORRIS *with interest.*]

Morris (*fumbling in his pocket*). It looks like just an ordinary little paw all dried up.

[*He pulls a mummified monkey's paw out of his pocket and holds it out.* MRS. WHITE *draws back in horror, but* HERBERT *takes the paw and looks at it curiously.*]

Mr. White. So what's so special about it? (*He takes the paw from* HERBERT *and examines it, then puts it down on the table.*)
Morris (*solemnly*). It had a spell put on it by an old holy man. He wanted to show that fate ruled people's lives, and that anyone who tried to interfere with fate would be sorry. He put a magic spell on the paw so that three people could each have three wishes from it.

[MR. WHITE *laughs uneasily.*]

Herbert. Well, why don't you wish on it, then?
Morris (*sadly*). I have.
Mrs. White. And did you really have your three wishes granted?
Morris. I did.
Mrs. White. And has anyone else wished on it?
Morris (*seriously*). The first owner had three wishes, yes. I don't know what the first two were for, but the third was for death. That's how I got the paw.
Mr. White (*after a pause*). If you've had your three wishes, that thing's no good to you now, then, Morris. What do you keep it for?
Morris (*shaking his head and shrugging*). No good reason, I guess. I did have some idea of selling it, but I don't think I will. It's caused enough trouble already. Besides, no one will

buy it. Some people think it's just a fairy tale, and the ones who do think anything of it want to try it first and pay me afterward.
Herbert. If you could have another three wishes, would you use them?
Morris. I don't know. (*Pauses*) I don't know. (*He takes the paw, dangles it between his finger and thumb, then suddenly throws it into the fire.*)
Mr. White. Hey! (*He jumps up and grabs the paw out of the fire before it starts to burn.*)
Morris (*solemnly*). Better let it burn.
Mr. White. If you don't want it, Morris, give it to me.
Morris (*stubbornly*). I won't. I threw it on the fire. If you keep it, don't blame me for what happens. If you're smart, you'll throw it back in the fire.
Mr. White (*shaking his head and looking closely at the paw*). How do you do it?
Morris. Hold it in your right hand and wish out loud. But I'm warning you, you won't like the consequences.
Mrs. White. Sounds like the *Arabian Nights.*[2] Why don't you wish for a few extra pairs of hands for me?

[*She gets up to set the table for supper.* MR. WHITE *starts to raise his arm, and* MORRIS, *alarmed, jumps forward to stop him. The three* WHITES *laugh.*]

Morris. If you must wish, for heaven's sake, wish for something sensible. But I don't want to be here to see it.

[*The four sit down and eat supper. The monkey's paw forgotten for the moment, the* WHITES *listen eagerly to more of* MORRIS*'s*

2. ***Arabian Nights:*** collection of ancient tales from Arabia, India, Persia, and other countries; also known as *The Thousand and One Nights.* Many of the stories involve wishes and magic.

Stranger. I—I was asked to come see you. I come from Maw and Meggins.

Mrs. White (*alarmed*). Is anything wrong? Has something happened to Herbert? What is it? What is it?

Mr. White. Now, now. Calm down. No point jumping to conclusions. (*Looking hopefully at the* STRANGER) I'm sure our visitor hasn't brought us any bad news.

Stranger. I'm sorry . . .

Mrs. White (*frantic*). Is he hurt?

Stranger (*nods*). Badly hurt. But he is not in any pain.

Mrs. White. Oh, thank goodness! Thank goodness for that! Thank——

[*She breaks off, suddenly understanding, and stares at the* STRANGER *in growing horror. The* STRANGER *looks at the floor.* MRS. WHITE *turns to her husband and takes his hand. There is a long pause.*]

Stranger (*in a low voice*). He was caught in the machinery.

Mr. White (*dazed*). Caught in the machinery. Yes. (*He squeezes his wife's hand and stares blankly out the window, then turns to the* STRANGER.)

Mr. White. He was our only child, you know. It is hard.

Stranger (*clearing his throat*). The company wants me to convey their sincere sympathy with you in your great loss. I hope you understand that I'm just doing my job. (*Pauses*) I'm supposed to tell you that Maw and Meggins disclaim all responsibility. They admit no liability,[4] but in consideration of your son's work, they would like to give you a certain sum as compensation.

Mr. White (*barely able to speak*). A certain sum . . . How much?

4. **liability** (lī′ə·bil′ə·tē): legal responsibility for damage or loss.

Stranger. Two hundred pounds.

[MRS. WHITE *screams.* MR. WHITE *holds out his hands and falls to the floor in a faint.*]

Scene 3 ▲

Nighttime, a week and a half later.

[MRS. WHITE *stands in the doorway, weeping as she looks out into the darkness.* MR. WHITE *comes downstairs. He goes to her and closes the door, then puts his arms around her.*]

Mr. White (*gently*). Come back to bed. It's cold out there tonight.

Mrs. White. It is colder for my son. (*She sobs. Suddenly she straightens and turns, clutching her husband's arms.*)

Mrs. White (*wildly*). The paw! The monkey's paw!

Mr. White. What? Where?

Mrs. White. I want it. You didn't get rid of it, did you?

Mr. White. It's upstairs, I think. Why?

Mrs. White (*crying and laughing hysterically*). I only just thought of it. Why didn't I think of it before? Why didn't you think of it?

Mr. White. Think of what?

Mrs. White. The other two wishes. We've only had one.

Mr. White (*fiercely*). Wasn't that enough?

Mrs. White. No! We'll have one more. Go get it down and wish our boy alive again.

Mr. White (*stepping back in horror*). You're insane!

Mrs. White. I want my son back. I want to see my son.

Mr. White. You don't know what you're saying.

Mrs. White. We had the first wish granted! Why not the second?

Mr. White. It was a coincidence.

Mrs. White. Go and get it and wish!

Mr. White (*facing her and taking her by the arms*). He's been dead ten days, and besides . . . I didn't want to tell you this, but I could only recognize him by his clothes. He was mangled in the machinery. If he was too terrible for you to see then, how would it be now?

Mrs. White. Bring him back! Do you think I would fear my own son?

[MR. WHITE *goes slowly upstairs, followed by his wife. He takes the paw and stares at it.*]

Mrs. White. Wish!
Mr. White (*weakly*). It is foolish and wicked.
Mrs. White. Wish!
Mr. White (*holding up the paw*). I wish my son alive again. ◆

[*He drops the paw and sinks trembling into a chair.* MRS. WHITE *runs to the window and stands looking out. The clock ticks. A stair creaks.* MRS. WHITE *comes and sits by her husband. Finally, a quiet knock is heard.* MRS. WHITE *jumps up.*]

Mrs. White. What's that?
Mr. White (*shakily*). A mouse. It's just a mouse in the wall.

[*Another knock, louder this time.*]

Mrs. White. It's Herbert! It's our son! (*She starts toward the stairs, but* MR. WHITE *grabs her by the arm.*)

Mr. White. What are you going to do?

Mrs. White. It's Herbert! What are you holding me for? Let go so I can open the door.

Mr. White (*hoarsely*). Don't let it in.

Mrs. White. How can you be afraid of your own son? Let me go.

[*The knocking is louder and louder. She breaks free and runs down to the door.*]

Mrs. White. I'm here, Herbert, I'm right here!

[*As she struggles with the lock,* MR. WHITE *falls to his knees. He picks up the monkey's paw from the floor and holds it up in his right hand. His lips move, but we can't hear him over the thunderous knocking. He drops the paw. At once the knocking stops, and the door springs open. There is a pause, and then a long, loud wail from* MRS. WHITE. *Beyond her, the road is empty.*] ✳

MEET THE WRITER

Escaping Captivity

The son of a dock manager on the River Thames in London, **William Wymark Jacobs** (1863–1943) grew up watching ships and listening to sailors' stories. Jacobs

referred to his civil-service job as "captivity" and wrote stories after work as an escape. Eventually his comic tales of seaside characters made him famous, and readers of the *Strand Magazine* eagerly awaited the next yarn. (The editors were eager too. Jacobs wrote slowly, in horrible handwriting that only one typist could decipher, and pushed deadlines to the minute.)

William Wymark Jacobs (1910) by Carton Moore-Park. Oil on canvas.

By courtesy of The National Portrait Gallery, London.

Still, the tardy Jacobs wrote more than 150 stories. While his seafaring stories overshadowed his tales of mystery and horror, "The Monkey's Paw" is a classic of the suspense genre and the reason he is still famous. (A rock band took the name Third Wish in Jacobs's honor.)

Whether writing about the sea or the spooky, Jacobs was a master of physical detail: 66 I get the idea of setting first. . . . If you begin by inventing a plot you have got to . . . see something mentally before you can possibly make a start. You can't begin from nowhere. 99

You'll find the beginning of Jacobs's original story version of "The Monkey's Paw" on pages 196 and 197.

from
The Monkey's Paw

W. W. Jacobs

Here is the beginning of W. W. Jacobs's original story version of "The Monkey's Paw." As you read the story, think about how it compares with the play.

Without, the night was cold and wet, but in the small parlor of Lakesnam Villa the blinds were drawn and the fire burned brightly. Father and son were at chess, the former, who possessed ideas about the game involving radical changes, putting his king into such sharp and unnecessary perils that it even provoked comment from the white-haired old lady knitting placidly by the fire.

"Hark at the wind," said Mr. White, who, having seen a fatal mistake after it was too late, was amiably[1] desirous of preventing his son from seeing it.

"I'm listening," said the latter, grimly surveying the board as he stretched out his hand. "Check."

"I should hardly think that he'd come tonight," said his father, with his hand poised over the board.

"Mate," replied the son.

"That's the worst of living so far out," bawled Mr. White, with sudden and unlooked-for violence; "of all the beastly, slushy, out-of-the-way places to live in, this is the worst. Pathway's a bog, and the road's a torrent. I don't know what people are thinking about. I suppose because only two houses on the road are let,[2] they think it doesn't matter."

"Never mind, dear," said his wife soothingly; "perhaps you'll win the next one."

Mr. White looked up sharply, just in time to intercept a knowing glance between mother and son. The words died away on his lips, and he hid a guilty grin in his thin gray beard.

"There he is," said Herbert White, as the gate banged to loudly and heavy footsteps came toward the door.

The old man rose with hospitable haste and, opening the door, was heard condoling[3] with the new arrival. The new arrival also condoled with himself, so that Mrs. White said, "Tut, tut!" and coughed gently as her husband entered the room, followed by a tall, burly man, beady of eye and rubicund of visage.[4]

"Sergeant Major Morris," he said, introducing him.

The sergeant major shook hands and, taking the proffered seat by the fire, watched contentedly while his host got out whiskey and tumblers and stood a small copper kettle on the fire.

At the third glass his eyes got brighter, and he began to talk, the little family circle regarding with eager interest this visitor from distant parts as he squared his broad shoulders in the chair and spoke of strange scenes and doughty[5] deeds, of wars and plagues and strange peoples.

1. **amiably:** good-naturedly.
2. **let:** rented.
3. **condoling:** expressing sympathy (here, about the bad weather).
4. **rubicund of visage** (viz′ij): red faced.
5. **doughty** (dout′ē): brave.

"Twenty-one years of it," said Mr. White, nodding at his wife and son. "When he went away, he was a slip of a youth in the warehouse. Now look at him."

"He don't look to have taken much harm," said Mrs. White politely.

"I'd like to go to India myself," said the old man, "just to look round a bit, you know."

"Better where you are," said the sergeant major, shaking his head. He put down the empty glass and, sighing softly, shook it again.

"I should like to see those old temples and fakirs[6] and jugglers," said the old man. "What was that you started telling me the other day about a monkey's paw or something, Morris?"

"Nothing," said the soldier hastily. "Leastways, nothing worth hearing."

"Monkey's paw?" said Mrs. White curiously.

"Well, it's just a bit of what you might call magic, perhaps," said the sergeant major offhandedly.

His three listeners leaned forward eagerly. The visitor absent-mindedly put his empty glass to his lips and then set it down again. His host filled it for him.

"To look at," said the sergeant major, fumbling in his pocket, "it's just an ordinary little paw, dried to a mummy."

He took something out of his pocket and proffered it. Mrs. White drew back with a grimace, but her son, taking it, examined it curiously.

"And what is there special about it?" inquired Mr. White, as he took it from his son and, having examined it, placed it upon the table.

"It had a spell put on it by an old fakir," said the sergeant major, "a very holy man. He wanted to show that fate ruled people's lives and that those who interfered with it did so to their sorrow. He put a spell on it so that three separate men could have three wishes from it."

His manner was so impressive that his hearers were conscious that their light laughter jarred somewhat.

"Well, why don't you have three, sir?" said Herbert White cleverly.

The soldier regarded him in the way that middle age is wont to regard presumptuous youth. "I have," he said quietly, and his blotchy face whitened.

"And did you really have the three wishes granted?" asked Mrs. White.

"I did," said the sergeant major, and his glass tapped against his strong teeth.

"And has anybody else wished?" inquired the old lady.

"The first man had his three wishes, yes," was the reply. "I don't know what the first two were, but the third was for death. That's how I got the paw."

His tones were so grave that a hush fell upon the group.

"If you've had your three wishes, it's no good to you now, then, Morris," said the old man at last. "What do you keep it for?"

The soldier shook his head. "Fancy,[7] I suppose," he said slowly. "I did have some idea of selling it, but I don't think I will. It has caused enough mischief already. Besides, people won't buy. They think it's a fairy tale, some of them, and those who do think anything of it want to try it first and pay me afterward."

"If you could have another three wishes," said the old man, eyeing him keenly, "would you have them?"

"I don't know," said the other. "I don't know." . . .

---

6. **fakirs** (fə·kirz′): Muslim or Hindu holy people, thought by some to perform miracles.

7. **Fancy:** here, whim or impulse.

MAKING MEANINGS

First Thoughts

1. Look at the **predictions** you made in your reading notes. Where did events turn out as you expected? What surprised you most in this play? What kept you in **suspense**—what did you want to find out?

Shaping Interpretations

2. Are the Whites' three wishes granted? Do they get what they really want? Explain.

3. What did the holy man want to prove to people by putting the spell on the paw? In your opinion, has the holy man made his point? Why or why not?

4. How could the first wish have been worded to avoid the tragic consequences? the second wish?

5. What things does the sergeant major say that **foreshadow,** or hint at, the Whites' fate?

6. Compare Mr. White's and Herbert's attitudes toward the monkey's paw. Why is it logical that Herbert would be the victim of the first wish?

7. Unlike Mr. White's first two wishes, the third wish doesn't seem to have unexpected disastrous consequences. Do you think the granting of the third wish will also produce a tragic outcome? If so, what might it be?

Reading Check

a. Explain how the monkey's paw got its powers.

b. What is the first wish, and who suggests it?

c. What seems to be the effect of the first wish?

d. What is the second wish, and why doesn't Mr. White want to make it?

e. What is the final wish? How do you know?

Connecting with the Text

8. Look again at your Quickwrite. Would you still make the same three wishes? How, if at all, would you change them? Explain.

Challenging the Text

9. Do you think it is believable that, knowing what he does, the sergeant major continues to carry the paw and then allows a friend to wish on it? Defend your position.

CHOICES: Building Your Portfolio

Writer's Notebook

1. Collecting Ideas for a Character Analysis

We learn about characters from
- what they do
- what they say
- what they think
- how they are described
- what other characters say about them

At different points in the play, each of the Whites has ideas about how to use the monkey's paw. Their ideas reveal a great deal about them. Jot down what you learn about Herbert, Mr. White, and Mrs. White from their reactions to the paw. At the right you'll see notes on a character from another story in this book.

WORK IN PROGRESS

Squeaky in "Raymond's Run" (page 3)
- what she does: cares a lot for her brother; defends her brother; runs
- what she says: use some quotes. She's really funny.
- what she thinks: hates girls who are phony

Performance

2. Acting Out the Paw

With several classmates, rehearse and perform *The Monkey's Paw*. Consider these questions:

- Who will play each part?
- What sound effects will you use?
- What costumes and props will you need? How will you create the main prop—the awful paw?
- What kind of set will you design?
- Will you keep the time period of the story, or will you reset it in the present day?

Comparing and Contrasting

3. Story to Stage

Read the opening section of the original short story by W. W. Jacobs (see **Connections** on page 196). Then, write a paragraph in which you compare and contrast the opening of the play version and the story version. What decisions did the dramatist make in adapting the story? Explain whether you prefer one version over the other, and why.

Creative Writing

4. Wish Carefully

The Monkey's Paw draws on a "formula" that is shared by dozens of world folk tales:

- An elderly couple is given three wishes.
- They make their first wish unintentionally, or it is granted in a way they didn't expect.
- The second wish is a stupid or hasty response to the problems created by the first wish.
- The third wish must be used to prevent the catastrophe caused by the first two wishes.

Write your own humorous or scary "three wishes" story. Use the basic **cause and effect structure** described above.

GRAMMAR LINK MINI-LESSON

Lie and Lay, Sit and Set, Rise and Raise

Language Handbook HELP

See Special Problems with Verbs, pages 760-761.

Technology HELP

See Language Workshop CD-ROM. Key word entry: confusing verbs.

Lie and *lay, sit* and *set,* and *rise* and *raise* are verb pairs that often cause confusion. Remember that the second verb in each pair expresses an action directed toward an object—a person or thing named in the sentence; the first verb simply expresses an action. (For example, you *lie* down, but you *lay* your school bag on the table first.) Below are some of the forms of these six verbs. Notice that the past tense of *lie* is *lay.*

Base Form	Present Participle	Past	Past Participle
lie	lying	lay	(have) lain
lay	laying	laid	(have) laid
sit	sitting	sat	(have) sat
set	setting	set	(have) set
rise	rising	rose	(have) risen
raise	raising	raised	(have) raised

Try It Out

Copy the following paragraph, choosing the correct verb from each underlined pair.

Mr. White (1) sat/set his chess piece down as he (2) raised/rose to answer the door. The sergeant major (3) laid/lay the shriveled paw on the table, then (4) sat/set down to begin his story. Soon after, Herbert (5) laid/lay lifeless beneath the ground.

VOCABULARY HOW TO OWN A WORD

Multiple Meanings: Which One Fits?

Have you noticed how many English words have **multiple meanings?** In fact, it's often the simplest, most common words that have several completely different meanings. (They can even be different parts of speech.) When Mr. White says, "It's just a *mouse* in the wall" (page 193), it's clear from the context that he's referring to "a small rodent," *not* "a hand-held computer device," or "a timid person."

Each of the words in the Word Bank is taken from the play. (Page numbers are given in parentheses.) Work with a dictionary and a partner to decide how people in at least three different professions might use the word to mean three different things. Put your findings in a chart something like this:

word	
mouse	**farmer:** A mouse is a "small rodent."
	computer user: A mouse is a "hand-held computer device."
	teacher: A mouse is a "child who is very shy."

Word Bank   *game* (page 187) • *smart* (page 189) • *mock* (page 190) • *pounds* (page 190) • *suit* (page 191)

Before You Read

THE TELL-TALE HEART

Make the Connection

Top Ten Terrors

Many people like a good scare now and then, which probably explains the popularity of everything from Stephen King's novels to amusement park rides and Halloween parties. Conduct a class poll to come up with a list of the "top ten terrors" in popular culture—choose from TV shows, movies, books, events—that tap into our craving for scary thrills.

Quickwrite

Jot down some ideas you have about the list the class came up with. Why do some people like being scared? (Can a good scare ever be healthy?)

Elements of Literature

Narrator

When we read a story, we rely on the **narrator** (the character telling the story) to let us know what is going on. What if the narrator can't be trusted, though? As you begin reading this story, decide if the narrator seems to be a reliable source of information.

> **A** **narrator** is a person or character who is telling a story.

go.hrw.com
LE0 8-3

Reading Skills and Strategies

Previewing: What's Ahead?

Before you begin reading the next story, try **previewing** the text by doing the following:

1. Look at the title.

2. Read the quotation in large type on the next page.

3. Glance at the story's illustrations.

On the basis of your preview, jot down in your reading notes your **predictions** of what will happen in the story.

THE TELL-TALE HEART

Edgar Allan Poe

*Why will you say
that I am mad?*

True!—nervous—very, very dreadfully nervous I had been and am; but why *will* you say that I am mad? The disease had sharpened my senses—not destroyed—not dulled them. Above all was the sense of hearing acute. I heard all things in the heaven and in the earth. I heard many things in hell. How, then, am I mad? Hearken! and observe how healthily—how calmly I can tell you the whole story.

It is impossible to say how first the idea entered my brain; but once conceived, it haunted me day and night. Object[1] there was none. Passion there was none. I loved the old man. He had never wronged me. He had never given me insult. For his gold I had no desire. I think it was his eye! Yes, it was this! One of his eyes resembled that of a vulture—a pale blue eye, with a film over it. Whenever it fell upon me, my blood ran cold; and so by degrees—very gradually—I made up my mind to take the life of the old man and thus rid myself of the eye forever.

Now this is the point. You fancy me mad. Madmen know nothing. But you should have seen *me*. You should have seen how wisely I proceeded—with what caution—with what foresight—with what dissimulation[2] I went to work! I was never kinder to the old man than during the whole week before I killed him. And every night, about midnight, I turned the latch of his door and opened it—oh, so gently! And then, when I had made an opening sufficient for my head, I put in a dark lantern, all closed, closed, so that no light shone out, and then I thrust in my head. Oh, you would have laughed to see how cunningly I thrust it in! I moved it slowly—very, very slowly, so that I might not disturb the old man's sleep.

It took me an hour to place my whole head within the opening so far that I could see him as he lay upon his bed. Ha! Would a madman have been so wise as this? And then, when my head was well in the room, I undid the lantern cautiously—oh, so cautiously—cautiously (for the hinges creaked)—I undid it just so much that a single thin ray fell upon the vulture eye. And this I did for seven long nights—every night just at midnight—but I found the eye always closed; and so it was impossible to do the work; for it was not the old man who vexed me, but his Evil Eye. And every morning, when the day broke, I went boldly into the chamber and spoke courageously to him, calling him by name in a hearty tone and inquiring how he had passed the night. So you see he would have been a very profound old man, indeed, to suspect that every night, just at twelve, I looked in upon him while he slept.

Upon the eighth night I was more than usually cautious in opening the door. A watch's minute hand moves more quickly than did mine. Never before that night had I *felt* the extent of my own powers—of my sagacity. I could scarcely contain my feelings of triumph. To think that there I was, opening the door, little by little, and he not even to dream of my secret deeds or thoughts. I fairly chuckled at the idea; and perhaps he heard me; for he moved on the bed suddenly, as if startled. Now you may think that I drew back—but no. His room was as black as pitch with the thick darkness (for the shutters were close fastened,

---

1. **object:** purpose or goal.
2. **dissimulation:** disguising of intentions or feelings. (Look for a similar word at the end of the story.)

WORDS TO OWN
acute (ə·kyōōt′) *adj.*: sharp; sensitive.
vexed (vekst) *v.*: disturbed; annoyed.
sagacity (sə·gas′ə·tē) *n.*: intelligence and good judgment.

through fear of robbers), and so I knew that he could not see the opening of the door, and I kept pushing it on steadily, steadily.

I had my head in, and was about to open the lantern, when my thumb slipped upon the tin fastening, and the old man sprang up in the bed, crying out—"Who's there?"

I kept quite still and said nothing. For a whole hour I did not move a muscle, and in the meantime I did not hear him lie down. He was still sitting up in the bed listening— just as I have done, night after night, hearkening to the deathwatches[3] in the wall.

Presently I heard a slight groan, and I knew it was the groan of mortal terror. It was not a groan of pain or of grief—oh, no!—it was the low, stifled sound that arises from the bottom of the soul when overcharged with awe. I knew the sound well. Many a night, just at midnight, when all the world slept, it has welled up from my own bosom, deepening, with its dreadful echo, the terrors that distracted me. I say I knew it well. I knew what the old man felt, and pitied him, although I chuckled at heart. I knew that he had been lying awake ever since the first slight noise, when he had turned in the bed. His fears had been ever since growing upon him. He had been trying to fancy them causeless but could not. He had been saying to himself—"It is nothing but the wind in the chimney—it is only a mouse crossing the floor," or "It is merely a cricket which has made a single chirp." Yes, he has been trying to comfort himself with these suppositions; but he had found all in vain. *All in vain;* because Death, in approaching

him, had stalked with his black shadow before him and enveloped the victim. And it was the mournful influence of the unperceived shadow that caused him to feel—although he neither saw nor heard—to *feel* the presence of my head within the room.

When I had waited a long time, very patiently, without hearing him lie down, I resolved to open a little—a very, very little crevice in the lantern. So I opened it—you cannot imagine how stealthily, stealthily— until, at length, a single dim ray, like the thread of the spider, shot from out the crevice and full upon the vulture eye.

It was open—wide, wide open— and I grew furious as I gazed upon it. I saw it with perfect distinctness—all a dull blue, with a hideous veil over it that chilled the very marrow in my bones; but I could see nothing else of the old man's face or person, for I had directed the ray, as if by instinct, precisely upon the damned spot.

And now have I not told you that what you mistake for madness is but overacuteness of the senses?—now, I say, there came to my ears a low, dull, quick sound, such as a watch makes when enveloped in cotton. I knew *that* sound well too. It was the beating of the old man's heart. It increased my fury, as the beating of a drum stimulates the soldier into courage.

But even yet I refrained and kept still. I scarcely breathed. I held the lantern motionless. I tried how steadily I could maintain the ray upon the eye. Meantime the hellish tattoo[4] of the heart increased. It

4. **tattoo:** steady beat.

3. **deathwatches:** beetles that burrow into wood and make tapping sounds, which some people believe are a sign of approaching death.

WORDS TO OWN
refrained (ri·frānd') v.: held back.

The illustrations on pages 205 and 206 are from a short movie based on "The Tell-Tale Heart."

grew quicker and quicker and louder and louder every instant. The old man's terror *must* have been extreme! It grew louder, I say, louder every moment!—do you mark me well? I have told you that I am nervous: So I am. And now at the dead hour of the night, amid the dreadful silence of that old house, so strange a noise as this excited me to uncontrollable terror. Yet for some minutes longer I refrained and stood still. But the beating grew louder, louder! I thought the heart must burst. And now a new anxiety seized me—the sound would be heard by a neighbor! The old man's hour had come! With a loud yell, I threw open the lantern and leaped into the room. He shrieked once—once only. In an instant I dragged him to the floor and pulled the heavy bed over him. I then smiled gaily to find the deed so far done. But, for many minutes, the heart beat on with a muffled sound. This, however, did not vex me; it would not be heard through the wall. At length it ceased. The old man was dead. I removed the bed and examined the corpse. Yes, he was stone, stone dead. I placed my hand upon the heart and held it there many minutes. There was no pulsation. He was stone dead. His eye would trouble me no more.

If still you think me mad, you will think no longer when I describe the wise precautions I took for the concealment of the body. The night waned, and I worked hastily but in silence. First of all I dismembered the corpse. I cut off the head and the arms and the legs.

I then took up three planks from the flooring of the chamber and deposited all between the scantlings.[5] I then replaced the boards so cleverly, so cunningly, that no human eye—not even *his*—could have detected anything wrong. There was nothing to wash out—no stain of any kind—no

5. **scantlings:** small beams of wood.

blood spot whatever. I had been too <u>wary</u> for that. A tub had caught all—ha! ha!

When I had made an end of these labors, it was four o'clock—still dark as midnight. As the bell sounded the hour, there came a knocking at the street door. I went down to open it with a light heart—for what had I *now* to fear? There entered three men, who introduced themselves, with perfect <u>suavity</u>, as officers of the police. A shriek had been heard by a neighbor during the

---

WORDS TO OWN

wary (wer′ē) *adj.:* cautious.
suavity (swäv′ə·tē) *n.:* smoothness; politeness.

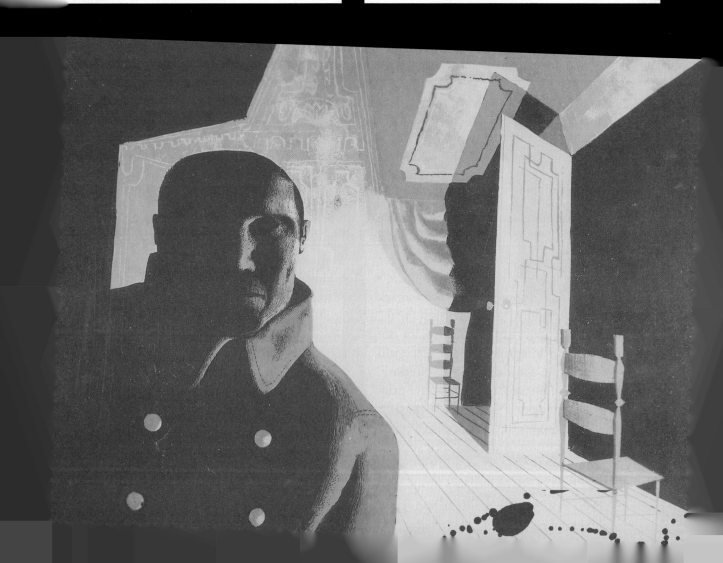

night; suspicion of foul play had been aroused; information had been lodged at the police office, and they (the officers) had been deputed[6] to search the premises.

I smiled—for *what* had I to fear? I bade the gentlemen welcome. The shriek, I said, was my own in a dream. The old man, I mentioned, was absent in the country. I took my visitors all over the house. I bade them search—search *well*. I led them, at length, to *his* chamber. I showed them his treasures, secure, undisturbed. In the enthusiasm of my confidence, I brought chairs into the room and desired them *here* to rest from their fatigues, while I myself, in the wild audacity of my perfect triumph, placed my own seat upon the very spot beneath which reposed the corpse of the victim.

The officers were satisfied. My *manner* had convinced them. I was singularly at ease. They sat, and while I answered cheerily, they chatted familiar things. But, ere long, I felt myself getting pale and wished them gone. My head ached, and I fancied a ringing in my ears; but still they sat and still chatted. The ringing became more distinct—it continued and became more distinct: I talked more freely to get rid of the feeling: but it continued and gained definitiveness—until, at length, I found that the noise was *not* within my ears.

No doubt I now grew *very* pale—but I talked more fluently and with a heightened voice. Yet the sound increased—and what could I do? It was *a low, dull, quick sound—much such a sound as a watch makes when enveloped in cotton.* I gasped for breath—and yet the officers heard it not. I talked more quickly—more vehemently; but the noise steadily increased. I

arose and argued about trifles, in a high key and with violent gesticulations, but the noise steadily increased. Why *would* they not be gone? I paced the floor to and fro with heavy strides, as if excited to fury by the observation of the men—but the noise steadily increased. Oh God! what *could* I do? I foamed—I raved—I swore! I swung the chair upon which I had been sitting and grated it upon the boards, but the noise arose over all and continually increased. It grew louder—louder—*louder!* And still the men chatted pleasantly, and smiled. Was it possible they heard not? Almighty God!—no, no! They heard!—they suspected!—they *knew!*—they were making a mockery of my horror!—this I thought, and this I think. But anything was better than this agony! Anything was more tolerable than this derision! I could bear those hypocritical smiles no longer! I felt that I must scream or die!—and now—again!—hark! louder! louder! louder! *louder!*—

"Villains!" I shrieked, "dissemble no more! I admit the deed!—tear up the planks!—here, here!—it is the beating of his hideous heart!"

WORDS TO OWN

audacity (ô·das′ə·tē) *n.*: boldness.
vehemently (vē′ə·mənt·lē) *adv.*: forcefully; passionately.
gesticulations (jes·tik′yōō·lā′shənz) *n.*: energetic gestures.
derision (di·rizh′ən) *n.*: contempt; ridicule.

---

6. **deputed** (dē·pyōōt′id): appointed.

MEET THE WRITER

The Dark Side

Born in Boston, **Edgar Allan Poe** (1809–1849) was the son of traveling actors. When Poe was a baby, his father deserted the family; his mother died before his third birthday. Poe was taken in by the wealthy Allan family of Richmond, Virginia, and given a first-class education. At the age of twelve, he had already written enough poems (mainly love poems to girls he knew) to fill a book. By the time he was twenty, he had published two volumes of poetry.

Poe constantly argued with his foster father, John Allan, about money. Allan eventually broke all ties with Poe, leaving him penniless. In 1831, Poe moved in with his aunt, Maria Clemm, and her children in Baltimore, probably in an attempt to find a new family. He married his young cousin Virginia Clemm five years later.

Poe became as celebrated for his tales of horror and mystery as for his poetry. Poe made very little money from his writing, though—one of his most famous poems, "The Raven," earned him only about fifteen dollars— and he seemed to live on the brink of disaster. His wife's death from

tuberculosis in 1847 brought on a general decline in his physical and emotional health. He was found lying unconscious in a Baltimore gutter on a rainy day in 1849; he died three days later of unknown causes.

More by Edgar Allan Poe

Poe was one of the first American writers to explore the dark side of the imagination. His horror tales include "The Masque of the Red Death," "The Pit and the Pendulum," and "The Fall of the House of Usher."

MAKING MEANINGS

First Thoughts

1. Go back to your reading notes. Did the story turn out the way you predicted? Did **previewing** the story help you make accurate predictions? Why or why not?

Shaping Interpretations

2. To whom might the narrator be telling his story? Where do you think he is as he tells it?

3. The narrator tries desperately to convince his listener that he is sane. What evidence does he give? How do his arguments actually demonstrate his madness?

4. How does the opening paragraph **foreshadow,** or hint at, the events of the story?

5. What is your explanation for the "heartbeat" noise that drives the narrator to confess? Draw on evidence from the text to support your opinion.

6. Why is this story called "The Tell-Tale Heart," in your opinion? (Can you think of more than one meaning for the title?)

7. The **mood,** or **atmosphere,** is the overall feeling in a story. For example, the mood might be happy or sad or scary. Writers create mood by piling up carefully chosen details. How would you describe the mood of this story? What details does Poe use to create that mood?

Connecting with the Text

8. Go back to your Quickwrite notes. What, if anything, did you find scary, unsettling, or otherwise memorable about this story? Explain what you think this story shares with other stories that scare people.

Edgar Allan Poe in a moment of writer's block.

> **Reading Check**
> Poe's story provides only limited information; some of the information is suspect because the only source is an unreliable **narrator.** Write down three questions you would like to ask a more reliable source. Explain how each question would help you better understand the **motivations** behind the murder.

CHOICES: Building Your Portfolio

Writer's Notebook

1. Collecting Ideas for a Character Analysis

What kind of person is the narrator? Reread the story looking for details that reveal the nature of this strange man. Gather your notes under headings such as these:

- what he says
- what he does
- what his conflicts are
- what his motivation seems to be

When you have gathered your details, make a generalization, and name at least three character traits you find in this person. Collect your data as if you were a psychiatrist who is trying to put together a profile of the murderer's personality.

At the right are a reader's notes on a different kind of character in this book.

Lemon Brown (page 93)

- **What he says:** everyone's got a treasure
- **What he does:** protects the boy
- **What his conflicts are:** not sure
- **What his motivation is:** he wants to help the boy
- **Traits:** kind, loving, troubled, fearful

Creative Writing

2. Scene of the Crime

Imagine that you are one of the police officers who responded to the neighbor's call. Write a **report** to be filed after you return to the station. Explain the circumstances of the investigation and what you found when you arrived on the scene. Include descriptions of the suspect's appearance and of your impressions. When did the suspect's behavior begin to strike you as odd?

Art

3. Hollywood Poe

Make a poster advertising a movie version of "The Tell-Tale Heart." Who will play each of these roles?

- the narrator
- the old man
- the police officers

Choose an exciting scene from the story to illustrate your poster. Will you use the original title or invent one that you think would attract a larger audience? What **mood** will your poster create?

Speaking and Listening

4. Crime and Punishment

With a group of classmates, stage a **mock trial** of the narrator for the murder of the old man. Will the defense plead guilty or not guilty? What witnesses will be called to the stand? These are other characters you may want to include:

- defense team
- prosecution team
- judge
- jury
- bailiff
- court reporter

GRAMMAR LINK   MINI-LESSON

Language Handbook HELP

See Consistency of Tense, page 759.

Technology HELP

See Language Workshop CD-ROM. Key word entry: consistency of tense.

Keeping Tense Consistent

Like most writers, Poe tells his story in the past tense; the events have already happened.

> "It grew louder—louder—*louder!* And still the men chatted pleasantly, and smiled. Was it possible they heard not?"

Writers sometimes choose to tell a story in the present tense instead, to make the reader feel as if the events are happening right now:

> It grows louder—louder—*louder!* And still the men chat pleasantly, and smile. Is it possible they hear not?

Whichever tense you choose to write in, use it consistently. Either the events happened before, or they're happening now. You'll confuse your reader if you switch tenses repeatedly:

> It grew louder—louder—*louder!* And still the men chat pleasantly, and smile. Was it possible they heard not?

When are the men chatting—after the story is over? By keeping tense consistent, you allow your reader to concentrate on the events of the story, rather than on trying to figure out when they occurred.

Try It Out

Select a story in this book, and rewrite its opening paragraph using a different tense. You might turn to "Raymond's Run" (page 3). How does the story sound when you rewrite the first paragraph in the *past* tense? How does "Broken Chain" (page 29) sound if you write the first paragraph in the *present* tense? After you rewrite your paragraph, exchange it for a partner's. Check to see that your partner used one tense consistently.

VOCABULARY   HOW TO OWN A WORD

WORD BANK

acute
vexed
sagacity
refrained
wary
suavity
audacity
vehemently
gesticulations
derision

Editing Edgar: Searching for Synonyms

Imagine that you are the editor of a magazine for teenagers. You want to include "The Tell-Tale Heart" in your Spooky Stories issue, but you think Poe's vocabulary is too hard and old-fashioned.

Divide the words in the Word Bank with a partner (five apiece). Find the sentences in the story in which your words appear (look for Words to Own), and copy the sentences onto a blank sheet of paper. Rewrite each sentence to make it easier. Substitute more commonly known words or phrases for the Word Bank words as well as for any other difficult words in the sentence. To locate **synonyms**—words with similar meanings—use a **thesaurus** (a dictionary of synonyms), a **synonym finder,** or a thesaurus that is part of your computer's **software.**

Elements of Literature

THE SHORT STORY: What Keeps Us Reading?

Plot: A Chain of Related Events

Plot is the chain of related events that make up a story. When a plot is well mapped out, it keeps us reading by making us curious about what will happen next.

Once upon a time, three well-to-do pigs came to the suburbs to build their dream homes. No sooner had they laid the foundations, however, than a black sedan pulled up. Out stepped Mr. Wolf, the building inspector, his eyes mean and shifty.

At once the storyteller stirs our curiosity by making us fear that a **conflict** will arise between the pigs and the wolf.

Mr. Wolf growled that the pigs didn't have the proper building permits. The pigs politely handed Mr. Wolf their paperwork, which he swallowed in one gulp. Then, sneering, he roared off in his black sedan.

Now **complications** develop. We fear that the wolf will wreck the pigs' plans. Also, since the wolf is a carnivore, there is a good chance the pigs will follow their permits down his throat.

The pigs rushed to complete their new homes. One pig built with straw, the second with wood, and the third with fiberglass and aluminum siding.

The **suspense** is building: What will happen next?

Just as the paint was drying, Mr. Wolf returned with a demolition crew. With a wrecking ball they knocked the first two houses down. The frightened pigs huddled in the fiberglass house, dialing a real estate lawyer on their cellular phone. Mr. Wolf huffed and he puffed, but he couldn't demolish that third house.

This is the plot's **climax,** or most exciting point, the moment at which the outcome of the conflict is decided. We are relieved that the space-age materials hold out against the enraged Mr. Wolf.

You may want to decide the **resolution,** or end, of the story for yourself. Does Mr. Wolf dynamite the last house? Will the pigs' lawyer arrive in time to stop him? The second outcome would make a satisfying resolution, at least for readers who favor the pigs. As you know, that's the way fairy tales usually end: happily ever after.

Suspense: The Page Turner

Conflict creates suspense in a story, and suspense is what keeps us turning those pages.

A *Writer on Plot*

"To me, the most important and difficult thing about writing is to find the plot. Good, original plots are very hard to come by. You never know when a lovely idea is going to flit suddenly into your mind, but by golly, when it does come along, you grab it with both hands and hang on to it tight. The trick is to write it down at once; otherwise you'll forget it."

—Roald Dahl, author of "The Landlady" (page 171)

by John Leggett

Writers use several methods to create suspense.

1. Foreshadowing

A writer may give clues—sometimes even false clues—that hint at a story's outcome. When we read in *The Monkey's Paw* (page 186) that the first owner of the magic paw wished for death after his first two wishes were granted, we expect that the new owners' wishes will also lead to misfortune.

2. Mystery

Writers sometimes create suspense by withholding information from the reader—for instance, *who* the murderer in a story is or *how* the crime was committed. Unusual or mysterious circumstances can also create suspense. In "The Landlady" (page 171), for example, why does the landlady open the door so quickly? Why is the last signature in the guest book over two years old? We read on to satisfy our curiosity.

3. Dilemma

Suspense is especially intense when a character we care about is in peril or must choose between two dangerous courses of action. At the end of *The Monkey's Paw,* we hold our breath as the old woman strains at the door. Will her husband stop her in time, and if not, what waits for her on the other side?

4. Reversal

A **reversal** is a sudden change in a character's situation from good to bad or vice versa. In "The Tell-Tale Heart" (page 202), it seems as if the narrator has gotten away with his crime. The corpse is hidden and the police suspect nothing—and then suddenly the narrator hears the sound of a heart beating. We worry about what lies ahead: Will there be another reversal for the narrator, or will things get even worse for him?

The word *suspense* is related to the word *suspended*. When a story keeps us in suspense, we feel almost as if we were suspended in midair. We may even hold our breath without realizing it as we read on eagerly to find out how the story ends.

Peanuts reprinted by permission of UFS, Inc.

Before You Read

THERE WILL COME SOFT RAINS

Make the Connection

Future Shock

Imagine the world of 2026. In what ways will it be different from the world of today? What kinds of new technologies, if any, will have changed the way people live? What would you find in a home of the future?

Quickwrite

Jot down your ideas on the pros and cons of technology. What benefits has technology brought us? What are its drawbacks?

Elements of Literature

Personification

Could a story about an empty house be interesting? Ray Bradbury thought so. As you read, notice how he uses **personification** to fill the empty house with life and action. Who—or what—are the "characters" in this story?

> **P**ersonification is a figure of speech in which an object or animal is spoken of as if it had human qualities.
>
> *For more on Personification, see pages 41–42 and the Handbook of Literary Terms.*

Reading Skills and Strategies

Using Chronology: Timing It Right

Have you ever asked a question like this after seeing a movie: "Did the holdup take place *before* or *after* the phone rang?" If you have, you were asking about chronology. **Chronology** is time order—what happens first, next, and last. A story written in **chronological order** presents events in the time sequence in which they occurred, one after the other.

As you read "There Will Come Soft Rains," use your reading notes to keep track of what's happening from hour to hour.

go.hrw.com

LEO 8-3

THERE WILL COME SOFT RAINS

Ray Bradbury

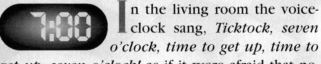

I n the living room the voice-clock sang, *Ticktock, seven o'clock, time to get up, time to get up, seven o'clock!* as if it were afraid that no-body would. The morning house lay empty. The clock ticked on, repeating and repeating its sounds into the emptiness. *Seven-nine, breakfast time, seven-nine!*

In the kitchen the breakfast stove gave a hissing sigh and ejected from its warm interior eight pieces of perfectly browned toast, eight eggs sunny side up, sixteen slices of bacon, and two coffees.

"Today is August 4, 2026," said a second voice from the kitchen ceiling, "in the city of Allendale, California." It repeated the date three times for memory's sake. "Today is Mr. Featherstone's birth-day. Today is the anniversary of Tilita's marriage. In-

The rain tapped on the empty house, echoing.

surance is payable, as are the water, gas, and light bills."

Somewhere in the walls, relays clicked, memory tapes glided under electric eyes.

8:01 *Eight-one, tick-tock, eight-one o'clock, off to school, off to work, run, run, eight-one!* But no doors slammed, no carpets took the soft tread of rubber heels. It was raining outside. The weather box on the front door sang quietly: "Rain, rain, go away; rubbers, raincoats for today . . ." And the rain tapped on the empty house, echoing.

Outside, the garage chimed and lifted its door to reveal the waiting car. After a long wait the door swung down again.

At eight-thirty the eggs were shriveled and the toast was like stone. An aluminum wedge scraped them into the sink, where hot water whirled them down a metal throat which digested and flushed them away to the distant sea. The dirty dishes were dropped into a hot washer and emerged twinkling dry.

Nine-fifteen, sang the clock, *time to clean.*

Out of warrens[1] in the wall, tiny robot mice darted. The rooms were acrawl with the small cleaning animals, all rubber and metal. They thudded against chairs, whirling their moustached runners, kneading the rug nap, sucking gently at hidden dust. Then, like mysterious invaders, they popped into their burrows. Their pink electric eyes faded. The house was clean.

10:00 *Ten o'clock.* The sun came out from behind the rain. The house stood alone in a city of rubble and ashes. This was the one house left standing. At night the ruined city gave off a radioactive glow which could be seen for miles.

Ten-fifteen. The garden sprinklers whirled up in golden founts, filling the soft morning air with scatterings of brightness. The water pelted windowpanes, running down the charred west side where the house had been burned evenly free of its white paint. The entire west face of the house was black, save for five places. Here the silhouette in paint of a man mowing a lawn. Here, as in a photograph, a woman bent to pick flowers. Still farther over, their images burned on wood in one titanic instant, a small boy, hands flung into the air; higher up, the image of a thrown ball, and opposite him a girl, hands raised to catch a ball which never came down.

The five spots of paint—the man, the woman, the children, the ball—remained. The rest was a thin charcoaled layer.

The gentle sprinkler rain filled the garden with falling light.

Until this day, how well the house had kept its peace. How carefully it had inquired, "Who goes there? What's the password?" and, getting no answer from lonely foxes and whining cats, it had shut up its windows and drawn shades in an old-maidenly preoccupation with self-protection which bordered on a mechanical paranoia.

It quivered at each sound, the house did. If a sparrow brushed a window, the shade snapped up. The bird, startled, flew off! No, not even a bird must touch the house!

The house was an altar with ten thousand attendants, big, small, servicing, attending, in choirs. But the gods had gone away, and the ritual of the religion continued senselessly, uselessly.

12:00 *Twelve noon.* A dog whined, shivering, on the front porch.

The front door recognized the dog voice and opened. The dog, once huge and fleshy, but

---

Words to Own

paranoia (par′ə·noi′ə) *n.:* mental disorder that often causes people to believe they are being persecuted; false suspicions.

---

1. **warrens:** small, crowded spaces.

now gone to bone and covered with sores, moved in and through the house, tracking mud. Behind it whirred angry mice, angry at having to pick up mud, angry at inconvenience.

For not a leaf fragment blew under the door but what the wall panels flipped open and the copper scrap rats flashed swiftly out. The offending dust, hair, or paper, seized in miniature steel jaws, was raced back to the burrows. There, down tubes which fed into the cellar, it was dropped into the sighing vent of an incinerator which sat like evil Baal[2] in a dark corner.

The dog ran upstairs, hysterically yelping to each door, at last realizing, as the house realized, that only silence was here.

It sniffed the air and scratched the kitchen door. Behind the door, the stove was making pancakes which filled the house with a rich baked odor and the scent of maple syrup.

The dog frothed at the mouth, lying at the door, sniffing, its eyes turned to fire. It ran wildly in circles, biting at its tail, spun in a frenzy, and died. It lay in the parlor for an hour.

Two o'clock, sang a voice.

Delicately sensing decay at last, the regiments of mice hummed out as softly as blown gray leaves in an electrical wind.

Two-fifteen.

The dog was gone.

In the cellar, the incinerator glowed suddenly and a whirl of sparks leaped up the chimney.

Two thirty-five.

Bridge tables sprouted from patio walls. Playing cards fluttered onto pads in a shower of pips.[3] Martinis manifested on an oaken bench with egg-salad sandwiches. Music played.

But the tables were silent and the cards untouched.

At four o'clock the tables folded like great butterflies back through the paneled walls.

2. **Baal** (bā′əl): in the Bible, the god of Canaan, whom the Israelites came to regard as a false god.
3. **pips:** figures on cards.

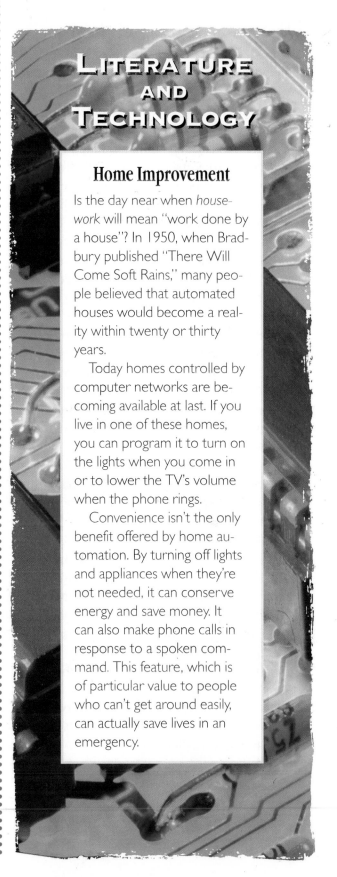

LITERATURE AND TECHNOLOGY

Home Improvement

Is the day near when *housework* will mean "work done by a house"? In 1950, when Bradbury published "There Will Come Soft Rains," many people believed that automated houses would become a reality within twenty or thirty years.

Today homes controlled by computer networks are becoming available at last. If you live in one of these homes, you can program it to turn on the lights when you come in or to lower the TV's volume when the phone rings.

Convenience isn't the only benefit offered by home automation. By turning off lights and appliances when they're not needed, it can conserve energy and save money. It can also make phone calls in response to a spoken command. This feature, which is of particular value to people who can't get around easily, can actually save lives in an emergency.

Four-thirty.

The nursery walls glowed. Animals took shape: yellow giraffes, blue lions, pink antelopes, lilac panthers cavorting in crystal substance. The walls were glass. They looked out upon color and fantasy. Hidden films clocked through well-oiled sprockets,[4] and the walls lived. The nursery floor was woven to resemble a crisp cereal[5] meadow. Over this ran aluminum roaches and iron crickets, and in the hot, still air butterflies of delicate red tissue wavered among the sharp aromas of animal spoors![6] There was the sound like a great matted yellow hive of bees within a dark bellows, the lazy bumble of a purring lion. And there was the patter of okapi[7] feet and the murmur of a fresh jungle rain, like other hoofs, falling upon the summer-starched grass. Now the walls dissolved into distances of parched weed, mile on mile, and warm endless sky. The animals drew away into thorn brakes[8] and water holes.

It was the children's hour.

Five o'clock. The bath filled with clear hot water.

Six, seven, eight o'clock. The dinner dishes manipulated like magic tricks, and in the study a *click.* In the metal stand opposite the hearth where a fire now blazed up warmly, a cigar popped out, half an inch of soft gray ash on it, smoking, waiting.

Nine o'clock. The beds warmed their hidden circuits, for nights were cool here.

Nine-five. A voice spoke from the study ceiling:

"Mrs. McClellan, which poem would you like this evening?"

The house was silent.

4. **sprockets:** wheels with points designed to fit into the holes along the edges of a filmstrip.
5. **cereal:** of grasses that produce grain.
6. **spoors:** tracks.
7. **okapi** (ō·kä′pē): African animal related to the giraffe but with a much shorter neck.
8. **thorn brakes:** clumps of thorns; thickets.

The voice said at last, "Since you express no preference, I shall select a poem at random." Quiet music rose to back the voice. "Sara Teasdale. As I recall, your favorite. . . .

> *There will come soft rains and the smell*
> *of the ground,*
> *And swallows circling with their shim-*
> *mering sound;*
>
> *And frogs in the pools singing at night,*
> *And wild plum trees in* tremulous *white;*
>
> *Robins will wear their feathery fire,*
> *Whistling their whims on a low fence-*
> *wire;*
>
> *And not one will know of the war, not*
> *one*
> *Will care at last when it is done.*

WORDS TO OWN
tremulous (trem′yo͞o·ləs) *adj.*: trembling. *Tremulous* also means "fearful" or "timid."

Not one would mind, neither bird nor tree,

If mankind perished utterly;

And Spring herself, when she woke at dawn
Would scarcely know that we were gone."

The fire burned on the stone hearth, and the cigar fell away into a mound of quiet ash on its tray. The empty chairs faced each other between the silent walls, and the music played.

10:00 At ten o'clock the house began to die.

The wind blew. A falling tree bough crashed through the kitchen window. Cleaning solvent,[9] bottled, shattered over the stove. The room was ablaze in an instant!

"Fire!" screamed a voice. The house lights flashed, water pumps shot water from the ceilings. But the solvent spread on the linoleum, licking, eating, under the kitchen door, while the voices took it up in chorus: "Fire, fire, fire!"

The house tried to save itself. Doors sprang tightly shut, but the windows were broken by the heat and the wind blew and sucked upon the fire.

The house gave ground as the fire in ten billion angry sparks moved with flaming ease from room to room and then up the stairs. While scurrying water rats squeaked from the walls, pistoled their water, and ran for more. And the wall sprays let down showers of mechanical rain.

But too late. Somewhere, sighing, a pump shrugged to a stop. The quenching rain ceased. The reserve water supply which had filled baths and washed dishes for many quiet days was gone.

The fire crackled up the stairs. It fed upon Picassos and Matisses[10] in the upper halls, like delicacies, baking off the oily flesh, tenderly crisping the canvases into black shavings.

Now the fire lay in beds, stood in windows, changed the colors of drapes!

And then, reinforcements.

From attic trapdoors, blind robot faces peered down with faucet mouths gushing green chemical.

The fire backed off, as even an elephant must at the sight of a dead snake. Now there were twenty snakes whipping over the floor, killing the fire with a clear cold venom of green froth.

But the fire was clever. It had sent flame outside the house, up through the attic to the pumps there. An explosion! The attic brain which directed the pumps was shattered into bronze shrapnel on the beams.

The fire rushed back into every closet and felt of the clothes hung there.

9. **solvent:** something that can dissolve something else (here, something that dissolves dirt). *Solvent, dissolve,* and *solution* have the same Latin root, *solvere,* which means "to loosen."

10. **Picassos and Matisses:** paintings by Pablo Picasso (1881–1973), a famous Spanish painter and sculptor who worked in France, and by Henri Matisse (än·rē' mȧ·tēs') (1869–1954), a famous French painter.

The house shuddered, oak bone on bone, its bared skeleton cringing from the heat, its wire, its nerves revealed as if a surgeon had torn the skin off to let the red veins and capillaries quiver in the scalded air. Help, help! Fire! Run, run! Heat snapped mirrors like the first brittle winter ice. And the voices wailed, Fire, fire, run, run, like a tragic nursery rhyme, a dozen voices, high, low, like children dying in a forest, alone, alone. And the voices fading as the wires popped their sheathings[11] like hot chestnuts. One, two, three, four, five voices died.

In the nursery the jungle burned. Blue lions roared, purple giraffes bounded off. The panthers ran in circles, changing color, and ten million animals, running before the fire, vanished off toward a distant steaming river. . . .

11. **sheathings:** protective coverings.

Ten more voices died. In the last instant under the fire avalanche, other choruses, oblivious, could be heard announcing the time, playing music, cutting the lawn by remote-control mower, or setting an umbrella frantically out and in, the slamming and opening front door, a thousand things happening, like a clock shop when each clock strikes the hour insanely before or after the other, a scene of maniac confusion, yet unity; singing, screaming, a few last cleaning mice darting bravely out to carry the horrid ashes away! And one voice, with sublime disregard for the situation, read poetry aloud in the fiery study, until all the film spools burned, until all the wires withered and the circuits cracked.

The fire burst the house and let it slam flat down, puffing out skirts of spark and smoke.

In the kitchen, an instant before the rain of fire and timber, the stove could be seen making breakfasts at a psychopathic[12] rate, ten dozen eggs, six loaves of toast, twenty dozen bacon strips, which, eaten by fire, started the stove working again, hysterically hissing!

The crash. The attic smashing into kitchen and parlor. The parlor into cellar, cellar into subcellar. Deep freeze, armchair, film tapes, circuits, beds, and all like skeletons thrown in a cluttered mound deep under.

Smoke and silence. A great quantity of smoke.

Dawn showed faintly in the east. Among the ruins, one wall stood alone. Within the wall, a last voice said, over and over again and again, even as the sun rose to shine upon the heaped rubble and steam:

"Today is August 5, 2026, today is August 5, 2026, today is . . ."

12. **psychopathic** (sī′kō·path′ik): insane.

WORDS TO OWN

oblivious (ə·bliv′ē·əs) *adj.:* unaware.
sublime (sə·blīm′) *adj.:* majestic; grand.

MEET THE WRITER

"My Stories Have Led Me Through My Life"

At the age of twelve, **Ray Bradbury** (1920–   ) wrote his first short stories, about the planet Mars, in pencil on brown wrapping paper. He's been writing stories—and novels, poems, plays, and screenplays—ever since. Their settings range from Mars and Venus to Ireland and Greentown, a fictional town based on his birthplace, Waukegan, Illinois. Much of Bradbury's writing, like "There Will Come Soft Rains," expresses his belief that advances in science and technology should never come at the expense of human beings. For another Bradbury favorite, see "The Drummer Boy of Shiloh" on page 581.

Bradbury advises young writers to keep writing:

Disney character © Disney Enterprises, Inc. Tophan/The Image Works.

66 If you write a hundred short stories and they're all bad, that doesn't mean you've failed. You fail only if you stop writing. I've written about two thousand short stories; I've only published about three hundred, and I feel I'm still learning. 99

He follows his own advice and writes nearly every day. Although he has been writing for over sixty years, he says he is still having fun.

66 Writing is supposed to be difficult, agonizing, a dreadful exercise, a terrible occupation. But, you see, my stories have led me through my life. They shout, I follow. They run up and bite me on the leg—I respond by writing down everything that goes on during the bite. When I finish, the idea lets go and runs off. 99

More by Ray Bradbury

Bradbury's best-known books include the short-story collections *The Martian Chronicles* (Bantam) and *The Illustrated Man* (Bantam) and the novel *Fahrenheit 451* (Ballantine). (The novel is about a future society in which books are burned because they are thought to contain dangerous ideas. The title is a reference to the temperature at which paper burns, 451° F.)

Experiment 023681

"They're still regressing," said Martak, as he raised his head from the viewing screen. He wore a look of disappointment on his face. "I can't see much use in the continued funding of Experiment 023681. We have others which are working much better."

"Very well," rumbled the deep voice of Martak's supervisor. "It's too bad, though. They seemed so promising."

"I know, I know. Disappointing, isn't it?" commented Martak. "But living conditions are horrible, they insist on killing each other in these petty little things called 'wars,' and look at their life span: on the outside, ninety-five of their 'years'!"

"I agree. OK. You now officially have permission to terminate Experiment 023681."

Johnny gazed on his mostly finished sand castle and felt all the pride a four-year-old could have. He noticed it was getting dark, though, so he proceeded at top speed.

Martak looked at the small mass of swirling blues, greens, and whites for one last time. Then he slowly pushed the red button and entered his access code.

"Request?" questioned a tinny voice from a grill in the wall.

"Terminate Experiment 023681."

"Request confirmed . . ."

Johnny looked up. Did he hear his mother calling him? He couldn't be sure, so he went back to playing in his sandbox.

"John!" screamed his mother from the house.

Johnny sighed and dropped his shovel as he slowly trudged toward his house. He knew his mother meant it when she just said "John." He looked up at the darkening sky and saw the first stars.

"*Now,* John!" yelled his mother.

"I'm coming!" he responded. He ambled to the porch, cleaned his shoes, and began to walk inside. On some unexplainable impulse, he turned and looked at the sky once more.

Man, that's a bright star up there! Hmmm, it seems to be growing larger! I guess it's an airplane, he decided. He opened the door and went in.

He then moved to the window and looked out. Man, it's even bigger! It looked like a big flashlight had been shone on the house.

He heard his mother yell at him to get away from the window, and his father yell something about invaders, but he was entranced.

Martak watched as the small, perfect sphere was engulfed in a yellow flame. The flame slowly turned orange, then red, then finally settled into a black cloud which died, leaving behind only dust. He sighed regretfully, as Johnny had done, and turned to the next experiment.

— Peter Leary
Athens Academy
Athens, Georgia

MAKING MEANINGS

First Thoughts

1. Complete any two of these statements:

   • As I read "There Will Come Soft Rains," I thought of . . .

   • This story interested/did not interest me because . . .

   • One question I have about the story is . . .

Shaping Interpretations

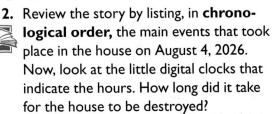

2. Review the story by listing, in **chronological order,** the main events that took place in the house on August 4, 2026. Now, look at the little digital clocks that indicate the hours. How long did it take for the house to be destroyed?

3. Go back to the text, and find three places in the story where the house, the fire, and the appliances are **personified**—that is, described as if they were living beings, even human.

4. Bradbury describes the house as "an altar with ten thousand attendants" (page 216). Who are the "gods" who are worshiped? What has happened to these "gods"?

5. What similarities and differences do you see between the visions of the future offered in Bradbury's story and those in Sara Teasdale's poem (pages 218–219)?

Connecting with the Text

6. Do you think there will ever be automated houses like the one in the story? Explain why or why not. How would you feel about living in one?

7. Turn back to your Quickwrite on the benefits and drawbacks of technology. What would you add to your list now that you have read "There Will Come Soft Rains"?

8. How old will you be and what do you think you'll be doing in the year 2026? How do you expect the world of 2026 to compare with the one Bradbury envisions?

Extending the Text

9. What warnings are Bradbury and Peter Leary (see page 222) trying to deliver through their stories? What do you think should be done to ensure that your generation's future is different from what is described in the stories?

Reading Check

a. As the story opens, what clues suggest that all is not well in the McClellan household?

b. What has happened to the family?

c. Explain why there is still activity in the house. Who or what controls the house?

d. Describe how the house is finally destroyed.

Writer's Notebook

1. Collecting Ideas for a Character Analysis

This story is remarkable because it doesn't have any human characters in it. Yet think of that house and the evil fire that ruins it. Take notes on one of them as a "character." What kind of person is the fire portrayed as? Take notes on the words used to describe the fire and on what it does. What kind of person is the house? How is it described? What does it do as its life is threatened and then destroyed? The notes at the right show how two nonhuman characters in this book are like people.

Gary Paulsen's dogs (page 277)
- Columbia—trait: sense of humor action: plays bone joke
- Obeah—trait: brave action: rescues Paulsen

Creative Writing

2. Dear Diary

Write a diary entry dated August 4, 2025, from the **point of view** of one of the McClellans—the mother, the father, the son, or the daughter. What happens to you on this day, one year before the events of the story? What are your hopes and fears?

Performance

3. It Pays to Advertise

Write a script for a thirty second TV or radio commercial advertising one of the devices mentioned in Bradbury's story. Perform your commercial for the class, videotaping or audiotaping it if possible.

Technology/Critical Thinking

4. The Cutting Edge

Invent a new toy or labor-saving appliance for Bradbury's world of 2026. Make a drawing of your invention, and attach a written explanation of what it does and how it works.

The Dog Wash Program is a machine with five cycles to make dog washing an easier chore. The eye protectors, flea shampoo, shampooing massage, dog positioners, and drying towel are the five cycles the dog goes through under running water to make your job much easier and clean the dog better.

—Kimberly Swift
  Canyon Vista Middle School
  Austin, Texas

GRAMMAR LINK MINI-LESSON

Don't or Doesn't?

Language Handbook HELP

See Problems in Agreement, page 750.

Technology HELP

See Language Workshop CD-ROM. *Key word entry: subject-verb agreement.*

The contractions *don't* and *doesn't* should agree with their subjects.

1. Use *don't* with plural subjects and with the pronouns *I* and *you.*

EXAMPLES   Science fiction <u>stories</u> <u>don't</u> always take place in the future.

<u>Don't</u> <u>you</u> wish your house would clean up after you?

2. Use *doesn't* with other singular subjects.

EXAMPLES   <u>Mrs. McClellan</u> <u>doesn't</u> hear her poetry reading that day.

<u>It</u> <u>doesn't</u> matter to the house that the dog is hungry.

If you're unsure whether to use *don't* or *doesn't* in a sentence, try substituting the phrases *do not* and *does not* for the contraction. For example, *she does not* is correct; *she do not* isn't.

Try It Out

Copy the following sentences, filling in each blank with the correct contraction, *don't* or *doesn't.*

1. The McClellans _____ live in the house anymore.

2. It seems as though the house _____ realize they are gone.

3. It _____ know how to stop cleaning, cooking, and reading poetry.

4. The amazing gadgets still work, but they _____ serve any purpose.

5. Bradbury seems to be saying that it _____ make sense to care more about technology than about human life.

VOCABULARY HOW TO OWN A WORD

WORD BANK

paranoia
tremulous
oblivious
sublime

Analogies

Complete each sentence by filling in the blank with the word that fits best from the Word Bank. Use each word only once. (You may want to review the explanation of analogies on page 76.)

1. *Weary* is to *tired* as *shaky* is to _____.

2. *Depression* is to *sadness* as _____ is to *suspicions*.

3. *Afraid* is to *frightened* as *majestic* is to _____.

4. *Hit* is to *miss* as *aware* is to _____.

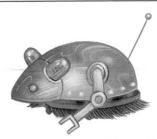

Before You Read

Make the Connection

Time Warp

What would you do if you awoke one day to find that you had slept for fifty years? Brainstorm the advantages and disadvantages of such a strange situation.

Quickwrite

If you woke up in the distant future, would you want to remain there or return to your own time? Why? Write briefly about your responses.

Elements of Literature

Framework Story

"The Inn of Lost Time" is a **framework story** with *two* **inner stories**—a short folk tale told by one of the characters to his children and a longer personal narrative told by another character. As you read the inner stories (which are indented on the page), keep in mind who is telling each story and who his audience is. Doing this will help you understand what is happening when you return to the **frame story.**

A **framework story** is a story that contains a **frame story** and an **inner story.** The inner story is often told by one of the characters in the frame story.

Reading Skills and Strategies

Drawing Inferences: Your Best Guess

Mystery stories invite you to make guesses, or **inferences,** that are based on carefully placed clues. When you draw inferences from a story, you go beyond what the text states directly. You make an educated guess based on what you read in the text combined with your own knowledge and experience. In a way, making inferences is like being a detective.

As you read this strange story, keep a notebook or piece of paper handy. Note clues that might help you solve the mystery before Zenta himself does.

go.hrw.com
LE0 8-3

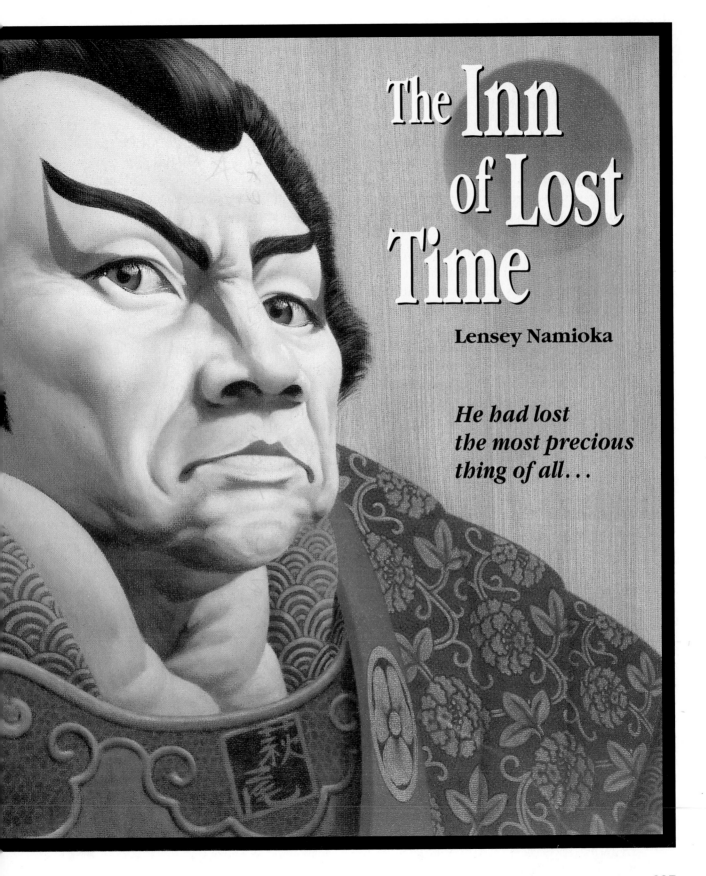

The Inn of Lost Time

Lensey Namioka

*He had lost
the most precious
thing of all...*

"Will you promise to sleep if I tell you a story?" said the father. He pretended to put on a stern expression.

"Yes! Yes!" the three little boys chanted in unison. It sounded like a nightly routine.

The two guests smiled as they listened to the exchange. They were wandering ronin, or unemployed samurai, and they enjoyed watching this cozy family scene.

The father gave the guests a helpless look. "What can I do? I have to tell them a story, or these little rascals will give us no peace." Clearing his throat, he turned to the boys. "All right. The story tonight is about Urashima Taro."

Instantly the three boys became still. Sitting with their legs tucked under them, the three little boys, aged five, four, and three, looked like a descending row of stone statuettes. Matsuzo, the younger of the two ronin, was reminded of the wayside half-body statues of Jizo, the God of Travelers and Protector of Children.

Behind the boys the farmer's wife took up a pair of iron chopsticks and stirred the ashes of the fire in the charcoal brazier.[1] A momentary glow brightened the room. The lean faces of the two ronin, lit by the fire, suddenly looked fierce and hungry.

The farmer knew that the two ronin were supposed to use their arms in defense of the weak. But in these troubled times, with the country torn apart by civil wars, the samurai didn't always live up to their honorable code.

Then the fire died down again and the subdued red light softened the features of the two ronin. The farmer relaxed and began his story.

The tale of Urashima Taro is familiar to every Japanese. No doubt the three little boys had heard their father tell it before—and more than once. But they listened with rapt attention.

Urashima Taro, a fisherman, rescued a turtle from some boys who were battering it with stones. The grateful turtle rewarded Taro by carrying him on his back to the bottom of the sea, where he lived happily with the Princess of the Undersea. But Taro soon became homesick for his native village and asked to go back on land. The princess gave him a box to take with him but warned him not to peek inside.

When Taro went back to his village, he found the place quite changed. In his home he found his parents gone, and living there was another old couple. He was stunned to learn that the aged husband was his own son, whom he had last seen as a baby! Taro thought he had spent only a pleasant week or two undersea with the princess. On land, seventy-two years had passed! His parents and most of his old friends had long since died.

Desolate, Taro decided to open the box given him by the princess. As soon as he looked inside, he changed in an instant from a young man to a decrepit old man of more than ninety.

At the end of the story the boys were close to tears. Even Matsuzo found himself deeply touched. He wondered why the farmer had told his sons such a poignant bedtime story. Wouldn't they worry all evening instead of going to sleep?

But the boys recovered quickly. They were soon laughing and jostling each other, and they made no objections when their mother shooed them toward bed. Standing in order of age, they bowed politely to the guests and then lay down on the mattresses spread out for them on

---

1. **brazier** (brā′zhər): metal container that holds burning coals or charcoal, used to warm a room or cook food.

WORDS TO OWN

desolate (des′ə·lit) *adj.*: lonely; miserable; deserted.
decrepit (dē·krep′it) *adj.*: broken down or worn out from old age or long use.
poignant (poin′yənt) *adj.*: causing sadness or pain; touching.

LITERATURE AND GEOGRAPHY

Samurai: Honor First

This story is set in sixteenth-century Japan. The story's main character, Zenta, is a samurai (sam′ə•rī′), a member of the warrior class. The samurai protected the feudal lords. They followed a code called Bushido, which required them to show absolute obedience and loyalty to their lords and to place their honor above anything else, including their own lives. The samurai class lost its privileges and began to die out when feudalism was abolished in Japan in 1871.

You may be surprised to hear that these disciplined warriors produced many of Japan's famous arts, including the tea ceremony and flower arrangement.

One of the great movies of the twentieth century is *The Seven Samurai* (1954), directed by Akira Kurosawa. In the movie, set in the sixteenth century, a group of samurai who are looking for work hire themselves out to protect a village threatened by bandits. The movie has been called an "eastern western" because the seven samurai remind people of the heroic cowboys of American western movies.

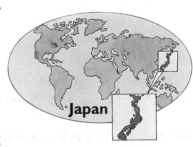
Japan

---

the floor. Within minutes the sound of their regular breathing told the guests that they were asleep.

Zenta, the older of the two ronin, sighed as he glanced at the peaceful young faces. "I wish I could fall asleep so quickly. The story of Urashima Taro is one of the saddest that I know among our folk tales."

The farmer looked proudly at his sleeping sons. "They're stout lads. Nothing bothers them much."

The farmer's wife poured tea for the guests and apologized. "I'm sorry this is only poor tea made from coarse leaves."

Zenta hastened to reassure her. "It's warm and heartening on a chilly autumn evening."

"You know what I think is the saddest part of the Urashima Taro story?" said Matsuzo, picking up his cup and sipping the tea. "It's that Taro lost not only his family and friends but a big piece of his life as well. He had lost the most precious thing of all: time."

The farmer nodded agreement. "I wouldn't sell even one year of my life for money. As for losing seventy-two years, no amount of gold will make up for that!"

Zenta put his cup down on the floor and looked curiously at the farmer. "It's interesting that you should say that. I had an opportunity once to observe exactly how much gold a person was willing to pay for some lost years of his life." He smiled grimly. "In this case the man went as far as one gold piece for each year he lost."

"That's bizarre!" said Matsuzo. "You never told me about it."

"It happened long before I met you," said Zenta. He drank some tea and smiled ruefully. "Besides, I'm not particularly proud of the part I played in that strange affair."

"Let's hear the story!" urged Matsuzo. "You've made us all curious."

The farmer waited expectantly. His wife sat down quietly behind her husband and folded her hands. Her eyes looked intently at Zenta.

"Very well, then," said Zenta. "Actually, my story bears some resemblance to that of Urashima Taro. . . ."

It happened about seven years ago, when I was a green, inexperienced youngster not quite eighteen years old. But I had had a good training in arms, and I was able to get a job as a bodyguard for a wealthy merchant from Sakai.

As you know, wealthy merchants are relatively new in our country. Traditionally the rich have been noblemen, landowners, and warlords with thousands of followers. Merchants, regarded as parasites in our society, are a despised class. But our civil wars have made people unusually mobile and stimulated trade between various parts of the country. The merchants have taken advantage of this to conduct business on a scale our fathers could not imagine. Some of them have become more wealthy than a warlord with thousands of samurai under his command.

The man I was escorting, Tokubei, was one of this new breed of wealthy merchants. He was trading not only with outlying provinces but even with the Portuguese[2] from across the sea. On this particular journey he was not carrying much gold with him. If he had, I'm sure he would have hired an older and more experienced bodyguard. But if the need should arise, he could always write a message to his clerks at home and have money forwarded to him. It's important to remember this.

The second day of our journey was a particularly grueling one, with several steep hills to climb. As the day was drawing to its close, we began to consider where we should spend the night. I knew that within an hour's walking was a hot-spring resort known to have several attractive inns.

But Tokubei, my employer, said he was already very tired and wanted to stop. He had heard of the resort and knew the inns there were expensive. Wealthy as he was, he did not want to spend more money than he had to.

While we stood talking, a smell reached our noses, a wonderful smell of freshly cooked rice. Suddenly I felt ravenous. From the way Tokubei swallowed, I knew he was feeling just as hungry.

We looked around eagerly, but the area was forested and we could not see very far in any direction. The tantalizing smell seemed to grow and I could feel the saliva filling my mouth.

"There's an inn around here somewhere," muttered Tokubei. "I'm sure of it."

We followed our noses. We had to leave the well-traveled highway and take a nar-

---

2. **Portuguese:** The Portuguese were the first Europeans to reach Japan, arriving in 1543. Until they were expelled, in the 1630s, they traded extensively with the Japanese.

WORDS TO OWN

ruefully (rōō′fəl·ē) *adv.*: with regret and embarrassment.

parasites (par′ə·sīts′) *n.*: people who live at others' expense without making any contribution. (In ancient Greece, *parasitos* was the term used for someone who flattered and amused a host in return for free meals.)

grueling (grōō′əl·iŋ) *adj.*: exhausting; extremely demanding.

ravenous (rav′ə·nəs) *adj.*: extremely hungry.

row, winding footpath. But the mouth-watering smell of the rice and the vision of fluffy, freshly aired cotton quilts drew us on.

The sun was just beginning to set. We passed a bamboo grove, and in the low evening light the thin leaves turned into little golden knives. I saw a gilded[3] clump of bamboo shoots. The sight made me think of the delicious dish they would make when boiled in soy sauce.

We hurried forward. To our delight we soon came to a clearing with a thatched house standing in the middle. The fragrant smell of rice was now so strong that we were certain a meal was being prepared inside.

Standing in front of the house was a pretty girl beaming at us with a welcoming smile. "Please honor us with your presence," she said, beckoning.

There was something a little unusual about one of her hands, but, being hungry and eager to enter the house, I did not stop to observe closely.

You will say, of course, that it was my duty as a bodyguard to be suspicious and to look out for danger. Youth and inexperience should not have prevented me from wondering why an inn should be found hidden away from the highway. As it was, my stomach growled, and I didn't even hesitate but followed Tokubei to the house.

Before stepping up to enter, we were given basins of water to wash our feet. As the girl handed us towels for drying, I saw what was unusual about her left hand: She had six fingers.

Tokubei had noticed it as well. When the girl turned away to empty the basins, he nudged me. "Did you see her left hand? She had——" He broke off in confusion as the girl turned around, but she didn't seem to have heard.

The inn was peaceful and quiet, and we soon discovered the reason why. We were the only guests. Again, I should have been suspicious. I told you that I'm not proud of the part I played.

Tokubei turned to me and grinned. "It seems that there are no other guests. We should be able to get extra service for the same amount of money."

The girl led us to a spacious room which was like the principal chamber of a private residence. Cushions were set out for us on the floor and we began to shed our traveling gear to make ourselves comfortable.

The door opened and a grizzled-haired man entered. Despite his vigorous-looking face his back was a little bent, and I guessed his age to be about fifty. After bowing and greeting us, he apologized in advance for the service. "We have not always been innkeepers here," he said, "and you may find the accommodations lacking. Our good intentions must make up for our inexperience. However, to compensate for our inadequacies, we will charge a lower fee than that of an inn with an established reputation."

Tokubei nodded graciously, highly pleased by the words of our host, and the evening began well. It continued well when the girl came back with some flasks of wine, cups, and dishes of salty snacks.

While the girl served the wine, the host looked with interest at my swords. From the few remarks he made, I gathered that he was a former samurai, forced by circumstances to turn his house into an inn.

Having become a bodyguard to a tight-fisted merchant, I was in no position to feel superior to a ronin-turned-innkeeper. Socially, therefore, we were more or less equal.

---

3. **gilded:** here, appearing to be coated with gold.

We exchanged polite remarks with our host while we drank and tasted the salty snacks. I looked around at the pleasant room. It showed excellent taste, and I especially admired a vase standing in the alcove.[4]

My host caught my eyes on it. "We still have a few good things that we didn't have to sell," he said. His voice held a trace of bitterness. "Please look at the panels of these doors. They were painted by a fine artist."

Tokubei and I looked at the pair of sliding doors. Each panel contained a landscape painting, the right panel depicting a winter scene and the left one the same scene in late summer. Our host's words were no idle boast. The pictures were indeed beautiful.

Tokubei rose and approached the screens for a closer look. When he sat down again, his eyes were calculating. No doubt he was trying to estimate what price the paintings would fetch.

After my third drink I began to feel very tired. Perhaps it was the result of drinking on an empty stomach. I was glad when the girl brought in two dinner trays and a lacquered[5] container of rice. Uncovering the rice container, she began filling our bowls.

Again I noticed her strange left hand with its six fingers. Any other girl would have tried to keep that hand hidden, but this girl made no effort to do so. If anything, she seemed to use that hand more than her other one when she served us. The extra little finger always stuck out from the hand, as if inviting comment.

The hand fascinated me so much that I kept my eyes on it and soon forgot to eat. After a while the hand looked blurry. And then everything else began to look blurry.

4. **alcove:** nook; hollow in a wall.
5. **lacquered** (lak′ərd): covered with lacquer, a varnish used to give a hard, smooth, shiny coating to wood.

Karaori. Japanese, Edo period (first half of the 18th century). Silk.

Museum of Art, Rhode Island School of Design. Gift of Lucy Truman Aldrich.

The last thing I remembered was the sight of Tokubei shaking his head, as if trying to clear it.

When I opened my eyes again, I knew that time had passed, but not how much time. My next thought was that it was cold. It was not only extremely cold but damp.

I rolled over and sat up. I reached immediately for my swords and found them safe on the ground beside me. *On the ground? What was I doing on the ground?* My last memory was of staying at an inn with a merchant called Tokubei.

The thought of Tokubei put me into a panic. I was his bodyguard, and instead of watching over him, I had fallen asleep and had awakened in a strange place.

I looked around frantically and saw that he was lying on the ground not far from where I was. Had he been killed?

I got up shakily, and when I stood up, my head was swimming. But my sense of urgency gave some strength to my legs. I stumbled over to my employer and to my great relief found him breathing—breathing heavily, in fact.

When I shook his shoulder, he grunted and finally opened his eyes. "Where am I?" he asked thickly.

It was a reasonable question. I looked

around and saw that we had been lying in a bamboo grove. By the light I guessed that it was early morning, and the reason I felt cold and damp was that my clothes were wet with dew.

"It's cold!" said Tokubei, shivering and climbing unsteadily to his feet. He looked around slowly, and his eyes became wide with disbelief. "What happened? I thought we were staying at an inn!"

His words came as a relief. One of the possibilities I had considered was that I had gone mad and that the whole episode with the inn was something I had imagined. Now I knew that Tokubei had the same memory of the inn. I had not imagined it.

But why were we out here on the cold ground, instead of on comfortable mattresses in the inn?

"They must have drugged us and robbed us," said Tokubei. He turned and looked at me furiously. "A fine bodyguard you are!"

There was nothing I could say to that. But at least we were both alive and unharmed. "Did they take all your money?" I asked.

Tokubei had already taken his wallet out of his sash and was peering inside. "That's funny! My money is still here!"

This was certainly unexpected. What did the innkeeper and his strange daughter intend to do by drugging us and moving us outside?

At least things were not as bad as we had feared. We had not lost anything except a comfortable night's sleep, although from the heaviness in my head I had certainly slept deeply enough—and long enough too. Exactly how much time had <u>elapsed</u> since we drank wine with our host?

All we had to do now was find the highway again and continue our journey. Tokubei suddenly chuckled. "I didn't even have to pay for our night's lodging!"

As we walked from the bamboo grove, I saw the familiar clump of bamboo shoots, and we found ourselves standing in the same clearing again. Before our eyes was the thatched house. Only it was somehow different. Perhaps things looked different in the daylight than at dusk.

But the difference was more than a change of light. As we approached the house slowly, like sleepwalkers, we saw that the thatching was much darker. On the previous evening the thatching had looked fresh and new. Now it was dark with age. Daylight should make things appear brighter, not darker. The plastering of the walls also looked more dingy.

Tokubei and I stopped to look at each other before we went closer. He was pale, and I knew that I looked no less frightened. Something was terribly wrong. I loosened my sword in its scabbard.[6]

We finally gathered the courage to go up to the house. Since Tokubei seemed unable to find his voice, I spoke out. "Is anyone there?"

After a moment we heard shuffling footsteps and the front door slid open. The face of an old woman appeared. "Yes?" she inquired. Her voice was creaky with age.

What set my heart pounding with panic, however, was not her voice. It was the sight of her left hand holding on to the frame of the door. The hand was wrinkled and crooked with the arthritis of old age— and it had six fingers.

I heard a gasp beside me and knew that Tokubei had noticed the hand as well.

The door opened wider and a man appeared beside the old woman. At first I

---

6. **scabbard:** case for the blade of a sword.

WORDS TO OWN

elapsed (ē·lapst′) v.: passed (said of time).

thought it was our host of the previous night. But this man was much younger, although the resemblance was strong. He carried himself straighter and his hair was black, while the innkeeper had been grizzled and slightly bent with age.

"Please excuse my mother," said the man. "Her hearing is not good. Can we help you in some way?"

Tokubei finally found his voice. "Isn't this the inn where we stayed last night?"

The man stared. "Inn? We are not inn-keepers here!"

"Yes, you are!" insisted Tokubei. "Your daughter invited us in and served us with wine. You must have put something in the wine!"

The man frowned. "You are serious? Are you sure you didn't drink too much at your inn and wander off?"

"No, I didn't drink too much!" said Tokubei, almost shouting. "I hardly drank at all! Your daughter, the one with six fingers on her hand, started to pour me a second cup of wine . . ." His voice trailed off, and he stared again at the left hand of the old woman.

"I don't have a daughter," said the man slowly. "My mother here is the one who has six fingers on her left hand, although I hardly think it polite of you to mention it."

"I'm getting dizzy," muttered Tokubei, and began to totter.

"I think you'd better come in and rest a bit," the man said to him gruffly. He glanced at me. "Perhaps you wish to join your friend. You don't share his delusion about the inn, I hope?"

"I wouldn't presume to contradict my elders," I said carefully. Since both Tokubei and the owner of the house were my elders, I wasn't committing myself. In truth, I didn't know what to believe, but I did want a look at the inside of the house.

The inside was almost the same as it was before but the differences were there when I looked closely. We entered the same room with the alcove and the pair of painted doors. The vase I had admired was no longer there, but the doors showed the same landscapes painted by a master. I peered closely at the pictures and saw that the colors looked faded. What was more, the left panel, the one depicting a winter scene, had a long tear in one corner. It had been painstakingly mended, but the damage was impossible to hide completely.

Tokubei saw what I was staring at and he became even paler. At this stage we had both considered the possibility that a hoax of some sort had been played on us. The torn screen convinced Tokubei that our host had not played a joke: The owner of a valuable painting would never vandalize it for a trivial reason.

As for me, I was far more disturbed by the sight of the sixth finger on the old woman's hand. Could the young girl have disguised herself as an old crone? She could put rice powder in her hair to whiten it, but she could not transform her pretty straight fingers into old fingers twisted with arthritis. The woman here with us now was genuinely old, at least fifty years older than the girl.

It was this same old woman who finally gave us our greatest shock. "It's interesting that you should mention an inn, gentlemen," she croaked. "My father used to operate an inn. After he died, my husband and I turned this back into a private residence. We didn't need the income, you see."

"Your . . . your . . . f-father?" stammered Tokubei.

"Yes," replied the old woman. "He was a ronin, forced to go into inn keeping when he lost his position. But he never liked the work. Besides, our inn had begun to acquire an unfortunate reputation. Some of our guests disappeared, you see."

Even before she finished speaking, a horrible suspicion had begun to dawn on me. Her *father* had been an innkeeper, she said, her father who used to be a ronin. The man who had been our host was a ronin-turned-innkeeper. Could this mean that this old woman was actually the same person as the young girl we had seen?

I sat stunned while I tried to absorb the implications. What had happened to us? Was it possible that Tokubei and I had slept while this young girl grew into a mature woman, got married, and bore a son, a son who was now an adult? If that was the case, then we had slept for fifty years!

The old woman's next words confirmed my fears. "I recognize you now! You are two of the lost guests from our inn! The other lost ones I don't remember so well, but I remember *you* because your disappearance made me so sad. Such a handsome youth, I thought; what a pity that he should have gone the way of the others!"

A high wail came from Tokubei, who began to keen[7] and rock himself back and forth. "I've lost fifty years! Fifty years of my life went by while I slept at this accursed inn!"

The inn was indeed accursed. Was the fate of the other guests similar to ours?

7. **keen:** wail.

Nuihaku. Japanese, Edo period (mid-18th century). Silk.

Museum of Art, Rhode Island School of Design. Gift of Lucy Truman Aldrich.

"Did anyone else return as we did, fifty years later?" I asked.

The old woman looked uncertain and turned to her son. He frowned thoughtfully. "From time to time wild-looking people have come to us with stories similar to yours. Some of them went mad with the shock."

Tokubei wailed again. "I've lost my business! I've lost my wife, my young and beautiful wife! We had been married only a couple of months!"

A gruesome chuckle came from the old woman. "You may not have lost your wife. It's just that she's become an old hag like me!"

That did not console Tokubei, whose keening became louder. Although my relationship with my employer had not been characterized by much respect on either side, I did begin to feel very sorry for him. He was right: He had lost his world.

As for me, the loss was less <u>traumatic</u>. I had left home under extremely painful circumstances and had spent the next three years wandering. I had no friends and no one I could call a relation. The only thing I had was my duty to my employer. Somehow, someway, I had to help him.

"Did no one find an explanation for these disappearances?" I asked. "Perhaps if we knew the reason why, we might find some way to reverse the process."

The old woman began to nod eagerly. "The priestess! Tell them about the shrine priestess!"

"Well," said the man, "I'm not sure if it would work in your case. . . ."

"What? What would work?" demanded Tokubei. His eyes were feverish.

"There was a case of one returning guest who consulted the priestess at our local shrine," said the man. "She went into a trance and revealed that there was an evil spirit dwelling in the bamboo grove here. This spirit would put unwary travelers into a long, unnatural sleep. They would wake up twenty, thirty, or even fifty years later."

"Yes, but you said something worked in his case," said Tokubei.

The man seemed reluctant to go on. "I don't like to see you cheated, so I'm not sure I should be telling you this."

"Tell me! Tell me!" demanded Tokubei. The host's reluctance only made him more impatient.

"The priestess promised to make a spell that would undo the work of the evil spirit," said the man. "But she demanded a large sum of money, for she said that she had to burn some very rare and costly incense before she could begin the spell."

At the mention of money Tokubei sat back. The hectic[8] flush died down on his face and his eyes narrowed. "How much money?" he asked.

The host shook his head. "In my opinion the priestess is a fraud and makes outrageous claims about her powers. We try to have as little to do with her as possible."

"Yes, but did her spell work?" asked Tokubei. "If it worked, she's no fraud!"

"At least the stranger disappeared again," cackled the old woman. "Maybe he went back to his own time. Maybe he walked into a river."

Tokubei's eyes narrowed further. "How much money did the priestess demand?" he asked again.

"I think it was one gold piece for every year lost," said the host. He hurriedly

8. **hectic:** feverish.

- -
WORDS TO OWN
traumatic (trô·mat′ik) *adj.*: emotionally painful; causing shock.
- -

added, "Mind you, I still wouldn't trust the priestess."

"Then it would cost me fifty gold pieces to get back to my own time," muttered Tokubei. He looked up. "I don't carry that much money with me."

"No, you don't," agreed the host.

Something alerted me about the way he said that. It was as if the host knew already that Tokubei did not carry much money on him.

Meanwhile Tokubei sighed. He had come to a decision. "I do have the means to obtain more money, however. I can send a message to my chief clerk and he will remit the money when he sees my seal."

"Your chief clerk may be dead by now," I reminded him.

"You're right!" moaned Tokubei. "My business will be under a new management and nobody will even remember my name!"

"And your wife will have remarried," said the old woman, with one of her chuckles. I found it hard to believe that the gentle young girl who had served us wine could turn into this dreadful harridan.[9]

"Sending the message may be a waste of time," agreed the host.

"What waste of time!" cried Tokubei. "Why shouldn't I waste time? I've wasted fifty years already! Anyway, I've made up my mind. I'm sending that message."

"I still think you shouldn't trust the priestess," said the host.

That only made Tokubei all the more determined to send for the money. However, he was not quite resigned to the amount. "Fifty gold pieces is a large sum. Surely the priestess can buy incense for less than that amount?"

"Why don't you try giving her thirty gold pieces?" cackled the old woman. "Then the priestess will send you back thirty years, and your wife will only be middle-aged."

While Tokubei was still arguing with himself about the exact sum to send for, I decided to have a look at the bamboo grove. "I'm going for a walk," I announced, rising and picking up my sword from the floor beside me.

The host turned sharply to look at me. For an instant a faint, rueful smile appeared on his lips. Then he looked away.

Outside, I went straight to the clump of shoots in the bamboo grove. On the previous night—or what I perceived as the previous night—I had noticed that clump of bamboo shoots particularly, because I had been so hungry that I pictured them being cut up and boiled.

The clump of bamboo shoots was still in the same place. That in itself proved nothing, since bamboo could spring up anywhere, including the place where a clump had existed fifty years earlier. But what settled the matter in my mind was that the clump looked almost exactly the way it did when I had seen it before, except that every shoot was about an inch taller. That was a reasonable amount for bamboo shoots to grow overnight.

Overnight. Tokubei and I had slept on the ground here overnight. We had not slept here for a period of fifty years.

Once I knew that, I was able to see another inconsistency: the door panels with the painted landscapes. The painting with the winter scene had been on the *right* last night and it was on the *left* this morning. It wasn't simply a case of the panels changing places, because the depressions in the

9. **harridan:** spiteful old woman.

WORDS TO OWN
remit (ri·mit′) v.: send as payment.

Karaori. Japanese, Edo period (early 19th century). Silk.

Museum of Art, Rhode Island School of Design. Gift of Lucy Truman Aldrich.

panel for the handholds had been reversed. In other words, what I saw just now was not a pair of paintings faded and torn by age. They were an entirely different pair of paintings.

But how did the pretty young girl change into an old woman? The answer was that if the screens could be different ones, so could the women. I had seen one woman, a young girl, last night. This morning I saw a different woman, an old hag.

The darkening of the thatched roof? Simply blow ashes over the roof. The grizzled-haired host of last night could be the same man who claimed to be his grandson today. It would be a simple matter for a young man to put gray in his hair and assume a stoop.

And the purpose of the hoax? To make Tokubei send for fifty pieces of gold, of course. It was clever of the man to accuse the shrine priestess of fraud and pretend reluctance to let Tokubei send his message.

I couldn't even feel angry toward the man and his daughter—or mother, sister, wife, whatever. He could have killed me and taken my swords, which he clearly admired. Perhaps he was really a ronin and felt sympathetic toward another one.

When I returned to the house, Tokubei was looking resigned. "I've decided to send for the whole fifty gold pieces." He sighed.

"Don't bother," I said. "In fact, we should be leaving as soon as possible. We shouldn't even stop here for a drink, especially not of wine."

Tokubei stared. "What do you mean? If I go back home, I'll find everything changed!"

"Nothing will be changed," I told him. "Your wife will be as young and beautiful as ever."

"I don't understand," he said. "Fifty years . . ."

"It's a joke," I said. "The people here have a peculiar sense of humor, and they've played a joke on us."

Tokubei's mouth hung open. Finally he closed it with a snap. He stared at the host, and his face became first red and then purple. "You—you were trying to swindle me!" He turned furiously to me. "And you let them do this!"

"I'm not letting them," I pointed out. "That's why we're leaving right now."

"Are you going to let them get away with this?" demanded Tokubei. "They might try to swindle someone else!"

"They only went to this much trouble when they heard of the arrival of a fine fat fish like you," I said. I looked deliberately at the host. "I'm sure they won't be tempted to try the same trick again."

"And that's the end of your story?" asked Matsuzo. "You and Tokubei just went away? How did you know the so-called innkeeper wouldn't try the trick on some other luckless traveler?"

Zenta shook his head. "I didn't know. I merely guessed that once the trick was exposed, they wouldn't take the chance of trying it again. Of course I thought about revisiting the place to check if the people there were leading an honest life."

"Why didn't you?" asked Matsuzo. "Maybe we could go together. You've made me curious about that family now."

"Then you can satisfy your curiosity," said Zenta, smiling. He held his cup out for more tea, and the farmer's wife came forward to pour.

Only now she used both hands to hold the pot, and for the first time Matsuzo saw her left hand. He gasped. The hand had six fingers.

"Who was the old woman?" Zenta asked the farmer's wife.

"She was my grandmother," she replied. "Having six fingers is something that runs in my family."

At last Matsuzo found his voice. "You mean this is the very house you visited? This is the inn where time was lost?"

"Where we *thought* we lost fifty years," said Zenta. "Perhaps I should have warned you first. But I was almost certain that we'd be safe this time. And I see that I was right."

He turned to the woman again. "You and your husband are farmers now, aren't you? What happened to the man who was the host?"

"He's dead," she said quietly. "He was my brother, and he was telling you the truth when he said that he was a ronin. Two years ago he found work with another warlord, but he was killed in battle only a month later."

Matsuzo was peering at the pair of sliding doors, which he hadn't noticed before. "I see that you've put up the faded set of paintings. The winter scene is on the left side."

The woman nodded. "We sold the newer pair of doors. My husband said that we're farmers now and that people in our position don't need valuable paintings. We used the money to buy some new farm implements."

She took up the teapot again. "Would you like another cup of tea?" she asked Matsuzo.

Staring at her left hand, Matsuzo had a sudden qualm. "I—I don't think I want any more."

Everybody laughed.

MEET THE WRITER

"I Didn't Have a Book; I Had a Short Story"

Although **Lensey Namioka** (1929–   ) was born in Beijing, China, several of her novels are set in feudal Japan and recount other adventures of Zenta and Matsuzo. "The Inn of Lost Time" was originally meant to be a novel as well, as she explains:

66 The story of Rip Van Winkle has always fascinated me. The Japanese version of the story, 'Urashima Taro,' is another favorite of mine. They are both sad stories, because the main character lost the most precious thing of all: time.

I had written several teenage books featuring Zenta and Matsuzo, a pair of jobless samurai wandering around Japan looking for work. When I needed an idea for a new book about the two samurai, I thought of using the theme of lost time. But I worked out a twist on the idea, to give the story a happy ending.

When I started work on the book, however, I couldn't get beyond the one central idea. Furthermore, it was necessary to have all the action take place in less than twenty-four hours. This did not give the characters an opportunity to grow and develop. I didn't have a book; I had a short story. 99

More by Lensey Namioka

- In *Island of the Ogres* (HarperCollins), Matsuzo and Zenta are sent to investigate strange doings on a mysterious island.

- *Who's Hu?* (Random House), a novel for young adults, is based on Namioka's experiences as a girl studying mathematics.

(Background) *Karaori.* Japanese, Edo period (second half of 18th century). Silk.
Museum of Art, Rhode Island School of Design. Gift of Lucy Truman Aldrich.

MAKING MEANINGS

First Thoughts

1. What **inferences** did you make that helped you to realize what was actually going on? (Who figured it out first, you or Zenta?)

Shaping Interpretations

Reading Check

Pretend that you are Tokubei. Write a short note to your wife, telling her about the trick that was played on you at the inn of lost time.

2. The **frame story** here is the story that contains two other stories. What is the frame story? What two stories are contained within the frame story?

3. How is Zenta's story like the story of Urashima Taro?

4. By the end of Zenta's story, what connection have you discovered between the inn in his story and the inn in the frame story?

5. In Zenta's story, what clues convince Zenta that he and Tokubei are the victims of a clever hoax?

6. Were you surprised to discover the identity of the farmer's wife in the frame story? Why did her family change their ways, in your opinion?

7. At the end of the story, what might Zenta be thinking when he holds out his cup for more tea? Why doesn't Matsuzo want any more?

Challenging the Text

8. Matsuzo calls time "the most precious thing of all." Challenge or defend his position. What do you believe is the most precious thing a person can have? Why?

Travellers in the Snow at Oi
(c. 1840) by Hiroshige. Japanese Oban color print.

The Granger Collection, New York.

Writer's Notebook

1. Collecting Ideas for a Character Analysis

When you analyze a character, you might want to compare him or her to another character, either in that story or in another story. There are several characters in this story, but the ones we learn the most about are Zenta and Tokubei. Draw a Venn diagram to help you compare Zenta and Tokubei. The Venn diagram at the right shows a comparison between the mother in Edna St. Vincent Millay's poem (page 108) and the grandfather in Leroy Quintana's poem (page 109).

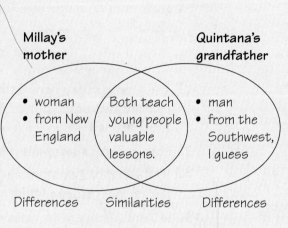

Millay's mother — Quintana's grandfather

- woman
- from New England

Both teach young people valuable lessons.

- man
- from the Southwest, I guess

Differences   Similarities   Differences

Creative Writing

2. The Motel of Lost Time?

Rewrite the story of "The Inn of Lost Time" to take place in the present-day United States. You might try writing it as a **progressive story:** Write the first half; then, exchange papers with a classmate, and finish your partner's story while he or she finishes yours.

Comparing Texts Across Cultures

3. Bedtime Stories

Find and read one of the following stories about a character who sleeps for many years and wakes up in an unfamiliar world:

- "Urashima Taro" (traditional Japanese)
- "Rip Van Winkle" (Washington Irving, American)
- "Oisin" (traditional Irish)

In a brief essay, compare your story with "The Inn of Lost Time." Consider:

- plot   • setting
- characters

Creative Writing

4. Lost in Time

Refer to the notes you made for the Quickwrite before you started this story. Then write a story of your own in which you wake up in the distant future. Tell what you miss about the past. What do you like about the future? How does your story end?

GRAMMAR LINK   MINI-LESSON

- ## Active and Passive Voice

Language Handbook HELP

See Voice, page 760.

When a verb is in the **active voice,** the subject of the verb does something. When a verb is in the **passive voice,** something is done to its subject.

ACTIVE   The father <u>told</u> a story to his sons. [The action is done *by* the subject, the father.]

PASSIVE   The sons <u>were told</u> a story by their father. [The action is done *to* the subject, the sons.]

The two sentences convey the same information, but with different emphases. The first sentence stresses the doer of the action; the second sentence stresses the receiver of the action.

You should use the active voice to give your writing a direct, lively tone. Use the passive voice sparingly, to emphasize the receiver of the action.

Try It Out

Take out a piece of your writing. Underline all the verbs in the active voice once and all the verbs in the passive voice twice. The number of single underlines should be much greater than the number of double underlines. If it isn't, rewrite some of the passive-voice sentences, putting them in the active voice.

VOCABULARY   HOW TO OWN A WORD

WORD BANK

desolate
decrepit
poignant
ruefully
parasites
grueling
ravenous
elapsed
traumatic
remit

- ## Mapping Words: Pinning Down Word Meanings

A **word map** can help you to clarify all the ways a word can be used. Study this sample word map for the word *desolate*.

What words describe a desolate house?
- empty
- abandoned
- run-down

When might a person feel desolate?
- best friend moves away
- pet is killed by car
- nothing to do on weekend

desolate

What words mean the opposite of desolate?
- cheerful
- joyful

What words mean the same as desolate?
- miserable
- wretched

With a partner, make a word map for each of the other words in the Word Bank. (You will need to make up some of your own questions.) Exchange your word maps with other teams. Can they think of new questions to ask about a word?

The Open Window

Saki

Somehow, in this restful country spot, tragedies seemed out of place.

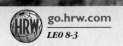

"My aunt will be down presently, Mr. Nuttel," said a very self-possessed young lady of fifteen; "in the meantime you must try and put up with me."

Framton Nuttel endeavored to say the correct something which should duly flatter the niece of the moment without unduly discounting the aunt that was to come. Privately he doubted more than ever whether these formal visits on a succession of total strangers would do much toward helping the nerve cure which he was supposed to be undergoing.

"I know how it will be," his sister had said when he was preparing to migrate to this rural retreat; "you will bury yourself down there and not speak to a living soul, and your nerves will be worse than ever from moping. I shall just give you letters of introduction to all the people I know there. Some of them, as far as I can remember, were quite nice."

Framton wondered whether Mrs. Sappleton, the lady to whom he was presenting one of the letters of introduction, came into the nice division.

"Do you know many of the people round here?" asked the niece, when she judged that they had had sufficient silent communion.

"Hardly a soul," said Framton. "My sister was staying here, at the rectory,[1] you know, some four years ago, and she gave me letters of introduction to some of the people here."

He made the last statement in a tone of distinct regret.

"Then you know practically nothing about my aunt?" pursued the self-possessed young lady.

"Only her name and address," admitted the caller. He was wondering whether Mrs. Sappleton was in the married or widowed state. An un-

---

1. **rectory:** house in which the minister of a parish lives.

definable something about the room seemed to suggest masculine habitation.

"Her great tragedy happened just three years ago," said the child; "that would be since your sister's time."

"Her tragedy?" asked Framton; somehow, in this restful country spot, tragedies seemed out of place.

"You may wonder why we keep that window wide open on an October afternoon," said the niece, indicating a large French window[2] that opened onto a lawn.

"It is quite warm for the time of the year," said Framton, "but has that window got anything to do with the tragedy?"

"Out through that window, three years ago to a day, her husband and her two young brothers went off for their day's shooting. They never came back. In crossing the moor to their favorite snipe-shooting[3] ground, they were all three engulfed in a treacherous piece of bog. It had been that dreadful wet summer, you know, and places that were safe in other years gave way suddenly without warning. Their bodies were never recovered. That was the dreadful part of it." Here the child's voice lost its self-possessed note and became falteringly human. "Poor aunt always thinks that they will come back someday, they and the little brown spaniel that was lost with them, and walk in at that window just as they used to do. That is why the window is kept open every evening till it is quite dusk. Poor dear aunt, she has often told me how they went out, her husband with his white waterproof coat over his arm, and Ronnie, her youngest brother, singing, 'Bertie, why do you bound?' as he always did to tease her, because she said it got on her nerves. Do you know, sometimes on still, quiet evenings like this, I almost get a creepy feeling that they will all walk in through that window——"

She broke off with a little shudder. It was a relief to Framton when the aunt bustled into the room with a whirl of apologies for being late in making her appearance.

"I hope Vera has been amusing you?" she said.

"She has been very interesting," said Framton.

"I hope you don't mind the open window," said Mrs. Sappleton briskly; "my husband and brothers will be home directly from shooting, and they always come in this way. They've been out for snipe in the marshes today, so they'll make a fine mess over my poor carpets. So like you menfolk, isn't it?"

She rattled on cheerfully about the shooting and the scarcity of birds and the prospects for duck in the winter. To Framton, it was all purely horrible. He made a desperate but only partially successful effort to turn the talk onto a less ghastly topic; he was conscious that his hostess was giving him only a fragment of her attention, and her eyes were constantly straying past him to the open window and the lawn beyond. It was certainly an unfortunate coincidence that he should have paid his visit on this tragic anniversary.

"The doctors agree in ordering me complete rest, an absence of mental excitement, and avoidance of anything in the nature of violent physical exercise," announced Framton, who labored under the tolerably widespread delusion that total strangers and chance acquaintances are hungry for the least detail of one's ailments and infirmities, their cause and cure. "On the matter of diet they are not so much in agreement," he continued.

"No?" said Mrs. Sappleton, in a voice which only replaced a yawn at the last moment. Then she suddenly brightened into alert attention—but not to what Framton was saying.

"Here they are at last!" she cried. "Just in

2. **French window:** pair of doors that have glass panes from top to bottom and open in the middle.
3. **snipe-shooting:** A snipe is a kind of bird that lives in swampy areas.

Miss Cicely Alexander: Harmony in Gray and Green (1872) by James McNeill Whistler. Oil on canvas.

time for tea, and don't they look as if they were muddy up to the eyes!"

Framton shivered slightly and turned toward the niece with a look intended to convey sympathetic comprehension. The child was staring out through the open window with dazed horror in her eyes. In a chill shock of nameless fear Framton swung round in his seat and looked in the same direction.

In the deepening twilight three figures were walking across the lawn toward the window; they all carried guns under their arms, and one of them was additionally burdened with a white coat hung over his shoulders. A tired brown spaniel kept close at their heels. Noiselessly they neared the house, and then a hoarse young voice chanted out of the dusk: "I said, Bertie, why do you bound?"

Framton grabbed wildly at his stick and hat; the hall door, the gravel drive, and the front gate were dimly noted stages in his headlong retreat. A cyclist coming along the road had to run into the hedge to avoid imminent collision.

"Here we are, my dear," said the bearer of the white mackintosh, coming in through the window, "fairly muddy, but most of it's dry. Who was that who bolted out as we came up?"

"A most extraordinary man, a Mr. Nuttel," said Mrs. Sappleton; "could only talk about his illnesses and dashed off without a word of goodbye or apology when you arrived. One would think he had seen a ghost."

"I expect it was the spaniel," said the niece calmly; "he told me he had a horror of dogs. He was once hunted into a cemetery somewhere on the banks of the Ganges[4] by a pack of pariah dogs[5] and had to spend the night in a newly dug grave with the creatures snarling and grinning and foaming just above him. Enough to make anyone lose their nerve."

Romance at short notice was her specialty.

4. **Ganges** (gan′jēz): river in northern India and Bangladesh.
5. **pariah** (pə·rī′ə) **dogs**: wild dogs.

MEET THE WRITER

Mischief and Mayhem

Saki is the pen name of Hector Hugh Munro (1870–1916). He was born in Burma (now called Myanmar), where his father, a Scottish military officer, was posted. Saki's mother died when he was a toddler, and he and his brother and sister were sent to England to be raised by their grandmother and two strict aunts.

Sickly as a child, Saki received little formal education before he was sent to boarding school at age fourteen. He spent most of his time with his brother and sister, developing the mischievous sense of humor that later made his writing famous.

Although Saki was forty-three when World War I broke out, he enlisted in the British Army. He was killed by a German sniper two years later on a dark morning in France. His last words before he was shot were "Put that bloody cigarette out."

More by Saki

If you liked Vera's imaginative stories in "The Open Window," you'll enjoy watching her have fun with a stuffy politician in "The Lull." You can find this story in *The Complete Stories of Saki* (Wordsworth). Also look for the mischief-making characters Reginald and Clovis.

READ ON

Valley of Fear

What would it be like to find yourself alone in a devastated world after a nuclear war? In Robert C. O'Brien's *Z for Zachariah* (Collier), sixteen-year-old Ann Burden has been left to survive on her own on her family's farm in a valley protected from radioactive winds. When a stranger appears one morning, Ann is happy to have a companion at last. Then she finds out there are worse things than loneliness.

Into the Fourth Dimension

Meg's father, a scientist, has disappeared while on secret government business. Now Meg, her friend Calvin, and her brilliant younger brother, Charles Wallace, must search for him through *A Wrinkle in Time* (Dell)—but can they save him from the dark terror beyond? (If you enjoy this novel by Madeleine L'Engle, you may also want to try the sequels, *A Wind in the Door* and *A Swiftly Tilting Planet*.)

The Water of Life

Have you ever wished you could live forever? In *Tuck Everlasting* by Natalie Babbitt (Farrar, Straus & Giroux), the members of the Tuck family are granted this wish when they drink from a hidden stream. (This title is available in the HRW Library.) Published in Spanish as *Tuck para siempre* (Farrar, Straus & Giroux).

Other Picks

- Isaac Asimov, *I, Robot* (Bantam). In nine short stories, a celebrated science fiction writer shows how robots of the future might be just a little *too* human.

- Robert Louis Stevenson, *The Strange Case of Dr. Jekyll and Mr. Hyde* (Dover). In this classic novel a kindhearted, respectable gentleman drinks a potion and unleashes his dark side.

- James M. Deem, *How to Catch a Flying Saucer* (Houghton Mifflin). This guide includes everything you need to know about those mysterious moving lights that some claim are visitors from other worlds—including how to assemble your own UFO sighting kit.

Speaking and Listening Workshop

ORAL INTERPRETATION

Reading Aloud: It's Not Just for Kids

When you present an **oral interpretation** of a literary work, you share with an audience your understanding of and feelings about the work. Oral interpretations can take a variety of forms, such as these:

- **Dramatic reading.** One person reads a work of literature aloud, using his or her voice, facial expressions, and gestures to convey the words and their meaning to the audience.

- **Choral reading.** A group presents a reading of a literary work, usually a poem. The group members may recite lines in unison, speak one at a time, or combine the two techniques.

- **Reader's theater.** A small group prepares and reads a script based on a scene from a narrative. The scene is generally one with a lot of dialogue and just a few characters. Usually a narrator gives background information about the setting, characters, and plot.

- **Creative enactment.** A creative enactment can be a pantomime, a skit, a monologue, or another kind of dramatic presentation of a literary work. An enactment can include the speaker's own words, the words of the text, or a combination of the two.

Planning: Get Ready, Get Set . . .

Follow these steps to prepare your oral interpretation:

1. Read the work of literature at least twice, either by yourself or aloud with a group. During your second reading, think about how to present the work, and jot down your ideas.

2. Write a script. You can either write out all the lines word for word or make a rough outline of what you plan to do and say—whichever works better for you. The script is used during rehearsal and can also be used during the actual presentation.

Try It Out

Use the instructions in this workshop to prepare and present an oral interpretation of one of the stories in this collection (or of another piece of literature approved by your teacher).

Try It Out

With two or three classmates as your audience, practice two different dramatic readings of a poem. Try varying your **pauses, tone, volume,** and **emphasis,** and ask for feedback from your listeners.

- Which reading did your audience prefer? Why?

- Which **vocal effects** did your listeners find most effective?

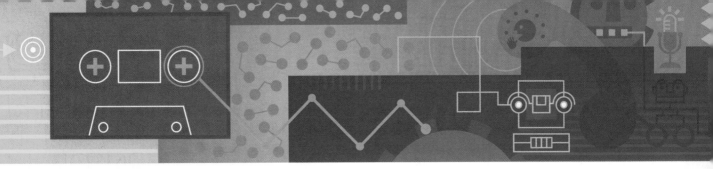

If you're preparing a script for a dramatic reading, make a copy of the original work. Then, add marks to guide you in your reading. For example, you can underline a word or phrase as a reminder to emphasize it and use a slash (/) as a signal to pause.

3. If your audience is unfamiliar with the piece, you may want to prepare a brief introduction, giving the title and author and any background information your audience will need to understand your presentation.

4. Hold at least one complete dress rehearsal with any props or costumes you plan to use. Time your presentation to make sure you don't exceed your time limit.

Presenting: Act Like You Mean It

Even if you're reading words written by someone else, it's up to *you* to bring those words to life through your presentation.

- Imagine that your listeners don't understand the language you speak. Ask yourself: How much meaning am I communicating through my **tone** of voice, **facial expressions,** and **gestures** alone? These signals should tell your audience whether you're asking a question or making a statement, for example, and whether the work of literature is funny or scary or sad.

- Try speaking twice as slowly and twice as loudly as you normally would, making your pauses twice as long and your gestures and expressions twice as forceful, putting twice as much feeling into each word. (If you think you might be overdoing it, ask someone to observe a rehearsal and comment on your reading.) Don't be afraid to be "bigger than life." You want everyone in your audience to get your message, even the people in the back of the room.

- Make sure to look at your audience, not at the floor.

How Did You Do?

Be sure to ask your audience for feedback after your performance. Which techniques and which parts of your interpretation were the most effective? Which were the least effective? Why?

Try It Out

Find a piece of writing with little emotional content—for example, a page in a dictionary or in an instructional manual. Read a short section aloud several times, using a different tone of voice or conveying a different mood with each reading. Try these:

spooky   sarcastic

happy   bored

suspenseful   soothing

amused   surprised

Sentence Workshop
H E L P

Combining sentences: page 259.

Proofreading Tip

Make a copy of your essay, and proofread it with a partner. As your partner reads aloud, read along silently. Stop when you come to an error in grammar, spelling, or punctuation, and correct it.

Communications Handbook
H E L P

See Proofreaders' Marks.

Publishing Tips

- Some Internet sites welcome reviews and essays. Check with your teacher before submitting your work on-line.

- Start a literary criticism (lit crit) club to print and discuss your essays.

Second, the narrator becomes increasingly nervous and strange after the officers come to his door. Then, he begins to hear the beating of the old man's heart. It isn't really there, but in his mind it is.

Finally, by the end of his story, the narrator can't take it anymore. He breaks down completely, shows the officers the body, and yells, "It is the beating of his hideous heart!" He has given himself away.

This story is very dark and eerie, like all of Poe's work. I enjoyed reading "The Tell-Tale Heart." It's classic Poe. The use of an insane narrator is also classic Poe.

—Taylor Roderick
Martin Junior High School
Austin, Texas

Second detail supporting thesis statement.

Third detail supporting thesis statement.

Summation of main idea.

Evaluating and Revising

1. Peer Response

Make copies of your essay, and exchange papers with two or three classmates. Before you read your partners' essays, discuss the Evaluation Criteria on page 257. Afterward, give your partners feedback. Be sure to point out passages in each essay that are unclear. Be sure also to tell the writer what you *liked* about the essay.

2. Self-Evaluation

Read your essay carefully. You may find it helpful to read it aloud into a tape recorder and listen to the results with a critical ear. Can you improve it by combining sentences or eliminating repetition? Can you do a better job of tying your ideas together? You may need to add some subordinating conjunctions (such as *after*, *because*, *though*, and *whenever*) and transitional words (such as *first*, *next*, and *finally*) to connect your ideas more logically.

Sentence Workshop

COMBINING SENTENCES

Consider these sentences:

> Poe's narrator was obsessed. He was obsessed with the old man's eye.

The sentences aren't incorrect, but the style seems awkward, doesn't it? The information could be conveyed more smoothly in a single sentence:

COMBINED   Poe's narrator was obsessed with the old man's eye.

How do you know when to combine sentences? Short, choppy sentences that express related ideas can often be combined. Look for repeated words or phrases.

ORIGINAL   The landlady opened the door. She opened it right away.

COMBINED   The landlady opened the door right away.

ORIGINAL   Tokubei was wealthy. Tokubei was also very miserly.

COMBINED   Tokubei was wealthy but very miserly.

Sentences that express related ideas don't always have to be combined. You may want to use repetition at times to emphasize a point.

Writer's Workshop Follow-up: Revising

Take out your essay, and underline every sentence containing words that also appear in the previous sentence. Circle the repeated words. (Don't circle words like *a* and *the*.) On a blank sheet of paper, write a combined sentence. Compare each new sentence with the original sentences. Which do you like better in each case?

Language Handbook
HELP

See Combining Sentences, pages 789-791.

Technology
HELP

See Language Workshop CD-ROM. *Key word entry: combining sentences.*

Try It Out

Combine each of the following pairs of sentences by adding the information in the second sentence to the first. You will need to make some changes, such as adding or deleting words.

1. Hector Munro was born in Burma. Hector was sent to live in England.

2. Hector's sister wrote about their childhood. His sister's name was Ethel.

3. Hector was a boy who liked to play tricks. Hector was mischievous.

4. He convinced children to misbehave. The children were usually well-behaved.

5. Vera is a character who appears in several of Saki's stories. She is a funny character.

Reading for Life

Taking Notes

Situation

After reading "The Inn of Lost Time," you're interested in learning more about Japanese samurai. You'd even like to try writing a samurai story of your own. You will have to take notes as you do your research.

Strategies

Get ready.

- Before you start, jot down questions to guide your reading. You'll think of other questions as you read.

- Use a different index card for each source you cite.

- If you are taking notes on a computer, use a different page for each source.

Get to the point.

- When you locate your sources, **skim** to find the sections that interest you. When you skim, you look over a page quickly, not reading every word. You look for key words and glance at headings and words in boldface.

- When you find an important section, **read closely** for main ideas. Take notes on the following: *Who* is this about? *What* happened? *When* and *where* did it happen?

> ronin= unemployed samurai, without masters. Ronin→farmers, monks—some wandered→bandits. Term ronin today=high school graduate, failed college entrance exam, waiting to try again.
> Columbia Encyclopedia, 5th ed., 1993, p. 2355. Columbia Univ. Press.

- Don't overlook important **supporting details.** Ask *why* and *how* this happened.

Get it in writing.

- As you read, **paraphrase** the writer's ideas (put them in your own words). Save time by using short phrases, abbreviations, and symbols.

- If you do want to use a direct quote, copy it exactly within quotation marks, and note its source.

Get organized.

- On each index card, record the author, the title, the date, the publisher (or Internet address), and the page(s) of the source you used.

- It's best to use only one side of an index card for notes.

- Consider making an **outline,** a **chart,** or a **time line** to summarize and organize the information.

Using the Strategies

1. What is the source for the notes above about ronin?

2. What symbol does the reader use to indicate a definition?

3. What do you think the arrows mean?

4. Are any words quoted directly from the source? How can you tell?

Extending the Strategies

Read and take notes on one of the Elements of Literature features in this book.

Learning for Life

Using Multiple Intelligences in a Group

Problem

Have you ever heard the expression "Two heads are better than one"? How can we pool our resources to accomplish more together than any one of us could achieve alone?

Project

Work with a group of classmates to create a response to a work of literature, using your combined abilities.

Preparation

Multiple intelligences. We're all intelligent in different ways: We each have different abilities and skills, learn best through different methods, and enjoy different types of activities. Listed below are seven types of intelligence. On a blank sheet of paper, copy them in the order you think best describes your own abilities. (That is, if you think working with music is your favorite activity or greatest talent, make *music* your first item.)

- people
- words (spoken or written)
- numbers or problem solving
- music
- sports or dance
- thoughts and feelings
- pictures

Then, with your teacher's help, form a group with several classmates whose top three items are different from yours. Your group's task is to create a presentation in which at least five of the seven intelligences are used.

Procedure

1. Select. Choose a work of literature that everyone in the group has read. Discuss possible choices until you reach a **consensus** (general agreement).

2. Review. If the work is a short story, an essay, or a poem, you may want to read it aloud with your group. If it's a longer work, such as a novel or a play, your group may want to simply review the characters, setting, and events.

3. Plan. Will you focus on

- the work's message?
- how it made you feel?
- its setting or mood?
- a character?
- another aspect of the work?

Presentation

Here are some things you might include in your presentation:

acting	photography
computers	science
dancing	sculpture
drawing	storytelling
graphics	talking
music	teaching
painting	videotape
pantomime	writing

Be prepared to explain to your teacher and classmates how your group has used five types of intelligence in its presentation. (Intelligences used in the planning stage count, too.) If possible, share your presentation with a wider audience, such as other classes.

Processing

If you would like to keep this project or a record of it in your portfolio, respond in writing to two or more of the following prompts:

- My most important contribution to this project was . . . because . . .
- The best/worst part of working in the group was . . . because . . .
- This project belongs in my portfolio because . . .

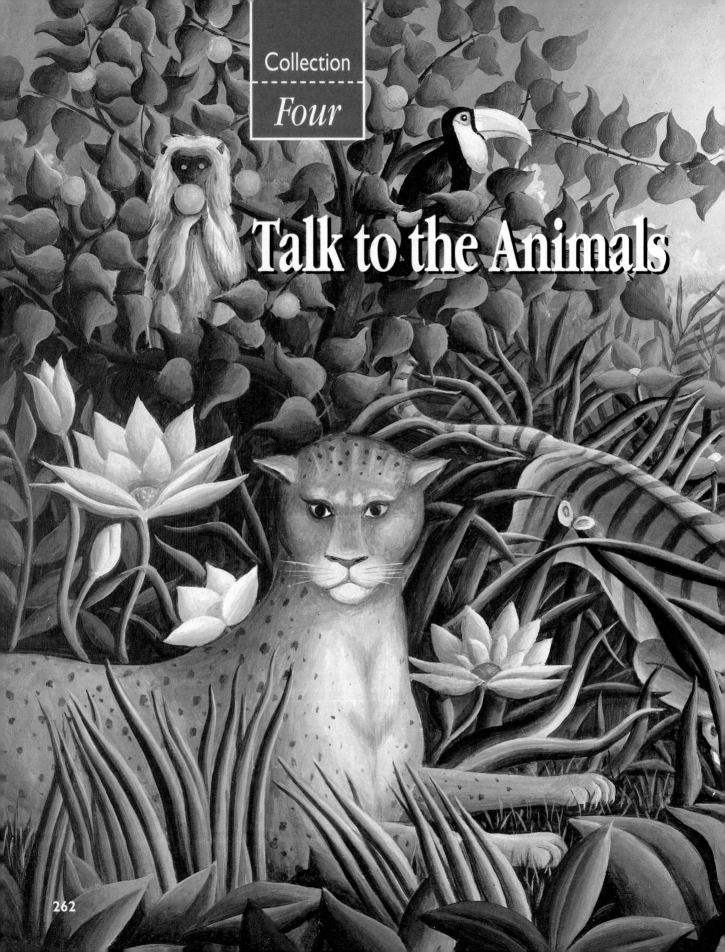

Talk to the Animals

But ask now the beasts, and they shall teach thee . . .

—Job 12:7, *The Bible*

Before You Read

WE ARE ALL ONE

Make the Connection

Sketch to Stretch

We are all one.

On a blank sheet of paper, draw a large circle to represent the earth. In the center, write *We are all one*. Then, fill in the circle with words and symbols that show what you think this statement means.

Share your drawing with your classmates, explaining your words and symbols.

Reading Skills and Strategies

Dialogue with the Text: Monitoring Your Comprehension

As you read this Chinese folk tale, keep your notebook or a sheet of paper handy to jot down your reactions. Look at the student's comments on the first page as an example, but remember that no two people read a story in exactly the same way.

HRW go.hrw.com
LEO 8-4

Painting of a man wearing a coat signifying that he is a fourth-degree military official. Leaf from a Manchu family album. Unidentified artist. Ch'ing Dynasty, probably K'ang-hsi period (1662–1723). Color and ink on paper.

Elements of Literature

Theme

While plot is what happens in a story, **theme** is the message—what the writer is saying about life.

A story's theme is usually implied, not stated directly. A story may have more than one theme, and different readers may find different themes in the same work.

> The **theme** of a work of literature is its message, or main idea about life.
>
> *For more on Theme, see the Handbook of Literary Terms.*

"We are one, you and I," a voice said faintly . . .

We Are All One

Laurence Yep

Long ago there was a rich man with a disease in his eyes. For many years, the pain was so great that he could not sleep at night. He saw every doctor he could, but none of them could help him.

"What good is all my money?" he groaned. Finally, he became so desperate that he sent criers[1] through the city offering a reward to anyone who could cure him.

Now in that city lived an old candy peddler. He would walk around with his baskets of candy, but he was so kind-hearted that he gave away as much as he sold, so he was always poor.

When the old peddler heard the announcement, he remembered something his mother had said. She had once told him about a magical herb that was good for the eyes. So he packed up his baskets and went back to the single tiny room in which his family lived.

When he told his plan to his wife, she scolded him, "If you go off on this crazy hunt, how are we supposed to eat?"

Usually the peddler gave in to his wife, but this time he was stubborn. "There are two baskets of candy," he said. "I'll be back before they're gone."

The next morning, as soon as the soldiers opened the gates, he was the first one to leave the city. He did not stop until he was deep inside the woods. As a boy, he had often wandered there. He had liked to pretend that the shadowy forest was a green sea and he was a fish slipping through the cool waters.

1. criers: people who called out public announcements in the streets of towns and villages before modern means of communication were invented.

As he examined the ground, he noticed ants scurrying about. On their backs were larvae[2] like white grains of rice. A rock had fallen into a stream, so the water now spilled into the ants' nest.

"We're all one," the kindhearted peddler said. So he waded into the shallow stream and put the rock on the bank. Then, with a sharp stick, he dug a shallow ditch that sent the rest of the water back into the stream.

Without another thought about his good deed, he began to search through the forest. He looked everywhere; but as the day went on, he grew sleepy. "Ho-hum. I got up too early. I'll take just a short nap," he decided, and lay down in the shade of an old tree, where he fell right asleep.

In his dreams, the old peddler found himself standing in the middle of a great city. Tall buildings rose high overhead. He couldn't see the sky even when he tilted back his head. An escort of soldiers marched up to him with a loud clatter of their black lacquer armor. "Our queen wishes to see you," the captain said.

The frightened peddler could only obey and let the fierce soldiers lead him into a shining palace. There, a woman with a high crown sat upon a tall throne. Trembling, the old peddler fell to his knees and touched his forehead against the floor.

But the queen ordered him to stand. "Like the great Emperor Yü of long ago, you tamed the great flood. We are all one now. You have only to ask, and I or any of my people will come to your aid."

The old peddler cleared his throat. "I am looking for a certain herb. It will cure any disease of the eyes."

The queen shook her head regretfully. "I have never heard of that herb. But you will surely find it if you keep looking for it."

And then the old peddler woke. Sitting up,

he saw that in his wanderings he had come back to the ants' nest. It was there he had taken his nap. His dream city had been the ants' nest itself.

"This is a good omen," he said to himself, and he began searching even harder. He was so determined to find the herb that he did not notice how time had passed. He was surprised when he saw how the light was fading. He looked all around then. There was no sight of his city—only strange hills. He realized then that he had searched so far he had gotten lost.

Night was coming fast and with it the cold. He rubbed his arms and hunted for shelter. In the twilight, he thought he could see the green tiles of a roof.

He stumbled through the growing darkness until he reached a ruined temple. Weeds grew through cracks in the stones and most of the roof itself had fallen in. Still, the ruins would provide some protection.

As he started inside, he saw a centipede with bright orange skin and red tufts of fur along its back. Yellow dots covered its sides like a dozen tiny eyes. It was also rushing into the temple as fast as it could, but there was a bird swooping down toward it.

The old peddler waved his arms and shouted, scaring the bird away. Then he put down his palm in front of the insect. "We are all one, you and I." The many feet tickled his skin as the centipede climbed onto his hand.

Inside the temple, he gathered dried leaves and found old sticks of wood, and soon he had a fire going. The peddler even picked some fresh leaves for the centipede from a bush near the temple doorway. "I may have to go hungry, but you don't have to, friend."

Stretching out beside the fire, the old peddler pillowed his head on his arms. He was so tired that he soon fell asleep, but even in his sleep he dreamed he was still searching in the woods. Suddenly he thought he heard footsteps near his head. He woke instantly and

2. **larvae** (lär′vē′): insects at an early stage of life.

looked about, but he saw only the brightly colored centipede.

"Was it you, friend?" The old peddler chuckled and, lying down, he closed his eyes again. "I must be getting nervous."

"We are one, you and I," a voice said faintly—as if from a long distance. "If you go south, you will find a pine tree with two trunks. By its roots, you will find a magic bead. A cousin of mine spat on it years ago. Dissolve that bead in wine and tell the rich man to drink it if he wants to heal his eyes."

The old peddler trembled when he heard the voice, because he realized that the centipede was magical. He wanted to run from the temple, but he couldn't even get up. It was as if he were glued to the floor.

But then the old peddler reasoned with himself: If the centipede had wanted to hurt me, it could have long ago. Instead, it seems to want to help me.

So the old peddler stayed where he was, but he did not dare open his eyes. When the first sunlight fell through the roof, he raised one eyelid cautiously. There was no sign of the centipede. He sat up and looked around, but the magical centipede was gone.

He followed the centipede's instructions when he left the temple. Traveling south, he kept a sharp eye out for the pine tree with two trunks. He walked until late in the afternoon, but all he saw was normal pine trees.

Wearily he sat down and sighed. Even if he found the pine tree, he couldn't be sure that he would find the bead. Someone else might even have discovered it a long time ago.

But something made him look a little longer. Just when he was thinking about turning back, he saw the odd tree. Somehow his tired legs managed to carry him over to the tree, and he got down on his knees. But the ground was covered with pine needles and his old eyes were too weak. The old peddler could have wept

Returning Through Snow to the Bamboo Retreat (Ming Dynasty) by Tai Chin (1388–1462). Ink on silk.

Twin Pines, Level Distance (Yuan Dynasty, c. 1310) by Chao Meng-fu. Handscroll; ink on paper.

with frustration, and then he remembered the ants.

He began to call, "Ants, ants, we are all one."

Almost immediately, thousands of ants came boiling out of nowhere. Delighted, the old man held up his fingers. "I'm looking for a bead. It might be very tiny."

Then, careful not to crush any of his little helpers, the old man sat down to wait. In no time, the ants reappeared with a tiny bead. With trembling fingers, the old man took the bead from them and examined it. It was colored orange and looked as if it had yellow eyes on the sides.

There was nothing very special about the bead, but the old peddler treated it like a fine jewel. Putting the bead into his pouch, the old peddler bowed his head. "I thank you and I thank your queen," the old man said. After the ants disappeared among the pine needles, he made his way out of the woods.

The next day, he reached the house of the rich man. However, he was so poor and ragged

that the gatekeeper only laughed at him. "How could an old beggar like you help my master?"

The old peddler tried to argue. "Beggar or rich man, we are all one."

But it so happened that the rich man was passing by the gates. He went over to the old peddler. "I said anyone could see me. But it'll mean a stick across your back if you're wasting my time."

The old peddler took out the pouch. "Dissolve this bead in some wine and drink it down." Then, turning the pouch upside down, he shook the tiny bead onto his palm and handed it to the rich man.

The rich man immediately called for a cup of wine. Dropping the bead into the wine, he waited a moment and then drank it down. Instantly the pain vanished. Shortly after that, his eyes healed.

The rich man was so happy and grateful that he doubled the reward. And the kindly old peddler and his family lived comfortably for the rest of their lives.

MEET THE WRITER

An Outsider

Laurence Yep (1948–   ) was born in San Francisco, California. He grew up in the mainly African American Fillmore District but attended a Catholic school in Chinatown. "As a result," he says, "I was always something of an outsider." Like his parents, who read four daily newspapers, Yep was an enthusiastic reader. The children's stories that were popular at the time failed to interest him, though:

66 When I was a child, there weren't any books about Chinese American children; but when I went to the library, I could never get interested in books about Homer Price or other such children. Every child had a bicycle and no one seemed to worry about locking their front doors. As a result, these and other such details seemed like fantasy to me.

Ironically, what seemed 'truer' to me were science fiction and fantasy because in those books, children were taken to other lands and other worlds, where they had to learn strange customs and languages—and that was something I did every time I got on and off the bus. **99**

More by Laurence Yep

"We Are All One" comes from *The Rainbow People* (HarperCollins). In this book, Yep retells folk tales originally recounted in the 1930s by Chinese immigrants to the United States. "When my father picked fruit in the Chinese orchards near Sacramento," he says, "the workers would gather in the shack after a hot, grueling workday; one of the ways that the old-timers would pass the time before sleep came was to tell stories."

Yep has also written fantasies, science fiction, and mysteries for children and for adults. His first published novel, *Sweetwater* (HarperCollins), is about the conflict between the human colonists on a planet called Harmony and the spiderlike Argans, the original inhabitants of the planet.

The Cormorant in My Bathtub

When I was about eight, I went to live with my grandparents at the beach. I had never seen the ocean before, and to this day the memory is vivid. We pulled into the driveway at dusk, and I could see behind the house an exciting expanse of untouched water. I shivered. Since my parents' death, I had not felt any emotion; I had been only a breathing vegetable. But now I could feel the blood beginning to pump through my veins. I felt warm and tingly. The colors of the horizon and the dying sun were a shimmer of pinks and purples. The sun, arrayed in its most beautiful gown, was ready to die valiantly. I was sure even the Garden of Eden could not have been more beautiful.

From that moment on I was madly in love with the ocean. I lay in the sand for hours watching the cormorants circling over the lapping waves. How I envied those birds their graceful black bodies circling and diving into the brilliant waters. They did not know fear or sadness; they knew only life, sun, and the ocean. They would plummet into the sea at tremendous speeds. But not once did they miss their prey. They always succeeded in

their world. There were no failures. Each one always emerged with a silver minnow speared on its beak.

Every day from sunup to sundown I haunted the beach. I never tried to make new friends; I was always alone. I dreaded the first day of school. I was always dreaming that I would become a cormorant and fly away over the ocean, never to be seen again.

It was a Wednesday night when the tanker sank. The rain was falling in solid sheets, the wind blowing at nearly fifty knots! All the power lines were out; even the glow of the lighthouse was not strong enough to pierce the storm. The captain of the tanker lost his course and ran aground on Lookout Point. The side of the tanker split on the rocks, spilling hundreds of thousands of gallons of oil into the raging sea.

The next day the ocean was calm, but the waves that lapped against the beach were tainted. Riding on the waves were the black re-

First appeared in *Merlyn's Pen: The National Magazines of Student Writing.*

mains of the oil tanker's cargo. I watched in horror as helpless seabirds struggled to stay afloat, flapping their wings in frenzied splashes as they tried desperately to free themselves from the clinging oil. Tears streamed down my cheeks as I dashed into the ocean and gathered up as many birds as I could capture. I returned to the house and filled the bathtub with clean, fresh water. Then I pried open as many beaks as I could. I watched helplessly as the birds surrendered to the clinging grease that clogged their nostrils and held fast their beaks. My whole body shook with grief. I lifted their limp bodies and tenderly set them on a towel. Among the dead were three gulls, two sandpipers, and one brown pelican.

One bird remained in the tub, a black bird who would not give up. He lay quietly in the tub, but his eyes were alert, and he was wide awake. He was a cormorant. To take my mind off the others, I picked him up and began to rub his back with tissue and detergent. It took hours, but the bird seemed to sense that I was trying to help. He lay still and allowed me to wipe every last drop of oil off his glossy back. When I placed him back in the tub he drank deeply, enjoying the strange, sweet taste of fresh water for the first time.

When my grandma found me, she did not scold me for hiding from her or for making a mess of her guest bathroom. She simply asked if I would like some help burying the dead birds. Without asking, I knew she would let the cormorant stay in her bathtub. The bird was clearly exhausted. He lay motionless with his head tucked under his wing. As we buried the six birds, I wondered what would happen to the seventh.

For a week my grandparents forbade me to visit the beach. I knew that the oil was still thick and that the white sand would never be quite as pure. We had numerous wildlife representatives visit our beach and collect water samples and gather up dead fish and birds.

They would often stop and look in on my bird, but they never tried to take him away. I fed him sardines and tuna fish. He ate greedily and slowly became stronger. Sadly I realized that my new friend would need to leave me.

A few kids in my neighborhood stopped by to see the bird. Grandma encouraged them to

stay for tea, and I was surprised at how much fun we had. The more time I spent with the neighborhood kids, the more I looked forward to the opening of school. The water was regaining its purity and soon it would be safe to let my bird go. He would once again be searching the sea for a school of minnows instead of splashing about in our bathtub. Still, I did not like to think about losing him.

Two weeks after the storm, school started. I was excited by new classes and new friends. I was spending very little time on the beach. Instead I had been playing baseball in the lot behind our house. I felt needed and wanted for the first time since my parents' death; the black bird in my bathtub needed me, and my friends wanted me to play third base and share adventures with them.

On the third day of school I returned home to find the bird gone. The door was shut tight, but the window was open and the curtain was blowing in the breeze. On the floor below the window a long black feather rested. I picked it up and stroked the smooth edge as I thought of all the bird had given me.

— Brooke Rogers
Charles Wright Academy
Tacoma, Washington

MAKING MEANINGS

First Thoughts

1. Take out the circle drawing you made before you read the story. Add any new ideas you have about the statement "We are all one." (You may want to refer to your reading notes.)

Shaping Interpretations

2. How does the peddler show that he believes "we are all one"?

3. Like almost all stories, "We Are All One" is built on a series of **causes** and **effects.** Think of how the peddler's good deeds affect what happens to him. Copy the chart below, adding other examples of the peddler's actions and their consequences.

Action (Cause)	Consequence (Effect)
1. Saves ants from flood.	1. Ant queen promises ants' help.
2. Saves centipede from bird.	2.
3. Etc.	3.

4. What message about life do you see in this folk tale? State this **theme** in a single sentence. (Be sure to think about the story's **title**.)

5. Do you believe the peddler would have gone on his journey if the rich man hadn't offered a reward? Why or why not?

6. How is the narrator of "The Cormorant in My Bathtub" (see pages 270–271) rewarded for kindness to animals?

Extending the Text

7. Do you believe that people who help their fellow creatures are always rewarded in some way? Explain your response.

8. Choose one of the following examples of people living today, or think of your own example. How might the person act on the belief that "we are all one"?

- an eighth-grader living in a big city
- the head of an international corporation
- a senator from your state

Reading Check

When the peddler comes home with the reward, his wife probably wants to know what happened to him. Make a list of questions she might ask him about his trip. Then, exchange papers with a classmate, and answer your partner's questions.

CHOICES: Building Your Portfolio

Writer's Notebook

1. Collecting Ideas for a How-To Essay

"We Are All One" shows how kind actions toward others can lead to a positive outcome. Try writing simple instructions on how to live life with the philosophy "we are all one." Base your how-to instructions on what you learned from the story as well as from your own experiences.

> —Don't wait to be asked; volunteer to help others.
> —Be considerate to everyone equally.
> —Cooperate with others; what goes around comes around.

Creative Writing

2. We Are *Not* All One

The peddler's wife doesn't seem as concerned about the welfare of others as her husband is. Imagine that she is the one who goes looking for the magic herb, hoping to receive the reward. Write a new version of the tale. Does the wife stop to help the ants and the centipede? What are the consequences of her actions? Is she rewarded or punished for her behavior?

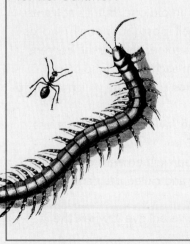

Art/Critical Thinking

3. Universal Lessons

Which of the proverbs below do you believe best expresses the **theme** of "We Are All One"?

* "It is not only giants that do great things."

    —traditional Liberian

* "Never do to others what you would not like them to do to you."

    —Confucius, *Analects*

* "The trees and all nature are witnesses of your thoughts and deeds."

    —traditional Winnebago

Make a drawing or a collage that connects the proverb you choose with the folk tale. Attach a note explaining your choice.

Creative Writing/ Technology

4. Literary Adventures

Write a "choose your own adventure" story, in book or hypermedia form, to teach the lesson "we are all one." Use the characters, settings, and events of the folk tale. On each page or screen, give readers a choice of actions to take (will they stop to help the ants or move on?); each action should lead to certain consequences. You may want to check a published "choose your own adventure" story for format.

GRAMMAR LINK   MINI-LESSON

Using Commas with Items in a Series

Language Handbook HELP

See Commas, pages 798-799.

Use commas to separate items in a series. The items may be single words or groups of words.

EXAMPLES   He slept, awoke, and began searching again.

He saw tall buildings, fierce soldiers, a shining palace, and a queen on a throne.

Without commas to separate the items, the words would slide together in a jumble. By showing where one item ends and another begins, commas help the reader make sense of a sentence.

When a series of adjectives all modify the same noun, don't use a comma *after* the last adjective.

INCORRECT   He had always loved the cool, dark, mysterious, forest.

(You wouldn't write *He had always loved the mysterious, forest,* would you?)

CORRECT   He had always loved the cool, dark, mysterious forest.

Hint: Use a comma where you could also use the word *and.* (You would not say "the mysterious *and* forest.")

Technology HELP

See Language Workshop CD-ROM. *Key word entry: commas.*

Try It Out

Copy the sentences below, adding commas to separate the items in a series.

1. The old peddler helped the ants the centipede and the rich man.

2. The centipede was orange red and yellow.

3. The peddler scared the bird away by running waving and shouting.

4. The kind gentle helpful peddler was rewarded in the end.

SPELLING   HOW TO OWN A WORD

Words with *ie* and *ei*

Language Handbook HELP

See Spelling Rules, page 812.

I before *e*,
Except after *c*,
Or when sounded like *a*,
As in *neighbor* and *weigh*.

The rhyme on the left is an old one, but it's still a useful device to help you spell most (but not all!) words with *ie* or *ei*. Using it as a guide, choose the correct spelling of the word from each underlined pair.

1. The candy peddler didn't mind the weight/wieght of his baskets.
2. He trembled when he saw the feirce/fierce ant soldiers.
3. The ant queen reigned/riegned with dignity.
4. The peddler laughed and called the centipede his freind/friend.
5. He could hardly beleive/believe it when the centipede answered him.

Before You Read

THE DOGS COULD TEACH ME

Make the Connection

Ask Now the Beasts . . .

How intelligent do you think animals are? On a piece of paper or in a notebook, rate each of the statements below with a number from 0 to 4.

disagree   0   1   2   3   4   agree

1. Animals know things that people don't.
2. Animals have a sense of humor.
3. Animals can teach us.
4. People are much smarter than animals.

Quickwrite

For each of the four statements, write the reason for your opinion.

Elements of Literature

Point of View

"The Dogs Could Teach Me" is told from the **first-person point of view,** that is, by a narrator using the pronoun *I*. In this true story the narrator is the writer, Gary Paulsen.

> **P**oint of view is the vantage point from which a story is told.
>
> *For more on Point of View, see pages 288–289 and the Handbook of Literary Terms.*

Reading Skills and Strategies

A Writer's Perspective: Be Aware of It!

Perspective simply means how a writer looks at a topic. Dogs, from Gary Paulsen's perspective, are wonderful. From your perspective, dogs might be something else. As you read this account, be aware of what Paulsen wants to tell you about dogs. If you love dogs, you will be glad to accept his conclusion. If you don't, you might question some of his reasoning. Whatever your perspective on dogs, Paulsen still can make you enjoy sharing his experiences.

Background

Literature and Real Life

This selection is taken from *Woodsong*, a book Gary Paulsen wrote about his adventures in northern Minnesota. When "The Dogs Could Teach Me" begins, Paulsen is trapping coyotes and beavers for Minnesota's predator control program. He had been covering the sixty miles of his route on foot or on skis until a friend gave him a team of four sled dogs.

go.hrw.com

LE0 8-4

I don't think I passed out so much as my brain simply exploded.

The Dogs Could Teach Me

from **Woodsong**

Gary Paulsen

Cold can be very strange. Not the cold felt running from the house to the bus or the car to the store, not the chill in the air on a fall morning, but deep cold.

Serious cold.

Forty, fifty, even sixty below zero—actual temperature, not wind chill—seems to change everything. Steel becomes brittle and breaks, shatters; breath taken straight into the throat will freeze the lining and burst blood vessels; eyes exposed too long will freeze; fingers and toes freeze, turn black, and break off. These are all known, normal parts of intense cold.

But it changes beauty as well. Things are steeped in a new clarity, a clear focus. Sound seems to ring and the very air seems to be filled with diamonds when ice crystals form.

On a river in Alaska, while training, I once saw a place where a whirlpool had frozen into a cone, open at the bottom, like a beautiful trap waiting to suck the whole team down. When I stopped to look at it, with the water roaring through at the bottom, the dogs became nervous and stared down into the center as if <u>mystified</u> and were very glad when we moved on.

After a time I stopped trapping. That change—as with many changes—occurred because of the dogs. As mentioned, I had hunted when I was young, trapping and killing many animals. I never thought it wrong until the dogs came. And then it was a simple thing, almost a silly thing, that caused the change.

Columbia had a sense of humor and I saw it.

In the summer the dogs live in the kennel area, each dog with his own house, on a chain that allows him to move in a circle. They can run only with the wheeled carts on cool nights, and sometimes they get bored being tied up. To <u>alleviate</u> the boredom, we give the dogs large beef bones to chew and play with. They get a new bone every other day or so. These bones are the center of much <u>contention</u>—we call them Bone Wars. Sometimes dogs clear across the kennel will hold their bones up in the air, look at each other, raise their hair, and start growling at each other, posturing and bragging about their bones.

But not Columbia.

Usually Columbia just chewed on his bone until the meat was gone. Then he buried it and waited for the next bone. I never saw him fight or get involved in Bone Wars and I always thought him a simple—perhaps a better word would be primitive—dog, basic and very wolflike, until one day when I was sitting in the kennel.

I had a notebook and I was sitting on the side of Cookie's roof, writing—the dogs are good company for working—when I happened to notice Columbia doing something strange.

He was sitting quietly on the outside edge of his circle, at the maximum length of his chain. With one paw he was pushing his bone—which still had a small bit of meat on it—out and away from him, toward the next circle.

Next to Columbia was a dog named Olaf. While Columbia was relatively passive, Olaf was very aggressive. Olaf always wanted to fight and he spent much time arguing over bones, females, the weather—anything and everything that caught his fancy. He was much scarred from fighting, with notched ears and lines on his muzzle, but he was a very good dog—strong and honest—and we liked him.

Being next to Columbia, Olaf had tried many times to get him to argue or bluster, but Columbia always ignored him.

Until this morning.

Carefully, slowly, Columbia pushed the bone toward Olaf's circle.

And of all the things that Olaf was—tough, strong, honest—he wasn't smart. As they say, some are smarter than others, and some are still not so smart, and then there was Olaf. It wouldn't be fair to call Olaf dumb—dogs don't measure those things like people—but even in the dog world he would not be known as a whip. Kind of a big bully who was also a bit of a doofus.

When he saw Columbia pushing the bone toward him, he began to reach for it. Straining against his chain, turning and trying to get farther and farther, he reached as far as he could

WORDS TO OWN
mystified (mis′tə·fīd′) v. used as *adj.*: puzzled.
alleviate (ə·lē′vē·āt′) v.: relieve; reduce.
contention (kən·ten′shən) n.: conflict; struggle. Paulsen is playing on the phrase *bone of contention,* meaning "subject about which there is disagreement."

with the middle toe on his right front foot, the claw going out as far as possible.

But not quite far enough. Columbia had measured it to the millimeter. He slowly pushed the bone until it was so close that Olaf's claw—with Olaf straining so hard his eyes bulged—just barely touched it.

Columbia sat back and watched Olaf straining and pushing and fighting, and when this had gone on for a long time—many minutes—and Olaf was still straining for all he was worth, Columbia leaned back and laughed.

"Heh, heh, heh . . ."

Then Columbia walked away.

And I could not kill or trap any longer.

It happened almost that fast. I had seen dogs with compassion for each other and their young and with anger and joy and hate and love, but this humor went into me more than the other things.

It was so complicated.

To make the joke up in his mind, the joke with the bone and the bully, and then set out to do it, carefully and quietly, to do it, then laugh and walk away—all of it was so complicated, so complex, that it triggered a chain reaction in my mind.

If Columbia could do that, I thought, if a dog could do that, then a wolf could do that. If a wolf could do that, then a deer could do that. If a deer could do that, then a beaver, and a squirrel, and a bird, and, and, and . . .

And I quit trapping then.

It was wrong for me to kill.

But I had this problem. I had gone over some kind of line with the dogs, gone back into some primitive state of exaltation that I wanted to study. I wanted to run them and learn from them. But it seemed to be wasteful (the word *immature* also comes to mind) to just run them. I thought I had to have a trap line to justify running the dogs, so I kept the line.

But I did not trap. I ran the country and camped and learned from the dogs and studied where I would have trapped if I were going to trap. I took many imaginary beaver and muskrat but I did no more sets and killed no more animals. I will not kill anymore.

Yet the line existed. Somehow in my mind—and until writing this I have never told another person about this—the line still existed and when I had "trapped" in one area, I would extend the line to "trap" in another, as is proper when you actually trap. Somehow the phony trapping gave me a purpose for running the dogs and would until I began to train them for the Iditarod, a dog-sled race across Alaska, which I had read about in *Alaska* magazine.

But it was on one of these "trapping" runs that I got my third lesson,[1] or awakening.

There was a point where an old logging trail went through a small, sharp-sided gully—a tiny canyon. The trail came down one wall of the gully—a drop of fifty or so feet—then scooted across a frozen stream and up the other side. It might have been a game trail that was slightly widened or an old foot trail that had not caved in. Whatever it was, I came onto it in the middle of January. The dogs were very excited. New trails always get them tuned up and they were fairly smoking as we came to the edge of the gully.

I did not know it was there and had been letting them run, not riding the sled brake to slow them, and we virtually shot off the edge.

The dogs stayed on the trail, but I immediately lost all control and went flying out into space with the sled. As I did, I kicked sideways, caught my knee on a sharp snag, and felt the wood enter under the kneecap and tear it loose.

1. **my third lesson:** The first lesson is described in the two previous chapters of *Woodsong*.

WORDS TO OWN
exaltation (eg′zôl·tā′shən) *n.:* great joy.

I may have screamed then.

The dogs ran out on the ice of the stream but I fell onto it. As these things often seem to happen, the disaster snowballed.

The trail crossed the stream directly at the top of a small frozen waterfall with about a twenty-foot drop. Later I saw the beauty of it, the falling lobes[2] of blue ice that had grown as the water froze and refroze, layering on itself. . . .

But at the time I saw nothing. I hit the ice of the stream bed like dropped meat, bounced once, then slithered over the edge of the waterfall and dropped another twenty feet onto the frozen pond below, landing on the torn and separated kneecap.

I have been injured several times running dogs—cracked ribs, a broken left leg, a broken left wrist, various parts frozen or cut or bitten while trying to stop fights—but nothing ever felt like landing on that knee.

I don't think I passed out so much as my brain simply exploded.

Again, I'm relatively certain I must have screamed or grunted, and then I wasn't aware of much for two, perhaps three minutes as I squirmed around trying to regain some part of my mind.

When things settled down to something I could control, I opened my eyes and saw that my snow pants and the jeans beneath were ripped in a jagged line for about a foot. Blood was welling out of the tear, soaking the cloth and the ice underneath the wound.

Shock and pain came in waves and I had to close my eyes several times. All of this was in minutes that seemed like hours, and I realized that I was in serious

2. **lobes:** rounded pieces that jut out.

trouble. Contrary to popular belief, dog teams generally do not stop and wait for a musher[3] who falls off. They keep going, often for many miles.

Lying there on the ice, I knew I could not walk. I didn't think I could stand without some kind of crutch, but I knew I couldn't walk. I was a good twenty miles from home, at least eight or nine miles from any kind of farm or dwelling.

It may as well have been ten thousand miles.

There was some self-pity creeping in, and not a little chagrin at being stupid enough to just let them run when I didn't know the country. I was trying to skootch myself up to the bank of the gully to get into a more comfortable position when I heard a sound over my head.

I looked up, and there was Obeah looking over the top of the waterfall, down at me.

I couldn't at first believe it.

He whined a couple of times, moved back and forth as if he might be going to drag the team over the edge, then disappeared from view. I heard some more whining and growling, then a scrabbling sound, and was amazed to see that he had taken the team back up the side of the gully and dragged them past the waterfall to get on the gully wall just over me.

They were in a horrible tangle, but he dragged them along the top until he was well below the waterfall, where he scrambled down the bank with the team almost literally falling on him. They dragged the sled up the frozen stream bed to where I was lying.

On the scramble down the bank Obeah had taken them through a thick stand of cockleburs. Great clumps of burrs wadded between their ears and down their backs.

He pulled them up to me, concern in his eyes and making a soft whine, and I reached into his ruff and pulled his head down and hugged him and was never so happy to see anybody probably in my life. Then I felt something and looked down to see one of the other dogs—named Duberry—licking the wound in my leg.

She was licking not with the excitement that prey blood would cause but with the gentle licking that she would use when cleaning a pup, a wound lick.

I brushed her head away, fearing infection, but she persisted. After a moment I lay back and let her clean it, still holding on to Obeah's ruff, holding on to a friend.

And later I dragged myself around and untangled them and unloaded part of the sled and crawled in and tied my leg down. We made it home that way, with me sitting in the sled; and later, when my leg was sewed up and healing and I was sitting in my cabin with the leg propped up on pillows by the wood stove; later, when all the pain was gone and I had all the time I needed to think of it . . . later I thought of the dogs.

How they came back to help me, perhaps to save me. I knew that somewhere in the dogs, in their humor and the way they thought, they had great, old knowledge; they had something we had lost.

And the dogs could teach me.

WORDS TO OWN

chagrin (shə·grin') *n.*: embarrassment and annoyance caused by disappointment or failure.

3. **musher** (mush'ər): person who travels over snow by dog sled.

MEET THE WRITER

"I Had Been Dying of Thirst"

Gary Paulsen (1939–   ) lived all over the United States, as well as in the Philippines, when he was growing up. His father was an army officer who moved the family with each new assignment. Paulsen calls his boyhood a "rough run":

66 The longest time I spent in one school was for about five months. I was an 'Army brat,' and it was a miserable life. School was a nightmare because I was unbelievably shy, and terrible at sports. I had no friends, and teachers ridiculed me. . . .

One day, as I was walking past the public library in twenty-below temperatures, I could see the reading room bathed in a beautiful golden light. I went in to get warm, and to my absolute astonishment the librarian walked up to me and asked if I wanted a library card. She didn't care if I looked right, wore the right clothes, dated the right girls, was popular at sports—none of those prejudices existed in the public library. When she handed me the card, she handed me the world. I can't even describe how liberating it was. She recommended westerns and science fiction but every now and then would slip in a classic. I roared through everything she gave me and in the summer read a book a day. It was as though I had been dying of thirst and the librarian had handed me a five-gallon bucket of water. I drank and drank. 99

More by Gary Paulsen

Woodsong is an autobiography, but Paulsen is best known for his young adult novels drawing on his own experiences. These are two of the most popular:

- *Hatchet* (Puffin), the adventures of a thirteen-year-old boy surviving alone in the Canadian wilderness.

- *Dogsong* (Puffin), about an Inuit youth's trek across Alaska by dog sled.

The Last Great Race on Earth

Diana Nyad

They call the Iditarod the Last Great Race on Earth, and for good reason. It's an experience beyond sport, a tribute really to the survival way of life familiar to many Alaskans. For ten days or so, no musher is allowed to accept any help from any individual—no dog food, no firewood, no one to carry even a pail of water, absolutely nothing. Each team runs with twelve to twenty dogs for four or five hours at a stretch, the unspoken law being that a musher jumps off and runs up every hill, often in hip-deep snow. At night, temperatures dipping to as low as sixty-five below zero, a musher might crouch on the runners behind the sled and doze as the dogs tread along a flat stretch, but those uncomfortable catnaps are virtually all the sleep the lead mushers take in ten days.

At the end of each running period, they pull the dogs up and start the tiring process of healing and feeding their team. They hurry, with swollen and partially numb fingers, to unhook all the dogs' leads and get them nestled on a ground cloth. They check paws for ice cuts, dress them with medicine and bandages and little protective booties. As the dogs sleep, they then hustle to build a fire and make hot gruel for their animals. Sometimes they have to chop down a tree for firewood.

By the time the dogs are fed and the sled is repacked, they rehook the team and run again. The musher hasn't even sat down during this three-hour rest period. If a moose attacks the team out on the trail and the musher must shoot the animal, he must also take the three or four hours necessary to skin the moose and bury its carcass in the snow. Disrespect for the wilderness is not tolerated in Alaska.

Yet as sturdy and as self-sufficient and as inspirational as the Iditarod mushers are, my most vibrant memory of the race is of the dogs. To me, watching the Alaskan husky in action is as thrilling as watching the magnificent thoroughbreds at Churchill Downs. These are the greatest endurance athletes in the world. Barely able to stand on wobbly legs in moments of extreme exhaustion, the husky will push headlong into a blizzard if his master asks him to.

I remember when Libby Riddles became the first woman to win the Last Great Race. She cried as she hugged her lead dog, and the first words that emanated from her blue lips were, "He would die for me out there, and I would die for him."

—from National Public Radio, *Morning Edition*

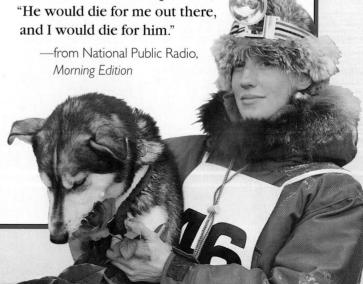

MAKING MEANINGS

First Thoughts

1. Go back to the ratings and opinions you recorded in your Quickwrite before you read "The Dogs Could Teach Me." Have any of your opinions changed? Note any changes and give reasons for them.

Shaping Interpretations

2. Make a rough diagram illustrating the trick Columbia plays on Olaf. What **cause-and-effect** relationships did Columbia need to understand to come up with his plan?

3. In your opinion, what is the most important sentence in "The Dogs Could Teach Me"? Explain your choice.

4. This account is told by Gary Paulsen himself, using the **first-person pronoun** *I*. What things does he tell you that no one else would know? Skim back through this book. What other accounts are told from the first-person point of view?

5. Think about Paulsen's and Libby Riddles's **perspectives** toward dogs (see the last paragraph of *Connections* on page 284). Do you think Paulsen would agree with Libby Riddles? Why or why not?

Connecting with the Text

6. About his decision to stop trapping, Paulsen says, "That change—as with many changes—occurred because of the dogs" (page 278). Give an example (from your own experience, if possible) of how a relationship with an animal might change someone.

Extending the Text

7. In "Mrs. Flowers" (page 20), Mrs. Flowers says that it is language that sets humans apart from other animals. Other people believe that only humans have souls or laugh. What do *you* believe makes people unique?

Challenging the Text

8. Go back to page 279, and reread the paragraph starting "If Columbia could do that. . . ." Do you agree with Paulsen's reasoning and the **conclusion** it leads him to? Why or why not?

CHOICES: Building Your Portfolio

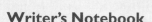

Writer's Notebook

1. Collecting Ideas for a How-To Essay

Suppose you would like to create a children's illustrated how-to guide to pet care. You could focus on one animal or make a general manual of pet care. You might get information from an animal shelter, pet owners, a veterinarian, or books on pet care. Take notes now on some of the basic kinds of information you'd like to cover. One writer's notes for a children's book about gerbils are shown at the right.

> How to Live with a Gerbil—illustrated, for little kids
> - Tell kids that gerbils don't have personalities.
> - Tell how to observe the gerbil.
> - Tell how to feed it.
> - Never let a gerbil run loose if you have a cat.

Supporting a Position

2. A Not-So-Great Race?

In "The Last Great Race on Earth," (see *Connections* on page 284), Diana Nyad celebrates the Iditarod, applauding the courage and endurance of the huskies and their mushers. Not everyone sees the race in a positive light, though. Some people feel that it should not be run because of the toll it takes in deaths and injuries among the dogs. What do you think? Write a letter to National Public Radio supporting or opposing Nyad's point of view. Do some research for evidence to back up your opinion.

Creative Writing

3. Let the Dogs Talk

How might one of the dogs describe the experiences Paulsen tells us about in this account? Rewrite one of the episodes so that one of the dogs tells the story from his or her **first-person point of view.** If you retell the story of how Columbia torments the doofus Olaf, let Columbia or Olaf tell the story, using *I*. If you retell the story of Paulsen's terrible accident, have Obeah tell the tale, using *I*. If the dogs tell the story, what will we know that Paulsen could not have known?

Creative Writing/Art

4. The Perfect Pet

Paulsen admires his sled dogs for their intelligence, strength, and loyalty. What would your ideal animal be like? Draw a picture of the perfect animal—it can be a member of a real species or one that you invent. Then, write a paragraph describing qualities the animal has that can't be shown in a picture. (Don't forget to give your imaginary animal a name.)

GRAMMAR LINK

Using Commas with Adjectives

Language Handbook HELP

See Commas, page 799.

Technology HELP

See Language Workshop CD-ROM. Key word entry: commas.

Sometimes an adjective and its noun are thought of as a unit, as in *orange juice, fried chicken,* or *mouse pad.* When you use adjectives to modify these pairs of words, you should not use a comma before the last adjective (*cold orange juice,* not *cold, orange juice*).

EXAMPLES   This is my favorite Paulsen book.

Brian eats raw, slimy turtle eggs.

You can use either of these methods to decide if you need to use a comma.

1. **Insert the word *and* between the adjectives in the series.** If *and* fits logically between the adjectives, use a comma between them. (In the first example above, *favorite and Paulsen book* doesn't make sense. In the second, *and* seems logical between *raw* and *slimy* but not between *slimy* and *turtle.*)

2. **Change the order of the adjectives.** If the phrase still makes sense when the order of the adjectives is reversed, use a comma between them. (*Slimy, raw turtle* eggs makes sense, but *turtle slimy* eggs and *Paulsen favorite book* don't).

Try It Out

Copy the following paragraph, adding commas where needed.

Hatchet is a popular adventure novel by Gary Paulsen. Its hero is a thirteen-year-old city boy who survives a terrifying disastrous plane crash. He learns to fend for himself in the harsh unforgiving Canadian wilderness.

By permission of Johnny Hart and Creators Syndicate, Inc.

VOCABULARY   HOW TO OWN A WORD

WORD BANK

mystified
alleviate
contention
exaltation
chagrin

All About Dogs

1. Name one thing that mystifies you about animals.
2. Name two things that might cause contention between a person and a dog.
3. How would you try to alleviate someone's fear of dogs?
4. How would a dog show chagrin? How would a dog show exaltation?

Elements of Literature

POINT OF VIEW: Who Tells the Story?

Who's Talking?

You've probably noticed, in your life as well as in books, that *who* is telling a story has a lot to do with *what* gets told.

> **Point of View**
>
> Thanksgiving dinner's sad
>   and thankless
> Christmas dinner's dark
>   and blue
> When you stop and try to
>   see it
> From the turkey's point of
>   view.
>
> Sunday dinner isn't sunny
> Easter feasts are just bad
>   luck
> When you see it from the
>   viewpoint
> Of a chicken or a duck.
>
> Oh how I once loved tuna
>   salad
> Pork and lobsters, lamb
>   chops too
> Till I stopped and looked
>   at dinner
> From the dinner's point
>   of view.
>
> —Shel Silverstein

The standpoint from which a story is told is called **point of view.** There are three points of view you're likely to come across in your reading and use in your writing: **omniscient** (äm·nish′ənt), **first person,** and **third-person limited.**

The Know-It-All

In a story told from the **omniscient** point of view, the narrator is outside the story and knows everything that happens and everything that goes on in the minds of all the characters:

As the musher lay trying to recover, he realized how much trouble he was in. "The dogs could be miles away by now," he thought, wincing.

Above the gully, Obeah growled and pulled the team around. He knew they had to get back to their musher—but how?

The omniscient narrator can describe the thoughts and feelings of different characters in the story. This narrator may also reveal information unknown to some or all of the characters—including what is happening in several places at the same time. This point of view reminds the reader of an important truth: that there is more than one side to every story.

Me, Me, Me, Me, Me

The **first-person** point of view is the "I" point of view. Writers normally use the first person when they tell stories about their own lives. If you've ever written a letter or kept a diary, you've almost certainly written in the first person.

Like nearly all autobiographies, Gary Paulsen's *Woodsong* is told from the first-person point of view of the writer:

"Shock and pain came in waves and I had to close my eyes several times. All of this was in minutes that seemed like hours, and I realized that I was in serious trouble." (pages 281–282)

In fiction narrated from the first-person point of view, the "I" who speaks is not the writer but a character in the

by John Leggett

story. That character is usually the main character, but not always. If Paulsen rewrote *Woodsong* as a novel, he might choose to tell it from the first-person point of view of his lead dog:

I was having the time of my life tearing down that new trail at the head of the team. All of a sudden I noticed how light the sled felt. I looked around, and there was our musher lying on the ice down in the gully.

He Said, She Said

In the **third-person limited** point of view, the story is also told from a single character's standpoint—but here the character is referred to in the third person, as *he* or *she*:

Shock and pain came in waves and Paulsen had to close his eyes several times. All of this was in minutes that seemed like hours, and he realized that he was in serious trouble.

This point of view is popular with fiction writers because it allows them to give the reader information that the character would be unlikely to provide—such as a description of his or her own appearance. ("I have beautiful, shiny black hair and big brown eyes with long lashes" sounds a little strange unless the character is supposed to be conceited.)

When you read a story told from the first-person or the third-person limited point of view, you share the thoughts and feelings of a single character and know only what he or she knows. Most writers of fiction published today tell their stories from the point of view of one character to help make the stories realistic. After all, we each go through life seeing things from only one person's point of view—our own.

A Writer on Point of View

"I sold my first story when I was eighteen, to a science fiction magazine, and I just kept on writing and publishing science fiction. I didn't realize until later that when I was writing these first-person narratives of aliens, I was really writing about myself."

— Laurence Yep, author of "We Are All One" (page 265)

IN OR OUT (DEPENDING ON YOUR POINT OF VIEW)

THAVES 9-6

FRANK & ERNEST reprinted by permission of Newspaper Enterprise Association, Inc.

Make the Connection

Lend a Helping Hand?

"Next time you see a bug on a sidewalk, help it out. Gently pick it up and move it out of the way, where no one will step on it. You've just saved a life!"

—The EarthWorks Group
50 Simple Things Kids Can Do to Save the Earth

Quickwrite

What do you think of the suggestion made above? Does it seem sensible? ridiculous? nice but impractical? Explain your opinion in a notebook or on a separate piece of paper.

Elements of Literature

Alliteration

Alliteration, like rhyme, can create musical effects in a poem. As you read "Birdfoot's Grampa" aloud, listen for the repeated *m, l, g, s,* and *t* sounds.

Alliteration is the repetition of consonant sounds in words that are close together.

For more on Alliteration, see the Handbook of Literary Terms.

go.hrw.com
LEO 8-4

Birdfoot's Grampa

Joseph Bruchac

The old man
must have stopped our car
two dozen times to climb out
and gather into his hands
5   the small toads blinded
by our lights and leaping,
live drops of rain.

The rain was falling,
a mist about his white hair
10   and I kept saying
you can't save them all
accept it, get back in
we've got places to go.

Zuni jar.

But, leathery hands full
15   of wet brown life,
      knee deep in the summer
      roadside grass,
      he just smiled and said
      they have places to go to
20   *too.*

Bowl by Elfa Boone, Zuni
Pueblo, New Mexico.

MEET THE WRITER

"One Lesson I Was Taught"

Joseph Bruchac (1942–   ) was
born in Saratoga Springs, New York,
and was raised there by his grandfather, a member of the Abenaki
people. Bruchac studied wildlife
conservation in college. Today he is
a well-known editor, publisher,
poet, and collector of folk tales.

Bruchac says that this poem

66 describes one lesson I was
taught in the way most good lessons
come to you—when you least expect them. **99**

Ode to a Toad

I was out one day for my usual jog
(I go kinda easy, rarely full-hog)
When I happened to see right there on the road
The squishy remains of a little green toad.

5   I thought to myself, where is his home?
Down yonder green valley, how far did he roam?
From out on the pond I heard sorrowful croaks,
Could that be the wailing of some of his folks?

I felt for the toad and his pitiful state,
10   But the day was now fading, and such was his fate.
In the grand scheme of things, now I confess,
What's one little froggie more or less?

        —Anne-Marie Wulfsberg
         Concord-Carlisle High School
         Concord, Massachusetts

First appeared in *Merlyn's Pen:
The National Magazines of Student Writing.*

MAKING MEANINGS

First Thoughts

1. Go back to your Quickwrite. How would Birdfoot's Grampa respond to the same question? How do you know?

Shaping Interpretations

2. What does Birdfoot's Grampa refuse to accept? What do you think of his attitude?

3. Whom does Bruchac seem to agree with: the speaker or Birdfoot's Grampa? How do you know?

4. Read the poem aloud. What uses of **alliteration** can you find in the poem? Which sounds in the poem do you like best?

Extending the Text

5. How is the jogger in Anne-Marie Wulfsberg's "Ode to a Toad" (see page 292) different from Birdfoot's Grampa? Whose attitude is closer to your own?

6. Many people, like Birdfoot's Grampa, believe that their actions can make a difference, even if they can't save everyone. Think of someone you know (or someone you know of) who has acted on this belief. What actions has this person taken?

CHOICES: Building Your Portfolio

Writer's Notebook

1. Collecting Ideas for a How-To Essay

The actions of Birdfoot's Grampa make a difference to the toads—and perhaps also to the speaker of the poem. If you were writing a how-to manual entitled "How to Make a Difference," what steps might you include? Freewrite your ideas.

WORK IN PROGRESS

Creative Writing

2. Places to Go

Write a short rhymed or unrhymed poem describing the incident in the road from the toads' **point of view**. Be sure to include the toads' feelings toward Birdfoot's Grampa. You might begin, "We were on our way to. . . ."

Role-Play

3. Gentle Persuasion

With a partner, role-play either a continuation of the conversation between the speaker of the poem and Birdfoot's Grampa or a discussion between Birdfoot's Grampa and the speaker of "Ode to a Toad."

Pipe from the Hopewell culture, which flourished from 300 B.C. to A.D. 500 in what is now southern Ohio.

VOCABULARY: USING CONTEXT CLUES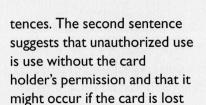

The **context** of a word—the words and sentences surrounding it—can help you figure out its meaning. Suppose someone in your family has just received a new credit card from a bank and asks you for help in reading the bank's terms of agreement. As you read, you come across an unfamiliar word, *unauthorized*.

> **UNAUTHORIZED USE.**
> You may be liable for unauthorized use of your credit card. If your card is lost or stolen, or if you think that someone is using your card without your permission, notify us immediately by telephone or in writing.

- From the context you know that the word must relate to credit cards.

- The fact that *unauthorized* comes before *use* tells you that it describes a kind of use of the card.

- You may find clues in the surrounding words and sentences. The second sentence suggests that unauthorized use is use without the card holder's permission and that it might occur if the card is lost or stolen.

Using context clues involves three things:

1. **Looking carefully at what is on the page.** Occasionally the **definition** of a term actually appears in a sentence: "I began to train them for the <u>Iditarod, a dog-sled race across Alaska</u>" ("The Dogs Could Teach Me," page 279). Other times the context provides clues that suggest the term's meaning by **comparing** or **contrasting** the term with other words. The information that context clues provide may be incomplete, but it's often enough to let you make an educated guess about the meaning of a word and go on with your reading.

2. **Using what you already know.**   The more you know about a topic, the more useful context is. Suppose you know a lot about electronics and nothing about cooking. You'll have an easier time using context to figure out an unknown word in a VCR manual than in a cookbook.

3. **Making the connection.** You can make the most of what's on the page and what you already know by asking yourself these questions:

   - Look at the word's placement in the sentence. What kind of word would fit: a noun? a verb? a modifier?

   - Do the surrounding words and sentences give clues to what the unknown word means?

   - Can I use my knowledge of **word structure** (word roots, prefixes, and suffixes) to figure out what the word might mean? In the case of *unauthorized,* for example, you should recognize *un–,* meaning "not."

Apply the strategy on the next page.

Before You Read

LET ME HEAR YOU WHISPER

Make the Connection

What Do You Know?

One of the main characters in the **teleplay** (play written for television) you are about to read is a dolphin. Dolphins are very intelligent; many scientists believe that they are smarter than chimpanzees, which are considered among the most intelligent animals.

What do you know about dolphins? With your classmates, recall as many facts as you can from your own experience and from reading, TV, and other sources.

Quickwrite

Suppose you woke up one day and discovered that you could speak the language of dolphins (or other animals). What would you do with your new ability?

Reading Skills and Strategies

Vocabulary: Using Context Clues

If you come across an unfamiliar word as you read *Let Me Hear You Whisper,* try using **context clues** (see the strategies discussed on page 294) to figure out what the word means. Then, check your guess against the word's definition at the bottom of the page, in the glossary, or in a dictionary. You can also use context to figure out which meaning of a word with **multiple meanings** is the best choice.

go.hrw.com
LEO 8-4

PAIN. PLEASURE.

ANGER. FEAR.

LET ME

JUST 'CAUSE IT DOESN'T TALK,

HEAR YOU

THEY'VE GOT TO KILL IT?

WHISPER

Paul Zindel

Characters

Helen, a cleaning woman
Miss Moray, her briskly efficient supervisor
Dr. Crocus, a dedicated lady of science
Mrs. Fridge, her assistant
Danielle, a talky porter[1]
A Dolphin, the subject of an experiment

Setting: The play is set in the laboratory of a building near the Hudson River in lower Manhattan—the home of the American Biological Association Development for the Advancement of Brain Analysis.

1. **porter:** person employed to perform such tasks as sweeping, cleaning, and running errands.

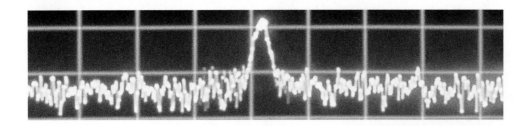

Scene 1

 Curtain rises on DR. CROCUS *and* MRS. FRIDGE, *conducting an experiment on the* DOLPHIN *in the laboratory. The* DOLPHIN *is in a long, narrow tank, with little room to move. A head sling lifting his blowhole[2] out of the water and several electrodes[3] implanted in his brain further the impression of a trapped and sad animal.* DR. CROCUS *is observing closely as* MRS. FRIDGE *presses various buttons on cue. An oscilloscope[4] is bleeping in the background.*

Dr. Crocus. Pain. (MRS. FRIDGE *presses a button. No response from the* DOLPHIN) Pleasure. (*Another button*) Anger. (*Another*) Fear.

[*There has been no satisfactory response from the* DOLPHIN, *but an automatic recorder starts to play a charming melody. When the accompanying vocal commences, however, it is an eerily precise enunciation of the words.*]

Record.
    Let me call you sweetheart,
    I'm in love with you.
    Let me hear you whisper,
    That you love me, too.

[*Disappointed at the lack of response,* DR. CROCUS *crosses toward* MRS. FRIDGE.]

---

2. **blowhole:** breathing hole in the top of the head.
3. **electrodes:** connecting devices through which electric current flows.
4. **oscilloscope** (ə·sil′ə·skōp′): screen displaying an electrical wave.

Dr. Crocus. Resistance to electrodic impulses. Possibly destroyed tissue. Continue impulse and auditory suggestion at intervals of seven minutes until end of week. If no response by Friday, termination.

[*The* DOLPHIN's *special discomfort at this word is unnoticed by others.* DR. CROCUS *and* MRS. FRIDGE *head toward elevator on other side of the stage. The elevator doors open and* MISS MORAY *emerges with* HELEN.]

Miss Moray. Dr. Crocus. Mrs. Fridge. I'm so glad we've run into you. I want you to meet Helen.
Helen. Hello.

[DR. CROCUS *and* MRS. FRIDGE *nod and get on elevator.*]

Miss Moray. Helen is the newest member of our Custodial Engineering Team. So if you two "coaches" have any suggestions, we'll be most grateful. We want everything to be perfect, don't we, Helen?
Helen. I do the best I can.
Miss Moray. Exactly. The doctor is one of the most remarkable . . . (*The elevator doors close and* MRS. FRIDGE *and* DR. CROCUS *are gone.*) Remarkable.
Helen. She looked remarkable.

[HELEN *looks like a peasant, kerchief and all. As they walk,* HELEN *begins to remove the ker-*

WORDS TO OWN

termination (tʉr′mə·nā′shən) *n.:* ending (here, of the experiment and perhaps of the dolphin's life).

WE WANT EVERYTHING TO BE PERFECT . . .

chief and she would like to fold it properly, for that to be her only activity, but she is distracted by a shopping bag she carries, a bulky coat, and the voice of MISS MORAY.]

Miss Moray. Dr. Crocus is the guiding heart here at the American Biological Association Development for the Advancement of Brain Analysis. We call it ABADABA, for short.
Helen. I guess you have to.

[They stop at a metal locker.]

Miss Moray. This will be your locker and your key. Mrs. Fridge has been with ABADABA only three months and already she's a much endeared part of our little family. Your equipment is in this closet. (*She opens a closet next to the locker.*)
Helen. I have to bring my own hangers, I suppose. . . .

Miss Moray. Although it was somewhat embarrassing to me, it was Mrs. Fridge's inventorial excellence that uncovered what Margaurita—your predecessor—did and why she had to leave us. She'd been drinking portions of the ethyl alcohol—there's a basin under the sink for rag rinsing—the denatured ethyl alcohol,[5] and she almost burned out her esophagus. (*Pause*) I wouldn't have minded so much if she had only asked. Didn't you find Personnel pleasant?

Helen. They asked a lot of crazy questions.

Miss Moray. For instance.

Helen. They wanted to know how I felt watching TV.

Miss Moray. What do you mean, *how you felt*?

Helen. They wanted to know what went on in my head when I'm watching television in my living room and the audience laughs. They asked if I ever thought the audience was laughing at *me*.

Miss Moray (*laughing*). My, oh my! What did you tell them?

Helen. I don't have a TV.

WHAT'S BEHIND THERE?

Miss Moray. I'm sorry.

Helen. I'm not.

Miss Moray. Yes. Now, it's really quite simple. That's our special soap solution. One tablespoon to a gallon of hot water for ordinary cleaning, if I may suggest. I so much prefer to act as an assist to the Custodial Engineering Staff. New ideas. Techniques. I try to keep myself open.

[*Her mouth pauses wide open.* HELEN *has been busy familiarizing herself with the con-*

---

5. **denatured** (dē·nā′chərd) **ethyl alcohol:** alcohol containing added substances that make it unfit to drink.

tents of the closet. She has culminated a series of small actions which have put things in order for her by running water into a pail which fits into a metal stand on wheels.]

Helen. She left a dirty mop.

Miss Moray. I beg your pardon?

Helen. The one that drank. She left a dirty mop.

Miss Moray. How ugly. I'll report it first thing in the morning. It may seem like a small point but if she ever tries to use us as a reference, she may be amazed at the specificity of our files.

Helen. It's not that dirty.

Miss Moray. I'll start you in the main laboratory area. We like it done first. The specimen section next. By that time we'll be well toward morning and if there are a few minutes left you can polish the brass strip. (*She points to brass strip which runs around halfway between ceiling and floor.*) Margaurita never once got to the brass strip. (HELEN *has completed her very professional preparations and looks impatient to get moving.*) Ready? Fine. (*They start moving toward the* DOLPHIN *area,* MISS MORAY *thumbing through papers on a clipboard.*) You were with one concern for fourteen years, weren't you? Fourteen years with the Metal Climax Building. That's next to the Radio City Music Hall, isn't it, dear?

Helen. Uh huh . . .

Miss Moray. They sent a marvelous letter of recommendation—how you washed the corridor on the seventeenth floor . . . and the Metal Climax Building is a very long building. My! Fourteen years on the seventeenth floor. You must be very proud. Why did you leave?

Helen. They put in a rug.

[MISS MORAY *leads* HELEN *into the laboratory area as* DANIELLE *enters.*]

Miss Moray. Danielle, Helen will be taking Margaurita's place. Danielle is the night porter for the fifth through ninth floors. Duties you might find distasteful.

Danielle. Hiya!

Helen. Hello. (HELEN *looks over the place.*)

Miss Moray. By the way, Danielle . . . there's a crock on nine you missed and the technicians on that floor have complained about the odor. . . . (*Back to* HELEN) You can be certain we'll assist in every way possible.

Helen. Maybe you could get me some hangers . . . ?

Danielle. I'll be glad to do anything. Just say the word and . . .

Helen. What's behind there? (*Opening the* DOLPHIN *area*)

Miss Moray. What? Oh, that's a dolphin, dear. But don't you worry about anything except the floor. Dr. Crocus prefers us not to touch either the equipment or the animals. That was another shortcoming of Margaurita's. Recently the doctor was . . . experimenting . . . with a colony of mice in that cage . . . (*She indicates cage.*) . . . and she was <u>incessantly</u> feeding them popcorn.

Danielle. Kinda a nice lady, though. Lived in the East Village.

Miss Moray. Yes, she did live in the East Village.

Helen (*attention still on the* DOLPHIN). Do you keep him cramped up in that all the time?

Miss Moray. We have a natatorium[6] for it to exercise in at Dr. Crocus's discretion.

Helen. He really looks cramped.

Miss Moray (*closing the* DOLPHIN *area*). Well, you must be anxious to begin. I'll make myself available at the reception desk in the hall for a few nights in case any questions arise. Although my hunch is that before you know it, I'll be coming to *you* with questions. . . . Coffee break at 2 and 6 A.M. Lunch at 4 A.M. All clear?

6. **natatorium** (nāt′ə·tôr′ē·əm): indoor swimming pool.

Helen. I don't need a coffee break.

Miss Moray. I beg your pardon?

Helen. I said I don't need a coffee break.

Miss Moray. Helen, we all need Perk-You-Ups. All of us. Perhaps you never liked them at the Metal Climax Building, but you'll learn to love them here. Perk-You-Ups make the employees much more efficient. Besides, Helen——

Helen. I don't want one.

Miss Moray. They're <u>compulsory</u>. Oh, Helen, I know you're going to fit right in with our little family. You're such a *nice* person.

[*She exits.* HELEN *immediately gets to work, moving her equipment into place and getting down on her hands and knees to scrub the floor.* DANIELLE *spots a ceiling bulb out and prepares to remove it by using a long stick with a grip on the end of it, designed to unscrew bulbs one cannot reach.*]

Danielle. Margaurita wasn't half as bad as Miss Moray thought she was.

Helen. I'm sure she wasn't.

Danielle. She was twice as bad. (*She laughs. Pause*) You live in the city? . . .

Helen. Yes.

Danielle. That's nice. . . . My husband died two years ago.

Helen. That's too bad.

Danielle. Yeah, two years in June. He blew up.

Helen. Oh, I'm sorry.

Danielle. When you want that water changed, just lemme know. I'll take care of it.

Helen. Thanks, but I just like to get the tem-

WORDS TO OWN

incessantly (in·ses′ənt·lē) *adv.*: constantly; continually.
compulsory (kəm·pul′sə·rē) *adj.*: required.

perature right so my hands don't get boiled. You must miss your husband.

Danielle. Biggest mistake I ever made, getting married. . . . You married?

Helen. No.

Danielle. Good, if a woman ain't suited for it, she shouldn't do it.

Helen. I didn't say I wasn't suited for it.

Danielle. My husband was set in his ways, too. . . .

Helen. If you'll excuse me, I have to get my work done.

Danielle. Guess I'd better see about that crock on nine. You don't like to talk, do you?

Helen. I'm used to working alone and that's the way I get my work done. (DANIELLE *exits. Not realizing she's already gone*) What do you mean, your husband blew up?

[*But* DANIELLE *is gone. She glances at the curtain shielding the* DOLPHIN, *then continues scrubbing. After a beat, the record begins to play.*]

Record.
> Let me call you sweetheart,
> I'm in love with you.
> Let me hear you whisper,
> That you love me, too.

[HELEN *eyes the automatic machinery with suspicion but goes on working. When the song is finished, she looks at the curtain again and again until her curiosity makes her pull the curtain open and look at the* DOLPHIN. *He is looking right back at her. She becomes uncomfortable and starts to close the curtain again. She decides to leave it partway open so that she can still see the* DOLPHIN *while she scrubs. She glances out of the corner of her eye after a few moments of scrubbing and notices that the* DOLPHIN *is looking at her. She pretends to look away and sings "Let Me Call You Sweetheart" to herself—missing a word or two here and there—but her eyes*

return to the DOLPHIN. *She becomes uncomfortable again under his stare and crawls on her hands and knees to the other side of the room; she scrubs there for a moment or two and then shoots a look at the* DOLPHIN. *He is still looking at her. She tries to ease her discomfort by playing peekaboo with the* DOLPHIN *for a moment. There is no response and she resumes scrubbing and humming. The* DOLPHIN *then lets out a bubble or two and moves in the tank to bring his blowhole to the surface. Any sounds he does make, including words, are like a haunting whisper and never enunciated so that they are absolute.*]

Dolphin. Youuuuuuuuuuuu. (HELEN *hears the sound, assumes she is mistaken, and goes on with her work.*) Youuuuuuuuuuuu.

[HELEN *has heard the sound more clearly this time. She is puzzled, contemplates a moment, and then decides to get up off the floor. She closes the curtain on the* DOLPHIN*'s tank and is quite disturbed. The elevator door suddenly opens and* MISS MORAY *enters.*]

Miss Moray. What is it, Helen?

Helen. The fish is making some kinda funny noise.

Miss Moray. Mammal, Helen. It's a mammal.

Helen. The mammal's making some kinda funny noise.

Miss Moray. Mammals are supposed to make funny noises.

Helen. Yes, Miss Moray.

[HELEN *hangs awkwardly a moment and then continues scrubbing.* MISS MORAY *exits* <u>officiously</u> *to another part of the floor. A moment later, from behind the curtain, the* DOLPHIN *is heard.*]

WORDS TO OWN

officiously (ə·fish′əs·lē) *adv.*: in a bossy and interfering way.

Dolphin. Youuuuuuuuuuuuuu. (HELEN *is quite worried.*) Youuuuuuuuuuuuuu.

[*She* <u>apprehensively</u> *approaches the curtain and opens it, when* DANIELLE *barges in. She goes to get her reaching pole and* HELEN *hurriedly returns to scrubbing the floor.*]

Danielle. Bulb out on ten.

Helen. What do they have that thing for?

Danielle. What thing?

Helen. That.

Danielle. Yeah, he's something, ain't he? They're tryin' to get it to talk.

Helen. Talk?

Danielle. Uh-huh, but this one don't. They had one last year that used to laugh. It'd go heh heh heh heh heh heh heh heh. I'd be in here doing something and it'd start heh heh heh heh heh hehing. He died a year ago May. Then they got another one that used to say "Yeah, it's four o'clock." Everybody took pictures of that one. All the magazines.

Helen. What'd it say "four o'clock" for?

Danielle. Nobody knows.

Helen. It just kept saying, "Yeah, it's four o'clock!"

Danielle. Until it died of pneumonia. (*Pause*) They talk outta their blowholes, when they can talk, that is. Did you see the blowhole?

Helen. No.

Danielle. Come on and take a look. Look at it.

Helen. I don't want to look at any blowhole.

Danielle. You can see it right there. (HELEN *gets up and goes to the tank. As she and* DANIELLE *stand at the tank, their backs are to one of the entrances, and they don't see* MISS MORAY *open the door and watch them.*) This one don't say anything at all. It bleeps, beeps, barks, and blats out of the mouth, but it don't talk out of the blowhole. They been playing that record every seven minutes for months and it can't learn beans.

Miss Moray. Helen? (HELEN *and* DANIELLE *turn around.*) Helen, would you mind stepping over here a moment?

Helen. Yes, Miss Moray.

Danielle. I was just showing her something.

Miss Moray. Have you attended to the crock on nine?

Danielle. Yes, ma'am.

Miss Moray. Then hadn't we better get on with our duties? (MISS MORAY *guides* HELEN *aside, putting her arm around her as though taking her into great confidence. She even whispers.*) Helen, I have to talk to you. Frankly, I need your help.

Helen. She was just showing me . . .

Miss Moray. It's something about Danielle I need your assistance with. I'm sure you've noticed that she . . .

Helen. Yes?

Miss Moray. Well, that she's the type of person who will do anything to breed idle chatter. Yes, an idle chatter breeder. How many times we've told her, "Danielle, this is a scientific atmosphere you're employed in and from Dr. Crocus all the way down to the most insignifi-

THIS IS A SCIENTIFIC ATMOSPHERE YOU'RE EMPLOYED IN . . .

WORDS TO OWN

apprehensively (ap′rē·hen′siv·lē) *adv.:* uneasily; fearfully.

---

cant member of the Custodial Engineering Staff we would appreciate a minimum of subjective intercourse." So—if you can help, Helen—and I'm sure you can, enormously—we'd be so grateful. This is science—and science means progress. You do want progress, don't you, dear?

Helen. Yes, Miss Moray.

Miss Moray. I knew you did.

Danielle. I just wanted to show her the blow-hole.

Miss Moray. I'm sure that's all it was, Danielle. (DANIELLE *exits.*) Helen, why don't you dust for a while? Vary your labors. (*She swings open a shelf area to reveal rather hideously pre-served specimens.* HELEN *looks ready to gag as she sees the jars of all sizes. Various animals and parts of animals are visible in their formaldehyde[7] baths.*) A feather duster—here—is marvelous for dusting, though a damp rag may be necessary for the glass surfaces. But whatever—do be careful. Margaurita once dropped a jar of assorted North Atlantic eels.

[MISS MORAY *smiles and exits in the elevator, leaving* HELEN *alone. She is most uncomfortable in the environment. The sound of music and voice from beyond the walls falls over.*]

7. **formaldehyde** (fôr·mal′də·hīd′): liquid used to kill germs and preserve laboratory specimens.

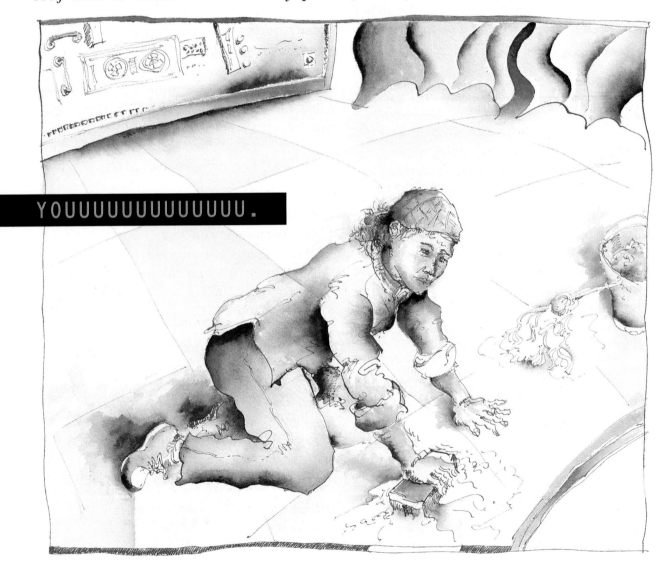

YOUUUUUUUUUUUUUU.

Record.

> Let me call you sweetheart,
> I'm in love with you.
> Let me hear you whisper,
> That you love me, too.

Scene 2

 It is the next evening.

HELEN gets off the elevator carrying a few hangers and still wearing her kerchief and coat. She looks around for anyone, realizes she is alone, and then proceeds to her locker. She takes her coat off and hangs it up. HELEN *pushes her equipment into the lab. The curtain on the* DOLPHIN*'s tank has been closed. She sets her items up, then goes to the tank and pulls the curtain open a moment. The* DOLPHIN *is looking at her. She closes the curtain and starts scrubbing. The thought of the* DOLPHIN *amuses her a moment, relieving the tension she feels about the mammal, and she appears to be in good spirits as she starts humming "Let Me Call You Sweetheart" and scrubs in rhythm to it. She sets a one-two-three beat for the scrub brush.*

This mood passes quickly and she opens the curtain so that she can watch the DOLPHIN *as she works. She and the* DOLPHIN *stare at each other and* HELEN *appears to be more curious than worried.*

Finally, she decides to try to imitate the sound she heard it make the night before:

Helen. Youuuuuuuuuuuuuu. (*She pauses, watches for a response.*) Youuuuuuuuuuuuuu. (*Still no response. She returns her attention to her scrubbing for a moment. Then*)

> Polly want a cracker?
> Polly want a cracker?

(*She wrings out a rag and resumes work.*) Yeah, it's four o'clock. Yeah, it's four o'clock.

(*When her expectation is unfulfilled, she is slightly disappointed. Then*) Polly want a cracker at four o'clock? (*She laughs at her own joke, then is reminded of the past success with laughter in working with dolphins. She can't resist trying it, so she goes to the* DOLPHIN*'s tank and notices how sad he looks. She is diverted from her initial intention by a guilty feeling of leaving the scrubbing. She bends down and looks directly into the* DOLPHIN*'s face. He lets out a bubble at her. She sticks her tongue out at him. She makes an exaggerated smile and is very curious about what his skin feels like. She reaches her hand in and just touches the top of his head. He squirms and likes it, but she's interested in drying off her finger. She even washes it in her soap solution. She returns to scrubbing for a minute, then can't resist more fully petting the* DOLPHIN. *This time he reacts even more enthusiastically. She is half afraid and half happy. She returns to scrubbing. Then, at the tank*) Heh heh heh heh heh heh heh heh heh. (*Beat*) Heh heh heh heh. (*Beat*) Heh heh heh heh heh heh . . .

[MISS MORAY *enters. She sees what's going on. Then says, with exaggerated praise*]

Miss Moray. Look how nicely the floor's coming along tonight! There's not a streak! Not a streak! You must have a special rinsing technique, Helen. You do, don't you? Why, you certainly do. I can smell something.

Helen. Just a little . . . vinegar in the rinse water.

Miss Moray. You brought that vinegar yourself just so the floors . . . they are sparkling, Helen. Sparkling! (*Jotting down in a pad*) This is going in your file, dear—and from now on, I'm going to requisition vinegar as a staple in the Custodial Engineering Department's supply list. (*She pauses—looks at the* DOLPHIN— *then at* HELEN.) It's marvelous, Helen, how well you've adjusted. . . .

Helen. Thank you, Miss Moray.

Miss Moray. Not everyone does, you know. Just last week I had a problem with a porter on five, who became too fond of a St. Bernard they . . . worked on . . . and . . . (*pause*) well, Helen, a lot of people can't seem——

Helen (*still scrubbing*). What do you mean, *worked on*?

Miss Moray. Well . . . well, even Margaurita. She had fallen in love with the mice. All three hundred of them. She seemed shocked when she found out Dr. Crocus was . . . using . . . them at the rate of twenty or so a day in connection with electrode implanting. She noticed them missing after a while and when I told her they'd been decapitated,[8] she seemed terribly upset. It made one wonder if she'd thought we'd been sending them away on vacations or something. But I'm sure you understand—you have such insight. (*She is at the tank.*) It's funny, isn't it? To look at these mammals, you'd never suspect they were such rapacious carnivori . . .[9]

Helen. What do they want with it?

[*The* Let Me Call You Sweetheart *record commences playing but* MISS MORAY *talks over it.*]

Miss Moray. Well, they may have an intelligence equal to our own. And if we can teach them our language—or learn theirs—we'll be able to communicate. (*Raising her voice higher over record*) Wouldn't that be wonderful, Helen? To be able to communicate?

Helen. I can't understand you.

Miss Moray (*louder*). Communicate! Wouldn't it be wonderful?

Helen. Oh, yeah.

Miss Moray (*with a cutting device*). When Margaurita found out they were using this . . . on the mice, she almost fainted. No end of trouble.

Helen. They chopped the heads off three hundred mice?

Miss Moray. Now, Helen, you wanted progress, remember?

Helen. That's horrible.

Miss Moray. Helen, over a thousand individual laboratories did the same study last year.

Helen. A thousand labs chopping off three hundred mice heads. Three hundred thousand mice heads chopped off? That's a lot of mouse heads. Couldn't one lab cut off a couple and then spread the word?

Miss Moray. Now, Helen, this is exactly what I mean. You will do best not to become fond of the subject animals. When you're here a little longer, you'll learn—well, there are some things in this world you have to accept on faith.

[*She exits. After a moment, the* DOLPHIN *starts in again.*]

Dolphin. Whisper . . .

Helen. What?

Dolphin. Whisper to me. . . .

[DANIELLE *barges in, pushing a hamper.*]

Danielle. Hi, Helen.

Helen. Hello.

Danielle (*emptying wastes into hamper*). Miss Moray said she's got almond horns for our Perk-You-Up tonight.

Helen. That thing never said anything to anybody?

Danielle. What thing?

Helen. That mammal fish.

Danielle. Nope.

Helen. Not one word?

Danielle. Nope.

Helen. Nothing that sounded like "Youuuuuuuuuuuuu."

Danielle. What?

Helen. "Youuuuuuuuuuuuuu?" Or "Whisper?"

Danielle. I don't know what you're talking about. I got here an hour too early so I sat

---

8. **decapitated** (dē·kap′ə·tāt′id): beheaded.
9. **carnivori** (kär·niv′ə·rī′): meat eaters.

down by the docks. You can see the moon in the river.

[*The record goes on again, and* DANIELLE *exits without the hamper.*]

Record.
>Let me call you sweetheart,
>I'm in love with you,
>Let me hear you whisper,
>That you love me, too.

[HELEN *opens the curtain to see the* DOLPHIN. *He is staring at her. It is as though the* DOLPHIN *is trying to tell her something, and she can almost suspect this from the intensity of his stare. She goes to her locker, unwraps a sandwich she brought, and takes a slice of ham from it. She approaches the tank and offers the ham. The* DOLPHIN *moves and startles her, but the ham falls to the bottom of the tank.*]

Dolphin. Hear . . .
Helen. Huh?
Dolphin. Hear me . . .

[DANIELLE *bursts back in, carrying a crock, and* HELEN *darts to her scrubbing.*]

Danielle. Ugh. This—gotta rinse this one out. Full of little gooey things.
Helen. What do they eat?
Danielle. What?
Helen. What do dolphins eat?
Danielle. Fish.
Helen. What kind of fish?
Danielle. These. (*She opens a freezer chest packed with fish.*) Fly 'em up from Florida. (DANIELLE *is at the* DOLPHIN*'s tank.*) Hiya, fella!

How are ya? That reminds me. Gotta get some formaldehyde jars set up by Friday.

[*She exits with hamper.* HELEN *returns to the* DOLPHIN, *apprehensive about leaving the piece of ham at the bottom of the tank. She begins to reach her hand into the tank.*]

Helen. You wouldn't bite Helen, would you? Helen's got to get that ham out of there. I wouldn't hurt you. You know that. Helen knows you talk. You do talk to Helen, don't you? Hear . . . hear me . . .
Dolphin. Hear . . .
Helen. That's a good boy. That's a goodie goodie boy.
Dolphin. Hear me . . .
Helen. Oh, what a pretty boy. Such a pretty boy.

[*At this point, the elevator doors zip open and* MISS MORAY *enters.*]

WHEN YOU'RE HERE A LITTLE LONGER, YOU'LL LEARN . . .

Miss Moray. What are you doing, Helen?

[HELEN *looks ready to cry.*]

Helen. I . . . uh . . .
Miss Moray. Never mind. Go on with your work. (MISS MORAY *surveys everything, and then sits on a stool and calms herself. As* HELEN *scrubs*) You know, Helen, you're such a sympathetic person. You have pets, I imagine? Cats? Lots of cats?
Helen. They don't allow them in my building.
Miss Moray. Then plants. I'm sure you have hundreds of lovely green things crawling up the windows?
Helen. If there were green things crawling up my windows, I'd move out.

Miss Moray. No plants, either?

Helen. Two gloxinias.

Miss Moray. Gloxinias! Oh, such trumpets! Such trumpets!

Helen. They never bloom. My apartment's too cold.

Miss Moray. Oh, that is a shame. (*Pause*) You live alone, don't you, Helen?

Helen (*almost hurt*). Yes. I live alone.

Miss Moray. But you have friends, of course. Other . . . custodial colleagues, perhaps . . . clubs you belong to . . . social clubs . . . activities?

Helen (*continuing to scrub*). I'm used to . . . being alone.

Miss Moray. Nothing . . . ?

Helen. I took a ceramic course . . . once.

Miss Moray. Isn't that nice. A ceramic course . . . (*Pause*) Oh, Helen, you're such a nice person. So nice. (*Pause*) It does seem unjust that so much more than that is required. You must feel overwhelmed by this environment here . . . of oscilloscopes and sonar and salinity meters. To have so many personal delicacies and then be forced to behold the complexity of an electronic and chemical world must be devastating. Nevertheless, I can't——

[DANIELLE *rushes in with several large jars on a wheeled table.*]

Danielle. 'Cuse me, but I figure I'll get the formaldehyde set up tonight so I'll only have to worry about the dissection stuff tomorrow.

Miss Moray. Very good, Danielle.

Danielle. I'm gonna need a twenty-liter one for the lungs and there ain't any on this floor.

Helen (*noticing that the* DOLPHIN *is stirring*). What's the formaldehyde for?

Miss Moray. That's what I'm trying to tell you, Helen . . . to make it easier on you. The experiment series on . . . the dolphin will . . . terminate . . . on Friday. Dr. Crocus left the orders with us tonight. That's why it has concerned me that you've apparently grown . . . fond . . . of the mammal.

Helen. They're gonna kill it?

Danielle. Gonna sharpen the handsaws now. Won't have any trouble getting through the skull on this one, no sir. Everything's gonna be perfect. (*She exits.*)

Helen. What for? Because it didn't say anything? Is that what they're killing it for?

Miss Moray (*so sweetly*). Of course, you wanted to be kind. You didn't know what harm you might have caused . . . what delicate rhythm you may have disturbed in the experiment. Helen, no matter how lovely our intentions, no matter how lonely we are and how much we want people or animals . . . to like us . . . we have no right to endanger the genius about us. Now, we've spoken about this before. And this time, we're going to remember, aren't you? Get your paraphernalia[10] ready. In a minute you're going upstairs to the main specimen room.

[HELEN *is dumbfounded as* MISS MORAY *exits in the direction* DANIELLE *went.* HELEN *gathers her equipment and looks at the* DOLPHIN, *who is staring desperately at her.*]

Dolphin. Help. Please help me.

[MISS MORAY *returns, pauses a moment, and then takes the mop to relieve* HELEN'*s burden.*]

Miss Moray. Come, Helen. Let me help you up to the main specimen room.

[*As they get into the elevator, the record plays again.*]

Record.
> Let me call you sweetheart,
> I'm in love with you.
> Let me hear you whisper . . .

---

10. **paraphernalia** (par'ə·fər·nāl'yə): equipment.

MAKING MEANINGS (SCENES 1 AND 2)

First Thoughts

1. Do you think the dolphin will be killed? Why or why not?

Shaping Interpretations

2. Why might Zindel have chosen the names he did for these characters?

   • Miss Moray

   • Dr. Crocus

   • Mrs. Fridge

3. In your opinion, why doesn't the dolphin have a name? What would you name him?

4. Skim back through the play, and find the places where Miss Moray tells Helen, "You're such a *nice* person." Think about what the word *nice* means. Use **context clues** (such as the other things Miss Moray says to and about Helen) to determine what Miss Moray *really* thinks of the cleaning woman.

5. We sense **irony** when we see a contrast between what we expect and the actual situation. What is ironic about the song that is played for the dolphin?

Connecting with the Text

6. Do you think you would catch on more quickly than Helen does to what is happening at ABADABA? Why or why not?

7. If Helen asked you for advice at the end of Scene 2, what would you tell her to do?

Extending the Text

8. Miss Moray tells Helen, "we have no right to endanger the genius about us" (page 308). What does she mean? What do you think of her statement? (When, if ever, do people have the right to question the actions of experts such as scientists, doctors, and politicians?)

Reading Check

a. Describe the experiment with the dolphin.

b. What instructions does Miss Moray give Helen regarding the dolphin?

c. Why does Helen begin paying attention to the dolphin?

d. What does Helen learn that makes her start to question what is happening at ABADABA?

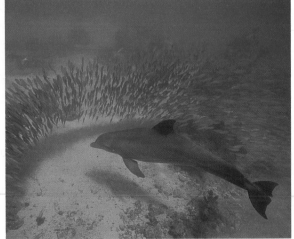

Scene 3

At rise, MISS MORAY *is walking with* DR. CROCUS *and* MRS. FRIDGE *to the elevator. She is jotting items down on a clipboard.*

Miss Moray. You can be assured the Custodial Engineering Staff is anxious to contribute in every nontechnical way possible. Every nontechnical way. (*The elevator doors open and* HELEN *gets off.*) Just a moment, Helen. I'd like to talk with you. (*To the others as they get on*) If you think of anything else between now and morning, please don't hesitate to call. Extra scalpels, dissection scissors, autoclaved glassware . . . Pleasant dreams. (*The doors close on* DR. CROCUS *and* MRS. FRIDGE, *and* MISS MORAY *turns to* HELEN.) I hope you're well this evening.

Helen. When they gonna kill it?

Miss Moray (*going with her to her locker*). Don't say "kill," Helen. You make it sound like murder. Besides, you won't have to go into the dolphin area at all this evening.

Helen. When they gonna do it?

Miss Moray. They'll be back, but don't worry. I've decided to let you go before they start, so . . . you won't have to be in the building when . . .

Helen. What do they do?

Miss Moray (*a hesitating laugh*). Why, what do you mean, what do they do?

Helen. How do they kill it?

Miss Moray. Nicotine mustard, Helen. Nicotine mustard. It's very humane. They inject it.

Helen. Just 'cause it don't talk, they've got to kill it?

Miss Moray. There's that word again.

Helen. Maybe he's a mute.

Miss Moray. Do you have all your paraphernalia?

Helen. Some human beings are mute, you know. Just because they can't talk, we don't kill them.

Miss Moray. It looks like you're ready to open a new box of steel wool.

Helen. Maybe he can type with his nose. Did they try that?

Miss Moray. Now, now, Helen . . .

Helen. Miss Moray, I don't mind doing the dolphin area.

Miss Moray. Absolutely not! I'm placing it off limits for your own good. You're too emotionally involved.

Helen. I'm not emotionally involved.

Miss Moray. Trust me, Helen. Trust me.

Helen. Yes, Miss Moray.

[MISS MORAY *exits and* HELEN *makes a beeline for the* DOLPHIN *area, which is closed off by portable walls. She opens the area enough to slide in. The lights are out and moonlight from the window casts many shadows.*]

Dolphin. Help. (HELEN *moves slowly toward the tank.*) Help me. (HELEN *opens the curtain. The* DOLPHIN *and she look at each other.*) Help me.

Helen. You don't need me. Just say something to them. Whatever you want. Say "Help." Any-

HELP. HELP ME.

thing. They just need to hear you say something. . . . (*She waits for a response, which doesn't come.*) You want me to tell 'em? I'll tell them. I'll just say I heard you say "Help." OK? I'll go tell them. (*She starts to leave the area, turning back to give opportunity for a response.*)

Dolphin. Noooooooooooo. (HELEN *stops. Moves back toward tank.*) Noooooooooooo.

Helen. They're gonna kill you! (*Puzzled,* HELEN *moves a bit closer to the tank. Pause*)

Dolphin. Boooooooooook.

SHE'S GONNA BE MAD.

Helen. What? (*There is a long pause. No response. She moves closer.*)
Dolphin. Booooooooooook.
Helen. Book?
Dolphin. Booooooooooook.
Helen. Booooooooooook? What book?

[DANIELLE *charges through a door and snaps on the light.*]

Danielle. Uh oh. Miss Moray said she don't want you in here. Said you have to not be in the lab and I'm not to talk to you about what they're gonna do because I make you nauseous.

[HELEN *goes to* DR. CROCUS's *desk in the lab and begins to look at various books on it.*]

Helen. Do you know anything about a book, Danielle?
Danielle. She's gonna be mad. What book?
Helen. Something to do with . . . (*She indicates the* DOLPHIN.)
Danielle. Hiya, fella! (*To* HELEN) Do I really make you nauseous?
Helen. About the dolphin . . .
Danielle. You talking about the experiment folder? They got an experiment folder they write in.
Helen. Where?
Danielle. I don't know.
Helen. Find it, please.
Danielle. I don't know where she keeps that stuff. Sometimes she puts it in the top and other times she puts it in the bottom.
Helen. Please find it. Please. (*She steps outside the area.*)
Danielle. I'll try. I'll try, but I got other things to do, you know. Can't spend time looking for what ain't any of my business anyway. I never knew I made anybody nauseous.

[DANIELLE *rummages through the desk, mumbling to herself, and finally finds the folder. She hands the folder out to* HELEN *as the elevator doors spring open and* MISS MORAY *enters.*]

DANIELLE *exits quickly through a door in the* DOLPHIN *area as* HELEN *conceals the folder.*]

Miss Moray. Helen?

Helen. Yes, Miss Moray?

Miss Moray. Would you feel better if we talked about it?

Helen. About what?

Miss Moray. Helen, you're such a nice person. I understand just what you're going through. Really, I do. And . . . well, I'm going to tell you something I've never told anyone else . . . my first week at ABADABA, I fell in love with an animal myself. An alley cat. Pussy Cat. That's what I called it—Pussy Cat.

Helen. Did they cut the head off it?

[MISS MORAY *removes a plastic covering from an object on a shelf to reveal an articulated[1] cat skeleton. As she talks, she sets it in view and gently dusts it with the feather duster.*]

Miss Moray. I sense a touch of bitterness in your voice, Helen, and don't think I wasn't bitter when I saw what had happened to Pussy Cat.

Helen. I'll bet it didn't sit well with Pussy Cat either.

Miss Moray. But when I thought about it for a while, I had to realize that I was just being selfish. Before . . . what happened to Pussy Cat happened, I was the only one benefiting from her—whereas now she's borrowed at least once a month. Last week she went to an anatomy seminar at St. Vincent's Medical School.

Helen. It's nice you let her out once in a while.

Miss Moray. In life, she was unnoticed and worthless except to me. Now she belongs to the ages. (*Then, solemnly*) I hope that's some comfort to you.

Helen. Oh, it's very comforting.

Miss Moray. Well, Perk-You-Up time will be here soon.

1. **articulated** (är·tik'yōo·lāt'id): here, with its joints connected.

Helen. Yes, Miss Moray.

Miss Moray. We have ladyfingers.

Helen. Oh, good.

Miss Moray. Such a strange thing to call a confectionery,[2] isn't it? It's almost <u>macabre</u>.

Helen. Miss Moray . . .

Miss Moray. Yes, Helen?

Helen. I was wondering . . .

Miss Moray. Yes?

Helen. I was wondering why they wanna talk with . . .

Miss Moray. Now now now! I was the same way about Pussy Cat. Right up to the final moment I kept asking, "What good is vivisection?"[3] "What good is vivisection?"

Helen. What good is vivisection?

Miss Moray. A *lot* of good, believe me.

Helen. Like what?

Miss Moray. Well, like fishing, Helen. If we could communicate with dolphins, they might be willing to herd fish for us. The fishing industry would be revolutionized. Millions of fish being rounded into nets by our little mammal friends.

Helen. Is that all?

Miss Moray. All? Heavens, no. They'd be a blessing to the human race. A blessing.

Helen. What kind?

Miss Moray. Oh. Why, oceanography. They would be worshiped in oceanography. Checking the Gulf Stream . . . taking water temperatures, depths, salinity readings. To say nothing of the contributions they could make in marine biology, navigation. Linguistics! Oh, Helen, it gives me the chills.

Helen. It'd be good if they talked?

Miss Moray. God's own blessing. God's own blessing. (MISS MORAY *exits and* HELEN *returns*

2. **confectionery** (kən·fek'shən·er'ē): sugary food.
3. **vivisection** (viv'ə·sek'shən): surgical operations and other experiments performed on living animals.

- -

WORDS TO OWN

macabre (mə·käb'rə) *adj.*: gruesome; horrible.

- -

to scrubbing for a moment. When she feels safe, she sets the folder in front of her and begins reading. Commence fantasy techniques to establish that the ensuing events are going on in HELEN*'s mind concerning the benevolent utilization[4] of dolphins. Relate to what* MISS MORAY *had told her about uses. Sound: Sonar beeping underwater. It has the urgency of a beating heart. Sweet strains of "Let Me Call You Sweetheart" in. Projection: Underwater shot, dolphins and fish gliding by. All voices echo. Doors open and* MISS MORAY, DR. CROCUS, *and* MRS. FRIDGE *appear phantasmagorically.)[5]* And if we could make friends with them, talk to them, they might be willing to herd all those fish for us. . . .

Dr. Crocus (*lovingly*). All right, little mammal friends—today we want swordfish. Fat, meaty ones suitable for controlled portion sizing. Go and get 'em!

[*Projection of dolphins swimming, a school of large fish panicking in the water*]

Mrs. Fridge. My dear dolphin friends. My dear, dear dolphin friends. We're most curious about seismographic readings at the bottom of the Mariana Trench. But do be careful. We're unsure of the weather above that area.

[*Projection of dolphins racing, deep underwater shots, sounding bell noises*]

Miss Moray (*sweetly*). Our linguistics lesson today will consider the most beautiful word in the English language: *love*. Love is a strong, complex emotion or feeling causing one to appreciate and promote the welfare of another. Do you have a word like it in dolphinese? A word similar to *love*? (*The fantasy disappears, leaving* MISS MORAY *and* HELEN *in the reality of the play.*) It has a nice sheen.

4. **benevolent utilization** (bə·nev′ə·lənt yo͞ot′′l·ĭ·zā′shən): use for the purpose of doing good.
5. **phantasmagorically** (fan·taz′mə·gôr′ə·klē): in a rapidly changing, dreamlike way.

Helen. What?
Miss Moray. It has a nice sheen. The floor. Up here where it's dried.
Helen. Thank you. Miss Moray . . . ?
Miss Moray. Yes, dear?
Helen. You sure it would be good for us if . . . dolphins talked?
Miss Moray. Helen, are you still thinking about that! Perhaps you'd better leave now. It's almost time.
Helen. No! I'm almost finished.

[DANIELLE *opens the* DOLPHIN *area and yells over* HELEN*'s head to* MISS MORAY.]

Danielle. I got everything except the head vise.
Miss Moray. I beg your pardon?
Danielle. The vise for the head. I can't find it. They can't saw through the skull bone without the head vise.
Miss Moray. Did you look on five? They had it there for . . . what they did to the St. Bernard . . . they had.

[*The record plays again and the others try to talk over it.*]

Record.
Let me call you sweetheart,
I'm in love with you.
Let me hear you whisper,
That you love me, too.

Danielle. Can't hear you.
Miss Moray. The St. Bernard. They used it for the St. Bernard.
Danielle. On five?
Miss Moray. That's what I said.
Danielle. I looked on five. I didn't see any head vise.
Miss Moray. You come with me. It must have been staring you in the face. Just staring you right in the face. (DANIELLE *tiptoes over the wet portion of the floor and she and* MISS MORAY *get on the elevator.*) We'll be right back, Helen.

[The doors close and HELEN *hurries into the* DOLPHIN *area. She stops just within the door and it is obvious that she is angry. There is a pause as she looks at the silhouette of the tank behind the closed curtain. Then]*

Dolphin. Booooooooooook.

*[*HELEN *charges to the curtain, pulls it open, and prepares to* reprimand *the* DOLPHIN.*]*

Helen. I looked at your book. I looked at your book all right!

Dolphin. Booooooooooook.

Helen. And you want to know what I think? I don't think much of you, that's what I think.

Dolphin. Booooooooooook.

Helen. Oh, shut up. Book book book book book. I'm not interested. You eat yourself silly—but to get a little fish for hungry humans is just too much for you. Well, I'm going to tell 'em you can talk. *(The* DOLPHIN *moves in the tank, lets out a few warning bubbles.)* You don't like that, eh? Well, I don't like lazy, selfish people, mammals, or animals. *(She starts away from the tank, half intending to go and half watching for a reaction. The* DOLPHIN *looks increasingly desperate and begins to make loud blat and beep sounds. He struggles a bit in the tank, starting to splash water.)* Oh, you'd do anything to avoid a little work, wouldn't you?

[In his most violent gyrations to date, the DOLPHIN *blasts at her.]*

Dolphin. Booooooooooook!

Helen. Cut it out; you're getting water all over the floor.

Dolphin. Booooooooooook!

*[*HELEN *is a little scared and stops moving toward the door. As she stops, the* DOLPHIN *calms down. She waits a moment and then moves closer to the tank again. They experience a sustained visual exchange.*[6] HELEN*'s anger*

and fear subside into frustration. When it appears the* DOLPHIN *is going to say nothing else,* HELEN *starts to leave the room. She turns around and looks back at the* DOLPHIN. *Then she looks at the folder on the desk. She is going to leave again when she decides to go to the folder once more. She picks it up, opens it, closes it, and sets it down again.]*

Helen. I guess you don't like us. *(Pause)* I guess you don't like us enough to . . . die rather than help us. . . .

Dolphin. Hate.

Helen *(picking up the folder and skimming reflexively)*. Yes.

Dolphin. Hate.

Helen. I guess you do hate us. . . . *(*HELEN *stops. She returns to the folder. Reading)* Military implications . . . plants mines in enemy waters . . . useful as antipersonnel self-directing weapons . . . war . . . deliver atomic warheads . . . war . . . nuclear torpedoes . . . attach bombs to submarines or surface vessels . . . terrorize enemy waters, beaches . . . war . . . war . . . war . . .

*[*HELEN*'s voice becomes echoed in the middle of the last speech, theatrical effects creeping in to establish fantasy sequence like the first except now the characters enter and appear sinister. Their requests are all war oriented.]*

Miss Moray *(demanding)*. And if we could talk to them, we'd get them to herd fish all right. One way or another, they'd do exactly as they were told!

["Let Me Call You Sweetheart" plays in background in a discordant *version, with projection of dolphins swimming.]*

---

6. **They experience a sustained visual exchange:** They look into each other's eyes for a long time.

WORDS TO OWN

reprimand (rep′rə·mand′) *v.*: scold; correct sharply.
discordant (dis·kôrd′'nt) *adj.*: harsh; disagreeable sounding; not in harmony.

Dr. Crocus. All right, you dolphins. Today we want you to herd fish. Herd all the fish you can away from the enemy's waters. Remove their food supply. Detonate underwater poison bombs and foul the enemy coastline. Make the water unfit for life of any kind.

[*A map is imposed over projection of dolphins.*]

Mrs. Fridge. Enemy fleets are located here and here and here. You'll have twenty-seven hours to attach the nuclear warheads before automatic detonation. Our objective: total annihilation.

[*Projection of dolphins racing off, deep underwater shots, frogmen[7] examining ships' hulls, planting mines*]

Miss Moray (*fanatically*). Our linguistics lesson today will consider the most basic word in the English language: *hate*. Hate is a strong emotion which means abhorrence, anger, animosity, detestation, hostility, malevolence, malice, malignity, odium, rancor, revenge, repugnance, and dislike. Do you have a word like it in dolphinese? If you don't, we'll teach you every <u>nuance</u> of ours. Every nuance of the word *hate*.

[*The fantasy sequence evaporates, leaving* HELEN *alone on stage with the* DOLPHIN. *She sadly closes the folder and moves slowly to the tank, a bit ashamed about the way she had reprimanded the* DOLPHIN. *They look sadly at each other. She reaches out her hand and just pets his head gently.*]

Helen. They're already thinking about ways to use you for . . . war. . . . Is that why you can't talk to them? What did you talk to me for? You won't talk to them but you . . . you talk to me because . . . you want something . . .

there's something . . . I can do? Something you want me to do?

Dolphin. Hamm . . .

Helen. What?

Dolphin. Hamm . . .

Helen. Ham? I thought you ate fish.

Dolphin (*moving with annoyance*). Ham . . . purrrrr.

Helen. Ham . . . purrrrr? I don't know what you're talking about?

Dolphin (*even more annoyed*). Ham . . . purrrrr.

Helen. Ham . . . purrrrr. What's a purrrrr?

[HELEN *is most upset and recalls that* MISS MORAY *is due back. Confused and scared, she returns to scrubbing the floor just as the doors of the elevator open, revealing* MISS MORAY, DANIELLE, *and* MRS. FRIDGE. DANIELLE *pushes a dissection table loaded with shiny instruments toward the lab.*]

Miss Moray. Clean the vise up, Danielle. Immediately.

Danielle. I didn't leave the blood on it.

Miss Moray. I'm not accusing you. I just said whoever was the porter the night they did you know what to the St. Bernard was . . . (*To* MRS. FRIDGE) It's the first dirty vise since I've led the Custodial Engineering Department! Is the good doctor in yet?

Mrs. Fridge. She's getting the nicotine mustard on eighteen. I'll have to see if she needs assistance.

Miss Moray. I'll come with you. Oh, Helen. You can go now. It's time. (*She smiles and the elevator doors close on* MRS. FRIDGE *and* MISS MORAY.)

Danielle (*pushing the dissection table into the* DOLPHIN *area*). I never left a dirty head vise. She's trying to say I left it like that. I know what she's getting at.

---

7. frogmen: people equipped to do exploration or other work underwater.

WORDS TO OWN

nuance (no͞o′äns′) *n*.: shade of meaning.

Helen. Did you ever hear of Ham . . . purrrrr?

Danielle. Wait'll I get my hands on Kazinski. Kazinski does the fifth floor and he should be cleaning this, not me. It's all caked up.

Helen. Would you listen a minute? Ham . . . purrrrr. Do you know what a ham . . . purrrrr is?

Danielle. The only hamper I ever heard of is out in the hall. (HELEN *looks toward an exit indicated by* DANIELLE.) Five scalpels, large clamps . . . small clamps . . . bone saws . . . scissors . . . dissection needles, two dozen . . . Kazinski left the high-altitude chamber dirty once and I got blamed for that, too. And that had mucus all over it. (DANIELLE *exits.*)

Helen (*rushing to the* DOLPHIN). You want me to do something with the hamper. What? To get it? To put—— You want me to put you in it?

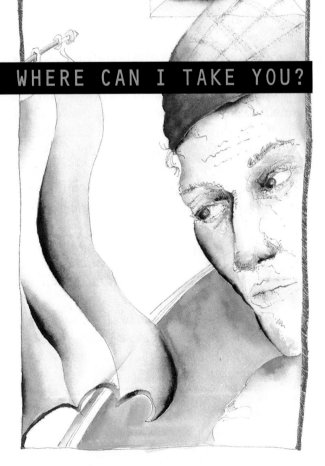

WHERE CAN I TAKE YOU?

. . . But what'll I do with you? Where can I take you?

Dolphin. Sea . . .

Helen. See? See what?

Dolphin. Sea . . . ham . . . purrrrr . . .

Helen. See ham—— I *saw* the hamper.

Dolphin. Sea . . .

Helen. See what? What do you want me to see? (*She walks about the room, mumbling, looking for what the* DOLPHIN *could want her to see. Finally, she looks out the window.*)

Dolphin. Sea . . . sea . . .

Helen. See? . . . The sea! That's what you're talking about! (*There is almost an atmosphere of celebration.*) The river . . . to the sea!

[*She darts into the hall and returns with hamper, pushes it next to the* DOLPHIN. *She pulls closed the curtain as . . .* MISS MORAY *gets off the elevator.* MISS MORAY *looks very calm. Everything is under control and on schedule from her point of view. She then notices that* HELEN *is not there, though her mop and pail are. She wonders if* HELEN *has gone and just carelessly left the items out.*]

Miss Moray (*sweetly*). Helen? (*When there is no response, she starts into the* DOLPHIN *area.*) Helen? (HELEN *is not there, though her coat is still hanging in her locker. She is little concerned at this point. For a second she assumes it is unlikely* HELEN *would be in there, since it was strictly placed off limits, but then she decides to investigate. She notices the closed curtain in front of the tank.*) Helen? Are you there? (*Pause*) Helen? Helen? (MISS MORAY *moves to the curtain and pulls it open. There is* HELEN, *with her arms around the front part of the* DOLPHIN, *lifting him a good part of the way out of the water.*) Helen, what do you think you're hugging?

[HELEN *gets so scared that she drops the* DOLPHIN *back into the tank, splattering* MISS MORAY *with water.* MISS MORAY *lets out a scream just as* DR. CROCUS *and* MRS. FRIDGE *enter.*]

Mrs. Fridge. Is anything wrong, Miss Moray? (MISS MORAY *is unable to answer at first.*) Is anything wrong?

Miss Moray (*not wishing to admit an irregularity*). No . . . nothing wrong. Nothing at all. (*She hurriedly composes herself, not wanting to hang any dirty wash of the Custodial Engineering Department.*) Just a little spilled water. Right, Helen? Just a little spilled water. Get those sponges, Helen. Immediately!

[HELEN *and* MISS MORAY *grab sponges from the lab sink and begin to get up some of the water around the tank.* DR. CROCUS *begins to occupy herself with filling a hypodermic syringe while* MRS. FRIDGE *expertly gets all equipment into place.* DANIELLE *enters.*]

Mrs. Fridge. Danielle, get the formaldehyde jars into position, please.

Danielle. I didn't spill anything. Don't try to blame *that* on me.

Miss Moray. I didn't say you did.

Danielle. You spilled something?

Miss Moray. Just do as Mrs. Fridge tells you. Hurry, Danielle, you're so slow.

Danielle. I'm tired of getting blame for Kazinski.

Mrs. Fridge. Would you like to get an encephalogram during the death process, Dr. Crocus?

Dr. Crocus. Why not?

[MRS. FRIDGE *begins to implant electrodes into the* DOLPHIN*'s head. The* DOLPHIN *commences making high-pitched distress signals, which send shivers up and down* HELEN*'s back.*]

Miss Moray. That'll do it. No harm done. Step outside, Helen. (*To the doctor*) I do hope everything is satisfactory, Doctor. (DR. CROCUS *looks at her, gives no reaction.*) The Custodial Engineering Staff has done everything in its power . . . (*She is still ignored.*) Come, Helen. I'll see you to the elevator. (HELEN *looks at the* DOLPHIN *as* MRS. FRIDGE *is sticking the elec-*

trodes into his head. His distress signals are pathetic, and HELEN *is terrified.*) Let's go now. (MISS MORAY *leads her out to the hall.* MISS MORAY *is trying to get control of herself, to resist yelling at* HELEN, *as she gets on her coat and kerchief.*) You can leave that.

Helen. I never left a dirty mop. Never.

[HELEN *gives the mop a quick rinse and puts the things in their place. Cuts to the lab door and the sounds coming out of it show where her attention is.*]

Miss Moray. Well, I hardly know what to say. Frankly, Helen, I'm deeply disappointed. I'd hoped that by being lenient with you—and heaven knows I have been—that you'd develop a heightened loyalty to our team. I mean, do you think for one minute that putting vinegar in rinse water really is more effective? If you ask me, it streaks. Streaks.

Helen (*bursting into tears and going to the elevator*). Leave me alone.

Miss Moray (*softening as she catches up to her*). You really are a nice person, Helen. A very nice person. But to be simple and nice in a world where great minds are giant-stepping the micro- and macrocosms, well—one would expect you'd have the humility to yield in unquestioning awe. I truly am very fond of you, Helen, but you're fired. Call Personnel after 9. And I was going to bring you in hangers. I want you to know that.

[*As* MISS MORAY *heads back toward the* DOLPHIN *area, the record starts to play.*]

Record.
>Let me call you sweetheart,
>I'm in love with you.
>Let me hear you whisper . . .

WORDS TO OWN
lenient (lēn'yənt) *adj.:* forgiving; not harsh in punishing.

LITERATURE AND SCIENCE

Animal Rights vs. Animal Research

Have you ever taken antibiotics? Have you been immunized against polio and whooping cough? Does anyone you know have a pacemaker or use insulin injections to control diabetes? Animal research made these and many other medical treatments possible.

Yet not everyone is in favor of animal research. Many people are troubled by reports of cruel or neglectful treatment of laboratory animals. In recent years, animal rights activists have repeatedly clashed with researchers. A number of scientists have responded by using fewer animals and new, less painful procedures in their experiments. Some scientists have developed research methods in which computer models and cell and tissue cultures, rather than living animals, are used.

Still, difficult questions persist: What rights, if any, do animals have? Should people's needs always come first? Where do we draw the line?

[*The record is roughly interrupted. What* HELEN *is contemplating at that moment causes the expression on her face to turn from sadness to thought to strength to anger and—as the elevator doors open—to fury. Instead of getting on the elevator, she whirls around and marches back to the* DOLPHIN *area.* MISS MORAY, MRS. FRIDGE, DANIELLE, *and* DR. CROCUS, *with hypodermic needle poised to stick the* DOLPHIN, *turn and look at her with surprise.*]

Helen. Who do you think you are? Who do you think you *are*? I think you're murderers, that's what I think.

Miss Moray. Doctor, I assure you this is the first psychotic outburst the Custodial Engineering Department has ever had.

Helen. I'm very tired of being a nice person, Miss Moray. You kept telling me how nice I was and now I know what you meant. (*Pause*) I'm going to report the bunch of you to the ASPCA—or somebody. Because . . . I've decided I don't like you cutting the heads off mice and sawing through skulls of St. Bernards . . . and if being a nice person is just not saying anything and letting you pack of butchers run around doing whatever you want, then I don't want to be nice anymore. You gotta be very stupid people to need an animal to talk before you know just from looking at it that it's saying something . . . that it knows what pain feels like. I'd like to see you all with a few electrodes stuck in your heads. I really would. (HELEN *starts crying, though her features won't give way to weakness.*) Being nice isn't any good. (*Looking at the* DOLPHIN) They just kill you off if you do that. And that's being a coward. You gotta talk back against what's wrong or you can't ever stop it. At least you've gotta try. (*She bursts into tears.*)

Miss Moray. Nothing like this has ever happened with a member of the Custodial Engineering . . . Helen, dear . . .

Helen. Get your hands off me. (*Yelling at the* DOLPHIN) You're a coward, that's what you are.

[*She turns and starts to leave. A sound comes from the* DOLPHIN'*s tank.*]

Dolphin (*whispering*). Loooooooooooveeeeee. (*Everyone turns to stare at the* DOLPHIN *and freezes for a second.*) Love.

Dr. Crocus. Get the recorder going.

[*The laboratory becomes a bustle of activity concerning the utterance of the* DOLPHIN. *Plans for dissection are obviously canceled and* HELEN *has a visual exchange with the* DOLPHIN. *Then she continues toward the elevator.*]

Dolphin. Love . . .

Dr. Crocus. Is the tape going?

Mrs. Fridge. Yes, Doctor.

Miss Moray. I'm enormously embarrassed about the incident, Doctor. Naturally, I've taken steps to see this won't . . .

Mrs. Fridge. He's opening the blowhole sphincter.

Dolphin. Love . . .

Dr. Crocus. That scrubwoman's got something to do with this. Get her back in here.

Miss Moray. She won't be any more trouble. I fired her.

Dolphin. Love . . .

Dr. Crocus. Just get her. (*To* MRS. FRIDGE) You're sure the machine's recording?

Miss Moray. Doctor, I'm afraid you don't understand. That woman was hugging the mammal . . .

Dr. Crocus. Try to get another word out of it.

Miss Moray. The water on the floor was her fault.

[*The record starts.*]

Dr. Crocus. Try the fear button.

Miss Moray. She could have damaged the rib cage if I hadn't stopped her.

Dr. Crocus. One more word . . . try anger.

Miss Moray. The last thing in the world I want is for our problems in Custodial Engineering to . . .

Dr. Crocus (*furious*). Will you shut up and get her back here?

[MISS MORAY *appears stunned momentarily.*]

Miss Moray. Immediately, Doctor. (*She hurries to* HELEN, *waiting for the elevator.*) Helen? Oh, Helen? (*She goes to* HELEN, *who refuses to pay any attention to her.*) Don't you want to hear what the dolphin has to say? He's so cute! Dr. Crocus thinks that his talking might have something to do with you. Wouldn't that be exciting? (*Pause*) Please, Helen. The doctor . . .

Helen. Don't talk to me, do you mind?

Miss Moray. It was only in the heat of argument that I distorted the ineffectiveness of the vinegar and . . . of course, you won't be discharged. All right? Please, Helen, you'll embarrass me . . . (*The elevator doors open and* HELEN *gets on to face* MISS MORAY. *She looks at her a moment and then lifts her hand to press the button for the ground floor.*) Don't you dare . . . Helen, the team needs you, don't you see? Everyone says the corridors have never looked so good. Ever. Helen, please. What will I do if you leave?

Helen. Why don't you put in a rug?

[*She presses the button. The elevator doors close.*]

MEET THE WRITER

"My Books Have a Secret"

Paul Zindel (1936–) was born in Staten Island, New York. Early in Zindel's childhood, his father left the family; his mother had to struggle to support Zindel and his older sister. Zindel wrote his first play, a version of "The Monkey's Paw" (another dramatization appears on page 186), when he was a teenager. He taught high school chemistry for ten years, then turned to writing plays and young adult novels full time.

When asked what he is trying to say to young people in his writing, Zindel responded:

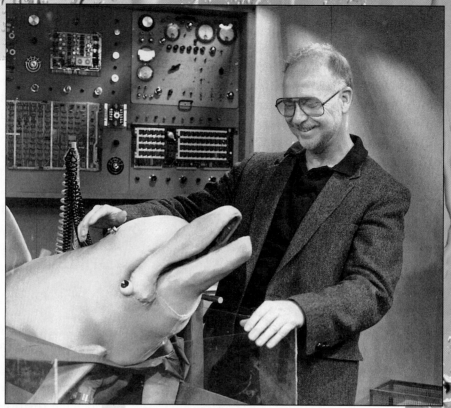

Zindel on the set of the off-Broadway stage production of *Let Me Hear You Whisper* with a dolphin puppet created and operated by Peter Baird.

66 I'm telling the kids that I love the underdog and sympathize with his struggle because that's what I was and am in many ways still. I want my kids to feel worthy, to search for hope against all odds as they travel the plots of my books. I'm trying to tell all kids that they don't have to consider themselves misfits, that they deserve hopes and dreams and the technique and patience to make those dreams reality. I tell the kids that my books have a secret—a very useful secret—and to read them to find the lessons they teach, or to examine the problems they pose. I ask the kids to provoke discussion among themselves, to share the books with their teachers and librarians and parents and see that there is a beautiful tomorrow for them. 99

More by Paul Zindel

Zindel won a Pulitzer Prize in drama in 1971 for his play *The Effect of Gamma Rays on Man-in-the-Moon Marigolds* (Bantam). The play is about a high school girl who finds happiness in spite of her troubled family life when she receives recognition for a science project. "I suspect it is autobiographical," Zindel says, "because whenever I see a production of it, I laugh and cry harder than anyone else in the audience."

from Touched by a Dolphin

ABC World of Discovery Special
ABC/Kane Productions International, Inc.

Pamela Stacey

What follows is an excerpt from the script of a television documentary. Sharon Lawrence, the on-screen host, guides viewers into the water world of the graceful, curious, and friendly dolphin.

Documentary Terms

video the images you see on-screen

audio the words and sounds you hear (The words in roman type are spoken by an unseen narrator; the words in *italic type* are spoken by someone on-screen.)

VO voice-over, the voice of an unseen narrator

on camera shown on the TV screen

c/u close-up shot

fade-out the gradual disappearance of an image from the screen

VIDEO	**AUDIO**
Dolphins swimming.	**Sharon VO:** Dolphins. What magical beings! Creatures born in the sea and yet so much like us. But until now, they've carried the secrets of their lives deep into their water world.
Sharon on camera.	*All of my life I've been fascinated by the sea and by dolphins. Hi. I'm Sharon Lawrence and I'm going to do something I've only dreamed of—see a dolphin eye to eye, face to face, hand to flipper, and on their terms in the wild.*

◆ ◆ ◆

	Sharon VO:
Coast of Brazil.	On the southern tip of Brazil, a dolphin culture and human culture have met.
Aerial view of channel.	In the coastal town of Laguna, an amazing partnership has formed.
Fishermen standing in line.	Almost every day, dozens of fishermen line up to wait for the dolphins.

VIDEO	AUDIO
Low angle of fishermen in line.	They stand in water so murky that only the dolphins, with their echolocation,[1] know if fish are there.
Dolphin moving toward camera.	The men wait for a signal as the dolphins herd fish to them.
Net throws.	Only when the dolphins signal and roll away in safety do they throw their nets.
	The dolphins wait for the fish, who try to escape the nets—only to be caught easily in their jaws.
Fishermen pull in fish. Fish in nets.	In this cooperative fishery, each fisherman catches more than forty pounds of fish to sell in the local markets.
	About one hundred families depend on this fishery to earn a living.
	And it's been happening here since 1847.
Fisherman throws net (over camera).	How it began is a mystery, unless you believe an intriguing myth . . . a love story.

Group singing folk song VO:

Canoe and fisherman.	No fish had been seen For a thousand days And the fisherman worried so.
Fisherman unloads boat with daughter.	Still, in joy she'd run to the water, The angel who was his daughter.
Over shoulder of stranger, girl looks up. Girl looks over c/u.	One morning the girl Met the steady gaze Of a stranger she seemed to know. Eyes that burned like the sky above him. She knew she was born to love him.
Fade-out on stranger.	There were stories of old That grandmothers told Of dolphins disguised. Their touch mesmerized Young girls, who fell prey To their passionate ways.
Girl and stranger dance. Men conspire.	The villagers whispered, A plan was made And the stranger thrown to the waves.

1. **echolocation** (ek′ō·lō·kā′shən): process by which dolphins and bats navigate and locate objects. The animals emit sound waves, which are reflected back as echoes.

VIDEO	AUDIO
Waves breaking.	Ahh ahh ah . . .
Girl walks at shore, finds hat.	She wept by the water The fisherman's heartbroken daughter.
	Ahh ahh ah . . .
Two dolphins jump in silhouette.	From her tears and her desolation Came a glorious transformation[2]
	Ahh ahh ah . . .
Fisherman stands up and enters water to fish. Dolphin c/u.	And the soul of a loving daughter Brought new life to the barren water. Ahh ahh ah . . .
	Sharon VO:
Net throws. Fishermen pulling in nets.	And so they have fished here for 150 years.
	Just as generations of fishermen have passed this tradition on to their children, so have the dolphins. Now fishermen and dolphins live here in a unique culture of cooperation.

2. **transformation:** change in form or appearance. The girl has turned into a dolphin.

Writing a Documentary: "A Little Like Poetry"

Pamela Stacey explains how she came to write this documentary:

"I was drawn to writing about the natural world out of a passionate belief that we must care for it as lovingly as we care for each other. Dolphins always fascinated me, and I read everything I could in scientific journals about new research. Because of the research and my experience as a writer, I was given the challenge to produce and write this film. The greatest fun was working with cameramen who know how to tell a story without words—through the images they capture on film.

In addition to constructing the story, the greatest challenge in writing a natural-history documentary is to blend the words with the images. A writer begins work only when the film is nearly complete but perfectly silent— no words, music, or sound effects. The writing becomes a little like poetry in its brevity and compression, and the information conveyed is always just the tip of the iceberg. To understand what it's like, turn off the sound on the television and imagine what you'd write. It's exhilarating and terrifying and a great privilege. Whatever the medium, the power of writing comes in part from paying careful attention to the world around you and what you can learn from it."

MAKING MEANINGS (SCENE 3)

First Thoughts

1. If you were Helen, would you leave the job or would you stay? Why?

Shaping Interpretations

2. Why does Miss Moray tell Helen to stop using the word *kill*?

3. Find three of Helen's sarcastic responses to Miss Moray's story about Pussy Cat. What does her sarcasm tell you about her feelings toward ABADABA?

4. How has Helen **changed** in the course of the teleplay?

5. What do you think happens to Helen after the teleplay ends?

6. In many stories, one **character** is cast as a hero, and one person is the villain. The hero is called the **protagonist.** The villain is called the **antagonist**—the one who tries to keep the hero from getting what he or she wants. In this play who is the hero, and who is the villain? In some stories the hero has both good and bad qualities, and the villain is not all bad. Discuss the way the hero and the villain are presented in this story— is one all good and one all bad? How do you feel about the way Zindel created the characters in this play?

Connecting with the Text

7. Which character in this play do you identify with—that is, which one do you feel is sort of like you? If you don't identify with anyone, explain why.

Extending the Text

8. Review the portion of the TV documentary "Touched by a Dolphin" (see *Connections* on pages 321–323). Discuss all the ways the documentary connects with Zindel's play. How do both the documentary and the play connect with the theme "Talk to the Animals"?

9. Describe Helen's two fantasies about the ways communication with dolphins could be used (pages 313 and 314–315). How do her ideas compare with what you wrote about in your Quickwrite (page 295)?

Challenging the Text

10. What do you think is Zindel's **perspective,** or **point of view,** on using animals in experiments? How is it different from or similar to yours?

Reading Check

a. On page 314, why does Helen become angry at the dolphin?

b. What does Helen find in the folder that makes her change her mind?

c. Why does Dr. Crocus want Helen to come back?

d. What does Helen decide to do?

CHOICES: Building Your Portfolio

Writer's Notebook

1. Collecting Ideas for a How-To Essay

In *Let Me Hear You Whisper,* Helen establishes a relationship with a dolphin. In other selections in this collection, "Talk to the Animals," you read about other relationships between humans and animals. Draw several comic-strip panels showing one or more steps in a how-to process suggested by one of the topics below. (If you don't enjoy drawing, simply describe the steps in the process.)

- how to be an animal's best friend
- how to go on a trip with your pet
- how to learn about life from an animal
- how to train your pet

Supporting a Position

2. To the Editor

Do you believe that people always have the right to kill animals? Is killing animals right only under certain circumstances, or is it always wrong to kill animals? Express your opinion in a letter to the editor of your school or local newspaper. Use arguments that appeal to logic and to emotion to persuade your readers to agree with you. For help in writing an essay supporting a position, see pages 160–164.

Research/Science

3. Fact and Fiction

Brainstorm a list of questions you have about dolphins after reading this teleplay. For example:

- How intelligent are dolphins?
- Can dolphins really learn to speak English?
- Have people ever studied dolphins for their possible usefulness to humans? How has the information been used?

Choose one or two questions to research. Present your findings to the class.

Expressing Your Response

4. Dear Mr. Zindel

On page 320 Paul Zindel tells us what he is trying to say to young people in his writing. Reread his comment, and decide what his **main idea** is. Then, think about the play you have just read. Write a letter to Zindel telling him how you feel about what he says on page 320 and how you feel about his play. Do you think he accomplishes what he says he'd like to accomplish? Be specific in telling him what you like (or dislike) about his work.

GRAMMAR LINK

Language Handbook HELP

See Commas, pages 799–800.

Technology HELP

See Language Workshop CD-ROM. *Key word entry: commas.*

Using Commas with Interrupters

A pair of commas can be used to set off an **interrupter**—a word, phrase, or clause in the middle of a sentence that could be omitted without changing the basic meaning of the sentence.

EXAMPLES Miss Moray asked Helen to clean the laboratory.

Miss Moray, <u>the supervisor,</u> asked Helen to clean the laboratory.

Dolphins nurse their young.

Dolphins, <u>which are mammals,</u> nurse their young.

Like parentheses, commas that set off interrupters always come in pairs. Make sure to put commas both before *and* after an interrupter.

Try It Out

Copy the following sentences, adding commas where needed before or after the interrupters.

1. Paul Zindel the writer of this teleplay, moved to a new town as a teenager.

2. His autobiography, *The Pigman and Me* tells the story of this move.

3. Zindel, who was shy didn't think anyone liked him.

4. Zindel despite his fears, did make friends at his new school.

VOCABULARY HOW TO OWN A WORD

WORD BANK

termination
incessantly
compulsory
officiously
apprehensively
macabre
reprimand
discordant
nuance
lenient

Context: Finding Clues to Meaning

When you come across an unfamiliar word, you can apply several strategies. (1) Search the **word's context** for specific clues. (2) **Sound the word out** to see if it sounds (and looks) like a word you are familiar with. (3) Look at the **word's structure** to see if you recognize any parts of the word. Of course, you should also determine the word's **part of speech.**

Go back to the text, and locate where each of the words in the Word Bank is used. Work with a partner to see if you can find any clues that would help you define the word (if it weren't already defined at the bottom of the page). The first word is done for you:

Word: *termination* (noun): "ending" (p. 298).
Clues: The dolphin is uncomfortable when he hears the word; the word looks and sounds like *terminal,* and a "terminal illness" is a fatal illness. Also, in the movie *The Terminator,* the title character "terminates" people.

The Naming of Cats

T. S. Eliot

The Naming of Cats is a difficult matter,
    It isn't just one of your holiday games;
You may think at first I'm as mad as a hatter
When I tell you, a cat must have THREE DIFFERENT NAMES.
5 First of all, there's the name that the family use daily,
    Such as Peter, Augustus, Alonzo or James,
Such as Victor or Jonathan, George or Bill Bailey—
    All of them sensible everyday names.
There are fancier names if you think they sound sweeter,
10   Some for the gentlemen, some for the dames:
Such as Plato, Admetus, Electra, Demeter—
    But all of them sensible everyday names.
But I tell you, a cat needs a name that's particular,
    A name that's peculiar, and more dignified,
15 Else how can he keep up his tail perpendicular,
    Or spread out his whiskers, or cherish his pride?
Of names of this kind, I can give you a quorum,°
    Such as Munkustrap, Quaxo, or Coricopat,
Such as Bombalurina, or else Jellylorum—
20   Names that never belong to more than one cat.
But above and beyond there's still one name left over,
    And that is the name that you never will guess;
The name that no human research can discover—
    But THE CAT HIMSELF KNOWS, and will never confess.
25 When you notice a cat in profound meditation,
    The reason, I tell you, is always the same;
His mind is engaged in a rapt contemplation
    Of the thought, of the thought, of the thought of his name:
      His ineffable° effable
30   Effanineffable
Deep and inscrutable° singular Name.

17. quorum (kwôr′əm): here, a select group.

29. ineffable (in·ef′ə·bəl): too awesome to be spoken.

31. inscrutable (in·skrōot′ə·bəl): mysterious; can't be understood.

MEET THE WRITER

The Poet's Secret Name Is . . .

"George Pushdragon." That's the alias **Thomas Stearns Eliot** (1888–1965) used when entering crossword competitions—it was also the name of one of his beloved cats. (Wiscus and Pittipaws were others.) Eliot, an American who moved to England in 1914 and later became a British citizen, was a truly revolutionary poet who won a Nobel Prize in 1948. Eliot composed the comic *Old Possum's Book of Practical Cats* for his godchildren—and perhaps for his father, who liked drawing cats. Eliot himself loved nonsense verse and music-hall shows, so he would probably have wanted a front-row seat for the smash Broadway hit *Cats,* which is based on his cat poems.

Drawing, 1930 by Powys Evans, The Granger Collection.

(HRW) go.hrw.com
LE0 8-4

Cat drawings by Edward Gorey from *Old Possum's Book of Practical Cats* by T. S. Eliot.

READ ON

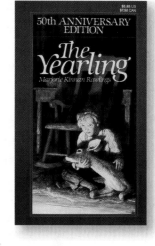

A Boy and His Fawn

Have you ever seen a baby animal in the wild and wanted to bring it home and raise it? Jody Baxter does in *The Yearling* (Macmillan)—but in the end he must decide his tamed fawn's fate. Marjorie Kinnan Rawlings won a Pulitzer Prize in 1939 for this novel, set near her home in rural Florida. (This title is available in the HRW Library.)

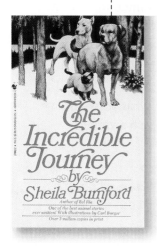

Homeward Bound

If you want to read more about how things might look from an animal's point of view, try *The Incredible Journey* by Sheila Burnford (Bantam). Two dogs and a cat brave the hazards of the wilderness to find their way back to the people they love. Compare the novel with Disney's 1993 film version, *Homeward Bound: The Incredible Journey.*

All the Answers

Does a frightened ostrich really hide its head in the sand? Just how fat was the fattest pig ever? What should you do if your cat runs away? You'll find answers to these questions and many more in *The Kids' World Almanac® of Animals and Pets* by Deborah G. Felder (World Almanac). This fact-packed book serves as both an introduction to the animal kingdom and a guide to pets and pet care.

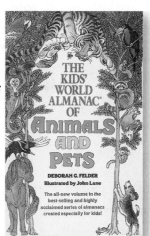

Other Picks

- Farley Mowat, *Never Cry Wolf* (Bantam). In this action-packed adventure, a Canadian conservationist travels to the Arctic to live among wolves and learn their ways.

- Wilson Rawls, *Where the Red Fern Grows* (Bantam). Set in the Ozark Mountains, this popular novel relates the adventures of a boy and his two hunting dogs. (This title is available in the HRW Library.)

- Sterling North, *Rascal* (Puffin). This nonfiction account tells the story of a boy and his best friend—a very unusual raccoon.

EXPOSITORY WRITING
HOW-TO ESSAY

ASSIGNMENT

Write an essay explaining, step-by-step, how to do something.

AIM

To inform; to explain.

AUDIENCE

Your teacher or other adults, your classmates, or younger children. (You choose.)

How do you make pizza? How can you put together a great Halloween costume for under ten dollars? How do you download data from the Internet or program a VCR? We often ask and answer questions like these: questions about how to *do* something or how to *use* something most effectively. Such questions are best answered through step-by-step instructions that explain a **process.**

When you give how-to instructions, you should use one or more of the following three approaches:

- **Demonstrate** the process as you explain what you're doing. You'd use this show-and-tell approach to teach a young cousin how to swing a baseball bat.

- Show the process using **pictures.** The cartoon below relies on pictures to explain a visual process. Someone who can't read or doesn't understand a word of English can follow these picture directions successfully.

- Explain the process using **words,** as in a set of written directions or instructions.

In this workshop you'll use the third approach: You'll write a **how-to essay** that provides clear, step-by-step instructions that tell how to perform a certain task.

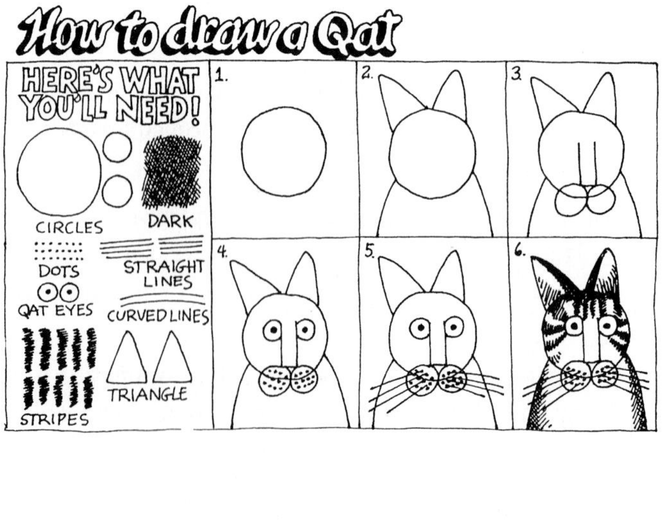

How to draw a Qat

From the book "Cat" by B. Kliban. Used by permission only. © J. K. Kliban.

The history
of the written
word is rich and

Page 1

Prewriting

1. Writer's Notebook

Look over your Writer's Notebook entries for
this collection. Does one of the how-to topics
you've come up with interest you enough to write about it? Do
you know enough about the process to explain it to someone else?

What I'm Good At
—winning at chess
—gymnastics (parallel bars)
—being a good friend
—cooking
—finding terrific bargains
Audience
—my classmates

2. Searching for Topic Ideas

One of these strategies may give you additional topic ideas:

- Ask friends or family members to name three things they
  think you do well. Then, add your own "best" activities.

- Keep a journal for a day. Write down everything you do.
  Do any of your ordinary activities suggest a topic?

- Take a walk through your home, and make a list of twenty
  pieces of equipment that you use regularly (such as a VCR).
  Do any of them suggest a process you'd like to explain?

3. Checking Your Topic

For each possible topic, ask yourself these questions:

- Is this something that I know well and can teach others to do?
- Can I break the process down into clear steps?
- Can I explain the activity in only three or four paragraphs?
- Will this process or activity interest my audience?

4. Organizing Your Essay

Once you've chosen a topic, think about these two questions:

- What are the different steps involved in the process?
- What materials, ingredients, equipment, or tools are needed?

You can organize your information in a chart like the one on
page 332. Be sure to list the steps of your process in **chronological order**—the exact order in time in which they must be
followed. (You can make the order clear by using words like
first, next, and *last*.)

**Strategies for
Elaboration**

*Exercise in
Observation*

Take notes as you
observe someone (or
yourself!) completing
a familiar process, such
as those listed below.
Try to break down the
process into its separate
steps. Note specific
details related to each
step.

- washing a car
- doing a load of laundry
- mowing a lawn
- making an omelet

Sentence Workshop
H E L P

Combining sentences: page 335.

Language/Grammar Link
H E L P

Using commas with items in a series: page 274. Using commas with adjectives: page 287. Using commas with interrupters: page 326.

How to Make a Cast of Animal Tracks	
Steps	**Materials and Comments**
1. Find animal tracks in dirt or mud.	(Explain what a plaster cast is.)
2. Brush away loose dirt or leaves.	(Remind readers to use a soft brush and to be careful not to disturb the track.)
3. Make cardboard ring, using paper clips to hold the ring in a circle.	cardboard strip approximately 2″ x 14″, scissors, 4 paper clips
4. Place ring around tracks.	
5. Mix plaster of Paris powder with water until mixture is slightly runny.	measuring cup, bowl, spoon, plaster of Paris powder, water (Explain where to get plaster of Paris powder. What's the ratio of powder to water?)
6. Pour plaster mixture over tracks; smooth out surface.	ruler or stick (to smooth the surface)
7. Let plaster mixture harden.	(How long does it take?)
8. Lift up hardened plaster cast and cardboard ring.	
9. Let dry for 24 hours. Then, remove cardboard ring.	

5. Elaborating Each Step

Think about the information you might add to your step-by-step summary of a process. What specific **details, definitions,** or **examples** would help someone carry out each step correctly? What **suggestions** or **warnings** might make the process go more smoothly—or more safely? As you are deciding what information to include, consider how much your audience already knows. Don't include unnecessary details.

Drafting

Your essay will need an **introduction, body,** and **conclusion** (see the framework on page 333). With your chart in front of you, start turning your numbered steps into sentences. Be as clear as you can, but don't worry about making your first draft perfect. You'll have time later to revise it. Consider adding some humor to make your essay more appealing.

HOW TO HAVE A SNAKE AS A PET

In this paper I am going to tell you, from experience, how to have a snake as a pet. I will tell you where to find a snake, what equipment you need, and how to take care of your snake. If you ever consider having a snake as a pet, take this advice seriously.

Introduction sets forth purpose of essay.

The first thing you have to do is get a snake. Finding the right snake is a hard task, but the best place to look for a snake is in a store that sells exotic animals. These animals include everything most people would <u>not</u> want for a pet, like lizards, frogs, turtles, and sometimes spiders. Not only is this the best place to buy snakes, but it is also a cool place to talk to interesting people. Some people you meet there might even want to sell their snakes for much, much less than the normal price.

Step 1: finding a snake.

Specific details.

Snakes can be expensive, so you might want to start with something small. Garter snakes go for about ten dollars each, but if you have the money to spend and feel strongly about having a snake, the ball python or any other type of python is a good choice. (Of course, you want a nice, nonpoisonous snake.)

Step 2: choosing a snake.

The next thing to do is to find a terrarium, which is a glass enclosed box. These are expensive, and the biggest problem in getting a large snake is that the bigger the terrarium (obviously), the more expensive your project will be. Next you need a water bowl for drinking and

Step 3: getting your equipment.

(continued on next page)

Framework for a How-To Essay

Introduction

- Grabs reader's attention
- Identifies process
- Lists equipment needed (unless the equipment is listed with each step in the body of the essay)

Body

- Step 1
  Equipment (if not listed in introduction)
- Step 2
  Equipment (if not listed in introduction)
- Step 3
  Equipment (if not listed in introduction)

[Add as many steps as you need.]

Conclusion

- Sums up the process
- May tell why the process is useful
- May explain how to solve possible problems

A good how-to essay

1. *has an introduction that identifies the process and grabs readers' interest*

2. *presents each step in chronological order*

3. *identifies all necessary materials or tools*

4. *uses transitions skillfully to show chronological order*

5. *is clear and easy to follow*

Proofreading Tip

As you proofread, check your use of commas

- with items in a series
- with interrupters
- with conjunctions that combine sentences

Communications Handbook HELP

See Proofreaders' Marks.

Publishing Tip

As a class, sort your papers into subject areas (science, art, sports, etc.). Bind the essays into how-to anthologies.

Student Model (continued)

for fish-eating snakes like the garter snake. You will also need bark for the ground and a heater pad to set up under the terrarium. All snakes have to have their terrariums at an exact temperature or they die. To find what temperature you need, ask the people at the store. The final thing that you need is a shelter or a place for the snakes to hide in.

Important point.

Finally, you should clean out your terrarium whenever it gets dirty and feed your snake about every two weeks.

Step 4: caring for your snake.

Overall, I think you will find that snakes are the coolest, the funniest, and the easiest animals to take care of.

Conclusion.

—Joshua Nichols
Pacific Academy Preparatory School
Richmond, California

Evaluating and Revising

1. Self Evaluation

Reread your first draft, checking to be sure you've met all the Evaluation Criteria on the left.

2. Peer Review

Exchange papers with a partner. As you read your partner's essay, imagine that you're actually doing the activity, or take the essay home and try to follow the steps yourself. Give your partner feedback: Were you successful in carrying out the process? Are there any steps or details that aren't absolutely clear? Do you have any unanswered questions?

Peanuts reprinted by permission of UFS, Inc.

Sentence Workshop

COMBINING SENTENCES

Two sentences that express closely related ideas can be connected with a comma and *and, but,* or *or.* By combining sentences in this way, you help your reader see their relationship.

ORIGINAL   The rich man saw all the doctors in the city. None of them could cure his disease.

COMBINED   The rich man saw all the doctors in the city, **but** none of them could cure his disease.

ORIGINAL   The sled flew off the edge of the gully. Paulsen fell onto the ice below.

COMBINED   The sled flew off the edge of the gully, **and** Paulsen fell onto the ice below.

ORIGINAL   Has the dolphin saved his life by talking? Will Dr. Crocus kill him anyway?

COMBINED   Has the dolphin saved his life by talking, **or** will Dr. Crocus kill him anyway?

Make sure you don't confuse your reader by combining sentences that are not closely related.

UNRELATED   I didn't like Zindel's play *Let Me Hear You Whisper,* but he also wrote the novel *The Pigman.*

RELATED   I didn't like Zindel's play *Let Me Hear You Whisper,* but his novel *The Pigman* is one of my favorite books.

Writer's Workshop Follow-up: Revising

Ask a classmate to read your how-to essay aloud to you. Listen to the sound of your writing: Do your sentences flow, or do they sound choppy? Ask your partner to point out sections that seem awkward. Then, look over your paper again. See if any sentences could be combined to improve the flow or make the connections between ideas clear.

Language Handbook
HELP

See Combining Sentences, pages 789-791.

Technology
HELP

See Language Workshop CD-ROM. *Key word entry: combining sentences.*

Try It Out

Combine each pair of sentences by adding a comma and *and, but,* or *or.*

1. Dolphins are very intelligent. Humans are learning more about them.

2. Do you know how dolphins use echolocation to communicate? Do you know how bats use echolocation?

3. T. S. Eliot wrote a book of poems about cats. He didn't know it would be turned into a Broadway musical.

4. Would you like a cat for a pet? Would you prefer either a dog, a bird, or a hamster?

Reading for Life

Understanding Induction and Deduction

Situation

Suppose that while reading a newspaper, you come across two letters to the editor about using animals in medical research. What strategies can you use to evaluate the arguments?

Strategies

Recognize a logical argument.

- A logical argument is based on correct reasoning. When you argue logically, you present reasons or opinions backed up by facts.

Recognize the writer's aim.

- Writers often use a logical argument to persuade you to think or act in a certain way.

Identify two common ways of organizing and presenting ideas to support arguments.

- **Understand induction.** Induction goes from the **specific to the general.** In inductive reasoning the writer starts with a series of specific facts or observations. From this evidence the writer makes a generalization—a general conclusion that covers many situations.

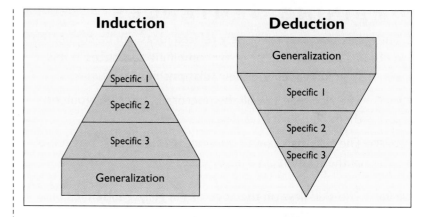

- Example of inductive reasoning:
  Supporting reasons: *Dolphins communicate messages to each other in a language of clicks, creaks, and other sounds. They can be trained to perform complicated tasks.*
  Generalization: *Dolphins are very intelligent animals.*

- **Understand deduction.** Deduction is just the reverse of induction—it goes from the **general to the specific.** In deductive reasoning the writer starts with a generalization, or broad statement. The writer then provides specific cases that reflect and support the generalization.

- Example of deductive reasoning:
  Generalization: *Dolphins*

are very intelligent animals.
Supporting reasons: *Dolphins communicate messages to each other in a language of clicks, creaks, and other sounds. They can be trained to perform complicated tasks.*

Using the Strategies

1. Pick an animal that interests you. Then, write a deductive argument about that animal. Use the diagram above and the example about dolphins on this page as a guide.

2. Turn the argument you wrote for question 1 into an example of inductive reasoning.

Extending the Strategies

Find several editorials in newspapers. Do the writers use inductive or deductive reasoning? How can you tell?

Learning for Life

Researching and Sharing Information About Animals

Problem

We humans aren't alone on this planet. We share it with millions of different species of animals and plants. How important are animals in our lives? How should we treat them? What can we learn from them?

Project

Research any topic about animals that interests you. Share your findings with your classmates and your community.

Preparation

1. Get together with a group, and brainstorm possible topics about animals, such as the following:

   • training animals for the movies

   • pets and older people

   • little-known facts about well-known animals

   • famous animals in literature

   • animal myths

2. Once you've selected a topic, brainstorm questions related to that topic.

3. Then, focus on one specific question that you'd enjoy researching, for instance, "What's a typical day in the life of an armadillo?"

4. Decide if you want to do this project on your own or with a group.

Procedure

1. Find reliable sources of information. You can discover information on the Internet, in TV documentaries, and in books and magazines. You might also interview an expert (a veterinarian or an animal trainer), conduct a survey, or call a government office.

2. Put it all together. Select a specific audience and a presentation format. Then, choose the most interesting, appropriate information for your audience. Consider preparing graphics (drawings, charts, graphs, maps, time lines, flowcharts) to convey some of your facts.

Presentation

Choose one of the following formats or another that your teacher approves.

1. Multimedia Presentation

Share your findings in a multimedia presentation combining sound (music, readings) and visuals (text, photos, drawings, other graphics). You might do a live performance or create an interactive computer presentation. (For help, see pages 719–721.)

2. Children's Book

Write an original animal story, a fable, or a nonfiction (factual) book. Write your book for children of a specific age group. Illustrate the book with drawings, photos, or cartoons.

3. All About Animals: A Guide for Owners

Illustrate and publish a guide for animal owners. You might include local animal regulations; a discussion of problems with animals, including stray dogs and cats; a directory of caregivers and organizations that deal with animals; and a list of recommended books and Internet sources.

Processing

Write a brief reflection on this project. You might use one of these starters:

• I discovered . . .

• The most fun was . . .

• The hardest part was . . .

I Still Believe

In spite of everything, I still believe that people are really good at heart.

—Anne Frank
July 15, 1944

Watercolor (1944) by Nely Silvínová, age 12, Theresienstadt Concentration Camp, Terezin, Czechoslovakia. The artist died before her thirteenth birthday.

Elements of Literature

DRAMA: Literature in Action *by* Robert Anderson

A Shared Experience

Literature of all kinds can help us see, explore, and come to know ourselves and our world. Drama speaks to us in a unique way: As "literature in action," it brings a story to life before our eyes.

Many people are involved in bringing a **playwright's** work to life in a theater. The **producer,** the **director,** the **actors,** the **set** and **lighting designers,** even the members of the **audience** share the act of creation with the writer.

The Basic Dramatic Principles

The first question to ask in thinking about a dramatic work (whether it's a play, a movie, or a TV program) is: Who wants what? You'll find that the character who wants something is opposed by another character or a force. This opposition is the source of the **conflict.** The person with the "want" drives the action of the play as he or she tries to resolve the conflict.

Additional problems, or **complications,** arise; then the **climax,** the moment of greatest emotional intensity, is reached. The climax is followed by the **resolution,** the final part of the play, where the conflict is resolved and the story is brought to a close. These steps—conflict, complications, climax, and resolution—are called the **basic dramatic principles.**

The Principles at Work

You can easily recognize these principles at work in TV shows and movies. Consider this typical plot.

Conflict

A lawyer who is down on her luck gets one last chance to prove her worth, by defending a shady-looking client. If she loses this case, she's through.

Complications

While hunting down important testimony, she finds that her life is threatened. At the same time she must overcome her own doubts about her client's innocence.

Climax

Finally, in a dramatic courtroom scene, she brilliantly cross-examines a witness and proves he is lying.

Resolution

The jury acquits her client. The conflict is resolved: The lawyer is back on top of her profession.

Characters in Crisis

Every play centers on a **crisis,** a situation of danger or difficulty that places at risk something of great value to the characters: life, love, family pride, anything that is precious to them. The crisis may arise because the characters want something for which they must struggle with someone else or with themselves. The crisis may also arise because the characters want to remove a threat to their safety or happiness.

Making a Change

Most plays are about **change,** both in the characters and in their relationships. These

changes come about as the characters work out their conflicts.

In the play you are about to read, *The Diary of Anne Frank*, several characters are in a dangerous situation. They are hiding from the Nazis in a small attic in Amsterdam during World War II. What is their primary "want"? They want to survive until the Nazis are driven out of the Netherlands.

Under the pressure of the situation, however, many more conflicts develop. We see several of the characters change as a result, some becoming wiser and more generous, others pettier and more self-centered.

Dramatic Irony: Knowing the Future

Irony is a contrast between expectation and reality. **Dramatic irony** occurs when the people watching a play know something that the characters onstage do not know—including, sometimes, what awaits them in the future.

Most people who see *The Diary of Anne Frank* performed know what happened to Anne and the others who shared her hiding place. (See pages 342–343.) This knowledge lends dramatic irony to everything that is said and done onstage—the conflicts and concerns that will vanish in the face of tragedy, the hopes and plans that will never become reality.

The Shock of Recognition

If a play succeeds, we feel what has been called "the shock of recognition." When the foolish behavior of a character onstage reminds us of ourselves or people we know, we laugh. When the anguish or sorrow expressed by a character calls to mind a painful memory, we cry. When we share in the laughter and tears of other people in the audience, we know we are not alone.

Stage Set for *The Diary of Anne Frank*

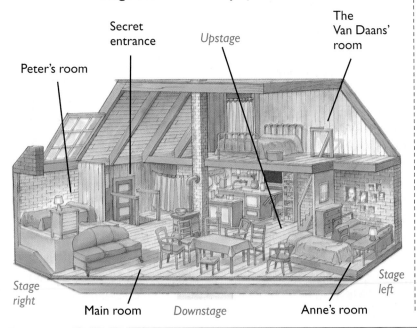

Peter's room

Secret entrance

Upstage

The Van Daans' room

Stage right

Main room

Downstage

Anne's room

Stage left

Before You Read

THE DIARY OF ANNE FRANK

Make the Connection

A True Story

❝ I hope I shall be able to confide in you completely, as I have never been able to do in anyone before, and I hope that you will be a great support and comfort to me. ❞

So begins the diary of a thirteen-year-old Jewish girl named Anne Frank. Anne's diary opens in 1942 with stories of boyfriends, parties, and school life. It closes two years later, just days before Anne is captured and imprisoned in a Nazi concentration camp.

Anne Frank was born in Frankfurt, Germany, in 1929. When she was four years old, her family immigrated to Amsterdam, the Netherlands, to escape the anti-Jewish measures being introduced in Germany. In Amsterdam, Otto Frank, Anne's father, managed a company that sold pectin, a substance used in making jams and jellies. Anne and her older sister, Margot, enjoyed a happy, carefree childhood until May 1940, when the Netherlands capitulated (surrendered) to the invading German Army. Anne wrote in her diary about the Nazi occupation that followed:

Anne Frank in 1942.

❝ After May 1940, good times rapidly fled: first the war, then the capitulation, followed by the arrival of the Germans, which is when the sufferings of us Jews really began. Anti-Jewish decrees followed each other in quick succession. Jews must wear a yellow star, Jews must hand in their bicycles, Jews are banned from trains and are forbidden to drive. Jews are only allowed to do their shopping between three and five o'clock and then only in shops which bear the placard 'Jewish shop.' Jews must be indoors by eight o'clock and cannot even sit in their own gardens after that hour. Jews are forbidden to visit theaters, cinemas, and other places of entertainment. Jews may not take part in public sports. Swimming baths, tennis courts, hockey fields, and other sports grounds are all prohibited to them. Jews may not visit Christians. Jews must go to Jewish schools, and many more restrictions of a similar kind.

So we could not do this and were forbidden to do that. But life went on in spite of it all. ❞

Soon, however, the situation in the Netherlands grew much worse. As in other German-occupied countries, the Nazis began rounding up Jews and transporting them to concentration camps and death camps, where prisoners died from overwork, starvation, or disease, or were murdered in gas chambers. Escaping Nazi-occupied territory became nearly impossible. Like many other Jews trapped in Europe at the time, Anne and her family went into hiding to avoid capture. Others were not so lucky, as Anne knew:

❝ Countless friends and acquaintances have gone to a terrible fate. Evening after evening the green and gray army lorries [trucks] trundle past. The Germans ring at every front door to inquire if

go.hrw.com

LEO 8-5

EUROPE DURING WORLD WAR II

Also see the maps on page 417.

Also see the maps on page 417.

there are any Jews living in the house. If there are, then the whole family has to go at once. If they don't find any, they go on to the next house. No one has a chance of evading them unless one goes into hiding. Often they go around with lists and only ring when they know they can get a good haul. Sometimes they let them off for cash—so much per head. It seems like the slave hunts of olden times. . . . In the evenings when it's dark, I often see rows of good, innocent people accompanied by crying children, walking on and on, in the charge of a couple of these chaps, bullied and knocked about until they almost drop. No one is spared—old people, babies, expectant mothers, the sick—each and all join in the march of death. **99**

The Frank family and four other Jews lived for more than two years hidden in a few cramped rooms (now known as "the Secret Annex") behind Mr. Frank's office and warehouse. In August 1944, the Nazi police raided their hiding place and sent all eight of its occupants to concentration camps. Of the eight, only Otto Frank survived. Anne died of typhus in a camp in Germany called Bergen-Belsen. She was fifteen years old.

When she began her diary, Anne didn't intend to show it to anyone unless she found a "real friend." Through its dozens of translations and the stage adaptation you are about to read, Anne's diary has found her generations of friends all over the world.

Elements of Literature

Flashback

Most of this play is told in the form of an extended **flashback,** framed by opening and closing scenes set at a later time. As you read Scene 1, notice how the frame gives the audience important background information about the characters and their situation.

> **A** flashback is an interruption in the present action of a plot to show events that happened at an earlier time.
>
> *For more on Flashback, see the Handbook of Literary Terms.*

Reading Skills and Strategies

Dialogue with the Text: Using Resources

This text includes many resources supplying facts about this true story. They include a map, a time line, historical photographs, and entries from Anne's diary.

As you read, jot down your thoughts and feelings about the characters and what is happening to them. Be sure to note where the background resources in the text help you to understand the play. The comments on page 348 show one student's thoughts.

ANNE FRANK'S LIFE

June 12: Anne Frank is born in Frankfurt, Germany.

Anne in 1933.

The Franks decide to leave Germany to escape Nazi persecution. While Mr. Frank looks for a new home in Amsterdam, the Netherlands, the rest of the family stays with relatives in Aachen, Germany.

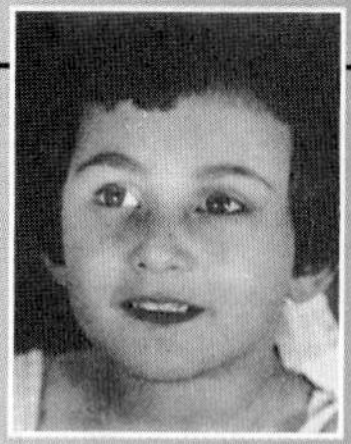

Anne with her father at Miep Santrouschitz and Jan Gies's wedding.

Summer: The Van Pels family (called the Van Daans in Anne's diary) flee Germany for the Netherlands.

December 8: Fritz Pfeffer (called Albert Dussel in Anne's diary) flees Germany for the Netherlands.

Anne playing with her friend Sanne Ledermann in Amsterdam.

The Granger Collection, New York.

WORLD EVENTS

1929

1930 – 1932

The National Socialist German Workers' (Nazi) party begins its rise to power. The Nazis proclaim the superiority of the German "master race" and blame Jews for the German defeat in World War I and for the troubled economy.

1933

January 30: The Nazi party leader, Adolf Hitler, becomes chancellor (head of the government) of Germany.

March 10: The first concentration camp is established by the Nazis, at Dachau, Germany.

April: The Nazis pass their first anti-Jewish law, banning the public employment of Jews.

Adolf Hitler.

1934

1935

September 15: The Nuremberg Laws are passed, denying Jews German citizenship and forbidding marriage between Jews and non-Jews.

1936

November 1: Germany and Italy form an alliance (the Axis).

1937

1938

March 12–13: The German Army invades and annexes Austria.

September 29–30: The Munich Agreement, granting Germany the right to annex part of Czechoslovakia, is drafted and signed by representatives from France, Great Britain, Italy, and Germany.

November 9–10: Kristallnacht (Night of the Broken Glass). Led by the SS, the Nazi special police, Germans beat and kill Jews, loot Jewish stores, and burn synagogues.

ANNE FRANK'S LIFE		WORLD EVENTS

ANNE FRANK'S LIFE

Anne, second from left, with friends on her tenth birthday.

The Granger Collection, New York.

June 12: Anne receives a diary for her thirteenth birthday.

July 6: The Franks go into hiding after Margot receives an order to appear for deportation to a labor camp in Germany. The Van Pels family joins them one week later.

November 16: Fritz Pfeffer becomes the eighth occupant of the Secret Annex.

August 4: Nazi police raid the Secret Annex; the occupants are sent to concentration camps.

September: Mr. Van Pels dies in Auschwitz.

December 20: Fritz Pfeffer dies in Neuengamme.

Anne's mother, Edith Frank, dies in Auschwitz. Three weeks later Otto Frank is freed when Auschwitz is liberated by the Soviet Army. Anne and Margot die in Bergen-Belsen a few weeks before British soldiers liberate the camp. Peter Van Pels dies in Mauthausen. Mrs. Van Pels dies in Theresienstadt.

WORLD EVENTS

1939

March: Germany invades and occupies most of Czechoslovakia.

September 1: Germany invades Poland. France and Great Britain declare war on Germany two days later.

1940

Spring: Germany invades Denmark, Norway, the Netherlands, Belgium, Luxembourg, and France.

September 27: Japan joins the Axis.

1941

June 22: Germany invades the Soviet Union.

December 8: The United States enters the war on the side of the Allied nations (including Great Britain, the Soviet Union, and other countries) after Japan attacks the U.S. naval base at Pearl Harbor.

1942

January: The "Final Solution" is secretly announced at a conference of Nazi officials: Europe's Jews are to be "exterminated," or murdered. Construction of death camps, equipped with gas chambers and huge incinerators for mass killing and cremation, begins in Poland. Millions of people (Jews and non-Jews) will die in these camps.

1943

1944

June 6: D-day. Allied forces land in Normandy, in northern France, and launch an invasion of western Europe.

Bombing of Hiroshima.

1945

May 8: The war in Europe ends with Germany's unconditional surrender to the Allies.

August 14: Japan surrenders after the United States drops atomic bombs on the Japanese cities of Hiroshima and Nagasaki.

Anne. Dear Diary, my name is Anne Frank. I am thirteen years old. Yesterday Father told me we were going into hiding.

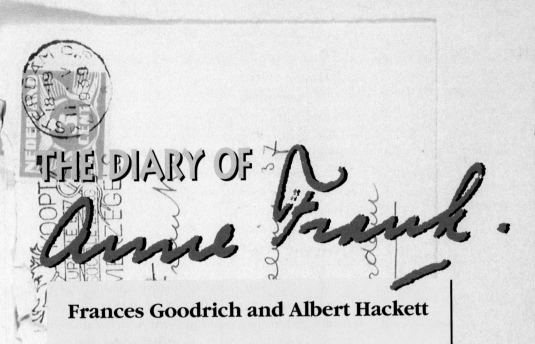

THE DIARY OF *Anne Frank*

Frances Goodrich and Albert Hackett

Characters

Occupants of the Secret Annex:
Anne Frank
Margot Frank, her older sister
Mr. Frank, their father
Mrs. Frank, their mother
Peter Van Daan
Mr. Van Daan, his father
Mrs. Van Daan, his mother
Mr. Dussel, a dentist

Workers in Mr. Frank's Business:
Miep Gies,[1] a young Dutchwoman
Mr. Kraler,[2] a Dutchman

Setting: Amsterdam, the Netherlands, July 1942 to August 1944; November 1945.

1. **Miep Gies** (mēp khēs).
2. **Kraler** (krä′lər).

Act One

■ SCENE 1

The scene remains the same throughout the play. It is the top floor of a warehouse and office building in Amsterdam, Holland. The sharply peaked roof of the building is outlined against a sea of other rooftops stretching away into the distance. Nearby is the belfry of a church tower, the Westertoren, whose carillon[3] rings out the hours. Occasionally faint sounds float up from below: the voices of children playing in the street, the tramp of marching feet, a boat whistle from the canal.[4]

The three rooms of the top floor and a small attic space above are exposed to our view. The largest of the rooms is in the center, with two small rooms, slightly raised, on either side. On the right is a bathroom, out of sight. A narrow, steep flight of stairs at the back leads up to the attic. The rooms are sparsely furnished, with a few chairs, cots, a table or two. The windows are painted over or covered with makeshift blackout curtains. In the main room there is a sink, a gas ring for cooking, and a wood-burning stove for warmth.

The room on the left is hardly more than a closet. There is a skylight in the sloping ceiling. Directly under this room is a small, steep stairwell, with steps leading down to a door. This is the only entrance from the building below. When the door is opened, we see that it has been concealed on the outer side by a bookcase attached to it.

The curtain rises on an empty stage. It is late afternoon, November 1945.

The rooms are dusty, the curtains in rags. Chairs and tables are overturned.

The door at the foot of the small stairwell swings open. MR. FRANK *comes up the steps into view. He is a gentle, cultured European in his middle years. There is still a trace of a German accent in his speech.*

He stands looking slowly around, making a supreme effort at self-control. He is weak, ill. His clothes are threadbare.

After a second he drops his rucksack on the couch and

---

3. **carillon** (kar'ə·län'): set of bells each of which produces a single tone.
4. **canal:** artificial waterway. Amsterdam, which was built on soggy ground, has more than one hundred canals, built to help drain the land. The canals are used like streets.

moves slowly about. He opens the door to one of the smaller rooms and then abruptly closes it again, turning away. He goes to the window at the back, looking off at the Westertoren as its carillon strikes the hour of six; then he moves restlessly on.

From the street below we hear the sound of a barrel organ and children's voices at play. There is a many-colored scarf hanging from a nail. MR. FRANK *takes it, putting it around his neck. As he starts back for his rucksack, his eye is caught by something lying on the floor. It is a woman's white glove. He holds it in his hand and suddenly all of his self-control is gone. He breaks down crying.*

We hear footsteps on the stairs. MIEP GIES *comes up, looking for* MR. FRANK. MIEP *is a Dutchwoman of about twenty-two. She wears a coat and hat, ready to go home. She is preg-*

The Secret Annex.

nant. Her attitude toward MR. FRANK *is protective, compassionate.*

Miep. Are you all right, Mr. Frank?

Mr. Frank (*quickly controlling himself*). Yes, Miep, yes.

Miep. Everyone in the office has gone home. . . . It's after six. (*Then, pleading*) Don't stay up here, Mr. Frank. What's the use of torturing yourself like this?

Mr. Frank. I've come to say goodbye . . . I'm leaving here, Miep.

Miep. What do you mean? Where are you going? Where?

Mr. Frank. I don't know yet. I haven't decided.

Miep. Mr. Frank, you can't leave here! This is your home! Amsterdam is your home. Your business is here, waiting for you. . . . You're needed here. . . . Now that the war is over, there are things that . . .

Mr. Frank. I can't stay in Amsterdam, Miep. It has too many memories for me. Everywhere, there's something . . . the house we lived in . . . the school . . . that street organ playing out there . . . I'm not the person you used to know, Miep. I'm a bitter old man. (*Breaking off*) Forgive me. I shouldn't speak to you like this . . . after all that you did for us . . . the suffering . . .

Miep. No. No. It wasn't suffering. You can't say we suffered. (*As she speaks, she straightens a chair which is overturned.*)

Mr. Frank. I know what you went through, you and Mr. Kraler. I'll remember it as long as I live. (*He gives one last look around.*) Come, Miep. (*He starts for the steps, then remembers his rucksack, going back to get it.*)

Miep (*hurrying up to a cupboard*). Mr. Frank, did you see? There are some of your papers here. (*She brings a bundle of papers to him.*) We found them in a heap of rubbish on the floor after . . . after you left.

Mr. Frank. Burn them. (*He opens his rucksack to put the glove in it.*)

Miep. But, Mr. Frank, there are letters, notes . . .

Mr. Frank. Burn them. All of them.

Miep. Burn *this*? (*She hands him a paperbound notebook.*)

Mr. Frank (*quietly*). Anne's diary. (*He opens the diary and begins to read.*) "Monday, the sixth of July, nineteen forty-two." (*To* MIEP) Nineteen forty-two. Is it possible, Miep? . . . Only three years ago. (*As he continues his reading, he sits down on the couch.*) "Dear Diary, since you and I are going to be great friends, I will start by telling you about myself. My name is Anne Frank. I am thirteen years old. I was born in Germany the twelfth of June, nineteen twenty-nine. As my family is Jewish, we emigrated to Holland when Hitler came to power."

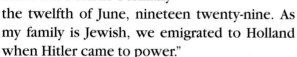

Miep Gies and Otto Frank.

[*As* MR. FRANK *reads on, another voice joins his, as if coming from the air. It is* ANNE's *voice.*]

Mr. Frank and Anne's Voice. "My father started a business, importing spice and herbs. Things went well for us until nineteen forty. Then the war came, and the Dutch capitulation, followed by the arrival of the Germans. Then things got very bad for the Jews."

[MR. FRANK's *voice dies out.* ANNE's *voice continues alone. The lights dim slowly to darkness. The curtain falls on the scene.*]

Anne's Voice. You could not do this and you could not do that. They forced Father out of his business. We had to wear yellow stars.[5] I had to turn in my bike. I couldn't go to a Dutch school anymore. I couldn't go to the movies or ride in an automobile or even on a streetcar, and a million other things. But somehow we children still managed to have fun. Yesterday Father told me we were going into hiding. Where, he wouldn't say. At five o'clock this morning Mother woke me and told me to hurry and get dressed. I was to put on as many clothes as I could. It would look too suspicious if we walked along carrying suitcases. It wasn't until we were on our way that I learned where we were going. Our hiding place was to be upstairs in the building where Father used to have his business. Three other people were coming in with us . . . the Van Daans and their son Peter . . . Father knew the Van Daans but we had never met them. . . .

[*During the last lines the curtain rises on the scene. The lights dim on.* ANNE's *voice fades out.*]

■ SCENE 2

It is early morning, July 1942. The rooms are bare, as before, but they are now clean and orderly.

MR. VAN DAAN, *a tall, portly man in his late forties, is in the main room, pacing up and down, nervously smoking a cigarette. His clothes and overcoat are expensive and well cut.*

MRS. VAN DAAN *sits on the couch, clutching her possessions: a hatbox, bags, etc. She is a pretty woman in her early forties. She wears a fur coat over her other clothes.*

PETER VAN DAAN *is standing at the window of the room on the right, looking down at the street below. He is a shy, awkward boy of sixteen. He wears a cap, a raincoat, and long*

---

5. yellow stars: The Nazis ordered all Jews to sew a large Star of David (a six-pointed star) on their outer clothing so that they could be easily recognized as Jews.

Dutch trousers, like plus fours.[6] *At his feet is a black case, a carrier for his cat.*

The yellow Star of David is <u>conspicuous</u> on all of their clothes.

Mrs. Van Daan (*rising, nervous, excited*). Something's happened to them! I know it!

Mr. Van Daan. Now, Kerli!

Mrs. Van Daan. Mr. Frank said they'd be here at seven o'clock. He said . . .

Mr. Van Daan. They have two miles to walk. You can't expect . . .

Mrs. Van Daan. They've been picked up. That's what's happened. They've been taken . . .

[MR. VAN DAAN *indicates that he hears someone coming.*]

6. **plus fours:** baggy trousers that end in cuffs just below the knees.

Mr. Van Daan. You see?

[PETER *takes up his carrier and his school bag, etc., and goes into the main room as* MR. FRANK *comes up the stairwell from below.* MR. FRANK *looks much younger now. His movements are brisk, his manner confident. He wears an overcoat and carries his hat and a small cardboard box. He crosses to the* VAN DAANS, *shaking hands with each of them.*]

Mr. Frank. Mrs. Van Daan, Mr. Van Daan, Peter. (*Then, in explanation of their lateness*) There were too many of the Green Police[7] on

7. **Green Police:** Nazi police, who wore green uniforms.

WORDS TO OWN

conspicuous (kən·spik′yo͞o·əs) *adj.:* obvious; noticeable.

Scene from the movie *The Diary of Anne Frank* (1959), starring Millie Perkins as Anne. Other scenes from the movie appear throughout the play.

the streets . . . we had to take the long way around.

[*Up the steps come* MARGOT FRANK, MRS. FRANK, MIEP *(not pregnant now), and* MR. KRALER. *All of them carry bags, packages, and so forth. The Star of David is conspicuous on all of the* FRANKS' *clothing.* MARGOT *is eighteen, beautiful, quiet, shy.* MRS. FRANK *is a young mother, gently bred, reserved. She, like* MR. FRANK, *has a slight German accent.* MR. KRALER *is a Dutchman, dependable, kindly.*

As MR. KRALER *and* MIEP *go upstage to put down their parcels,* MRS. FRANK *turns back to call* ANNE.]

Mrs. Frank. Anne?

[ANNE *comes running up the stairs. She is thirteen, quick in her movements, interested in everything, mercurial*[8] *in her emotions. She wears a cape and long wool socks and carries a school bag.*]

Mr. Frank (*introducing them*). My wife, Edith. Mr. and Mrs. Van Daan (MRS. FRANK *hurries over, shaking hands with them.*) . . . their son, Peter . . . my daughters, Margot and Anne.

[ANNE *gives a polite little curtsy as she shakes* MR. VAN DAAN's *hand. Then she immediately starts off on a tour of investigation of her new home, going upstairs to the attic room.*

MIEP *and* MR. KRALER *are putting the various things they have brought on the shelves.*]

Mr. Kraler. I'm sorry there is still so much confusion.

Mr. Frank. Please. Don't think of it. After all, we'll have plenty of leisure to arrange everything ourselves.

Miep (*to* MRS. FRANK). We put the stores of food you sent in here. Your drugs are here . . . soap, linen here.

Mrs. Frank. Thank you, Miep.

Miep. I made up the beds . . . the way Mr. Frank and Mr. Kraler said. (*She starts out.*) Forgive me. I have to hurry. I've got to go to the other side of town to get some ration books[9] for you.

Mrs. Van Daan. Ration books? If they see our names on ration books, they'll know we're here.

Mr. Kraler. There isn't anything . . .

Miep. Don't worry. Your names won't be on them. (*As she hurries out*) I'll be up later.

} *Together*

Mr. Frank. Thank you, Miep.

Mrs. Frank (*to* MR. KRALER). It's illegal, then, the ration books? We've never done anything illegal.

Mr. Frank. We won't be living here exactly according to regulations.

[*As* MR. KRALER *reassures* MRS. FRANK, *he takes various small things, such as matches and soap, from his pockets, handing them to her.*]

Mr. Kraler. This isn't the black market,[10] Mrs. Frank. This is what we call the white market . . . helping all of the hundreds and hundreds who are hiding out in Amsterdam.

[*The carillon is heard playing the quarter-hour before eight.* MR. KRALER *looks at his watch.* ANNE *stops at the window as she comes down the stairs.*]

Anne. It's the Westertoren!

Mr. Kraler. I must go. I must be out of here and downstairs in the office before the workmen get here. (*He starts for the stairs leading out.*) Miep or I, or both of us, will be up each day to bring you food and news and find out

---

8. **mercurial** (mər·kyoor′ē·əl): changeable.

9. **ration books:** books of stamps or coupons issued by the government during wartime. People could purchase scarce items such as food, clothing, and gasoline only with these coupons.
10. **black market:** place or system for buying and selling goods illegally, without ration stamps.

what your needs are. Tomorrow I'll get you a better bolt for the door at the foot of the stairs. It needs a bolt that you can throw yourself and open only at our signal. (*To* MR. FRANK) Oh . . . You'll tell them about the noise?

Mr. Frank. I'll tell them.

Mr. Kraler. Goodbye, then, for the moment. I'll come up again, after the workmen leave.

Mr. Frank. Goodbye, Mr. Kraler.

Mrs. Frank (*shaking his hand*). How can we thank you?

[*The others murmur their goodbyes.*]

Mr. Kraler. I never thought I'd live to see the day when a man like Mr. Frank would have to go into hiding. When you think——

[*He breaks off, going out.* MR. FRANK *follows him down the steps, bolting the door after him. In the interval before he returns,* PETER *goes over to* MARGOT, *shaking hands with her. As* MR. FRANK *comes back up the steps,* MRS. FRANK *questions him anxiously.*]

Mrs. Frank. What did he mean, about the noise?

Mr. Frank. First let us take off some of these clothes.

[*They all start to take off garment after garment. On each of their coats, sweaters, blouses, suits, dresses is another yellow Star of David.* MR. *and* MRS. FRANK *are underdressed quite simply. The others wear several things: sweaters, extra dresses, bathrobes, aprons, nightgowns, etc.*]

Mr. Van Daan. It's a wonder we weren't arrested, walking along the streets . . . Petronella with a fur coat in July . . . and that cat of Peter's crying all the way.

Anne (*as she is removing a pair of panties*). A cat?

Mrs. Frank (*shocked*). Anne, please!

Anne. It's all right. I've got on three more.

[*She pulls off two more. Finally, as they have all removed their surplus clothes, they look to* MR. FRANK, *waiting for him to speak.*]

Mr. Frank. Now. About the noise. While the men are in the building below, we must have complete quiet. Every sound can be heard down there, not only in the workrooms but in the offices too. The men come at about eight-thirty and leave at about five-thirty. So, to be perfectly safe, from eight in the morning until six in the evening we must move only when it is necessary, and then in stockinged feet. We must not speak above a whisper. We must not run any water. We cannot use the sink or even, forgive me, the w.c.[11] The pipes go down through the workrooms. It would be heard. No trash . . . (MR. FRANK *stops abruptly as he hears the sound of marching feet from the street below. Everyone is motionless, paralyzed with fear.* MR. FRANK *goes quietly into the room on the right to look down out of the window.* ANNE *runs after him, peering out with him. The tramping feet pass without stopping. The tension is relieved.* MR. FRANK, *followed by* ANNE, *returns to the main room and resumes his instructions to the group.*) . . . No trash must ever be thrown out which might reveal that someone is living up here . . . not even a potato paring. We must burn everything in the stove at night. This is the way we must live until it is over, if we are to survive.

[*There is silence for a second.*]

Mrs. Frank. Until it is over.

Mr. Frank (*reassuringly*). After six we can move about . . . we can talk and laugh and have our supper and read and play games . . .

11. **w.c.:** short for "water closet," or toilet.

just as we would at home. (*He looks at his watch.*) And now I think it would be wise if we all went to our rooms, and were settled before eight o'clock. Mrs. Van Daan, you and your husband will be upstairs. I regret that there's no place up there for Peter. But he will be here, near us. This will be our common room, where we'll meet to talk and eat and read, like one family.

Mr. Van Daan. And where do you and Mrs. Frank sleep?

Mr. Frank. This room is also our bedroom.

Mrs. Van Daan. That isn't right. We'll sleep here and you take the room upstairs. $\left.\vphantom{\begin{array}{c}a\\b\\c\end{array}}\right\}$ *Together*

Mr. Van Daan. It's your place.

Mr. Frank. Please. I've thought this out for weeks. It's the best arrangement. The only arrangement.

Mrs. Van Daan (*to* MR. FRANK). Never, never can we thank you. (*Then, to* MRS. FRANK) I don't know what would have happened to us, if it hadn't been for Mr. Frank.

Mr. Frank. You don't know how your husband helped me when I came to this country . . . knowing no one . . . not able to speak the language. I can never repay him for that. (*Going to* MR. VAN DAAN) May I help you with your things?

Mr. Van Daan. No. No. (*To* MRS. VAN DAAN) Come along, liefje.[12]

Mrs. Van Daan. You'll be all right, Peter? You're not afraid?

Peter (*embarrassed*). Please, Mother.

[*They start up the stairs to the attic room above.* MR. FRANK *turns to* MRS. FRANK.]

Mr. Frank. You too must have some rest, Edith. You didn't close your eyes last night. Nor you, Margot.

Anne. I slept, Father. Wasn't that funny? I

12. **liefje** (lēf′hyə): Dutch for "little dear one."

Anne. I love cats. I have one . . .

knew it was the last night in my own bed, and yet I slept soundly.

Mr. Frank. I'm glad, Anne. Now you'll be able to help me straighten things in here. (*To* MRS. FRANK *and* MARGOT) Come with me. . . . You and Margot rest in this room for the time being. (*He picks up their clothes, starting for the room on the right.*)

Mrs. Frank. You're sure . . . ? I could help . . . And Anne hasn't had her milk . . .

Mr. Frank. I'll give it to her. (*To* ANNE *and* PETER) Anne, Peter . . . it's best that you take off your shoes now, before you forget. (*He leads the way to the room, followed by* MARGOT.)

Mrs. Frank. You're sure you're not tired, Anne?

Anne. I feel fine. I'm going to help Father.

Mrs. Frank. Peter, I'm glad you are to be with us.

Peter. Yes, Mrs. Frank.

[MRS. FRANK *goes to join* MR. FRANK *and* MARGOT.

During the following scene MR. FRANK *helps* MARGOT *and* MRS. FRANK *to hang up their clothes. Then he persuades them both to lie down and rest. The* VAN DAANS, *in their room above, settle themselves. In the main room* ANNE *and* PETER *remove their shoes.* PETER *takes his cat out of the carrier.*]

Anne. What's your cat's name?

Peter. Mouschi.[13]

Anne. Mouschi! Mouschi! Mouschi! (*She picks up the cat, walking away with it. To* PETER) I love cats. I have one . . . a darling little cat. But they made me leave her behind. I left some food and a note for the neighbors to take care of her. . . . I'm going to miss her terribly. What is yours? A him or a her?

Peter. He's a tom. He doesn't like strangers. (*He takes the cat from her, putting it back in its carrier.*)

Anne (*unabashed*). Then I'll have to stop being a stranger, won't I? Is he fixed?

Peter (*startled*). Huh?

Anne. Did you have him fixed?

Peter. No.

Anne. Oh, you ought to have him fixed—to keep him from—you know, fighting. Where did you go to school?

Peter. Jewish Secondary.

Anne. But that's where Margot and I go! I never saw you around.

Peter. I used to see you . . . sometimes . . .

Anne. You did?

Peter Van Pels
("Peter Van Daan").

Peter. . . . in the schoolyard. You were always in the middle of a bunch of kids. (*He takes a penknife from his pocket.*)

Anne. Why didn't you ever come over?

Peter. I'm sort of a lone wolf. (*He starts to rip off his Star of David.*)

Anne. What are you doing?

Peter. Taking it off.

Anne. But you can't do that. They'll arrest you if you go out without your star.

[*He tosses his knife on the table.*]

Peter. Who's going out?

Anne. Why, of course! You're right! Of course we don't need them anymore. (*She picks up his knife and starts to take her star off.*) I wonder what our friends will think when we don't show up today?

Peter. I didn't have any dates with anyone.

Anne. Oh, I did. I had a date with Jopie to go and play ping-pong at her house. Do you know Jopie de Waal?[14]

Peter. No.

Anne. Jopie's my best friend. I wonder what she'll think when she telephones and there's no answer? . . . Probably she'll go over to the house. . . . I wonder what she'll think . . . we left everything as if we'd suddenly been called away . . . breakfast dishes in the sink . . . beds not made . . . (*As she pulls off her star, the cloth underneath shows clearly the color and form of the star.*) Look! It's still there! (PETER *goes over to the stove*

14. **Jopie de Waal** (yō′pē də väl′).

WORDS TO OWN

unabashed (un′ə·basht′) *adj.:* unembarrassed; unashamed.

---

13. **Mouschi** (mo͞o·shē).

with his star.) What're you going to do with yours?

Peter. Burn it.

Anne. (*She starts to throw hers in, and cannot.*) It's funny, I can't throw mine away. I don't know why.

Peter. You can't throw . . . ? Something they branded you with . . . ? That they made you wear so they could spit on you?

Anne. I know. I know. But after all, it *is* the Star of David, isn't it?

[*In the bedroom, right,* MARGOT *and* MRS. FRANK *are lying down.* MR. FRANK *starts quietly out.*]

Peter. Maybe it's different for a girl.

[MR. FRANK *comes into the main room.*]

Mr. Frank. Forgive me, Peter. Now let me see. We must find a bed for your cat. (*He goes to a cupboard.*) I'm glad you brought your cat. Anne was feeling so badly about hers. (*Getting a used small washtub*) Here we are. Will it be comfortable in that?

Peter (*gathering up his things*). Thanks.

Mr. Frank (*opening the door of the room on the left*). And here is your room. But I warn you, Peter, you can't grow anymore. Not an inch, or you'll have to sleep with your feet out of the skylight. Are you hungry?

Peter. No.

Mr. Frank. We have some bread and butter.

Peter. No, thank you.

Mr. Frank. You can have it for luncheon then. And tonight we will have a real supper . . . our first supper together.

Peter. Thanks. Thanks. (*He goes into his room. During the following scene he arranges his possessions in his new room.*)

Mr. Frank. That's a nice boy, Peter.

Anne. He's awfully shy, isn't he?

Mr. Frank. You'll like him, I know.

Anne. I certainly hope so, since he's the only boy I'm likely to see for months and months.

[MR. FRANK *sits down, taking off his shoes.*]

Mr. Frank. Annele,[15] there's a box there. Will you open it?

[*He indicates a carton on the couch.* ANNE *brings it to the center table. In the street below, there is the sound of children playing.*]

Anne (*as she opens the carton*). You know the way I'm going to think of it here? I'm going to think of it as a boardinghouse. A very peculiar summer boardinghouse, like the one that we—— (*She breaks off as she pulls out some photographs.*) Father! My movie stars! I was wondering where they were! I was looking for them this morning . . . and Queen Wilhelmina![16] How wonderful!

Mr. Frank. There's something more. Go on. Look further. (*He goes over to the sink, pouring a glass of milk from a thermos bottle.*)

Anne (*pulling out a pasteboard-bound book*). A diary! (*She throws her arms around her father.*) I've never had a diary. And I've always longed for one. (*She looks around the room.*) Pencil, pencil, pencil, pencil. (*She starts down the stairs.*) I'm going down to the office to get a pencil.

Mr. Frank. Anne! No! (*He goes after her, catching her by the arm and pulling her back.*)

Anne (*startled*). But there's no one in the building now.

Mr. Frank. It doesn't matter. I don't want you ever to go beyond that door.

Anne (*sobered*). Never . . . ? Not even at nighttime, when everyone is gone? Or on Sundays? Can't I go down to listen to the radio?

Mr. Frank. Never. I am sorry, Anneke.[17] It isn't safe. No, you must never go beyond that door.

[*For the first time* ANNE *realizes what "going into hiding" means.*]

---

15. Annele (än′ə·lə): Yiddish for "little Anne" (like "Annie").

16. Queen Wilhelmina (vil′hel·mē′nä) (1880–1962): queen of the Netherlands from 1890 to 1948.

17. Anneke (än′ə·kə): another affectionate nickname for Anne.

Anne. I've never had a diary. And I've always longed for one.

Anne. I see.

Mr. Frank. It'll be hard, I know. But always remember this, Anneke. There are no walls, there are no bolts, no locks that anyone can put on your mind. Miep will bring us books. We will read history, poetry, mythology. (*He gives her the glass of milk.*) Here's your milk. (*With his arm about her, they go over to the couch, sitting down side by side.*) As a matter of fact, between us, Anne, being here has certain advantages for you. For instance, you remember the battle you had with your mother the other day on the subject of overshoes? You said you'd rather die than wear overshoes? But in the end you had to wear them? Well now, you see, for as long as we are here, you will never have to wear overshoes! Isn't that good? And the coat that you inherited from Margot, you won't have to wear that anymore. And the piano! You won't have to practice on the piano. I tell you, this is going to be a fine life for you!

[ANNE's *panic is gone.* PETER *appears in the doorway of his room, with a saucer in his hand. He is carrying his cat.*]

Peter. I . . . I . . . I thought I'd better get some water for Mouschi before . . .
Mr. Frank. Of course.

[*As he starts toward the sink, the carillon begins to chime the hour of eight. He tiptoes to the window at the back and looks down at the street below. He turns to* PETER, *indicating in pantomime that it is too late.* PETER *starts back for his room. He steps on a creaking board. The three of them are frozen for a minute in fear. As* PETER *starts away again,* ANNE *tiptoes over to him and pours some of the milk from her glass into the saucer for the cat.* PETER *squats on the floor, putting the milk before the cat.* MR. FRANK *gives* ANNE *his fountain pen and then goes into the room at the right. For a second* ANNE *watches the cat; then she goes over to the center table and opens her diary.*

In the room at the right, MRS. FRANK *has sat up quickly at the sound of the carillon.* MR. FRANK *comes in and sits down beside her on the settee,[18] his arm comfortingly around her.*

Upstairs, in the attic room, MR. *and* MRS. VAN DAAN *have hung their clothes in the closet and are now seated on the iron bed.* MRS. VAN DAAN *leans back, exhausted.* MR. VAN DAAN *fans her with a newspaper.*

ANNE *starts to write in her diary. The lights dim out; the curtain falls.*

In the darkness ANNE's *voice comes to us again, faintly at first and then with growing strength.*]

Anne's Voice. I expect I should be describing what it feels like to go into hiding. But I really don't know yet myself. I only know it's funny never to be able to go outdoors . . . never to breathe fresh air . . . never to run and shout

18. **settee** (se·tē′): small couch.

and jump. It's the silence in the nights that frightens me most. Every time I hear a creak in the house or a step on the street outside, I'm sure they're coming for us. The days aren't so bad. At least we know that Miep and Mr. Kraler are down there below us in the office. Our protectors, we call them. I asked Father what would happen to them if the Nazis found out they were hiding us. Pim[19] said that they would suffer the same fate that we would. . . . Imagine! They know this, and yet when they come up here, they're always cheerful and gay, as if there were nothing in the world to bother them. . . . Friday, the twenty-first of August, nineteen forty-two. Today I'm going to tell you our general news. Mother is unbearable. She insists on treating me like a baby, which I loathe. Otherwise things are going better. The weather is . . .

[*As* ANNE's *voice is fading out, the curtain rises on the scene.*]

■ SCENE 3

It is a little after six o'clock in the evening, two months later.

MARGOT *is in the bedroom at the right, studying.* MR. VAN DAAN *is lying down in the attic room above.*

The rest of the "family" is in the main room. ANNE *and* PETER *sit opposite each other at the center table, where they have been doing their lessons.* MRS. FRANK *is on the couch.* MRS. VAN DAAN *is seated with her fur coat, on which she has been sewing, in her lap. None of them are wearing their shoes.*

Their eyes are on MR. FRANK, *waiting for him to give them the signal which will release*

19. **Pim:** family nickname for Mr. Frank.

- -

WORDS TO OWN
loathe (lōth) *v.:* hate.

- -

them from their day-long quiet. MR. FRANK, *his shoes in his hand, stands looking down out of the window at the back, watching to be sure that all of the workmen have left the building below.*

After a few seconds of motionless silence, MR. FRANK *turns from the window.*

Mr. Frank (*quietly, to the group*). It's safe now. The last workman has left.

[*There is an immediate stir of relief.*]

Anne (*Her pent-up energy explodes.*). WHEE!
Mrs. Frank (*startled, amused*). Anne!
Mrs. Van Daan. I'm first for the w.c.

[*She hurries off to the bathroom.* MRS. FRANK *puts on her shoes and starts up to the sink to prepare supper.* ANNE *sneaks* PETER's *shoes from under the table and hides them behind her back.* MR. FRANK *goes into* MARGOT's *room.*]

Mr. Frank (*to* MARGOT). Six o'clock. School's over.

[MARGOT *gets up, stretching.* MR. FRANK *sits down to put on his shoes. In the main room* PETER *tries to find his.*]

Peter (*to* ANNE). Have you seen my shoes?
Anne (*innocently*). Your shoes?
Peter. You've taken them, haven't you?
Anne. I don't know what you're talking about.
Peter. You're going to be sorry!
Anne. Am I?

[PETER *goes after her.* ANNE, *with his shoes in her hand, runs from him, dodging behind her mother.*]

Mrs. Frank (*protesting*). Anne, dear!
Peter. Wait till I get you!
Anne. I'm waiting! (PETER *makes a lunge for her. They both fall to the floor.* PETER *pins her down, wrestling with her to get the shoes.*) Don't! Don't! Peter, stop it. Ouch!
Mrs. Frank. Anne! . . . Peter!

[*Suddenly* PETER *becomes self-conscious. He grabs his shoes roughly and starts for his room.*]

Anne (*following him*). Peter, where are you going? Come dance with me.
Peter. I tell you I don't know how.
Anne. I'll teach you.
Peter. I'm going to give Mouschi his dinner.
Anne. Can I watch?
Peter. He doesn't like people around while he eats.
Anne. Peter, please.
Peter. No!

[*He goes into his room.* ANNE *slams his door after him.*]

Mrs. Frank. Anne, dear, I think you shouldn't play like that with Peter. It's not dignified.
Anne. Who cares if it's dignified? I don't want to be dignified.

[MR. FRANK *and* MARGOT *come from the room on the right.* MARGOT *goes to help her mother.* MR. FRANK *starts for the center table to correct* MARGOT's *school papers.*]

Mrs. Frank (*to* ANNE). You complain that I don't treat you like a grown-up. But when I do, you resent it.
Anne. I only want some fun . . . someone to laugh and clown with . . . After you've sat still all day and hardly moved, you've got to have some fun. I don't know what's the matter with that boy.
Mr. Frank. He isn't used to girls. Give him a little time.
Anne. Time? Isn't two months time? I could cry. (*Catching hold of* MARGOT) Come on, Margot . . . dance with me. Come on, please.
Margot. I have to help with supper.
Anne. You know we're going to forget how to dance. . . . When we get out, we won't remember a thing.

[*She starts to sing and dance by herself.* MR.

FRANK *takes her in his arms, waltzing with her.* MRS. VAN DAAN *comes in from the bathroom.*]

Mrs. Van Daan. Next? (*She looks around as she starts putting on her shoes.*) Where's Peter?

Anne (*as they are dancing*). Where would he be!

Mrs. Van Daan. He hasn't finished his lessons, has he? His father'll kill him if he catches him in there with that cat and his work not done. (MR. FRANK *and* ANNE *finish their dance. They bow to each other with extravagant formality.*) Anne, get him out of there, will you?

Anne (*at* PETER's *door*). Peter? Peter?

Peter (*opening the door a crack*). What is it?

Anne. Your mother says to come out.

Peter. I'm giving Mouschi his dinner.

Mrs. Van Daan. You know what your father says. (*She sits on the couch, sewing on the lining of her fur coat.*)

Peter. For heaven's sake, I haven't even looked at him since lunch.

Mrs. Van Daan. I'm just telling you, that's all.

Anne. I'll feed him.

Peter. I don't want you in there.

Mrs. Van Daan. Peter!

Peter (*to* ANNE). Then give him his dinner and come right out, you hear?

[*He comes back to the table.* ANNE *shuts the door of* PETER's *room after her and disappears behind the curtain covering his closet.*]

Mrs. Van Daan (*to* PETER). Now is that any way to talk to your little girlfriend?

Peter. Mother . . . for heaven's sake . . . will you please stop saying that?

Mrs. Van Pels ("Mrs. Van Daan").

Mrs. Van Daan. Look at him blush! Look at him!

Peter. Please! I'm not . . . anyway . . . let me alone, will you?

Mrs. Van Daan. He acts like it was something to be ashamed of. It's nothing to be ashamed of, to have a little girlfriend.

Peter. You're crazy. She's only thirteen.

Mrs. Van Daan. So what? And you're sixteen. Just perfect. Your father's ten years older than I am. (*To* MR. FRANK) I warn you, Mr. Frank, if this war lasts much longer, we're going to be related and then . . .

Mr. Frank. Mazel tov![20]

Mrs. Frank (*deliberately changing the conversation*). I wonder where Miep is. She's usually so prompt.

[*Suddenly everything else is forgotten as they hear the sound of an automobile coming to a screeching stop in the street below. They are tense, motionless in their terror. The car starts away. A wave of relief sweeps over them. They pick up their occupations again.* ANNE *flings open the door of* PETER's *room, making a dramatic entrance. She is dressed in* PETER's *clothes.* PETER *looks at her in fury. The others are amused.*]

Anne. Good evening, everyone. Forgive me if I don't stay. (*She jumps up on a chair.*) I have a friend waiting for me in there. My friend Tom. Tom Cat. Some people say that we look alike. But Tom has the most beautiful whiskers, and I have only a little fuzz. I am hoping . . . in time . . .

Peter. All right, Mrs. Quack Quack!

Anne (*outraged—jumping down*). Peter!

Peter. I heard about you . . . how you talked

---

20. Mazel tov! (mä′zəl tōv′): Yiddish expression meaning "Congratulations!"

so much in class they called you Mrs. Quack Quack. How Mr. Smitter made you write a composition . . . "'Quack, quack,' said Mrs. Quack Quack."

Anne. Well, go on. Tell them the rest. How it was so good he read it out loud to the class and then read it to all his other classes!

Peter. Quack! Quack! Quack . . . Quack . . . Quack . . .

[ANNE *pulls off the coat and trousers.*]

Anne. You are the most intolerable, insufferable boy I've ever met!

[*She throws the clothes down the stairwell.* PETER *goes down after them.*]

Peter. Quack, quack, quack!

Mrs. Van Daan (*to* ANNE). That's right, Anneke! Give it to him!

Anne. With all the boys in the world . . . why I had to get locked up with one like you! . . .

Peter. Quack, quack, quack, and from now on stay out of my room!

[*As* PETER *passes her,* ANNE *puts out her foot, tripping him. He picks himself up and goes on into his room.*]

Mrs. Frank (*quietly*). Anne, dear . . . your hair. (*She feels* ANNE's *forehead.*) You're warm. Are you feeling all right?

Anne. Please, Mother. (*She goes over to the center table, slipping into her shoes.*)

Mrs. Frank (*following her*). You haven't a fever, have you?

Anne (*pulling away*). No. No.

Mrs. Frank. You know we can't call a doctor here, ever. There's only one thing to do . . . watch carefully. Prevent an illness before it comes. Let me see your tongue.

Anne. Mother, this is perfectly absurd.

Mrs. Frank. Anne, dear, don't be such a baby. Let me see your tongue. (*As* ANNE *refuses,* MRS. FRANK *appeals to* MR. FRANK.) Otto . . . ?

Mr. Frank. You hear your mother, Anne.

[ANNE *flicks out her tongue for a second, then turns away.*]

Mrs. Frank. Come on—open up! (*As* ANNE *opens her mouth very wide*) You seem all right . . . but perhaps an aspirin . . .

Mrs. Van Daan. For heaven's sake, don't give that child any pills. I waited for fifteen minutes this morning for her to come out of the w.c.

Anne. I was washing my hair!

Mr. Frank. I think there's nothing the matter with our Anne that a ride on her bike or a visit with her friend Jopie de Waal wouldn't cure. Isn't that so, Anne?

[MR. VAN DAAN *comes down into the room. From outside we hear faint sounds of bombers going over and a burst of ack-ack.*][21]

Mr. Van Daan. Miep not come yet?

Mrs. Van Daan. The workmen just left, a little while ago.

Mr. Van Daan. What's for dinner tonight?

Mrs. Van Daan. Beans.

Mr. Van Daan. Not again!

Mrs. Van Daan. Poor Putti! I know. But what can we do? That's all that Miep brought us.

[MR. VAN DAAN *starts to pace, his hands behind his back.* ANNE *follows behind him, imitating him.*]

Anne. We are now in what is known as the "bean cycle." Beans boiled, beans en casserole, beans with strings, beans without strings . . .

[PETER *has come out of his room. He slides into his place at the table, becoming immediately absorbed in his studies.*]

Mr. Van Daan (*to* PETER). I saw you . . . in there, playing with your cat.

Mrs. Van Daan. He just went in for a second, putting his coat away. He's been out here all the time, doing his lessons.

21. **ack-ack:** slang for "antiaircraft gunfire."

Mr. Frank (*looking up from the papers*). Anne, you got an "excellent" in your history paper today . . . and "very good" in Latin.

Anne (*sitting beside him*). How about algebra?

Mr. Frank. I'll have to make a confession. Up until now I've managed to stay ahead of you in algebra. Today you caught up with me. We'll leave it to Margot to correct.

Anne. Isn't algebra vile, Pim!

Mr. Frank. Vile!

Margot (*to* MR. FRANK). How did I do?

Anne (*getting up*). Excellent, excellent, excellent, excellent!

Mr. Frank (*to* MARGOT). You should have used the subjunctive here. . . .

Margot. Should I? . . . I thought . . . look here . . . I didn't use it here. . . .

[*The two become absorbed in the papers.*]

Anne. Mrs. Van Daan, may I try on your coat?

Mrs. Frank. No, Anne.

Mrs. Van Daan (*giving it to* ANNE). It's all right . . . but careful with it. (ANNE *puts it on and struts with it.*) My father gave me that the year before he died. He always bought the best that money could buy.

Anne. Mrs. Van Daan, did you have a lot of boyfriends before you were married?

Mrs. Frank. Anne, that's a personal question. It's not courteous to ask personal questions.

Mrs. Van Daan. Oh, I don't mind. (*To* ANNE) Our house was always swarming with boys. When I was a girl, we had . . .

Mr. Van Daan. Oh, God. Not again!

Mrs. Van Daan (*good-humored*). Shut up! (*Without a pause, to* ANNE. MR. VAN DAAN *mimics* MRS. VAN DAAN, *speaking the first few words in unison with her.*) One summer we had a big house in Hilversum. The boys came buzzing round like bees around a jam pot. And when I was sixteen! . . . We were wearing our skirts very short those days and I had good-looking legs. (*She pulls up her skirt, going to* MR.

FRANK.) I still have 'em. I may not be as pretty as I used to be, but I still have my legs. How about it, Mr. Frank?

Mr. Van Daan. All right. All right. We see them.

Mrs. Van Daan. I'm not asking you. I'm asking Mr. Frank.

Peter. Mother, for heaven's sake.

Mrs. Van Daan. Oh, I embarrass you, do I? Well, I just hope the girl you marry has as good. (*Then, to* ANNE) My father used to worry about me, with so many boys hanging round. He told me, if any of them gets fresh, you say to him . . . "Remember, Mr. So-and-So, remember I'm a lady."

Anne. "Remember, Mr. So-and-So, remember I'm a lady." (*She gives* MRS. VAN DAAN *her coat.*)

Mr. Van Daan. Look at you, talking that way in front of her! Don't you know she puts it all down in that diary?

Mrs. Van Daan. So, if she does? I'm only telling the truth!

[ANNE *stretches out, putting her ear to the floor, listening to what is going on below. The sound of the bombers fades away.*]

Mrs. Frank (*setting the table*). Would you mind, Peter, if I moved you over to the couch?

Anne (*listening*). Miep must have the radio on.

[PETER *picks up his papers, going over to the couch beside* MRS. VAN DAAN.]

Mr. Van Daan (*accusingly, to* PETER). Haven't you finished yet?

Peter. No.

Mr. Van Daan. You ought to be ashamed of yourself.

Peter. All right. All right. I'm a dunce. I'm a hopeless case. Why do I go on?

Mrs. Van Daan. You're not hopeless. Don't talk that way. It's just that you haven't anyone to help you, like the girls have. (*To* MR. FRANK) Maybe you could help him, Mr. Frank?

Mr. Frank. I'm sure that his father . . . ?

Mr. Van Daan. Not me. I can't do anything with him. He won't listen to me. You go ahead . . . if you want.

Mr. Frank (*going to* PETER). What about it, Peter? Shall we make our school coeducational?

Mrs. Van Daan (*kissing* MR. FRANK). You're an angel, Mr. Frank. An angel. I don't know why I didn't meet you before I met that one there. Here, sit down, Mr. Frank . . . (*She forces him down on the couch beside* PETER.) Now, Peter, you listen to Mr. Frank.

Mr. Frank. It might be better for us to go into Peter's room.

[PETER *jumps up eagerly, leading the way.*]

Mrs. Van Daan. That's right. You go in there, Peter. You listen to Mr. Frank. Mr. Frank is a highly educated man.

[*As* MR. FRANK *is about to follow* PETER *into his room,* MRS. FRANK *stops him and wipes the lipstick from his lips. Then she closes the door after them.*]

Anne (*on the floor, listening*). Shh! I can hear a man's voice talking.

Mr. Van Daan (*to* ANNE). Isn't it bad enough here without your sprawling all over the place?

[ANNE *sits up.*]

Mrs. Van Daan (*to* MR. VAN DAAN). If you didn't smoke so much, you wouldn't be so bad-tempered.

Mr. Van Daan. Am I smoking? Do you see me smoking?

Mrs. Van Daan. Don't tell me you've used up all those cigarettes.

Mr. Van Daan. One package. Miep only brought me one package.

Mrs. Van Daan. It's a filthy habit anyway. It's a good time to break yourself.

Mr. Van Daan. Oh, stop it, please.

Mrs. Van Daan. You're smoking up all our money. You know that, don't you?

Mr. Van Daan. Will you shut up? (*During this,* MRS. FRANK *and* MARGOT *have studiously kept their eyes down. But* ANNE, *seated on the floor, has been following the discussion interestedly.* MR. VAN DAAN *turns to see her staring up at him.*) And what are you staring at?

Anne. I never heard grown-ups quarrel before. I thought only children quarreled.

Mr. Van Daan. This isn't a quarrel! It's a discussion. And I never heard children so rude before.

Anne (*rising, indignantly*). I, rude!

Mr. Van Daan. Yes!

Mrs. Frank (*quickly*). Anne, will you get me my knitting? (ANNE *goes to get it.*) I must remember, when Miep comes, to ask her to bring me some more wool.

Margot (*going to her room*). I need some hairpins and some soap. I made a list. (*She goes into her bedroom to get the list.*)

Mrs. Frank (*to* ANNE). Have you some library books for Miep when she comes?

Anne. It's a wonder that Miep has a life of her own, the way we make her run errands for us. Please, Miep, get me some starch. Please take my hair out and have it cut. Tell me all the latest news, Miep. (*She goes over, kneeling on the couch beside* MRS. VAN DAAN.) Did you know she was engaged? His name is Dirk, and Miep's afraid the Nazis will ship him off to Germany to work in one of their war plants. That's what they're doing with some of the young Dutchmen . . . they pick them up off the streets——

Mr. Van Daan (*interrupting*). Don't you ever get tired of talking? Suppose you try keeping still for five minutes. Just five minutes.

[*He starts to pace again. Again* ANNE *follows him, mimicking him.* MRS. FRANK *jumps up*

WORDS TO OWN

indignantly (in·dig′nənt·lē) *adv.:* with anger caused by something felt to be unjust.

and takes her by the arm up to the sink and gives her a glass of milk.]

Mrs. Frank. Come here, Anne. It's time for your glass of milk.

Mr. Van Daan. Talk, talk, talk. I never heard such a child. Where is my . . . ? Every evening it's the same, talk, talk, talk. (*He looks around.*) Where is my . . . ?

Mrs. Van Daan. What're you looking for?

Mr. Van Daan. My pipe. Have you seen my pipe?

Mrs. Van Daan. What good's a pipe? You haven't got any tobacco.

Mr. Van Daan. At least I'll have something to hold in my mouth! (*Opening* MARGOT'*s bedroom door*) Margot, have you seen my pipe?

Margot. It was on the table last night.

[ANNE *puts her glass of milk on the table and picks up his pipe, hiding it behind her back.*]

Mr. Van Daan. I know. I know. Anne, did you see my pipe? . . . Anne!

Mrs. Frank. Anne, Mr. Van Daan is speaking to you.

Anne. Am I allowed to talk now?

Mr. Van Daan. You're the most aggravating . . . The trouble with you is, you've been spoiled. What you need is a good old-fashioned spanking.

Anne (*mimicking* MRS. VAN DAAN). "Remember, Mr. So-and-So, remember I'm a lady." (*She thrusts the pipe into his mouth, then picks up her glass of milk.*)

Mr. Van Daan (*restraining himself with difficulty*). Why aren't you nice and quiet like your sister Margot? Why do you have to show off all the time? Let me give you a little advice, young lady. Men don't like that kind of thing in a girl. You know that? A man likes a girl who'll listen to him once in a while . . . a domestic girl, who'll keep her house shining for her husband . . . who loves to cook and sew and . . .

Anne. I'd cut my throat first! I'd open my

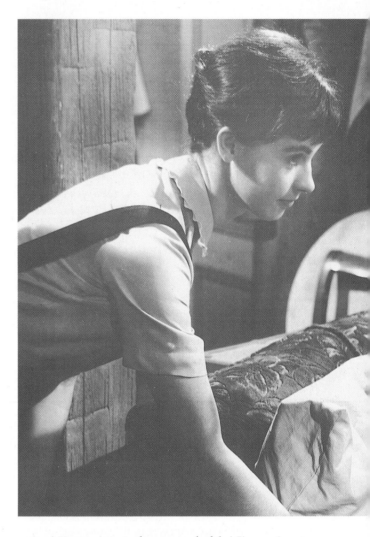

veins! I'm going to be remarkable! I'm going to Paris . . .

Mr. Van Daan (*scoffingly*). Paris!

Anne. . . . to study music and art.

Mr. Van Daan. Yeah! Yeah!

Anne. I'm going to be a famous dancer or singer . . . or something wonderful.

[*She makes a wide gesture, spilling the glass of milk on the fur coat in* MRS. VAN DAAN'*s lap.* MARGOT *rushes quickly over with a towel.* ANNE *tries to brush the milk off with her skirt.*]

Mrs. Van Daan. Now look what you've done . . . you clumsy little fool! My beautiful fur coat my father gave me . . .

Anne. I'm so sorry.

Mrs. Van Daan. Now look what you've done!

Mrs. Frank. I don't mean that. I mean the answering back. You must not answer back. They are our guests. We must always show the greatest courtesy to them. We're all living under terrible tension. (*She stops as* MARGOT *indicates that* MR. VAN DAAN *can hear. When he is gone, she continues.*) That's why we must control ourselves. . . . You don't hear Margot getting into arguments with them, do you? Watch Margot. She's always courteous with them. Never familiar. She keeps her distance. And they respect her for it. Try to be like Margot.

Anne. And have them walk all over me, the way they do her? No, thanks!

Mrs. Frank. I'm not afraid that anyone is going to walk all over you, Anne. I'm afraid for other people, that you'll walk on them. I don't know what happens to you, Anne. You are wild, self-willed. If I had ever talked to my mother as you talk to me . . .

Anne. Things have changed. People aren't like that anymore. "Yes, Mother." "No, Mother." "Anything you say, Mother." I've got to fight things out for myself! Make something of myself!

Mrs. Frank. It isn't necessary to fight to do it. Margot doesn't fight, and isn't she . . . ?

Anne (*violently rebellious*). Margot! Margot! Margot! That's all I hear from everyone . . . how wonderful Margot is . . . "Why aren't you like Margot?"

Margot (*protesting*). Oh, come on, Anne, don't be so . . .

Anne (*paying no attention*). Everything she does is right, and everything I do is wrong! I'm the goat around here! . . . You're all against me! . . . And you worst of all!

[*She rushes off into her room and throws herself down on the settee, stifling her sobs.* MRS. FRANK *sighs and starts toward the stove.*]

Mrs. Van Daan. What do you care? It isn't yours. . . . So go on, ruin it! Do you know what that coat cost? Do you? And now look at it! Look at it!

Anne. I'm very, very sorry.

Mrs. Van Daan. I could kill you for this. I could just kill you!

[MRS. VAN DAAN *goes up the stairs, clutching the coat.* MR. VAN DAAN *starts after her.*]

Mr. Van Daan. Petronella . . . liefje! Liefje! . . . Come back . . . the supper . . . come back!

Mrs. Frank. Anne, you must not behave in that way.

Anne. It was an accident. Anyone can have an accident.

Mrs. Frank (*to* MARGOT). Let's put the soup on the stove . . . if there's anyone who cares to eat. Margot, will you take the bread out? (MARGOT *gets the bread from the cupboard.*) I don't know how we can go on living this way. . . . I can't say a word to Anne . . . she flies at me . . .

Margot. You know Anne. In half an hour she'll be out here, laughing and joking.

Mrs. Frank. And . . . (*She makes a motion upward, indicating the* VAN DAANS.) . . . I told your father it wouldn't work . . . but no . . . no . . . he had to ask them, he said . . . he owed it to him, he said. Well, he knows now that I was right! These quarrels! . . . This bickering!

Margot (*with a warning look*). Shush. Shush.

[*The buzzer for the door sounds.* MRS. FRANK *gasps, startled.*]

Mrs. Frank. Every time I hear that sound, my heart stops!

Margot (*starting for* PETER'S *door*). It's Miep. (*She knocks at the door.*) Father?

[MR. FRANK *comes quickly from* PETER'S *room.*]

Mr. Frank. Thank you, Margot. (*As he goes down the steps to open the outer door*) Has everyone his list?

Margot. I'll get my books. (*Giving her mother a list*) Here's your list. (MARGOT *goes into her and* ANNE'S *bedroom on the right.* ANNE *sits up, hiding her tears, as* MARGOT *comes in.*) Miep's here.

[MARGOT *picks up her books and goes back.* ANNE *hurries over to the mirror, smoothing her hair.*]

Mr. Van Daan (*coming down the stairs*). Is it Miep?

Margot. Yes. Father's gone down to let her in.

Mr. Van Daan. At last I'll have some cigarettes!

Mrs. Frank (*to* MR. VAN DAAN). I can't tell you how unhappy I am about Mrs. Van Daan's coat. Anne should never have touched it.

Mr. Van Daan. She'll be all right.

Mrs. Frank. Is there anything I can do?

Mr. Van Daan. Don't worry.

[*He turns to meet* MIEP. *But it is not* MIEP *who comes up the steps. It is* MR. KRALER, *followed by* MR. FRANK. *Their faces are grave.* ANNE *comes from the bedroom.* PETER *comes from his room.*]

Mrs. Frank. Mr. Kraler!

Mr. Van Daan. How are you, Mr. Kraler?

Margot. This is a surprise.

Mrs. Frank. When Mr. Kraler comes, the sun begins to shine.

Mr. Van Daan. Miep is coming?

Mr. Kraler. Not tonight. (MR. KRALER *goes to* MARGOT *and* MRS. FRANK *and* ANNE, *shaking hands with them.*)

Mrs. Frank. Wouldn't you like a cup of coffee? . . . Or, better still, will you have supper with us?

Mr. Frank. Mr. Kraler has something to talk over with us. Something has happened, he says, which demands an immediate decision.

Mrs. Frank (*fearful*). What is it?

[MR. KRALER *sits down on the couch. As he talks he takes bread, cabbages, milk, etc., from his briefcase, giving them to* MARGOT *and* ANNE *to put away.*]

Mr. Kraler. Usually, when I come up here, I try to bring you some bit of good news. What's the use of telling you the bad news when there's nothing that you can do about it? But today something has happened. . . . Dirk . . . Miep's Dirk, you know, came to me just now. He tells me that he has a Jewish friend living near him. A dentist. He says he's in trouble. He begged me, could I do anything for this man? Could I find him a hiding place? . . . So I've come to you . . . I know it's a terrible thing to ask of you, living as you are, but would you take him in with you?

Mr. Frank. Of course we will.

Mr. Kraler (*rising*). It'll be just for a night or two . . . until I find some other place. This happened so suddenly that I didn't know where to turn.

Mr. Frank. Where is he?

Mr. Kraler. Downstairs in the office.

Mr. Frank. Good. Bring him up.

Mr. Kraler. His name is Dussel[22] . . .

Mr. Frank. Dussel . . . I think I know him.

Mr. Kraler. I'll get him.

[*He goes quickly down the steps and out.* MR. FRANK *suddenly becomes conscious of the others.*]

Mr. Frank. Forgive me. I spoke without consulting you. But I knew you'd feel as I do.

Mr. Van Daan. There's no reason for you to consult anyone. This is your place. You have a right to do exactly as you please. The only thing I feel . . . there's so little food as it is . . . and to take in another person . . .

[PETER *turns away, ashamed of his father.*]

Mr. Frank. We can stretch the food a little. It's only for a few days.

Mr. Van Daan. You want to make a bet?

Mrs. Frank. I think it's fine to have him. But, Otto, where are you going to put him? Where?

Peter. He can have my bed. I can sleep on the floor. I wouldn't mind.

Mr. Frank. That's good of you, Peter. But your room's too small . . . even for *you*.

Anne. I have a much better idea. I'll come in here with you and Mother, and Margot can take Peter's room and Peter can go in our room with Mr. Dussel.

Margot. That's right. We could do that.

Mr. Frank. No, Margot. You mustn't sleep in that room . . . neither you nor Anne. Mouschi has caught some rats in there. Peter's brave. He doesn't mind.

Anne. Then how about *this*? I'll come in here with you and Mother, and Mr. Dussel can have my bed.

Mrs. Frank. No. No. *No!* Margot will come in here with us and he can have her bed. It's the only way. Margot, bring your things in here. Help her, Anne.

[MARGOT *hurries into her room to get her things.*]

Anne (*to her mother*). Why Margot? Why can't I come in here?

Mrs. Frank. Because it wouldn't be proper for Margot to sleep with a . . . Please, Anne. Don't argue. Please.

[ANNE *starts slowly away.*]

Mr. Frank (*to* ANNE). You don't mind sharing your room with Mr. Dussel, do you, Anne?

Anne. No. No, of course not.

Mr. Frank. Good. (ANNE *goes off into her bedroom, helping* MARGOT. MR. FRANK *starts to search in the cupboards.*) Where's the cognac?[23]

Mrs. Frank. It's there. But, Otto, I was saving it in case of illness.

Mr. Frank. I think we couldn't find a better time to use it. Peter, will you get five glasses for me?

[PETER *goes for the glasses.* MARGOT *comes out of her bedroom, carrying her possessions, which she hangs behind a curtain in the main room.* MR. FRANK *finds the cognac and pours it into the five glasses that* PETER *brings him.* MR. VAN DAAN *stands looking on sourly.* MRS. VAN DAAN *comes downstairs and looks around at all the bustle.*]

Mrs. Van Daan. What's happening? What's going on?

Mr. Van Daan. Someone's moving in with us.

Mrs. Van Daan. In here? You're joking.

Margot. It's only for a night or two . . . until Mr. Kraler finds him another place.

22. **Dussel** (dŏo′səl).

23. **cognac** (kän′yak′): type of brandy (distilled wine).

Mr. Van Daan. Yeah! Yeah!

[MR. FRANK *hurries over as* MR. KRALER *and* DUSSEL *come up.* DUSSEL *is a man in his late fifties, meticulous, finicky . . . bewildered now. He wears a raincoat. He carries a briefcase, stuffed full, and a small medicine case.*]

Mr. Frank. Come in, Mr. Dussel.
Mr. Kraler. This is Mr. Frank.
Dussel. Mr. Otto Frank?
Mr. Frank. Yes. Let me take your things. (*He takes the hat and briefcase, but* DUSSEL *clings to his medicine case.*) This is my wife, Edith . . . Mr. and Mrs. Van Daan . . . their son, Peter . . . and my daughters, Margot and Anne.

[DUSSEL *shakes hands with everyone.*]

Mr. Kraler. Thank you, Mr. Frank. Thank you all. Mr. Dussel, I leave you in good hands. Oh . . . Dirk's coat.

[DUSSEL *hurriedly takes off the raincoat, giving it to* MR. KRALER. *Underneath is his white dentist's jacket, with a yellow Star of David on it.*]

Dussel (*to* MR. KRALER). What can I say to thank you . . . ?
Mrs. Frank (*to* DUSSEL). Mr. Kraler and Miep . . . They're our lifeline. Without them we couldn't live.
Mr. Kraler. Please. Please. You make us seem very heroic. It isn't that at all. We simply don't like the Nazis. (*To* MR. FRANK, *who offers him a drink*) No, thanks. (*Then, going on*) We don't like their methods. We don't like . . .
Mr. Frank (*smiling*). I know. I know. "No one's going to tell us Dutchmen what to do with our damn Jews!"

Mr. Kraler (*to* DUSSEL). Pay no attention to Mr. Frank. I'll be up tomorrow to see that they're treating you right. (*To* MR. FRANK) Don't trouble to come down again. Peter will bolt the door after me, won't you, Peter?
Peter. Yes, sir.
Mr. Frank. Thank you, Peter. I'll do it.
Mr. Kraler. Good night. Good night.
Group. Good night, Mr. Kraler. We'll see you tomorrow. (*Etc., etc.*)

[MR. KRALER *goes out with* MR. FRANK. MRS. FRANK *gives each one of the "grown-ups" a glass of cognac.*]

Mrs. Frank. Please, Mr. Dussel, sit down.

[DUSSEL *sinks into a chair.* MRS. FRANK *gives him a glass of cognac.*]

Dussel. I'm dreaming. I know it. I can't believe my eyes. Mr. Otto Frank here! (*To* MRS. FRANK) You're not in Switzerland, then? A woman told me . . . She said she'd gone to your house . . . the door was open, everything was in disorder, dishes in the sink. She said she found a piece of paper in the wastebasket with an address scribbled on it . . . an address in Zurich.[24] She said you must have escaped to Zurich.
Anne. Father put that there purposely . . . just so people would think that very thing!
Dussel. And you've been *here* all the time?
Mrs. Frank. All the time . . . ever since July.

[ANNE *speaks to her father as he comes back.*]

Anne. It worked, Pim . . . the address you left! Mr. Dussel says that people believe we escaped to Switzerland.

Fritz Pfeffer ("Dussel").

24. **Zurich** (zoor´ik): Switzerland's largest city. Because Switzerland remained neutral during World War II, many refugees sought safety there.

Mr. Frank. I'm glad. . . . And now let's have a little drink to welcome Mr. Dussel. (*Before they can drink,* DUSSEL *bolts his drink.* MR. FRANK *smiles and raises his glass.*) To Mr. Dussel. Welcome. We're very honored to have you with us.

Mrs. Frank. To Mr. Dussel, welcome.

[*The* VAN DAANS *murmur a welcome. The "grown-ups" drink.*]

Mrs. Van Daan. Um. That was good.

Mr. Van Daan. Did Mr. Kraler warn you that you won't get much to eat here? You can imagine . . . three ration books among the seven of us . . . and now you make eight.

[PETER *walks away, humiliated. Outside, a street organ is heard dimly.*]

Dussel (*rising*). Mr. Van Daan, you don't realize what is happening outside that you should warn me of a thing like that. You don't realize what's going on. . . . (*As* MR. VAN DAAN *starts his characteristic pacing,* DUSSEL *turns to speak to the others.*) Right here in Amsterdam every day hundreds of Jews disappear. . . . They surround a block and search house by house. Children come home from school to find their parents gone. Hundreds are being deported . . .[25] people that you and I know . . . the Hallensteins . . . the Wessels . . .

Mrs. Frank (*in tears*). Oh, no. No!

Dussel. They get their call-up notice . . . come to the Jewish theater on such and such a day and hour . . . bring only what you can carry in a rucksack. And if you refuse the call-up notice, then they come and drag you from your home and ship you off to Mauthausen. The death camp!

Mrs. Frank. We didn't know that things had got so much worse.

Dussel. Forgive me for speaking so.

---

25. **deported:** forcibly sent away (to concentration camps and death camps).

Anne (*coming to* DUSSEL). Do you know the de Waals? . . . What's become of them? Their daughter Jopie and I are in the same class. Jopie's my best friend.

Dussel. They are gone.

Anne. Gone?

Dussel. With all the others.

Anne. Oh, no. Not Jopie!

[*She turns away, in tears.* MRS. FRANK *motions to* MARGOT *to comfort her.* MARGOT *goes to* ANNE, *putting her arms comfortingly around her.*]

Mrs. Van Daan. There were some people called Wagner. They lived near us . . . ?

Mr. Frank (*interrupting, with a glance at* ANNE). I think we should put this off until later. We all have many questions we want to ask. . . . But I'm sure that Mr. Dussel would like to get settled before supper.

Dussel. Thank you. I would. I brought very little with me.

Mr. Frank (*giving him his hat and briefcase*). I'm sorry we can't give you a room alone. But I hope you won't be too uncomfortable. We've had to make strict rules here . . . a schedule of hours . . . We'll tell you after supper. Anne, would you like to take Mr. Dussel to his room?

Anne (*controlling her tears*). If you'll come with me, Mr. Dussel? (*She starts for her room.*)

Dussel (*shaking hands with each in turn*). Forgive me if I haven't really expressed my gratitude to all of you. This has been such a shock to me. I'd always thought of myself as Dutch. I was born in Holland. My father was born in Holland, and my grandfather. And now . . . after all these years . . . (*He breaks off.*) If you'll excuse me.

[DUSSEL *gives a little bow and hurries off after* ANNE. MR. FRANK *and the others are subdued.*]

Anne (*turning on the light*). Well, here we are.

[DUSSEL *looks around the room. In the main room* MARGOT *speaks to her mother.*]

Margot. The news sounds pretty bad, doesn't it? It's so different from what Mr. Kraler tells us. Mr. Kraler says things are improving.

Mr. Van Daan. I like it better the way Kraler tells it.

[*They resume their occupations, quietly.* PETER *goes off into his room. In* ANNE's *room,* ANNE *turns to* DUSSEL.]

Anne. You're going to share the room with me.

Dussel. I'm a man who's always lived alone. I haven't had to adjust myself to others. I hope you'll bear with me until I learn.

Anne. Let me help you. (*She takes his brief-case.*) Do you always live all alone? Have you no family at all?

Dussel. No one. (*He opens his medicine case and spreads his bottles on the dressing table.*)

Anne. How dreadful. You must be terribly lonely.

Dussel. I'm used to it.

Anne. I don't think I could ever get used to it. Didn't you even have a pet? A cat, or a dog?

Dussel. I have an allergy for fur-bearing animals. They give me asthma.

Anne. Oh, dear. Peter has a cat.

Dussel. Here? He has it here?

Anne. Yes. But we hardly ever see it. He keeps it in his room all the time. I'm sure it will be all right.

Dussel. Let us hope so. (*He takes some pills to fortify himself.*)

Anne. That's Margot's bed, where you're going to sleep. I sleep on the sofa there. (*Indicating the clothes hooks on the wall*) We cleared these off for your things. (*She goes over to the window.*) The best part about this room . . . you can look down and see a bit of the street and the canal. There's a houseboat . . . you can see the end of it . . . a bargeman lives there with his family . . . They have a baby and he's just beginning to walk and I'm so afraid he's going to fall into the canal someday. I watch him . . .

Dussel (*interrupting*). Your father spoke of a schedule.

Anne (*coming away from the window*). Oh, yes. It's mostly about the times we have to be quiet. And times for the w.c. You can use it now if you like.

Dussel (*stiffly*). No, thank you.

Anne. I suppose you think it's awful, my talking about a thing like that. But you don't know how important it can get to be, especially when you're frightened. . . . About this room, the way Margot and I did . . . she had it to herself in the afternoons for studying, reading . . . lessons, you know . . . and I took the mornings. Would that be all right with you?

Dussel. I'm not at my best in the morning.

Anne. You stay here in the mornings, then. I'll take the room in the afternoons.

Dussel. Tell me, when you're in here, what happens to me? Where am I spending my time? In there, with all the people?

Anne. Yes.

Dussel. I see. I see.

Anne. We have supper at half past six.

Dussel (*going over to the sofa*). Then, if you don't mind . . . I like to lie down quietly for ten minutes before eating. I find it helps the digestion.

Anne. Of course. I hope I'm not going to be too much of a bother to you. I seem to be able to get everyone's back up.

[DUSSEL *lies down on the sofa, curled up, his back to her.*]

Dussel. I always get along very well with children. My patients all bring their children to me, because they know I get on well with them. So don't you worry about that.

[ANNE *leans over him, taking his hand and shaking it gratefully.*]

WORDS TO OWN
fortify (fôrt'ə·fī') *v*.: strengthen.

Anne.
Nothing is right about me . . .

Anne. Thank you. Thank you, Mr. Dussel.

[*The lights dim to darkness. The curtain falls on the scene.* ANNE*'s voice comes to us, faintly at first and then with increasing power.*]

Anne's Voice. . . . And yesterday I finished Cissy Van Marxvelt's latest book. I think she is a first-class writer. I shall definitely let my children read her. Monday, the twenty-first of September, nineteen forty-two. Mr. Dussel and I had another battle yesterday. Yes, Mr. Dussel! According to him, nothing, I repeat . . . nothing is right about me . . . my appearance, my character, my manners. While he was going on at me, I thought . . . sometime I'll give you such a smack that you'll fly right up to the ceiling! Why is it that every grown-up thinks he knows the way to bring up children? Particularly the grown-ups that never had any. I keep wishing that Peter was a girl instead of a boy. Then I would have someone to talk to. Margot's a darling, but she takes everything too seriously. To pause for a moment on the subject of Mrs. Van Daan. I must tell you that her attempts to flirt with Father are getting her nowhere. Pim, thank goodness, won't play.

[*As she is saying the last lines, the curtain rises on the darkened scene.* ANNE*'s voice fades out.*]

MAKING MEANINGS (ACT ONE, SCENES 1–3)

First Thoughts

1. What do you think would be the hardest part of life in the Secret Annex: the fear of discovery, the need to keep silent for hours at a time, the sharing of cramped quarters with strangers, or some other aspect? Explain. (If you've been taking notes as you read, look them over for ideas.)

Shaping Interpretations

2. Do Anne and Peter seem to have typical teenage attitudes toward their families? Go back to the text for examples to support your response.

3. List the **conflicts** that have developed among the characters by the end of Scene 3. Why are these conflicts dangerous for the people in the Secret Annex? What other conflicts do you **predict** might arise?

4. **Compare** Mr. Frank's and Mr. Van Daan's reactions to the arrival of Albert Dussel. Which seems like the right way to respond? Why?

5. When the play opens, only months have passed since Otto Frank was freed from Auschwitz. What do you think makes him return to Amsterdam and revisit the place where he and his family were captured by the Nazis? Would you do the same? Explain.

Connecting with the Text

6. If you were going into hiding and could take only as many items as you could carry in a single trip, what would they be? List the contents of your bags, and explain why you chose them.

Extending the Text

7. Mr. Frank tells Anne, "There are no walls, there are no bolts, no locks that anyone can put on your mind" (page 357). What does he mean? Do you agree? Support your opinion with examples from your own experience or knowledge.

Reading Check

a. What do we learn about the basic situation of the characters in the play from Scene 1, before the **flashback** begins?

b. By the end of Scene 3, we have met all ten **characters** who appear in the play. List these characters, and choose two or three adjectives to describe each character.

c. When does Anne begin to understand what going into hiding will mean? Describe some of the ways life in the Secret Annex is different from life outside.

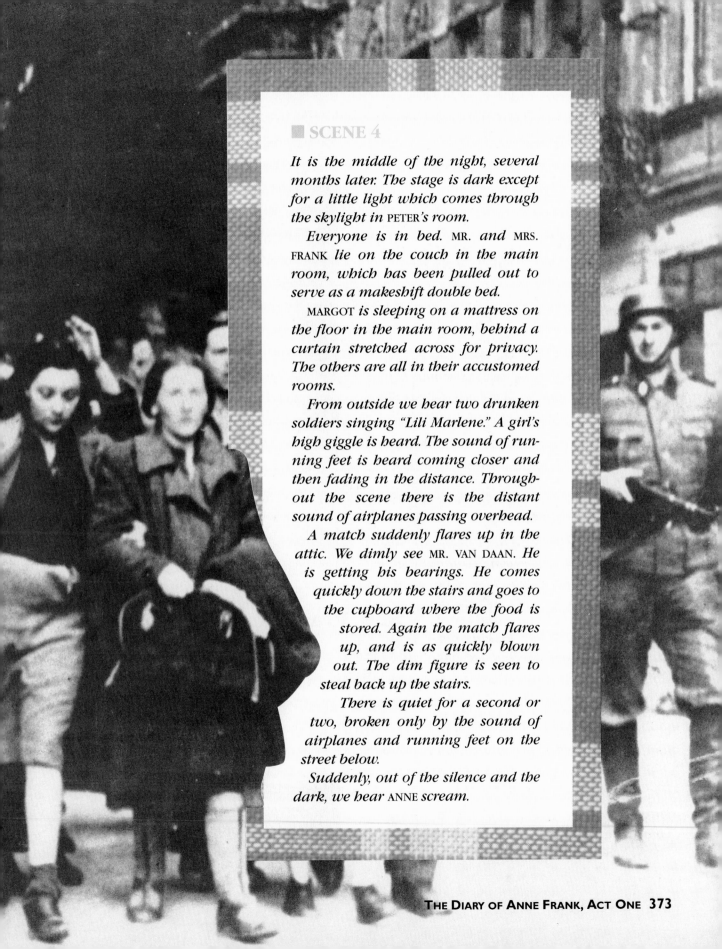

■ SCENE 4

It is the middle of the night, several months later. The stage is dark except for a little light which comes through the skylight in PETER's *room.*

Everyone is in bed. MR. *and* MRS. FRANK *lie on the couch in the main room, which has been pulled out to serve as a makeshift double bed.*

MARGOT *is sleeping on a mattress on the floor in the main room, behind a curtain stretched across for privacy. The others are all in their accustomed rooms.*

From outside we hear two drunken soldiers singing "Lili Marlene." A girl's high giggle is heard. The sound of running feet is heard coming closer and then fading in the distance. Throughout the scene there is the distant sound of airplanes passing overhead.

A match suddenly flares up in the attic. We dimly see MR. VAN DAAN. *He is getting his bearings. He comes quickly down the stairs and goes to the cupboard where the food is stored. Again the match flares up, and is as quickly blown out. The dim figure is seen to steal back up the stairs.*

There is quiet for a second or two, broken only by the sound of airplanes and running feet on the street below.

Suddenly, out of the silence and the dark, we hear ANNE *scream.*

Anne (*screaming*). No! No! Don't . . . don't take me!

[*She moans, tossing and crying in her sleep. The other people wake, terrified.* DUSSEL *sits up in bed, furious.*]

Dussel. Shush! Anne! Anne, for God's sake, shush!

Anne (*still in her nightmare*). Save me! Save me!

[*She screams and screams.* DUSSEL *gets out of bed, going over to her, trying to wake her.*]

Dussel. For God's sake! Quiet! Quiet! You want someone to hear?

[*In the main room* MRS. FRANK *grabs a shawl and pulls it around her. She rushes in to* ANNE, *taking her in her arms.* MR. FRANK *hurriedly gets up, putting on his overcoat.* MARGOT *sits up, terrified.* PETER's *light goes on in his room.*]

Mrs. Frank (*to* ANNE, *in her room*). Hush, darling, hush. It's all right. It's all right. (*Over her shoulder, to* DUSSEL) Will you be kind enough to turn on the light, Mr. Dussel? (*Back to* ANNE) It's nothing, my darling. It was just a dream.

[DUSSEL *turns on the light in the bedroom.* MRS. FRANK *holds* ANNE *in her arms. Gradually* ANNE *comes out of her nightmare, still trembling with horror.* MR. FRANK *comes into the room, and goes quickly to the window, looking out to be sure that no one outside has heard* ANNE's *screams.* MRS. FRANK *holds* ANNE, *talking softly to her. In the main room* MARGOT *stands on a chair, turning on the center hanging lamp. A light goes on in the* VAN DAANS' *room overhead.* PETER *puts his robe on, coming out of his room.*]

Dussel (*to* MRS. FRANK, *blowing his nose*). Something must be done about that child, Mrs. Frank. Yelling like that! Who knows but there's

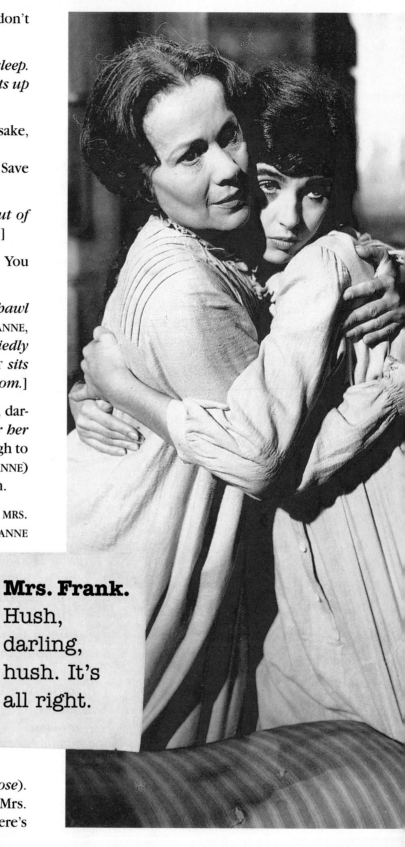

Mrs. Frank. Hush, darling, hush. It's all right.

somebody on the streets? She's endangering all our lives.

Mrs. Frank. Anne, darling.

Dussel. Every night she twists and turns. I don't sleep. I spend half my night shushing her. And now it's nightmares!

[MARGOT *comes to the door of* ANNE's *room, followed by* PETER. MR. FRANK *goes to them, indicating that everything is all right.* PETER *takes* MARGOT *back.*]

Mrs. Frank (*to* ANNE). You're here, safe, you see? Nothing has happened. (*To* DUSSEL) Please, Mr. Dussel, go back to bed. She'll be herself in a minute or two. Won't you, Anne?

Dussel (*picking up a book and a pillow*). Thank you, but I'm going to the w.c. The one place where there's peace!

[*He stalks out.* MR. VAN DAAN, *in underwear and trousers, comes down the stairs.*]

Mr. Van Daan (*to* DUSSEL). What is it? What happened?

Dussel. A nightmare. She was having a nightmare!

Mr. Van Daan. I thought someone was murdering her.

Dussel. Unfortunately, no.

[*He goes into the bathroom.* MR. VAN DAAN *goes back up the stairs.* MR. FRANK, *in the main room, sends* PETER *back to his own bedroom.*]

Mr. Frank. Thank you, Peter. Go back to bed.

[PETER *goes back to his room.* MR. FRANK *follows him, turning out the light and looking out the window. Then he goes back to the main room, and gets up on a chair, turning out the center hanging lamp.*]

Mrs. Frank (*to* ANNE). Would you like some water? (ANNE *shakes her head.*) Was it a very bad dream? Perhaps if you told me . . . ?

Anne. I'd rather not talk about it.

Mrs. Frank. Poor darling. Try to sleep, then. I'll sit right here beside you until you fall asleep. (*She brings a stool over, sitting there.*)

Anne. You don't have to.

Mrs. Frank. But I'd like to stay with you . . . very much. Really.

Anne. I'd rather you didn't.

Mrs. Frank. Good night, then. (*She leans down to kiss* ANNE. ANNE *throws her arm up over her face, turning away.* MRS. FRANK, *hiding her hurt, kisses* ANNE's *arm.*) You'll be all right? There's nothing that you want?

Anne. Will you please ask Father to come.

Mrs. Frank (*after a second*). Of course, Anne dear. (*She hurries out into the other room.* MR. FRANK *comes to her as she comes in.*) Sie verlangt nach Dir![1]

Mr. Frank (*sensing her hurt*). Edith, Liebe, schau . . .[2]

Mrs. Frank. Es macht nichts! Ich danke dem lieben Herrgott, dass sie sich wenigstens an Dich wendet, wenn sie Trost braucht! Geh hinein, Otto, sie ist ganz hysterisch vor Angst.[3] (*As* MR. FRANK *hesitates*) Geh zu ihr.[4] (*He looks at her for a second and then goes to get a cup of water for* ANNE. MRS. FRANK *sinks down on the bed, her face in her hands, trying to keep from sobbing aloud.* MARGOT *comes over to her, putting her arms around her.*) She wants nothing of me. She pulled away when I leaned down to kiss her.

Margot. It's a phase . . . You heard Father . . . Most girls go through it . . . they turn to their fathers at this age . . . they give all their love to their fathers.

Mrs. Frank. You weren't like this. You didn't shut me out.

Margot. She'll get over it. . . .

---

1. **Sie . . . Dir!:** German for "She's asking for you!"
2. **Liebe, schau:** "dear, look."
3. **Es . . . Angst:** "It doesn't matter! I thank the dear Lord that she turns at least to you when she needs comfort! Go to her, Otto, she's completely hysterical with fear."
4. **Geh zu ihr:** "Go to her."

[*She smooths the bed for* MRS. FRANK *and sits beside her a moment as* MRS. FRANK *lies down. In* ANNE*'s room* MR. FRANK *comes in, sitting down by* ANNE. ANNE *flings her arms around him, clinging to him. In the distance we hear the sound of ack-ack.*]

Anne. Oh, Pim. I dreamed that they came to get us! The Green Police! They broke down the door and grabbed me and started to drag me out the way they did Jopie.

Mr. Frank. I want you to take this pill.

Anne. What is it?

Mr. Frank. Something to quiet you.

[*She takes it and drinks the water. In the main room* MARGOT *turns out the light and goes back to her bed.*]

Mr. Frank (*to* ANNE). Do you want me to read to you for a while?

Anne. No. Just sit with me for a minute. Was I awful? Did I yell terribly loud? Do you think anyone outside could have heard?

Mr. Frank. No. No. Lie quietly now. Try to sleep.

Anne. I'm a terrible coward. I'm so disappointed in myself. I think I've conquered my fear . . . I think I'm really grown-up . . . and then something happens . . . and I run to you like a baby. . . . I love you, Father. I don't love anyone but you.

Mr. Frank (*reproachfully*). Annele!

Anne. It's true. I've been thinking about it for a long time. You're the only one I love.

Mr. Frank. It's fine to hear you tell me that you love me. But I'd be happier if you said you loved your mother as well. . . . She needs your help so much . . . your love . . .

Anne. We have nothing in common. She doesn't understand me. Whenever I try to explain my views on life to her, she asks me if I'm constipated.

Mr. Frank. You hurt her very much just now. She's crying. She's in there crying.

Anne. I can't help it. I only told the truth. I didn't want her here . . . (*Then, with sudden change*) Oh, Pim, I was horrible, wasn't I? And the worst of it is, I can stand off and look at myself doing it and know it's cruel and yet I can't stop doing it. What's the matter with me? Tell me. Don't say it's just a phase! Help me.

Mr. Frank. There is so little that we parents can do to help our children. We can only try to set a good example . . . point the way. The rest you must do yourself. You must build your own character.

Anne. I'm trying. Really I am. Every night I think back over all of the things I did that day that were wrong . . . like putting the wet mop in Mr. Dussel's bed . . . and this thing now with Mother. I say to myself, that was wrong. I make up my mind, I'm never going to do that again. Never! Of course, I may do something worse . . . but at least I'll never do *that* again! . . . I have a nicer side, Father . . . a sweeter, nicer side. But I'm scared to show it. I'm afraid that people are going to laugh at me if I'm serious. So the mean Anne comes to the outside and the good Anne stays on the inside, and I keep on trying to switch them around and have the good Anne outside and the bad Anne inside and be what I'd like to be . . . and might be . . . if only . . . only . . .

[*She is asleep.* MR. FRANK *watches her for a moment and then turns off the light, and starts out. The lights dim out. The curtain falls on the scene.* ANNE*'s voice is heard, dimly at first and then with growing strength.*]

Anne's Voice. . . . The air raids[5] are getting worse. They come over day and night. The noise is terrifying. Pim says it should be music to our ears. The more planes, the sooner will come the end of the war. Mrs. Van Daan pre-

---

5. air raids: Allied aircraft conducted air raids, or bombing attacks on ground targets, in the Netherlands because the country was occupied by the Germans.

tends to be a fatalist.[6] What will be, will be. But when the planes come over, who is the most frightened? No one else but Petronella! . . . Monday, the ninth of November, nineteen forty-two. Wonderful news! The Allies have landed in Africa. Pim says that we can look for an early finish to the war. Just for fun, he asked each of us what was the first thing we wanted to do when we got out of here. Mrs. Van Daan longs to be home with her own things, her needlepoint chairs, the Bechstein piano her father gave her . . . the best that money could buy. Peter would like to go to a movie. Mr. Dussel wants to get back to his dentist's drill. He's afraid he is losing his touch. For myself, there are so many things . . . to ride a bike again . . . to laugh till my belly aches . . . to have new clothes from the skin out . . . to have a hot tub filled to overflowing and wallow in it for hours . . . to be back in school with my friends . . .

[*As the last lines are being said, the curtain rises on the scene. The lights dim on as* ANNE*'s voice fades away.*]

■ SCENE 5

It is the first night of the Hanukkah[7] celebration. MR. FRANK *is standing at the head of the table on which is the menorah.[8] He lights the shamas, or servant candle, and holds it as he says the blessing. Seated, listening, are all of the "family," dressed in their best. The men wear hats;* PETER *wears his cap.*

Mr. Frank (*reading from a prayer book*). "Praised be Thou, oh Lord our God, Ruler of the universe, who has sanctified us with Thy commandments and bidden us kindle the Hanukkah lights. Praised be Thou, oh Lord our God, Ruler of the universe, who has wrought wondrous deliverances for our fathers in days of old. Praised be Thou, oh Lord our God, Ruler of the universe, that Thou has given us life and sustenance and brought us to this happy season." (MR. FRANK *lights the one candle of the menorah as he continues.*) "We kindle this Hanukkah light to celebrate the great and wonderful deeds wrought through the zeal with which God filled the hearts of the heroic Maccabees, two thousand years ago. They fought against indifference, against tyranny and oppression, and they restored our Temple to us. May these lights remind us that we should ever look to God, whence cometh our help." Amen. (*Pronounced "o-mayn"*)
All. Amen.

[MR. FRANK *hands* MRS. FRANK *the prayer book.*]

Mrs. Frank (*reading*). "I lift up mine eyes unto the mountains, from whence cometh my help. My help cometh from the Lord who made heaven and earth. He will not suffer thy foot to be moved. He that keepeth thee will not slumber. He that keepeth Israel doth neither slumber nor sleep. The Lord is thy keeper. The Lord is thy shade upon thy right hand. The sun shall not smite thee by day, nor the moon by night. The Lord shall keep thee from all evil.

---

6. fatalist (fāt′l·ist): person who believes that all events are determined by fate and therefore cannot be prevented or affected by people's actions.
7. Hanukkah (khä′noo·kä′): joyous eight-day Jewish holiday, usually falling in December, celebrating the rededication of the holy Temple in Jerusalem in 165 B.C. The Temple had been taken over by the Syrians, who had conquered Jerusalem. The Maccabee family led the Jews in a successful rebellion against the Syrians and retook the Temple.
8. menorah: Hebrew for "candleholder." Mr. Frank is lighting a menorah that holds nine candles: eight candles, one for each of the eight nights of Hanukkah, and the shamas, the candle used to light the others.

WORDS TO OWN
zeal (zēl) *n.*: great enthusiasm; devotion to a cause.
tyranny (tir′ə·nē) *n.*: cruel and unjust rule or use of power.

He shall keep thy soul. The Lord shall guard thy going out and thy coming in, from this time forth and forevermore."[9] Amen.

All. Amen.

[MRS. FRANK *puts down the prayer book and goes to get the food and wine.* MARGOT *helps her.* MR. FRANK *takes the men's hats and puts them aside.*]

Dussel (*rising*). That was very moving.
Anne (*pulling him back*). It isn't over yet!

9. Mrs. Frank is reading Psalm 121 from the Bible.

> **Mr. Frank.**
> They fought against indifference, against tyranny and oppression . . .

Mrs. Van Daan. Sit down! Sit down!

Anne. There's a lot more, songs and presents.

Dussel. Presents?

Mrs. Frank. Not this year, unfortunately.

Mrs. Van Daan. But always on Hanukkah everyone gives presents . . . everyone!

Dussel. Like our St. Nicholas's Day.[10]

[*There is a chorus of "no"s from the group.*]

Mrs. Van Daan. No! Not like St. Nicholas! What kind of a Jew are you that you don't know Hanukkah?

Mrs. Frank (*as she brings the food*). I remember particularly the candles . . . First, one, as we have tonight. Then, the second night, you light two candles, the next night three . . . and so on until you have eight candles burning. When there are eight candles, it is truly beautiful.

Mrs. Van Daan. And the potato pancakes.

Mr. Van Daan. Don't talk about them!

Mrs. Van Daan. I make the best latkes[11] you ever tasted!

Mrs. Frank. Invite us all next year . . . in your own home.

Mr. Frank. God willing!

Mrs. Van Daan. God willing.

Margot. What I remember best is the presents we used to get when we were little . . . eight days of presents . . . and each day they got better and better.

Mrs. Frank (*sitting down*). We are all here, alive. That is present enough.

Anne. No, it isn't. I've got something. . . . (*She rushes into her room, hurriedly puts on a little hat improvised from the lampshade, grabs a satchel bulging with parcels, and comes running back.*)

Mrs. Frank. What is it?

---

10. **St. Nicholas's Day:** Christian holiday celebrated in the Netherlands and other European countries on December 6, on which small gifts are given, especially to children.

11. **latkes** (lät′kəz): potato pancakes, a traditional Hanukkah food.

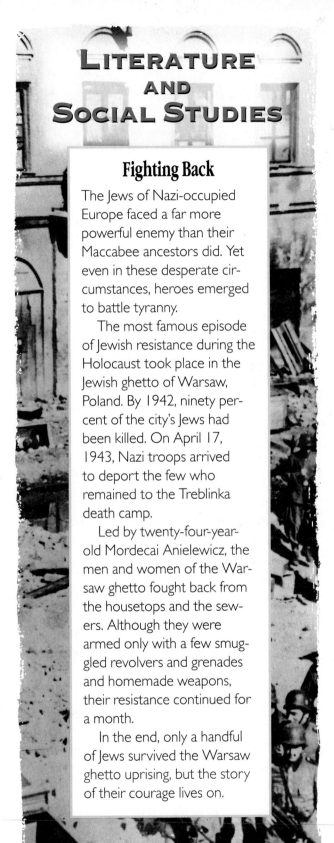

LITERATURE AND SOCIAL STUDIES

Fighting Back

The Jews of Nazi-occupied Europe faced a far more powerful enemy than their Maccabee ancestors did. Yet even in these desperate circumstances, heroes emerged to battle tyranny.

The most famous episode of Jewish resistance during the Holocaust took place in the Jewish ghetto of Warsaw, Poland. By 1942, ninety percent of the city's Jews had been killed. On April 17, 1943, Nazi troops arrived to deport the few who remained to the Treblinka death camp.

Led by twenty-four-year-old Mordecai Anielewicz, the men and women of the Warsaw ghetto fought back from the housetops and the sewers. Although they were armed only with a few smuggled revolvers and grenades and homemade weapons, their resistance continued for a month.

In the end, only a handful of Jews survived the Warsaw ghetto uprising, but the story of their courage lives on.

Anne. Presents!

Mrs. Van Daan. Presents!

Dussel. Look!

Mr. Van Daan. What's she got on her head?

Peter. A lampshade!

Anne. (*She picks out one at random.*) This is for Margot. (*She hands it to* MARGOT, *pulling her to her feet.*) Read it out loud.

Margot (*reading*).

> You have never lost your temper.
> You never will, I fear,
> You are so good.
> But if you should,
> Put all your cross words here.

(*She tears open the package.*) A new crossword puzzle book! Where did you get it?

Anne. It isn't new. It's one that you've done. But I rubbed it all out, and if you wait a little and forget, you can do it all over again.

Margot (*sitting*). It's wonderful, Anne. Thank you. You'd never know it wasn't new.

[*From outside we hear the sound of a streetcar passing.*]

Anne (*with another gift*). Mrs. Van Daan.

Mrs. Van Daan (*taking it*). This is awful . . . I haven't anything for anyone . . . I never thought . . .

Mr. Frank. This is all Anne's idea.

Mrs. Van Daan (*holding up a bottle*). What is it?

Anne. It's hair shampoo. I took all the odds and ends of soap and mixed them with the last of my toilet water.[12]

Mrs. Van Daan. Oh, Anneke!

Anne. I wanted to write a poem for all of them, but I didn't have time. (*Offering a large box to* MR. VAN DAAN) Yours, Mr. Van Daan, is *really* something . . . something you want more than anything. (*As she waits for him to open it*) Look! Cigarettes!

Mr. Van Daan. Cigarettes!

12. **toilet water:** cologne.

Anne. Two of them! Pim found some old pipe tobacco in the pocket lining of his coat . . . and we made them . . . or rather, Pim did.

Mrs. Van Daan. Let me see . . . Well, look at that! Light it, Putti! Light it.

[MR. VAN DAAN *hesitates.*]

Anne. It's tobacco, really it is! There's a little fluff in it, but not much.

[*Everyone watches intently as* MR. VAN DAAN *cautiously lights it. The cigarette flares up. Everyone laughs.*]

Peter. It works!

Mrs. Van Daan. Look at him.

Mr. Van Daan (*spluttering*). Thank you, Anne. Thank you.

[ANNE *rushes back to her satchel for another present.*]

Anne (*handing her mother a piece of paper*). For Mother, Hanukkah greeting. (*She pulls her mother to her feet.*)

Mrs. Frank (*she reads*).

> Here's an IOU that I promise to pay.
> Ten hours of doing whatever you say.
> Signed, Anne Frank.

(MRS. FRANK, *touched, takes* ANNE *in her arms, holding her close.*)

Dussel (*to* ANNE). Ten hours of doing what you're told? *Anything* you're told?

Anne. That's right.

Dussel. You wouldn't want to sell that, Mrs. Frank?

Mrs. Frank. Never! This is the most precious gift I've ever had!

[*She sits, showing her present to the others.* ANNE *hurries back to the satchel and pulls out a scarf, the scarf that* MR. FRANK *found in the first scene.*]

Anne (*offering it to her father*). For Pim.

Mr. Frank. Anneke . . . I wasn't supposed to

have a present! (*He takes it, unfolding it and showing it to the others.*)

Anne. It's a muffler . . . to put round your neck . . . like an ascot, you know. I made it myself out of odds and ends. . . . I knitted it in the dark each night, after I'd gone to bed. I'm afraid it looks better in the dark!

Mr. Frank (*putting it on*). It's fine. It fits me perfectly. Thank you, Annele.

[ANNE *hands* PETER *a ball of paper with a string attached to it.*]

Anne. That's for Mouschi.

Peter (*rising to bow*). On behalf of Mouschi, I thank you.

Anne (*hesitant, handing him a gift*). And . . . this is yours . . . from Mrs. Quack Quack. (*As he holds it <u>gingerly</u> in his hands*) Well . . . open it . . . Aren't you going to open it?

Peter. I'm scared to. I know something's going to jump out and hit me.

Anne. No. It's nothing like that, really.

Mrs. Van Daan (*as he is opening it*). What is it, Peter? Go on. Show it.

Anne (*excitedly*). It's a safety razor!

Dussel. A what?

Anne. A razor!

Mrs. Van Daan (*looking at it*). You didn't make that out of odds and ends.

Anne (*to* PETER). Miep got it for me. It's not new. It's second-hand. But you really do need a razor now.

Dussel. For what?

Anne. Look on his upper lip . . . you can see the beginning of a moustache.

Dussel. He wants to get rid of that? Put a little milk on it and let the cat lick it off.

Peter (*starting for his room*). Think you're funny, don't you.

Dussel. Look! He can't wait! He's going in to try it!

Peter. I'm going to give Mouschi his present! (*He goes into his room, slamming the door behind him.*)

Mr. Van Daan (*disgustedly*). Mouschi, Mouschi, Mouschi.

[*In the distance we hear a dog persistently barking.* ANNE *brings a gift to* DUSSEL.]

Anne. And last but never least, my roommate, Mr. Dussel.

Dussel. For me? You have something for me? (*He opens the small box she gives him.*)

Anne. I made them myself.

Dussel (*puzzled*). Capsules! Two capsules!

Anne. They're earplugs!

Dussel. Earplugs?

Anne. To put in your ears so you won't hear me when I thrash around at night. I saw them advertised in a magazine. They're not real ones. . . . I made them out of cotton and candle wax. Try them . . . See if they don't work . . . See if you can hear me talk . . .

Dussel (*putting them in his ears*). Wait now until I get them in . . . so.

Anne. Are you ready?

Dussel. Huh?

Anne. Are you ready?

Dussel. Good God! They've gone inside! I can't get them out! (*They laugh as* DUSSEL *jumps about, trying to shake the plugs out of his ears. Finally he gets them out. Putting them away*) Thank you, Anne! Thank you!

Margot Frank.

WORDS TO OWN

gingerly (jin′jər′lē) *adv.:* carefully; cautiously.

Mr. Van Daan. A real Hanukkah! ⎫

Mrs. Van Daan. Wasn't it cute of her? ⎬ *Together*

Mrs. Frank. I don't know when she did it. ⎭

Margot. I love my present.

Anne (*sitting at the table*). And now let's have the song, Father . . . please . . . (*to* DUSSEL) Have you heard the Hanukkah song, Mr. Dussel? The song is the whole thing! (*She sings*) "Oh, Hanukkah! Oh, Hanukkah! The sweet celebration . . ."

Mr. Frank (*quieting her*). I'm afraid, Anne, we shouldn't sing that song tonight. (*To* DUSSEL) It's a song of jubilation, of rejoicing. One is apt to become too enthusiastic.

Anne. Oh, please, please. Let's sing the song. I promise not to shout!

Mr. Frank. Very well. But quietly, now . . . I'll keep an eye on you and when . . .

[*As* ANNE *starts to sing, she is interrupted by* DUSSEL, *who is snorting and wheezing.*]

Dussel (*pointing to* PETER). You . . . You! (PETER *is coming from his bedroom, ostentatiously holding a bulge in his coat as if he were holding his cat, and dangling* ANNE's *present before it.*) How many times . . . I told you . . . Out! Out!

Mr. Van Daan (*going to* PETER). What's the matter with you? Haven't you any sense? Get that cat out of here.

Peter (*innocently*). Cat?

Mr. Van Daan. You heard me. Get it out of here!

Peter. I have no cat.

[*Delighted with his joke, he opens his coat and pulls out a bath towel. The group at the table laugh, enjoying the joke.*]

Dussel (*still wheezing*). It doesn't need to be the cat . . . his clothes are enough . . . when he comes out of that room . . .

Mr. Van Daan. Don't worry. You won't be bothered anymore. We're getting rid of it.

Dussel. At last you listen to me. (*He goes off into his bedroom.*)

Mr. Van Daan (*calling after him*). I'm not doing it for you. That's all in your mind . . . all of it! (*He starts back to his place at the table.*) I'm doing it because I'm sick of seeing that cat eat all our food.

Peter. That's not true! I only give him bones . . . scraps . . .

Mr. Van Daan. Don't tell me! He gets fatter every day! Damn cat looks better than any of us. Out he goes tonight!

Peter. No! No!

Anne. Mr. Van Daan, you can't do that! That's Peter's cat. Peter loves that cat.

Mrs. Frank (*quietly*). Anne.

Peter (*to* MR. VAN DAAN). If he goes, I go.

Mr. Van Daan. Go! Go!

Mrs. Van Daan. You're not going and the cat's not going! Now please . . . this is Hanukkah . . . Hanukkah . . . this is the time to celebrate . . . What's the matter with all of you? Come on, Anne. Let's have the song.

Anne (*singing*).

Oh, Hanukkah! Oh, Hanukkah!
The sweet celebration.

Mr. Frank (*rising*). I think we should first blow out the candle . . . then we'll have something for tomorrow night.

Margot. But, Father, you're supposed to let it burn itself out.

Mr. Frank. I'm sure that God understands shortages. (*Before blowing it out*) "Praised be Thou, oh Lord our God, who hast sustained us and permitted us to celebrate this joyous festival."

- -

WORDS TO OWN

ostentatiously (äs′tən·tā′shəs·lē) *adv.*: in a showy or exaggerated way.

- -

[*He is about to blow out the candle when suddenly there is a crash of something falling below. They all freeze in horror, motionless. For a few seconds there is complete silence.* MR. FRANK *slips off his shoes. The others noiselessly follow his example.* MR. FRANK *turns out a light near him. He motions to* PETER *to turn off the center lamp.* PETER *tries to reach it, realizes he cannot, and gets up on a chair. Just as he is touching the lamp, he loses his balance. The chair goes out from under him. He falls. The iron lampshade crashes to the floor. There is a sound of feet below running down the stairs.*]

Mr. Van Daan (*under his breath*). God Almighty! (*The only light left comes from the Hanukkah candle.* DUSSEL *comes from his room.* MR. FRANK *creeps over to the stairwell and stands listening. The dog is heard barking excitedly.*) Do you hear anything?

Mr. Frank (*in a whisper*). No. I think they've gone.

Mrs. Van Daan. It's the Green Police. They've found us.

Mr. Frank. If they had, they wouldn't have left. They'd be up here by now.

Mrs. Van Daan. I know it's the Green Police. They've gone to get help. That's all. They'll be back!

Mr. Van Daan. Or it may have been the Gestapo,[13] looking for papers . . .

Mr. Frank (*interrupting*). Or a thief, looking for money.

Mrs. Van Daan. We've got to do something . . . Quick! Quick! Before they come back.

Mr. Van Daan. There isn't anything to do. Just wait.

[MR. FRANK *holds up his hand for them to be quiet. He is listening intently. There is complete silence as they all strain to hear any sound from below. Suddenly* ANNE *begins to sway. With a low cry she falls to the floor in a faint.* MRS. FRANK *goes to her quickly, sitting beside her on the floor and taking her in her arms.*]

Mrs. Frank. Get some water, please! Get some water!

[MARGOT *starts for the sink.*]

Mr. Van Daan (*grabbing* MARGOT). No! No! No one's going to run water!

Mr. Frank. If they've found us, they've found us. Get the water. (MARGOT *starts again for the sink.* MR. FRANK, *getting a flashlight*) I'm going down.

[MARGOT *rushes to him, clinging to him.* ANNE *struggles to consciousness.*]

Margot. No, Father, no! There may be someone there, waiting. . . . It may be a trap!

Mr. Frank. This is Saturday. There is no way for us to know what has happened until Miep or Mr. Kraler comes on Monday morning. We cannot live with this uncertainty.

Margot. Don't go, Father!

Mrs. Frank. Hush, darling, hush. (MR. FRANK *slips quietly out, down the steps, and out through the door below.*) Margot! Stay close to me.

[MARGOT *goes to her mother.*]

Mr. Van Daan. Shush! Shush!

[MRS. FRANK *whispers to* MARGOT *to get the water.* MARGOT *goes for it.*]

Mrs. Van Daan. Putti, where's our money? Get our money. I hear you can buy the Green Police off, so much a head. Go upstairs quick! Get the money!

Mr. Van Daan. Keep still!

Mrs. Van Daan (*kneeling before him, pleading*). Do you want to be dragged off to a concentration camp? Are you going to stand there and wait for them to come up and get you? Do something, I tell you!

---

13. **Gestapo** (gə·stä′pō): Nazi secret police.

Mr. Van Daan (*pushing her aside*). Will you keep still!

[*He goes over to the stairwell to listen.* PETER *goes to his mother, helping her up onto the sofa. There is a second of silence; then* ANNE *can stand it no longer.*]

Anne. Someone go after Father! Make Father come back!
Peter (*starting for the door*). I'll go.
Mr. Van Daan. Haven't you done enough?

[*He pushes* PETER *roughly away. In his anger against his father* PETER *grabs a chair as if to hit him with it, then puts it down, burying his face in his hands.* MRS. FRANK *begins to pray softly.*]

Anne. Please, please, Mr. Van Daan. Get Father.
Mr. Van Daan. Quiet! Quiet!

[ANNE *is shocked into silence.* MRS. FRANK *pulls her closer, holding her protectively in her arms.*]

Mrs. Frank (*softly, praying*). "I lift up mine eyes unto the mountains, from whence cometh my help. My help cometh from the Lord who made heaven and earth. He will not suffer thy foot to be moved . . . He that keepeth thee will not slumber . . ."

[*She stops as she hears someone coming. They all watch the door tensely.* MR. FRANK *comes quietly in.* ANNE *rushes to him, holding him tight.*]

Mr. Frank. It was a thief. That noise must have scared him away.
Mrs. Van Daan. Thank God.
Mr. Frank. He took the cash box. And the radio. He ran away in such a hurry that he didn't stop to shut the street door. It was swinging wide open. (*A breath of relief sweeps over them.*) I think it would be good to have some light.
Margot. Are you sure it's all right?

Mr. Frank. The danger has passed. (MARGOT *goes to light the small lamp.*) Don't be so terrified, Anne. We're safe.
Dussel. Who says the danger has passed? Don't you realize we are in greater danger than ever?
Mr. Frank. Mr. Dussel, will you be still! (MR. FRANK *takes* ANNE *back to the table, making her sit down with him, trying to calm her.*)
Dussel (*pointing to* PETER). Thanks to this clumsy fool, there's someone now who knows we're up here! Someone now knows we're up here, hiding!
Mrs. Van Daan (*going to* DUSSEL). Someone knows we're here, yes. But who is the someone? A thief! A thief! You think a thief is going to go to the Green Police and say . . . "I was robbing a place the other night and I heard a noise up over my head?" You think a thief is going to do that?
Dussel. Yes. I think he will.
Mrs. Van Daan (*hysterically*). You're crazy! (*She stumbles back to her seat at the table.* PETER *follows protectively, pushing* DUSSEL *aside.*)
Dussel. I think someday he'll be caught and then he'll make a bargain with the Green Police . . . if they'll let him off, he'll tell them where some Jews are hiding!

[*He goes off into the bedroom. There is a second of* appalled *silence.*]

Mr. Van Daan. He's right.
Anne. Father, let's get out of here! We can't stay here now . . . Let's go . . .
Mr. Van Daan. Go! Where?
Mrs. Frank (*sinking into her chair at the table*). Yes. Where?
Mr. Frank (*rising, to them all*). Have we lost all faith? All courage? A moment ago we

---

WORDS TO OWN
appalled (ə·pôld') *v.* used as *adj.*: horrified; shocked.

Anne. We can't stay here now . . .

thought that they'd come for us. We were sure it was the end. But it wasn't the end. We're alive, safe. (MR. VAN DAAN *goes to the table and sits.* MR. FRANK *prays*) "We thank Thee, oh Lord our God, that in Thy infinite mercy Thou hast again seen fit to spare us." (*He blows out the candle, then turns to* ANNE.) Come on, Anne. The song! Let's have the song! (*He starts to sing.* ANNE *finally starts falteringly to sing, as* MR. FRANK *urges her on. Her voice is hardly audible at first.*)

Anne (*singing*).

Oh, Hanukkah! Oh, Hanukkah!
The sweet . . . celebration . . .

[*As she goes on singing, the others gradually join in, their voices still shaking with fear.* MRS. VAN DAAN *sobs as she sings.*]

Group.

Around the feast . . . we . . . gather
In complete . . . jubilation . . .
Happiest of sea . . . sons
Now is here.
Many are the reasons for good cheer.

[DUSSEL *comes from the bedroom. He comes over to the table, standing beside* MARGOT, *listening to them as they sing.*]

Together
We'll weather
Whatever tomorrow may bring.

[*As they sing on with growing courage, the lights start to dim.*]

So hear us rejoicing
And merrily voicing
The Hanukkah song that we sing.
Hoy!

[*The lights are out. The curtain starts slowly to fall.*]

Hear us rejoicing
And merrily voicing
The Hanukkah song that we sing.

[*They are still singing as the curtain falls.*]

Curtain

MAKING MEANINGS (ACT ONE, SCENES 4–5)

First Thoughts

1. Now that you've read Scenes 4 and 5, how have your feelings about Anne and the other characters changed? (Check the notes you made while reading.)

Shaping Interpretations

2. Go back to the list of **characters** you made after you read Scenes 1–3. Which adjectives, if any, would you change now? Why?

3. Anne is a **dynamic character;** that is, she changes in the course of the play. What does Anne's gift giving reveal about her? How do her gifts to her mother and Peter show that she has changed?

4. Describe the **reversal**—the sudden change in the characters' fortunes—that is central to Scene 5. How did it make you feel?

5. Imagine that you are watching this play in a theater. What questions do you have as the curtain comes down on Act One? What do you **predict** will happen in Act Two?

Connecting with the Text

6. Reread Anne's conversation with her father on page 376. What does she say that reminds you the most—or the least—of yourself? Explain.

Challenging the Text

7. The play's version of events differs in many ways from what actually happened. (Check the time line for some of the actual facts.) For example:

- In real life, Anne was given the diary as a present for her thirteenth birthday, several weeks before her family went into hiding.

- The Frank family moved into the Secret Annex a week before the Van Pels family did. (Anne made up names. She called the Van Pels family the Van Daans.)

- Margot was sixteen, not eighteen, when the Franks went into hiding.

- The occupants of the Secret Annex often ventured to the lower floors of the office building after working hours.

Why might the writers have chosen to change each of these details? Do you think the changes make the play more effective? Explain.

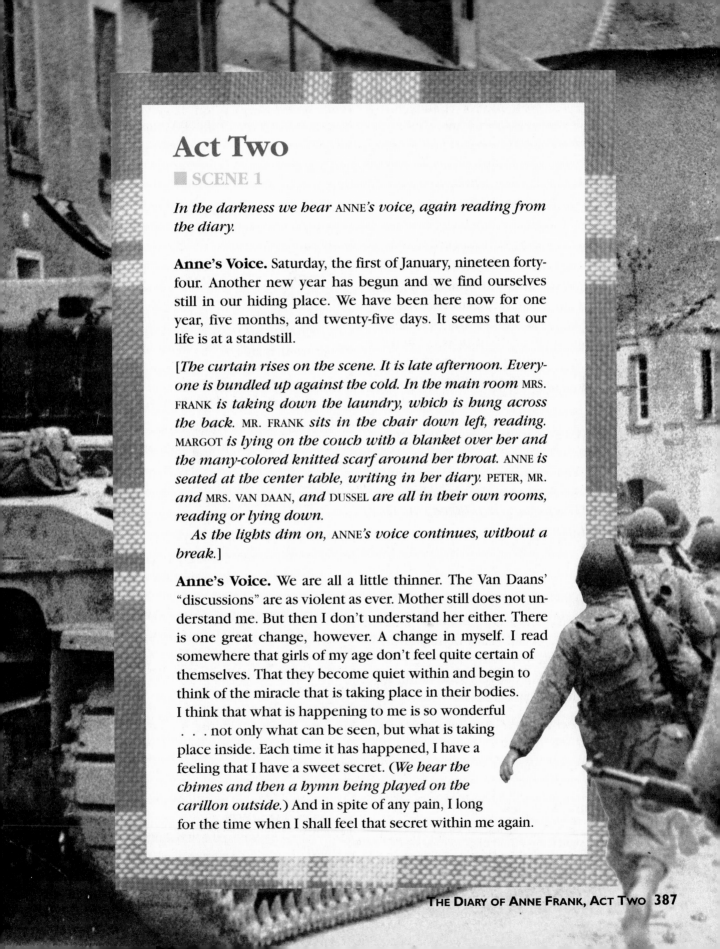

Act Two

■ SCENE 1

In the darkness we hear ANNE's *voice, again reading from the diary.*

Anne's Voice. Saturday, the first of January, nineteen forty-four. Another new year has begun and we find ourselves still in our hiding place. We have been here now for one year, five months, and twenty-five days. It seems that our life is at a standstill.

[*The curtain rises on the scene. It is late afternoon. Everyone is bundled up against the cold. In the main room* MRS. FRANK *is taking down the laundry, which is hung across the back.* MR. FRANK *sits in the chair down left, reading.* MARGOT *is lying on the couch with a blanket over her and the many-colored knitted scarf around her throat.* ANNE *is seated at the center table, writing in her diary.* PETER, MR. *and* MRS. VAN DAAN, *and* DUSSEL *are all in their own rooms, reading or lying down.*

   As the lights dim on, ANNE's *voice continues, without a break.*]

Anne's Voice. We are all a little thinner. The Van Daans' "discussions" are as violent as ever. Mother still does not understand me. But then I don't understand her either. There is one great change, however. A change in myself. I read somewhere that girls of my age don't feel quite certain of themselves. That they become quiet within and begin to think of the miracle that is taking place in their bodies. I think that what is happening to me is so wonderful . . . not only what can be seen, but what is taking place inside. Each time it has happened, I have a feeling that I have a sweet secret. (*We hear the chimes and then a hymn being played on the carillon outside.*) And in spite of any pain, I long for the time when I shall feel that secret within me again.

[*The buzzer of the door below suddenly sounds. Everyone is startled.* MR. FRANK *tiptoes cautiously to the top of the steps and listens. Again the buzzer sounds, in* MIEP'S *V-for-victory signal.*][1]

Mr. Frank. It's Miep!

[*He goes quickly down the steps to unbolt the door.* MRS. FRANK *calls upstairs to the* VAN DAANS *and then to* PETER.]

Mrs. Frank. Wake up, everyone! Miep is here! (ANNE *quickly puts her diary away.* MARGOT *sits up, pulling the blanket around her shoulders.* DUSSEL *sits on the edge of his bed, listening, disgruntled.* MIEP *comes up the steps, followed by* MR. KRALER. *They bring flowers, books, newspapers, etc.* ANNE *rushes to* MIEP, *throwing her arms affectionately around her.*) Miep . . . *and* Mr. Kraler . . . What a delightful surprise!
Mr. Kraler. We came to bring you New Year's greetings.
Mrs. Frank. You shouldn't . . . you should have at least one day to yourselves. (*She goes quickly to the stove and brings down teacups and tea for all of them.*)
Anne. Don't say that, it's so wonderful to see them! (*Sniffing at* MIEP'S *coat*) I can smell the wind and the cold on your clothes.
Miep (*giving her the flowers*). There you are. (*Then, to* MARGOT, *feeling her forehead*) How are you, Margot? . . . Feeling any better?
Margot. I'm all right.
Anne. We filled her full of every kind of pill so she won't cough and make a noise.

[*She runs into her room to put the flowers in water.* MR. *and* MRS. VAN DAAN *come from upstairs. Outside there is the sound of a band playing.*]

Mrs. Van Daan. Well, hello, Miep. Mr. Kraler.

Mr. Kraler (*giving a bouquet of flowers to* MRS. VAN DAAN). With my hope for peace in the New Year.
Peter (*anxiously*). Miep, have you seen Mouschi? Have you seen him anywhere around?
Miep. I'm sorry, Peter. I asked everyone in the neighborhood had they seen a gray cat. But they said no.

[MRS. FRANK *gives* MIEP *a cup of tea.* MR. FRANK *comes up the steps, carrying a small cake on a plate.*]

Mr. Frank. Look what Miep's brought for us!
Mrs. Frank (*taking it*). A cake!
Mr. Van Daan. A cake! (*He pinches* MIEP'S *cheeks gaily and hurries up to the cupboard.*) I'll get some plates.

[DUSSEL, *in his room, hastily puts a coat on and starts out to join the others.*]

Mrs. Frank. Thank you, Miepia. You shouldn't have done it. You must have used all of your sugar ration for weeks. (*Giving it to* MRS. VAN DAAN) It's beautiful, isn't it?
Mrs. Van Daan. It's been ages since I even saw a cake. Not since you brought us one last year. (*Without looking at the cake, to* MIEP) Remember? Don't you remember, you gave us one on New Year's Day? Just this time last year? I'll never forget it because you had "Peace in nineteen forty-three" on it. (*She looks at the cake and reads*) "Peace in nineteen forty-four!"
Miep. Well, it has to come sometime, you know. (*As* DUSSEL *comes from his room*) Hello, Mr. Dussel.
Mr. Kraler. How are you?
Mr. Van Daan (*bringing plates and a knife*). Here's the knife, liefje. Now, how many of us are there?

---

1. **V-for-victory signal:** three short rings and one long ring, Morse code for the letter *V,* the Allied symbol for victory.

WORDS TO OWN
disgruntled (dis·grunt''ld) *v.* used as *adj.*: displeased; annoyed.

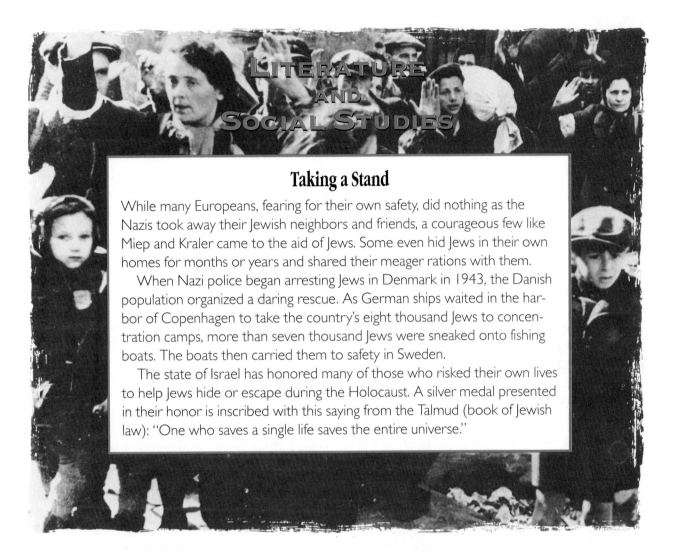

Taking a Stand

While many Europeans, fearing for their own safety, did nothing as the Nazis took away their Jewish neighbors and friends, a courageous few like Miep and Kraler came to the aid of Jews. Some even hid Jews in their own homes for months or years and shared their meager rations with them.

When Nazi police began arresting Jews in Denmark in 1943, the Danish population organized a daring rescue. As German ships waited in the harbor of Copenhagen to take the country's eight thousand Jews to concentration camps, more than seven thousand Jews were sneaked onto fishing boats. The boats then carried them to safety in Sweden.

The state of Israel has honored many of those who risked their own lives to help Jews hide or escape during the Holocaust. A silver medal presented in their honor is inscribed with this saying from the Talmud (book of Jewish law): "One who saves a single life saves the entire universe."

Miep. None for me, thank you.

Mr. Frank. Oh, please. You must.

Miep. I couldn't.

Mr. Van Daan. Good! That leaves one . . . two . . . three . . . seven of us.

Dussel. Eight! Eight! It's the same number as it always is!

Mr. Van Daan. I left Margot out. I take it for granted Margot won't eat any.

Anne. Why wouldn't she!

Mrs. Frank. I think it won't harm her.

Mr. Van Daan. All right! All right! I just didn't want her to start coughing again, that's all.

Dussel. And please, Mrs. Frank should cut the cake.

Mr. Van Daan. What's the difference?

Mrs. Van Daan. It's not Mrs. Frank's cake, is it, Miep? It's for all of us.

} *Together*

Dussel. Mrs. Frank divides things better.

Mrs. Van Daan (*going to* DUSSEL). What are you trying to say?

Mr. Van Daan. Oh, come on! Stop wasting time!

} *Together*

Mrs. Van Daan (*to* DUSSEL). Don't I always give everybody exactly the same? Don't I?

Mr. Van Daan. Forget it, Kerli.

Mrs. Van Daan. No. I want an answer! Don't I?

Dussel. Yes. Yes. Everybody gets exactly the same . . . except Mr. Van Daan always gets a little bit more.

[MR. VAN DAAN *advances on* DUSSEL, *the knife still in his hand.*]

Mr. Van Daan. That's a lie!

[DUSSEL *retreats before the onslaught of the* VAN DAANS.]

Mr. Frank. Please, please! (*Then, to* MIEP) You see what a little sugar cake does to us? It goes right to our heads!

Mr. Van Daan (*handing* MRS. FRANK *the knife*). Here you are, Mrs. Frank.

Mrs. Frank. Thank you. (*Then, to* MIEP, *as she goes to the table to cut the cake*) Are you sure you won't have some?

Miep (*drinking her tea*). No, really, I have to go in a minute.

[*The sound of the band fades out in the distance.*]

Peter (*to* MIEP). Maybe Mouschi went back to our house . . . they say that cats . . . Do you ever get over there . . . ? I mean . . . do you suppose you could . . . ?

Miep. I'll try, Peter. The first minute I get, I'll try. But I'm afraid, with him gone a week . . .

Dussel. Make up your mind, already someone has had a nice big dinner from that cat!

[PETER *is furious,* inarticulate. *He starts toward* DUSSEL *as if to hit him.* MR. FRANK *stops him.* MRS. FRANK *speaks quickly to ease the situation.*]

Mrs. Frank (*to* MIEP). This is delicious, Miep!

Mrs. Van Daan (*eating hers*). Delicious!

Mr. Van Daan (*finishing it in one gulp*). Dirk's in luck to get a girl who can bake like this!

Miep (*putting down her empty teacup*). I have to run. Dirk's taking me to a party tonight.

Anne. How heavenly! Remember now what everyone is wearing and what you have to eat and everything, so you can tell us tomorrow.

Miep. I'll give you a full report! Goodbye, everyone!

Mr. Van Daan (*to* MIEP). Just a minute. There's something I'd like you to do for me. (*He hurries off up the stairs to his room.*)

Mrs. Van Daan (*sharply*). Putti, where are you going? (*She rushes up the stairs after him, calling hysterically.*) What do you want? Putti, what are you going to do?

Miep (*to* PETER). What's wrong?

Peter (*his sympathy is with his mother*). Father says he's going to sell her fur coat. She's crazy about that old fur coat.

Dussel. Is it possible? Is it possible that anyone is so silly as to worry about a fur coat in times like this?

Peter. It's none of your darn business . . . and if you say one more thing . . . I'll, I'll take you and I'll . . . I mean it . . . I'll . . .

[*There is a piercing scream from* MRS. VAN DAAN, *above. She grabs at the fur coat as* MR. VAN DAAN *is starting downstairs with it.*]

Mrs. Van Daan. No! No! No! Don't you dare take that! You hear? It's mine! (*Downstairs* PETER *turns away, embarrassed, miserable.*) My father gave me that! You didn't give it to me. You have no right. Let go of it . . . you hear?

[MR. VAN DAAN *pulls the coat from her hands and hurries downstairs.* MRS. VAN DAAN *sinks to the floor, sobbing. As* MR. VAN DAAN *comes into the main room, the others look away, embarrassed for him.*]

Mr. Van Daan (*to* MR. KRALER). Just a little—

WORDS TO OWN

inarticulate (in′är·tik′yo͞o·lit) *adj.:* unable to speak. *Inarticulate* also means "unable to speak understandably or effectively."

---

discussion over the advisability of selling this coat. As I have often reminded Mrs. Van Daan, it's very selfish of her to keep it when people outside are in such desperate need of clothing. . . . (*He gives the coat to* MIEP.) So if you will please to sell it for us? It should fetch a good price. And by the way, will you get me cigarettes. I don't care what kind they are . . . get all you can.

Miep. It's terribly difficult to get them, Mr. Van Daan. But I'll try. Goodbye.

[*She goes.* MR. FRANK *follows her down the steps to bolt the door after her.* MRS. FRANK *gives* MR. KRALER *a cup of tea.*]

Mrs. Frank. Are you sure you won't have some cake, Mr. Kraler?

Mr. Kraler. I'd better not.

Mr. Van Daan. You're still feeling badly? What does your doctor say?

Mr. Kraler. I haven't been to him.

Mrs. Frank. Now, Mr. Kraler! . . .

Mr. Kraler (*sitting at the table*). Oh, I tried. But you can't get near a doctor these days . . . they're so busy. After weeks I finally managed to get one on the telephone. I told him I'd like an appointment . . . I wasn't feeling very well. You know what he answers . . . over the telephone . . . "Stick out your tongue!" (*They laugh. He turns to* MR. FRANK *as* MR. FRANK *comes back.*) I have some contracts here . . . I wonder if you'd look over them with me . . .

Mr. Frank (*putting out his hand*). Of course.

Mr. Kraler (*he rises*). If we could go downstairs . . . (MR. FRANK *starts ahead;* MR. KRALER *speaks to the others.*) Will you forgive us? I won't keep him but a minute. (*He starts to follow* MR. FRANK *down the steps.*)

Margot (*with sudden foreboding*). What's happened? Something's happened! Hasn't it, Mr. Kraler?

[MR. KRALER *stops and comes back, trying to reassure* MARGOT *with a pretense of casualness.*]

Mr. Kraler. No, really. I want your father's advice . . .

Margot. Something's gone wrong! I know it!

Mr. Frank (*coming back, to* MR. KRALER). If it's something that concerns us here, it's better that we all hear it.

Mr. Kraler (*turning to him, quietly*). But . . . the children . . . ?

Mr. Frank. What they'd imagine would be worse than any reality.

[*As* MR. KRALER *speaks, they all listen with intense apprehension.* MRS. VAN DAAN *comes down the stairs and sits on the bottom step.*]

Mr. Kraler. It's a man in the storeroom . . . I don't know whether or not you remember him . . . Carl, about fifty, heavyset, nearsighted . . . He came with us just before you left.

Mr. Frank. He was from Utrecht?

Mr. Kraler. That's the man. A couple of weeks ago, when I was in the storeroom, he closed the door and asked me . . . "How's Mr. Frank? What do you hear from Mr. Frank?" I told him I only knew there was a rumor that you were in Switzerland. He said he'd heard that rumor too, but he thought I might know something more. I didn't pay any attention to it . . . but then a thing happened yesterday . . . He'd brought some invoices to the office for me to sign. As I was going through them, I looked up. He was standing staring at the bookcase . . . your bookcase. He said he thought he remembered a door there . . . Wasn't there a door there that used to go up to the loft? Then he told me he wanted more money. Twenty guilders[2] more a week.

Mr. Van Daan. Blackmail!

Mr. Frank. Twenty guilders? Very modest blackmail.

Mr. Van Daan. That's just the beginning.

Dussel (*coming to* MR. FRANK). You know what I think? He was the thief who was down there

2. **guilders** (gil′dərz): Dutch money.

that night. That's how he knows we're here.

Mr. Frank (*to* MR. KRALER). How was it left? What did you tell him?

Mr. Kraler. I said I had to think about it. What shall I do? Pay him the money? . . . Take a chance on firing him . . . or what? I don't know.

Dussel (*frantic*). For God's sake, don't fire him! Pay him what he asks . . . keep him here where you can have your eye on him.

Mr. Frank. Is it so much that he's asking? What are they paying nowadays?

Mr. Kraler. He could get it in a war plant. But this isn't a war plant. Mind you, I don't know if he really knows . . . or if he doesn't know.

Mr. Frank. Offer him half. Then we'll soon find out if it's blackmail or not.

Dussel. And if it is? We've got to pay it, haven't we? Anything he asks we've got to pay!

Mr. Frank. Let's decide that when the time comes.

Mr. Kraler. This may be all my imagination. You get to a point, these days, where you suspect everyone and everything. Again and again . . . on some simple look or word, I've found myself . . .

[*The telephone rings in the office below.*]

Mrs. Van Daan (*hurrying to* MR. KRALER). There's the telephone! What does that mean, the telephone ringing on a holiday?

Mr. Kraler. That's my wife. I told her I had to go over some papers in my office . . . to call me there when she got out of church. (*He starts out.*) I'll offer him half, then. Goodbye . . . we'll hope for the best!

[*The group call their goodbyes halfheartedly.* MR. FRANK *follows* MR. KRALER *to bolt the door below. During the following scene,* MR. FRANK *comes back up and stands listening, disturbed.*]

Dussel (*to* MR. VAN DAAN). You can thank your son for this . . . smashing the light! I tell you,

it's just a question of time now. (*He goes to the window at the back and stands looking out.*)

Margot. Sometimes I wish the end would come . . . whatever it is.

Mrs. Frank (*shocked*). Margot!

[ANNE *goes to* MARGOT, *sitting beside her on the couch with her arms around her.*]

Margot. Then at least we'd know where we were.

Mrs. Frank. You should be ashamed of yourself! Talking that way! Think how lucky we are! Think of the thousands dying in the war, every day. Think of the people in concentration camps.

Anne (*interrupting*). What's the good of that? What's the good of thinking of misery when you're already miserable? That's stupid!

Mrs. Frank. Anne!

[*As* ANNE *goes on raging at her mother,* MRS. FRANK *tries to break in, in an effort to quiet her.*]

Anne. We're young, Margot and Peter and I! You grown-ups have had your chance! But look at us . . . If we begin thinking of all the horror in the world, we're lost! We're trying to hold on to some kind of ideals . . . when everything . . . ideals, hopes . . . everything is being destroyed! It isn't our fault that the world is in such a mess! We weren't around when all this started! So don't try to take it out on us! (*She rushes off to her room, slamming the door after her. She picks up a brush from the chest and hurls it to the floor. Then she sits on the settee, trying to control her anger.*)

Mr. Van Daan. She talks as if we started the war! Did we start the war? (*He spots* ANNE's *cake. As he starts to take it,* PETER *anticipates him.*)

Peter. She left her cake. (*He starts for* ANNE's *room with the cake. There is silence in the main room.* MRS. VAN DAAN *goes up to her room, followed by* MR. VAN DAAN. DUSSEL *stays*

Peter. You know just how to talk to them.

looking out the window. MR. FRANK *brings* MRS. FRANK *her cake. She eats it slowly, without relish.* MR. FRANK *takes his cake to* MARGOT *and sits quietly on the sofa beside her.* PETER *stands in the doorway of* ANNE's *darkened room, looking at her, then makes a little movement to let her know he is there.* ANNE *sits up quickly, try-*

ing to hide the signs of her tears. PETER *holds out the cake to her.*) You left this.
Anne (*dully*). Thanks.

[PETER *starts to go out, then comes back.*]

Peter. I thought you were fine just now. You know just how to talk to them. You know just how to say it. I'm no good . . . I never can think . . . especially when I'm mad . . . That Dussel . . . when he said that about Mouschi . . . someone eating him . . . all I could think is . . . I wanted to hit him. I wanted to give him such a . . . a . . . that he'd . . . That's what I used to do when there was an argument at school. . . . That's the way I . . . but here . . . And an old man like that . . . it wouldn't be so good.
Anne. You're making a big mistake about me. I do it all wrong. I say too much. I go too far. I hurt people's feelings. . . .

[DUSSEL *leaves the window, going to his room.*]

Peter. I think you're just fine . . . What I want to say . . . if it wasn't for you around here, I don't know. What I mean . . .

[PETER *is interrupted by* DUSSEL's *turning on the light.* DUSSEL *stands in the doorway, startled to see* PETER. PETER *advances toward him forbiddingly.* DUSSEL *backs out of the room.* PETER *closes the door on him.*]

Anne. Do you mean it, Peter? Do you really mean it?
Peter. I said it, didn't I?
Anne. Thank you, Peter!

[*In the main room* MR. *and* MRS. FRANK *collect the dishes and take them to the sink, washing them.* MARGOT *lies down again on the couch.* DUSSEL, *lost, wanders into* PETER's *room and takes up a book, starting to read.*]

Peter (*looking at the photographs on the wall*). You've got quite a collection.
Anne. Wouldn't you like some in your room? I

could give you some. Heaven knows you spend enough time in there . . . doing heaven knows what . . .

Peter. It's easier. A fight starts, or an argument . . . I duck in there.

Anne. You're lucky, having a room to go to. His Lordship is always here . . . I hardly ever get a minute alone. When they start in on me, I can't duck away. I have to stand there and take it.

Peter. You gave some of it back just now.

Anne. I get so mad. They've formed their opinions . . . about everything . . . but we . . . we're still trying to find out . . . We have problems here that no other people our age have ever had. And just as you think you've solved them, something comes along and bang! You have to start all over again.

Peter. At least you've got someone you can talk to.

Anne. Not really. Mother . . . I never discuss anything serious with her. She doesn't understand. Father's all right. We can talk about everything . . . everything but one thing. Mother. He simply won't talk about her. I don't think you can be really intimate with anyone if he holds something back, do you?

Peter. I think your father's fine.

Anne. Oh, he is, Peter! He is! He's the only one who's ever given me the feeling that I have any sense. But anyway, nothing can take the place of school and play and friends of your own age . . . or near your age . . . can it?

Peter. I suppose you miss your friends and all.

Anne. It isn't just . . . (*She breaks off, staring up at him for a second.*) Isn't it funny, you and I? Here we've been seeing each other every minute for almost a year and a half, and this is the first time we've ever really talked. It helps a lot to have someone to talk to, don't you think? It helps you to let off steam.

Peter (*going to the door*). Well, any time you want to let off steam, you can come into my room.

Anne (*following him*). I can get up an awful lot of steam. You'll have to be careful how you say that.

Peter. It's all right with me.

Anne. Do you mean it?

Peter. I said it, didn't I?

[*He goes out.* ANNE *stands in her doorway looking after him. As* PETER *gets to his door, he stands for a minute looking back at her. Then he goes into his room.* DUSSEL *rises as he comes in, and quickly passes him, going out. He starts across for his room.* ANNE *sees him coming and pulls her door shut.* DUSSEL *turns back toward* PETER'*s room.* PETER *pulls his door shut.* DUSSEL *stands there, bewildered,* <u>forlorn</u>.

The scene slowly dims out. The curtain falls on the scene. ANNE'*s voice comes over in the darkness . . . faintly at first and then with growing strength.*]

Anne's Voice. We've had bad news. The people from whom Miep got our ration books have been arrested. So we have had to cut down on our food. Our stomachs are so empty that they rumble and make strange noises, all in different keys. Mr. Van Daan's is deep and low, like a bass fiddle. Mine is high, whistling like a flute. As we all sit around waiting for supper, it's like an orchestra tuning up. It only needs Toscanini[3] to raise his baton and we'd be off in the "Ride of the Valkyries."[4] Monday, the sixth of March, nineteen forty-four. Mr. Kraler is in the hospital. It seems he has ulcers. Pim says we are his ulcers. Miep has to run the business and us too. The Americans have landed on the southern tip of Italy. Father looks for a quick finish to the

3. **Toscanini** (täs′kə·nē′nē): Arturo Toscanini (1867–1957), a famous orchestra conductor.
4. **"Ride of the Valkyries"** (val·kir′ēz): lively piece of music from an opera by the German composer Richard Wagner (1813–1883).

WORDS TO OWN
forlorn (fôr·lôrn′) *adj.:* abandoned and lonely.

---

war. Mr. Dussel is waiting every day for the warehouse man to demand more money. Have I been skipping too much from one subject to another? I can't help it. I feel that spring is coming. I feel it in my whole body and soul. I feel utterly confused. I am longing . . . so longing . . . for everything . . . for friends . . . for someone to talk to . . . someone who understands . . . someone young, who feels as I do . . .

[*As these last lines are being said, the curtain rises on the scene. The lights dim on.* ANNE's *voice fades out.*]

▮ SCENE 2

It is evening, after supper. From outside we hear the sound of children playing. The "grown-ups," with the exception of MR. VAN DAAN, *are all in the main room.* MRS. FRANK *is doing some mending.* MRS. VAN DAAN *is reading a fashion magazine.* MR. FRANK *is going over business accounts.* DUSSEL, *in his dentist's jacket, is pacing up and down, impatient to get into his bedroom.* MR. VAN DAAN *is upstairs working on a piece of embroidery in an embroidery frame.*

In his room PETER *is sitting before the mirror, smoothing his hair. As the scene goes on, he puts on his tie, brushes his coat and puts it on, preparing himself meticulously for a visit from* ANNE. *On his wall are now hung some of* ANNE's *motion picture stars.*

In her room ANNE *too is getting dressed. She stands before the mirror in her slip, trying various ways of dressing her hair.* MARGOT *is seated on the sofa, hemming a skirt for* ANNE *to wear.*

In the main room DUSSEL *can stand it no longer. He comes over, rapping sharply on the door of his and* ANNE's *bedroom.*

Anne (*calling to him*). No, no, Mr. Dussel! I am not dressed yet. (DUSSEL *walks away, furious, sitting down and burying his head in his*

hands. ANNE *turns to* MARGOT.) How is that? How does that look?
Margot (*glancing at her briefly*). Fine.
Anne. You didn't even look.
Margot. Of course I did. It's fine.
Anne. Margot, tell me, am I terribly ugly?
Margot. Oh, stop fishing.
Anne. No. No. Tell me.
Margot. Of course you're not. You've got nice eyes . . . and a lot of <u>animation</u>, and . . .
Anne. A little vague, aren't you?

[*She reaches over and takes a brassiere out of* MARGOT's *sewing basket. She holds it up to herself, studying the effect in the mirror. Outside,* MRS. FRANK, *feeling sorry for* DUSSEL, *comes over, knocking at the girls' door.*]

Mrs. Frank (*outside*). May I come in?
Margot. Come in, Mother.
Mrs. Frank (*shutting the door behind her*). Mr. Dussel's impatient to get in here.
Anne (*still with the brassiere*). Heavens, he takes the room for himself the entire day.
Mrs. Frank (*gently*). Anne, dear, you're not going in again tonight to see Peter?
Anne (*dignified*). That is my intention.
Mrs. Frank. But you've already spent a great deal of time in there today.
Anne. I was in there exactly twice. Once to get the dictionary, and then three quarters of an hour before supper.
Mrs. Frank. Aren't you afraid you're disturbing him?
Anne. Mother, I have some intuition.
Mrs. Frank. Then may I ask you this much, Anne. Please don't shut the door when you go in.
Anne. You sound like Mrs. Van Daan! (*She throws the brassiere back in* MARGOT's *sewing basket and picks up her blouse, putting it on.*)

WORDS TO OWN
animation (an'i·mā'shən) *n.*: liveliness.

Mrs. Frank. No. No. I don't mean to suggest anything wrong. I only wish that you wouldn't expose yourself to criticism . . . that you wouldn't give Mrs. Van Daan the opportunity to be unpleasant.

Anne. Mrs. Van Daan doesn't need an opportunity to be unpleasant!

Mrs. Frank. Everyone's on edge, worried about Mr. Kraler. This is one more thing . . .

Anne. I'm sorry, Mother. I'm going to Peter's room. I'm not going to let Petronella Van Daan spoil our friendship.

[MRS. FRANK *hesitates for a second, then goes out, closing the door after her. She gets a pack of playing cards and sits at the center table, playing solitaire. In* ANNE's *room* MARGOT *hands the finished skirt to* ANNE. *As* ANNE *is putting it on,* MARGOT *takes off her high-heeled shoes and stuffs paper in the toes so that* ANNE *can wear them.*]

Margot (*to* ANNE). Why don't you two talk in the main room? It'd save a lot of trouble. It's hard on Mother, having to listen to those remarks from Mrs. Van Daan and not say a word.

Anne. Why doesn't she say a word? I think it's ridiculous to take it and take it.

Margot. You don't understand Mother at all, do you? She can't talk back. She's not like you. It's just not in her nature to fight back.

Anne. Anyway . . . the only one I worry about is you. I feel awfully guilty about you. (*She sits on the stool near* MARGOT, *putting on* MARGOT's *high-heeled shoes.*)

Margot. What about?

Anne. I mean, every time I go into Peter's room, I have a feeling I may be hurting you. (MARGOT *shakes her head.*) I know if it were me, I'd be wild. I'd be desperately jealous, if it were me.

Margot. Well, I'm not.

Anne. You don't feel badly? Really? Truly? You're not jealous?

Margot. Of course I'm jealous . . . jealous that

you've got something to get up in the morning for . . . But jealous of you and Peter? No.

[ANNE *goes back to the mirror.*]

Anne. Maybe there's nothing to be jealous of. Maybe he doesn't really like me. Maybe I'm just taking the place of his cat . . . (*She picks up a pair of short white gloves, putting them on.*) Wouldn't you like to come in with us?

Margot. I have a book.

[*The sound of the children playing outside fades out. In the main room* DUSSEL *can stand it no longer. He jumps up, going to the bedroom door and knocking sharply.*]

Dussel. Will you please let me in my room!

Anne. Just a minute, dear, dear Mr. Dussel. (*She picks up her mother's pink stole and adjusts it elegantly over her shoulders, then gives a last look in the mirror.*) Well, here I go . . . to run the gantlet.[5] (*She starts out, followed by* MARGOT.)

Dussel (*as she appears—sarcastic*). Thank you so much.

[DUSSEL *goes into his room.* ANNE *goes toward* PETER's *room, passing* MRS. VAN DAAN *and her parents at the center table.*]

Mrs. Van Daan. My God, look at her! (ANNE *pays no attention. She knocks at* PETER's *door.*) I don't know what good it is to have a son. I never see him. He wouldn't care if I killed myself. (PETER *opens the door and stands aside for* ANNE *to come in.*) Just a minute, Anne. (*She goes to them at the door.*) I'd like to say a few words to my son. Do you mind? (PETER *and* ANNE *stand waiting.*) Peter, I don't want you staying up till all hours tonight. You've got to have your sleep. You're a growing boy. You hear?

Mrs. Frank. Anne won't stay late. She's going to bed promptly at nine. Aren't you, Anne?

---

5. **run the gantlet** (gônt'lit): proceed while under attack from both sides.

Anne. Yes, Mother . . . (*To* MRS. VAN DAAN) May we go now?

Mrs. Van Daan. Are you asking me? I didn't know I had anything to say about it.

Mrs. Frank. Listen for the chimes, Anne dear.

[*The two young people go off into* PETER'S *room, shutting the door after them.*]

Mrs. Van Daan (*to* MRS. FRANK). In my day it was the boys who called on the girls. Not the girls on the boys.

Mrs. Frank. You know how young people like to feel that they have secrets. Peter's room is the only place where they can talk.

Mrs. Van Daan. Talk! That's not what they called it when I was young.

[MRS. VAN DAAN *goes off to the bathroom.* MARGOT *settles down to read her book.* MR. FRANK *puts his papers away and brings a chess game to the center table. He and* MRS. FRANK *start to play. In* PETER'S *room,* ANNE *speaks to* PETER, *indignant, humiliated.*]

Anne. Aren't they awful? Aren't they impossible? Treating us as if we were still in the nursery.

[*She sits on the cot.* PETER *gets a bottle of pop and two glasses.*]

Peter. Don't let it bother you. It doesn't bother me.

Anne. I suppose you can't really blame them . . . they think back to what *they* were like at our age. They don't realize how much more advanced we are. . . . When you think what wonderful discussions we've had! . . . Oh, I forgot. I was going to bring you some more pictures.

Peter. Oh, these are fine, thanks.

Mrs. Frank.

Anne. Don't you want some more? Miep just brought me some new ones.

Peter. Maybe later. (*He gives her a glass of pop and, taking some for himself, sits down facing her.*)

Anne (*looking up at one of the photographs*). I remember when I got that . . . I won it. I bet Jopie that I could eat five ice-cream cones. We'd all been playing ping-pong . . . We used to have heavenly times . . . we'd finish up with ice cream at the Delphi or the Oasis, where Jews were allowed . . . there'd always be a lot of boys . . . we'd laugh and joke . . . I'd like to go back to it for a few days or a week. But after that I know I'd be bored to death. I think more seriously about life now. I want to be a journalist . . . or something. I love to write. What do you want to do?

Peter. I thought I might go off someplace . . . work on a farm or something . . . some job that doesn't take much brains.

Anne. You shouldn't talk that way. You've got the most awful inferiority complex.

Peter. I know I'm not smart.

Anne. That isn't true. You're much better than I am in dozens of things . . . arithmetic and algebra and . . . well, you're a million times better than I am in algebra. (*With sudden directness*) You like Margot, don't you? Right from the start you liked her, liked her much better than me.

Peter (*uncomfortably*). Oh, I don't know.

[*In the main room* MRS. VAN DAAN *comes from the bathroom and goes over to the sink, polishing a coffeepot.*]

Anne. It's all right. Everyone feels that way. Margot's so good. She's sweet and bright and beautiful and I'm not.

Peter. I wouldn't say that.

Anne. Oh, no, I'm not. I know that. I know quite well that I'm not a beauty. I never have been and never shall be.

Peter. I don't agree at all. I think you're pretty.

Anne. That's not true!

Peter. And another thing. You've changed . . . from at first, I mean.

Anne. I have?

Peter. I used to think you were awful noisy.

Anne. And what do you think now, Peter? How have I changed?

Peter. Well . . . er . . . you're . . . quieter.

[*In his room* DUSSEL *takes his pajamas and toilet articles and goes into the bathroom to change.*]

Anne. I'm glad you don't just hate me.

Peter. I never said that.

Anne. I bet when you get out of here, you'll never think of me again.

Peter. That's crazy.

Anne. When you get back with all of your friends, you're going to say . . . now what did I ever see in that Mrs. Quack Quack.

Peter. I haven't got any friends.

Anne. Oh, Peter, of course you have. Everyone has friends.

Peter. Not me. I don't want any. I get along all right without them.

Anne. Does that mean you can get along without me? I think of myself as your friend.

Peter. No. If they were all like you, it'd be different.

[*He takes the glasses and the bottle and puts them away. There is a second's silence and then* ANNE *speaks, hesitantly, shyly.*]

Anne. Peter, did you ever kiss a girl?

Peter. Yes. Once.

Anne. (*to cover her feelings*). That picture's crooked. (PETER *goes over, straightening the photograph.*) Was she pretty?

Peter. I've always thought that when two people . . .

Peter. Huh?

Anne. The girl that you kissed.

Peter. I don't know. I was blindfolded. (*He comes back and sits down again.*) It was at a party. One of those kissing games.

Anne (*relieved*). Oh. I don't suppose that really counts, does it?

Peter. It didn't with me.

Anne. I've been kissed twice. Once a man I'd never seen before kissed me on the cheek when he picked me up off the ice and I was crying. And the other was Mr. Koophuis, a friend of Father's, who kissed my hand. You wouldn't say those counted, would you?

Peter. I wouldn't say so.

Anne. I know almost for certain that Margot would never kiss anyone unless she was engaged to them. And I'm sure too that Mother never touched a man before Pim. But I don't know . . . things are so different now . . . What do you think? Do you think a girl shouldn't kiss anyone except if she's engaged or something? It's so hard to try to think what to do, when here we are with the whole world falling around our ears and you think . . . well . . . you don't know what's going to happen tomorrow and . . . What do you think?

Peter. I suppose it'd depend on the girl. Some girls, anything they do's wrong. But others . . . well . . . it wouldn't necessarily be wrong with them. (*The carillon starts to strike nine o'clock.*) I've always thought that when two people . . .

Anne. Nine o'clock. I have to go.

Peter. That's right.

Anne (*without moving*). Good night.

[*There is a second's pause; then* PETER *gets up and moves toward the door.*]

Peter. You won't let them stop you coming?

Anne. No. (*She rises and starts for the door.*) Sometime I might bring my diary. There are so many things in it that I want to talk over with you. There's a lot about you.

Peter. What kind of thing?

Anne. I wouldn't want you to see some of it. I thought you were a nothing, just the way you thought about me.

Peter. Did you change your mind, the way I changed my mind about you?

Anne. Well . . . You'll see . . .

[*For a second* ANNE *stands looking up at* PETER, *longing for him to kiss her. As he makes no move, she turns away. Then suddenly* PETER *grabs her awkwardly in his arms, kissing her on the cheek.* ANNE *walks out dazed. She stands for a minute, her back to the people in the main room. As she regains her poise, she goes to her mother and father and* MARGOT, *silently kissing them. They murmur their good nights to her. As she is about to open her bedroom door, she catches sight of* MRS. VAN DAAN. *She goes quickly to her, taking her face in her hands and kissing her, first on one cheek and then on the other. Then she hurries off into her room.* MRS. VAN DAAN *looks after her and then looks over at* PETER'*s room. Her suspicions are confirmed.*]

Mrs. Van Daan (*she knows*). Ah hah!

[*The lights dim out. The curtain falls on the scene. In the darkness* ANNE'*s voice comes, faintly at first and then with growing strength.*]

Anne's Voice. By this time we all know each other so well that if anyone starts to tell a story, the rest can finish it for him. We're having to cut down still further on our meals. What makes it worse, the rats have been at work again. They've carried off some of our precious food. Even Mr. Dussel wishes now that Mouschi was here. Thursday, the twentieth of April, nineteen forty-four. Invasion fever is mounting every day. Miep tells us that people outside talk of nothing else. For myself, life has become much more pleasant. I often go to Peter's room after supper. Oh, don't think I'm in love, because I'm not. But it does make life more bearable to have someone with whom you can exchange views. No more tonight. P.S. . . . I must be honest. I must confess that I actually live for the next meeting. Is there anything lovelier than to sit under the skylight and feel the sun on your cheeks and have a darling boy in your arms? I admit now that I'm glad the Van Daans had a son and not a daughter. I've outgrown another dress. That's the third. I'm having to wear Margot's clothes after all. I'm working hard on my French and am now reading *La Belle Nivernaise*.[6]

[*As she is saying the last lines, the curtain rises on the scene. The lights dim on as* ANNE'*s voice fades out.*]

■ SCENE 3

It is night, a few weeks later. Everyone is in bed. There is complete quiet. In the VAN DAANS' *room a match flares up for a moment and then is quickly put out.* MR. VAN DAAN, *in bare feet, dressed in underwear and trousers, is dimly seen coming stealthily down the stairs and into the main room, where* MR. *and* MRS. FRANK *and* MARGOT *are sleeping. He goes to the food safe and again lights a match. Then he cautiously opens the safe, taking out a half loaf of bread. As he closes the safe, it creaks. He stands rigid.* MRS. FRANK *sits up in bed. She sees him.*

Mrs. Frank (*screaming*). Otto! Otto! Komme schnell![7]

[*The rest of the people wake, hurriedly getting up.*]

Mr. Frank. Was ist los? Was ist passiert?[8]

[DUSSEL, *followed by* ANNE, *comes from his room.*]

Mrs. Frank (*as she rushes over to* MR. VAN DAAN). Er stiehlt das Essen![9]

6. *La Belle Nivernaise* (nē·ver′nez′): children's story by the French writer Alphonse Daudet (1840-1897).
7. **Komme schnell!:** German for "Come quickly!"
8. **Was . . . passiert?:** "What's going on? What happened?"
9. **Er . . . Essen!:** "He is stealing the food!"

Dussel (*grabbing* MR. VAN DAAN). You! You! Give me that.
Mrs. Van Daan (*coming down the stairs*). Putti . . . Putti . . . what is it?
Dussel (*his hands on* MR. VAN DAAN'*s neck*). You dirty thief . . . stealing food . . . you good-for-nothing . . .
Mr. Frank. Mr. Dussel! For God's sake! Help me, Peter!

[PETER *comes over, trying, with* MR. FRANK, *to separate the two struggling men.*]

Peter. Let him go! Let go!

[DUSSEL *drops* MR. VAN DAAN, *pushing him away. He shows them the end of a loaf of bread that he has taken from* MR. VAN DAAN.]

Dussel. You greedy, selfish . . . !

[MARGOT *turns on the lights.*]

Mrs. Van Daan. Putti . . . what is it?

[*All of* MRS. FRANK'*s gentleness, her self-control, is gone. She is outraged, in a frenzy of indignation.*]

Mrs. Frank. The bread! He was stealing the bread!
Dussel. It was you, and all the time we thought it was the rats!
Mr. Frank. Mr. Van Daan, how could you!
Mr. Van Daan. I'm hungry.
Mrs. Frank. We're all of us hungry! I see the children getting thinner and thinner. Your own son Peter . . . I've heard him moan in his sleep, he's so hungry. And you come in the night and steal food that should go to them . . . to the children!
Mrs. Van Daan (*going to* MR. VAN DAAN *protectively*). He needs more food than the rest of us. He's used to more. He's a big man.

[MR. VAN DAAN *breaks away, going over and sitting on the couch.*]

Mrs. Frank (*turning on* MRS. VAN DAAN). And

you . . . you're worse than he is! You're a mother, and yet you sacrifice your child to this man . . . this . . . this . . .

Mr. Frank. Edith! Edith!

[MARGOT *picks up the pink woolen stole, putting it over her mother's shoulders.*]

Mrs. Frank (*paying no attention, going on to* MRS. VAN DAAN). Don't think I haven't seen you! Always saving the choicest bits for him! I've watched you day after day and I've held my tongue. But not any longer! Not after this! Now I want him to go! I want him to get out of here!

Mr. Frank. Edith!

Mr. Van Daan. Get out of here? }

Mrs. Van Daan. What do you mean? } *Together*

Mrs. Frank. Just that! Take your things and get out!

Mr. Frank (*to* MRS. FRANK). You're speaking in anger. You cannot mean what you are saying.

Mrs. Frank. I mean exactly that!

[MRS. VAN DAAN *takes a cover from the* FRANKS' *bed, pulling it about her.*]

Mr. Frank. For two long years we have lived here, side by side. We have respected each other's rights . . . we have managed to live in peace. Are we now going to throw it all away? I know this will never happen again, will it, Mr. Van Daan?

Mr. Van Daan. No. No.

Mrs. Frank. He steals once! He'll steal again!

[MR. VAN DAAN, *holding his stomach, starts for the bathroom.* ANNE *puts her arms around him, helping him up the step.*]

Mr. Frank. Edith, please. Let us be calm. We'll all go to our rooms . . . and afterwards we'll sit down quietly and talk this out . . . we'll find some way . . .

Mrs. Frank. No! No! No more talk! I want them to leave!

Mrs. Van Daan. You'd put us out, on the streets?

Mrs. Frank. There are other hiding places.

Mrs. Van Daan. A cellar . . . a closet. I know. And we have no money left even to pay for that.

Mrs. Frank. I'll give you money. Out of my own pocket I'll give it gladly. (*She gets her purse from a shelf and comes back with it.*)

Mrs. Van Daan. Mr. Frank, you told Putti you'd never forget what he'd done for you when you came to Amsterdam. You said you could never repay him, that you . . .

Mrs. Frank (*counting out money*). If my husband had any obligation to you, he's paid it, over and over.

Mr. Frank. Edith, I've never seen you like this before. I don't know you.

Mrs. Frank. I should have spoken out long ago.

Dussel. You can't be nice to some people.

Mrs. Van Daan (*turning on* DUSSEL). There would have been plenty for all of us, if *you* hadn't come in here!

Mr. Frank. We don't need the Nazis to destroy us. We're destroying ourselves.

[*He sits down, with his head in his hands.* MRS. FRANK *goes to* MRS. VAN DAAN.]

Mrs. Frank (*giving* MRS. VAN DAAN *some money*). Give this to Miep. She'll find you a place.

Anne. Mother, you're not putting *Peter* out. Peter hasn't done anything.

Mrs. Frank. He'll stay, of course. When I say I must protect the children, I mean Peter too.

[PETER *rises from the steps where he has been sitting.*]

Peter. I'd have to go if Father goes.

[MR. VAN DAAN *comes from the bathroom.* MRS. VAN DAAN *hurries to him and takes him to the couch. Then she gets water from the sink to bathe his face.*]

Mrs. Frank (*while this is going on*). He's no father to you . . . that man! He doesn't know what it is to be a father!

Peter (*starting for his room*). I wouldn't feel right. I couldn't stay.

Mrs. Frank. Very well, then. I'm sorry.

Anne (*rushing over to* PETER). No, Peter! No! (PETER *goes into his room, closing the door after him.* ANNE *turns back to her mother, crying.*) I don't care about the food. They can have mine! I don't want it! Only don't send them away. It'll be daylight soon. They'll be caught . . .

Margot (*putting her arms comfortingly around* ANNE). Please, Mother!

Mrs. Frank. They're not going now. They'll stay here until Miep finds them a place. (*To* MRS. VAN DAAN) But one thing I insist on! He must never come down here again! He must never come to this room where the food is stored! We'll divide what we have . . . an equal share for each! (DUSSEL *hurries over to get a sack of potatoes from the food safe.* MRS. FRANK *goes on, to* MRS. VAN DAAN) You can cook it here and take it up to him.

[DUSSEL *brings the sack of potatoes back to the center table.*]

Margot. Oh, no. No. We haven't sunk so far that we're going to fight over a handful of rotten potatoes.

Dussel (*dividing the potatoes into piles*). Mrs. Frank, Mr. Frank, Margot, Anne, Peter, Mrs. Van Daan, Mr. Van Daan, myself . . . Mrs. Frank . . .

[*The buzzer sounds in* MIEP's *signal.*]

Mr. Frank. It's Miep! (*He hurries over, getting his overcoat and putting it on.*)

Margot. At this hour?

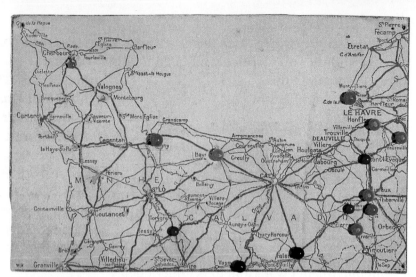

Map kept by Mr. Frank after the Allied invasion of Normandy. Colored pins show the progress of the Allied forces.

Mrs. Frank. It is trouble.

Mr. Frank (*as he starts down to unbolt the door*). I beg you, don't let her see a thing like this!

Dussel (*counting without stopping*). . . . Anne, Peter, Mrs. Van Daan, Mr. Van Daan, myself . . .

Margot (*to* DUSSEL). Stop it! Stop it!

Dussel. . . . Mr. Frank, Margot, Anne, Peter, Mrs. Van Daan, Mr. Van Daan, myself, Mrs. Frank . . .

Mrs. Van Daan. You're keeping the big ones for yourself! All the big ones . . . Look at the size of that! . . . And that! . . .

[DUSSEL *continues with his dividing.* PETER, *with his shirt and trousers on, comes from his room.*]

Margot. Stop it! Stop it!

[*We hear* MIEP's *excited voice speaking to* MR. FRANK *below.*]

Miep. Mr. Frank . . . the most wonderful news! . . . The invasion[10] has begun!

10. **the invasion:** On June 6, 1944, Allied forces landed in Normandy, a region of northern France, to launch a military campaign against the Germans.

Mr. Frank. Go on, tell them! Tell them!

[MIEP *comes running up the steps, ahead of* MR. FRANK. *She has a man's raincoat on over her nightclothes and a bunch of orange-colored flowers in her hand.*]

Miep. Did you hear that, everybody? Did you hear what I said? The invasion has begun! The invasion!

[*They all stare at* MIEP, *unable to grasp what she is telling them.* PETER *is the first to recover his wits.*]

Peter. Where?
Mrs. Van Daan. When? When, Miep?
Miep. It began early this morning . . .

[*As she talks on, the realization of what she has said begins to dawn on them. Everyone goes crazy. A wild demonstration takes place.* MRS. FRANK *hugs* MR. VAN DAAN.]

Mrs. Frank. Oh, Mr. Van Daan, did you hear that?

[DUSSEL *embraces* MRS. VAN DAAN. PETER *grabs a frying pan and parades around the room, beating on it, singing the Dutch national anthem.* ANNE *and* MARGOT *follow him, singing, weaving in and out among the excited grown-ups.* MARGOT *breaks away to take the flowers from* MIEP *and distribute them to everyone. While this pandemonium is going on,* MRS. FRANK *tries to make herself heard above the excitement.*]

Mrs. Frank (*to* MIEP). How do you know?
Miep. The radio . . . The BBC![11] They said they landed on the coast of Normandy!
Peter. The British?
Miep. British, Americans, French, Dutch, Poles, Norwegians . . . all of them! More than

four thousand ships! Churchill[12] spoke, and General Eisenhower![13] D-day, they call it!
Mr. Frank. Thank God, it's come!
Mrs. Van Daan. At last!
Miep (*starting out*). I'm going to tell Mr. Kraler. This'll be better than any blood transfusion.
Mr. Frank (*stopping her*). What part of Normandy did they land, did they say?
Miep. Normandy . . . that's all I know now . . . I'll be up the minute I hear some more! (*She goes hurriedly out.*)
Mr. Frank (*to* MRS. FRANK). What did I tell you? What did I tell you?

[MRS. FRANK *indicates that he has forgotten to bolt the door after* MIEP. *He hurries down the steps.* MR. VAN DAAN, *sitting on the couch, suddenly breaks into a convulsive sob. Everybody looks at him, bewildered.*]

Mrs. Van Daan (*hurrying to him*). Putti! Putti! What is it? What happened?
Mr. Van Daan. Please. I'm so ashamed.

[MR. FRANK *comes back up the steps.*]

Dussel. Oh, for God's sake!
Mrs. Van Daan. Don't, Putti.
Margot. It doesn't matter now!
Mr. Frank (*going to* MR. VAN DAAN). Didn't you hear what Miep said? The invasion has come! We're going to be liberated! This is a time to celebrate! (*He embraces* MRS. FRANK *and then hurries to the cupboard and gets the cognac and a glass.*)
Mr. Van Daan. To steal bread from children!
Mrs. Frank. We've all done things that we're ashamed of.
Anne. Look at me, the way I've treated Mother . . . so mean and horrid to her.

11. **BBC:** British Broadcasting Corporation. People listened to the BBC, illegally, for news of the war that was more accurate than what German-controlled broadcasters offered.

12. **Churchill:** Sir Winston Churchill (1874–1965), British prime minister during World War II.
13. **General Eisenhower:** Dwight D. Eisenhower (1890–1969), commander of the Allied forces in western Europe. He later became president of the United States (1953–1961).

Mrs. Frank. No, Anneke, no.

[ANNE *runs to her mother, putting her arms around her.*]

Anne. Oh, Mother, I was. I was awful.

Mr. Van Daan. Not like me. No one is as bad as me!

Dussel (*to* MR. VAN DAAN). Stop it now! Let's be happy!

Mr. Frank (*giving* MR. VAN DAAN *a glass of cognac*). Here! Here! Schnapps![14] L'chaim![15]

[MR. VAN DAAN *takes the cognac. They all watch him. He gives them a feeble smile.* ANNE *puts up her fingers in a V-for-victory sign. As* MR. VAN DAAN *gives an answering V sign, they are startled to hear a loud sob from behind them. It is* MRS. FRANK, *stricken with* remorse. *She is sitting on the other side of the room.*]

Mrs. Frank (*through her sobs*). When I think of the terrible things I said . . .

[MR. FRANK, ANNE, *and* MARGOT *hurry to her, trying to comfort her.* MR. VAN DAAN *brings her his glass of cognac.*]

Mr. Van Daan. No! No! You were right!

Mrs. Frank. That I should speak that way to you! . . . Our friends! . . . Our guests! (*She starts to cry again.*)

Dussel. Stop it, you're spoiling the whole invasion!

[*As they are comforting her, the lights dim out. The curtain falls.*]

Anne's Voice (*faintly at first and then with growing strength*). We're all in much better spirits these days. There's still excellent news of the invasion. The best part about it is that I have a feeling that friends are coming. Who knows? Maybe I'll be back in school by fall. Ha, ha! The joke is on us! The warehouse man doesn't know a thing and we are paying him all that money! . . . Wednesday, the second of July, nineteen forty-four. The invasion seems temporarily to be bogged down. Mr. Kraler has to have an operation, which looks bad. The Gestapo have found the radio that was stolen. Mr. Dussel says they'll trace it back and back to the thief, and then, it's just a matter of time till they get to us. Everyone is low. Even poor Pim can't raise their spirits. I have often been downcast myself . . . but never in despair. I can shake off everything if I write. But . . . and that is the great question . . . will I ever be able to write well? I want to so much. I want to go on living even after my death. Another birthday has gone by, so now I am fifteen. Already I know what I want. I have a goal, an opinion.

[*As this is being said, the curtain rises on the scene, the lights dim on, and* ANNE'*s voice fades out.*]

■ SCENE 4

It is an afternoon a few weeks later. . . . Everyone but Margot is in the main room. There is a sense of great tension.

Both MRS. FRANK *and* MR. VAN DAAN *are nervously pacing back and forth.* DUSSEL *is standing at the window, looking down fixedly at the street below.* PETER *is at the center table, trying to do his lessons.* ANNE *sits opposite him, writing in her diary.* MRS. VAN DAAN *is seated on the couch, her eyes on* MR. FRANK *as he sits reading.*

The sound of a telephone ringing comes from the office below. They all are rigid, listening tensely. DUSSEL *rushes down to* MR. FRANK.

---

14. **schnapps** (shnäps): strong liquor.
15. **L'chaim!** (lə·khä´yim): Hebrew toast meaning "To life!"

WORDS TO OWN
remorse (ri·môrs´) *n*.: deep feeling of guilt.

Dussel. There it goes again, the telephone! Mr. Frank, do you hear?

Mr. Frank (*quietly*). Yes. I hear.

Dussel (*pleading, insistent*). But this is the third time, Mr. Frank! The third time in quick succession! It's a signal! I tell you it's Miep, trying to get us! For some reason she can't come to us and she's trying to warn us of something!

Mr. Frank. Please. Please.

Mr. Van Daan (*to* DUSSEL). You're wasting your breath.

Dussel. Something has happened, Mr. Frank. For three days now Miep hasn't been to see us! And today not a man has come to work. There hasn't been a sound in the building!

Mrs. Frank. Perhaps it's Sunday. We may have lost track of the days.

Mr. Van Daan (*to* ANNE). You with the diary there. What day is it?

Dussel (*going to* MRS. FRANK). I don't lose track of the days! I know exactly what day it is! It's Friday, the fourth of August. Friday, and not a man at work. (*He rushes back to* MR. FRANK, *pleading with him, almost in tears.*) I tell you Mr. Kraler's dead. That's the only explanation. He's dead and they've closed down the building, and Miep's trying to tell us!

Mr. Frank. She'd never telephone us.

Dussel (*frantic*). Mr. Frank, answer that! I beg you, answer it!

Mr. Frank. No.

Mr. Van Daan. Just pick it up and listen. You don't have to speak. Just listen and see if it's Miep.

Dussel (*speaking at the same time*). For God's sake . . . I ask you.

Mr. Frank. No. I've told you, no. I'll do nothing that might let anyone know we're in the building.

Peter. Mr. Frank's right.

Mr. Van Daan. There's no need to tell us what side you're on.

Mr. Frank. If we wait patiently, quietly, I believe that help will come.

[*There is silence for a minute as they all listen to the telephone ringing.*]

Dussel. I'm going down. (*He rushes down the steps.* MR. FRANK *tries ineffectually to hold him.* DUSSEL *runs to the lower door, unbolting it. The telephone stops ringing.* DUSSEL *bolts the door and comes slowly back up the steps.*) Too late.

[MR. FRANK *goes to* MARGOT *in* ANNE's *bedroom.*]

Mr. Van Daan. So we just wait here until we die.

Mrs. Van Daan (*hysterically*). I can't stand it! I'll kill myself! I'll kill myself!

Mr. Van Daan. For God's sake, stop it!

[*In the distance, a German military band is heard playing a Viennese waltz.*]

Mrs. Van Daan. I think you'd be glad if I did! I think you want me to die!

Mr. Van Daan. Whose fault is it we're here? (MRS. VAN DAAN *starts for her room. He follows, talking at her.*) We could've been safe somewhere . . . in America or Switzerland. But no! No! You wouldn't leave when I wanted to. You couldn't leave your things. You couldn't leave your precious furniture.

Mrs. Van Daan. Don't touch me!

[*She hurries up the stairs, followed by* MR. VAN DAAN. PETER, *unable to bear it, goes to his room.* ANNE *looks after him, deeply concerned.* DUSSEL *returns to his post at the window.* MR. FRANK *comes back into the main room and takes a book, trying to read.* MRS. FRANK *sits near the sink, starting to peel some potatoes.* ANNE *quietly goes to* PETER's *room, closing the door after her.* PETER *is lying face down on the cot.* ANNE *leans over him, holding him in her arms, trying to bring him out of his despair.*]

Anne. Look, Peter, the sky. (*She looks up through the skylight.*) What a lovely, lovely day! Aren't the clouds beautiful? You know what I do when it seems as if I couldn't stand being cooped up for one more minute? I *think* myself out. I think myself on a walk in the park where I used to go with Pim. Where the jonquils and the crocuses and the violets grow down the slopes. You know the most wonderful part about *thinking* yourself out? You can have it any way you like. You can have roses and violets and chrysanthemums all blooming at the same time. . . . It's funny . . . I used to take it all for granted . . . and now I've gone crazy about everything to do with nature. Haven't you?

Peter. I've just gone crazy. I think if something doesn't happen soon . . . if we don't get out of here . . . I can't stand much more of it!

Anne (*softly*). I wish you had a religion, Peter.

Peter. No, thanks! Not me!

Anne. Oh, I don't mean you have to be Orthodox . . . [16] or believe in Heaven and Hell and Purgatory and things . . . I just mean some religion . . . it doesn't matter what. Just to believe in something! When I think of all that's out there . . . the trees . . . and flowers . . . and sea gulls . . . When I think of the dearness of you, Peter . . . and the goodness of the people we know . . . Mr. Kraler, Miep, Dirk, the vegetable man, all risking their lives for us every day . . . When I think of these good things, I'm not afraid anymore . . . I find myself, and God, and I . . .

[PETER *interrupts, getting up and walking away.*]

Peter. That's fine! But when I begin to think, I get mad! Look at us, hiding out for two years. Not able to move! Caught here like . . . waiting for them to come and get us . . . and all for what?

Anne. We're not the only people that've had to suffer. There've always been people that've had

to . . . sometimes one race . . . sometimes another . . . and yet . . .

Peter. That doesn't make me feel any better!

Anne (*going to him*). I know it's terrible, trying to have any faith . . . when people are doing such horrible . . . But you know what I sometimes think? I think the world may be going through a phase, the way I was with Mother. It'll pass, maybe not for hundreds of years, but someday . . . I still believe, in spite of everything, that people are really good at heart.

Peter. I want to see something now . . . not a thousand years from now! (*He goes over, sitting down again on the cot.*)

Anne. But, Peter, if you'd only look at it as part of a great pattern . . . that we're just a little minute in the life . . . (*She breaks off.*) Listen to us, going at each other like a couple of stupid grown-ups! Look at the sky now. Isn't it lovely? (*She holds out her hand to him.* PETER *takes it and rises, standing with her at the window looking out, his arms around her.*) Someday, when we're outside again, I'm going to . . .

[*She breaks off as she hears the sound of a car, its brakes squealing as it comes to a sudden stop. The people in the other rooms also become aware of the sound. They listen tensely. Another car roars up to a screeching stop.* ANNE *and* PETER *come from* PETER's *room.* MR. *and* MRS. VAN DAAN *creep down the stairs.* DUSSEL *comes out from his room. Everyone is listening, hardly breathing. A doorbell clangs again and again in the building below.* MR. FRANK *starts quietly down the steps to the door.* DUSSEL *and* PETER *follow him. The others stand rigid, waiting, terrified.*

In a few seconds DUSSEL *comes stumbling back up the steps. He shakes off* PETER's *help and goes to his room.* MR. FRANK *bolts the door below and comes slowly back up the steps. Their eyes are all on him as he stands there*

---

16. **Orthodox:** Orthodox Jews strictly observe Jewish traditions.

for a minute. They realize that what they feared has happened. MRS. VAN DAAN *starts to whimper.* MR. VAN DAAN *puts her gently in a chair and then hurries off up the stairs to their room to collect their things.* PETER *goes to comfort his mother. There is a sound of violent pounding on a door below.*]

Mr. Frank (*quietly*). For the past two years we have lived in fear. Now we can live in hope.

[*The pounding below becomes more insistent. There are muffled sounds of voices, shouting commands.*]

Men's Voices. Aufmachen! Da drinnen! Aufmachen! Schnell! Schnell! Schnell![17] (*Etc., etc.*)

[*The street door below is forced open. We hear the heavy tread of footsteps coming up.* MR. FRANK *gets two school bags from the shelves and gives one to* ANNE *and the other to* MARGOT. *He goes to get a bag for* MRS. FRANK. *The sound of feet coming up grows louder.* PETER *comes to* ANNE, *kissing her goodbye; then he goes to his room to collect his things. The buzzer of their door starts to ring.* MR. FRANK *brings* MRS. FRANK *a bag. They stand together, waiting. We hear the thud of gun butts on the door, trying to break it down.*

ANNE *stands, holding her school satchel, looking over at her father and mother with a soft, reassuring smile. She is no longer a child, but a woman with courage to meet whatever lies ahead.*

The lights dim out. The curtain falls on the scene. We hear a mighty crash as the door is shattered. After a second ANNE'*s voice is heard.*]

Anne's Voice. And so it seems our stay here is over. They are waiting for us now. They've allowed us five minutes to get our things. We can each take a bag and whatever it will hold of

Anne's Voice. And so it seems our stay here is over.

17. **Aufmachen! . . . Schnell!:** German for "Open up! You in there! Open up! Quickly! Quickly! Quickly!"

clothing. Nothing else. So, dear Diary, that means I must leave you behind. Goodbye for a while. P.S. Please, please, Miep, or Mr. Kraler, or anyone else. If you should find this diary, will you please keep it safe for me, because someday I hope . . .

[*Her voice stops abruptly. There is silence. After a second the curtain rises.*]

■ SCENE 5

It is again the afternoon in November 1945. The rooms are as we saw them in the first scene. MR. KRALER *has joined* MIEP *and* MR. FRANK. *There are coffee cups on the table. We see a great change in* MR. FRANK. *He is calm now. His bitterness is gone. He slowly turns a few pages of the diary. They are blank.*

Mr. Frank. No more. (*He closes the diary and puts it down on the couch beside him.*)

Miep. I'd gone to the country to find food. When I got back, the block was surrounded by police . . .

Mr. Kraler. We made it our business to learn how they knew. It was the thief . . . the thief who told them.

[MIEP *goes up to the gas burner, bringing back a pot of coffee.*]

Mr. Frank (*after a pause*). It seems strange to say this, that anyone could be happy in a concentration camp. But Anne was happy in the camp in Holland where they first took us. After two years of being shut up in these rooms, she could be out . . . out in the sunshine and the fresh air that she loved.

Miep (*offering the coffee to* MR. FRANK). A little more?

Mr. Frank (*holding out his cup to her*). The news of the war was good. The British and Americans were sweeping through France. We felt sure that they would get to us in time. In September we were told that we were to be shipped to Poland. . . . The men to one camp. The women to another. I was sent to Auschwitz. They went to Belsen. In January we were freed, the few of us who were left. The war wasn't yet over, so it took us a long time to get home. We'd be sent here and there behind the lines where we'd be safe. Each time our train would stop . . . at a siding or a crossing . . . we'd all get out and go from group to group . . . Where were you? Were you at Belsen? At Buchenwald? At Mauthausen? Is it possible that you knew my wife? Did you ever see my husband? My son? My daughter? That's how I found out about my wife's death . . . of Margot, the Van Daans . . . Dussel. But Anne . . . I still hoped . . . Yesterday I went to Rotterdam. I'd heard of a woman there . . . She'd been in Belsen with Anne . . . I know now.

[*He picks up the diary again and turns the pages back to find a certain passage. As he finds it, we hear* ANNE's *voice.*]

Anne's Voice. In spite of everything, I still believe that people are really good at heart.

[MR. FRANK *slowly closes the diary.*]

Mr. Frank. She puts me to shame.

[*They are silent.*]

Curtain

MEET THE WRITERS

The Making of a Masterpiece

Frances Goodrich (1890–1984) and **Albert Hackett** (1900–1995) both started out as actors. They began writing plays and screenplays together in the 1920s and were married soon after. Working at desks facing in opposite directions in the same room, they would each write a version of a scene, then read and comment on the other's version before revising. In this way, Goodrich and Hackett created the scripts for many hit movies, including *Easter Parade, Father of the Bride*, and *It's a Wonderful Life*.

The Diary of Anne Frank is considered their masterpiece. Before they wrote the play, the playwrights spent ten days in Amsterdam visiting the Secret Annex, studying the neighborhood, and questioning Otto Frank (who came from Switzerland to help) on his memories and impressions. It took them two years and eight drafts to complete the play, which opened on Broadway in 1955 to great acclaim. The play won a Pulitzer Prize in 1956 and has since been performed countless times in countries around the world.

The cast of *The Diary of Anne Frank* on Broadway, in a 1997 adaptation by Wendy Kesselman. Anne (center, on table) is smiling at Mr. Frank.

More About Anne Frank

In addition to her diary, Anne wrote many short stories and autobiographical sketches during her time in hiding. You'll find a selection of these in *Anne Frank's Tales from the Secret Annex* (Bantam).

Anne Frank Remembered (Simon & Schuster) is the story of Anne and the other occupants of the Secret Annex as told by their helper and protector Miep Gies.

from The Diary of a Young Girl

Anne Frank

Wednesday, 3 May, 1944

. . . Since Saturday we've changed over, and have lunch at half past eleven in the mornings, so we have to last out with one cupful of porridge; this saves us a meal. Vegetables are still very difficult to obtain; we had rotten boiled lettuce this afternoon. Ordinary lettuce, spinach, and boiled lettuce, there's nothing else. With these we eat rotten potatoes, so it's a delicious combination!

As you can easily imagine, we often ask ourselves here despairingly: "What, oh, what is the use of the war? Why can't people live peacefully together? Why all this destruction?"

Anne in 1940.

The question is very understandable, but no one has found a satisfactory answer to it so far. Yes, why do they make still more gigantic planes, still heavier bombs, and, at the same time, prefabricated houses for reconstruction? Why should millions be spent daily on the war and yet there's not a penny available for medical services, artists, or poor people?

Why do some people have to starve while there are surpluses rotting in other parts of the world? Oh, why are people so crazy?

I don't believe that the big men, the politicians and the capitalists alone, are guilty of the war. Oh no, the little man is just as guilty; otherwise the peoples of the world would have risen in revolt long ago! There's in people simply an urge to destroy, an urge to kill, to murder and rage, and until all mankind, without exception, undergoes a great change, wars will be waged, everything that has been built up, cultivated, and grown will be destroyed and disfigured, after which mankind will have to begin all over again.

I have often been downcast, but never in despair; I regard our hiding as a dangerous adventure, romantic and interesting at the same time. In my diary I treat all the privations° as amusing. I have made up my mind now to lead a different life from other girls and, later on, different from ordinary housewives. My start has been so very full of

° **privations** (prī·vā′shənz): hardships.

interest, and that is the sole reason why I have to laugh at the humorous side of the most dangerous moments.

I am young and I possess many buried qualities; I am young and strong and am living a great adventure; I am still in the midst of it and can't grumble the whole day long. I have been given a lot: a happy nature, a great deal of cheerfulness and strength. Every day I feel that I am developing inwardly, that the liberation is drawing nearer, and how beautiful nature is, how good the people are about me, how interesting this adventure is! Why, then, should I be in despair?

Yours,

Anne

Saturday, 15 July, 1944

. . . "For in its innermost depths youth is lonelier than old age." I read this saying in some book and I've always remembered it, and found it to be true. Is it true, then, that grown-ups have a more difficult time here than we do? No. I know it isn't. Older people have formed their opinions about everything and don't waver before they act. It's twice as hard for us young ones to hold our ground and maintain our opinions in a time when all ideals are being shattered and destroyed, when people are showing their worst side and do not know whether to believe in truth and right and God.

Anyone who claims that the older ones have a more difficult time here certainly doesn't realize to what extent our problems weigh down on us, problems for which we are probably much too young but which thrust themselves upon us continually, until, after a long time, we think we've found a solution, but the solution doesn't seem able to resist the facts which reduce it to nothing again. That's the difficulty in these times: Ideals, dreams, and cherished hopes rise within us, only to meet the horrible truth and be shattered.

It's really a wonder that I haven't dropped all my ideals, because they seem so absurd and impossible to carry out. Yet I keep them, because in spite of everything I still believe that people are really good at heart. I simply can't build up my hopes on a foundation consisting of confusion, misery, and death. I see the world gradually being turned into a wilderness, I hear the ever approaching thunder, which will destroy us too, I can feel the sufferings of millions, and yet, if I look up into the heavens, I think that it will all come right, that this cruelty too will end, and that peace and tranquility will return again.

In the meantime, I must uphold my ideals, for perhaps the time will come when I shall be able to carry them out.

Yours,

Anne

MAKING MEANINGS (ACT TWO)

- ## First Thoughts

    1. Do you agree with Anne that "people are really good at heart"? Does the play offer any evidence to support this statement?

  ## Shaping Interpretations

    2. In your opinion, is Mrs. Frank justified in demanding that the Van Daans leave the Secret Annex? (Why or why not?) What do you think would have happened if Miep hadn't come in with news of the invasion?

    3. The **climax** of a play is its moment of greatest tension. What is this play's climax?

    4. In Act One, Scene 4, Mr. Frank tells Anne, "You must build your own character" (page 376). Do you think she has succeeded in doing this by the end of the play? Explain.

    5. On page 404, Anne says, "I want to go on living even after my death." Do you think her wish has come true? Explain.

    6. What do you think is the main **conflict** in the play? Is it the conflict between the occupants of the Secret Annex and the Nazis, or is it something else?

  ## Extending the Text

    7. Now that you have finished the play, think about the resources that accompany it—for example, Anne's diary entries, the historical photographs, the time line. Which resources did you find most helpful? Are there other resources you wish had been included? Explain your answers.

    8. Before *The Diary of Anne Frank* was first performed, Otto Frank wrote in a letter to the actor who would portray him, "Please don't play me as a 'hero.' . . . Nothing happened to me that did not happen to thousands upon thousands of other people." Do you see anyone in the play as a hero? What qualities or actions make someone a hero?

  ## Challenging the Text

    9. There is no evidence in Anne's diary that Mr. Van Daan stole food; the playwrights may have invented this incident for dramatic effect. What do you think of such changes in fiction or drama that is based on real events?

> ## Reading Check
>
> a. Miep and Mr. Kraler's visit in Act Two, Scene 1, sets off two **conflicts:** one over a cake, the other over a coat. Describe each conflict.
>
> b. How does Anne and Peter's relationship change in Act Two, Scene 1? In Scene 2, how do Mrs. Frank and Mrs. Van Daan respond to this change?
>
> c. At the beginning of Act Two, Scene 4, what is causing tension and fear in the household?

Students visiting the Treblinka death camp.

CHOICES: Building Your Portfolio

Writer's Notebook

1. Collecting Ideas for a Comparison-Contrast Essay

Whenever you **compare** two people or things, you tell how they're alike. When you **contrast** them, you point out their differences. Choose any two characters in this play who have at least one thing in common (the two sisters, for instance, or the two mothers or fathers). Think about how they're alike and different, and jot down your ideas in a Venn diagram like the one begun at right. List the ways your characters are alike where the circles overlap.

Mr. Frank
- cultured
- gentle

Both
- fathers
- businessmen

Mr. Van Daan
- nervous
- smokes

Art

2. Setting the Stage

The stage set shown on page 341 is just one possible design. Using the **stage directions** on page 348, make a diorama of a **stage set** for the play. Remember that all action taking place onstage must be visible from every point in the audience.

Creative Writing

3. "I Am" Anne

Write an "I Am" **poem** for Anne Frank, using this framework:

I am . . .
I hear . . .
I see . . .
I say . . .
I cry . . .
I am . . .

I am . . .
I feel . . .
I try . . .
I dream . . .
I am . . .

Analyzing a Play

4. Is It a Tragedy?

A **tragedy** is a serious play in which the main character meets with failure or death. The main character in a tragedy, however, is admirable and very self aware. When this character is defeated, we feel horror and sadness, but we also feel triumphant because something good has appeared in our world.

There are several types of tragedy. One type involves "the destruction of innocence." In this kind of tragedy the hero is not responsible for his or her disaster. We feel great pity at the loss of this hero because an innocent person is destroyed by cruel outside forces. Does this play about Anne Frank meet these criteria for a tragedy? Write your answer in a brief essay. Be sure to cite details from the play in your response.

(continued on next page)

Anne's diary.

CHOICES: Building Your Portfolio

(continued from previous page)

Role-Play

5. Issues and Answers

How do you think Anne would feel about the fact that her diary has been read by millions of strangers? What influence has the diary had that might justify Mr. Frank's decision to have it published? With a partner, role-play a **dialogue** between Anne and her father about the publication of the diary.

Creative Writing

6. Points of View

Much of the play is based on accounts of conversations and events that Anne Frank recorded in her diary. As a result, the play reflects her **point of view.** From the point of view of one of the other occupants of the Secret Annex, write a **diary entry** describing an event in the play as that character saw it. (In fact, Margot Frank also kept a diary during their time in hiding, but it was lost.)

Art

7. What's the Story?

Make a **storyboard** of the play. Divide a large sheet of paper into six equal sections by drawing two lines down and one across. Choose what you think are the six most important events in the play. In each section of the paper, draw an illustration of one of the events on your list. Share your storyboard with your classmates, explaining why you chose the six events you did.

Supporting an Opinion

8. The Real Anne?

Reread the excerpts from Anne Frank's diary (see pages 342–343 and *Connections* on pages 410–411). Based on these entries, do you feel that the play captures the "real Anne," or do you think important aspects of her personality are missing from the character in the play? Write one or two paragraphs in which you clearly state your opinion on the question. Cite evidence from the play or the diary entries to support your opinion.

Performance

9. The Play's the Thing

With a group of classmates, rehearse and perform a **scene** or part of a scene from the play. Here are some questions to consider:

- How many **characters** appear in this scene?

- What **props** will you need? (Read the **dialogue** and **stage directions** closely to find out.)

- What offstage **sound effects** will be heard, and how will you produce them?

Research/Social Studies

10. Past and Present

How does the Holocaust continue to affect the world today? Using the Internet and print sources in a library, research one of the following topics or another topic of your choice:

- the work of the Anne Frank Foundation

- the creation of the United States Holocaust Memorial Museum in Washington, D.C.

Present what you have learned to your class.

GRAMMAR LINK

Dangling and Misplaced Modifiers

Language Handbook HELP

See Placement of Modifiers, pages 768-769.

Technology HELP

See Language Workshop *CD-ROM.* Key word entry: dangling modifiers.

A modifying phrase or clause that doesn't clearly modify a word in a sentence is called a **dangling modifier.**

DANGLING   Peeking out the window, the church tower could be seen.

The church tower isn't peeking out the window. Rearranging and adding or changing words in the sentence can make the meaning clear.

CLEAR   Peeking out the window, Anne could see the church tower.

A **misplaced modifier** causes confusion because it seems to modify the wrong word in a sentence.

MISPLACED   My grandmother told me about her experiences in Nazi-occupied Europe last week.

CLEAR   My grandmother told me last week about her experiences in Nazi-occupied Europe.

The best way to catch dangling and misplaced modifiers, as with any error that causes confusion for readers, is to ask other people to read your drafts.

Try It Out

Each of the following sentences contains a dangling or misplaced modifier. Rewrite each sentence so that it makes sense.

1. Anne watched the canal boats hiding in the Secret Annex.

2. Coughing and sneezing, Peter's cat was a problem for Dussel.

3. Hoping for a better future, the cake read "Peace in 1944."

4. Miep discovered the diary in the Secret Annex, which had been thrown on the floor.

VOCABULARY   HOW TO OWN A WORD

WORD BANK

conspicuous
unabashed
loathe
indignantly
fortify
zeal
tyranny
gingerly

ostentatiously
appalled
disgruntled
inarticulate
forlorn
animation
remorse

Dear Diary

Divide the list of words in the Word Bank with two classmates. Write down your five words; then, match each one with the name of a character or an event you think Anne might apply the word to in her diary. Read your list of characters and events to your partners, and have them guess which of your vocabulary words goes with each item on the list.

Reading Skills and Strategies

USING PRIOR KNOWLEDGE

You Already Know a Lot

When we read, we apply our knowledge of and beliefs about a topic. Without this prior knowledge, we could never create meaning from a text. Suppose you saw the item below on the front page of a newspaper.

INSIDE

Never Again. In Holocaust Remembrance Day speech, community leader urges students to help wipe out racial prejudice and violence.

You probably wouldn't have any trouble understanding this information. In fact, from your knowledge of history and your understanding of current events, you'd probably have some idea of what to expect in the article. If you could read the article, your knowledge would affect your interpretation of the words on the page.

Imagine what would happen, though, if someone who lived a hundred years ago hopped out of a time machine and picked up the paper. This visitor from the past would never have heard of the Holocaust and would probably find the article difficult to understand.

Drawing Inferences: Making the Connection

Prior knowledge allows you to draw **inferences**—conclusions based on information in the text combined with what you already know. An inference is an educated guess.

Drawing inferences when you read is important because writers don't always tell you everything they mean. For example, in the article you'll read next, "A Tragedy Revealed: A Heroine's Last Days," Ernst Schnabel writes, "Ironically enough, the occupants of the Secret Annex had grown optimistic in the last weeks of their self-imposed confinement" (page 423). Schnabel doesn't

explain why this optimism is ironic. He expects us to connect his statement with our knowledge that the occupants would soon be captured by the Nazis and taken to death camps. From this connection we can infer that the irony lies in the contrast between their rising hopes and their actual fate.

Focusing on What You Know

The more you know about the topic of a text, of course, the easier it is to understand the text. You can sharpen your awareness of what you already know by thinking and writing about a topic before you read. You might ask yourself:

- What do I already know about this topic?

- When I think about this topic, what words and ideas come to mind?

- Do I expect to agree or disagree with the ideas expressed in this text? Why?

Apply the strategy on the next page.

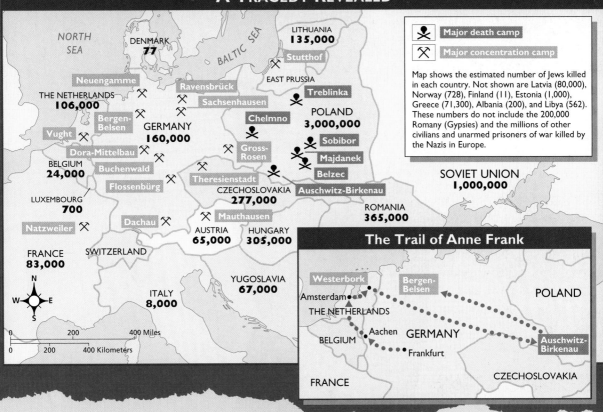

A TRAGEDY REVEALED

NORTH SEA

DENMARK **77**

BALTIC SEA

LITHUANIA **135,000**

☠ **Stutthof**

EAST PRUSSIA

THE NETHERLANDS **106,000**

⚒ **Ravensbrück**

⚒ **Sachsenhausen**

☠ **Treblinka**

Bergen-Belsen ⚒

GERMANY **160,000**

⚒ **Chelmno** ☠

POLAND **3,000,000**

⚒ **Vught**

⚒ **Dora-Mittelbau**

BELGIUM **24,000**

⚒ **Buchenwald**

Gross-Rosen ⚒

☠ **Sobibor**

☠ **Majdanek**

⚒ **Flossenbürg**

Theresienstadt ⚒

☠ **Belzec**

LUXEMBOURG **700**

Auschwitz-Birkenau ☠

CZECHOSLOVAKIA **277,000**

SOVIET UNION **1,000,000**

⚒ **Natzweiler**

⚒ **Dachau** ⚒

⚒ **Mauthausen**

ROMANIA **365,000**

FRANCE **83,000**

SWITZERLAND

AUSTRIA **65,000**

HUNGARY **305,000**

ITALY **8,000**

YUGOSLAVIA **67,000**

N W E S

0 200 400 Miles
0 200 400 Kilometers

☠ Major death camp

⚒ Major concentration camp

Map shows the estimated number of Jews killed in each country. Not shown are Latvia (80,000), Norway (728), Finland (11), Estonia (1,000), Greece (71,300), Albania (200), and Libya (562). These numbers do not include the 200,000 Romany (Gypsies) and the millions of other civilians and unarmed prisoners of war killed by the Nazis in Europe.

The Trail of Anne Frank

Westerbork

Bergen-Belsen

Amsterdam

THE NETHERLANDS

POLAND

Aachen GERMANY

BELGIUM

Frankfurt

Auschwitz-Birkenau

FRANCE

CZECHOSLOVAKIA

Before You Read

A TRAGEDY REVEALED: A HEROINE'S LAST DAYS

The article you're about to read, which was published in *Life* magazine in 1958, starts where Anne Frank's diary and the play adaptation leave off— with the discovery of the Secret Annex and the arrest of its occupants.

go.hrw.com

LEO 8-5

Quickwrite

If you could interview survivors of the Holocaust who knew Anne Frank, what would you ask them? Jot down some of your questions.

Reading Skills and Strategies

Using Prior Knowledge

Make a **KWL chart** like the one that follows. In the K column, jot down what you already know about Anne Frank's life. In the W column, write down what you want to know about Anne's fate after the discovery of the Secret Annex.

Then, as you read, make a note in the L column of any new information that adds to or contradicts your **prior knowledge.** In your W column, check off any questions that are answered in the text.

K	W	L

Statue of Anne Frank by
Pieter L'Hont, Utrecht, the
Netherlands.

A Tragedy Revealed:
A Heroine's Last Days

Ernst Schnabel

Last year in Amsterdam I found an old reel of movie film on which Anne Frank appears. She is seen for only ten seconds and it is an accident that she is there at all.

The film was taken for a wedding in 1941, the year before Anne Frank and seven others went into hiding in their "Secret Annex." It has a flickering, Chaplinesque[1] quality, with people popping suddenly in and out of doorways, the nervous smiles and hurried waves of the departing bride and groom.

---

1. **Chaplinesque** (chap′lin·esk′): like the old silent movies starring Charlie Chaplin (1889–1977).

Then, for just a moment, the camera seems uncertain where to look. It darts to the right, then to the left, then whisks up a wall, and into view comes a window crowded with people waving after the departing automobiles. The camera swings farther to the left, to another window. There a girl stands alone, looking out into space. It is Anne Frank.

Just as the camera is about to pass on, the child moves her head a trifle. Her face flits more into focus, her hair shimmers in the sun. At this moment she discovers the camera, discovers the photographer, discovers us watching seventeen years later, and laughs at all of us, laughs with sudden

Last year I set out to follow the fading trail of this girl who has become a legend.

merriment and surprise and embarrassment all at the same time.

I asked the projectionist to stop the film for a moment so that we could stand up to examine her face more closely. The smile stood still, just above our heads. But when I walked forward close to the screen, the smile ceased to be a smile. The face ceased to be a face, for the canvas screen was granular and the beam of light split into a multitude of tiny shadows, as if it had been scattered on a sandy plain.

Anne Frank, of course, is gone too, but her spirit has remained to stir the conscience of the world. Her remarkable diary has been read in almost every language. I have seen a letter from a teenaged girl in Japan who says she thinks of Anne's Secret Annex as her second home. And the play based on the diary has been a great success wherever it is produced. German audiences, who invariably greet the final curtain of *The Diary of Anne Frank* in stricken silence, have jammed the theaters in what seems almost a national act of penance.

Last year I set out to follow the fading trail of this girl who has become a legend. The trail led from Holland to Poland and back to Germany, where I visited the moss-grown site of the old Bergen-Belsen concentration camp at the village of Belsen and saw the common graves shared by Anne Frank and thirty thousand others. I interviewed forty-two people who knew Anne or who survived the ordeal that killed her. Some had known her intimately in those last tragic months. In the recollections of others she appears only for a moment. But even these fragments fulfill a promise. They make explicit a truth implied in the diary. As we somehow knew she must be, Anne Frank, even in the most frightful extremity, was indomitable.

The known story contained in the diary is a simple one of human relationships, of the poignant maturing of a perceptive girl who is thirteen when her diary begins and only fifteen when it ends. It is a story without violence, though its background is the most dreadful act of violence in the history of man, Hitler's annihilation of six million European Jews.

In the summer of 1942, Anne Frank, her father, her mother, her older sister, Margot, and four others were forced into hiding during the Nazi occupation of Holland. Their refuge was a tiny apartment they called the Secret Annex, in the back of an Amsterdam office building. For twenty-five months the Franks, the Van Daan family, and later a dentist, Albert Dussel,[2] lived in the Secret Annex, protected from the Gestapo[3] only by a swinging bookcase which masked the entrance to their hiding place and by the heroism of a few Christians who knew they were there. Anne Frank's diary recounts the daily pressures of their cramped existence: the hushed silences when strangers were in the building, the diminishing food supply, the fear of fire from the incessant Allied air raids, the hopes for an early invasion, above all the dread of capture by the pitiless men who were hunting Jews from house to house and sending them to concentration camps. Anne's diary also describes with sharp insight and youthful humor the bickerings, the wounded pride, the tearful reconciliations of the eight human beings in the Secret Annex. It tells of Anne's wishes for the understanding of her adored father, of her despair at the gulf between her mother and herself, of her tremulous and growing love for young Peter Van Daan.

2. In her diary, Anne made up names. The Van Daan family were really named Van Pels, and Albert Dussel was really Fritz Pfeffer.
3. Gestapo (gə·stä′pō): Nazi secret police force, known for its use of terror.

WORDS TO OWN

indomitable (in·däm′i·tə·bəl) *adj.*: unconquerable.
annihilation (ə·nī′ə·lā′shən) *n.*: destruction; killing.
refuge (ref′yo͞oj) *n.*: place of safety.
reconciliations (rek′ən·sil′ē·ā′shənz) *n.*: acts of making up after arguments or disagreements.

The actual diary ends with an entry for August 1, 1944, in which Anne Frank, addressing her imaginary friend Kitty, talks of her impatience with her own unpredictable personality. The stage version goes further: It attempts to reconstruct something of the events of August 4, 1944, the day the Secret Annex was violated and its occupants finally taken into a captivity from which only one returned.

What really happened on that August day fourteen years ago was far less dramatic than what is now depicted on the stage. The automobiles did not approach with howling sirens, did not stop with screaming brakes in front of the house on the Prinsengracht canal in Amsterdam. No rifle butt pounded against the door until it reverberated, as it now does in the theater every night somewhere in the world. The truth was, at first, that no one heard a sound.

It was midmorning on a bright summer day. In the hidden apartment behind the secret bookcase there was a scene of relaxed domesticity. The Franks, the Van Daans, and Mr. Dussel had finished a poor breakfast of ersatz coffee[4] and bread. Mrs. Frank and Mrs. Van Daan were about to clear the table. Mr. Van Daan, Margot Frank, and Mr. Dussel were resting or reading. Anne Frank was very likely at work on one of the short stories she often wrote when she was not busy with her diary or her novel. In Peter Van Daan's tiny attic room Otto Frank was chiding the eighteen-year-old boy for an error in his English lesson. "Why, Peter," Mr. Frank was saying, "you know that *double* is spelled with only one *b*."

In the main part of the building four other people, two men and two women, were working at their regular jobs. For more than two years these four had risked their lives to protect their friends in the hide-out, supplied them with food, and brought them news of a

world from which they had disappeared. One of the women was Miep, who had just got married a few months earlier. The other was Elli, a pretty typist of twenty-three. The men were Kraler and Koophuis, middle-aged spice merchants who had been business associates of Otto Frank's before the occupation. Mr. Kraler was working in one office by himself. Koophuis and the two women were in another.

I spoke to Miep, Elli, and Mr. Koophuis in Amsterdam. The two women had not been arrested after the raid on the Secret Annex. Koophuis had been released in poor health after a few weeks in prison, and Kraler, who now lives in Canada, had eventually escaped from a forced labor camp.

Elli, now a mother, whose coloring and plump good looks are startlingly like those of the young women painted by the Dutch masters,[5] recalled: "I was posting entries in the receipts book when a car drove up in front of the house. But cars often stopped, after all. Then the front door opened, and someone came up the stairs. I wondered who it could be. We often had callers. Only this time I could hear that there were several men. . . ."

Miep, a delicate, intelligent, still young-looking woman, said: "The footsteps moved along the corridor. Then a door creaked, and a moment later the connecting door to Mr. Kraler's office opened, and a fat man thrust his head in and said in Dutch: 'Quiet. Stay in your seats.' I started and at first did not know what was happening. But then, suddenly, I knew."

Mr. Koophuis is now in very poor health, a gaunt, white-haired man in his sixties. He added: "I suppose I did not hear them because

4. **ersatz** (er'zäts') **coffee:** artificial coffee. Regular coffee beans were unavailable because of severe wartime shortages.

5. **Dutch masters:** seventeenth-century painters including Rembrandt, Frans Hals (fräns häls), and Jan Vermeer (yän vər·mir').

WORDS TO OWN

gaunt (gônt) *adj.*: thin and bony; hollow-eyed.

---

of the rumbling of the spice mills in the warehouse. The fat man's head was the first thing I knew. He came in and planted himself in front of us. 'You three stay here, understand?' he barked. So we stayed in the office and listened as someone else went upstairs, and doors rattled, and then there were footsteps everywhere. They searched the whole building."

Mr. Kraler wrote me this account from Toronto: "A uniformed staff sergeant of the Occupation Police[6] and three men in civilian clothes entered my office. They wanted to see the storerooms in the front part of the building. All will be well, I thought, if they don't want to see anything else. But after the sergeant had looked at everything, he went out into the corridor, ordering me again to come along. At the end of the corridor they drew their revolvers all at once and the sergeant or-

in the Secret Annex, he is the only survivor. A handsome, soft-spoken man of obviously great intelligence, he regularly answers correspondence that comes to him about his daughter from all over the world. He recently went to Hollywood for consultation on the movie version of *The Diary of Anne Frank.* About the events of that August morning in 1944 Mr. Frank told me: "I was showing Peter Van Daan his spelling mistakes when suddenly someone came running up the stairs. The steps creaked, and I started to my feet, for it was morning, when everyone was supposed to be quiet. But then the door flew open and a man stood before us holding his pistol aimed at my chest.

"In the main room the others were already assembled. My wife and the children and Van Daans were standing there with raised hands. Then Albert Dussel came in, followed by an-

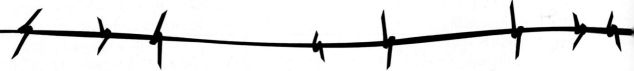

"It yielded and the secret door was exposed."

dered me to push aside the bookcase and open the door behind it. I said: 'But there's only a bookcase there!' At that he turned nasty, for he knew everything. He took hold of the bookcase and pulled. It yielded and the secret door was exposed. Perhaps the hooks had not been properly fastened. They opened the door and I had to precede them up the steps. The policemen followed me. I could feel their pistols in my back. I was the first to enter the Franks' room. Mrs. Frank was standing at the table. I made a great effort and managed to say: 'The Gestapo is here.'"

Otto Frank, now sixty-eight, has remarried and lives in Switzerland. Of the eight who lived

other stranger. In the middle of the room stood a uniformed policeman. He stared into our faces.

"'Where are your valuables?' he asked. I pointed to the cupboard where my cash box was kept. The policeman took it out. Then he looked around and his eye fell on the leather briefcase where Anne kept her diary and all her papers. He opened it and shook everything out, dumped the contents on the floor so that Anne's papers and notebooks and loose sheets lay scattered at our feet. No one spoke, and the policeman didn't even glance at the mess on the floor as he put our valuables into the briefcase and closed it. He asked us whether we had any weapons. But we had none, of course. Then he said, 'Get ready.'"

Who betrayed the occupants of the Secret

6. **Occupation Police:** police organized by the German forces while they occupied the Netherlands.

Bookcase hiding the entrance to the Secret Annex.

Annex? No one is sure, but some suspicion centers on a man I can only call M., whom the living remember as a crafty and disagreeable sneak. He was a warehouse clerk hired after the Franks moved into the building, and he was never told of their presence. M. used to come to work early in the mornings, and he once found a locked briefcase which Mr. Van Daan had carelessly left in the office, where he sometimes worked in the dead of night. Though Kraler claimed it was his own briefcase, it is possible the clerk suspected. Little signs lead to bigger conclusions. In the course of the months he had worked in the building, M. might have gathered many such signs: the dial on the office radio left at BBC[7] by nocturnal lis-

teners, slight rearrangements in the office furniture, and, of course, small <u>inexplicable</u> sounds from the back of the building.

M. was tried later by a war crimes court, denied everything, and was acquitted. No one knows where he is now. I made no effort to find him. Neither did I search out Silberthaler, the German police sergeant who made the arrest. The betrayers would have told me nothing.

Ironically enough, the occupants of the Secret Annex had grown optimistic in the last weeks of their self-imposed confinement. The

7. **BBC:** British Broadcasting Corporation.

WORDS TO OWN

inexplicable (in·eks′pli·kə·bəl) *adj.:* incapable of being explained.

errors of those first nights had largely faded. Even the German army communiqués[8] made clear that the war was approaching an end. The Russians were well into Poland. On the Western front Americans had broken through at Avranches and were pouring into the heart of France. Holland must be liberated soon. In her diary Anne Frank wrote that she thought she might be back in school by fall.

Now they were all packing. Of the capture Otto Frank recalled: "No one wept. Anne was very quiet and composed, only just as dispirited as the rest of us. Perhaps that was why she did not think to take along her notebooks, which lay scattered about on the floor. But maybe she too had the premonition that all was lost now, everything, and so she walked back and forth and did not even glance at her diary."

As the captives filed out of the building, Miep sat listening. "I heard them going," she said, "first in the corridor and then down the stairs. I could hear the heavy boots and the footsteps, and then the very light footsteps of Anne. Through the years she had taught herself to walk so softly that you could hear her only if you knew what to listen for. I did not see her, for the office door was closed as they all passed by."

At Gestapo headquarters the prisoners were interrogated only briefly. As Otto Frank pointed out to his questioners, it was unlikely, after twenty-five months in the Secret Annex, that he would know the whereabouts of any other Jews who were hiding in Amsterdam.

The Franks, the Van Daans, and Dussel were kept at police headquarters for several days, the men in one cell, the women in the other. They were relatively comfortable there. The food was better than the food they had had in the Secret Annex and the guards left them alone.

Suddenly, all eight were taken to the railroad station and put on a train. The guards named their destination: Westerbork, a concentration camp for Jews in Holland, about eighty miles from Amsterdam. Mr. Frank said: "We rode in a regular passenger train. The fact that the door was bolted did not matter very much. We were together and had been given a little food for the journey. We were actually cheerful. Cheerful, at least, when I compare that journey to our next. We had already anticipated the possibility that we might not remain in Westerbork to the end. We knew what was happening to Jews in Auschwitz. But weren't the Russians already deep into Poland? We hoped our luck would hold.

"As we rode, Anne would not move from the window. It was summer outside. Meadows, stubble fields, and villages flew by. The telephone wires along the right of way curved up and down along the windows. After two years it was like freedom for her. Can you understand that?"

Among the names given me of survivors who had known the Franks at Westerbork was that of a Mrs. de Wiek, who lives in Apeldoorn, Holland. I visited Mrs. de Wiek in her home. A lovely, gracious woman, she told me that her family, like the Franks, had been in hiding for months before their capture. She said: "We had been at Westerbork three or four weeks when the word went around that there were new arrivals. News of that kind ran like wildfire through the camp, and my daughter Judy came running to me, calling, 'New people are coming, Mama!'

"The newcomers were standing in a long

---

8. **communiqués** (kə·myoo'ni·kāz'): official bulletins.

row in the mustering square,[9] and one of the clerks was entering their names on a list. We looked at them, and Judy pressed close against me. Most of the people in the camp were adults, and I had often wished for a young friend for Judy, who was only fifteen. As I looked along the line, fearing I might see someone I knew, I suddenly exclaimed, 'Judy, see!'

"In the long line stood eight people whose faces, white as paper, told you at once that they had been hiding and had not been in the open air for years. Among them was this girl. And I said to Judy, 'Look, there is a friend for you.'

"I saw Anne Frank and Peter Van Daan every day in Westerbork. They were always together, and I often said to my husband, 'Look at those two beautiful young people.'

"Anne was so radiant that her beauty flowed over into Peter. Her eyes glowed and her movements had a lilt to them. She was very pallid at first, but there was something so attractive about her frailty and her expressive face that at first Judy was too shy to make friends.

"Anne was happy there, incredible as it seems. Things were hard for us in the camp. We 'convict Jews' who had been arrested in hiding places had to wear blue overalls with a red bib and wooden shoes. Our men had their heads shaved. Three hundred people lived in each barracks. We were sent to work at five in the morning, the children to a cable workshop and the grown-ups to a shed where we had to break up old batteries and salvage the metal and the carbon rods. The food was bad, we were always kept on the run, and the guards all screamed 'Faster, faster!' But Anne was happy.

9. **mustering square:** place of assembly for inspection and roll call.

It was as if she had been liberated. Now she could see new people and talk to them and could laugh. She could laugh while the rest of us thought nothing but: Will they send us to the camps in Poland? Will we live through it?

"Edith Frank, Anne's mother, seemed numbed by the experience. She could have been a mute. Anne's sister Margot spoke little and Otto Frank was quiet too, but his was a reassuring quietness that helped Anne and all of us. He lived in the men's barracks, but once when Anne was sick, he came over to visit her every evening and would stand beside her bed for hours, telling her stories. Anne was so like him. When another child, a twelve-year-old boy named David, fell ill, Anne stood by his bed and talked to him. David came from an Orthodox family, and he and Anne always talked about God."

Anne Frank stayed at Westerbork only three weeks. Early in September a thousand of the "convict Jews" were put on a freight train, seventy-five people to a car. Brussels fell to the Allies, then Antwerp, then the Americans reached Aachen. But the victories were coming too late. The Franks and their friends were already on the way to Auschwitz, the camp in Poland where four million Jews died.

"As we rode, Anne would not move from the window. After two years it was like freedom for her."

Mrs. de Wiek was in the same freight car as the Franks on that journey from Westerbork to Auschwitz. "Now and then when the train stopped," she told me, "the SS guards[10] came to the door and held out their caps and we had to toss our money and valuables into the caps. Anne and Judy sometimes pulled themselves up to the small barred window of the car and described the villages we were passing through. We made the children repeat the addresses where we could meet after the war if we became separated in the camp. I remember that the Franks chose a meeting place in Switzerland.

"I sat beside my husband on a small box. On the third day in the train, my husband suddenly took my hand and said, 'I want to thank you for the wonderful life we have had together.'

"I snatched my hand away from his, crying, 'What are you thinking about? It's not over!'

"But he calmly reached for my hand again and took it and repeated several times, 'Thank you. Thank you for the life we have had together.' Then I left my hand in his and did not try to draw it away."

On the third night, the train stopped, the doors of the car slid violently open, and the first the exhausted passengers saw of Auschwitz was the glaring searchlights fixed on the train. On the platform, kapos (criminal convicts who were assigned to positions of authority over the other prisoners) were running back and forth shouting orders. Behind them, seen distinctly against the light, stood the SS officers, trimly built and smartly uniformed, many of them with huge dogs at their sides. As the people poured out of the train, a loudspeaker roared, "Women to the left! Men to the right!"

Mrs. de Wiek went on calmly: "I saw them all as they went away, Mr. Van Daan and Mr. Dussel and Peter and Mr. Frank. But I saw no sign of my husband. He had vanished. I never saw him again.

"'Listen!' the loudspeaker bawled again. 'It is an hour's march to the women's camp. For the children and the sick there are trucks waiting at the end of the platform.'

"We could see the trucks," Mrs. de Wiek said. "They were painted with big red crosses. We all made a rush for them. Who among us was not sick after those days on the train? But we did not reach them. People were still hanging on to the backs of the trucks as they started off. Not one person who went along on that ride ever arrived at the women's camp, and no one has ever found any trace of them."

Mrs. de Wiek, her daughter, Mrs. Van Daan, Mrs. Frank, Margot, and Anne survived the brutal pace of the night march to the women's camp at Auschwitz. Next day their heads were shaved; they learned that the hair was useful as packing for pipe joints in U-boats.[11] Then the women were put to work digging sods of grass, which they placed in great piles. As they labored each day, thousands of others were dispatched with maniacal efficiency in the gas chambers, and smoke rising from the stacks of the huge crematoriums[12] blackened the sky.

Mrs. de Wiek saw Anne Frank every day at Auschwitz. "Anne seemed even more beautiful there," Mrs. de Wiek said, "than she had at Westerbork. Of course her long hair was gone, but now you could see that her beauty was in her eyes, which seemed to grow bigger as she grew thinner. Her gaiety had vanished, but she was still alert and sweet, and with her charm she sometimes secured things that the rest of us had long since given up hoping for.

"For example, we each had only a gray sack to wear. But when the weather turned cold, Anne came in one day wearing a suit of men's

10. **SS guards:** Nazi special police, who ran the concentration camps.

11. **U-boats:** submarines.
12. **crematoriums:** furnaces in which prisoners' bodies were cremated (burned to ashes).

Train destination sign.

long underwear. She had begged it somewhere. She looked screamingly funny with those long white legs but somehow still delightful.

"Though she was the youngest, Anne was the leader in her group of five people. She also gave out the bread to everyone in the barracks and she did it so fairly there was none of the usual grumbling.

"We were always thirsty at Auschwitz, so thirsty that at roll call we would stick out our tongues if it happened to be raining or snowing, and many became sick from bad water. Once, when I was almost dead because there was nothing to drink, Anne suddenly came to me with a cup of coffee. To this day I don't know where she got it.

"In the barracks many people were dying, some of starvation, others of weakness and despair. It was almost impossible not to give up hope, and when a person gave up, his face became empty and dead. The Polish woman doctor who had been caring for the sick said to me, 'You will pull through. You still have your face.'

"Anne Frank, too, still had her face, up to the very last. To the last also she was moved by the dreadful things the rest of us had somehow become hardened to. Who bothered to look when the flames shot up into the sky at night from the crematoriums? Who was troubled that every day new people were being selected and gassed? Most of us were beyond feeling. But not Anne. I can still see her standing at the door and looking down the camp street as a group of naked Gypsy girls were driven by on their way to the crematorium. Anne watched them going and cried. And she also cried when we marched past the Hungarian children who had been waiting half a day in the rain in front of the gas chambers. And Anne nudged me and said, 'Look, look! Their eyes!' Anne cried. And you cannot imagine how soon most of us came to the end of our tears."

Late in October the SS selected the healthiest of the women prisoners for work in a munitions factory in Czechoslovakia. Judy de Wiek was taken from her mother, but Anne and her sister Margot were rejected because they had contracted scabies.[13] A few days later there

13. **scabies:** skin disease that causes severe itching.

Prisoners arriving at Auschwitz.

was another selection for shipment from Auschwitz. Stripped, the women waited naked for hours on the mustering ground outside the barracks. Then, one by one, they filed into the barracks, where a battery of powerful lights had been set up and an SS doctor waited to check them over. Only those able to stand a trip and do hard work were being chosen for this new shipment, and many of the women lied about their age and condition in the hope that they would escape the almost certain death of Auschwitz. Mrs. de Wiek was rejected and so was Mrs. Frank. They waited, looking on.

"Next it was the turn of the two girls, Anne and Margot," Mrs. de Wiek recalled. "Even under the glare of that light Anne still had her face, and she encouraged Margot, and Margot walked erect into the light. There they stood for a moment, naked and shaven-headed, and Anne looked at us with her unclouded face, looked straight and stood straight, and then they were approved and passed along. We could not see what was on the other side of the light. Mrs. Frank screamed, 'The children! Oh, God!'"

The chronicle of most of the other occupants of the Secret Annex ends at Auschwitz. Mrs. Frank died there of malnutrition two months later. Mr. Frank saw Mr. Van Daan marched to the gas chambers. When the SS fled Auschwitz before the approaching Russians in January 1945, they took Peter Van Daan with them. It was bitter cold and the roads were covered with ice and Peter Van Daan, Anne Frank's shy beloved, was never heard of again.

From Auschwitz, Mr. Dussel, the dentist, was shipped to a camp in Germany, where he died. Only Otto Frank remained there alive until liberation. Anne Frank and Mrs. Van Daan and Margot had been selected for shipment to Bergen-Belsen.

Last year I drove the 225 miles from Amsterdam to Belsen and spent a day there walking over the heath.[14] The site of the old camp is near the city of Hannover, in the state of Lower Saxony. It was June when I arrived, and lupine was in flower in the scrubland.

My guide first showed me the cemetery where fifty thousand Russian prisoners of war, captured in one of Hitler's great early offensives, were buried in 1941. Next to them is a cemetery for Italians. No one knows exactly whether there are three hundred or three thousand in that mass grave.

"Even under the glare of that light Anne still had her face . . ."

About a mile farther we came to the main site of the Bergen-Belsen camp. Amid the low growth of pine and birches many large rectangular patches can be seen on the heath. The barracks stood on these, and between them the worn tracks of thousands of bare feet are still visible. There are more mass graves nearby, low mounds overgrown with heath grass or new-planted dwarf pines. Boards bearing the numbers of the dead stand beside some mounds, but others are unmarked and barely discernible. Anne Frank lies there.

The train that carried Anne from Auschwitz to Belsen stopped at every second station

14. **heath** (hēth): area of open wasteland covered with low-growing plants.

...ause of air raids. At Bergen-Belsen there ...re no roll calls, no organization, almost no ...gn of the SS. Prisoners lived on the heath without hope. The fact that the Allies had reached the Rhine encouraged no one. Prisoners died daily—of hunger, thirst, sickness.

The Auschwitz group had at first been assigned to tents on the Bergen-Belsen heath, tents which, one survivor recalls, gave an oddly gay, carnival aspect to the camp. One night that fall a great windstorm brought the tents crashing down, and their occupants were then put in wooden barracks. Mrs. B. of Amsterdam remembered about Anne: "We lived in the same block and saw each other often. In fact, we had a party together at Christmastime. We had saved up some stale bread, and we cut this up and put onions and boiled cabbage on the pieces. Over our feast we nearly forgot our misery for a few hours. We were almost happy. I know that it sounds ghastly now, but we really were a little happy in spite of everything."

One of Anne Frank's dearest childhood friends in Amsterdam was a girl named Lies Goosens.[15] Lies is repeatedly mentioned in the diary. She was captured before the Franks were found in the Secret Annex, and Anne wrote of her great fears for the safety of her friend. Now the slim and attractive wife of an Israeli army officer, Lies lives in Jerusalem. But she was in Bergen-Belsen in February 1945, when she heard that a group of Dutch Jews had been moved into the next compound.

Lies said, "I waited until night. Then I stole out of the barracks and went over to the barbed wire which separated us from the newcomers. I called softly into the darkness, 'Is anyone there?'

"A voice answered, 'I am here. I am Mrs. Van Daan.'

"We had known the Van Daans in Amsterdam. I told her who I was and asked whether Margot or Anne could come to the fence. Mrs. Van Daan answered in a breathless voice that Margot was sick but that Anne could probably come and that she would go look for her.

"I waited, shivering in the darkness. It took a long time. But suddenly I heard a voice: 'Lies? Lies? Where are you?'

"I ran in the direction of the voice, and then I saw Anne beyond the barbed wire. She was in rags. I saw her <u>emaciated</u>, sunken face in the darkness. Her eyes were very large. We cried and cried as we told each other our sad news, for now there was only the barbed wire between us, nothing more, and no longer any difference in our fates.

"But there was a difference after all. My block still had food and clothing. Anne had nothing. She was freezing and starving. I called to her in a whisper, 'Come back tomorrow. I'll bring you something.'

"And Anne called across, 'Yes, tomorrow. I'll come.'

"I saw Anne again when she came to the fence on the following night," Lies continued. "I had packed up a woolen jacket and some zwieback[16] and sugar and a tin of sardines for her. I called out, 'Anne, watch now!' Then I threw the bundle across the barbed wire.

"But I heard only screams and Anne crying. I shouted, 'What's happened?' And she called back, weeping, 'A woman caught it and won't give it to me.' Then I heard rapid footsteps as the woman ran away. Next night I had only a pair of stockings and zwieback, but this time Anne caught it."

In the last weeks at Bergen-Belsen, as Ger-

---

16. **zwieback** (tsvē′bäk′): sweetened bread that is sliced and toasted after it is baked.

WORDS TO OWN
emaciated (ē·mā′shē·ā′tid) v. used as adj.: extremely thin, as from starvation or illness. *Emaciated* and *gaunt* are synonyms.

---

15. **Lies Goosens** (lēs khō′sins).

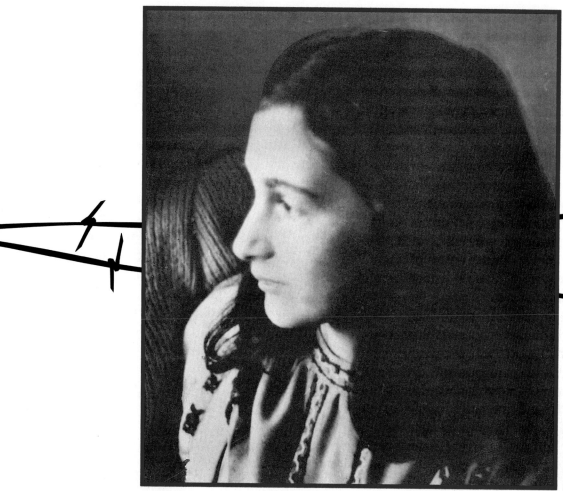

Anne in 1942. This may be the last photograph ever taken of her.

many was strangled between the Russians and the Western Allies, there was almost no food at all. The roads were blocked, the railroads had been bombed, and the SS commander of the camp drove around the district trying unsuccessfully to requisition supplies. Still, the crematoriums worked night and day. And in the midst of the starvation and the murder there was a great epidemic of typhus.

Both Anne and Margot Frank contracted the disease in late February or early March of 1945. Margot lay in a coma for several days. Then, while unconscious, she somehow rolled from her bed and died. Mrs. Van Daan also died in the epidemic.

The death of Anne Frank passed almost with-

out notice. For Anne, as for millions of others, it was only the final anonymity, and I met no one who remembers being with her in that moment. So many were dying. One woman said, "I feel certain she died because of her sister's death. Dying is easy for anyone left alone in a concentration camp." Mrs. B., who had shared the pitiful Christmastide feast with Anne, knows a little more: "Anne, who was very sick at the time, was not informed of her sister's death. But a few days later she sensed it and soon afterward she died, peacefully."

Three weeks later British troops liberated Bergen-Belsen.

Miep and Elli, the heroic young women who had shielded the Franks for two years, found

e's papers during the week after the police
id on the Secret Annex. "It was terrible when
. went up there," Miep recalled. "Everything
had been turned upside down. On the floor lay
clothes, papers, letters, and school notebooks.
Anne's little wrapper hung from a hook on the
wall. And among the clutter on the floor lay a
notebook with a red-checked cover. I picked it
up, looked at the pages, and recognized Anne's
handwriting."

Elli wept as she spoke to me: "The table was
still set. There were plates, cups, and spoons,
but the plates were empty, and I was so frightened I scarcely dared take a step. We sat down
on the floor and leafed through all the papers.
They were all Anne's, the notebooks and the
colored duplicate paper from the office too.
We gathered all of them and locked them up in
the main office.

"A few days later M. came into the office, M.
who now had the keys to the building. He said
to me, 'I found some more stuff upstairs,' and
he handed me another sheaf of Anne's papers.
How strange, I thought, that *he* should be the
one to give these to me. But I took them and
locked them up with the others."

Miep and Elli did not read the papers they
had saved. The red-checked diary, the office account books into which it overflowed, the 312
tissue-thin sheets of colored paper filled with
Anne's short stories and the beginnings of a
novel about a young girl who was to live in
freedom—all these were kept in the safe until
Otto Frank finally returned to Amsterdam
alone. Thus Anne Frank's voice was preserved
out of the millions that were silenced. No
louder than a child's whisper, it speaks for
those millions and has outlasted the <u>raucous</u>
shouts of the murderers, soaring above the
clamorous voices of passing time.

WORDS TO OWN

raucous (rô′kəs) *adj.:* harsh sounding; loud.

MEET THE WRITER

Following the Trail

As a young man, **Ernst Schnabel** (1913–1986) left his birthplace of
Zittau, Germany, to become a sailor and travel the world. He served
in the German Marines during World War II, then gave up the seafaring life for a writing career. He was well-known in Germany for his
radio plays, tales of his adventures at sea, and books linking classical
mythology with modern-day situations. Schnabel's adventures didn't
end when he began writing: In 1951, he flew around the world in
nine days, then turned his experience into a novel.

More by Ernst Schnabel

"I have followed the trail of Anne Frank. It leads out of Germany
and back into Germany, for there was no escape." So begins *Anne
Frank: A Portrait in Courage* (1958). Based on interviews with
forty-two people whose lives touched Anne's, this book enlarges on the story told in the article.

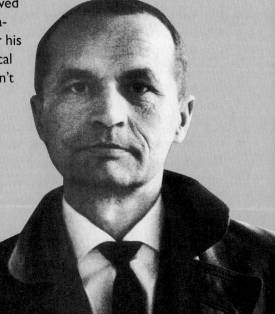

Walking with Living Feet

I had a very unusual fifteenth birthday. During my birthday week, at the end of April, I was traveling with five thousand high school students from around the world, visiting concentration camps in Poland. I learned more there than I learned during my entire life in school; once I stepped out of a gas chamber, I became a different person. When I turned fifteen, I discovered that no matter how much you read about the Holocaust, nothing can ever be like seeing it with your own eyes. The day after my fifteenth birthday was the turning point of my life. I was at Majdanek, one of the largest Nazi concentration camps. And I will never forget it.

Majdanek has been left exactly as it was when it was in use, so intact that if it were to be "plugged in," it could start gassing people tomorrow.

I stood in a gas chamber there, at Majdanek. I saw the blue stains of Zyklon B streaking the ceilings and walls, the poison used to kill the people who were crushed into this tiny, gray cement room. I could see how their fingers had scraped off the white paint, trying to escape. The cement floor that I sat on was cold and clammy; the air in the room seemed made of chills. When I first sat down, I did not notice, but soon those chilling waves were seeping into my skin, like so many tiny fingers trying to pull at my nerves and make my bones quiver. All around me, kids were crying hysterically, yet the chills that rankled the air around me hadn't reached my mind, and I could not feel. I hated myself for it. Anger, fear, pain, and shock—I could have felt all of those and more, but instead I felt nothing. That void was far worse: All the other emotions around me showed the presence of human hearts, but I was almost not there at all. I wanted to feel; I hated the guilt I had at my lack of reaction as much as I hated what happened there. Only my squirming skin could attest to my surroundings, and the crawling air made my lungs tighten. I wished I could cry, but I couldn't break down my mental blockade. Why?

The camp of Majdanek extends for miles, but one of the worst things about it is that it's right in a town, almost a city, called Lublin. There are actually houses right next to the barbed wire, the fence with its thorns that stabbed my frightened eyes, enough to separate a universe. The people of that city would have had to be dead not to notice the death which struck daily, right behind their back yards, where I saw children playing. People marched through Lublin from the train station, entered through the same barbed wire gate that I did, and left through the chimney. Nobody in Lublin noticed, because if they had, their fate would have been the same. And today the camp's long gray, barnlike barracks still extend forever, in endless rows, the sky a leaden weight blocking the colors that grace free life. Gray is the color of hell.

Inside each of the barracks is a new horror. Some are museum exhibits, with collections of people's toothbrushes (they were told that they were being "relocated" and to bring one suitcase, the contents of which were confiscated) and people's hair. All of the walls in one barracks are covered with people's hats, hanging in rows. But the worst were the shoes.

About five of the barracks are filled with nothing but the shoes of some of the people who were killed there—over 850,000 pairs. In one barracks, I sat on a platform about five feet off the ground, and surrounding it was an ocean of shoes, five feet deep. In the gas chamber I could not feel, but in that room filled with shoes, my mental blockade cracked. The photographs meant nothing to me, the history lessons and names and numbers were never strong enough. But here each shoe is different, a different size and shape: a high heel, a sandal, a baby's shoe so tiny that its owner couldn't have been old enough to walk, and shoes like mine. Each pair of those shoes walked a path all its own, guided its owner through his or her life and to all of their deaths. Thousands and thousands of shoes, each pair different, each pair silently screaming someone's murdered dreams. No book can teach me what I saw there with my own eyes!

I glanced at my own shoe, expecting it to be far different from those in that ocean of death, and my breath caught in my throat as I saw that my shoe seemed to be almost the same style as one, no, two, three, of the shoes I saw; it seemed as if every shoe there was my shoe. I touched the toe of one nearby and felt its dusty texture, certain that mine would be different. But as I touched my own toe, tears welled in my eyes as my fingers traced the edges of my dusty, living shoes. Eight hundred and fifty thousand pairs of shoes, but now I understood: They weren't numbers; they were people.

Soon I was crying, but for someone else: for the child whose mother's sandals rested on that pile, for the woman whose husband's shoes swam motionless in that sea, like the tears that streaked my face, for the girl whose best friend's slippers were buried in that ocean of grayness and silence. I was lost to the shoes there. I wished I could throw my shoes into that pile, to grasp and feel each shoe, to jump into the sea of shoes, to become a part of it, to take it with me. I wanted to add my own shoes to that ocean, but all I could leave there were my salty tears. My feet clumped on the wooden platform as I left, and I had never been more conscious of how my shoes fit my living feet.

At the very end of the camp was another gas chamber and the crematorium, its smokestack jutting through the leaden sky. This gas chamber did not have the blue poison stains that streaked the walls in the one I saw first, or maybe it did: The only light in that cement room was from dozens of memorial candles. It was too dark to see. The air inside was damp and suffocating, like a burial cave, and yet the air was savagely alive. It crawled down my neck and compressed me as the walls and ceiling seemed to move closer. No words can express how it felt to step out of that gas chamber alive, wearing my living shoes.

And I saw the crematorium where the corpses were burned, ovens shaped to fit a person. As I touched the brick furnaces with trembling fingers, my tears froze in my eyes and I could not cry. It was here that I felt my soul go up in flames, leaving me an empty shell.

Majdanek reeks of death everywhere. Even the reminders and signs of life that exist in a cemetery, like a footprint or rustling leaves, are absent here, every image of life erased. Even the wind does not ruffle the grass, which never used to grow here because the prisoners would eat it. But in the crematorium, I felt something I cannot express. No words exist to describe how I felt. It was someone else's nightmare, a nightmare that turned real before I even noticed it. It was a stark and chilling reality that struck me there, standing where people were slaughtered and burned, and my mind simply stopped. Have you ever been to Planet Hell? My people are numbers here, struck from a list and sent out the chimney, their children's bodies roasting. And I was there. You cannot visit this planet through any film or book; photographs cannot bring you here. Planet Hell is beyond the realm of tears. This is why I could not cry.

I left the camp. How many people, who had walked in those 850,000 pairs of shoes, once dreamed of doing what I had just done? And did they, too, forget how to cry?

In Israel I planted a tree with soil I had taken from concentration camps. In the soil were white specks, human bone ash. I am fifteen years old, and I know I can never forget.

—Dara Horn
Millburn High School
Millburn, New Jersey

First appeared in *Merlyn's Pen: The National Magazines of Student Writing.*

MAKING MEANINGS

First Thoughts

1. Did reading the pieces by Ernst Schnabel and Dara Horn change your feelings about Anne Frank's story or help you understand the events in the play? Explain.

Reading Check

Fill in the L column of your **KWL chart.** Then, choose one or two interesting or surprising items, and share them with a partner. Discuss your reactions.

Shaping Interpretations

2. Which description of the concentration camps did you find more effective, Schnabel's or Horn's? Why?

3. Schnabel says that Anne Frank was indomitable. Find three examples of her behavior that Schnabel uses to support this characterization.

4. How closely does the Anne that Mrs. de Wiek describes resemble the character of Anne in the play? Explain.

5. Reread Otto Frank's comments on Anne's mood and actions during the final moments in the Secret Annex (page 424). What do *you* think was Anne's reason for leaving her diary behind?

6. Choose two quotations from the people Schnabel interviewed, and write the question you think he asked to get each response. Are any of these questions similar to ones you wrote in your Quickwrite notes?

Connecting with the Text

7. Now that you've read Schnabel's article, how do you feel about Anne's statement that "people are really good at heart"? Explain whether your reading of the article tends to support or contradict Anne's belief.

Extending the Text

8. Who else do you know of whose "spirit has remained to stir the conscience of the world"? Describe the lasting influence this person has had.

Challenging the Text

9. Do you agree that the discovery of the Secret Annex as described by Schnabel is "far less dramatic" than the play's version? Why or why not?

CHOICES: Building Your Portfolio

Writer's Notebook

1. Collecting Ideas for a Comparison-Contrast Essay

Use a chart like the one on the right to compare Schnabel's description of the final moments in the Secret Annex (pages 421–424) with the corresponding scene in the play *The Diary of Anne Frank* (pages 404–408). List three ways in which the two versions differ; then, jot down your thoughts on the comparison. How do you account for the differences? Which version do you think you will remember longer? (Save your notes for the Writer's Workshop on page 442.)

Article	Play
1. no one hears anything at first	1. squealing brakes, loud pounding
2.	2.
3.	3.

Supporting an Opinion

2. Cutting Copy

Imagine that you are a textbook editor working on the next edition of this textbook. Unfortunately, you don't have room for both *The Diary of Anne Frank* and "A Tragedy Revealed: A Heroine's Last Days." Which do you keep? Write a **memo** to your boss to persuade him or her that you have chosen the better piece.

Speaking and Listening

3. Talking with Anne

What if Anne Frank had survived the Holocaust? Where would she be today? What would she have done with her life? With a partner, **role-play** a **dialogue** between Anne Frank and a TV interviewer. You may want to prepare a script in question-and-answer format, or you could perform your role-play impromptu.

Writing an Evaluation

4. Dear Author

Pick one of the books about the Holocaust or World War II from the Read On list on page 439. After you've read the book, write a letter to the author giving your evaluation of it. Be specific about what you did and did not like. Be sure to take into account the **prior knowledge** you now have about the Holocaust from reading about Anne Frank. If you like, do this assignment with one or two partners, giving the author your combined reactions.

GRAMMAR LINK

Language Handbook HELP

See Comparison of Modifiers, pages 766-768.

Technology HELP

See Language Workshop CD-ROM. Key word entry: double comparisons.

Avoiding Double Comparisons

In general, one-syllable modifiers add -*er* and -*est* to form their comparative and superlative degrees. Modifiers of three or more syllables add *more* and *most*. Comparisons of some two-syllable modifiers are formed by adding -*er* or -*est*. Other two-syllable modifiers are formed by adding *more* or *most*.

A **double comparison** is incorrect because it contains both -*er* and *more* or both -*est* and *most*. A comparison should be formed in one of these ways, not both.

NONSTANDARD	I think Schnabel's article stays more closer to the facts than the play does.
STANDARD	I think Schnabel's article stays closer to the facts than the play does.
NONSTANDARD	Anne Frank's diary is the most movingest book I ever read.
STANDARD	Anne Frank's diary is the most moving book I ever read.

Try It Out

Take out a piece of your writing, and underline the words *more* and *most* and the suffixes -*er* and -*est*. If you find any double comparisons, circle the correct form and cross out the unneeded part.

VOCABULARY   HOW TO OWN A WORD

WORD BANK

indomitable
annihilation
refuge
reconciliations
gaunt
inexplicable
dispirited
premonition
emaciated
raucous

Word Ratings: Connotations

Connotations are the feelings associated with a word, feelings that go beyond its strict dictionary definition, or **denotation.** Often, connotations show shades of meaning or intensity. Use the symbols + or − to show how the words in each of the following pairs compare in intensity. Use + if the word on the left seems stronger and − if it seems weaker. Use a dictionary for help. (Try this exercise with a partner. You may not agree!)

1. indomitable   (   ) strong
2. annihilation   (   ) ruin
3. refuge   (   ) shelter
4. reconciliations   (   ) agreements
5. gaunt   (   ) thin
6. inexplicable   (   ) mysterious
7. dispirited   (   ) hopeless
8. premonition   (   ) dread
9. emaciated   (   ) skinny
10. raucous   (   ) noisy

READ ON

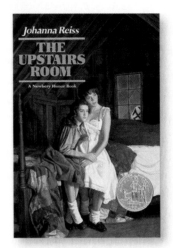

Under Cover

The Netherlands, World War II. Anne and Margot Frank go into hiding with their parents. Meanwhile, another pair of Jewish sisters escape to the country to live through the war with a Dutch family in their farmhouse. *The Upstairs Room* (HarperCollins) and its sequel, *The Journey Back* (Harper-Collins), tell Johanna Reiss's true story.

Real-Life Heroes

Under Nazi rule, even to be seen talking to a Jew was dangerous—yet all over Europe, non-Jews risked their lives to save neighbors and friends from the death camps. In *Rescue: The Story of How Gentiles Saved Jews in the Holocaust* (Harper-Collins), Milton Meltzer tells of their heroism.

Perilous Mission

How far would you go to save a friend's life? In *Number the Stars* by Lois Lowry (Dell), Annemarie Johansen and Ellen Rosen, best friends living in peaceful Copenhagen, Denmark, don't concern themselves with questions like this—until the Nazis come for Ellen.

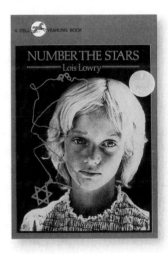

Other Picks

- Jane Yolen, *The Devil's Arithmetic* (Puffin). In this novel a contemporary Jewish girl opens the door one day to find herself facing Nazi soldiers in a Polish village of the 1940s.

- Steven Spielberg, *Survivors: Testimonies of the Holocaust.* This CD-ROM contains annotated excerpts from interviews of Holocaust survivors filmed by Spielberg. The disk is narrated by Leonardo DiCaprio and Winona Ryder.

- Hanna Volavková, ed., *I Never Saw Another Butterfly: Children's Drawings and Poems from Terezin Concentration Camp, 1942–1944* (Schocken).

Speaking and Listening Workshop

PERSUASIVE COMMUNICATION

Why Should I?

Persuasive communication is the use of words or images to get people to believe something or to do something. Different people respond to different approaches. You can increase your chances of success by using the right persuasive technique for your audience.

Persuasive Techniques

1. **Appeals to logic** are arguments that emphasize reason and clear thinking. Evidence such as statistics, examples, and anecdotes (short true stories) is used in logical appeals.

   > "You should do your homework because Department of Labor statistics show that well-educated people earn more than less-educated people."

2. **Appeals to emotion** are arguments that stir an audience's feelings and cause a gut-level response.

   > "How will you feel when you watch all your friends go on to high school and you've been held back a year?"

3. **Appeals to credibility** ask an audience to believe in *you* (and therefore in what you say).

   > "I know that teacher, and she won't pass you if you haven't done your work. I'm only thinking of you."

Consider Your Audience

Knowing your listeners' opinions on your topic before you begin speaking will help you choose an effective approach.

- Do they agree with you already and just need to be prodded into action?
- Do they oppose your point of view and need to be persuaded even to listen to you?
- Are they uninformed or uninterested? Do they need to be presented with basic facts and persuaded that the subject is important?

Try It Out

Try this movie-critics skit with a partner. Choose a movie that one of you liked and the other didn't. Take turns presenting to each other three arguments supporting your position: one logical appeal, one appeal to credibility, and one emotional appeal.

- Perform your skit for the class. Ask whose arguments they find more persuasive, and why.
- Then, ask the class to analyze each argument to identify the three different appeals.

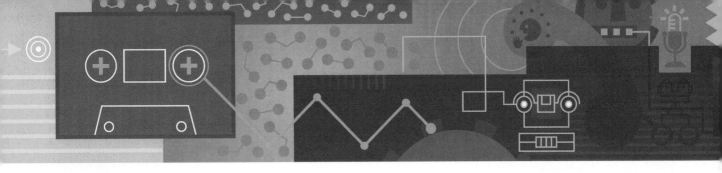

Critical Listening

People are constantly trying to persuade us to do things—to go somewhere, to buy something, to think a certain way. You need to evaluate these messages carefully and decide for yourself in each case whether you should be persuaded. Ask yourself:

1. Is the evidence presented **believable**? Does it contain **facts**? Don't accept a statement as fact simply because someone says it's so. Numbers, words, and pictures can be altered, taken out of context, or used in other misleading ways. If in doubt, check it out—with a reliable neutral source. Is the evidence **opinions** rather than facts?

2. Is the evidence presented **relevant** to the argument and to you? An advertiser may say that a pair of sneakers has soles made of the most durable rubber available—but does that matter if you outgrow your shoes long before they wear out?

3. Does the argument rely on **faulty reasoning**, such as false assumptions, generalizations based on too little evidence, or far-fetched comparisons?

4. Does the argument use **loaded words** (word or phrases with strong positive or negative connotations) to appeal to your emotions? For example, a politician who calls herself *cautious* may be described by her opponent as *wishy-washy*. Be aware of who is using the loaded words and what they want their listeners to do or think.

5. Are you being swayed by **propaganda**—persuasive techniques that deliberately discourage people from thinking for themselves? Look for these common, often hidden messages:

   - **Bandwagon:** "Everybody's doing it."
   - **Transfer:** "Buy this product and you'll be beautiful, popular, happy, rich . . ."
   - **Testimonial:** "I'm a glamorous celebrity, and I use this product. Don't you want to be just like me?"
   - **Card stacking:** "I'll just tell you half the truth—the half that supports what I want you to believe."

EXPOSITORY WRITING

COMPARISON-CONTRAST ESSAY

You do it all the time. You meet someone who reminds you of someone else, or you realize that the latest disaster movie is a lot like last summer's disaster movie. What you're doing is **comparing** (seeing similarities) and **contrasting** (seeing differences). In this workshop you'll compare and contrast two characters, literary works, or movies.

Watch the Wording

Compare means "to point out similarities." *Contrast* means "to point out differences." Sometimes, the word *compare* is used to mean *both* to compare and to contrast. Whenever you see just the word *compare* in a test question or essay assignment, find out if you're expected to do both: compare *and* contrast.

Professional Model

This paragraph is from a review of Parallel Journeys *by Eleanor H. Ayer, a book of personal narratives.*

They grew up a few miles apart in Nazi Germany. Helen Waterford was Jewish; Alfons Heck was an ardent member of the Hitler Youth. . . . While she was crammed in a cattle car bound for Auschwitz, he was a teenage commander of front line troops, ready to fight and die for the glory of Hitler and the Fatherland. Their postwar experiences in the U.S. are just as compelling: Helen trying to pick up the pieces of her shattered self; Alfons awakening to what he'd been part of, determined now to warn the world about it. . . . Both Germans speak quietly and honestly, without hand wringing, cover-up, or self-pity.	*Similarity #1.* *Difference #1.* *Difference #2.* *Difference #3.* *Similarity #2.*

—Hazel Rochman, *Booklist*

The history
of the written
word is rich and
Once upon a time
Page 1

Prewriting

1. Choosing a Topic

Check your Writer's Notebook for notes about possible subjects that have at least one thing in common. Sometimes the most interesting comparison-contrast essays show how two subjects that seem to be similar are in fact quite different; or how two subjects that seem to be different are really similar.

A good way to find stories with a common **subject** or **theme** is to choose two selections from any one of the collections in this book. For example, all the selections in Collection Four are about the relationship between humans and animals. The works you choose do not have to be in the same form. You can, for instance, compare and contrast two works such as the following:

- Anne Frank's diary and the play version you just read
- a memoir (or a movie) and a novel about the same subject

2. Finding Similarities and Differences

Your next step is to decide which **features,** or **qualities,** to compare and contrast. For example, suppose you were writing an article for the school newspaper about pizzerias in your town. You might compare and contrast any of these features: overall taste (highly subjective!), freshness, type of crust, variety of toppings, price, and service. When you compare and contrast two short stories, you'll probably discuss the elements of fiction (plot, conflict, character, point of view, setting, and so on). If you're comparing and contrasting characters, you might discuss each character's appearance, traits, motivation, and actions.

Use a **Venn diagram** (see page 444) to collect ideas about how your subjects are alike and different. In the overlapping part of the circles, jot down your ideas about the features they share—their similarities. Note their differences in the outer part of each circle.

Strategies for Elaboration

Exercises in Observation and Description

Carefully observe two objects that are similar but not identical: a pen and a pencil, for example, or two trees. Draw a line down the middle of a blank sheet of paper. On the left side, list every similarity you see between the two objects; on the right side, list their differences. Circle the details that you think would be the most significant in a comparison-contrast essay of these two objects.

Anne Frank		Margot Frank
• Mind of her own (Mrs. Van Daan's fur coat) • Outgoing • Optimistic	• Sisters—same parents • Situation—in hiding • Strength to endure	• Always obedient and polite • Very shy • Felt betrayed; mistrustful
Differences	Similarities	Differences

3. Elaborating with Supporting Details

Try to provide **specific details** and **examples** to back up your general statements. The Student Model writer, for instance, refers to a specific incident in the play to support a statement about Anne's behavior. Search for passages to quote and specific incidents to elaborate the statements you make.

4. Organizing Your Information

There are two basic ways to organize a comparison-contrast essay (see the two charts at the left).

- **Block Method.** Discuss all of the features of Subject 1 first; then, all of the features of Subject 2. For each subject, discuss the same features in the same order.

- **Point-by-Point Method.** Discuss one feature at a time. First talk about Subject 1; then discuss the same feature in Subject 2. Both the Professional and Student Models use this method.

Drafting

Think of your essay as having these three parts:

- **Introduction:** Briefly describe the two subjects. (If they are characters or stories, identify them by author and title.) Add a sentence that **summarizes** your **main idea** about the subjects' similarities and differences.

- **Body:** Discuss the two or three most important similarities and differences. Use either the block method or the point-by-point method.

- **Conclusion:** Leave your readers with a sense of completeness by restating your main ideas. You might also add a personal response or comment, as in the Student Model.

Block Method	
Subject 1:	Anne Frank
Feature 1:	Behavior
Feature 2:	Personality
Feature 3:	Feelings
Subject 2:	Margot Frank
Feature 1:	Behavior
Feature 2:	Personality
Feature 3:	Feelings

Point-by-Point Method	
Feature 1:	Behavior
Subject 1:	Anne
Subject 2:	Margot
Feature 2:	Personality
Subject 1:	Anne
Subject 2:	Margot
Feature 3:	Feelings
Subject 1:	Anne
Subject 2:	Margot

Thirteen-year-old Anne Frank and eighteen-year-old Margot Frank are sisters growing up in Amsterdam during World War II. Anne and Margot are alike and different in many ways, and in the play version of *The Diary of Anne Frank*, they are often compared to each other.

Margot is a mature, beautiful young lady. Even through the hardest times in the war, she would keep quiet. She was always obedient and polite; she did everything that she was told, like helping with supper and setting the table. Anne, on the other hand, had a mind of her own. She did not need people to tell her what to do. She was often active, loud, and curious. Anne was a daydreamer, and sometimes her dreams caused people to see her as a troublemaker. A perfect example is when Anne tried on Mrs. Van Daan's fur coat. While pretending she was a young Mrs. Van Daan, Anne spilled milk all over the coat.

Mrs. Frank would always compare Anne and Margot, which sometimes made Anne feel insecure. Margot was always known as the ladylike one, whereas Anne was known as the childish one. I do not think that Anne was treated like other girls her age because of Margot's maturity.

Anne was always outgoing. She had many school friends and grew to be Peter Van Daan's good friend. Margot was charming and polite, but very shy, so it was hard for her

Identifies characters.

States main idea.

Identifies title.

Paragraph elaborates difference #1: their behavior.

Uses transition and point-by-point method.

Cites specific example.

Summarizes a character's views of two girls.

Paragraph elaborates difference #2: their personalities.

(continued on next page)

Transition Words

Words that show similarities: also, both, similarly, like, in addition, too, another, just as, in the same way
Words that show differences: but, although, however, yet, still, instead, unlike, in contrast, in spite of, on the other hand

---

■ *Evaluation Criteria*

A good comparison-contrast essay

1. *has an introduction that identifies the subjects and states the essay's main idea*

2. *has a body that discusses at least two similarities or differences*

3. *is clearly organized, using either the block method or the point-by-point method*

4. *includes specific details and examples to support general statements*

5. *concludes with a summary of the main ideas*

Proofreading Tip

Check your essay for dangling and misplaced modifiers. Also look for problems with comparative and superlative forms of modifiers, particularly double comparisons.

Sentence Workshop
H E L P

Stringy sentences: page 447.

Communications Handbook
H E L P

See Proofreaders' Marks.

Publishing Tip

Place copies of your essays in a binder to be filed in your school library or media center for other students' reference.

Student Model (continued)

to be sociable. When Anne went to see Peter, Margot would always stay in her room and read a book.

Throughout the play Anne was usually cheerful and peppy. It might have been her way of making the war less painful. Though she would never say it, I think that Margot felt like she had been betrayed and had trouble trusting people. I also think that she felt that she should keep quiet and let others sort things out.

Paragraph elaborates difference #3: their feelings.

All in all, I believe that Anne and Margot are different, but they do share one thing: the strength to survive through the harsh times in the Secret Annex. I think they should have forgotten their petty differences and concentrated on what they believed in because they were all fighting for the same reasons.

Conclusion.

Similarity.

Personal response.

—Hanna Jamal
United Nations International School
New York, New York

Evaluating and Revising

1. Self-Evaluation

Revise your draft to make sure your essay measures up to the Evaluation Criteria on page 445. To help your readers follow your ideas, look for places where you can insert transitions. (Review the box of transition words on page 445.) As you revise, check for stringy sentences that have too many independent clauses.

2. Peer Response

Trade essays with a partner, and answer these questions:

- Did I present enough specific examples to support what I wrote about the similarities and differences?

- Were you confused by anything? How could I be clearer?

Use your partner's comments to help revise your paper.

Sentence Workshop

STRINGY SENTENCES

Stringy sentences are sentences that just go on and on. They have too many independent clauses strung together with words like *and, but,* or *so.* (An **independent clause** is a group of words that expresses a complete thought and can stand alone as a sentence.)

STRINGY   Jane Elliot was a third-grade teacher in Iowa, and she wanted her students to understand why prejudice is wrong, so she began treating blue-eyed students differently from brown-eyed students, and at first blue-eyed students got better treatment, but then brown-eyed students got better treatment, and when the experiment ended, all the third-graders knew how it felt to be discriminated against.

To fix a stringy sentence, you can break it into two or more sentences. You can also add words to make the relationships between ideas clearer.

REVISED   Jane Elliot was a third-grade teacher in Iowa who wanted her students to understand why prejudice is wrong. She began treating blue-eyed students differently from brown-eyed students. At first blue-eyed students got better treatment; then brown-eyed students got better treatment. When the experiment ended, all the third-graders knew how it felt to be discriminated against.

Writer's Workshop Follow-up: Revising

To check your essay for stringy sentences, quietly read your paper aloud. If you find that a sentence goes on and on (maybe even making you run out of breath before you reach the end), you probably have a stringy sentence. Consider breaking it into shorter sentences to give your reader a chance to pause between ideas.

Language Handbook
H E L P

See Improving Sentence Style, page 791.

Technology
H E L P

See Language Workshop CD-ROM. *Key word entry: stringy sentences.*

Try It Out

Revise the following sentences to eliminate stringiness.

The Wave is a TV movie, and it is based on real events in a high school class in California, and the story was also made into a book.

The movie is about a history teacher, and he wanted students to understand how something like the Holocaust could happen, so he invented a group called The Wave, and it had rules and slogans and a special salute, and he told the members they were better than everyone else.

The teacher said that The Wave was part of a national youth movement, and its leader would address the students at a rally, but when they arrived they were shocked to see a film of Adolf Hitler giving a speech.

Reading for Life

Using Text Organizers

Situation

Suppose you want to learn more about World War II, now that you've read about Anne Frank. You can use these strategies when you read a history book on the subject.

Strategies

Focus your search.

- Write down the questions you want to answer.

- List the key words in your questions, such as names and places.

Skim the table of contents.

- Note what topics are covered and how they are organized. Is the book divided into **sections**? How are the **chapters** arranged—chronologically (in time order), by geographical region, or by another method? Do the chapters begin with an **overview** and end with a **summary**?

- Note any **special features** listed. For example, does the book include excerpts from **primary sources**, such as diaries, letters, and speeches? Does it include **graphic organizers** (such as **maps, charts, tables,**

From *Call to Freedom*, Sterling Stuckey and Linda Kerrigan Salvucci (Holt, Rinehart and Winston, © 2000).

time lines, and **graphs**) or **photographs**? Is there a **glossary** or an **appendix**?

Scan the index.

- *Scanning* is rapidly searching for key words.

- Jot down the numbers of the pages where your subject is discussed.

Preview the presentation.

- **Skim** the chapter, noting the **headings** and **subheadings.**

- Notice how color or special type styles, such as **boldface** and *italic,* are used.

Using the Strategies

1. What are the five main sections of Chapter 25 (above)?

2. Which sections include special-interest material?

3. Does the book help you focus your reading?

4. Scan the index. What page covers the Blitzkrieg?

Extending the Strategies

Make up three questions about the text organizers in this book, *Elements of Literature*. Trade papers, and answer a partner's questions.

Reading Focus

Why was the Allies' North Africa campaign so important?

What were the major turning points of the war in Europe?

Learning for Life

Media Literacy

Problem

TV, movies, radio, newspapers, and magazines don't just entertain and inform us. The media send messages about what we should believe and how we should live. How can we increase our awareness of the messages we receive, both positive and negative?

Project

Analyze and evaluate the mass media's content and messages.

Preparation

With a group of classmates, discuss how the mass media influence your lives.

1. How much TV do you watch in a day? a month?

2. Who is your favorite celebrity? What do you like or admire about him or her?

3. Have you ever bought a product because of an advertisement? Why?

Procedure

To analyze a product of the mass media, ask yourself:

1. Who created the product? Who is the intended audience?

2. What messages—intended or unintended—are being conveyed?

3. What's missing? What images, information, or points of view weren't included?

Presentation

Demonstrate what you have learned by completing one of the activities that follow.

1. Letter from Earth

Imagine that you are an alien circling Earth in your spaceship, picking up TV signals to learn about how Earth people live and about their customs and beliefs. Write a letter home about a TV program, explaining what you've learned about Earth people from it. Try these starters:

• Earth people care most about . . .

• A typical day on Earth includes . . .

• The strangest thing about Earth people is . . .

2. The Anti-Commercial

Choose an advertisement from TV, a newspaper, or a magazine, and analyze it. What product is it selling? What words and images does it use, and why were they chosen? Then, create an "anti-commercial" for the same product, using words and images to persuade people *not* to buy the product.

3. As Time Goes By

View two movies of the same genre—for example, adventure, romantic comedy, or horror—one made recently and one at least twenty years old. (You may find it interesting to watch a classic movie and a modern remake.) Write a short essay **comparing** and **contrasting** the values reflected in the two movies. Who are the heroes and the villains in each? How are men and women expected to behave? How violent is each movie?

Processing

Discuss with your classmates:

• Does everyone "hear" the same messages in a particular TV show, movie, song?

• Were the messages that you found mainly positive or negative? What messages surprised you?

• If you could influence the mass media, what changes would you make?

It is true that you may fool all the people some of the time; you can even fool some of the people all the time; but you can't fool all of the people all the time.

—Abraham Lincoln

Sneaky Tricks
and
Whopping Lies

BRER POSSUM'S DILEMMA

Make the Connection

SNAKE!

Picture this: You're walking down a quiet country road when suddenly you look down and see at your feet—a hissing snake. What do you do? With your classmates, discuss your reactions and any experiences you've had with snakes.

Sketch to stretch. Draw a large outline of a snake on the chalkboard or on a sheet of paper. Fill it in with words and phrases that come to mind when you think of snakes.

Elements of Literature

Dialect

Jackie Torrence tells "Brer Possum's Dilemma" in the **dialect** spoken by her family and by other African Americans living in the South. ("Brer," for example, is a Southern way of saying "brother.") Dialect is often used in written versions of folk tales as a way of capturing on paper the voices of the people who first told the tales.

Black and Tan (1939–1942) by Bill Traylor. Pencil, crayon, and gouache on paper.

A **dialect** is a way of speaking that is characteristic of a certain geographical area or a certain group of people.

For more on Dialect, see the Handbook of Literary Terms.

Reading Skills and Strategies

Dialogue with the Text: Paraphrasing (In Your Own Words)

Paraphrasing means restating a passage in your own words. Paraphrasing is a good way to see if you understand something you've read, especially if it's hard or uses unfamiliar language.

As you read this comical tale, jot down your thoughts, and try paraphrasing sections you have trouble understanding—perhaps the passages in dialect. Look at the example on the first page of the tale. It contains one student's comments.

go.hrw.com
LEO 8-6

Now, ol' Brer Possum was kind and gentle, but he was also nosy . . .

Brer Possum's Dilemma

*traditional African American,
retold by* **Jackie Torrence**

Back in the days when the animals could talk, there lived ol' Brer Possum. He was a fine feller. Why, he never liked to see no critters in trouble. He was always helpin' out, a-doin' somethin' for others.

Ever' night, ol' Brer Possum climbed into a persimmon tree, hung by his tail, and slept all night long. And each mornin', he climbed outa the tree and walked down the road to sun 'imself.

One mornin', as he walked, he come to a big hole in the middle of the road. Now, ol' Brer Possum was kind and gentle, but he was also nosy, so he went over to the hole and looked in. All at once, he stepped back, 'cause layin' in the bottom of that hole was ol' Brer Snake with a brick on his back.

Brer Possum said to 'imself, "I best git on outa here, 'cause ol' Brer Snake is mean and evil and lowdown, and if I git to stayin' around 'im, he jist might git to bitin' me."

So Brer Possum went on down the road.

But Brer Snake had seen Brer Possum, and he commenced to callin' for 'im.

"Help me, Brer Possum."

Brer Possum stopped and turned around. He said to 'imself, "That's ol' Brer Snake a-callin' me. What do you reckon he wants?"

Well, ol' Brer Possum was kindhearted, so he went back down the road to the hole, stood at the edge, and looked down at Brer Snake.

"Was that you a-callin' me? What do you want?"

Brer Snake looked up and said, "I've been down here in this hole for a mighty long time with this brick on my back. Won't you help git it offa me?"

Brer Possum thought.

"Now listen here, Brer Snake. I knows you. You's mean and evil and lowdown, and if'n I was to git down in that hole and git to liftin' that brick offa your back, you wouldn't do nothin' but bite me."

Ol' Brer Snake just hissed.

"Maybe not. Maybe not. Maaaaaaaybe not."

Brer Possum said, "I ain't sure 'bout you at all. I jist don't know. You're a-goin' to have to let me think about it."

So ol' Brer Possum thought—he thought high, and he thought low—and jist as he was thinkin', he looked up into a tree and saw a dead limb a-hangin' down. He climbed into the tree, broke off the limb, and with that ol' stick, pushed that brick offa Brer Snake's back. Then he took off down the road.

Brer Possum thought he was away from ol' Brer Snake when all at once he heard somethin'.

"Help me, Brer Possum."

Brer Possum said, "Oh, no, that's him agin."

But bein' so kindhearted, Brer Possum turned around, went back to the hole, and stood at the edge.

"Brer Snake, was that you a-callin' me? What do you want now?"

Ol' Brer Snake looked up outa the hole and hissed.

"I've been down here for a mighty long time, and I've gotten a little weak, and the sides of this ol' hole are too slick for me to climb. Do you think you can lift me outa here?"

Brer Possum thought.

"Now, you jist wait a minute. If'n I was to git down into that hole and lift you outa there, you wouldn't do nothin' but bite me."

Brer Snake hissed.

"Maybe not. Maybe not. Maaaaaaaybe not."

Brer Possum said, "I jist don't know. You're a-goin' to have to give me time to think about this."

So ol' Brer Possum thought.

And as he thought, he jist happened to look down there in that hole and see that ol' dead limb. So he pushed the limb underneath ol' Brer Snake and he lifted 'im outa the hole, way up into the air, and throwed 'im into the high grass.

Brer Possum took off a-runnin' down the road.

Well, he thought he was away from ol' Brer Snake when all at once he heard somethin'.

"Help me, Brer Possum."

Brer Possum thought, "That's him agin."

But bein' so kindhearted, he turned around, went back to the hole, and stood there a-lookin' for Brer Snake. Brer Snake crawled outa the high grass just as slow as he could, stretched 'imself out across the road, rared up, and looked at ol' Brer Possum.

Then he hissed. "I've been down there in that ol' hole for a mighty long time, and I've gotten a little cold 'cause the sun didn't shine. Do you think you could put me in your pocket and git me warm?"

Brer Possum said, "Now you listen here, Brer Snake. I knows you. You's mean and evil and lowdown, and if'n I put you in my pocket you wouldn't do nothin' but bite me."

Brer Snake hissed.

Snake (1939–1942) by Bill Traylor. Pencil, crayon, and gouache on paper.

"Maybe not. Maybe not. Maaaaaaaybe not."

"No, sireee, Brer Snake. I knows you. I jist ain't a-goin' to do it."

But jist as Brer Possum was talkin' to Brer Snake, he happened to git a real good look at 'im. He was a-layin' there lookin' so pitiful, and Brer Possum's great big heart began to feel sorry for ol' Brer Snake.

"All right," said Brer Possum. "You must be cold. So jist this once I'm a-goin' to put you in my pocket."

So ol' Brer Snake coiled up jist as little as he could, and Brer Possum picked 'im up and put 'im in his pocket.

Brer Snake laid quiet and still—so quiet and still that Brer Possum even forgot that he was a-carryin' 'im around. But all of a sudden, Brer Snake commenced to crawlin' out, and he turned and faced Brer Possum and hissed.

"I'm a-goin' to bite you."

But Brer Possum said, "Now wait a minute. Why are you a-goin' to bite me? I done took that brick offa your back, I got you outa that hole, and I put you in my pocket to git you warm. Why are you a-goin' to bite me?"

Brer Snake hissed.

"You knowed I was a snake before you put me in your pocket."

And when you're mindin' your own business and you spot trouble, don't never trouble trouble 'til trouble troubles you.

MEET THE WRITER

"She Told Me This Story"

A professional storyteller, **Jackie Torrence** (1944–   ) learned her art by telling Bible stories in church and entertaining small children at the public library where she worked. Many of her most popular stories are traditional African American tales she heard while growing up on a farm near Salisbury, North Carolina, with a family that loved storytelling. Torrence has her aunt Mildred to thank for "Brer Possum's Dilemma," as she explains:

❝ When I was in high school, my best friend promised for months to buy me a sweater. 'I'm goin' to git you that sweater for Christmas,' she told me. 'I've done laid it away.' Her mother was a teacher and her father was a professional band director, and I knew that she could afford to buy me the sweater.

Then she took me shopping downtown and showed me a bracelet and ring that she wanted. Since she had promised me the sweater, I knew that I had to give her something just as nice. The bracelet and ring cost $25, and I begged Aunt Mildred to help me buy it for my friend for Christmas. We were poor, and Aunt Mildred refused.

'I've got to get that bracelet for her!'

Aunt Mildred just said, 'I know her and I know her mama, and she's not goin' to git you that sweater. She's jist talkin'.'

I spent nights awake, wondering where I was going to get the money to buy that jewelry, and finally I persuaded my uncle Nesbit to give me $25. And I bought the bracelet and ring.

Christmas came, and I couldn't wait to get my sweater. Sure enough, my friend called.

'I'm comin' to see you with your Christmas present.'

I said, 'That's great, 'cause I've got your present too.'

But when she walked into my house, I didn't see a box. I looked at her, puzzled.

She said, 'I've got your gift right here.'

And from her purse, she pulled a little box and gave it to me. I ripped it open, and instead of the sweater, I found rocks glued to a piece of paper—something you could buy for fifty cents.

I gave her the bracelet and ring. And when she left, I cried. But Aunt Mildred took me in her arms and said, 'I warned you of her nature.' And she told me this story. ❞

MAKING MEANINGS

First Thoughts

1. Go back to the notes you took as you read. Were you surprised when Brer Snake announced that he was going to bite Brer Possum? Do you think Brer Possum deserved to get bitten? Explain.

Shaping Interpretations

2. **Paraphrase** (rewrite in your own words) the last sentence of "Brer Possum's Dilemma." Compare your paraphrase with that of one or more classmates. How are your paraphrases different?

3. A **fable** is a brief story, usually about talking animals, that ends with a **moral,** or lesson about life. The moral of "Brer Possum's Dilemma" is in the last sentence. Do you think it is a good lesson for this fable? Do you think it is a good lesson at all? Why or why not?

4. Reread Torrence's comments in Meet the Writer. Why do you think her aunt Mildred told her this particular story? (What is the connection between Brer Possum's dilemma and Jackie's problem with her friend?)

Connecting with the Text

5. Describe an occasion when it would have been appropriate for you to tell someone this story—or for someone to tell it to you. (Make up an event or situation if you can't think of a real one you'd like to share.)

Extending the Text

6. What other stories do you know in which a snake is the bad guy? How do you think snakes got their bad reputation?

Reading Check

The number three often appears in folk literature—three little pigs, three blind mice, three wishes. What happens three times in this tale? What happens the third time to make it different from the first two?

Writer's Notebook

1. Collecting Ideas for Observational Writing

WORK IN PROGRESS

Brer Snake and Brer Possum had real-life models—the animals found in the rural areas where the creators of the folk tales lived. Choose one of the two photographs below, and look at it closely. In your Writer's Notebook, write down what you see in the picture— colors, shapes, every detail you notice. (If you prefer, find another nature photograph to observe.)

—fuzzy opossum
—pink nose and toes
—white face
—alert expression

Creative Writing

2. Learning a Lesson

"Brer Possum's Dilemma" illustrates the saying "Never trouble trouble 'til trouble troubles you." Write a short animal **fable** ending with one of the following sayings (or another that you know).

- "Nothing ventured, nothing gained."

- "Look before you leap."

- "Easy come, easy go."

If you like, write the fable in a local **dialect,** and use the kinds of animals that live in your area as characters. You might read your fable to your classmates and then ask them to guess what the lesson, or moral, is.

Role-Play

3. I'll See You in Court

Imagine that Brer Possum survives Brer Snake's bite and sues him for damages. With two classmates, act out a scene in which Brer Possum makes his complaint to a judge, Brer Snake defends his behavior, and the judge delivers a decision.

Research/Science

4. A Snake in the Grass

What are snakes really like? Using the Internet and the library, research snakes to find out whether they've earned their reputation for being mean and sneaky. Think of questions you have. Use the following ones to get started:

- How many species of snakes are poisonous?

- Are snakes ever useful to humans?

Share your findings, especially any interesting visuals.

GRAMMAR LINK   MINI-LESSON

Personal Pronouns

Language Handbook HELP

See Case, pages 762-764.

Technology HELP

See Language Workshop CD-ROM. Key word entry: case.

Here are some rules for choosing between the personal pronoun forms *I* and *me, she* and *her, he* and *him, we* and *us,* and *they* and *them.*

1. When the pronoun is the **subject** of the verb in a sentence, use *I, she, he, we,* or *they.*

EXAMPLES   I don't like snakes.

They can be poisonous.

Also use *I, she, he, we,* or *they* when the pronoun follows a linking verb (such as *is, am, are, was,* or *were*) and refers to the subject.

EXAMPLE   The owner thinks I am she.

2. When the pronoun is the **object of the verb** (the receiver of an action) or the **object of a preposition** in a sentence, use *me, her, him, us,* or *them.*

EXAMPLES   Brer Snake wouldn't have fooled me.

Will you read another story to us?

3. Most problems with personal pronouns come in sentences containing compound constructions, such as "The prize went to Dude and I/me." In such cases, it helps to try just the pronoun alone.

EXAMPLES   The prize went to me.

The prize went to Dude and me.

Try It Out

For each of the following sentences, choose the correct pronoun from the underlined pair.

1. Gilda and <u>she/her</u> worked the crowd.

2. Gilda and <u>I/me</u> don't get along.

3. Everyone believed it was <u>he/him</u>.

4. I gave the books to Sue and <u>she/her</u>.

5. Sue and <u>he/him</u> are listening to CDs.

SPELLING   HOW TO OWN A WORD

Homonyms: Spelling Checkers Won't Help!

Homonyms are words that sound the same but are spelled differently, such as *to* and *too; hear* and *here;* and *their, there,* and *they're.* A computer spelling checker won't help you if you mistake one homonym for another. The word isn't misspelled; it just isn't the word you want. You can help yourself remember the difference between homonyms by making up and using *mnemonics,* or memory aids. For example:

- You <u>hear</u> with your <u>ear</u>.

- Wh<u>ere</u> is the place—h<u>ere</u> or th<u>ere</u>? (All three place words are spelled with *e-r-e.*)

- *They're* is *they are* with an <u>a</u>postrophe instead of an *<u>a</u>.*

To make sure you've chosen the word you want, check in a dictionary.

Elements of Literature

FOLK TALES: Stories of a People

Telling Tales

Stories of all kinds have always been an important part of the American experience. Native American peoples began our storytelling tradition, using tales to teach as well as to entertain. When other groups of people came to America, they brought their own tales with them from their homelands. As these groups adapted to life in this country, the stories changed to reflect their new circumstances. The African trickster Hare became Brer Rabbit, the wily hero of the plantation.

Folk tales like these are traditionally passed along by word of mouth. Over time they have changed as tellers added, omitted, and altered details to suit their listeners. Folk tales have no single author; they are the creations of an entire culture and belong to everyone in it.

A **fable** is a kind of folk tale that usually uses talking animal characters to teach us practical lessons about life.

A Writer on Folk Tales

"The telling of black folk tales, and indeed tales of all cultures, was a social event bringing together adults and children. . . . Traditionally, tales were told by adults to adults. If the children were quiet, they might be allowed to listen."

—Julius Lester, author of "Brer Rabbit and Brer Lion" (page 466)

Myths: A Matter of Belief

Myths, a society's oldest stories, reflect some of its deep religious traditions and beliefs. Nearly every culture has **creation myths,** stories that explain how the world came to be or how human beings were created. Other myths explain different aspects of life and the natural world. For example, the Zuni myth "Coyote Steals the Sun and Moon" (page 463) explains the origin of winter.

Legends: The Historical Connection

Legends come from a society's more recent past; most were inspired by real people and real events. Pocahontas, Gregorio Cortez, Annie Oakley, and Davy Crockett did exist, like many other Americans whose names became legendary. Yet the abilities and achievements of the folk heroes often bear little resemblance to those of the people on whom they are based. Some of these legendary figures have been immortalized in **tall tales,** humorous, highly exaggerated stories that are not even meant to be believed.

"This Really Happened": Urban Legends

Folk tales aren't just stories from long ago, told by people to pass the time before TV was invented. Folk tales are being created all the time— and you may have participated in passing them on without even realizing it. Have you ever heard a story about

by David Adams Leeming

someone who found a rat in an order of fried chicken? How about stories about alligators in the sewers, or the tale of the hitchhiker who vanishes like a ghost?

These and other modern-day tales of the bizarre, horrible, spooky, or hilarious, many of which seem believable, are known as **urban legends.**

Motif: The Common Thread

Although a tale reflects the culture of the group of people that created it, certain elements, called **motifs** (mō·tēfs′), appear in stories from all over the world. Many folk tales, myths, and legends include such motifs as the perilous journey or the door or box that should not be opened.

How did these common threads come to run through so many different cultures? Actual events may have played a part. For example, many societies tell of a tremendous flood. Because this motif is so widespread, a number of

Peanuts reprinted by permission of UFS, Inc.

scholars believe that a real flood caused damage to civilizations across the ancient world.

Some motifs may reflect universal ideas or patterns of thought that every human being is born with—clever, mischievous **trickster** characters, for example, seem to appear in every culture. Another explanation is that stories were shared when there was contact between cultures, such as through trade or migration. The tales may have spread in this way from one society to the next, with each new group of tellers adapting the tales to fit their own tradi-

tions and experiences. The story of Cinderella may have traveled this way; there are hundreds of versions of the story, each with a different name and with details reflecting the culture in which it is told.

Modern works of literature and popular culture often draw on traditional motifs. The sneaky, foolish cartoon character Wile E. Coyote is a trickster in the classic mold. With each voyage into space, the starship captains of *Star Trek* reenact the journey of the hero. These motifs are as effective today as they were centuries ago.

Before You Read

Make the Connection

Trick or Treat?

The tales you are about to read are both **trickster tales.** Below, Richard Erdoes and Alfonso Ortiz, the writers of "Coyote Steals the Sun and Moon," discuss the figure of the trickster:

66 Stories about tricks and pranks, especially when played by the lowly, small, and poor on the proud, big, and rich, have delighted audiences from the dawn of storytelling. . . . The trickster is a rebel against authority and the breaker of all taboos. He is what the best-behaved person may secretly wish to be. He is, especially in the western areas of North America, at the same time imp and hero—the great culture bringer who can also make mischief beyond belief, turning quickly from clown to creator and back again. 99

Quickwrite

Using what you already know and what you've just read, work with a group of classmates to complete a "trickster" word map like the one above. Save your map—you'll refer to it later.

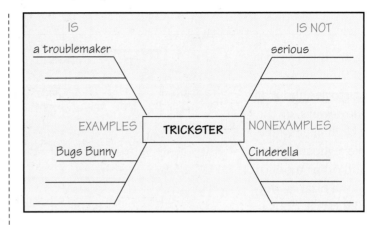

	IS			IS NOT	
	a troublemaker			serious	
	EXAMPLES		TRICKSTER	NONEXAMPLES	
	Bugs Bunny			Cinderella	

Elements of Literature

Motif

The figure of the **trickster** is a **motif** that has appeared in different forms throughout history and in oral traditions all over the world.

The sly Coyote is a familiar figure in Native American folklore. "Coyote Steals the Sun and Moon" is told by the Zuni people of the southwestern United States. Brer Rabbit, a mischievous underdog who often outwits bigger, stronger animals, is Coyote's counterpart in the African American tradition.

> **A** **motif** is a character, event, image, or theme that appears in the literature of many cultures.
>
> *For more on Motif, see pages 460–461 and the Handbook of Literary Terms.*

Reading Skills and Strategies

Comparing Oral Traditions: The Trickster

The next two tales come from different oral traditions: Native American and African American. Yet both use the trickster **motif.** As you read, think of how the tricksters

Coyote (Native American) and Brer Rabbit (African American) are alike—and how they are different.

go.hrw.com

LEO 8-6

"They have all the light we need. Let's steal it."

Coyotes Howling at the Moon (c. 1985) by Alonzo Jimenez. Cottonwood and latex house paint.

Coyote Steals the Sun and Moon

traditional Zuni, retold by **Richard Erdoes and Alfonso Ortiz**

Coyote is a bad hunter who never kills anything. Once he watched Eagle hunting rabbits, catching one after another—more rabbits than he could eat. Coyote thought, "I'll team up with Eagle so I can have enough meat." Coyote is always up to something.

"Friend," Coyote said to Eagle, "we should hunt together. Two can catch more than one."

"Why not?" Eagle said, and so they began to hunt in partnership. Eagle caught many rabbits, but all Coyote caught was some little bugs.

Original art by Sergio Bustamante and Clint Clemens.

At this time the world was still dark; the sun and moon had not yet been put in the sky. "Friend," Coyote said to Eagle, "no wonder I can't catch anything; I can't see. Do you know where we can get some light?"

"You're right, friend, there should be some light," Eagle said. "I think there's a little toward the west. Let's try and find it."

And so they went looking for the sun and moon. They came to a big river, which Eagle flew over. Coyote swam, and swallowed so much water that he almost drowned. He crawled out with his fur full of mud, and Eagle asked, "Why don't you fly like me?"

"You have wings; I just have hair," Coyote said. "I can't fly without feathers."

At last they came to a pueblo,[1] where the Kachinas[2] happened to be dancing. The people invited Eagle and Coyote to sit down and have something to eat while they watched the sacred dances. Seeing the power of the Kachi-

nas, Eagle said, "I believe these are the people who have light."

Coyote, who had been looking all around, pointed out two boxes, one large and one small, that the people opened whenever they wanted light. To produce a lot of light, they opened the lid of the big box, which contained the sun. For less light they opened the small box, which held the moon.

Coyote nudged Eagle. "Friend, did you see that? They have all the light we need in the big box. Let's steal it."

"You always want to steal and rob. I say we should just borrow it."

"They won't lend it to us."

"You may be right," said Eagle. "Let's wait till they finish dancing and then steal it."

After a while the Kachinas went home to sleep, and Eagle scooped up the large box and flew off. Coyote ran along trying to keep up, panting, his tongue hanging out. Soon he yelled up to Eagle, "Ho, friend, let me carry the box a little way."

"No, no," said Eagle, "you never do anything right."

He flew on, and Coyote ran after him. After a while Coyote shouted again: "Friend, you're my chief, and it's not right for you to carry the box; people will call me lazy. Let me have it."

"No, no, you always mess everything up." And Eagle flew on and Coyote ran along.

So it went for a stretch, and then Coyote started again. "Ho, friend, it isn't right for you to do this. What will people think of you and me?"

"I don't care what people think. I'm going to carry this box."

Again Eagle flew on and again Coyote ran after him. Finally Coyote begged for the fourth time: "Let me carry it. You're the chief, and I'm just Coyote. Let me carry it."

Eagle couldn't stand any more pestering. Also, Coyote had asked him four times, and if someone asks four times, you'd better give him

---

1. **pueblo** (pweb′lō): Native American village in the southwestern United States.
2. **Kachinas** (kə·chē′nəz): gods or spirits of ancestors. In the Pueblo cultures of the southwestern United States, masked dancers imitate the Kachinas in sacred rituals.

what he wants. Eagle said, "Since you won't let up on me, go ahead and carry the box for a while. But promise not to open it."

"Oh, sure, oh yes, I promise." They went on as before, but now Coyote had the box. Soon Eagle was far ahead, and Coyote lagged behind a hill where Eagle couldn't see him. "I wonder what the light looks like, inside there," he said to himself. "Why shouldn't I take a peek? Probably there's something extra in the box, something good that Eagle wants to keep to himself."

And Coyote opened the lid. Now, not only was the sun inside, but the moon also. Eagle had put them both together, thinking that it would be easier to carry one box than two.

As soon as Coyote opened the lid, the moon escaped, flying high into the sky. At once all the plants shriveled up and turned brown. Just as quickly, all the leaves fell off the trees, and it was winter. Trying to catch the moon and put it back in the box, Coyote ran in pursuit as it skipped away from him. Meanwhile the sun flew out and rose into the sky. It drifted far away, and the peaches, squashes, and melons shriveled up with cold.

Eagle turned and flew back to see what had delayed Coyote. "You fool! Look what you've done!" he said. "You let the sun and moon escape, and now it's cold." Indeed, it began to snow, and Coyote shivered. "Now your teeth are chattering," Eagle said, "and it's your fault that cold has come into the world."

It's true. If it weren't for Coyote's curiosity and mischief making, we wouldn't have winter; we could enjoy summer all the time.

MEET THE WRITERS

"Common Elements and Rich Diversity"

Richard Erdoes (1912–   ) was born in Vienna, Austria.
Alfonso Ortiz (1939–1997) was born in San Juan, a Tewa pueblo in New Mexico. Having studied and written about Native American cultures, Erdoes and Ortiz together edited *American Indian Myths and Legends* (1984), from which "Coyote Steals the Sun and Moon" is taken. They asked readers to notice "both the common elements that run through stories told at opposite ends of the continent and the rich diversity of detail":

Alfonso Ortiz

66 Legends, of course, vary according to a people's way of life, the geography and the climate in which they live, the food they eat and the way they obtain it. The nomadic buffalo hunters of the Plains tell stories very different from those of Eastern forest dwellers. To the Southwestern planters and harvesters, the coming of corn and the changing of seasons are of primal concern, while people of the Northwest who make their living from the sea fill their tales with ocean monsters, swift harpooners, and powerful boat builders. All tribes have spun narratives as well for the features of their landscape: how this river came to be, when these mountains were formed, how our coastline was carved. 99

Richard Erdoes

Brer Rabbit and Brer Lion

traditional African American,
retold by **Julius Lester**

Illustration (1987) by Jerry Pinkney.

Brer Rabbit was in the woods one afternoon when a great wind came up. It blew on the ground and it blew in the tops of the trees. It blew so hard that Brer Rabbit was afraid a tree might fall on him, and he started running.

He was trucking through the woods when he ran smack into Brer Lion. Now, don't come telling me ain't no lions in the United States. Ain't none here now. But back in yonder times, all the animals lived everywhere. The lions and tigers and elephants and foxes and what 'nall run around with each other like they was family. So that's how come wasn't unusual for Brer Rabbit to run up on Brer Lion like he done that day.

"What's your hurry, Brer Rabbit?"

"Run, Brer Lion! There's a hurricane coming."

Brer Lion got scared. "I'm too heavy to run, Brer Rabbit. What am I going to do?"

"Lay down, Brer Lion. Lay down! Get close to the ground!"

Brer Lion shook his head. "The wind might pick me up and blow me away."

"Hug a tree, Brer Lion! Hug a tree!"

"But what if the wind blows all day and into the night?"

> *Brer Rabbit was trucking through the woods when he ran smack into Brer Lion.*

"Let me tie you to the tree, Brer Lion. Let me tie you to the tree."

Brer Lion liked that idea. Brer Rabbit tied him to the tree and sat down next to it. After a while, Brer Lion got tired of hugging the tree.

"Brer Rabbit? I don't hear no hurricane."

Brer Rabbit listened. "Neither do I."

"Brer Rabbit? I don't hear no wind."

Brer Rabbit listened. "Neither do I."

"Brer Rabbit? Ain't a leaf moving in the trees."

Brer Rabbit looked up. "Sho' ain't."

"So untie me."

"I'm afraid to, Brer Lion."

Brer Lion began to roar. He roared so loud and so long, the foundations of the Earth started shaking. Least that's what it seemed like, and the other animals came from all over to see what was going on.

When they got close, Brer Rabbit jumped up and began strutting around the tied-up Brer Lion. When the animals saw what Brer Rabbit had done to Brer Lion, you'd better believe it was the forty-eleventh of Octorerarry before they messed with him again.

Meet the Writer

"Trust the Tale"

Julius Lester (1939–   ) was born in St. Louis, Missouri, but lived in Kansas, Tennessee, and Arkansas as a child and a teenager. Lester says he "absorbed so much of Southern rural black traditions, particularly music and stories," from his father, a Methodist minister. Growing up in the segregated South of the 1940s and 1950s shaped Lester's goals and beliefs. He became a political activist and folk musician in the 1960s, then turned to writing for young people as a way of passing on African American history and traditions.

"The tales will live only if they flow through your voice," Lester tells his readers.

❝ If the language you speak is different from the language I speak, tell the tale in your language. Tell the tale as you would, not I, and believe in the tale. It will communicate its riches and its wonders, regardless of who you are. Trust the tale. Trust your love for the tale. That is all any good storyteller can do. ❞

More by Julius Lester

"Brer Rabbit and Brer Lion" appears in *The Tales of Uncle Remus* (Dial). The adventures of Brer Rabbit and his friends continue in *More Tales of Uncle Remus, Further Tales of Uncle Remus,* and *The Last Tales of Uncle Remus* (all Dial).

Wooden Rabbit (1981) by Felipe Archuleta. Cottonwood, sisal, and latex house paint.

MAKING MEANINGS

- **First Thoughts**

    1. Who do you think deserves a tougher punishment for his mischievous behavior, Coyote or Brer Rabbit? Why?

Shaping Interpretations

    2. Explain how Coyote upsets the order of the world by opening the box. Can you see any good coming from Coyote's actions, or has he just made a mess of things, as Eagle said he would?

Reading Check

Tell a partner about the trick played by Coyote *or* Brer Rabbit and its consequences. Then, listen as your partner tells you about the other character's trick and its effects.

    3. In what ways are Coyote and Brer Rabbit similar? In what ways are they different? Fill in a Venn diagram like the one below with words and phrases describing the personalities and actions of the two tricksters. (You'll use this information in question 4.)

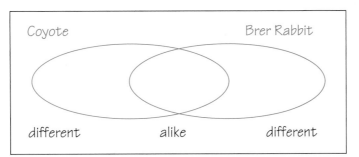

Coyote   Brer Rabbit

different   alike   different

    4. Go back to the "trickster" word map you made before you read the two tales. Does Coyote have the qualities you expected to find in a trickster? Does Brer Rabbit? Explain.

Connecting with the Text

    5. Erdoes and Ortiz suggest that even the best-behaved people secretly want to be tricksters sometimes (page 462). Do you agree? What do you like, or dislike, most about the **motif** of the trickster?

Extending the Text

    6. Erdoes and Ortiz say that the stories people tell are influenced by where and how they live (page 465). Choose one of the two tales. Then, drawing on the details of the text, describe one thing the tale tells you about the environment or the way of life of the people who originated the tale.

CHOICES: Building Your Portfolio

Writer's Notebook

1. Collecting Ideas for Observational Writing

Coyote and Brer Rabbit are both tricksters, yet each has unique **traits** (qualities or characteristics). Similarly, a person may resemble other people in some ways but still have traits that set him or her apart. Picture a person you see frequently but don't know well. Jot down all the details you can think of that make this person special.

Kyle:
—loves bicycle racing
—makes everyone laugh in class
—wears shorts even when it's cold

Creative Writing/Art

2. Brer Lion's Revenge

Brer Lion must have been furious about falling for Brer Rabbit's trick. Write a **sequel** (a continuation of the story) in which Brer Lion tries to get even with Brer Rabbit. Does he get his revenge or just more embarrassment?

If you prefer to draw, design your sequel in comic-strip form.

Cottonwood Lion (c. 1985) by Alonzo Jimenez. Cottonwood, unraveled hemp, and latex house paint.

Performance/Art

3. Do Not Open

Many stories use the **motif** of characters who are forbidden to open a box—and, of course, do. Some examples:

- "Coyote Steals the Sun and Moon" (Zuni)
- "Pandora's Box" (Greek)
- "Urashima Taro" (Japanese)

Use one of these stories, or a story of your own, to write a **script** for a **puppet show.** Make puppets and perform your show for your class or for a group of children. Don't forget the most important prop—a box containing a picture or symbol of the secret contents.

Research/Summary

4. Myth Hunt

A **creation myth** is a story from a particular culture that explains how the world came to be. "Coyote Steals the Sun and Moon" is a Zuni myth about the origin of winter. Research a myth from another culture that explains the origin of one of the seasons. Start your search on the Internet or in the library. What key words will you use in your search? Once you've found a myth, summarize it briefly. You might want to illustrate a character or setting in the myth. Collect your summaries in a booklet. Be sure to list your sources at the back.

GRAMMAR LINK MINI-LESSON

Two Pronoun Problems

Language Handbook HELP

See Pronouns with appositives, page 765. Case, pages 762–764.

Technology HELP

See Language Workshop CD-ROM. *Key word entry: case.*

1. Sometimes a pronoun is followed directly by a noun that identifies it ("we students," "us players"). Such a noun is called an **appositive.** If you don't know which pronoun to use **before an appositive,** remove the appositive and try each form of the pronoun separately.

   EXAMPLES   <u>We/Us</u> students are collecting myths.

   The trophy went to <u>we/us</u> players.

   You wouldn't say, "Us are collecting myths." Therefore, *We* must be correct. You also wouldn't say, "The trophy went to we," so *us* must be correct.

   EXAMPLES   <u>We</u> students are collecting myths.

   The trophy went to <u>us</u> players.

2. Sometimes it's hard to know which pronoun to use **following a preposition.** The answer is simple: Always use a pronoun in the objective case. In the following example, *between* is the preposition. It should be followed by a pronoun in the objective case.

   EXAMPLE   Just between <u>you</u> and <u>me</u>, the dinner was a disaster.

   With *between,* people often use a nominative-case pronoun because they think it sounds correct. "Between you and I" is not correct, however. The correct form is "between you and me" or "between him [or her] and me."

Try It Out

Choose the correct pronoun from each underlined pair.

1. The work continued without Ted and <u>I/me</u>.

2. <u>Us/we</u> players put our reputations on the line.

3. The opposition wanted to crush <u>us/we</u> guards.

4. Everyone ate cake except Jackie and <u>I/me</u>.

5. The deal is between Fran and <u>he/him</u>.

VOCABULARY HOW TO OWN A WORD

Regional and Cultural Sayings: What Do *You* Call It?

What do you call a piece of playground equipment that consists of a long board balanced on a support in the middle and on which two people may sit at either end? Depending on where you live, you might call it a *seesaw,* a *teeter-totter,* or a *teeterboard.* Many of our words and sayings reflect the regions and cultures we come from. Read the sentences below, and tell what the underlined words and phrases mean. Then, tell how you would express the same idea if you were talking to a friend.

1. "So it went for a <u>stretch</u>, and then Coyote started again." (page 464)
2. "He was <u>trucking</u> through the woods when he ran <u>smack</u> into <u>Brer</u> Lion." (page 467)
3. "But back in <u>yonder</u> times, all the animals lived everywhere." (page 467)
4. "The lions and tigers and elephants and foxes and <u>what 'nall</u> run around with each other. . . ." (page 467)

Before You Read

Make the Connection

Here Comes Trouble

You've probably never seen Brer Rabbit or Coyote walking down the hall between classes, but you may have come across a trickster like Shirley Jackson's "Charles." As Julius Lester (author of "Brer Rabbit and Brer Lion," page 466) explains, tricksters don't just appear in folk tales:

66 Teachers and parents know Trickster well, because there is one in every classroom and every large family. Trickster is the class clown, the child who seems to have a genius for walking a thin line between fun and trouble, the child who is always 'up to something,' but you can never punish him or her because what he or she does is disruptive but never rebellious or serious enough to merit severe punishment. And it is always entertaining because Trickster is charming and likable. 99

Quickwrite

Do you know anyone who matches Lester's description of a trickster? Freewrite about this real-life trickster.

(If you prefer, write about a character from a TV sitcom or a movie.)

Reading Skills and Strategies

Comparing the Trickster Motif

As you read "Charles":
- Look for similarities between the **trickster** in this story, set in modern-day America, and Brer Rabbit and Coyote.
- Think about why the trickster is so popular across cultures.

Elements of Literature

Plot Twist

Humor writing often includes sudden turnarounds that startle us, then make us laugh. As you read "Charles," watch for an unexpected turn in the story.

> **A plot twist** is an unexpected development or turn of events.
>
> *For more on Plot, see pages 212–213 and the Handbook of Literary Terms.*

go.hrw.com
LE0 8-6

Charles

Shirley Jackson

"Well, Charles was bad again today."

The day Laurie started kindergarten, he renounced corduroy overalls with bibs and began wearing bluejeans with a belt; I watched him go off the first morning with the older girl next door, seeing clearly that an era of my life was ended, my sweet-voiced nursery-school tot replaced by a long-trousered, swaggering character who forgot to stop at the corner and wave goodbye to me.

He came home the same way, the front door slamming open, his cap on the floor, and the voice suddenly become raucous shouting, "Isn't anybody *here*?"

At lunch he spoke insolently to his father, spilled Jannie's milk, and remarked that his teacher said that we were not to take the name of the Lord in vain.

WORDS TO OWN

renounced (ri·nounsd') *v.*: gave up; abandoned.
insolently (in'sə·lənt·lē) *adv.*: with bold disrespect.

"How *was* school today?" I asked, elaborately casual.

"All right," he said.

"Did you learn anything?" his father asked.

Laurie regarded his father coldly. "I didn't learn nothing," he said.

"Anything," I said. "Didn't learn anything."

"The teacher spanked a boy, though," Laurie said, addressing his bread and butter. "For being fresh," he added with his mouth full.

"What did he do?" I asked. "Who was it?"

Laurie thought. "It was Charles," he said. "He was fresh. The teacher spanked him and made him stand in a corner. He was awfully fresh."

"What did he do?" I asked again, but Laurie slid off his chair, took a cookie, and left, while his father was still saying, "See here, young man."

The next day Laurie remarked at lunch, as soon as he sat down, "Well, Charles was bad again today." He grinned enormously and said, "Today Charles hit the teacher."

"Good heavens," I said, mindful of the Lord's name, "I suppose he got spanked again?"

"He sure did," Laurie said. "Look up," he said to his father.

"What?" his father said, looking up.

"Look down," Laurie said. "Look at my thumb. Gee, you're dumb." He began to laugh insanely.

"Why did Charles hit the teacher?" I asked quickly.

"Because she tried to make him color with red crayons," Laurie said. "Charles wanted to color with green crayons so he hit the teacher and she spanked him and said nobody play with Charles but everybody did."

The third day—it was Wednesday of the first week—Charles bounced a seesaw onto the head of a little girl and made her bleed and the teacher made him stay inside all during recess. Thursday Charles had to stand in a corner during story time because he kept pounding his feet on the floor. Friday Charles was deprived of blackboard privileges because he threw chalk.

On Saturday I remarked to my husband, "Do you think kindergarten is too unsettling for Laurie? All this toughness and bad grammar, and this Charles boy sounds like such a bad influence."

"It'll be all right," my husband said reassuringly. "Bound to be people like Charles in the world. Might as well meet them now as later."

On Monday Laurie came home late, full of news. "Charles," he shouted as he came up the hill; I was waiting anxiously on the front steps, "Charles," Laurie yelled all the way up the hill, "Charles was bad again."

"Come right in," I said, as soon as he came close enough. "Lunch is waiting."

"You know what Charles did?" he demanded, following me through the door. "Charles yelled so in school they sent a boy in from first grade to tell the teacher she had to make Charles keep quiet, and so Charles had to stay after school. And so all the children stayed to watch him."

"What did he do?" I asked.

"He just sat there," Laurie said, climbing into his chair at the table. "Hi Pop, y'old dust mop."

"Charles had to stay after school today," I told my husband. "Everyone stayed with him."

"What does this Charles look like?" my husband asked Laurie. "What's his other name?"

"He's bigger than me," Laurie said. "And he

doesn't have any rubbers and he doesn't even wear a jacket."

Monday night was the first Parent-Teachers meeting, and only the fact that Jannie had a cold kept me from going; I wanted passionately to meet Charles's mother. On Tuesday Laurie remarked suddenly, "Our teacher had a friend come see her in school today."

"Charles's mother?" my husband and I asked simultaneously.

"Naaah," Laurie said scornfully. "It was a man who came and made us do exercises. Look." He climbed down from his chair and squatted down and touched his toes. "Like this," he said. He got solemnly back into his chair and said, picking up his fork, "Charles didn't even *do* exercises."

"That's fine," I said heartily. "Didn't Charles want to do exercises?"

"Naaah," Laurie said. "Charles was so fresh to the teacher's friend he wasn't *let* do exercises."

"Fresh again?" I said.

"He kicked the teacher's friend," Laurie said. "The teacher's friend told Charles to touch his toes like I just did and Charles kicked him."

"What are they going to do about Charles, do you suppose?" Laurie's father asked him.

Laurie shrugged elaborately. "Throw him out of school, I guess," he said.

Wednesday and Thursday were routine; Charles yelled during story hour and hit a boy in the stomach and made him cry. On Friday Charles stayed after school again and so did all the other children.

With the third week of kindergarten Charles was an institution in our family; Jannie was being a Charles when she cried all afternoon; Laurie did a Charles when he filled his wagon full of mud and pulled it through the kitchen; even my husband, when he caught his elbow in the telephone cord and pulled telephone, ash tray, and a bowl of flowers off the table, said, after the first minute, "Looks like Charles."

During the third and fourth weeks there

"He kicked the teacher's friend."

seemed to be a reformation in Charles; Laurie reported grimly at lunch on Thursday of the third week, "Charles was so good today the teacher gave him an apple."

"What?" I said, and my husband added warily, "You mean Charles?"

"Charles," Laurie said. "He gave the crayons around and he picked up the books afterward and the teacher said he was her helper."

"What happened?" I asked incredulously.

"He was her helper, that's all," Laurie said, and shrugged.

"Can this be true, about Charles?" I asked my husband that night. "Can something like this happen?"

"Wait and see," my husband said cynically. "When you've got a Charles to deal with, this may mean he's only plotting."

He seemed to be wrong. For over a week Charles was the teacher's helper; each day he handed things out and he picked things up; no one had to stay after school.

- -

WORDS TO OWN

warily (wer′ə·lē) *adv.*: cautiously.
incredulously (in·krej′oo·ləs·lē) *adv.*: unbelievingly.

- -

"The PTA meeting's next week again," I told my husband one evening. "I'm going to find Charles's mother there."

"Ask her what happened to Charles," my husband said. "I'd like to know."

"I'd like to know myself," I said.

On Friday of that week things were back to normal. "You know what Charles did today?" Laurie demanded at the lunch table, in a voice slightly awed. "He told a little girl to say a word and she said it and the teacher washed her mouth out with soap and Charles laughed."

"What word?" his father asked unwisely, and Laurie said, "I'll have to whisper it to you, it's so bad." He got down off his chair and went around to his father. His father bent his head down and Laurie whispered joyfully. His father's eyes widened.

"Did Charles tell the little girl to say *that*?" he asked respectfully.

"She said it *twice*," Laurie said. "Charles told her to say it *twice*."

"What happened to Charles?" my husband asked.

"Nothing," Laurie said. "He was passing out the crayons."

Monday morning Charles abandoned the little girl and said the evil word himself three or four times, getting his mouth washed out with soap each time. He also threw chalk.

My husband came to the door with me that evening as I set out for the PTA meeting. "Invite her over for a cup of tea after the meeting," he said. "I want to get a look at her."

"If only she's there," I said prayerfully.

"She'll be there," my husband said. "I don't see how they could hold a PTA meeting without Charles's mother."

At the meeting I sat restlessly, scanning each comfortable matronly face, trying to determine which one hid the secret of Charles. None of them looked to me haggard enough. No one stood up in the meeting and apologized for the way her son had been acting. No one mentioned Charles.

After the meeting I identified and sought out Laurie's kindergarten teacher. She had a plate with a cup of tea and a piece of chocolate cake; I had a plate with a cup of tea and a piece of marshmallow cake. We maneuvered up to one another cautiously and smiled.

"I've been so anxious to meet you," I said. "I'm Laurie's mother."

"We're all so interested in Laurie," she said.

"Well, he certainly likes kindergarten," I said. "He talks about it all the time."

"We had a little trouble adjusting, the first week or so," she said primly, "but now he's a fine little helper. With lapses, of course."

"Laurie usually adjusts very quickly," I said. "I suppose this time it's Charles's influence."

"Charles?"

"Yes," I said, laughing, "you must have your hands full in that kindergarten, with Charles."

"Charles?" she said. "We don't have any Charles in the kindergarten."

WORDS TO OWN

haggard (hag'ərd) *adj.*: looking worn-out and exhausted.

MEET THE WRITER

From Horror to Humor and Back Again

Shirley Jackson (1919–1965) was born in San Francisco, California. If you've ever read her most famous story, "The Lottery," you may be surprised to learn that the writer of this bone-chilling tale of horror is the same Shirley Jackson who wrote "Charles" and other comically exaggerated accounts of life with her husband and four children. Jackson's keen sense of irony, the thread that runs through all her writing, is evident in this mock questionnaire she wrote for fellow suffering mothers:

Shirley Jackson reading one of her stories in a classroom.

66 At breakfast I raise a considerable howl about the general sloppy condition of the back porch and the yard. Laurie, Joanne, Sally, and Barry promise that after school there will be a monumental cleaning-up and I will find the yard and porch immaculate. (1) Who has to stay after school to finish his chemistry notebook? (2) Who forgot that today was Girl Scouts? (3) Who calls from the library to say she will be home later? (4) Who stops off at David's house to see David's new steam engine and has to be sent for at five o'clock? (5) Who raises another howl the next morning at breakfast?

My husband has to catch a train for New York in twenty minutes. (1) Where will his clean shirts be? (2) Who forgot to call the laundry?

Barry has been waiting all day for two things: the arrival of his grandparents for a visit, and a particular television program on which one of his friends will be visible in the audience. The television program goes on at five-fifteen and lasts till five-thirty. (1) What time will the grandparents arrive? (2) What will be the general tone of the remarks about little children who are so mad for television they can't even say hello properly? (3) Who will eat dinner in dignified silence? 99

More by Shirley Jackson

"Charles" comes from *Life Among the Savages* (Amereon). The adventures of Laurie and the rest of the Jackson family continue in *Raising Demons* (Academy Chicago).

MAKING MEANINGS

First Thoughts

1. What is the **plot twist** at the end of the story? Did it surprise you? Explain.

Shaping Interpretations

2. What clues does Jackson give to Charles's identity?

3. In your opinion, why does Laurie invent Charles?

4. Do you think Laurie's parents should have realized the truth about Charles sooner? Explain.

5. Reread Julius Lester's comments on page 472. Do you think Laurie qualifies as a trickster? Why or why not?

Connecting with the Text

6. How would you have felt about Laurie if he had been in *your* kindergarten class? Would you have wanted to be friends with him? Explain your response.

Reading Check

a. Describe how Laurie's behavior at home changes after he begins school.

b. According to Laurie, what is Charles like?

c. How does Laurie's mother learn the truth about Charles?

CHOICES: Building Your Portfolio

Writer's Notebook

1. Collecting Ideas for Observational Writing

Have you ever known a class clown, trickster, or troublemaker? Describe how this person looks and acts and what you think of him or her. (Either expand on your Quickwrite or choose a new subject.)

Creative Writing

2. First Day of School

What do you remember about *your* first days (or weeks) of school? Write about your own experiences beginning elementary school or starting over at a new school. Try writing five or six sentences beginning *I remember . . .*; then, choose one to write about further.

Writing a Response

3. Dear Laurie

Shirley Jackson based the character of Laurie on her own son (see page 477). Write a letter to her now-grown son Laurie, telling him how you responded to "Charles." Did you think it was funny? silly? true to life? How does knowing that the story is about Laurie affect what you will say to him?

GRAMMAR LINK MINI-LESSON

Pronoun Reference

Language Handbook HELP

See Agreement of Pronoun and Antecedent, page 751.

When you use pronouns in your writing, make sure their **antecedents** (the words they refer to) are clear.

UNCLEAR | Shirley Jackson and her daughter Jannie went to the store to buy her new shoes. [Who needed shoes, Shirley or her daughter?]

CLEAR | Shirley Jackson took her daughter Jannie to the store to buy Jannie new shoes.

UNCLEAR | Jannie wanted a pair of high-heeled black sandals, but it didn't please her mother at all. [What does *it* refer to?]

CLEAR | Jannie wanted a pair of high-heeled black sandals, but they didn't meet with her mother's approval.

Jannie wanted a pair of high-heeled black sandals, but this choice didn't please her mother at all.

Try It Out

Number each line of a piece of writing you've been working on, and exchange papers with a classmate. On a separate sheet of paper, list by line number every pronoun your partner used, and identify its antecedent. If you can't tell, put a question mark on your list next to the pronoun. Switch papers again, and revise any sentences with unclear pronoun references.

VOCABULARY HOW TO OWN A WORD

Synonyms and Antonyms

WORD BANK

renounced
insolently
warily
incredulously
haggard

Complete each of the sentences below by choosing the word that fits best from the Word Bank. (Use each word only once.) Then, write *S* next to the word if it is a **synonym** (word with a similar meaning) or *A* if it is an **antonym** (word with the opposite meaning) of the underlined word.

1. "There is no Charles in the class?" Laurie's father said _____, looking at his wife <u>unbelievingly</u>.
2. "Maybe the teacher forgot," he continued _____. "Don't jump to conclusions; it's best to approach these matters <u>cautiously</u>."
3. "Well," she replied, "it's hard to believe that my son, who used to behave so <u>politely</u> at home, behaves _____ at school."
4. "Anyway, I'm sure I'll hear at the next PTA meeting that he has _____ any bad habits he's <u>adopted</u> in kindergarten."
5. "I'm <u>exhausted</u>," her husband said, looking _____. "Now I know how Charles's parents must feel."

Elements of Literature

HUMOR: Getting a Laugh

What Is Humor?

What *is* humor? We recognize it when we see it, but it's hard to explain why something is funny—and if you've ever tried to explain a joke to someone, you know that's the surest way to drain every bit of humor out of it. Yet the people who make their living by making us laugh don't rely on instinct alone. Like scientists analyzing the results of an experiment, professional humorists analyze successful humor for the elements that get a laugh. Humor is usually central to **comedy,** a play or other literary work that ends happily and often makes us laugh.

Surprise!

The essence of humor is **surprise.** Not every surprise is funny, but nothing is funny without being surprising. We laugh at an unexpected choice of words or combination of ideas or a twist on a seemingly predictable situation.

Why is a joke funny to people of one culture, generation, or social group but not another? In part it's because they have different expectations of what is ordinary and predictable. It is those expectations that make the humor of the unexpected possible.

Expect the Unexpected: Three Types of Irony

Irony is a contrast between expectation and reality. Irony can be tragic or profound; it can also be funny.

Verbal irony involves a contrast between what is said and what is really meant. Someone who says "Speak up!" to a person who is shouting is using verbal irony.

Situational irony occurs when what happens is very different from what we expect. A puppy outwitting humans on a TV sitcom gets laughs because of situational irony: We expect people to be smarter than their pets.

Dramatic irony occurs when the audience or the reader knows something a character does not know. Dramatic irony is what makes us laugh at Elmer Fudd trying to sneak up on Bugs Bunny when *we* know that Elmer is going to meet an angry bear, not a delicious rabbit.

More or Less?

Another comic technique is **exaggeration,** or overstatement. "My schoolbooks are heavy enough to sink a ship" is an example of exaggeration. **Tall tales** get their humor from exaggeration; so do caricatures, which exaggerate a person's most noticeable features for comic effect. The opposite of exaggeration is **understatement**—saying less than what is meant. The action hero clinging to a roof by his fingernails who politely mentions that he could use a hand up is using understatement to get a laugh.

A Writer on Humor

"Wit is the sudden marriage of ideas which, before their union, were not perceived to have any relation."

— Mark Twain

Before You Read

THE RANSOM OF RED CHIEF

Make the Connection

Tales of the Unexpected

What do you predict this story will be about? Look at the story's title and pictures. Look at the quotations from the story that are "pulled out" and placed next to some illustrations.

Quickwrite

Take notes on what you think this story will be about. Organize your notes like this: Where is the story set? Who are the characters? What do they want? What problems will they face? How will the story end?

Think-pair-share. Tell your story to a classmate, and listen to his or her story.

Elements of Literature

Irony

Much of the humor in "The Ransom of Red Chief" comes from O. Henry's skillful use of **irony.** Look for examples of the three types of irony you've learned about:

*   **verbal irony,** where what is said is the opposite of what is meant
*   **situational irony,** where what happens is very different from what we expect
*   **dramatic irony,** where we know something a character doesn't

> **I**rony is a contrast between expectation and reality.
>
> *For more on Irony, see page 480 and the Handbook of Literary Terms.*

Reading Skills and Strategies

Drawing Inferences: Finding Clues

An inference is a guess you make based on your own experiences and on clues in the story. When writers use irony, they are counting on you to make inferences as you read. They expect that you'll infer that certain things will happen next. Then they surprise you by making something else happen instead. As you read "The Ransom of Red Chief," think about the things that you guess will happen. What happens instead?

HRW go.hrw.com
LEO 8-6

I t looked like a good thing: but wait till I tell you. We were down South, in Alabama—Bill Driscoll and myself—when this kidnapping idea struck us. It was, as Bill afterward expressed it, "during a moment of temporary mental apparition";[1] but we didn't find that out till later.

I was awakened

There was a town down there, as flat as a flannel cake, and called Summit, of course. It contained inhabitants of as undeleterious[2] and self-satisfied a class of peasantry as ever clustered around a Maypole.

Bill and me had a joint capital of about six hundred dollars, and we needed just two thousand dollars more to pull off a

by a series of

fraudulent town-lot scheme in Western Illinois with. We talked it over on the front steps of the Hotel. Philoprogenitiveness,[3] says we, is strong in semirural communities; therefore, and for other reasons, a kidnapping project ought to do better there than in the radius[4] of newspapers that send reporters out in plain

awful screams . . .

clothes to stir up talk about such things. We knew that Summit couldn't get after us with anything stronger than constables and, maybe, some lackadaisical bloodhounds and a <u>diatribe</u> or two in the *Weekly Farmers' Budget.* So, it looked good.

1. **apparition** (ap′ə·rish′ən): appearance of a ghost. Bill means *aberration* (ab′ər·ā′shən), a departure from what is normal.
2. **undeleterious** (un·del′ə·tir′ē·əs): harmless.
3. **philoprogenitiveness** (fil′ō·prō·jen′ə·tiv·nis): parents' love for their children.
4. **radius:** range; area of activity.

WORDS TO OWN

diatribe (dī′ə·trīb′) *n.:* condemnation; harsh, abusive criticism.

The Ransom of Red Chief

O. Henry

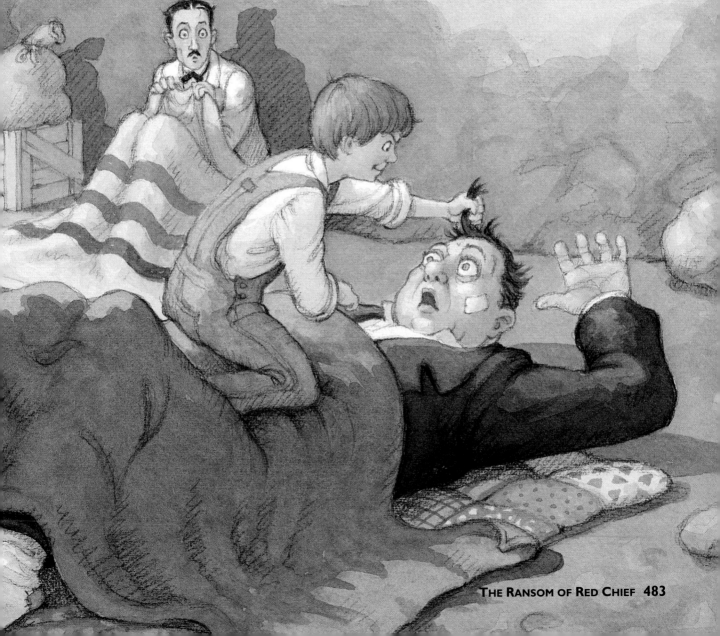

We selected for our victim the only child of a prominent citizen named Ebenezer Dorset. The father was respectable and tight, a mortgage fancier and a stern, upright collection-plate passer and forecloser. The kid was a boy of ten, with bas-relief[5] freckles and hair the color of the cover of the magazine you buy at the newsstand when you want to catch a train. Bill and me figured that Ebenezer would melt down for a ransom of two thousand dollars to a cent. But wait till I tell you.

About two miles from Summit was a little mountain, covered with a dense cedar brake.[6] On the rear elevation of this mountain was a cave. There we stored provisions.

One evening after sundown, we drove in a buggy past old Dorset's house. The kid was in the street, throwing rocks at a kitten on the opposite fence.

"Hey, little boy!" says Bill, "would you like to have a bag of candy and a nice ride?"

The boy catches Bill neatly in the eye with a piece of brick.

"That will cost the old man an extra five hundred dollars," says Bill, climbing over the wheel.

That boy put up a fight like a welterweight cinnamon bear; but, at last, we got him down in the bottom of the buggy and drove away. We took him up to the cave, and I hitched the horse in the cedar brake. After dark I drove the buggy to the little village, three miles away, where we had hired it, and walked back to the mountain.

Bill was pasting court plaster[7] over the scratches and bruises on his features. There was a fire burning behind the big rock at the entrance of the cave, and the boy was watching a pot of boiling coffee, with two buzzard tail feathers stuck in his red hair. He points a stick at me when I come up, and says:

"Ha! cursed paleface, do you dare to enter the camp of Red Chief, the terror of the plains?"

"He's all right now," says Bill, rolling up his trousers and examining some bruises on his shins. "We're playing Indian. We're making Buffalo Bill's show look like magic-lantern views[8] of Palestine in the town hall. I'm Old Hank, the Trapper, Red Chief's captive, and I'm to be scalped at daybreak. By Geronimo! that kid can kick hard."

Yes, sir, that boy seemed to be having the time of his life. The fun of camping out in a cave had made him forget that he was a captive himself. He immediately christened me Snake-eye, the Spy, and announced that when his braves returned from the warpath, I was to be broiled at the stake at the rising of the sun.

Then we had supper; and he filled his mouth full of bacon and bread and gravy and began to talk. He made a during-dinner speech something like this:

"I like this fine. I never camped out before; but I had a pet 'possum once, and I was nine last birthday. I hate to go to school. Rats ate up sixteen of Jimmy Talbot's aunt's speckled hen's eggs. Are there any real Indians in these woods? I want some more gravy. Does the trees moving make the wind blow? We had five puppies. What makes your nose so red, Hank? My father has lots of money. Are the stars hot? I whipped Ed Walker twice, Saturday. I don't like girls. You dassent[9] catch toads unless with a string. Do oxen make any noise? Why are oranges round? Have you got beds to sleep on in this cave? Amos Murray has got six toes. A parrot can talk, but a monkey or a fish can't. How many does it take to make twelve?"

---

5. bas-relief (bä′ri·lēf′): slightly raised. *Bas-relief* usually refers to a kind of sculpture in which figures are carved in a flat surface so that they project only slightly from the background.
6. brake: clump of trees or bushes.
7. court plaster: cloth that sticks to the skin, used for covering cuts and scratches.

8. magic-lantern views: slides. A magic lantern was an early type of projector.
9. dassent: dare not.

Every few minutes he would remember that he was a pesky redskin, and pick up his stick rifle and tiptoe to the mouth of the cave to rubber[10] for the scouts of the hated paleface. Now and then he would let out a war whoop that made Old Hank the Trapper shiver. That boy had Bill terrorized from the start.

"Red Chief," says I to the kid, "would you like to go home?"

"Aw, what for?" says he. "I don't have any fun at home. I hate to go to school. I like to camp out. You won't take me back home again, Snake-eye, will you?"

"Not right away," says I. "We'll stay here in the cave awhile."

"All right!" says he. "That'll be fine. I never had such fun in all my life."

We went to bed about eleven o'clock. We spread down some wide blankets and quilts and put Red Chief between us. We weren't afraid he'd run away. He kept us awake for three hours, jumping up and reaching for his rifle and screeching: "Hist! pard," in mine and Bill's ears, as the fancied crackle of a twig or the rustle of a leaf revealed to his young imagination the stealthy approach of the outlaw band. At last, I fell into a troubled sleep, and dreamed that I had been kidnapped and chained to a tree by a ferocious pirate with red hair.

Just at daybreak, I was awakened by a series of awful screams from Bill. They weren't yells, or howls, or shouts, or whoops, or yawps, such as you'd expect from a manly set of vocal organs—they were simply indecent, terrifying, humiliating screams, such as women emit when they see ghosts or caterpillars. It's an awful thing to hear a strong, desperate, fat man scream incontinently in a cave at daybreak.

I jumped up to see what the matter was. Red Chief was sitting on Bill's chest, with one hand twined in Bill's hair. In the other he had the sharp case knife we used for slicing bacon; and he was industriously and realistically trying to take Bill's scalp, according to the sentence that had been pronounced upon him the evening before.

I got the knife away from the kid and made him lie down again. But, from that moment, Bill's spirit was broken. He laid down on his side of the bed, but he never closed an eye again in sleep as long as that boy was with us. I dozed off for a while, but along toward sunup I remembered that Red Chief had said I was to be burned at the stake at the rising of the sun. I wasn't nervous or afraid; but I sat up and lit my pipe and leaned against a rock.

"What you getting up so soon for, Sam?" asked Bill.

"Me?" says I. "Oh, I got a kind of pain in my shoulder. I thought sitting up would rest it."

"You're a liar!" says Bill. "You're afraid. You was to be burned at sunrise, and you was afraid he'd do it. And he would, too, if he could find a match. Ain't it awful, Sam? Do you think anybody will pay out money to get a little imp like that back home?"

"Sure," said I. "A rowdy kid like that is just the kind that parents dote on. Now, you and the Chief get up and cook breakfast, while I go up on the top of this mountain and reconnoiter."

I went up on the peak of the little mountain and ran my eye over the contiguous vicinity.[11] Over toward Summit I expected to see the sturdy yeomanry of the village armed with scythes and pitchforks beating the countryside for the dastardly kidnappers. But what I saw was a peaceful landscape dotted with one man plowing with a dun mule. Nobody was dragging the creek; no couriers dashed hither and yon, bringing tidings of no news to the distracted parents. There was a sylvan[12] attitude

---

10. **rubber:** short for *rubberneck*, meaning "stretch the neck to look at something curiously." Traffic reports often mention delays caused by rubbernecking—drivers slow down to stare at accidents and create jams.

11. **contiguous vicinity:** nearby area.
12. **sylvan** (sil′vən): like a forest.

of <u>somnolent</u> sleepiness pervading that section of the external outward surface of Alabama that lay exposed to my view. "Perhaps," says I to myself, "it has not yet been discovered that the wolves have borne away the tender lambkin from the fold. Heaven help the wolves!" says I, and I went down the mountain to breakfast.

When I got to the cave, I found Bill backed up against the side of it, breathing hard, and the boy threatening to smash him with a rock half as big as a coconut.

"He put a red-hot boiled potato down my back," explained Bill, "and then mashed it with his foot; and I boxed his ears. Have you got a gun about you, Sam?"

I took the rock away from the boy and kind of patched up the argument. "I'll fix you," says the kid to Bill. "No man ever yet struck the Red Chief but he got paid for it. You better beware!"

After breakfast the kid takes a piece of leather with strings wrapped around it out of his pocket and goes outside the cave unwinding it.

"What's he up to now?" says Bill, anxiously. "You don't think he'll run away, do you, Sam?"

"No fear of it," says I. "He don't seem to be much of a homebody. But we've got to fix up some plan about the ransom. There don't seem to be much excitement around Summit on account of his disappearance; but maybe they haven't realized yet that he's gone. His folks may think he's spending the night with Aunt Jane or one of the neighbors. Anyhow, he'll be missed today. Tonight we must get a message to his father demanding the two thousand dollars for his return."

Just then we heard a kind of war whoop, such as David might have emitted when he knocked out the champion Goliath. It was a

"I'll fix you," says the kid to Bill.

sling that Red Chief had pulled out of his pocket, and he was whirling it around his head.

I dodged, and heard a heavy thud and a kind of a sigh from Bill, like a horse gives out when you take his saddle off. A rock the size of an egg had caught Bill just behind his left ear. He loosened himself all over and fell in the fire across the frying pan of hot water for washing the dishes. I dragged him out and poured cold water on his head for half an hour.

By and by, Bill sits up and feels behind his

WORDS TO OWN
somnolent (säm′nə·lənt) *adj.*: drowsy.

ear and says: "Sam, do you know who my favorite Biblical character is?"

"Take it easy," says I. "You'll come to your senses presently."

"King Herod,"[13] says he. "You won't go away and leave me here alone, will you, Sam?"

I went out and caught that boy and shook him until his freckles rattled.

"If you don't behave," says I, "I'll take you straight home. Now, are you going to be good, or not?"

"I was only funning," says he, sullenly. "I didn't mean to hurt Old Hank. But what did he

---

13. **King Herod** (her′əd): Herod the Great, ruler of Judea from 37 to 4 B.C., ordered the killing of all boys in Bethlehem less than two years old (Matthew 2:16).

hit me for? I'll behave, Snake-eye, if you won't send me home and if you'll let me play the Black Scout today."

"I don't know the game," says I. "That's for you and Mr. Bill to decide. He's your playmate for the day. I'm going away for a while, on business. Now, you come in and make friends with him and say you are sorry for hurting him, or home you go, at once."

I made him and Bill shake hands, and then I took Bill aside and told him I was going to Poplar Grove, a little village three miles from the cave, and find out what I could about how the kidnapping had been regarded in Summit. Also, I thought it best to send a peremptory letter to old man Dorset that day, demanding the ransom and dictating how it should be paid.

"You know, Sam," says Bill, "I've stood by you without batting an eye in earthquakes, fire, and flood—in poker games, dynamite outrages, police raids, train robberies, and cyclones. I never lost my nerve yet till we kidnapped that two-legged skyrocket of a kid. He's got me going. You won't leave me long with him, will you, Sam?"

"I'll be back sometime this afternoon," says I. "You must keep the boy amused and quiet till I return. And now we'll write the letter to old Dorset."

Bill and I got paper and pencil and worked on the letter while Red Chief, with a blanket wrapped around him, strutted up and down, guarding the mouth of the cave. Bill begged me tearfully to make the ransom fifteen hundred dollars instead of two thousand. "I ain't attempting," says he, "to decry[14] the celebrated moral aspect of parental affection, but we're dealing with humans, and it ain't human for

---

14. **decry:** undervalue.

- -

WORDS TO OWN

peremptory (pər·emp′tə·rē) *adj.:* commanding; allowing no debate or delay.

- -

anybody to give up two thousand dollars for that forty-pound chunk of freckled wildcat. I'm willing to take a chance at fifteen hundred dollars. You can charge the difference up to me."

So, to relieve Bill, I acceded, and we collaborated a letter that ran this way:

EBENEZER DORSET, ESQ.:

We have your boy concealed in a place far from Summit. It is useless for you or the most skillful detectives to attempt to find him. Absolutely the only terms on which you can have him restored to you are these: We demand fifteen hundred dollars in large bills for his return; the money to be left at midnight tonight at the same spot and in the same box as your reply—as hereinafter described. If you agree to these terms, send your answer in writing by a solitary messenger tonight at half-past eight o'clock. After crossing Owl Creek on the road to Poplar Grove, there are three large trees about a hundred yards apart, close to the fence of the wheat field on the right-hand side. At the bottom of the fence post, opposite the third tree, will be found a small pasteboard box.

The messenger will place the answer in this box and return immediately to Summit.

If you attempt any treachery or fail to comply with our demand as stated, you will never see your boy again.

If you pay the money as demanded, he will be returned to you safe and well within three hours. These terms are final, and if you do not accede to them, no further communication will be attempted.

TWO DESPERATE MEN

I addressed this letter to Dorset and put it in my pocket. As I was about to start, the kid comes up to me and says:

"Aw, Snake-eye, you said I could play the Black Scout while you was gone."

"Play it, of course," says I. "Mr. Bill will play with you. What kind of a game is it?"

"I'm the Black Scout," says Red Chief, "and I have to ride to the stockade to warn the settlers that the Indians are coming. I'm tired of playing Indian myself. I want to be the Black Scout."

"All right," says I. "It sounds harmless to me. I guess Mr. Bill will help you foil the pesky savages."

"What am I to do?" asks Bill, looking at the kid suspiciously.

"You are the hoss," says Black Scout. "Get down on your hands and knees. How can I ride to the stockade without a hoss?"

"You'd better keep him interested," said I, "till we get the scheme going. Loosen up."

Bill gets down on his all fours, and a look comes in his eye like a rabbit's when you catch it in a trap.

"How far is it to the stockade, kid?" he asks, in a husky manner of voice.

"Ninety miles," says the Black Scout. "And you have to hump[15] yourself to get there on time. Whoa, now!"

The Black Scout jumps on Bill's back and digs his heels in his side.

"For Heaven's sake," says Bill, "hurry back, Sam, as soon as you can. I wish we hadn't made the ransom more than a thousand. Say, you quit kicking me or I'll get up and warm you good."

I walked over to Poplar Grove and sat around the post office and store, talking with the chaw-bacons that came in to trade. One whiskerando says that he hears Summit is all upset on account of Elder Ebenezer Dorset's boy having been lost or stolen. That was all I wanted to know. I bought some smoking tobacco, referred casually to the price of

15. **hump:** here, hurry.

WORDS TO OWN

acceded (ak·sēd′id) v.: gave in; consented.

---

black-eyed peas, posted my letter surreptitiously, and came away. The postmaster said the mail carrier would come by in an hour to take the mail to Summit.

When I got back to the cave, Bill and the boy were not to be found. I explored the vicinity of the cave and risked a yodel or two, but there was no response.

So I lighted my pipe and sat down on a mossy bank to await developments.

In about half an hour I heard the bushes rustle, and Bill wabbled out into the little glade in front of the cave. Behind him was the kid, stepping softly like a scout, with a broad grin on his face. Bill stopped, took off his hat, and wiped his face with a red handkerchief. The kid stopped about eight feet behind him.

"Sam," says Bill, "I suppose you'll think I'm a renegade, but I couldn't help it. I'm a grown person with masculine proclivities and habits of self-defense, but there is a time when all systems of egotism and predominance fail. The boy is gone. I sent him home. All is off. There was martyrs in old times," goes on Bill, "that suffered death rather than give up the particular graft they enjoyed. None of 'em ever was subjugated to such supernatural tortures as I have been. I tried to be faithful to our articles of depredation;[16] but there came a limit."

"What's the trouble, Bill?" I asks him.

"I was rode," says Bill, "the ninety miles to the stockade, not barring an inch. Then, when the settlers was rescued, I was given oats. Sand ain't a palatable substitute. And then, for an hour I had to try to explain to him why there was nothin' in holes, how a road can run both ways, and what makes the grass green. I tell you, Sam, a human can only stand so much. I takes him by the neck of his clothes and drags him down the mountain. On the way he kicks my legs black and blue from the knees down;

16. **depredation** (dep′rə·dā′shən): robbery; looting. The phrase *articles of depredation* is a pun on *Articles of Confederation*, the name of the first U.S. constitution.

and I've got to have two or three bites on my thumb and hand cauterized.[17]

"But he's gone"—continues Bill—"gone home. I showed him the road to Summit and kicked him about eight feet nearer there at one kick. I'm sorry we lose the ransom; but it was either that or Bill Driscoll to the madhouse."

Bill is puffing and blowing, but there is a look of ineffable peace and growing content on his rose-pink features.

"Bill," says I, "there isn't any heart disease in your family, is there?"

"No," says Bill, "nothing chronic except malaria and accidents. Why?"

"Then you might turn around," says I, "and have a look behind you."

Bill turns and sees the boy, and loses his complexion and sits down plump on the ground and begins to pluck aimlessly at grass and little sticks. For an hour I was afraid of his mind. And then I told him that my scheme was to put the whole job through immediately and that we would get the ransom and be off with it by midnight if old Dorset fell in with our proposition. So Bill braced up enough to give the kid a weak sort of a smile and a promise to play the Russian in a Japanese war with him as soon as he felt a little better.

I had a scheme for collecting that ransom without danger of being caught by counterplots that ought to commend itself to professional kidnappers. The tree under which the

17. **cauterized:** burned to prevent infection.

- -

WORDS TO OWN

surreptitiously (sʉr′əp·tish′əs·lē) *adv.*: in a secret or sneaky way.

renegade (ren′ə·gād′) *n.*: traitor; person who abandons a cause and goes over to the other side.

proclivities (prō·kliv′ə·tēz) *n.*: natural tendencies.

palatable (pal′ə·tə·bəl) *adj.*: fit to eat; acceptable.

ineffable (in·ef′ə·bəl) *adj.*: indescribable; too great to describe.

proposition (präp′ə·zish′ən) *n.*: proposal; suggested plan.

- -

I had a scheme

for collecting

that ransom . . .

answer was to be left—and the money later on—was close to the road fence, with big, bare fields on all sides. If a gang of constables should be watching for anyone to come for the note, they could see him a long way off crossing the fields or in the road. But no, sirree! At half-past eight I was up in that tree as well hidden as a tree toad, waiting for the messenger to arrive.

Exactly on time, a half-grown boy rides up the road on a bicycle, locates the pasteboard box at the foot of the fence post, slips a folded piece of paper into it, and pedals away again back toward Summit.

I waited an hour and then concluded the thing was square. I slid down the tree, got the note, slipped along the fence till I struck the woods, and was back at the cave in another half an hour. I opened the note, got near the lantern, and read it to Bill. It was written with a pen in a crabbed hand,[18] and the sum and substance of it was this:

TWO DESPERATE MEN:

Gentlemen: I received your letter today by post, in regard to the ransom you ask for the return of my son. I think you are a little high in your demands, and I hereby make you a counterproposition, which I am inclined to believe you will accept. You bring Johnny home and pay me two hundred and fifty dollars in cash, and I agree to take him off your hands. You had better come at night, for the neighbors believe he is lost, and I couldn't be responsible for what they would do to anybody they saw bringing him back. Very respectfully,

EBENEZER DORSET

"Great Pirates of Penzance," says I; "of all the impudent——"

But I glanced at Bill, and hesitated. He had the most appealing look in his eyes I ever saw on the face of a dumb or a talking brute.

"Sam," says he, "what's two hundred and fifty dollars, after all? We've got the money. One more night of this kid will send me to a bed in Bedlam.[19] Besides being a thorough gentleman, I think Mr. Dorset is a spendthrift for making us such a liberal offer. You ain't going to let the chance go, are you?"

"Tell you the truth, Bill," says I, "this little he–ewe lamb has somewhat got on my nerves too. We'll take him home, pay the ransom, and make our getaway."

We took him home that night. We got him to go by telling him that his father had bought a silver-mounted rifle and a pair of moccasins for him and we were to hunt bears the next day.

It was just twelve o'clock when we knocked at Ebenezer's front door. Just at the moment when I should have been abstracting the fifteen hundred dollars from the box under the tree, according to the original proposition, Bill was counting out two hundred and fifty dollars into Dorset's hand.

When the kid found out we were going to leave him at home, he started up a howl like a calliope[20] and fastened himself as tight as a leech to Bill's leg. His father peeled him away gradually, like a porous plaster.

"How long can you hold him?" asks Bill.

"I'm not as strong as I used to be," says old Dorset, "but I think I can promise you ten minutes."

"Enough," says Bill. "In ten minutes I shall cross the Central, Southern, and Middle Western States and be legging it trippingly for the Canadian border."

And as dark as it was, and as fat as Bill was, and as good a runner as I am, he was a good mile and a half out of Summit before I could catch up with him.

---

18. **crabbed** (krab′id) **hand:** handwriting that is hard to read.

19. **Bedlam:** an insane asylum.
20. **calliope** (kə·lī′ə·pē′): keyboard instrument like an organ, with a series of whistles sounded by steam or compressed air.

MEET THE WRITER

"I Have to Get a Story off My Chest"

O. Henry is the pen name of William Sydney Porter (1862–1910), who wrote almost three hundred short stories in his relatively brief life. O. Henry grew up in Greensboro, North Carolina. His mother died when he was young, and his aunt, who ran a private school, took over his education.

When he was twenty years old, O. Henry moved to Texas. In 1896, facing charges of embezzling money from a bank where he had worked, he fled the country and sailed to Honduras. He returned to Texas because of his wife's illness and was obliged to stand trial. Convicted of embezzlement, he was sent to jail for three years. Some people believe that he took his pen name from the name of a prison guard, Orrin Henry; others say that he found the name in a book.

O. Henry (1918–1919) by W. D. Stokes. Oil on canvas.

O. Henry moved to New York in 1902. He took to life in the city, prowling streets, cafes, and stores and recording snatches of conversation. He turned many of his experiences into fiction, often locking himself in a room for three or four days to write. When a friend expressed amazement at this habit, he responded:

““ I have to get a story off my chest as soon as possible. . . . I have to top it off while my interest is still hot. Once I begin a yarn, I must finish it without stopping or it kinda goes dead on me. ””

More by O. Henry

"The Ransom of Red Chief" and other popular stories by O. Henry, including "A Retrieved Reformation" and "After Twenty Years," appear in his *Selected Stories* (Penguin).

MAKING MEANINGS

First Thoughts

1. Rate this story's **humor** on a scale of one to five, with five being the funniest. Share and discuss your rating with your classmates. What made the story funny or not funny to you?

Shaping Interpretations

2. What is Johnny doing when we first meet him? How do his actions **foreshadow,** or hint at, the trouble he will make for his kidnappers?

3. Name two **inferences** about the kidnappers' plan that you made early in the story. What did you think would happen? Why? What actually happened?

4. Go back to the text, and find at least one example of each of the three kinds of **irony** discussed on page 480. Which example do you like best? Why?

5. O. Henry spent several years in jail (see Meet the Writer), and many of his stories include likable criminal characters. Whom does he seem to sympathize with most in this story? Do you think he is too forgiving of criminal behavior? Explain.

Connecting with the Text

6. Whom did you sympathize with *most* as you read this story—Johnny, his father, or Bill and Sam? Whom did you like *least*? Why?

7. Go back to your Quickwrite notes. How close did your predictions come to what happened in the story? What details in the story surprised you the most?

Extending the Text

8. What could the kidnappers have done to escape their "victim" without paying his father to take him back? Outline a "plan B" that Bill and Sam could have followed.

9. What do you think would happen if Johnny met Laurie (from "Charles," page 473)? How would they get along?

10. Does "The Ransom of Red Chief" qualify as a trickster tale? a tall tale? both? neither? Give reasons for your opinion.

> ### Reading Check
> Imagine that the local police chief comes over for dinner with the Dorsets the day after the kidnapping and notices (as who wouldn't) that Johnny isn't there. With a partner, make up the chief's questions and Mr. Dorset's responses. Be sure to mention the contents of the ransom note and Mr. Dorset's surprising reply.

CHOICES: Building Your Portfolio

Writer's Notebook

1. Collecting Ideas for Observational Writing

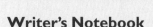

Although O. Henry exaggerates them for comic effect, the qualities that allow Johnny to get the best of his kidnappers are those of real children: energy and curiosity, love of make-believe, and an ability to cause endless trouble.

Observe a child you know—perhaps a younger relative, a friend's brother or sister, or a neighbor—engaging in everyday activities. Take notes on your observations and impressions.

> Kendra:
> —loves to climb on things and ride her bicycle
> —always teasing her baby sister
> —cute smile
> —does the exact opposite of whatever her mother says to do

Creative Writing

2. Thanks So Much

Write one of the following **ironic** thank-you notes:

- from Johnny to Bill and Sam, for taking him on a camping trip
- from Bill and Sam to Ebenezer Dorset, for taking his son back
- from the Dorsets to Bill and Sam, inviting them to come back and spend more time with the boy

Art

3. Vacation Snapshots

Design a photo album with pictures showing Johnny Dorset's adventure with his kidnappers. Choose what you think are the three or four funniest moments in the story, and draw "snapshots" of them. Label the pictures with captions Johnny might have written.

Creative Writing

4. By Any Other Name?

Pick a character from the story, and write a "name poem" for him. In a **name poem** the first letters of the lines spell out a name, as in this example:

Silly
Afraid of Johnny
Money-hungry

Writing About Comedy

5. Now That's Funny!

What is a **comedy**?
- A comedy is a story that ends happily.
- Usually, comedies make us laugh.
- One popular comic plot involves a young character who uses all sorts of tricks and schemes to triumph over an older character.
- Comedies often involve reversals—the bad guy becomes a hero, or the loser becomes the big winner.

In a brief essay, tell why "The Ransom of Red Chief" is a comedy. Be sure to mention the ways in which O. Henry makes you laugh. (Review the essay on humor on page 480.)

GRAMMAR LINK

Pronoun-Antecedent Agreement

Language Handbook HELP

See Agreement of Pronoun and Antecedent, pages 751-753.

Technology HELP

See Language Workshop CD-ROM. *Key word entry: pronoun-antecedent agreement.*

A pronoun should agree with its antecedent in **number** (singular or plural) and **gender** (masculine or feminine).

EXAMPLES Johnny did not want to return to his family. [A masculine singular pronoun is used to refer to a masculine singular antecedent.]

Do you think Mr. and Mrs. Dorset were happy to see their son? [A plural pronoun is used to refer to a plural antecedent.]

Singular pronouns are used to refer to *anybody, anyone, each, either, everybody, everyone, neither, nobody, no one, one, somebody,* and *someone.*

EXAMPLES Neither of the girls brought her book.

Is anyone ready to present his or her project?

You can often avoid the awkward *his or her* construction by rephrasing sentences, using plural pronouns and antecedents:

AWKWARD Each student read his or her story to the class.

BETTER All the students read their stories to the class.

Try It Out

Take out a draft you've written. Underline each pronoun, and write above it *S* (singular) or *P* (plural). Then, draw arrows from the pronouns to their antecedents, and write *S* or *P* above each antecedent. If you have an *S* paired with a *P,* rewrite your sentence to make the pronoun agree with its antecedent.

VOCABULARY   HOW TO OWN A WORD

WORD BANK

diatribe
somnolent
peremptory
acceded
surreptitiously
renegade
proclivities
palatable
ineffable
proposition

Synonyms: Word Twins (But Not Identical)

A **synonym** is a word that has the same or nearly the same meaning as another word. For example, *peaceful* and *calm,* and *fix* and *repair* are synonyms—word twins. For practice with a standardized test format, choose the *best* synonym for each word in capital letters.

1. SOMNOLENT: (a) nightmarish (b) sleepy (c) awake
2. SURREPTITIOUSLY: (a) openly (b) carefully (c) secretly
3. PROPOSITION: (a) schedule (b) problem (c) plan
4. PROCLIVITIES: (a) tendencies (b) objections (c) fears
5. PALATABLE: (a) unpleasant (b) acceptable (c) unlikely
6. INEFFABLE: (a) inexpressible (b) humorous (c) annoying
7. DIATRIBE: (a) condemnation (b) praise (c) speech
8. RENEGADE: (a) newcomer (b) traitor (c) patriot
9. ACCEDED: (a) argued (b) refused (c) agreed
10. PEREMPTORY: (a) weak (b) angry (c) commanding

Before You Read

THEY HAVE YARNS

Make the Connection

That's Outrageous

What's the most outrageous, most ridiculous, most unbelievable story you've ever heard?

Quickwrite

Summarize the story in two or three sentences. If you like, share it with your classmates.

Elements of Literature

Tall Tales

"They Have Yarns" is a list of yarns, or **tall tales,** from around the United States. As you read, see if you recognize any of the stories Sandburg refers to—or if they remind you of any others you've heard.

A **tall tale** is an exaggerated, far-fetched story that is obviously untrue but is told as though it should be believed.

For more on Tall Tales, see pages 460–461 and the Handbook of Literary Terms.

go.hrw.com
LEO 8-6

They Have Yarns

from **The People, Yes**

Carl Sandburg

They have yarns
Of a skyscraper so tall they had to put hinges
On the two top stories so to let the moon go by,
Of one corn crop in Missouri when the roots
5   Went so deep and drew off so much water
The Mississippi riverbed that year was dry,
Of pancakes so thin they had only one side,
Of "a fog so thick we shingled the barn and six feet out on the fog,"
Of Pecos Pete° straddling a cyclone in Texas and riding it to the west
    coast where "it rained out under him,"

9. Pecos Pete is more commonly known as Pecos Bill (see page 502).

Of the man who drove a swarm of bees across the Rocky Mountains and
    the Desert "and didn't lose a bee,"
10
Of a mountain railroad curve where the engineer in his cab can touch
    the caboose and spit in the conductor's eye,
Of the boy who climbed a cornstalk growing so fast he would have
    starved to death if they hadn't shot biscuits up to him,
Of the old man's whiskers: "When the wind was with him his whiskers
    arrived a day before he did,"
Of the hen laying a square egg and cackling, "Ouch!" and of hens laying
    eggs with the dates printed on them,
15
Of the ship captain's shadow: it froze to the deck one cold winter night,
Of mutineers on that same ship put to chipping rust with rubber
    hammers,
Of the sheep counter who was fast and accurate: "I just count their feet
    and divide by four,"
Of the man so tall he must climb a ladder to shave himself,
Of the runt so teeny-weeny it takes two men and a boy to see him,
20
Of mosquitoes: one can kill a dog, two of them a man,
Of a cyclone that sucked cookstoves out of the kitchen, up the chimney
    flue,° and on to the next town,
Of the same cyclone picking up wagon-tracks in Nebraska and dropping
    them over in the Dakotas,
Of the hook-and-eye snake unlocking itself into forty pieces, each piece
    two inches long, then in nine seconds flat snapping itself together
    again,
Of the watch swallowed by the cow—when they butchered her a year
    later the watch was running and had the correct time,
Of horned snakes, hoop snakes that roll themselves where they want to
25
    go, and rattlesnakes carrying bells instead of rattles on their tails,
Of the herd of cattle in California getting lost in a giant redwood tree
    that had hollowed out,
Of the man who killed a snake by putting its tail in its mouth so it
    swallowed itself,
Of railroad trains whizzing along so fast they reach the station before
    the whistle,
Of pigs so thin the farmer had to tie knots in their tails to keep them
    from crawling through the cracks in their pens,
Of Paul Bunyan's big blue ox, Babe, measuring between the eyes forty-
30
    two ax-handles and a plug of Star tobacco exactly,
Of John Henry's hammer and the curve of its swing and his singing of
    it as "a rainbow round my shoulder."

21. flue (flo͞o): tube through which smoke can pass.

MEET THE WRITER

What Is Poetry?

The son of Swedish immigrants, Carl Sandburg (1878–1967) was born in Galesburg, Illinois. He left school at the age of fourteen and went to work as a milk wagon driver. (Years later he went to college and earned a degree.) He then began to travel around the Midwest, working at dozens of jobs, including washing dishes, painting houses, firefighting, and door-to-door sales. These early experiences influenced his writing, which often celebrates American workers.

Sandburg was interested in everything about America—its history, its folklore, its leaders, its ordinary people. A talented guitarist, he traveled around the country singing folk songs and reciting his poems to large, enthusiastic audiences. Sandburg spent thirty years researching and writing a six-volume biography of his hero, Abraham Lincoln. He won a Pulitzer Prize for history in 1940 and one for poetry in 1951.

Some critics have argued that Sandburg's free-verse lines aren't really poetry. In *Good Morning, America* (1928), Sandburg sets forth his own definitions of poetry:

> 66 Poetry is a series of explanations of life, fading off into horizons too swift for explanations. . . .
>
> Poetry is a search for syllables to shoot at the barriers of the unknown and the unknowable. . . .
>
> Poetry is a sliver of the moon lost in the belly of a golden frog. . . .
>
> Poetry is the opening and closing of a door, leaving those who look through to guess about what is seen during a moment. . . .
>
> Poetry is a packsack of invisible keepsakes. 99

More by Carl Sandburg

- *Abe Lincoln Grows Up* (Harcourt Brace), a biography of Lincoln for young readers
- *The American Songbag* (Harcourt Brace), a collection of folk songs, both serious and funny

MAKING MEANINGS

First Thoughts

1. Did the poem remind you of any **tall tales** you've heard before? Describe one, *or* state which yarn in the poem is your favorite and why.

Shaping Interpretations

2. Each of the yarns in the poem takes something real, such as thick fog or sharp curves in a railroad, and **exaggerates** it. Choose two of the yarns, and identify the real things they exaggerate.

3. The long poem that these lines come from is called *The People, Yes*. Which of the adjectives below could describe the people who tell these tall tales?
   - boastful • bold • frightened
   - humorous • imaginative • serious
   - independent • lively • meek • proud

North Woods Lumber Camp by Nancy Travers. Oil on plywood.

CHOICES: Building Your Portfolio

Writer's Notebook

1. Collecting Ideas for Observational Writing

What's the most amazing thing you've ever seen? Freewrite for two or three minutes, describing everything you remember about it.

Creative Writing

2. More Yarns

Write four or five lines to add to the end of "They Have Yarns." Try to make your yarns even more ridiculous, outrageous, and humorous than Sandburg's. You could either go back to your Quickwrite for an idea or start from scratch.

Art

3. Tall Drawing

Draw a **cartoon** illustrating one or more of the unbelievable situations Sandburg describes. You could either copy the relevant lines from the poem as a caption or leave them off and let your classmates guess which lines inspired your drawing.

Oral Performance

4. Tell It Proud

Get together with a group interested in performing Sandburg's poem. Decide how you want to present the poem: You could read it as a chorus or with individual voices, or you could mix the two. You might want to use props or even background music in your performance.

VOCABULARY: PREFIXES AND SUFFIXES

A **prefix** is a word part added to the beginning of a word. A **suffix** is a word part added to the end of a word. Some common prefixes and suffixes are listed in the boxes at the right.

The more prefixes and suffixes you know, the more unfamiliar words you'll be able to figure out. For example, if you know the words *pay, judge,* and *heat,* learning the prefix *pre–* will help you guess what *prepay, prejudge,* and *preheat* mean. Similarly, if you know the words *happy* and *like* and the suffixes *–ly* and *–en,* you can guess what *happily* and *liken* mean. Even if the prefix or suffix is the *only* part of an unknown word you understand, knowing it and using context clues may help you guess the word's meaning.

Prefixes	Meanings	Examples
bi–	two	bilingual; bicycle
co–	with; together	coexist; coauthor
dis–	away; off; opposing	disagree; disregard
fore–	before; front part of	forepaws; foreshadow
mis–	badly; not; wrongly	misbehave; misspell
non–	not	nontoxic; nonfat
post–	after; following	postwar; postgraduate
pre–	before	preview; prehistoric
re–	back; again	rebuild; reelect
sub–	under; beneath	subway; sublease
un–	not; reverse of	uncommon; uncover

Suffixes	Meanings	Examples
Noun –ance, –ancy, –ence, –ity, –tion, –ty	act; quality; state; condition	admittance; constancy; excellence; reality; continuation; safety
Verb –ate, –en, –fy, –ize	become; cause; make	activate; deepen; simplify; socialize
Adjective –able, –ible –ous	able; likely characterized by	comparable; flexible dangerous; mutinous
Adverb –ly	to a certain degree; in a certain way; at a certain time	firmly; angrily

Apply the strategy on the next page.

PECOS BILL AND THE MUSTANG

Make the Connection

My Hero!

Heroes are just like anyone else, only better—bigger, stronger, smarter, braver, craftier. The more fantastic they are, the better. The hero of a **tall tale,** like Pecos Bill, can do anything and everything—all in a larger-than-life way.

With your classmates, brainstorm ideas for the greatest superhero ever.

Quickwrite

Use details from your class brain-storm and your own imagi-nation to invent a hero. Give your hero a name, and de-scribe him or her. What does your hero look like? What superhuman powers does he or she have?

Elements of Literature

Protagonist

The **protagonist** is the main character of a story— the one who gets the action going. The protagonist is usually the hero. Look at the title and the first sentence of the next selection. Who is the protagonist? How do you know?

> A **protagonist** is the main character in a work of literature.
>
> *For more on Protagonist, see the Handbook of Literary Terms.*

Reading Skills and Strategies

Understanding Words by Using Prefixes: Great Starts

A **prefix** is a word part added to the beginning of a word. The prefix *super–,* for example, means "above, beyond, greater than, or better than." Know-ing what a hero is, can you figure out what a superhero is? Knowing what a human is, can you figure out what *superhuman* means?

Background

Literature and Social Studies

Mustangs were horses that ran wild on the plains of the American West. Cowboys would capture and "break" them—tame them for riding. They then rode the mustangs while herding cattle.

MEET THE WRITER

"Big Shoes to Fill"

66 If Bill's tale seems slightly tall here and there, it may be well to recall that the whole story of America is a tall tale, a tale of seem-ingly impossible obstacles overcome. . . . So there is a little bit of the great Pecos Bill in each of us. **99**

That's the way **Harold W. Felton** (1902–   ) introduces his "biography" of Pecos Bill—a collection of hundreds of tales and whoppers about the king of the cowboys. Felton worked as a lawyer in New York City long before he started writing, but he won fame as a folklorist and writer of history books. Felton be-lieves ordinary people can possess larger-than-life spirits, too.

go.hrw.com
LEO 8-6

Pecos Bill and the Mustang

Harold W. Felton

Did you ever hear of Pecos Bill? He was a cowboy. The first cowboy. He invented cowboys and everything about them and he became the hero of all the other rootin'-tootin', high-falootin', straight-shootin' cowboys.

He could shoot a bumblebee in the eye at sixty paces, and he was a man who was not afraid to shake hands with lightning.

But before he became a man, he was a boy, and before he was a boy, he was a baby.

That seems only reasonable, doesn't it?

Bill was born a long time ago, away out in the wild and woolly west.

It was so long ago the sun was only about the size of a dime. Of course, money went farther in those days, so naturally a dime was bigger than it is now.

Bill always obeyed his parents. They used to say he was the best child they ever saw, and that was quite a compliment because he had seventeen brothers and sisters.

One day, Bill's family saw smoke from a new neighbor's chimney. It was beyond the river and two hills but Bill's paw allowed the country was getting too crowded. Bill's maw agreed. They liked plenty of elbowroom, so they decided to move farther west.

So they loaded their wagon with all their household goods and their eighteen children, and off they went over the Texas plains, across the rivers, and over the mountains and the valleys.

They came to the Pecos River and crossed it. Then the left hind wheel hit a prairie-dog hole. The wagon lurched, and Bill fell out.

He landed headfirst on a rock. The rock broke into a thousand pieces, and Bill's head was bruised, a little.

The wagon juggled and rumbled away into the distance, toward the setting sun.

When Bill came to, he didn't know where he was or who he was. He didn't know what to do or how to do it.

He didn't remember a single thing about his life, his maw and paw, or his seventeen brothers and sisters.

He was all alone on the west bank of the Pecos River in West Texas.

He didn't know his age, either, so no one

HE BECAME THE HERO OF ALL THE OTHER ROOTIN'-TOOTIN', HIGH-FALOOTIN', STRAIGHT-SHOOTIN' COWBOYS.

knows exactly how old he was. But he was a little shaver, only about half as high as the withers° of a pinto pony.

An old coyote rescued him. The coyote's name was El Viejo, which means "old man" in Spanish.

El Viejo didn't know what the little boy's name was or what to call him. Finally, he called him Pecos Bill, and took him to live with the coyotes.

So Pecos Bill grew up with the coyotes. He learned to walk like a coyote. He learned to talk like a coyote. He thought he *was* a coyote. That was only natural, considering that he had lost his memory when he fell out of the wagon and broke the rock into a thousand pieces and bruised his head, a little.

His playmates were coyote pups. He wrestled with them and they yipped and yapped and growled playfully at him and nipped each other.

Bill learned to howl at the moon. He learned to scratch his ear with his foot, and he could run fast enough to catch a rabbit.

When he got older he could run down an antelope without losing his breath.

Then, one day, Pecos Bill met a *man*. The man said, "Who are you?"

"I'm a coyote pup," Bill growled.

"You don't look like a coyote to me," said the man. "You look like a human."

°**withers:** highest part of a horse's back.

"I am not a human," Bill snarled. "I'm a coyote and that's all there is to it!"

"If you're a coyote, where is your tail?" the man asked with a grin.

Bill looked over his shoulder. He couldn't see a tail. He must have a tail. All the coyotes Bill knew had long, bushy tails.

He must have a tail. He must. After all, he was a coyote, wasn't he? At least he thought he was.

Bill looked around again, this time under his arm. He couldn't see a tail. Not even a little one.

There must be some mistake!

He backed up to a stream and looked at his reflection in the water.

It was true! He didn't have a tail! No tail at all!

If he didn't have a tail, he couldn't be a coyote.

If he wasn't a coyote, he must be a human.

And that is how Pecos Bill discovered he was a human and not a coyote.

Then he decided that if he wasn't a coyote, he shouldn't be living with coyotes.

So he barked "goodbye" to El Viejo and he yipped "so long pals" to his coyote pup friends and started off with the man.

"As long as I'm a human, I'm going to be a cowboy," he said. "And if I'm going to be a *cowboy,* I'll need a horse."

"What's a cowboy?" the man asked.

"That's easy. He's a man who rounds up cattle," Bill answered.

"You won't need a horse," the man said. "We only have tame cows and you don't need a horse for tame cows."

"There are wild longhorn cattle around these parts," said Bill. "There are wild horses and other wild critters. No sir! I'll need a horse because I aim to round up and catch those wild longhorns!"

But Pecos Bill was too big for an ordinary horse.

The biggest animal in that part of the country was a mountain lion. A long-haired, long-tailed, long-toothed mountain lion.

Bill captured the mountain lion and broke him to ride.

The mountain lion didn't like it much, at first. He was quite peevish about it. He was as peevish as a bee with a boil.

But he soon learned to like Pecos Bill and became quite friendly.

He liked to have Pecos scratch him behind the ears. That made him purr. When Bill's mountain lion purred, he sounded like a freight train rumbling by.

By this time, Bill was almost full grown, and he was big. No one knows exactly *how* big, but he was big enough to chase bears with a switch.

Bill slept on a gravel bed, between sandpaper sheets. He used a soft rock for a pillow. On cold nights, he pulled a blanket of fog over him.

He shaved with his bowie knife. Not with the knife itself—it was too sharp. He used its shadow to shave, as it was quite sharp enough.

One day, a rattlesnake bit him. It was a tough, mean rattlesnake and challenged Bill to a fight.

Pecos Bill was a gentle man. He didn't like to fight, but the rattler insisted.

Bill won that fight, too, and he used the rattlesnake for a *quirt,* or riding whip. The rattler liked the job. It was something not every rattlesnake got a chance to do.

It was quite a sight to see Pecos Bill riding his mountain lion on a dead run, kicking up a cloud of dust and sandburs and using the rattler for a quirt.

But Pecos Bill wanted a horse. To be exact, he wanted the Famous Pacing Mustang of the Prairies.

No one had ever been able to catch the mustang and ride him. They said even bullets could not stop him. Few men had ever even seen him.

Pecos Bill thought the Famous Pacing Mustang of the Prairies was the horse for him.

He rode far out on the prairie until he found the herd of wild horses led by the great Pacing Mustang.

He gasped when he saw the horse. He was a palomino. His shining coat was the color of a new-minted gold coin. His mane and tail were snowy white. He had four white stockings and a white blaze between the eyes, and Bill made up his mind to capture him that very day.

HE WAS AS PEEVISH AS A BEE WITH A BOIL.

THERE WAS PIN WHEELING, HIGH DIVING, SUN FISHING, HIGH FLYING.

Bill mounted his mountain lion. He lifted his quirt and his rattlesnake rattled.

The mountain lion roared and dug his claws in the ground. Cactus and tumbleweed swirled up in the dusty air as he shot forward like a bullet.

The Famous Pacing Mustang of the Prairies saw them coming and began to run away. But it was too late. Bill's galloping mountain lion rushed toward the mustang. They were running side by side.

In another instant, the mustang would draw ahead. There was no time to lose. Bill had to act! At once!

The mountain lion roared. The rattlesnake rattled. Pecos Bill dropped his quirt and sprang from the mountain lion to the back of the Famous Pacing Mustang of the Prairies!

No one had ever been astride the mustang before.

The mustang jumped and bucked and twisted and turned. But Pecos Bill kept his seat.

"Yippee!" Bill yelled.

The mustang ran and kicked. Bill stayed on.

The mustang reared and pawed the air. Bill could not be thrown off.

The horse covered the land from the Platte River in Nebraska to the Pecos River in Texas, from the Mississippi River to the Pacific Ocean.

There was pin wheeling, high diving, sun fishing, high flying, and all the other tricks of a bucking bronco.

But Bill stayed astride, waving his hat and shouting at the top of his voice, "Yippee-ee-ee!"

Pecos thought the mustang would never stop bucking, so he spoke to him. He told the horse how he wanted to be a cowboy, how he wanted to ride the range and lasso wild longhorn cattle and drive them to market.

He told the mustang he needed a good horse to help him. If he didn't have a horse that was good enough he might quit trying to be a cowboy and go back to being a coyote again.

"I won't argue with you anymore," Pecos said. "I won't try to break you anymore. If you don't want to help me, you go your way, and I'll go mine."

Bill turned away and lay down to drink from the river.

The Famous Pacing Mustang of the Prairies came to his side. He put his big nose in the water and he drank with Bill.

It was a sign that the mustang wanted to belong to Pecos Bill.

They both drank. They drank so much the river went down three inches.

Pecos Bill had a horse at last!

And that is how Pecos Bill got his first horse and became the first cowboy.

Before You Read

PAUL BUNYAN

Make the Connection

Talk About *That*

*Talk about workin', when he
    swung his axe
You could hear it ring for a mile
    and a half.*

That's the writer Shel Silverstein "talking about" the legendary logger—and **tall-tale** superhero—Paul Bunyan. Now, you're probably thinking that saying someone could swing an ax so hard you could hear it a mile away is a pretty big **exaggeration**—but Silverstein's just getting warmed up. Wait until you see what else he has to say about the great Paul Bunyan.

Quickwrite

Use the phrase "Talk about . . . " in a few exaggerations of your own. Here are some starters:

- Talk about big . . .
- Talk about popular . . .
- Talk about running . . .
- Talk about climbing . . .

 go.hrw.com
LEO 8-6

Elements of Literature

Standard English

Standard English is the most widely accepted form of English. It's the kind of English we hear in evening newscasts, for example. In contrast, **dialect** is the kind of language used in a particular region or by a certain group of people.

In this poem you'll see many words and phrases that aren't part of standard English, like *ain't* and *talkin'*. Notice how these spellings create the sound of a tale told aloud.

> **S**tandard English is the form of English that is most widely accepted in the United States.
>
> *For more on Standard English, see the Handbook of Literary Terms.*

Reading Skills and Strategies

Understanding Words with Suffixes: The End

A **suffix** is a word part added to the end of a word. One common suffix is *–ing*. The suffix *–ing* at the end of a verb indicates that action is being taken. *Talk* becomes *talking, walk* becomes *walking,* and so on.

Sometimes writers leave the *g* off *–ing* to make a word sound the way some people say it—*talkin'* or *walkin'*. The apostrophe at the end indicates that the *g* has been left off. See how many words like these you can spot as you read "Paul Bunyan."

Paul and Babe at Rest (1992) by Nancy Travers. Oil on plywood.

PAUL BUNYAN

Shel Silverstein

He rode through the woods on a big blue ox,
He had fists as hard as choppin' blocks,
Five hundred pounds and nine feet tall . . . that's Paul.

Talk about workin', when he swung his axe
5   You could hear it ring for a mile and a half.
Then he'd yell "Timber!" and down she'd fall . . . for Paul.

Talk about drinkin', that man's so mean
That he'd never drink nothin' but kerosene,
And a five-gallon can is a little bit small . . . for Paul.

10 Talk about tough, well he once had a fight
With a thunderstorm on a cold dark night.
I ain't sayin' who won,
But it don't storm at all . . . 'round here . . . thanks to Paul.

He was ninety years old when he said with a sigh,
15 "I think I'm gonna lay right down and die
'Cause sunshine and sorrow, I've seen it all" . . . says Paul.

He says, "There ain't no man alive can kill me,
Ain't no woman 'round can thrill me,
And I think heaven just might be a ball" . . . says Paul.

20 So he died . . . and we cried.

It took eighteen men just to bust the ground,
It took twenty-four more just to lower him down.
And we covered him up and we figured that was all . . . for Paul.

But late one night the trees started shakin',
25 The dogs started howlin' and the earth started quakin',
And out of the ground with a "Hi, y'all" . . . come Paul!

He shook the dirt from off of his clothes,
He scratched his butt and he wiped his nose.
"Y'know, bein' dead wasn't no fun at all" . . . says Paul.

30 He says, "Up in heaven they got harps on their knees,
They got clouds and wings but they got no trees.
I don't think that's much of a heaven at all" . . . says Paul.

So he jumps on his ox with a fare-thee-well,
He says, "I'll find out if they's trees in hell."
35 And he rode away, and that was all . . . we ever seen . . . of Paul.

But the next time you hear a "Timber!" yell
That sounds like it's comin' from the pits of hell,
Then a weird and devilish ghostly wail
Like somebody choppin' on the devil's tail,
40 Then a shout, a call, a crash, a fall—
That ain't no mortal man at all . . . that's Paul!

MEET THE WRITER

"The Wonderful Stuff . . . in Life"

Like Paul Bunyan, **Shel Silverstein** (1932–1999) had a huge
appetite for life, an amazing array of talents, and an independent
streak a mile long. He once said:

66 I want to go everywhere, look and listen to everything. You
can go crazy with some of the wonderful stuff there is in life. 99

Silverstein said he turned to writing and drawing because he
wasn't good at sports, dancing, or attracting girls. He grew up to be good at
singing, cartooning, acting, and writing songs, poetry, and plays. His best-selling
collections of poetry and drawings, *Where the Sidewalk Ends* (Harper) and
A Light in the Attic (Harper), are read by young and old.

Silverstein was fiercely private and once said:

66 I won't go on television, because who am I talking to? Johnny Carson?
The camera? Twenty million people I can't see? Uh-uh. And I won't give any
more interviews. 99

That 1975 quote is one of the last that he gave any reporter.

MAKING MEANINGS
PECOS BILL AND THE MUSTANG
PAUL BUNYAN

First Thoughts

1. What comic-book or storybook superheroes do Pecos Bill and Paul Bunyan remind you of?

Shaping Interpretations

2. **Protagonists** usually have to face **antagonists,** people or forces that oppose them. What antagonists do Pecos Bill and Paul Bunyan meet? Which antagonist is Paul still fighting?

3. Richard Erdoes (author of "Coyote Steals the Sun and Moon," page 463) says that the essence of American legends, especially of Western tales, is **exaggeration.** Read aloud your favorite exaggeration from "Pecos Bill and the Mustang" or "Paul Bunyan." Explain why it's an exaggeration and why you like it.

4. **Tall tales,** like **myths,** often tell of superheroes who create natural features of the earth or think up key inventions. In one story, for example, Paul Bunyan digs out the Great Lakes because he needs watering troughs for his giant blue ox, Babe. What does Pecos Bill invent?

Extending the Text

5. Traditional stories in many cultures feature a hero raised by wild animals. Which of the heroes in these two selections is raised by wild creatures? What other stories do you know of in which the hero is raised by animals? (What special things might the hero learn from animals?)

6. Think of what you know about life on the American frontier. In your opinion, why would settlers create **tall-tale** heroes like Pecos Bill or Paul Bunyan? Do we tell tales about superheroes like them today?

Challenging the Text

7. Read either "Pecos Bill and the Mustang" or "Paul Bunyan" again. Would you describe the way it's written as funny, babyish, or something else? Give examples from the story to support your opinion.

> **Reading Check**
>
> Have a partner time you as you retell the story of Pecos Bill in two minutes or less. Then, time your partner as he or she retells the story of Paul Bunyan in one minute or less. When you're finished, check to see if you forgot any details.

CHOICES: Building Your Portfolio

Writer's Notebook

1. Collecting Ideas for Observational Writing

Much of the color and interest of "Pecos Bill and the Mustang" and "Paul Bunyan" comes from the writers' language, which you may find more fun to read than **standard English.** Their stories sound just like people talking. Listen to people you know—your friends, your family, even yourself. Jot down some of the words and expressions you hear in casual conversation.

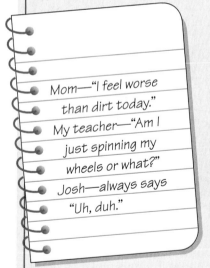

Mom—"I feel worse than dirt today."
My teacher—"Am I just spinning my wheels or what?"
Josh—always says "Uh, duh."

Creative Writing

2. A Super Superhero

Using ideas from your Quickwrites (see pages 501 and 506), write your own story about a superhero. You might begin the way Felton does: *"Did you ever hear of _____? He/she was a _____, the first _____.*" Fill in the first blank with your hero's name and the second and third with his or her occupation. Remember that exaggeration is a must.

Art

3. Supertoons

Tell the adventures of one of these superheroes in the form of a series of cartoons. Use quotes from the story as your captions. Remember to exaggerate your hero's looks and adventures.

Debate

4. American Made

Choose Pecos Bill, Paul Bunyan, or another American tall-tale hero (maybe John Henry, Captain Stormalong, or Davy Crockett). Debate this question with a partner: Could this hero have come from another country, or is he or she uniquely American? Use examples of the hero's personality, speech, and behavior to support your position.

Art/Language

5. It's a Bird, It's a Plane—Wait, It *Is* a Bird

If a superhero is superhuman, what would a superbird be? How about a superpuppy, supergiraffe, or superworm? Draw your own superanimal, and describe its supercharacteristics. Use a dictionary or another reference work to help you invent an adjective for your superanimal. (For example, a superdog would be super-canine.)

Language Study

6. She's *Fabulous!*

Working with a partner or a small group, draw up a list of adjectives that could be used to describe a superhero. Here's the catch: Each adjective must contain a **prefix** or a **suffix** (or both), which you should underline. (For help, check the lists of prefixes and suffixes on pages 500, 727, and 728.) Use these adjectives to get started: *unconquerable, monstrous, invincible.* You might use your adjectives in your own story or cartoon (see Choices 2 and 3).

GRAMMAR LINK   MINI-LESSON

Don't Double Your Subject with a Pronoun

What's wrong with these sentences?

INCORRECT   Pecos Bill he was the first cowboy.

One day, Bill's family they saw smoke from a new neighbor's chimney.

The wagon it juggled and rumbled away into the distance.

The problem is that in each sentence an unnecessary pronoun is used after the subject. This error is called a **double subject.** Here is one way to correct the sentences:

CORRECTED   Pecos Bill ~~he~~ was the first cowboy.

One day, Bill's family ~~they~~ saw smoke from a new neighbor's chimney.

The wagon ~~it~~ juggled and rumbled away into the distance.

In what other way could each sentence be corrected? (Remember that only one subject—either a noun or a pronoun—is needed.)

Try It Out
Edit the following paragraph to correct the double subjects.

Some people they say that the tall tale was invented in America. Many of these stories they began in the frontier. Davy Crockett he is a tall-tale hero, as are John Henry and Pecos Bill. Pecos Bill he was created by cowboys. African Americans they created John Henry. Paul Bunyan he was a hero of the Northern lumber camps.

VOCABULARY   HOW TO OWN A WORD

Specialized Vocabulary: All About Horses

➤ In history, science, and math—in fact, in all your classes—you learn specialized vocabulary. For example, you might learn the words underlined in the sentences below in a science or biology class. You might also find these words in an encyclopedia article about horses or in a novel or movie with a Western setting. Use a **dictionary** to look up every underlined word you can't define or explain. Then, answer each question.

1. How can you tell a palomino from a pinto?
2. True or false: All horses have withers, but only some have stockings and a blaze. Define these words.
3. Which would you rather ride—a pacing horse or a bucking one? Why?
4. How is a mustang different from a bronco—or is it?

➤ With a partner, make up five questions about special terms from a subject you have studied. Then, exchange papers with another team, and answer their questions.

Before You Read

THE CREMATION OF SAM MCGEE

Make the Connection

Going to Extremes

It was so hot, you could fry an egg on the sidewalk.

Spinners of tall tales love to amaze and amuse their listeners with exaggerated claims like that one. Can you top it?

Quickwrite

Choose two of the starters below, and make up your own humorous exaggerations.

- It was so cold . . .
- It rained so hard . . .
- The snow was so deep . . .

Elements of Literature

Exaggeration

The key element of all **tall tales** is **exaggeration**— stretching the truth as high and wide as it will go. As you read this tall tale in rhyme, notice how exaggeration is used to create a **mood,** or feeling, that may not be quite what you expected. (*Cremation* is the burning of a body to ashes.)

Exaggeration is the use of overstatement, usually to create a comic effect.

For more on Exaggeration, see page 480 and the Handbook of Literary Terms.

Reading Skills and Strategies

Describing Mental Images: Appealing to the Senses

When writers describe something, they use words that appeal to the senses. When you read, you use those sensory details to make **mental images,** or imagined pictures. As you read Robert Service's poem, notice how you use his words to help you picture the frozen Klondike.

When you read descriptive writing, note that

- most images are visual, but images often appeal to several senses at once

- writers often choose details that show how they feel about what they describe

Background

Literature and Geography

In 1896, thousands of fortune hunters rushed north, braving bitter cold and deep snow. Gold had been found in northwestern Canada, in the Klondike region of the Yukon Territory. The town of Dawson, at the center of the region, became the Yukon's capital.

Like many other gold seekers, Sam McGee was unprepared for the Klondike's seven-month winter, when the temperature sometimes falls as low as -68° F. This poem tells his story.

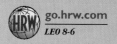

go.hrw.com
LEO 8-6

The Cremation of Sam McGee

Robert W. Service

> There are strange things done in the midnight sun
>   By the men who moil° for gold;
> The Arctic trails have their secret tales
>   That would make your blood run cold;
> 5 The Northern Lights have seen queer sights,
>   But the queerest they ever did see
> Was that night on the marge° of Lake Lebarge
>   I cremated Sam McGee.

2. **moil:** labor.

7. **marge:** edge.

Now Sam McGee was from Tennessee, where the
    cotton blooms and blows.
Why he left his home in the South to roam 'round the
10   Pole, God only knows.
He was always cold, but the land of gold seemed to
    hold him like a spell;
Though he'd often say in his homely way that he'd
    "sooner live in hell."

On a Christmas Day we were mushing our way over the
    Dawson trail.
Talk of your cold! through the parka's fold it stabbed
    like a driven nail.
If our eyes we'd close, then the lashes froze till some-
15   times we couldn't see;
It wasn't much fun, but the only one to whimper was
    Sam McGee.

And that very night, as we lay packed tight in our robes
    beneath the snow,
And the dogs were fed, and the stars o'erhead were
    dancing heel and toe,
He turned to me, and "Cap," says he, "I'll cash in this
    trip, I guess;
And if I do, I'm asking that you won't refuse my last
20   request."

Well, he seemed so low that I couldn't say no; then he
    says with a sort of moan:
"It's the cursèd cold, and it's got right hold till I'm
    chilled clean through to the bone.
Yet 'tain't being dead—it's my awful dread of the icy
    grave that pains;
So I want you to swear that, foul or fair, you'll cremate
    my last remains."

A pal's last need is a thing to heed, so I swore I would
25   not fail;
And we started on at the streak of dawn; but God! he
    looked ghastly pale.
He crouched on the sleigh, and he raved all day of his
    home in Tennessee;
And before nightfall a corpse was all that was left of
    Sam McGee.

Sunlit Nights and Northern Lights

If you went to the Yukon, you might see some strange sights your-self. During the summer the tilt of the earth's axis increases the North Pole's exposure to the sun. As a result, areas close to the pole have very long summer days. The regions north of the Arctic Circle have twenty-four hours of continuous daylight at least one day a year, during which the sun actually shines at midnight.

If you visited during the winter, you could view another Arctic wonder: the northern lights (aurora borealis). These are red and green displays of light that appear in the night sky, caused by electrical disturbances in the atmosphere above the North Pole.

There wasn't a breath in that land of death, and I
    hurried, horror-driven,
With a corpse half hid that I couldn't get rid, because
30   of a promise given;
It was lashed to the sleigh, and it seemed to say: "You
    may tax your brawn and brains,
But you promised true, and it's up to you to cremate
    those last remains."

Now a promise made is a debt unpaid, and the trail has
    its own stern code.
In the days to come, though my lips were dumb, in my
    heart how I cursed that load.
In the long, long night, by the lone firelight, while the
35   huskies, round in a ring,
Howled out their woes to the homeless snows——
    O God! how I loathed the thing.

And every day that quiet clay seemed to heavy and
    heavier grow;
And on I went, though the dogs were spent and the
    grub was getting low;

The trail was bad, and I felt half mad, but I swore I
    would not give in;
And I'd often sing to the hateful thing, and it
40   hearkened° with a grin.

Till I came to the marge of Lake Lebarge, and a derelict°
    there lay;
It was jammed in the ice, but I saw in a trice it was
    called the "Alice May."
And I looked at it, and I thought a bit, and I looked at
    my frozen chum;
Then "Here," said I, with a sudden cry, "is my cre-ma-
    tor-ium."

Some planks I tore from the cabin floor, and I lit the
45   boiler fire;
Some coal I found that was lying around, and I heaped
    the fuel higher;
The flames just soared, and the furnace roared—such a
    blaze you seldom see;
And I burrowed a hole in the glowing coal, and I
    stuffed in Sam McGee.

Then I made a hike, for I didn't like to hear him sizzle
    so;
And the heavens scowled, and the huskies howled, and
50   the wind began to blow.
It was icy cold, but the hot sweat rolled down my
    cheeks, and I don't know why;
And the greasy smoke in an inky cloak went streaking
    down the sky.

I do not know how long in the snow I wrestled with
    grisly° fear;
But the stars came out and they danced about ere again
    I ventured near;
I was sick with dread, but I bravely said: "I'll just take a
55   peep inside.
I guess he's cooked, and it's time I looked"; . . . then
    the door I opened wide.

And there sat Sam, looking cool and calm, in the heart
    of the furnace roar;
And he wore a smile you could see a mile, and he said:

40. hearkened (härk′ənd):
listened carefully.

41. derelict (der′ə·likt′):
abandoned ship.

53. grisly: here, caused by
something horrible.

"Please close that door.
It's fine in here, but I greatly fear you'll let in the cold
    and storm——
Since I left Plumtree, down in Tennessee, it's the first
60   time I've been warm."

There are strange things done in the midnight sun
    By the men who moil for gold;
The Arctic trails have their secret tales
    That would make your blood run cold;
65   *The Northern Lights have seen queer sights,*
    But the queerest they ever did see
Was that night on the marge of Lake Lebarge
    I cremated Sam McGee.

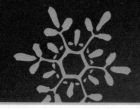

MEET THE WRITER

"A Story Jack London Never Got"

Born in Lancashire, England, **Robert W. Service** (1874–1958) immigrated to Canada at the age of twenty. After traveling along the Canadian Pacific coast, he took a job with a bank and was transferred to the Yukon Territory. He wrote his most popular poems there, including "The Cremation of Sam McGee." The poem was inspired by a story Service heard at a party where he was feeling awkward and out of place:

66 I was staring gloomily at a fat fellow across the table. He was a big mining man from Dawson, and he scarcely acknowledged his introduction to a little bank clerk. Portly and important, he was smoking a big cigar with a gilt band. Suddenly he said: 'I'll tell you a story Jack London never got.' Then he spun a yarn of a man who cremated his pal. It had a surprise climax which occasioned much laughter. I did not join, for I had a feeling that here was a decisive moment of destiny. I still remember how a great excitement usurped me. Here was a perfect ballad subject. The fat man who ignored me went his way to bankruptcy, but he had pointed me the road to fortune. 99

Service left the party and spent the next six hours wandering through the frozen woods in the bright moonlight, writing verse after verse in his head. When he finally went to bed, the poem was complete and Service was satisfied; he didn't even put it on paper until the next day.

More by Robert W. Service

You'll find "The Cremation of Sam McGee," along with "The Shooting of Dan McGrew" and other poems, in *The Best of Robert Service* (Perigee).

Maiden-Savin' Sam: A Ballad

In the wild ol' West there lived a man,
A man by the title of "Maiden-Savin' Sam."
Saving maidens was his hobby and he did it very well,
Bragged about his victories—great stories did he tell.

> CHORUS:
> *Sam, Sam, Maiden-Savin' Sam,*
> *Greatest maiden saver in all of the land.*
> *Saved all the short ones, all the tall ones, too,*
> *With his hat on his head and spurs on his shoes.*

"One day a herd of buffalo crossed the land,
Biggest gaw-darned herd in all the land!
I was a-watchin' them, watchin' was I,"
Sam began the story, with a twinkle in his eye.

> CHORUS:
> *Sam, Sam, Maiden-Savin' Sam . . .*

"Now as I was watchin'—'Uh-oh,' says I,
'In the herd's way a pretty maiden does lie.
She's gonna get trampled,' I thought to myself.
'No longer will she be in such radiatin' health.'"

> CHORUS:
> *Sam, Sam, Maiden-Savin' Sam . . .*

"I looked all around, and what did I see?
A big, shiny pitchfork just a-waitin' for me.
I picked it up, threw it far and wide,
And now them buffalo are buffalo hide."

> CHORUS:
> *Sam, Sam, Maiden-Savin' Sam . . .*

Sam now lies deep in his grave,
Chased one too many bears into a cave.
But never we'll forget him—he was the very best
Of all the maiden savers in all of the West!

—Jenny Ellison
Webb School of Knoxville
Knoxville, Tennessee

MAKING MEANINGS

First Thoughts

1. What did you like best (or least) about "The Cremation of Sam McGee"? Why has it been popular for so long, in your opinion?

Shaping Interpretations

2. Pick your favorite two or three sensory details that help you picture the frozen landscape or feel the cold. Describe the **mental images** these words put into your head.

3. This poem uses both end rhymes and **internal rhymes**—rhymes contained within lines, such as *done* and *sun* in the first line. List three more pairs of internal rhymes in the poem. How do they help to give it rhythm?

Reading Check

a. Why is Sam McGee in the Klondike?

b. What does Sam ask the speaker to do? Why?

c. What surprise does the speaker meet with when he carries out Sam's request?

Connecting with the Text

4. Do you feel that all promises must be kept? If you were the speaker, would you keep this one? Explain.

CHOICES: Building Your Portfolio

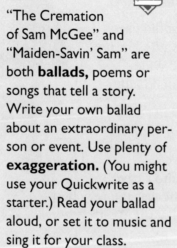

Writer's Notebook

1. Collecting Ideas for Observational Writing

In "The Cremation of Sam McGee," Service helps us see and feel the frozen **setting.** Think of a *place* where you've been or a *natural event* you've witnessed or experienced (such as an earthquake or a heat wave). Jot down all the details you remember that might help readers feel as if they were there.

Creative Writing/Music

2. Boggling Ballad

"The Cremation of Sam McGee" and "Maiden-Savin' Sam" are both **ballads,** poems or songs that tell a story. Write your own ballad about an extraordinary person or event. Use plenty of **exaggeration.** (You might use your Quickwrite as a starter.) Read your ballad aloud, or set it to music and sing it for your class.

Oral Interpretation

3. Rhyme and Reason

Rehearse and perform a dramatic reading of "The Cremation of Sam McGee." What **mood,** or feeling, will your reading create?

Research/Geography

4. Freeze or Fry

Using the Internet or the library, research one of the coldest or hottest places on earth. How do people survive there?

Davy Is Born

from **Yankee Thunder: The Legendary Life of Davy Crockett**

Irwin Shapiro

"I can ride a streak o' lightnin', hug a bear too close for comfort, and whip my weight in wildcats!"

The morning Davy Crockett was born, Davy's Pa came busting out of his cabin in Tennessee alongside the Nola-chucky River. He fired three shots into the air, gave a whoop, and said, "I've got me a son. His name is Davy Crockett, and he'll be the greatest hunter in all creation."

When he said that, the sun rose up in the sky like a ball of fire. The wind howled riproariously. Thunder boomed, and all the critters and varmints of the forest let out a moan.

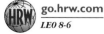 go.hrw.com
LEO 8-6

MEET THE WRITER

"Which Davy Crockett?"

Irwin Shapiro (1911–1981) studied painting in college, but his interest in American folklore led him to a career in writing. He wrote more than forty books, including a collection of tall tales and books for children about such legendary figures as John Henry, Paul Bunyan, and Daniel Boone. In his introductory note to *Yankee Thunder: The Legendary Life of Davy Crockett,* he writes:

❝ The biographer of Davy Crockett is immediately confronted with a problem: Which Davy Crockett shall he write about? For if there ever was a man of multiple identity, that man was Davy Crockett.

First of all there was—or at least there exists some fairly reliable evidence to that effect—the flesh-and-blood Crockett, the frontiersman and hunter of early Tennessee. There was the historical Crockett, with his heroic exploits at the Alamo duly recorded in history. There was the political Crockett, a figure alternately built up and deflated by the Jacksonites and anti-Jacksonites. . . . And then there was the mythical Crockett, the Crockett of legend and folksay, of the tall tales and fireside yarns and almanac stories—the veritable yaller blossom of the forest, half horse, half alligator, with a little touch of snapping turtle, the ring-tailed roarer who could bring a coon out of a tree, ride a streak of lightning, wade the Mississippi, and come down off the Peak o' Day with a piece of sunrise in his pocket.

It was to this last Crockett, in the grand American tradition of Paul Bunyan, John Henry, Old Stormalong, and Pecos Bill, that I turned as being obviously the most credible, authentic, significant, and true. **❞**

READ ON

Women of Valor

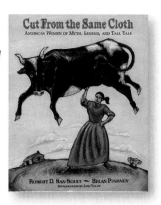

In *Cut From the Same Cloth: American Women of Myth, Legend, and Tall Tale* (Philomel), Robert D. San Souci proves that males aren't the only ones with a gift for sneaky tricks and whopping lies. Here are the adventures of Molly Cotton-Tail, Brer Rabbit's clever wife; Sister Fox, the brains behind Brother Coyote; and others including the Star Maiden, Annie Christmas, and Sweet Betsey from Pike.

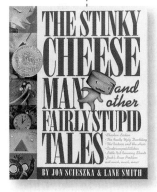

Fractured Folklore

You may have heard the stories of the ugly duckling, the frog prince, and Cinderella more times than you'd like to remember—but what about the *really* ugly duckling, the *other* frog prince, and Cinderumpelstiltskin, "the girl who really blew it"? You'll find these and more in Jon Scieszka and Lane Smith's *The Stinky Cheese Man and Other Fairly Stupid Tales* (Viking).

Trickster Treats

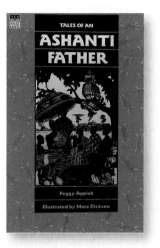

In *Tales of an Ashanti Father* (Beacon Press), Peggy Appiah reveals how the great trickster Ananse the Spider outwits the python and how he's punished for his bad manners. You'll also find out why the lizard stretches his neck, why the leopard has spots, and more in this collection of tales from Ghana.

Other Picks

- Mark Twain, *The Adventures of Tom Sawyer* (available in the HRW library). Tom gets in and out of more trouble than you can imagine in this comic novel set in frontier America.

- Joseph Bruchac, *Hoop Snakes, Hide Behinds, & Side-Hill Winders: Adirondack Tall Tales* (Crossing Press). Read about a mosquito the size of a cow, the pit bulltrout, and other unlikely forms of wildlife.

- Richard Chase, *American Folk Tales and Songs* (Dover). Sample Appalachian humor and culture with "Jack tales" (about the trickster hero of "Jack and the Beanstalk" fame), tall tales, ballads, and jokes.

Writer's Workshop

**Technology
H E L P**

See Writer's Workshop 1
CD-ROM. *Assignment:
Observational Writing.*

ASSIGNMENT

**Write an essay de-
scribing something
you've observed.**

AIM

To inform.

AUDIENCE

**Your teacher and
classmates.**

DESCRIPTIVE WRITING

OBSERVATIONAL WRITING

For your **observational writing** assignment, you'll observe your
subject closely and write a detailed **description** of what you see.

Professional Model

*In this excerpt, Mark Twain describes an unusual
person he observed in 1861 while traveling through
Kansas by stagecoach with his brother.*

After supper a woman got in who
lived about fifty miles further on, and
we three had to take turns at sitting
outside with the driver and conductor. Apparently she was not a talka-
tive woman. She would sit there in
the gathering twilight and fasten her
steadfast eyes on a mosquito rooting
into her arm, and slowly she would
raise her other hand till she had got
his range, and then she would launch
a slap at him that would have jolted a
cow; and after that she would sit and
contemplate the corpse with tranquil
satisfaction—for she never missed
her mosquito; she was a dead shot at
short range. She never removed a
carcass, but left them there for bait. I
sat by this grim Sphinx and watched
her kill thirty or forty mosquitoes—
watched her, and waited for her to
say something, but she never did.

*Writer clearly
identifies the
subject of the
observation.*

*Writer helps the
reader picture
the subject by
presenting a
detailed
description of
her behavior.*

*Writer's choice
of words and
selection of
details reveal his
attitude toward
the subject: He
finds her odd
and comical.*

—Mark Twain, from *Roughing It*

Prewriting

1. Writer's Notebook

Go back to the notes you made in your Writer's Notebook for this collection. Is there a person, a place, or a thing mentioned in one of your entries you'd like to explore further? Does one of the assignments give you an idea for a different subject? If not, try responding to the Freewriting prompt below.

2. Freewriting

Write whatever comes to mind about three of these topics:

*   someone you see frequently but don't know very well
*   someone you see frequently but don't know at all
*   a place where you went on vacation
*   a place where you go every day
*   a place where you used to spend a lot of time
*   the roughest weather you've ever seen
*   what you see from a classroom window (or from a window at home)
*   your room
*   an animal you have observed (ant, worm, bird, cat, gerbil)
*   a scientific experiment you've observed (if you want to be a scientist, you should be skilled at observational writing)

3. Choosing a Subject

Before deciding on your subject, ask yourself these questions:

a. Can I observe this subject directly? If not, can I picture it clearly enough to write a vivid description of it?

b. Do I find it interesting? Would it interest a reader?

c. Does the subject provide enough sensory details for a good description?

> *Early every morning, woman in apt. 2C— long red hair, long skirts—tosses peanuts under trees, calls squirrels by name*

What I recall: Her smile, lilting voice; squirrels hurrying to her; out in rain, winter dark, snow

What I observe: From my window—she holds wicker basket with different kinds of nuts; dog walkers say hi but keep their dogs away

To polish your observational skills, practice on the most difficult subject to see objectively—yourself. Picture yourself as you appear right now. What do you look like? How are you dressed? If you were observed by a stranger, what would he or she be able to tell about you from your appearance? Take notes on your observations.

Sensory Details

Sight: face like a rosy apple

Hearing: drip of water from faucet

Smell: sour smell of old milk

Taste: sweet flavor of ice cream

Feeling: scratchy wool sweater

4. Gathering Details

Gather as many details about your subject as you can, either by observing your subject directly or by drawing on your memory. You may find it helpful to use a chart like the one below.

Sensory Details	Events	Impressions
—sound of huge drums pounding —sight of bright cloth —feeling of tropical heat	acrobats making the dragon dance, jumping over bridges	It was fantastic!

An occasional **figure of speech,** or imaginative comparison, can add color to your writing and help your reader picture the subject of your observation. In the Professional Model on page 526, for example, Mark Twain describes a woman killing mosquitoes as a "dead shot," as if she were a big-game hunter, and calls her a "Sphinx," comparing her to the mysterious creature in Greek mythology. (To review figures of speech, go back to pages 41–42.)

5. Organizing

Here are three common ways of organizing ideas and structuring your observational essays.

a. **Spatial order,** describing details according to location—near to far or far to near, left to right or right to left, top to bottom or bottom to top, clockwise or counterclockwise. Spatial order helps readers see an entire scene. It is often used in descriptions of places. (The word *spatial* comes from the Latin word for "space." When spatial order is used, things are described as they are arranged "in a space.")

b. **Order of importance,** putting the most important details at the beginning or at the end for emphasis. Writers may use order of importance to help convey their feelings about a subject. This type of organization works well in descriptions of people and objects.

c. **Chronological order,** arranging details in the order in which they occur or the order in which you notice them as you observe your subject. Chronological order usually works best in descriptions of events. For example, if you were to write about what you observed happening in a scientific experiment, you would probably use chronological order.

Drafting

Before you start your first draft, decide how to arrange your ideas. You can use one of the three patterns of organizing described on page 528 or come up with your own arrangement—whatever works best for your subject and details.

Student Model

In this piece the writer describes an event he observed while celebrating the Chinese New Year with his family in Singapore.

A dragon dance was held, starting in the front yard and gradually making its way inside. This procession was to drive all spirits of evil away from my grandma's house. It was fantastic! In the corner the huge drums were pounded over and over again in steady rhythm as the dragon was dancing around. The dragon was made of a long piece of cloth in a bright design of colors. At the front was a wooden headpiece of a dragon. Two acrobatic professionals would man the dragon, one in the front and one in the back. The headpiece had special features; it could be made to blink and open or close its mouth. The dragon danced around, performing daring feats such as the front part jumping onto the back part and jumping over miniature bridges. The warm weather of the tropics shone down immensely, the dancers sweating, the heat on my back as I stood watching the dancers from the porch.

Writer introduces his subject and gives his opinion of it.

Sensory details (sounds and sights) are used to help the reader imagine the scene.

Writer moves from a close-up on the dragon's head to a description of the dance.

Writer specifies the setting and his position as observer.

—Chris Hoe
San Jose, California

Language/Grammar Link
H E L P

Personal pronouns: page 459. Two pronoun problems: page 471. Pronoun reference: page 479. Pronoun-antecedent agreement: page 495. Don't double your subject with a pronoun: page 511.

Sentence Workshop
H E L P

Varying sentence length: page 531.

Proofreading Tip

Check your pronouns: Have you used the correct form (*I* or *me*, *she* or *her*)? Are antecedents clear? Does the pronoun match its antecedent in number and gender?

Communications Handbook
H E L P

See Proofreaders' Marks.

Evaluating and Revising

1. Peer Response

a. Read your first draft aloud to a classmate. Afterward, ask your partner these questions:

- What did you picture as I was reading?
- What detail can you recall most clearly?
- What confused you?

b. Exchange papers with your partner. Find places in his or her paper where you think details should be added. Write in pencil or attach stick-on notes. (For example, "I'd like to know more about what the fish you caught looked and felt like.") Check to make sure that all pronouns have been used correctly. Exchange papers with your partner again, and use your partner's comments to help you write your second draft.

2. Revising Sentence and Paragraph Length

Look over your essay one last time, **scanning** (reading very quickly) to check sentence and paragraph length.

- Are many of your sentences about the same length? Consider combining some of the short sentences into longer ones or splitting long sentences into shorter ones.

- Are your paragraphs too long? Give your reader a break by dividing long paragraphs into shorter ones, each focusing on one **main idea.**

- Are your paragraphs short and choppy? You may want to add more details to a choppy paragraph or combine it with another paragraph.

"So, then . . . Would that be 'us the people' or 'we the people?'"

Sentence Workshop

VARYING SENTENCE LENGTH

In earlier Sentence Workshops, you learned how to develop a sentence fragment into a full sentence and how to divide a run-on sentence into two or more sentences. You learned how to combine short sentences to create longer ones and how to divide a long sentence into shorter sentences. At this point you may be wondering, how long is a sentence *supposed* to be, anyway?

In fact, there is no one "right" length for a sentence. Paragraphs that include sentences of different lengths make for more interesting reading than paragraphs made up of sentences that are all the same length.

> "At the meeting I sat restlessly, scanning each comfortable matronly face, trying to determine which one hid the secret of Charles. **[21 words.]** None of them looked to me haggard enough. **[8 words.]** No one stood up in the meeting and apologized for the way her son had been acting. **[17 words.]** No one mentioned Charles. **[4 words.]**"
>
> —Shirley Jackson, "Charles" (page 476)

> "Philoprogenitiveness, says we, is strong in semirural communities; therefore, and for other reasons, a kidnapping project ought to do better there than in the radius of newspapers that send reporters out in plain clothes to stir up talk about such things. **[41 words.]** We knew that Summit couldn't get after us with anything stronger than constables and, maybe, some lackadaisical bloodhounds and a diatribe or two in the *Weekly Farmers' Budget*. **[28 words.]** So, it looked good. **[4 words.]**"
>
> —O. Henry, "The Ransom of Red Chief" (page 482)

Writer's Workshop Follow-up: Revising

Count the words in each sentence of your observational writing piece. If most of your sentences are similar in length, try adding variety to your paragraphs by splitting up some of the longer sentences or combining some of the shorter sentences.

Try It Out

Rewrite the following paragraph, changing some of the sentences to vary sentence length. Be sure to compare your rewritten versions in class. Are any two versions alike?

Some of my favorite novels have tricksters as their main characters. Tom Sawyer is an example of a famous trickster in fiction. He is always playing tricks and getting into trouble. Once, his aunt Polly tells him to whitewash the fence. He tricks other children into doing it for him. Another time Tom gives his medicine to his cat. Tom is a troublemaker, but he has a good heart.

Reading for Life

Reading for Different Purposes

Situation

Suppose you are in a library and have a reading list for middle school students. (See the sample list at the right.) Here are strategies to help you select and read a book.

Strategies

Recognize your own purpose for reading.

- Are you searching for information? Do you want to be entertained? Are you choosing a book for a book report or another project?

Identify the main purpose of the book you are examining.

- Skim the book's jacket copy (the copy on the cover) or introduction. Is the book fiction or nonfiction? Is its **main purpose** to **inform,** to **entertain,** or to **influence** (persuade)?

Preview your choice.

- If you are reading a nonfiction book for **information,** scan the table of contents. Skim the book's headings and subheadings. Note if the book has illustrations or **graphic organizers,** such as maps, charts, and time lines.

Reading List

E = easy	A = average	C = challenging
F = fiction	P = poetry	NF = nonfiction

Bombeck, Erma. *Family: The Ties That Bind . . . and Gag* **E, NF**
These wise and witty essays about family life are fun for all ages to read.

Macaulay, David. *The Way Things Work* **C, NF**
This clearly written text explains complicated machinery in a fascinating way.

Silverstein, Shel. *Where the Sidewalk Ends* and *A Light in the Attic* **E, P**
Both of these collections are more popular than the fiction books at many libraries. This poet seems to know exactly how to appeal to young people.

Soto, Gary. *Baseball in April* **E, NF**
These stories are based on Soto's experiences growing up Latino in central California.

- If you are selecting a book to read for **enjoyment,** read the blurb on the back cover to get an idea of what the book is about. Note the author. Have you read other books by this writer? Did you enjoy them? What do you like about this writer's style?

Adjust your reading rate to suit your purpose.

- If you are reading nonfiction to get information on a subject, read closely. **Reread** any passages you don't understand. Use **context clues** or a **glossary** or **dictionary** to find the meanings of unfamiliar words. Take notes.
- If reading for enjoyment, use a comfortable rate.

- For poetry especially, **read aloud** to hear the sounds.

Using the Strategies

1. Which book from the list above would you read to learn new facts?

2. Which book would you be likely to read aloud?

3. What do you think is the main purpose of Erma Bombeck's book on family?

4. Which book would you recommend to a struggling reader?

Extending the Strategies

Use these strategies to select a book for outside reading. Report to your reading group on how useful the strategies are. Would you add any?

Learning for Life

Community Folklore

Problem

Folklore includes many kinds of cultural traditions: customs, jokes, expressions, anecdotes, recipes, objects with special meanings. Even small groups, such as families, schools, and local communities, have their own culture and folklore. As time passes, though, much of this unique material may be lost or forgotten. How can we preserve our folklore?

Project

Collect and record folklore from a community you belong to, such as your family, school, local community, or state.

Preparation

Choose a group you belong to and ask yourself:

- Are there any expressions or jokes that are unique to this group? How did they start?

- Which holidays or special events are most important to my community? How do we celebrate them? (Think about food, clothing, and activities.)

- Are there any objects of special significance to the group? What are the stories behind them?

As you **brainstorm,** take notes on your memories and ideas.

Procedure

To expand your collection of community folklore, **interview** two members of the group. What can they tell you about the origins of the traditions? What details or comments can they add to your descriptions?

You might also ask other questions. For example, if you're interviewing a family member, you could ask if the person knows any interesting stories about the following:

- how your family came to this country

- how your parents or other relatives met and married

- unusual people in your family's history

- the effect of any world events on your family

Presentation

Present what you have learned to your classmates in one of the following formats (or another that your teacher approves).

1. Flat Scrapbook

Make a "flat scrapbook": Tape photographs or drawings of traditional ceremonies or objects to a poster. Write captions for the pictures.

2. Time-Capsule Report

Write two or three paragraphs describing a single item of community folklore in as much detail as possible. Assume that your report will be put in a time capsule for future generations to discover.

3. Oral History

Record yourself on audiotape or videotape talking about your community folklore. Focus on one or two items. You might, instead, record an interview with someone who has special knowledge about your community folklore.

Processing

Round robin. With a small group of classmates, share your responses to these questions.

1. What is one new thing you learned from someone you interviewed?

2. What is the most interesting thing you learned from a classmate's presentation?

The American Hero: Myth and Reality

*I love the story of
Paul Revere,
whether he rode
or not.*
*—U.S. President
Warren G. Harding*

Midnight Ride of Paul Revere (1931) by Grant Wood. Oil on composition board.

PAUL REVERE'S RIDE

Make the Connection

What Is a Hero?

Who are your heroes? Make a list of the people you consider heroes. Write down the qualities or actions that make each person a hero.

Round robin. Share what you have written with a small group of class-mates. Work with your group to create a definition of a hero. Consider:

- Does a hero have to be famous?
- Can a fictional character be a hero?
- Does a hero have to help others?

Present your definition to the class, and compare it with other groups' definitions.

Reading Skills and Strategies

Dialogue with the Text: Monitoring Your Comprehension

Generations of readers have enjoyed this poem's exciting story line, dramatic images, and memorable rhythm. The fact that many people like a poem, though, doesn't mean you have to like it (or dislike it). As you read the poem and record your thoughts in your notebook, pretend you're the first person ever to read "Paul Revere's Ride." One student's responses appear on the first page as an example.

Background

Literature and Social Studies

This poem is based loosely on historical events. On the night of April 18, 1775, Paul Revere and two other men set out from Boston to warn the American colonists of a planned British raid on Concord, Massachusetts. The next day armed volunteers known as minutemen confronted the British at Lexington and Concord in the first battles of the American Revolution.

Elements of Literature

Rhythm

The rhythm of this poem reflects its subject—a long, fast ride on horse-back. The *clippety-clop* of the horse's hoofs is heard in the opening line and then echoes through every stanza.

Rhythm is a rise and fall of the voice produced by repeated sound patterns.

For more on Rhythm, see pages 544–545 and the Handbook of Literary Terms.

go.hrw.com
LEO 8-7

Paul Revere's Ride

Henry Wadsworth Longfellow

Listen, my children, and you shall hear
Of the midnight ride of Paul Revere,
On the eighteenth of April, in Seventy-five;
Hardly a man is now alive
5 Who remembers that famous day and year.

He said to his friend, "If the British march
By land or sea from the town tonight,
Hang a lantern aloft in the belfry arch
Of the North Church tower as a signal light—
10 One, if by land, and two, if by sea;
And I on the opposite shore will be,
Ready to ride and spread the alarm
Through every Middlesex village and farm,
For the country folk to be up and to arm."

15 Then he said, "Good night!" and with muffled oar
Silently rowed to the Charlestown shore,
Just as the moon rose over the bay,
Where swinging wide at her moorings° lay
The Somerset, British man-of-war;
20 A phantom ship, with each mast and spar°
Across the moon like a prison bar,
And a huge black hulk, that was magnified
By its own reflection in the tide.

Meanwhile, his friend, through alley and street,
25 Wanders and watches with eager ears,
Till in the silence around him he hears
The muster° of men at the barrack door,
The sound of arms, and the tramp of feet,
And the measured tread of the grenadiers,°
30 Marching down to their boats on the shore.

18. **moorings:** cables holding a ship in place so that it doesn't float away.
20. **mast and spar:** poles supporting a ship's sails.
27. **muster:** assembly; gathering.
29. **grenadiers** (gren′ə·dirz′): foot soldiers who carry and throw grenades.

Dialogue with the Text

So the poem was written much after the happening.

How can they MARCH by sea?

Nice rhyming.

Rhyming pattern changes here.

Militia, or just old men with muskets?

Ah! They're trying to sneak around.

Obviously a warship.

Symbolizing how the British "imprison" the colonists?

Cory Rockliff

—Cory Rockliff
Solomon Schechter Day School
West Orange, New Jersey

Then he climbed the tower of the Old North Church,
By the wooden stairs, with stealthy tread,
To the belfry chamber overhead,
And startled the pigeons from their perch
35 On the somber rafters, that round him made
Masses and moving shapes of shade—
By the trembling ladder, steep and tall,
To the highest window in the wall,
Where he paused to listen and look down
40 A moment on the roofs of the town,
And the moonlight flowing over all.

Beneath, in the churchyard, lay the dead,
In their night encampment on the hill,
Wrapped in silence so deep and still
45 That he could hear, like a sentinel's° tread,
The watchful night wind, as it went
Creeping along from tent to tent,
And seeming to whisper, "All is well!"
A moment only he feels the spell
50 Of the place and the hour, and the secret dread
Of the lonely belfry and the dead;
For suddenly all his thoughts are bent
On a shadowy something far away,
Where the river widens to meet the bay—
55 A line of black that bends and floats
On the rising tide, like a bridge of boats.

Meanwhile, impatient to mount and ride,
Booted and spurred, with a heavy stride
On the opposite shore walked Paul Revere.
60 Now he patted his horse's side,
Now gazed at the landscape far and near,
Then, impetuous,° stamped the earth,
And turned and tightened his saddle girth;
But mostly he watched with eager search
65 The belfry tower of the Old North Church,
As it rose above the graves on the hill,
Lonely and spectral° and somber and still.
And lo! as he looks, on the belfry's height
A glimmer, and then a gleam of light!

45. **sentinel's:** guard's.
62. **impetuous** (im·pech′o͞o·əs): impulsive; eager.
67. **spectral:** ghostly.

The Midnight Ride of Paul Revere (detail) (1985) by Barbara Olsen. Oil on canvas.

70   He springs to the saddle, the bridle he turns,
       But lingers and gazes, till full on his sight
       A second lamp in the belfry burns!

       A hurry of hoofs in a village street,
       A shape in the moonlight, a bulk in the dark,
75   And beneath, from the pebbles, in passing, a spark
       Struck out by a steed flying fearless and fleet:
       That was all! And yet, through the gloom and the light,
       The fate of a nation was riding that night;
       And the spark struck out by that steed, in his flight,
80   Kindled the land into flame with its heat.

He has left the village and mounted the steep,
And beneath him, tranquil and broad and deep,
Is the Mystic, meeting the ocean tides;
And under the alders that skirt its edge,
85   Now soft on the sand, now loud on the ledge,
Is heard the tramp of his steed as he rides.

It was twelve by the village clock,
When he crossed the bridge into Medford town.
He heard the crowing of the cock,
90   And the barking of the farmer's dog,
And felt the damp of the river fog,
That rises after the sun goes down.

It was one by the village clock,
When he galloped into Lexington.
95   He saw the gilded weathercock
Swim in the moonlight as he passed,
And the meetinghouse windows, blank and bare,
Gaze at him with a spectral glare,
As if they already stood aghast
100   At the bloody work they would look upon.

It was two by the village clock,
When he came to the bridge in Concord town.
He heard the bleating of the flock,
And the twitter of birds among the trees,
105   And felt the breath of the morning breeze
Blowing over the meadows brown.
And one was safe and asleep in his bed
Who at the bridge would be first to fall,
Who that day would be lying dead,

110 Pierced by a British musket ball.
You know the rest. In the books you have read,
How the British Regulars fired and fled—
How the farmers gave them ball for ball,
From behind each fence and farmyard wall,
115 Chasing the redcoats down the lane,
Then crossing the fields to emerge again
Under the trees at the turn of the road,
And only pausing to fire and load.

So through the night rode Paul Revere;
120 And so through the night went his cry of alarm
To every Middlesex village and farm—
A cry of defiance and not of fear,
A voice in the darkness, a knock at the door,
And a word that shall echo forevermore!
125 For, borne on the night wind of the Past,
Through all our history, to the last,
In the hour of darkness and peril and need,
The people will waken and listen to hear
The hurrying hoofbeats of that steed,
130 And the midnight message of Paul Revere.

Henry Wadsworth Longfellow (1871) by Theodore Wust. Watercolor on ivory.

MEET THE WRITER

"Footprints on the Sands of Time"

If you went to school a hundred years ago, you and all your friends would probably be able to recite by heart several of the poems of **Henry Wadsworth Longfellow** (1807–1882). Born in Portland, Maine, Longfellow became the most popular poet of his day, at a time when it was common for families to entertain themselves by reading poetry aloud in the evening by the fireside. (In fact, Longfellow was one of a group of writers known as the Fireside Poets.) Even today many lines and phrases from his poems are used in writing and conversation: "the patter of little feet," "the forest primeval," "ships that pass in the night," "Into each life some rain must fall."

Many of Longfellow's poems, such as *Evangeline* (1847), *The Song of Hiawatha* (1855), and *The Courtship of Miles Standish* (1858), were inspired by people and events in American history. As "Paul Revere's Ride" shows, Longfellow believed that one person's actions could make a difference. In an early piece of verse, he wrote:

   66 Lives of great men all remind us
We can make our lives sublime.
And, departing, leave behind us
Footprints on the sands of time. 99

MAKING MEANINGS

First Thoughts

1. Do you think Paul Revere is a hero? Is his friend? Explain why or why not.

Shaping Interpretations

2. What does the poet mean when he says "The fate of a nation was riding that night" (line 78)? What does he mean by saying that the spark struck by the horse's hoof "kindled the land into flame" (line 80)?

3. Read aloud the first line of each stanza, clapping out its **rhythm**. What feeling does the rhythm give you? What is happening in the story when the rhythm is broken?

4. What do you think the word or words are "that shall echo forevermore" (line 124)? Write what Revere might have said as he knocked on each door.

5. Reread the last five lines of the poem. Why does the poet believe that "in the hour of darkness and peril and need," Americans will remember Paul Revere's message? What significance do you think this story has today?

Extending the Text

6. What other "Paul Reveres," from history or living today, have rallied their people with cries "of defiance and not of fear" (line 122)?

Challenging the Text

7. Imagine that this poem was just written today. Do you think it would deserve to become famous? Do you think it's important that the poem be included in schoolbooks? Why?

Reading Check

a. What is the purpose of Paul Revere's ride?

b. Describe the system of signals Revere arranges with his friend. What signal does he finally see?

c. How does Revere spread the alarm?

d. According to Longfellow, what were the results of Revere's midnight ride?

Foxtrot © Bill Amend. Reprinted with permission of Universal Press Syndicate. All rights reserved.

CHOICES: Building Your Portfolio

Writer's Notebook

1. Collecting Ideas for an Informative Report

Like many literary works inspired by historical events, Longfellow's account of Paul Revere's ride is not entirely accurate. Key details have been left out or changed, and yet this is the version that many people accept as the truth. Find a factual account of the midnight ride in an article, a book, or an encyclopedia. Use a chart like the one on the right to **compare** details of the ride in Longfellow's poem with those in the historical account. Be sure to find the answers to these questions:

- Who were Samuel Prescott and William Dawes?

- Who else helped Paul Revere spread the alarm?

- Did Revere ever reach Concord that night?

Before you fill in the left-hand column, you may find it helpful to go over the notes you took while reading.

Myth	Reality
In the poem, Revere rows himself from Boston to Charlestown.	A group of boatmen helped him slip by the British ships.

Writing a Reflection

2. Footprints in Time

Write a paragraph or two responding to the quotation by Longfellow in Meet the Writer. You might start by considering these questions:

- What historical figures or people living today remind you that people can accomplish great things?

- What do you hope to do in your own life to make "footprints on the sands of time"?

Oral Interpretation

3. And You Shall Hear

With a group of classmates, prepare a **dramatic reading** of "Paul Revere's Ride." Decide how the parts will be divided. For example, you and your partners could take turns reading stanzas solo, or you can split into two groups and perform a **choral reading,** alternating stanzas. Look for points where you may want to add sound effects. (For help, see pages 252–253.)

Creative Writing/Art

4. Colonial Times

Using Longfellow's poem (and if you wish, your historical research) as a source, design a page for a newspaper dated April 19, 1775. Be sure to include an illustrated news article about the events of the previous night. (Don't forget to give it a headline.) You could also include features such as letters to the editor, classified ads, and a weather forecast.

Elements of Literature

SOUND EFFECTS: The Music of Language

Playing with Words

Children love the music of language. They'll repeat nursery rhymes, jump-rope jingles, and tongue twisters over and over because they enjoy hearing the sounds. As we grow older, we find that language has the power to please our minds as well as our ears when sound and sense are skillfully combined.

The Music of Meter

Whether it's in a popular song, a humorous greeting card, or a stirring sermon, **rhythm** comes from the repetition of sounds. One way to create rhythm is with **meter,** a regular pattern of stressed and unstressed syllables. In these lines from "Paul Revere's Ride" (page 537), the stressed syllables are marked with an accent (´) and the unstressed syllables are

marked with a cup (˘). Read this verse aloud to hear the regular rise and fall of your voice as you say the words.

In the hour of darkness and
    peril and need,
The people will waken and
    listen to hear
The hurrying hoofbeats of
    that steed,
And the midnight message of
    Paul Revere.

You can see that Longfellow varied his meter, so that his verse isn't singsong; instead, it echoes the rhythmic but slightly irregular "hurrying hoofbeats" of Revere's horse.

A Writer on Sound Effects

"Music is the universal language of mankind—poetry their universal pastime and delight."

—Henry Wadsworth Longfellow, author of "Paul Revere's Ride" (page 537)

A Different Drummer: Free Verse

Free verse is so called because it is not written in meter; instead, it imitates the natural rhythms of speech. Free

verse has its own kind of music. The following lines are from "I Hear America Singing" by Walt Whitman. Read them aloud to hear how Whitman creates a strong rhythm in free verse just by repeating sentence patterns.

I hear America singing, the
    varied carols I hear,
Those of mechanics, each one
    singing his as it should be
    blithe and strong,
The carpenter singing his as
    he measures his plank or
    beam,
The mason singing his as he
    makes ready for work, or
    leaves off work . . .

Rhyme and Reason

The chiming effect of **rhyme** adds to the musical quality of a poem. The **rhyme scheme** (pattern of rhymes) helps give structure to a poem and acts as a memory aid. Rhyme can also be used to emphasize certain words or ideas.

Most rhymes in poetry are **end rhymes:** The rhyming words appear at the ends of lines, as in "Paul Revere's

by John Malcolm Brinnin

Ride." Rhymes can also occur within lines. Such rhymes are called **internal rhymes.**

Rhymes involving sounds that are similar but not exactly the same are called **approximate rhymes** (or **near rhymes, off rhymes, slant rhymes,** or **imperfect rhymes**). *Cut* and *rat, bat* and *bit,* and *cat* and *catch* are approximate rhymes. This kind of rhyme is popular with many modern poets. They believe it sounds less artificial and more like real speech than exact rhymes do. Another reason poets use approximate rhymes is that it is difficult to come up with exact rhymes that haven't already been used many times.

Other Sound Effects

The use of words whose sounds imitate or suggest their meaning is called **onomatopoeia** (än′ō·mat′ō·pē′ə). When we say that a bell *clangs* or *tinkles* or that bacon *sizzles,* we are using onomatopoeia. A poet can use a whole series of words to imitate a sound. For example, in this line from his poem "The Raven," Edgar Allan Poe uses words with *s* sounds to suggest the sound of wind blowing through curtains: "And the silken, sad, uncertain rustling of each purple curtain."

This line is also an example of **alliteration,** the repetition of sounds, usually consonants, in several words that are close together. (The repeti-tion of vowel sounds is called **assonance.**) Alliteration and assonance aren't used only to imitate natural sounds. Sometimes the repeated sounds just help to create a mood or rhythm.

Giving a Poem Voice

Whenever possible, read a poem aloud at least once to combine its sound with its sense.

1. Be aware of **punctuation,** especially **periods** and **commas.** Periods signal the ends of sentences (which are not always at the ends of lines).

2. If a line of poetry doesn't end with punctuation, do not make a full stop. Pause very briefly, and continue reading until you reach a mark of punctuation.

3. If the poem has a regular rhythm—*da-DUM, da-DUM, da-DUM, da-DUM,* for example—don't read it in a singsong way. Try to read the poem in a natural voice and let the music come through on its own.

"I think that I shall never see, a poem as lovely as a bee, flea, sea, ski, pea, key..."

Before You Read

TOO SOON A WOMAN

Make the Connection

A Typical Teenager

Work with a small group to create a profile of a typical teenager. Fill in a circle with words and symbols showing what you think teenagers are like inside: their likes and dislikes, hopes and worries. Outside the circle, write what teenagers are like on the outside: appearance, activities, how they are perceived by adults, and so on.

Quickwrite

How are teenagers today similar to and different from teenagers in the past? Jot down your ideas in your notebook.

go.hrw.com
LEO 8-7

Elements of Literature

Motivation

What makes people do the things they do? In literature, as in life, a person's **motivation** is not always obvious. As you read this story, decide whether the characters' actions make sense to you. Does each character's motivation become clearer as the story continues?

> **M**otivation is the reasons for a character's behavior.
>
> *For more on Motivation, see the Handbook of Literary Terms.*

Reading Skills and Strategies

Summarizing: Keep It Simple

A summary is a short restatement of the main events and essential ideas in a work. When you **summarize** a story, briefly identify the major characters. Then, in your own words, describe the characters' problems, state the main events, and explain how the problems are finally resolved. Remember to keep your summary simple and to leave out minor details. As you read "Too Soon a Woman," think about which events you would include if you had to summarize it for a friend.

She had run away from somewhere that she wouldn't tell.

Too Soon a Woman

Dorothy M. Johnson

We left the home place behind, mile by slow mile, heading for the mountains, across the prairie where the wind blew forever.

At first there were four of us with the one-horse wagon and its skimpy load. Pa and I walked, because I was a big boy of eleven. My two little sisters romped and trotted until they got tired and had to be boosted up into the wagon bed.

That was no covered Conestoga,[1] like Pa's folks came West in, but just an old farm wagon, drawn by one weary horse, creaking and rumbling westward to the mountains, toward the little woods town where Pa thought he had an old uncle who owned a little two-bit sawmill.

Two weeks we had been moving when we picked up Mary, who had run away from somewhere that she wouldn't tell. Pa didn't want her along, but she stood up to him with no fear in her voice.

1. **Conestoga** (kän′əs·tō′gə): covered wagon with wide wheels, used by American settlers to cross the prairies.

"I'd rather go with a family and look after kids," she said, "but I ain't going back. If you won't take me, I'll travel with any wagon that will."

Pa scowled at her, and her wide blue eyes stared back.

"How old are you?" he demanded.

"Eighteen," she said. "There's teamsters[2] come this way sometimes. I'd rather go with you folks. But I won't go back."

"We're prid'near out of grub," my father told her. "We're clean out of money. I got all I can handle without taking anybody else." He turned away as if he hated the sight of her. "You'll have to walk," he said.

So she went along with us and looked after the little girls, but Pa wouldn't talk to her.

On the prairie, the wind blew. But in the mountains, there was rain. When we stopped at little timber claims along the way, the homesteaders[3] said it had rained all summer. Crops among the blackened stumps were rotted and spoiled. There was no cheer anywhere, and little hospitality. The people we talked to were past worrying. They were scared and desperate.

So was Pa. He traveled twice as far each day as the wagon, ranging through the woods with his rifle, but he never saw game. He had been depending on venison,[4] but we never got any except as a grudging gift from the homesteaders.

He brought in a porcupine once, and that was fat meat and good. Mary roasted it in chunks over the fire, half crying with the smoke. Pa and I rigged up the tarp[5] sheet for shelter to keep the rain from putting the fire clean out.

The porcupine was long gone, except for some of the tried-out fat[6] that Mary had saved, when we came to an old, empty cabin. Pa said we'd have to stop. The horse was wore out, couldn't pull anymore up those grades on the deep-rutted roads in the mountains.

At the cabin, at least there was shelter. We had a few potatoes left and some cornmeal. There was a creek that probably had fish in it, if a person could catch them. Pa tried it for half a day before he gave up. To this day I don't care for fishing. I remember my father's sunken eyes in his gaunt, grim face.

He took Mary and me outside the cabin to talk. Rain dripped on us from branches overhead.

"I think I know where we are," he said. "I calculate to get to old John's and back in about four days. There'll be grub in the town, and they'll let me have some whether old John's still there or not."

He looked at me. "You do like she tells you," he warned. It was the first time he had admitted Mary was on earth since we picked her up two weeks before.

"You're my pardner," he said to me, "but it might be she's got more brains. You mind what she says."

He burst out with bitterness, "There ain't anything good left in the world, or people to care if you live or die. But I'll get grub in the town and come back with it."

He took a deep breath and added, "If you get too all-fired hungry, butcher the horse. It'll be better than starvin'."

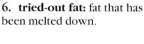

2. **teamsters:** people who drive teams of horses.
3. **homesteaders:** settlers living on and farming pieces of land granted to them by the U.S. government.
4. **venison** (ven′i·zən): deer meat.
5. **tarp:** short for *tarpaulin* (tär·pô′lin), or waterproof canvas.
6. **tried-out fat:** fat that has been melted down.

He kissed the little girls goodbye and plodded off through the woods with one blanket and the rifle.

The cabin was moldy and had no floor. We kept a fire going under a hole in the roof, so it was full of blinding smoke, but we had to keep the fire so as to dry out the wood.

The third night we lost the horse. A bear scared him. We heard the racket, and Mary and I ran out, but we couldn't see anything in the pitch dark.

In gray daylight I went looking for him, and I must have walked fifteen miles. It seemed like I had to have that horse at the cabin when Pa came or he'd whip me. I got plumb lost two or three times and thought maybe I was going to die there alone and nobody would ever know it, but I found the way back to the clearing.

That was the fourth day, and Pa didn't come. That was the day we ate up the last of the grub.

The fifth day, Mary went looking for the horse. My sisters whimpered, huddled in a quilt by the fire, because they were scared and hungry.

I never did get dried out, always having to bring in more damp wood and going out to yell to see if Mary would hear me and not get lost. But I couldn't cry like the little girls did, because I was a big boy, eleven years old.

It was near dark when there was an answer to my yelling, and Mary came into the clearing.

Mary didn't have the horse—we never saw hide nor hair of that old horse again—but she was carrying something big and white that looked like a pumpkin with no color to it.

She didn't say anything, just looked around and saw Pa wasn't there yet, at the end of the fifth day.

"What's that thing?" my sister Elizabeth demanded.

"Mushroom," Mary answered. "I bet it hefts[7] ten pounds."

"What are you going to do with it now?" I sneered. "Play football here?"

"Eat it—maybe," she said, putting it in a corner. Her wet hair hung over her shoulders. She huddled by the fire.

My sister Sarah began to whimper again. "I'm hungry!" she kept saying.

"Mushrooms ain't good eating," I said. "They can kill you."

"Maybe," Mary answered. "Maybe they can. I don't set up to know all about everything, like some people."

"What's that mark on your shoulder?" I asked her. "You tore your dress on the brush."

"What do you think it is?" she said, her head bowed in the smoke.

"Looks like scars," I guessed.

"'Tis scars. They whipped me. Now mind your own business. I want to think."

Elizabeth whimpered, "Why don't Pa come back?"

"He's coming," Mary promised. "Can't come in the dark. Your pa'll take care of you soon's he can."

She got up and rummaged around in the grub box.

"Nothing there but empty dishes," I growled. "If there was anything, we'd know it."

Mary stood up. She was holding the can with the porcupine grease.

"I'm going to have something to eat," she said coolly. "You kids can't have any yet. And I don't want any squalling, mind."

It was a cruel thing, what she did then. She sliced that big, solid mushroom and heated grease in a pan.

The smell of it brought the little girls out of

their quilt, but she told them to go back in so fierce a voice that they obeyed. They cried to break your heart.

I didn't cry. I watched, hating her.

I endured the smell of the mushroom frying as long as I could. Then I said, "Give me some."

"Tomorrow," Mary answered. "Tomorrow, maybe. But not tonight." She turned to me with a sharp command: "Don't bother me! Just leave me be."

She knelt there by the fire and finished frying the slice of mushroom.

If I'd had Pa's rifle, I'd have been willing to kill her right then and there.

She didn't eat right away. She looked at the brown, fried slice for a while and said, "By tomorrow morning, I guess you can tell whether you want any."

The little girls stared at her as she ate. Sarah was chewing an old leather glove.

When Mary crawled into the quilts with them, they moved away as far as they could get.

I was so scared that my stomach heaved, empty as it was.

Mary didn't stay in the quilts long. She took a drink out of the water bucket and sat down by the fire and looked through the smoke at me.

She said in a low voice, "I don't know how it will be if it's poison. Just do the best you can with the girls. Because your pa will come back, you know. . . . You better go to bed. I'm going to sit up."

And so would you sit up. If it might be your last night on earth and the pain of death might seize you at any moment, you would sit up by the smoky fire, wide awake, remembering whatever you had to remember, savoring life.

We sat in silence after the girls had gone to sleep. Once I asked, "How long does it take?"

7. **hefts:** weighs.

"I never heard," she answered. "Don't think about it."

I slept after a while, with my chin on my chest. Maybe Peter dozed that way at Gethsemane as the Lord knelt praying.[8]

Mary's moving around brought me wide awake. The black of night was fading.

"I guess it's all right," Mary said. "I'd be able to tell by now, wouldn't I?"

I answered gruffly, "I don't know."

Mary stood in the doorway for a while, looking out at the dripping world as if she found it beautiful. Then she fried slices of the mushroom while the little girls danced with anxiety.

We feasted, we three, my sisters and I, until Mary ruled, "That'll hold you," and would not cook any more. She didn't touch any of the mushroom herself.

That was a strange day in the moldy cabin. Mary laughed and was gay; she told stories, and we played "Who's Got the Thimble?" with a pine cone.

In the afternoon we heard a shout, and my sisters screamed and I ran ahead of them across the clearing.

The rain had stopped. My father came plunging out of the woods leading a pack horse—and well I remember the treasures of food in that pack.

He glanced at us anxiously as he tore at the ropes that bound the pack.

"Where's the other one?" he demanded.

Mary came out of the cabin then, walking sedately. As she came toward us, the sun began to shine.

My stepmother was a wonderful woman.

8. **Maybe Peter . . . knelt praying:** According to Matthew 26:36–46, Jesus spent an entire night praying in the Garden of Gethsemane, outside Jerusalem, knowing he would be arrested in the morning. He asked Peter and two other followers to stay awake with him, but they kept falling asleep.

MEET THE WRITER

Kills-Both-Places

Dorothy M. Johnson (1905–1984) was born in McGregor, Iowa, but made the West her home—in both a physical and a literary sense. After graduating from the University of Montana, she moved to New York City to work as a magazine editor but eventually returned to Montana to write the stories that would make her famous. Johnson is known for her sensitive, realistic portrayals of the American West. Three of her stories—"The Hanging Tree," "The Man Who Shot Liberty Valance," and "A Man Called Horse"—were made into movies.

The Blackfoot people of Montana made Johnson an honorary member and gave her the name Kills-Both-Places.

MAKING MEANINGS

First Thoughts

1. Reread your Quickwrite. Does Mary seem like a typical teenager? Explain.

Shaping Interpretations

2. List three **conflicts** (internal or external) in this story. Which conflict seems to be the main one? Why?

3. Explain the **title** of the story. In what way is Mary "too soon a woman"?

4. In your opinion, does the eleven-year-old narrator become "too soon a man" as well? Why or why not?

5. Is Mary a hero? What heroic qualities does she display? (You may want to look at the definition of a hero you created with your group—see page 536.)

6. Explain the character's **motivation** for each of these actions:
   • At the beginning of the story, why does Pa refuse to talk to Mary?
   • Why does Mary refuse to give the children any of the mushroom at first?
   • Why does Pa ask about Mary when he returns?

Connecting with the Text

7. Would you have done what Mary did if you were in her place? Explain. (As Mary, can you think of a way to save the children without risking your own life?)

8. Have you ever been given more responsibility than is usual for someone your age? Describe your experience being "too soon a woman" or "too soon a man." How did it change you? (If you prefer, describe an experience someone you know or know about has had.)

Challenging the Text

9. "Too Soon a Woman" has also been published under the title "The Day the Sun Came Out." Which title do you like better? Why?

10. Do you think this story presents a realistic picture of life for Western settlers in the nineteenth century? Why or why not?

Reading Check

Summarize the main events of the story, using the story map below to help you. Remember to include the main events only.

Characters	
Their problems	
Main events	
Resolution	

Writer's Notebook

1. Collecting Ideas for an Informative Report

Choose a teenager in your community, in the national news, or from history who did something heroic. Find out three things about his or her actions. What makes this person a hero? Why would people be interested in reading about him or her?

> Ryan White:
> —just a kid
> —courageously battled AIDS
> —went to court to fight to attend school
> —educated others about the disease

Creative Writing

2. Travels with Mary

What happens to the narrator's family as they continue to travel west with Mary? Write a short **sequel** to the story, describing their next adventure. How do Mary's courage and resourcefulness help her face

- an angry bear?
- a pack of hungry wolves?
- a raging river?
- another dangerous situation (your idea)?

Graphic Organizer/ Analyzing a Character

3. A Well-Rounded Character?

Make an **attribute wheel** for Mary or one of the other characters in the story. (An *attribute* is a characteristic or personal quality, such as shyness or rudeness.) Draw a simple wagon wheel like the one below. In the center, write the character's name. On each spoke, write a word or phrase describing the character. In the space between the spokes, give evidence from the text that supports each attribute.

Performance

4. Secret Thoughts

Divide the roles of Mary and the narrator with a partner. Then, write an **interior monologue** for your character at the moment that Mary is frying the slice of mushroom. What is she thinking as she kneels by the fire? What is the narrator thinking as he watches her? (If you like, choose another pair of characters and another scene, such as the one with Mary and Pa at the very end of the story.) With your partner, perform the monologues for your class.

GRAMMAR LINK

Language Handbook HELP

See Colons, page 803.

Technology HELP

See Language Workshop CD-ROM. Key word entry: colons.

Using Colons Before Lists

Use a colon to show your reader that a list of items follows.

EXAMPLES   When Pa returned, we had a feast**:** salt pork, beans, and biscuits with molasses.

There were now five people in our family**:** Pa, Mary, my two sisters, and me.

Don't use a colon before a list or a series that follows a verb or a preposition.

EXAMPLES   When Pa returned, we ate salt pork, beans, and biscuits with molasses.

Our family now consisted of Pa, Mary, my two sisters, and me.

The children were wet, hungry, and frightened.

Try It Out

Write a sentence listing your four favorite writers (or foods or TV shows), using a colon correctly.

EXAMPLE
These are my favorite writers: Robert Cormier, Sandra Cisneros, O. Henry, and Maya Angelou.

Exchange papers with a classmate, and check his or her work.

SPELLING   HOW TO OWN A WORD

Consonant and Vowel Sounds

Someone once suggested that *fish* could be spelled *g-h-o-t-i: gh* as in *laugh, o* as in *women,* and *ti* as in *motion.*

Because English has borrowed words from so many other languages, each with its own system of spelling, many sounds in English can be spelled several ways. For that reason there are many ear rhymes that aren't eye rhymes, such as *sigh* and *buy.*

For each of the following words from the story, write down a rhyme that uses a different spelling for the same sound. The first one is done for you as an example.

prairie	meat	road	grease	creek
horse	smoke	wood	water	bear

EXAMPLE   prairie—scary

Reading Skills and Strategies

PREVIEWING AND REVIEWING

When you preview and review a text, strategic reading starts even before you read and continues after you've finished reading. Previewing and reviewing are especially useful study strategies when you're reading for information, but they can help you monitor your understanding of any kind of text—even one you're reading strictly for enjoyment.

Previewing: Where Are You Going?

Before you begin to read a text, take a few minutes to flip through the pages and do a quick survey. Previewing will help you determine what you'll find in the text and decide on your reading rate. When you skim and scan, you're not reading every word. You're glancing at the text to get an overall view or to look for particular information. You'll probably make some **predictions** about what the text will be like based on your skimming and scanning.

1. **Skim** for a general overview:

    *   **Title and subtitles.** What is the text about? Is the information or story line broken up with subheads?

    *   **Length.** How long is the text? Is the type easy to read?

    *   **Visuals.** Are there any pictures, charts, diagrams, maps, or other visuals to help you make sense of the information?

2. **Scan** for important information:

    *   **Introductions and conclusions.** When you are reading to get information, look at the first and last chapters of a book, the first and last paragraphs of a chapter, or the first and last sentences of a paragraph. Often (though not always) you'll find the most important information in a text there.

    *   **Key words.** Do certain words keep popping up? If

you scan "Harriet Tubman" (pages 557–566), for example, you'll notice that the words *slaves* and *runaways* are repeated many times. Key words are clues to what the text is about. You'll need to know them to understand the text, so you may want to look up unfamiliar ones before you begin reading.

Reviewing: Where Have You Been?

Reviewing and rereading portions of a text help you

*   check to see if you've understood a text

*   check to see if you've remembered the main ideas

One way to review is to **summarize** the text. Restate its main ideas in your own words; leave out minor details. Going over any notes you took as you read will help you recall the major points of an expository piece or the major events of a narrative.

Apply the strategy on the next page.

Before You Read

HARRIET TUBMAN

Make the Connection

History Round Table

Working with a small group of classmates, write each of the following phrases at the top of a separate slip of paper:

- Harriet Tubman
- the Abolitionist movement
- the Underground Railroad

Take one of the slips of paper, and write down anything you know (or can guess) about the topic. Then, pass it to another member of your group, and take a second slip. Continue until everyone has had the chance to write on all slips. With your classmates, compile a chart of the class's combined knowledge on the topics; you'll refer to it after you read the selection.

Quickwrite

Respond to one of the following prompts:

- How do you define *freedom?* What does it mean in your life?

- Is there anything you can imagine giving up your freedom for? Is there anything you would refuse to do for freedom?

go.hrw.com
LEO 8-7

Reading Skills and Strategies

Previewing and Reviewing: Before and After

Before you read Harriet Tubman's story, **skim** and **scan** it to decide how to approach the text. (How fast will you read? Are there any key words you want to look up before you start? Do you want to look at the map on page 562 first or wait until you've read the text?)

As you read, take notes on any important information. You'll use these notes later to write a **summary.**

Background

Literature and Religion

In the Biblical Book of Exodus, Moses is chosen by God to lead the people of Israel out of slavery in Egypt. Pursued by the Egyptians, Moses takes his people on a long, perilous desert journey and leads them to the Promised Land.

As you read about Harriet Tubman, ask yourself: Why was she called "the Moses of her people"?

Collection of Mr. and Dr. Payson Wolff/Courtesy Heritage Gallery, Los Angeles, California.

If they were caught, she would probably be hanged.

from *Harriet Tubman*

Conductor on the Underground Railroad

Ann Petry

Roots (1964) by Charles White. Chinese ink.

The Railroad Runs to Canada

Along the Eastern Shore of Maryland, in Dorchester County, in Caroline County, the masters kept hearing whispers about the man named Moses, who was running off slaves. At first they did not believe in his existence. The stories about him were fantastic, unbelievable. Yet they watched for him. They offered rewards for his capture.

They never saw him. Now and then they heard whispered rumors to the effect that he was in the neighborhood. The woods were searched. The roads were watched. There was never anything to indicate his whereabouts. But a few days afterward, a goodly number of slaves would be gone from the plantation. Neither the master nor the overseer had heard or seen anything unusual in the quarter.[1] Sometimes one or the other would vaguely remember having heard a whippoorwill call somewhere in the woods, close by, late at night. Though it was the wrong season for whippoorwills.

1. **quarter:** area in a plantation where enslaved Africans lived. It consisted of windowless, one-room cabins made of logs and mud.

CAUTION!!
COLORED PEOPLE
OF BOSTON, ONE & ALL,
You are hereby respectfully CAUTIONED and advised, to avoid conversing with the
Watchmen and Police Officers of Boston,
For since the recent ORDER OF THE MAYOR & ALDERMEN, they are empowered to act as
KIDNAPPERS
AND
Slave Catchers,
And they have already been actually employed in KIDNAPPING, CATCHING, AND KEEPING SLAVES. Therefore, if you value your LIBERTY, and the *Welfare of the Fugitives* among you, *Shun* them in every possible manner, as so many *HOUNDS* on the track of the most unfortunate of your race.
Keep a Sharp Look Out for KIDNAPPERS, and have TOP EYE open.
APRIL 24, 1851.
THEODORE PARKER'S PLACARD

Sometimes the masters thought they had heard the cry of a hoot owl, repeated, and would remember having thought that the intervals between the low moaning cry were wrong, that it had been repeated four times in succession instead of three. There was never anything more than that to suggest that all was not well in the quarter. Yet, when morning came, they invariably discovered that a group of the finest slaves had taken to their heels.

Unfortunately, the discovery was almost always made on a Sunday. Thus a whole day was lost before the machinery of pursuit could be set in motion. The posters offering rewards for

the fugitives could not be printed until Monday. The men who made a living hunting for runaway slaves were out of reach, off in the woods with their dogs and their guns, in pursuit of four-footed game, or they were in camp meetings saying their prayers with their wives and families beside them.

Harriet Tubman could have told them that there was far more involved in this matter of running off slaves than signaling the would-be runaways by imitating the call of a whippoorwill, or a hoot owl, far more involved than a matter of waiting for a clear night when the North Star[2] was visible.

In December 1851, when she started out with the band of fugitives that she planned to take to Canada, she had been in the vicinity of the plantation for days, planning the trip, carefully selecting the slaves that she would take with her.

She had announced her arrival in the quarter by singing the forbidden spiritual[3]—"Go down, Moses, 'way down to Egypt Land"— singing it softly outside the door of a slave cabin, late at night. The husky voice was beautiful even when it was barely more than a murmur borne on the wind.

Once she had made her presence known, word of her coming spread from cabin to cabin. The slaves whispered to each other, ear to mouth, mouth to ear, "Moses is here." "Moses has come." "Get ready. Moses is back again." The ones who had agreed to go North with her put ashcake[4] and salt herring in an old bandanna, hastily tied it into a bundle, and then waited patiently for the signal that meant it was time to start.

There were eleven in this party, including one of her brothers and his wife. It was the largest group that she had ever conducted, but she was determined that more and more slaves should know what freedom was like.

She had to take them all the way to Canada. The Fugitive Slave Law[5] was no longer a great many incomprehensible words written down on the country's lawbooks. The new law had become a reality. It was Thomas Sims, a boy, picked up on the streets of Boston at night and shipped back to Georgia. It was Jerry and Shadrach, arrested and jailed with no warning.

She had never been in Canada. The route beyond Philadelphia was strange to her. But she could not let the runaways who accompanied her know this. As they walked along, she told them stories of her own first flight; she kept painting vivid word pictures of what it would be like to be free.

But there were so many of them this time.

4. **ashcake:** cornmeal bread baked in hot ashes.
5. **Fugitive Slave Law:** harsh federal law passed in 1850 stating that slaves who escaped to free states could be forced to return to their owners. As a result, those who escaped were safe only in Canada. The law also made it a crime for a free person to help slaves escape or to prevent their return.

2. **North Star:** Runaways fleeing north used the North Star (Polaris) to help them stay on course.
3. **forbidden spiritual:** Spirituals are religious songs, some of which are based on the Biblical story of the Israelites' escape from slavery in Egypt. Plantation owners feared that the singing of spirituals might lead to rebellion.

WORDS TO OWN

fugitives (fyōō′ji·tivz) *n*.: people fleeing from danger.
incomprehensible (in′käm′prē·hen′sə·bəl) *adj*.: impossible to understand.

She knew moments of doubt, when she was half afraid and kept looking back over her shoulder, imagining that she heard the sound of pursuit. They would certainly be pursued. Eleven of them. Eleven thousand dollars' worth of flesh and bone and muscle that belonged to Maryland planters. If they were caught, the eleven runaways would be whipped and sold South, but she—she would probably be hanged.

They tried to sleep during the day but they never could wholly relax into sleep. She could tell by the positions they assumed, by their restless movements. And they walked at night. Their progress was slow. It took them three nights of walking to reach the first stop. She had told them about the place where they would stay, promising warmth and good food, holding these things out to them as an <u>incentive</u> to keep going.

When she knocked on the door of a farmhouse, a place where she and her parties of runaways had always been welcome, always been given shelter and plenty to eat, there was no answer. She knocked again, softly. A voice from within said, "Who is it?" There was fear in the voice.

She knew instantly from the sound of the voice that there was something wrong. She said, "A friend with friends," the password on the Underground Railroad.

The door opened, slowly. The man who stood in the doorway looked at her coldly, looked with unconcealed astonishment and fear at the eleven <u>disheveled</u> runaways who were standing near her. Then he shouted, "Too many, too many. It's not safe. My place was searched last week. It's not safe!" and slammed the door in her face.

She turned away from the house, frowning. She had promised her passengers food and rest and warmth, and instead of that, there would be hunger and cold and more walking over the frozen ground. Somehow she would have to <u>instill</u> courage into these eleven people, most of them strangers, would have to feed them on hope and bright dreams of freedom instead of the fried pork and corn bread and milk she had promised them.

They stumbled along behind her, half dead for sleep, and she urged them on, though she was as tired and as discouraged as they were. She had never been in Canada, but she kept painting wondrous word pictures of what it would be like. She managed to <u>dispel</u> their fear of pursuit so that they would not become hysterical, panic-stricken. Then she had to bring some of the fear back, so that they would stay awake and keep walking though they drooped with sleep.

Yet, during the day, when they lay down deep in a thicket, they never really slept, because if a twig snapped or the wind sighed in the branches of a pine tree, they jumped to their feet, afraid of their own shadows, shiver-

---

WORDS TO OWN

incentive (in·sent′iv) *n.*: reason to do something; motivation.
disheveled (di·shev′əld) *adj.*: untidy; rumpled.
instill (in·stil′) *v.*: gradually put in (an idea or feeling). *Stilla* is Latin for "drop"; *instill* literally means "put in drop by drop."
dispel (di·spel′) *v.*: scatter; drive away.

ing and shaking. It was very cold, but they dared not make fires because someone would see the smoke and wonder about it.

She kept thinking, eleven of them. Eleven thousand dollars' worth of slaves. And she had to take them all the way to Canada. Sometimes she told them about Thomas Garrett, in Wilmington.[6] She said he was their friend even though he did not know them. He was the friend of all fugitives. He called them God's poor. He was a Quaker[7] and his speech was a little different from that of other people. His clothing was different, too. He wore the wide-brimmed hat that the Quakers wear.

She said that he had thick white hair, soft, almost like a baby's, and the kindest eyes she had ever seen. He was a big man and strong, but he had never used his strength to harm anyone, always to help people. He would give all of them a new pair of shoes. Everybody. He always did. Once they reached his house in Wilmington, they would be safe. He would see to it that they were.

She described the house where he lived, told them about the store where he sold shoes. She said he kept a pail of milk and a loaf of bread in the drawer of his desk so that he would have food ready at hand for any of God's poor who should suddenly appear before him, fainting with hunger. There was a hidden room in the store. A whole wall swung open, and behind it was a room where he could hide fugitives. On the wall there were shelves filled with small boxes—boxes of shoes—so that

Wanted Poster Series #17 (1971) by Charles White. Oil wash.

6. **Wilmington:** city in Delaware.
7. **Quaker:** member of the Society of Friends, a religious group active in the movement to end slavery.

The Underground Railroad runs to Canada.

you would never guess that the wall actually opened.

While she talked, she kept watching them. They did not believe her. She could tell by their expressions. They were thinking. New shoes, Thomas Garrett, Quaker, Wilmington—what foolishness was this? Who knew if she told the truth? Where was she taking them anyway?

That night they reached the next stop—a farm that belonged to a German. She made the runaways take shelter behind trees at the edge of the fields before she knocked at the door. She hesitated before she approached the door, thinking, suppose that he too should refuse shelter, suppose—— Then she thought, *Lord, I'm going to hold steady on to You and You've got to see me through*—and knocked softly.

She heard the familiar guttural voice say, "Who's there?"

She answered quickly, "A friend with friends."

He opened the door and greeted her warmly. "How many this time?" he asked.

"Eleven," she said and waited, doubting, wondering.

He said, "Good. Bring them in."

He and his wife fed them in the lamp-lit kitchen, their faces glowing as they offered food and more food, urging them to eat, saying there was plenty for everybody, have more milk, have more bread, have more meat.

They spent the night in the warm kitchen. They really slept, all that night and until dusk the next day. When they left, it was with reluctance. They had all been warm and safe and well-fed. It was hard to exchange the security offered by that clean, warm kitchen for the darkness and the cold of a December night.

"Go On or Die"

Harriet had found it hard to leave the warmth and friendliness, too. But she urged them on. For a while, as they walked, they seemed to carry in them a measure of contentment; some of the serenity and the cleanliness of that big, warm kitchen lingered on inside them. But as they walked farther and farther away from the warmth and the light, the cold and the darkness entered into them. They fell silent, sullen, suspicious. She waited for the moment when some one of them would turn <u>mutinous</u>. It did not happen that night.

Two nights later, she was aware that the feet behind her were moving slower and slower. She heard the irritability in their voices, knew that soon someone would refuse to go on.

She started talking about William Still and the Philadelphia Vigilance Committee.[8] No one commented. No one asked any questions. She told them the story of William and Ellen Craft and how they escaped from Georgia. Ellen was so fair that she looked as though she were white, and so she dressed up in a man's clothing and she looked like a wealthy young planter. Her husband, William, who was dark, played the role of her slave. Thus they traveled from Macon, Georgia, to Philadelphia, riding on the trains, staying at the finest hotels. Ellen pretended to be very ill—her right arm was in a sling and her right hand was bandaged be-

cause she was supposed to have rheumatism.[9] Thus she avoided having to sign the register at the hotels, for she could not read or write. They finally arrived safely in Philadelphia and then went on to Boston.

No one said anything. Not one of them seemed to have heard her.

She told them about Frederick Douglass, the most famous of the escaped slaves, of his <u>eloquence</u>, of his magnificent appearance. Then she told them of her own first, vain effort at running away, evoking the memory of that miserable life she had led as a child, reliving it for a moment in the telling.

But they had been tired too long, hungry too long, afraid too long, footsore too long. One of them suddenly cried out in despair, "Let me go back. It is better to be a slave than to suffer like this in order to be free."

She carried a gun with her on these trips. She had never used it—except as a threat. Now, as she aimed it, she experienced a feeling of guilt, remembering that time, years ago, when she had prayed for the death of Edward Brodas, the Master, and then, not too long afterward, had heard that great wailing cry that came from the throats of the field hands, and knew from the sound that the Master was dead.

9. **rheumatism** (r$\overline{oo}$′mə·tiz′əm): painful swelling and stiffness of the joints or muscles.

WORDS TO OWN

mutinous (my$\overline{oo}$t′n·əs) *adj.*: rebellious. *Mutiny* usually refers to a revolt of soldiers or sailors against their officers.

eloquence (el′ə·kwəns) *n.*: ability to write or speak gracefully and convincingly.

8. **Philadelphia Vigilance Committee:** group that offered help to people escaping slavery. **Still,** a free African American, was chairman of the committee.

Harriet (1972) by Charles White. Oil drawing.

One of the runaways said again, "Let me go back. Let me go back," and stood still, and then turned around and said, over his shoulder, "I am going back."

She lifted the gun, aimed it at the despairing slave. She said, "Go on with us or die." The husky, low-pitched voice was grim.

He hesitated for a moment and then he joined the others. They started walking again. She tried to explain to them why none of them could go back to the plantation. If a runaway returned, he would turn traitor; the master and the overseer would force him to turn traitor. The returned slave would disclose the stopping places, the hiding places, the corn stacks they had used with the full knowledge of the owner of the farm, the name of the German farmer who had fed them and sheltered them. These people who had risked their own security to help runaways would be ruined, fined, imprisoned.

She said, "We got to go free or die. And freedom's not bought with dust."

This time she told them about the long agony of the Middle Passage[10] on the old slave ships, about the black horror of the holds, about the chains and the whips. They too knew these stories. But she wanted to remind them of the long, hard way they had come, about the long, hard way they had yet to go. She told them about Thomas Sims, the boy picked up on the streets of Boston and sent back to Georgia. She said when they got him back to Savannah, got

him in prison there, they whipped him until a doctor who was standing by watching said, "You will kill him if you strike him again!" His master said, "Let him die!"

Thus she forced them to go on. Sometimes she thought she had become nothing but a voice speaking in the darkness, cajoling, urging, threatening. Sometimes she told them things to make them laugh; sometimes she sang to them and heard the eleven voices behind her blending softly with hers, and then she knew that for the moment all was well with them.

She gave the impression of being a short, muscular, indomitable woman who could never be defeated. Yet at any moment she was liable to be seized by one of those curious fits of sleep, which might last for a few minutes or for hours.[11]

Even on this trip, she suddenly fell asleep in the woods. The runaways, ragged, dirty, hungry, cold, did not steal the gun as they might have and set off by themselves or turn back. They sat on the ground near her and waited patiently until she awakened. They had come to trust her implicitly, totally. They, too, had come to believe her repeated statement, "We got to go free or die." She was leading them into freedom, and so they waited until she was ready to go on.

11. Harriet's losses of consciousness were caused by a serious head injury that she had suffered as a teenager. Harriet had tried to protect another slave from punishment, and an enraged overseer threw a two-pound weight at her head.

10. **Middle Passage:** route traveled by ships carrying captured Africans across the Atlantic Ocean to the Americas. The captives endured the horrors of the Middle Passage crammed into **holds,** airless cargo areas below decks.

WORDS TO OWN
cajoling (kə·jōl′iŋ) *v.* used as *adj.*: coaxing.

Finally, they reached Thomas Garrett's house in Wilmington, Delaware. Just as Harriet had promised, Garrett gave them all new shoes, and provided carriages to take them on to the next stop.

By slow stages they reached Philadelphia, where William Still hastily recorded their names, and the plantations whence they had come, and something of the life they had led in slavery. Then he carefully hid what he had written, for fear it might be discovered. In 1872 he published this record in book form and called it *The Underground Railroad.* In the foreword to his book he said: "While I knew the danger of keeping strict records, and while I did not then dream that in my day slavery would be blotted out, or that the time would come when I could publish these records, it used to afford me great satisfaction to take them down, fresh from the lips of fugitives on the way to freedom, and to preserve them as they had given them."

William Still, who was familiar with all the station stops on the Underground Railroad, supplied Harriet with money and sent her and her eleven fugitives on to Burlington, New Jersey.

Harriet felt safer now, though there were danger spots ahead. But the biggest part of her job was over. As they went farther and farther north, it grew colder; she was aware of the wind on the Jersey ferry and aware of the cold damp in New York. From New York they went on to Syracuse,[12] where the temperature was even lower.

In Syracuse she met the Reverend J. W. Loguen, known as "Jarm" Loguen. This was the beginning of a lifelong friendship. Both Harriet and Jarm Loguen were to become friends and supporters of Old John Brown.[13]

From Syracuse they went north again, into a colder, snowier city—Rochester. Here they almost certainly stayed with Frederick Douglass, for he wrote in his autobiography:

"On one occasion I had eleven fugitives at the same time under my roof, and it was necessary for them to remain with me until I could collect sufficient money to get them to Canada. It was the largest number I ever had at any one time, and I had some difficulty in providing so many with food and shelter, but, as may well be imagined, they were not very <u>fastidious</u> in either direction, and were well content with very plain food, and a strip of carpet on the floor for a bed, or a place on the straw in the barn loft."

Late in December 1851, Harriet arrived in St. Catharines, Canada West (now Ontario), with the eleven fugitives. It had taken almost a month to complete this journey.

13. Old John Brown (1800–1859): abolitionist (opponent of slavery) who was active in the Underground Railroad. In 1859, Brown led a raid on the federal arsenal at Harpers Ferry, Virginia, in hopes of inspiring a slave uprising. The local militia overpowered Brown and his followers, and Brown was convicted of treason and hanged.

12. Syracuse: city in central New York.

WORDS TO OWN
fastidious (fas·tid′ē·əs) *adj.:* fussy; hard to please.

MEET THE WRITER

"A Message in the Story"

A native of Old Saybrook, Connecticut, **Ann Petry** (1908–1997) was the grand-daughter of a man who escaped from slavery on a Virginia plantation and came north by way of the Underground Railroad. As a young woman she worked as a pharmacist in her family's drugstores before moving to New York, where she became a writer of books for young people and adults. About her writing she said:

66 My writing has, of course, been influenced by the books I've read but it has been much more influenced by the circumstances of my birth and my growing up, by my family. . . .

We always had relatives visiting us. They added excitement to our lives. They brought with them the aura and the customs of a very different world. They were all storytellers, spinners of yarns. So were my mother and my father.

Some of these stories had been handed down from one generation to the next, improved, embellished, embroidered. Usually there was a message in the story, a message for the young, a message that would help a young black child survive, help convince a young black child that black is truly beautiful. 99

More by Ann Petry

Tituba of Salem Village (HarperCollins) is based on the true story of another heroic woman of African descent, who was accused of witchcraft in 1692.

Go Down, Moses

traditional African American

Thus saith the Lord, bold Moses said
Let my people go
If not I'll smite your firstborn dead
Let my people go

> CHORUS:
> *Go down, Moses . . .*

No more shall they in bondage toil
Let my people go
Let them come out with Egypt's spoil
Let my people go

> CHORUS:
> *Go down, Moses . . .*

We need not always weep and mourn
Let my people go
And wear those slavery's chains forlorn
Let my people go

> CHORUS:
> *Go down, Moses . . .*

The devil thought he had us fast
Let my people go
But we thought we'd break his chains at last
Let my people go

> CHORUS:
> *Go down, Moses . . .*

Freedom Walk

A fictional diary based on "Harriet Tubman."

December 10, 1851

The sun is setting and is spraying pretty colors on the horizon. It's getting dark out, and the stars are starting to come out. Moses called us, singing, "Go down, Moses, way down to Egypt land." Me and my brother, Philip, are only packing hard bread and salted fish. Maybe a little water. I learned to write and read from the master's only white maid. She taught me in her spare time. Master Anderson never knew. If he found out, I would be whipped, and she would have to leave. God bring us luck, so that we don't get caught.

Sarah

December 18, 1851

We have a day's head start under our belts, more than we do food. Our leader, Harriet Tubman, said that there was a house that we could stop at for a warm place to sleep and a good meal. We've been sleeping on cold, hard earth. If anything makes the slightest noise, we're up and ready to run to the next county. We're almost there. The house she promised we would be able to stay in is not far from here. We can see some of the windows lit up with candles. Harriet went up to the house, and they wouldn't let us in. They got scared and said they might get caught. My brother is very doubtful and wants to turn back. I tell him we're almost there—only a little while more. I don't know if that's true or not. She had one of her sleeping spells. It lasted for an hour or so, but she insisted she was fine. God help us.

Sarah

—Heather Melchert
Moscow Junior High School
Moscow, Idaho

Making Meanings

- ## First Thoughts

  1. Why might someone like Harriet Tubman, who was already free, risk her life to lead other people to freedom? What do you think of her actions?

- ## Shaping Interpretations

  2. How was Tubman like the Moses of the Bible? What was her Promised Land?

  3. We sense **irony** when we notice that something is the opposite of what it should be. Why do we sense irony when we read that the men who hunted fugitives for money said prayers with their families on Sundays (page 559)? Can you find any other examples of irony in Petry's account?

  4. Go back to the text, and find two **primary sources** (firsthand accounts) mentioned by Petry. What other sources might she have used to get information on her topic?

  5. In Meet the Writer, Petry says that the stories her family told usually had a message for young people. What **main idea,** or message, do you see in the story of Harriet Tubman? Put it in your own words.

  6. What do you think is the difference between a leader and a hero? Was Harriet Tubman a leader or a hero or both? Explain.

  7. Do the runaways who followed Tubman qualify as heroes, in your opinion? Were the people on the Underground Railroad who broke the law and risked imprisonment heroes? Find examples to support your opinion.

- ## Connecting with the Text

  8. One of the fugitives says, "It is better to be a slave than to suffer like this in order to be free." What does Tubman think of this attitude? What do you think of it? (Reread your Quickwrite before you answer.)

- ## Extending the Text

  9. What other people do you know of who have had to flee their homeland or take other risks so that they could be free?

Reading Check

a. What did you notice when you **previewed** the text by **skimming** and **scanning**? In what ways did previewing help you understand the text?

b. Using the notes you took while reading, write two or three sentences **summarizing** this part of Tubman's story. If you need to, **review** or **reread** parts of the text.

c. Go back to the chart you made with your class before you read. What have you learned about these topics from Petry's account? Add the new information to the chart.

CHOICES: Building Your Portfolio

Writer's Notebook

1. Collecting Ideas for an Informative Report

Like most historical accounts, Petry's account suggests many topics for further investigation. Choose one of the following topics or another that your teacher approves. Make a list of questions about your topic. Then, research your topic on the Internet or in the library. Record the *three* most interesting facts you find.

- Tubman's early life
- Tubman's later life
- Frederick Douglass
- code songs and spirituals
- Thomas Garrett
- the Philadelphia Vigilance Committee
- the Middle Passage and the slave trade

"Follow the Drinking Gourd":
—code song giving directions to runaways fleeing north
—"drinking gourd": another name for the Big Dipper, a group of stars used by runaways to find the North Star
—safe houses had real drinking gourds hanging outside as a signal

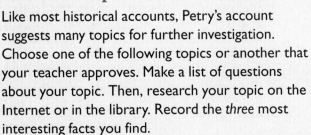

The Granger Collection, New York.

Creative Writing

2. Living History

In "Freedom Walk" you read entries from an imaginary diary kept by one of the eleven runaways. Write your own **diary entry** or **letter** from the point of view of one of the following people in Petry's account:

- the man who wants to return to the plantation
- the plantation owner
- Harriet Tubman
- the farmer who turns the group away

Music

3. Spirituals

With a group, plan a musical event for the class or for a group of family members. You'll need people in your group who can sing, research music, read music, and guide singers. Practice and perform the spiritual "Go Down, Moses" (see *Connections* on page 568) along with other spirituals or freedom songs. Ask the audience to rate your group's performance.

Geography/Art

4. That Lonely Road

The eleven fugitives from Maryland in the story were escaping from the northernmost slave state. Find out which states allowed slavery in 1851, and choose a location in one of those states. Draw a **map** showing a route a fugitive could take to reach freedom from that location. (Look at the map on page 562 as a model.) Be sure to take natural features such as rivers and mountains into account.

GRAMMAR LINK   MINI-LESSON

Joining Independent Clauses

Language Handbook HELP

See The Conjunction, page 746; Semicolons, pages 801–802.

Technology HELP

See Language Workshop CD-ROM. *Key word entries: conjunctions; semicolons.*

To join two **independent clauses** that are closely related in meaning, either use a comma and a coordinating conjunction (*and, but, or, nor, for, so,* or *yet*) or use a semicolon. (An independent clause expresses a complete thought and can stand by itself as a sentence.)

EXAMPLES

The first farmer turned the fugitives away**,** **but** the second welcomed them.

The first farmer turned the fugitives away**;** the second welcomed them.

If there are commas within the clauses, use a semicolon to prevent confusion.

CONFUSING

Harriet Tubman, Thomas Garrett, and William Still were important figures in the fight against slavery**, and** Harriet Beecher Stowe, who is not mentioned by Petry, was also important.

CLEAR

Harriet Tubman, Thomas Garrett, and William Still were important figures in the fight against slavery**;** and Harriet Beecher Stowe, who is not mentioned by Petry, was also important.

Try It Out

Combine each pair of independent clauses, using either a comma and a coordinating conjunction or a semicolon.

1. Harriet Tubman never learned to read or write she helped free hundreds of people from slavery.

2. One of the runaways wanted to turn back the others were ready to continue despite the danger.

3. Tubman talked about Canada she had never been there herself.

4. The fugitives were tired, cold, and hungry they were glad to eat, drink, and sleep.

VOCABULARY   HOW TO OWN A WORD

WORD BANK

fugitives
incomprehensible
incentive
disheveled
instill
dispel
mutinous
eloquence
cajoling
fastidious

Word Maps: Make Your Own

Draw a "map" of each word in the Word Bank. Provide a definition of the word, and then answer at least one question about the word. You will have to make up different questions for each word. You might want to work with a partner. Here is a map of *fugitives*:

fugitives: "people fleeing from danger"

Who is a fugitive?	**Who is *not* a fugitive?**
• escaped convict	• person safe at home
• person fleeing slavery	
• person fleeing persecution	

Before You Read

THE PEOPLE COULD FLY

Make the Connection

Reaching for the Stars

"Once you have flown, you will walk the earth with your eyes turned skyward, for there you have been, and there you long to return."

—Leonardo da Vinci

Many ancient myths tell of humans attaining—and then losing—the power of flight.

With your classmates, brainstorm common expressions relating to flight (for example, "The sky's the limit" or "walking on air"). What do these expressions tell you about the attitude toward flight of the people who came up with them?

Quickwrite

Imagine waking up one morning and discovering that you can fly! How does it feel? What's the first thing you do? Write for two or three minutes in your notebook.

go.hrw.com
LEO 8-7

Elements of Literature

Style

Style comes mainly from a writer's choice of words and the way he or she puts sentences together. The writer of this folk tale uses an informal style to create the impression of a story-teller speaking. She also uses **figures of speech** to bring out the wonder of the tale.

> **S**tyle is the way a writer uses language.
>
> *For more on Style, see the Handbook of Literary Terms.*

Reading Skills and Strategies

Comparing and Contrasting Texts: Alike and Different

When you **compare** and **contrast** two works, you look for the ways they are alike and different. As you read "The People Could Fly," a folk tale, think about how it is like and different from the biography of Harriet Tubman. Focus on these elements:

- characters
- setting
- theme, or main idea
- author's purpose
- the work's effect on you

The People Could Fly

Virginia Hamilton

They forgot about flyin when they could no longer breathe the sweet scent of Africa.

They say the people could fly. Say that long ago in Africa, some of the people knew magic. And they would walk up on the air like climbin up on a gate. And they flew like blackbirds over the fields. Black, shiny wings flappin against the blue up there.

Then, many of the people were captured for Slavery. The ones that could fly shed their wings. They couldn't take their wings across the water on the slave ships. Too crowded, don't you know.

The folks were full of misery, then. Got sick with the up and down of the sea. So they forgot about flyin when they could no longer breathe the sweet scent of Africa.

Say the people who could fly kept their power, although they shed their wings. They kept their secret magic in the land of slavery. They looked the same as the other people from Africa who had been comin over, who had dark skin. Say you couldn't tell anymore one who could fly from one who couldn't.

One such who could was an old man, call him Toby. And standin tall, yet afraid, was a young woman who once had wings. Call her Sarah. Now Sarah carried a babe tied to her back. She trembled to be so hard worked and scorned.

The slaves labored in the fields from sunup to sundown. The owner of the slaves callin himself their Master. Say he was a hard lump of clay. A hard, glinty coal. A hard rock pile, wouldn't be moved. His Overseer on horseback pointed out the slaves who were slowin down. So the one called Driver cracked his whip over the slow ones to make them move faster. That whip was a slice-open cut of pain. So they did move faster. Had to.

Sarah hoed and chopped the row as the babe on her back slept.

Say the child grew hungry. That babe started up bawlin too loud. Sarah couldn't stop to feed it. Couldn't stop to soothe and quiet it down. She let it cry. She didn't want to. She had no heart to croon to it.

"Keep that thing quiet," called the Overseer. He pointed his finger at the babe. The woman scrunched low. The Driver cracked his whip across the babe anyhow. The babe hollered like any hurt child, and the woman fell to the earth.

The old man that was there, Toby, came and helped her to her feet.

"I must go soon," she told him.

"Soon," he said.

Sarah couldn't stand up straight any longer. She was too weak. The sun burned her face. The babe cried and cried, "Pity me, oh, pity me," say it sounded like. Sarah was so sad and starvin, she sat down in the row.

"Get up, you black cow," called the Overseer. He pointed his hand, and the Driver's whip snarled around Sarah's legs. Her sack dress tore into rags. Her legs bled onto the earth. She couldn't get up.

Toby was there where there was no one to help her and the babe.

"Now, before it's too late," panted Sarah. "Now, Father!"

"Yes, Daughter, the time is come," Toby answered. "Go, as you know how to go!"

He raised his arms, holdin them out to her. "Kum . . . yali, kum buba tambe," and more magic words, said so quickly, they sounded like whispers and sighs.

The young woman lifted one foot on the air. Then the other. She flew clumsily at first, with the child now held tightly in her arms. Then she felt the magic, the African mystery. Say she rose just as free as a bird. As light as a feather.

The Overseer rode after her, hollerin. Sarah flew over the fences. She flew over the woods. Tall trees could not snag her. Nor could the Overseer. She flew like an eagle now, until she was gone from sight. No one dared speak about it. Couldn't believe it. But it was, because they that was there saw that it was.

Say the next day was dead hot in the fields. A young man slave fell from the heat. The Driver come and whipped him. Toby come over and spoke words to the fallen one. The words of ancient Africa once heard are never remembered completely. The young man forgot them as soon as he heard them. They went way inside him. He got up and rolled over on the air. He rode it awhile. And he flew away.

Another and another fell from the heat. Toby was there. He cried out to the fallen and reached his arms out to them. "Kum kunka yali, kum . . . tambe!" Whispers and sighs. And they too rose on the air. They rode the hot breezes. The ones flyin were black and shinin sticks, wheelin above the head of the Overseer. They crossed the rows, the fields, the fences, the streams, and were away.

"Seize the old man!" cried the Overseer. "I heard him say the magic *words*. Seize him!"

The one callin himself Master come runnin. The Driver got his whip ready to curl around old Toby and tie him up. The slaveowner took his hip gun from its place. He meant to kill old, black Toby.

But Toby just laughed. Say he threw back his head and said, "Hee, hee! Don't you know who I am? Don't you know some of us in this field?" He said it to their faces. "We are ones who fly!"

And he sighed the ancient words that were a dark promise. He said them all around to the others in the field under the whip, ". . . buba yali . . . buba tambe. . . ."

There was a great outcryin. The bent backs straightened up. Old and young who were called slaves and could fly joined hands. Say like they would ring-sing. But they didn't shuffle in a circle. They didn't sing. They rose on the air.

They flew in a flock that was black against the heavenly blue. Black crows or black shadows. It didn't matter, they went so high. Way above the plantation, way over the slavery land. Say they flew away to *Free-dom.*

And the old man, old Toby, flew behind them, takin care of them. He wasn't cryin. He wasn't laughin. He was the seer. His gaze fell on the plantation where the slaves who could not fly waited.

"Take us with you!" Their looks spoke it but they were afraid to shout it. Toby couldn't take them with him. Hadn't the time to teach them to fly. They must wait for a chance to run.

"Goodie-bye!" The old man called Toby

spoke to them, poor souls! And he was flyin gone.

So they say. The Overseer told it. The one called Master said it was a lie, a trick of the light. The Driver kept his mouth shut.

The slaves who could not fly told about the people who could fly to their children.

When they were free. When they sat close before the fire in the free land, they told it. They did so love firelight and *Freedom,* and tellin.

They say that the children of the ones who could not fly told their children. And now, me, I have told it to you.

MEET THE WRITER

"I Wanted You to Understand the Horrors of Slavery"

Virginia Hamilton (1936–   ) grew up in Yellow Springs, Ohio, an Underground Railroad stop where her grandfather had settled after escaping from slavery in Virginia. Hamilton grew up to be a celebrated writer of books for children and young adults, including the award-winning folk tale collection *The People Could Fly: American Black Folktales* (1986). "I wrote this tale," she tells readers, "because I wanted you to understand the horrors of slavery and to be touched by these courageous human beings."

66 'The People Could Fly' is one of the most extraordinary, moving tales in black folklore. It almost makes us believe that the people *could* fly. There are numerous separate accounts of flying Africans and slaves in the black folk tale literature. Such accounts are often combined with tales of slaves disappearing. A plausible explanation might be the slaves running away from slavery, slipping away while in the fields or under cover of darkness. In code language murmured from one slave to another, 'Come fly away!' might have been the words used. Another explanation is the wish-fulfillment motif.

'The People Could Fly' is a detailed fantasy of suffering, of magic power exerted against the so-called Master and his underlings. Finally, it is a powerful testament to the millions of slaves who never had the opportunity to 'fly' away. They remained slaves, as did their children. 'The People Could Fly' was first told and retold by those who had only their imaginations to set them free. 99

MAKING MEANINGS

First Thoughts

1. How did you feel about this folk tale? (Consider **style**—the way it's told—as well as content.)

Shaping Interpretations

2. The people who could fly have forgotten how to use their power. What do you think makes them remember?

3. Were you surprised that Toby didn't stay behind to help everyone escape? Do you think he made the right decision? Explain.

4. Why would the people left behind in slavery continue to tell this story even after winning their freedom? Why is the story still told today, in your opinion? (What purpose does the telling serve?)

Connecting with the Text

5. Describe a story that is told and retold in your family, your religious community, or another group you belong to. What is its message?

6. You've now read both a biography about an escape from slavery ("Harriet Tubman," page 557) and a folk tale. Which did you find more effective? Why?

CHOICES: Building Your Portfolio

Writer's Notebook

1. Collecting Ideas for an Informative Report

Read Meet the Writer on page 577, and learn about Virginia Hamilton, a famous American novelist and "teller" of folk tales. Write down at least three questions you could use to guide your research on Virginia Hamilton's life and work or on black American folklore in general.

WORK IN PROGRESS

Creative Writing

2. Up, Up, and Away

If you had the power to fly, how would you use it? Would you help others, like Toby in the folk tale or Superman? Write a **journal entry** describing your imaginary adventures in flight. (You may want to use your Quickwrite as a starter.)

Comparing and Contrasting

3. Toby vs. Tubman

Both Toby and Harriet Tubman led people out of slavery into freedom. What other similarities can you find between Toby and Tubman? How are they different? Name three ways in which the two characters are alike or different. You might begin by collecting details in a Venn diagram.

GRAMMAR LINK | MINI-LESSON

Joining Independent Clauses

Language Handbook HELP

See Semi-colons, pages 801-802.

Technology HELP

See Language Workshop CD-ROM. *Key word entry: semi-colons.*

Use a semicolon between independent clauses joined by such words as these:

after all • besides • for example • for instance • furthermore • however • in fact • instead • meanwhile • nevertheless • on the other hand • otherwise • still • therefore • to begin with • unfortunately

EXAMPLES   Toby couldn't take the other people with him**; after all**, they didn't know how to fly.

It would probably have taken too long to teach them**; still**, he could have tried.

(Notice that the connecting words are always followed by a comma.)

Try It Out

Copy the following sentences, adding semicolons and commas where they're needed.

1. Many cultures have tales of people flying for example the ancient Greeks told the story of Daedalus and his son, Icarus.

2. Daedalus wanted to free himself and Icarus from imprisonment therefore he created wings of feathers and wax.

3. Icarus didn't listen to his father's warnings instead he flew away to try his wings.

4. Icarus flew higher and higher unfortunately he flew so high that the sun melted his wings.

SPELLING/VOCABULARY | HOW TO OWN A WORD

Verbs with *–cede, –ceed,* and *–sede*

Only one verb in English ends in *–sede: supersede*. Only three verbs end in *–ceed: exceed, proceed,* and *succeed.* All other verbs that end with this sound have *–cede* as their final letters. Complete each of the following sentences by filling in the blank with the best choice from the words below. (Use each word once.) You may want to use a dictionary.

concede   intercede   precede   secede   succeed

1. Frederick Douglass was born into slavery in Maryland only a few years before Harriet Tubman, but his escape would _____ hers by more than a decade.

2. Many people, both black and white, defied the Fugitive Slave Law of 1850 and continued to _____ on behalf of runaway slaves.

3. In its 1857 Dred Scott decision, the Supreme Court refused to _____ any rights to African Americans, whether free or enslaved.

4. John Brown hoped to march south and arm slaves for an uprising, but he did not _____; he was captured after he attacked a federal arsenal.

5. After Abraham Lincoln was elected president in 1860, six Southern states voted to _____ from the Union.

Before You Read

THE DRUMMER BOY OF SHILOH

Make the Connection

You Are There

It is a warm April night in Tennessee. The year is 1862, during the Civil War. You are only fourteen years old, but you are in the army. Your job is to beat a drum for the soldiers as they march into battle. You lie awake beneath a tree, surrounded by thousands of sleeping soldiers. You're thinking about the battle that will take place the next day.

Quickwrite

Now write. What are you thinking? How do you feel? What do you notice around you? What do you hear? smell? Can you see by the moon, or is it too dark? Record your impressions as if you were there.

go.hrw.com
LE0 8-1

Elements of Literature

Figures of Speech: Seeing Things in New Ways

Figures of speech are comparisons between two unlike things. When Bradbury says the drum has a "lunar face," he is using a figure of speech; he is comparing the drum to a moon. As you read this story, be aware of the figures of speech—comparisons that help you visualize the night scene and the terrible battle that will take place the next day.

> **A** **figure of speech** compares one thing to something very different. A figure of speech often helps us see things in unusual ways.
>
> *For more on Figures of Speech, see pages 41–42 and the Handbook of Literary Terms.*

Reading Skills and Strategies

Describing Mental Images

Mental images are the pictures we form in our minds as we read. Two people reading the same text can form very different mental images. That's because readers combine their own personal knowledge and experience with the writer's descriptions. You'll probably notice, for example, that the mental images you form as you read the next story will be affected by the thinking and writing you just did.

Data Bank

The Battle of Shiloh

Date April 6–7, 1862

Location In Tennessee near the Mississippi border beside the Tennessee River (Shiloh was a nearby church.)

Generals
- Union—Ulysses S. Grant with 45,000 troops
- Confederate—Albert Sidney Johnston with 65,000 troops

Casualties 23,746 Largest, bloodiest battle of the Civil War to that point (Larger battles, like Gettysburg, were still to come.)

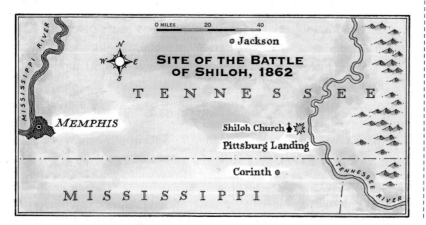

The Drummer Boy of Shiloh

*"I'm the one of all the rest who won't die.
I'll live through it."*

Ray Bradbury

In the April night, more than once, blossoms fell from the orchard trees and lighted with rustling taps on the drumhead. At midnight a peach stone, left miraculously on a branch through winter, flicked by a bird, fell swift and unseen; it struck once, like panic, and jerked the boy upright. In silence he listened to his own heart ruffle away, away—at last gone from his ears and back in his chest again.

After that he turned the drum on its side, where its great lunar face peered at him whenever he opened his eyes.

His face, alert or at rest, was solemn. It was a solemn time and a solemn night for a boy just turned fourteen in the peach orchard near Owl Creek, not far from the church at Shiloh.

". . . thirty-one . . . thirty-two . . . thirty-three." Unable to see, he stopped counting.

Beyond the thirty-three familiar shadows, forty thousand men, exhausted by nervous expectation and unable to sleep for romantic dreams of battles yet unfought, lay crazily askew[1] in their uniforms. A mile farther on, another army was strewn helter-skelter, turning slowly, basting themselves with the thought of what they would do when the time came—a leap, a yell, a blind plunge their strategy, raw youth their protection and benediction.

Now and again the boy heard a vast wind come up that gently stirred the air. But he knew what it was—the army here, the army there, whispering to itself in the dark. Some men talking to others, others murmuring to themselves, and all so quiet it was like a natural element arisen from South or North with the motion of the earth toward dawn.

What the men whispered the boy could only guess, and he guessed that it was "Me, I'm the one, I'm the one of all the rest who won't die. I'll live through it. I'll go home. The band will play. And I'll be there to hear it."

"Yes," thought the boy, "that's all very well for them, they can give as good as they get!"

For with the careless bones of the young men, harvested by night and bindled[2] around campfires, were the similarly strewn steel bones of their rifles with bayonets fixed like eternal lightning lost in the orchard grass.

"Me," thought the boy, "I got only a drum, two sticks to beat it, and no shield."

There wasn't a man-boy on this ground tonight who did not have a shield he cast, riveted, or carved himself on his way to his first attack, compounded of remote but nonetheless firm and fiery family devotion, flag-blown patriotism, and cocksure immortality, strengthened by the touchstone of very real gunpowder, ramrod, Minié ball,[3] and flint. But without

these last, the boy felt his family move yet farther off in the dark, as if one of those great prairie-burning trains had chanted them away, never to return—leaving him with this drum, which was worse than a toy in the game to be played tomorrow or someday much too soon.

The boy turned on his side. A moth brushed his face, but it was peach blossom. A peach blossom flicked him, but it was a moth. Nothing stayed put. Nothing had a name. Nothing was as it once was.

If he stayed very still when the dawn came up and the soldiers put on their bravery with their caps, perhaps they might go away, the war with them, and not notice him lying small here, no more than a toy himself.

"Well, by thunder now," said a voice. The boy shut his eyes to hide inside himself, but it was too late. Someone, walking by in the night, stood over him. "Well," said the voice quietly, "here's a soldier crying before the fight. Good. Get it over. Won't be time once it all starts."

And the voice was about to move on when the boy, startled, touched the drum at his elbow. The man above, hearing this, stopped. The boy could feel his eyes, sense him slowly bending near. A hand must have come down out of the night, for there was a little *rat-tat* as the fingernails brushed and the man's breath fanned the boy's face.

"Why, it's the drummer boy, isn't it?"

The boy nodded, not knowing if his nod was seen. "Sir, is that you?" he said.

"I assume it is." The man's knees cracked as he bent still closer. He smelled as all fathers should smell, of salt-sweat, tobacco, horse and

---

1. **askew** (ə·skyo͞o′): crookedly; not in straight lines.
2. **bindled:** bundled together.
3. **Minié** (min′ē) **ball:** cone-shaped rifle bullet, used in the 1800s.

- -
WORDS TO OWN
benediction (ben′ə·dik′shən) *n.*: blessing.
- -

boot leather, and the earth he walked upon. He had many eyes. No, not eyes, brass buttons that watched the boy.

He could only be, and was, the general. "What's your name, boy?" he asked.

"Joby, sir," whispered the boy, starting to sit up.

"All right, Joby, don't stir." A hand pressed his chest gently, and the boy relaxed. "How long you been with us, Joby?"

"Three weeks, sir."

"Run off from home or join legitimate, boy?" Silence.

"Darn-fool question," said the general. "Do you shave yet, boy? Even more of a fool. There's your cheek, fell right off the tree overhead. And the others here, not much older. Raw, raw, darn raw, the lot of you. You ready for tomorrow or the next day, Joby?"

"I think so, sir."

"You want to cry some more, go on ahead. I did the same last night."

"You, sir?"

"God's truth. Thinking of everything ahead. Both sides figuring the other side will just give up, and soon, and the war done in weeks and us all home. Well, that's not how it's going to be. And maybe that's why I cried."

"Yes, sir," said Joby.

The general must have taken out a cigar now, for the dark was suddenly filled with the Indian smell of tobacco—unlighted yet, but chewed as the man thought what next to say.

"It's going to be a crazy time," said the general. "Counting both sides, there's a hundred thousand men—give or take a few thousand—out there tonight, not one as can spit a sparrow off a tree or knows a horse clod from a Minié ball. Stand up, bare the breast, ask to be a target, thank them, and sit down, that's us, that's them. We should turn tail and train four

months; they should do the same. But here we are, taken with spring fever and thinking it blood lust, taking our sulfur with cannons instead of with molasses,[4] as it should be—going to be a hero, going to live forever. And I can see all them over there nodding agreement, save the other way around. It's wrong, boy, it's wrong as a head put on hind-side front and a man marching backward through life. Sometime this week more innocents will get shot out of pure Cherokee enthusiasm than ever got shot before. Oil Creek was full of boys splashing around in the noonday sun just a few hours ago. I fear it will be full of boys again, just floating, at sundown tomorrow, not caring where the current takes them."

The general stopped and made a little pile of winter leaves and twigs in the dark, as if he might at any moment strike fire to them to see his way through the coming days when the sun might not show its face because of what was happening here and just beyond.

The boy watched the hand stirring the leaves and opened his lips to say something, but did not say it. The general heard the boy's breath and spoke himself.

"Why am I telling you this? That's what you wanted to ask, eh? Well, when you got a bunch of wild horses on a loose rein somewhere, somehow you got to bring order, rein them in. These lads, fresh out of the milkshed, don't know what I know; and I can't tell them—men actually die in war. So each is his own army. I got to make one army of them. And for that, boy, I need you."

"Me!" The boy's lips barely twitched.

"You, boy," said the general quietly. "You are

---

4. Sulfur and molasses was used to treat constipation and other illnesses.

the heart of the army. Think about that. You are the heart of the army. Listen to me, now."

And lying there, Joby listened. And the general spoke. If he, Joby, beat slow tomorrow, the heart would beat slow in the men. They would lag by the wayside. They would drowse in the fields on their muskets. They would sleep forever after that—in those same fields, their hearts slowed by a drummer boy and stopped by enemy lead.

But if he beat a sure, steady, ever-faster rhythm, then, then, their knees would come up in a long line down over that hill, one knee after the other, like a wave on the ocean shore. Had he seen the ocean ever—seen the waves rolling in like a well-ordered cavalry charge to the sand? Well, that was it, that's what he wanted; that's what was needed. Joby was his right hand and his left. He gave the orders, but Joby set the pace.

So bring the right knee up and the right foot out and the left knee up and the left foot out, one following the other in good time, in brisk time. Move the blood up the body, and make the head proud and the spine stiff and the jaw resolute. Focus the eye and set the teeth; flare the nostril and tighten the hands; put steel armor all over the men, for blood moving fast in them does indeed make men feel as if they'd put on steel. He must keep at it, at it! Long and steady, steady and long! Then, even though shot or torn, those wounds got in hot blood—in blood he'd helped stir—would feel less pain. If their blood was cold, it would be more than slaughter: It would be murderous nightmare and pain best not told and no one to guess.

The general spoke and stopped, letting his breath slack off. Then, after a moment, he said, "So there you are, that's it. Will you do that, boy? Do you know now you're general of the army when the general's left behind?"

The boy nodded mutely.

"You'll run them through for me then, boy?"

"Yes, sir."

"Good. And, God willing, many nights from tonight, many years from now, when you're as old or far much older than me, when they ask you what you did in this awful time, you will tell them—one part humble and one part proud—I was the drummer boy at the battle of Owl Creek or of the Tennessee River, or maybe they'll just name it after the church there. I was the drummer boy at Shiloh. Good grief, that has a beat and sound to it fitting for Mr. Longfellow.[5] 'I was the drummer boy at Shiloh.' Who will ever hear those words and not know you, boy, or what you thought this night, or what you'll think tomorrow or the next day when we must get up on our legs and move."

The general stood up. "Well, then, God bless you, boy. Good night."

"Good night, sir." And tobacco, brass, boot polish, salt-sweat, and leather, the man moved away through the grass.

Joby lay for a moment staring, but unable to see where the man had gone. He swallowed. He wiped his eyes. He cleared his throat. He settled himself. Then, at last, very slowly and firmly, he turned the drum so it faced up toward the sky.

He lay next to it, his arm around it, feeling the tremor, the touch, the muted thunder as all the rest of the April night in the year 1862, near the Tennessee River, not far from the Owl Creek, very close to the church named Shiloh, the peach blossoms fell on the drum.

---

5. **Mr. Longfellow:** Henry Wadsworth Longfellow (1807–1882), popular American poet who was known for writing poems with strong, regular rhythms. (See "Paul Revere's Ride," page 537.)

- -

WORDS TO OWN
resolute (rez′ə·loot′) *adj.:* purposeful; determined.
tremor (trem′ər) *n.:* quiver; vibration.

- -

For a biography of Ray Bradbury, see page 221.

MAKING MEANINGS

First Thoughts

1. Go back to your Quickwrite notes. How did your feelings compare with the boy's feelings at the start of the story? How do you feel now?

Shaping Interpretations

2. The general says that the boy is the "heart of the army." What does he mean? Do you think it is true, or is he just trying to help the boy?

3. Find the place in the story where Joby thinks of fathers. What could this tell you about Joby's feelings?

4. After the Battle of Shiloh, the orchards and fields near Owl Creek were littered with the bodies of over 23,000 young men. Find passages where the general indicates that he knows the battle will be a bad one. Do you think the drummer boy survives? Why, or why not?

5. How do you think the writer wants you to feel about the drummer boy and the general and the war itself?

6. Bradbury's story is rich in **figures of speech**. On page 583 the general uses a figure of speech when he says to the boy: "There's your cheek, fell right off the tree overhead." What comparison is the general making? Skim back through the story, and find other places where Bradbury uses comparisons to help you see things in new ways. What **image** from the story do you think you will remember most?

> **Reading Check**
>
> a. Where and when does this story take place?
>
> b. How old is the drummer boy?
>
> c. What will happen the next day?
>
> d. Why is the boy so afraid? (What do the soldiers have that he does not have?)
>
> e. According to the general, why does he need the drummer boy?

Connecting with the Text

7. There really were drummer boys in both armies during the Civil War. Many of them were runaways or homeless boys. What clue in the story tells you that Joby is probably a runaway? After reading this story, how do you feel about the practice of using boys as drummers?

Challenging the Text

8. Bradbury never tells us which side the drummer boy is on—Union or Confederate. Why do you think he left that out of the story? Was it a good decision? Explain why or why not.

For Choices activities, a Grammar Link activity, and a Vocabulary activity based on this story, see pages 599–600.

Before You Read

THE DESERTER

Make the Connection

Deserter!

What does the word *deserter* mean to you? When have you heard the word used? Would you want to be called a deserter?

Quickwrite

With your class-mates, brainstorm all the things the word *deserter* brings to mind. If you're stuck, you could start by finding a definition in a dictionary. Record the group's ideas on the board in a cluster map.

Elements of Literature

Historical Fiction: But Is It True?

Irene Hunt wrote this novel to give readers a personal knowledge of the Civil War. The novel is historical because it is set in a real historical era and features real historical peo-ple (in this section, President Lincoln). It is fiction because it also includes made-up charac-ters—Jethro, Eb, and all the members of their family. The best writers of historical fiction try to depict the customs of the time. They try to help us see how people of that time thought and felt and what their problems were.

Ray Bradbury's "The Drum-mer Boy of Shiloh" (page 581) is also a good example of his-torical fiction. It helps us see the Civil War from the point of view of a young drummer boy.

> **H**istorical fiction is set during a real histori-cal era. It includes both historical characters and fictional characters.
>
> *For more on Historical Fiction, see the Handbook of Literary Terms.*

Reading Skills and Strategies

Using Prior Knowledge: You Know a Lot Already

Prior knowledge is what you already know—the information you have in your head that helps you understand a text. When you brainstormed and wrote about the word *deserter,* you were tapping into your prior knowledge and experi-ence. What you already know about the American Civil War will help you make connections as you read the next story.

 go.hrw.com
LEO 8-7

Background

Literature and Social Studies

During Lincoln's presidency, the Civil War dramatically divided the nation as states declared their allegiance either to the Union or to the Confederacy. Families, too, were sometimes divided when individual members chose to support different sides. In "The Deserter" eleven-year-old Jethro Creighton lives with his family on a farm in southern Illinois. His brothers Tom and John; his sister Jenny's boy-friend, Shad; and his cousin Eb are fighting in the Union army. Bill, his favorite brother, has disappeared, presumably to fight for the Confederacy. In 1863, when this story opens, the number of deserters from both the Union and Confederate armies was alarmingly high—and still growing.

THE DESERTER

from **Across Five Aprils**

Irene Hunt

Then a skeleton came out from among the trees.

One night in February of '63, as the family sat around the open fire, a wagon clattered down the road from the north and stopped in front of the house. Opening the door, Jethro saw three young men jump down from the wagon and stride up to the porch.

"Is this the home of Matthew Creighton?" one of them asked. Jethro noticed the crispness of the voice—an upstate voice, he thought.

"Yes, sir, my father's right here. Will you come indoors?"

They came inside with a great clatter of heavy boots. Jenny stood, wide-eyed, beside her father's chair; Nancy and Ellen held the small boys tightly in their arms. Matt tried to rise.

"Stay seated, sir. We're here to ask you a few questions." The young man who spoke threw back his coat to show his uniform and insignia. "We are representatives of the Federal Registrars; we are charged with hunting down deserters from the United States Army."

"Will you take chairs, gentlemen?" Matt said evenly, but Jethro noticed the sudden paleness of his father's face.

"Thank you, no. We are here to inquire if this is the home of Ebenezer Carron, 17th Illinois Infantry, Army of Tennessee."

"It is. This has bin Eb's home since he was a lad of ten or so."

"Have you seen him lately?"

"Why, no. Him and my son Thomas left together for the Army in August of '61. My own boy was kilt at Pittsburg Landing;[1] we ain't heered from Eb but once since then."

"You know the penalty for shielding a deserter from the United States Army?"

"I do. Air you tellin' me that Eb is a deserter?"

"His commanding officer has reason to believe that he is and that he has been making his way toward this part of the state—we assume toward his home."

Matt lifted a shaking hand and covered his eyes. Jenny glanced at him anxiously and then suddenly blazed out at the questioner.

"We haven't seen Eb. He's not here, and I'll thank you not to worry my father with more of this talk. If you want to look through this house——"

"We do, Miss—this house and all other buildings around here."

Jenny grasped the kerosene lamp with a firm hand. "Jeth, you come with me. We'll show these soldiers through the house; they can hunt outside for themselves."

---

1. **Pittsburg Landing:** site of the Battle of Shiloh (April 6–7, 1862). See "The Drummer Boy of Shiloh," page 580.

Her anger made Jenny a very grand lady, Jethro thought. He had never seen her more beautiful than she was that night, with her cheeks flaming and her eyes large and black with mixed anger and fear.

The soldiers grinned a little among themselves and followed her and Jethro to the sleeping rooms in the loft, then down to the kitchen and pantry, where Jenny took down the big key to the smokehouse and handed it to one of the men.

"We lock the smokehouse these nights. It's true there are deserters in these parts, and there's thievin' around everywhere. But we're not shieldin' anyone. Go look in the smokehouse for yourselves; go through the barn, the grainery, everywhere you think someone might be hidin'. After that I could say you'd best go down to the Point Prospect campground. The talk is that there are plenty of deserters there."

The Federal Registrars looked uncomfortable.

"Yes, we've heard," one of them muttered.

Jenny nodded. "It is easier to come to a house and upset a sick old man and scared womenfolk. Nobody in this neighborhood thinks it's healthy to go down to Point Prospect, but you sounded so brave just now—I thought you might want to do your duty down there."

The man who had done the questioning bowed mockingly before Jenny.

"We'll see to our duty, Miss, and if we find Ebenezer Carron on this place, we'll take him back with us—and maybe you, too." He turned toward Jethro. "Will you get a lantern, young man, and light us out back?"

Jethro took down the lantern that hung on the outside wall of the kitchen and started down the path toward the barn. The Federal Registrars followed, laughing with one another. One of them fell into step with Jethro after a time.

"Is that girl your sister?"

"Yes, sir."

"Well, she's quite a little beauty."

Jethro did not answer. His silence seemed to provoke the young man.

"I said that your sister is quite a little beauty, did you hear me?"

"She's spoke fer," Jethro answered shortly.

The young man shrugged and called out to the others. "I've just come upon some very interesting information: The beautiful little spitfire up at the ancestral mansion is 'spoke fer.' "

They laughed a great deal over that, and exaggerating the southern Illinois drawl and the backwoods diction, they made considerable sport over the boy's remark. Jethro felt his face burn with anger, but something new had been pointed up to him, something in the long process of learning to which he would be sensitive for the rest of his days. Until then he had not thought of his speech as being subject to ridicule.

The soldiers searched the place thoroughly and then started back to their wagon. One of them spoke sternly to Jethro on the way.

"If this man, Ebenezer Carron, turns up, you know what to do?"

"No, sir."

"Then you'd better listen. You get word to the Office of the Federal Registrars in Chicago right away, telling them where the man is or expects to be. You fail to report him, and you and your family will be up to your necks in trouble. Do you understand?"

Jethro nodded briefly. He was deeply antagonized by these men, but he knew they were simply carrying out a job assigned to them. Anyway, he was glad when the wagon carried them away—to the north. Evidently they were not going down to the deserters' camp at Point Prospect, not that night anyway.

There was an early spring that year. By the first of March the weather was warm, and the higher fields were dry enough for plowing. Jethro carried a rifle with him when he went down to John's place to work; Ellen fretted a great deal about it, but Matt insisted. Jethro had learned how to handle a gun properly, and it was always possible that he might bring down some kind of wild game for the table, or that he would have need to defend himself against a desperate man.

The field he plowed that day in early March was bordered on the east by dense woods, and Jethro became conscious that each time he approached the woods side of the field, the sharp, harsh call of a wild turkey would sound out with a strange kind of insistence—almost as if some stupid bird demanded that he stop and listen. Once when he halted his team and walked a little distance toward the woods, the calls came furiously, one after the other; then when he returned to his team and moved toward the west, they stopped until he had made the round of the field.

After several repetitions of this pattern, Jethro tethered his team and, taking up his rifle, walked into the woods. His heart beat fast as he walked, and his slim brown hand clutching the rifle was wet with sweat. Ed Turner was giving him a day's help in the field across the road, but Jethro chose not to call him although he had a guilty feeling that he was taking a foolish and dangerous chance.

He walked slowly and carefully, pausing now and then to listen. The calls stopped for a while, and he was half convinced that they had actually come from a wild bird; he made no move for a few minutes, and they began again, softer now and more certainly coming from the throat of a man.

Jethro stood quite still. "Hello," he called finally. "What is it you want of me?"

There was no answer. Then the call came again, softly, insistently, from a clump of trees, one of which was a tremendous old oak—long since hollowed out, first by lightning and then by decay.

Jethro walked closer, his gun raised, and after a minute, the human voice which he had been half expecting to hear called out to him.

"Put yore gun down, Jeth; I ain't aimin' to hurt ye. I didn't dast take the chancet of Ed Turner hearin' me call to ye."

He thought joyfully of Bill at first. He shouldn't have; almost every night he heard his parents talking of Eb and of what uncertainties they would face if he were really a deserter and if he should suddenly appear. But Jethro had forgotten Eb for the moment; the possibility of Bill's return was always a hope far back in his mind.

"Who is it?" he asked again. "Come out and let me see your face."

Then a skeleton came out from among the trees. It was the skeleton of a Union soldier, though the uniform it wore was so ragged and filthy it was difficult to identify. The sunken cheeks were covered with a thin scattering of fuzz; the hair was lank and matted. It fell over the skeleton's forehead and down into its eyes. The boy stared at it without speaking.

"Jeth, you've growed past all believin'. I've bin watchin' you from fur off, and I couldn't git over it—how you've growed."

Then Jethro realized who it was. "Eb," he exclaimed in a voice hardly above a whisper. "It's Eb, ain't it?"

There was utter despair in the soldier's voice.

"Yes," he said, "I reckon it's Eb—what there's left of him."

For a few seconds Jethro forgot the Federal Registrars and the fact that not only the word which preceded Eb, but his method of announcing himself gave credence to[2] the suspicion that he was a deserter. But for those first few seconds Jethro could only remember that this was Eb, a part of the family, the boy who had been close to Tom, the soldier who would have more vivid stories to tell of the war than ever a newspaper would be able to publish. He held out his hand.

"Eb, it's good—it's so good to see you. Pa

2. **gave credence to:** made believable.

and Ma will be——" he stopped suddenly. He noticed that Eb ignored his outstretched hand.

"Yore pa and ma will be scairt—that's what you mean, ain't it? Scairt fer themselves and ashamed of me." He paused for a second and then added defiantly, "I deserted, you know; I up and left Ol' Abe's Army of the United States."

Jethro could only stare at his cousin; he could find no words.

"Desertin' ain't a purty word to you, is it? Well, I done it—I don't jest know why. We'd had another skirmish and there was dead boys that we had to bury the next day—and we'd bin licked agin. All at oncet I knowed I couldn't stand it no longer, and I jest up and left. Oncet a man has left, he's done fer. I've bin a long time gittin' home, and now that I'm here, it ain't no comfort."

"Eb, couldn't you just come up to the house and see them for a few hours or so? Couldn't you have a good meal and get cleaned up and tell the folks all you know about Tom?"

"I cain't. I could git 'em into awful trouble. Besides, they would prob'ly jest as soon not set eyes on the likes of me agin."

"But, Eb, if you can't come up to the house, what *did* you come for?"

Eb's face showed quick anger. "I come because I couldn't help myself, that's why. *You*

don't know what it's like—you that was allus the baby and the pet of the fam'ly. There be things that air too terr'ble to talk about—and you want to see the fields where you used to be happy, you want to smell the good air of old Illinois so much that you fergit—you go crazy fer an hour or so—and then you don't dare go back."

He shivered and leaned back against a tree trunk as if just talking had taken more strength than he had to spend.

"Have you been down to the Point Prospect camp?" Jethro asked after a while.

"A couple days. It's worse than the war down there, with fellers afraid and gittin' meaner as they git more afraid. I didn't come back to be with soldiers anyway. I'm sick of soldiers, livin' and dead; I'm sick of all of 'em." He threw himself down on a thick padding of dead leaves and motioned Jethro to do the same.

"I want ye to tell me about 'em, Jeth—Uncle Matt and Aunt Ellen, Jenny . . ."

"You knew Pa had a heart attack; he's not been himself since. Ma's tolerable, and Jenny's fine. We do the work of the farm together, Jenny and me."

"And John, Shad—where air they? They jined up, didn't they?"

"Yes, John's in Tennessee under a general named Rosecrans. And Shad's in the East with the Army of the Potomac. He was at Antietam Creek and Fredericksburg;[3] you heard of them two battles, didn't you?"

"We hear precious little except what's happenin' in the part of the country we're in. I've heered of Ol' Abe kickin' out that fine McClellan;[4] it's a pity he don't kick out a passel of 'em out in the West." Eb seemed absorbed in his angry thoughts for a while; then he looked up at Jethro again.

"And Bill, did ever you hear from him?"

"Not a word," Jethro replied in a voice that was hardly audible.

"I guess you took that hard. You was allus a pet of Bill's."

"All of us took it hard."

"Yore pa wrote Tom and me about it. Tom tried to pretend he didn't keer, but I know he did. He cried oncet—I wouldn't tell that 'cept now it's no matter."

"No," Jethro agreed dully, "now it's no matter."

Eb took a dry twig and broke it up into a dozen pieces, aimlessly.

"How did you git the word about Tom?" he asked finally.

"Dan Lawrence was home on sick leave. His pa brought him over; he told us all about it."

"I was at Pittsburg Landing too, but I didn't know about Tom—not fer two or three days. I wanted to write, but somehow I couldn't do it. Tom and me had bin in swimmin' the day before the Rebs su'prised us; we was both of us in good spirits then, laughin' and carryin' on like we done in the old days back home. Somehow all the spirit in me has bin gone ever since. I could stand things as long as I had Tom along with me."

He ran his hand across his eyes as if to shut out a picture or a memory. "Tell me about little Jenny; is she still in love with Shad Yale?"

"More than ever, I guess. She writes to him a lot; he sets great store by her letters."

"He ought to. A man needs a girl's nice letters when he's sufferin' with the homesick. I wisht I'd had a girl like Jenny to write to me, but there ain't many such as her, I reckon."

Jethro studied Eb's sunken cheeks and dull eyes.

"How do you manage to eat, Eb?"

"I don't do it reg'lar, that's shore. I live off the land—steal a little, shoot me a rabbit or squirrel and cook 'em over a low fire late at night. It ain't good eatin', but nothin's good these days like it used to be."

---

3. **Antietam** (an·tēt′əm) **Creek and Fredericksburg:** The battle fought at Antietam, in western Maryland, on September 17, 1862, was one of the bloodiest of the war, leaving more than 23,000 dead or wounded. The battle fought at Fredericksburg, Virginia, on December 13, 1862, ended in a major Confederate victory.

4. **McClellan:** George B. McClellan (1826–1885), Union general removed by Lincoln in November 1862 for being too cautious and slow to act.

Jethro's insides twisted in sympathy. "Are you hungry now, Eb?"

"I'm allus hungry. Ye git used to it after a while."

"Nancy fixed me some grub to bring to the field with me; I'll go get it for you."

He ran to the fencerow where he had left two pieces of bread and the cuts from a particularly tender haunch of beef that Nancy had wrapped in a white cloth for him. Ordinarily he would have eaten the snack by midafternoon, but the wild-turkey calls had made him forget it. He returned to Eb minutes later with the food and a jug of water.

They sat together in the shadows, while Eb ate with an appetite that was like a hungry animal's.

"Eb, I've got to tell you," Jethro said quietly after a while. "The soldiers that call themselves the Federal Registrars was at the house lookin' for you last month."

Eb seemed to shrink within himself. He looked at his hands carefully, as if he really cared about inspecting them, and his mouth worked in a strange, convulsive <u>grimace</u>. He wouldn't look at Jethro when he finally spoke.

"I was an awful fool—at least you got a chancet in battle—maybe it's one in a hunderd, but it's a chancet. This way, I got none. There's no place on this earth fer me to go. Even the

camps of deserters don't want fellers as weak and sick as I am; they let me know that quick at Point Prospect. I'll either freeze or starve—or be ketched. I'd give just about anythin' if I could walk back to my old outfit and pitch into the fightin' agin. A soldier don't have to feel ashamed."

Jethro sat for a while trying to think of some way out of the situation; it appeared more hopeless the more he thought. He was frightened—for the despairing man in front of him, for himself and his family. When he finally spoke, he tried hard to sound reassuring, but the pounding of his heart made his voice shake.

"Well, you stay here till we can think of somethin', Eb. I'm goin' to get you some quilts and things from Nancy's place; I'll bring you what grub I can lay hands on—I can always get eggs and a chicken for you. I think you'd best eat all you can and rest for a spell; we'll think of what's to be done when once you get a little stronger."

Eb looked up then. "You all but fool me into believin' that somethin' *kin* be done, Jeth, but I know better. You ner no one else kin help me now—not even Ol' Abe hisself."

Ol' Abe. Mr. Lincoln. Mr. President.

"I ought to go back to work now, Eb."

"I guess so," Eb looked at him with a suggestion of a smile. "I cain't git used to it—you bein' big enough to handle a team alone. You seem almost a man these days, Jeth; even yore hair ain't quite as yaller and curly as it used to be."

Jethro turned away. "I'll bring you a quilt from Nancy's before I go in for the night," he said shortly.

He walked back to his waiting team; there was still time to plow a dozen furrows before sunset—and to think.

He had faced sorrow when Bill left and fear the night Guy Wortman tried to pull him down from the wagon; he had felt a terrible empti-

---

WORDS TO OWN

grimace (grim'is) *n.:* twisting of the face expressing pain or disgust.

---

ness the day Shadrach and John went away and deep anger the night he watched the barn burn at the hands of the county ruffians. But in his eleven years he had never been faced with the responsibility of making a fearful decision like the one confronting him.

The authority of the law loomed big in his mind; he remembered, "You and your family will be in serious trouble." Loyalty to his brother Tom and the many thousands who had fought to the last ditch at Pittsburg Landing, at Antietam, Fredericksburg, and all the other places that were adding length to the long list—how could loyalty to these men be true if one were going to harbor and give comfort to a man who simply said, "I quit."

But, on the other hand, how did one feel at night if he awoke and remembered, "I'm the one that sent my cousin to his death." Eb was not a hero, certainly—not now, anyway. People scorned the likes of Eb; sure, so did Jethro, and yet—

"How do I know what *I'd* be like if I was sick and scared and hopeless; how does Ed Turner or Mr. Milton or *any* man know that ain't been there? We got to remember that Eb has been in battles for two years; maybe he's been a hero in them battles, and maybe to go on bein' a hero in a war that has no end in sight is too much to ask . . . . Sure, deep down in me, I want Eb to get out, to leave me free of feelin' that I'm doin' wrong to give him grub, or takin' the risk of keepin' it a secret that he's here. Yes, it would leave me free if he'd just move on—but no, it wouldn't—I ain't goin' to be free when he moves on; I can't set down to a table and forget that someone sick as Eb looks to be is livin' off the land, that he's livin' scared like a wild animal that's bein' hunted.

"But what's it goin' to be like if more and more soldiers quit and go into the woods and leave the fightin' to them that won't quit? What do you say to yourself when you remember that you fed and helped someone like Eb and maybe you get a letter from the East that Shad is killed and you see Jenny grievin', or that John is killed and Nancy and her little boys is left all alone—how do you feel when things like that come up?

"Of course, right now I could say to Pa 'I leave it up to you'—and then what could he do? Why, he'd be caught in the same trap I'm in now; I'd wriggle out of it and leave the decidin' to a sick old man; I'd put him in the spot where any way he decided would be bad—hurtful to a man's conscience. No, there ain't an answer that's any plainer to an old man than it is to me. And what was it that man said the day of the barn-raisin'? 'It's good that you're a boy and don't have to worry yourself about this war.' Why yes, no doubt about it, eleven-year-old boys ain't got a thing to worry about; this year of 1863 is a fine, carefree time for eleven-year-old boys. . . ."

Jenny noticed his <u>preoccupation</u> at supper that night. She waited until the others were out of the kitchen and she and Jethro were left alone.

"What is it that's on your mind, Jeth?"

"Nothin'. Just tired." He threw himself down in front of the fireplace and closed his eyes. He knew it would be hard to deceive his sister; there was a determination about Jenny.

"You'd better tell me, Jeth. I'll find out, you know."

"You don't give me any worry; there's nothin' to find out."

"Jeth, have you had some news about Shad or John?"

"No, how could I? You know what mail has come."

"You might ha' talked to someone."

"Well, I ain't. Not to anyone that knows a word about Shad or John."

She worked at her dishpan for a while in silence; then she walked over and poked him a little with the toe of her shoe.

"There's somethin', Jeth. Nancy noticed it too. Now I want to know—is it somethin' about Eb? Is he here with the deserters?"

WORDS TO OWN

preoccupation (prē·ăk′yōō·pā′shən) *n.*: state of being absorbed in thought.

He turned his head away from her; he couldn't remember when he had lied to Jenny, and he wasn't sure that he could do it well.

"Jenny, you vex me when I'm not feelin' so well. Can't I have an upset stummick without you firin' a passel of questions at me?"

She stood looking down at him thoughtfully for a while, and then an idea stemming from experience with older brothers suddenly struck her. She dropped down beside him and whispered her suspicion gleefully in his ear.

"Jeth Creighton, have you been smokin' on the sly? Is *that* what's givin' you an upset stummick?"

He kept his eyes closed and did not answer, knowing his silence would confirm her guess. Jenny was triumphant.

"That's it! I know without your sayin' it," she crowed. "You look white, the way Tom and Eb did once when they tried it."

It was very simple to lie without words; he merely opened his eyes and grinned sheepishly at her.

"I'm su'prised you would be that silly, Jeth. With so much spring work to do, you don't have the time to get sick over smokin'." She shook her head. "How do you expect to keep goin' when you didn't more than touch your meal tonight?"

He seized the opportunity to get some food for Eb without detection. "Would you fix me a little bread and meat and slip it up to my room later on, Jenny? I'll likely feel better after a while, and I'm goin' to be hungry when I do."

She sighed, but with a certain satisfaction. There was an adventurous streak in Jenny; she would have liked to try smoking herself if she had dared, and she was a little amused that her sober young brother had been tempted in this direction of most young males.

Jethro lay awake in his room that night and wrestled with his problem. He wondered if, after all, it wouldn't be better to ask his father's advice, but he decided against that almost immediately and as firmly as he had rejected the idea that afternoon. He wondered about Ross

Milton, but there was little chance to make a trip to Newton at this time of year. What about Ed Turner, staunch, levelheaded neighbor? No, Ed had two sons in the army; it wouldn't do to lay this responsibility upon Ed's shoulders. He thought of Eb's words. "You ner no one else kin help me now—not even Ol' Abe hisself."

Ol' Abe. Mr. Lincoln. Mr. President. Not even Mr. Lincoln himself!

Jethro turned restlessly in his bed. What if one put it up to Mr. Lincoln? What if one said, "I will abide by the word of him who is highest in this land"? But wasn't that word already known? Wasn't the word from the highest in the land just this: Turn in deserters or there will be terrible trouble for you and your family?

But Mr. Lincoln was a man who looked at problems from all sides. Mr. Lincoln was not a faraway man like General McClellan or Senator Sumner[5] or Secretary of State Seward.[6] Mr. Lincoln had plowed fields in Illinois; he had thought of the problems men came up against; he was not ready to say, "Everything on this side of the line is right, and everything on the other side is wrong."

But would one dare? A nobody, a boy on a southern Illinois farm—would he dare? Mr. Lincoln held the highest office in the land; what would he think? Would it vex him that a boy from southern Illinois could be so bold? And anyway, how could one say it? What manner of words could one use so as not to be too forward, too lacking in respect toward the President of the United States?

Jeth realized he was not going to be able to go to sleep. There was a candle in his room; there was some ink and an old pen that Bill had sometimes used. There was also Ross Milton's book—the book on English usage. Jethro got up in the quiet of the night, lighted his candle, opened Ross Milton's book and began to write on a piece of rough lined paper.

5. **Senator Sumner:** Charles Sumner (1811-1874), U.S. senator from Massachusetts from 1851 to 1874.
6. **Secretary of State Seward:** William Henry Seward (1801-1872), U.S. secretary of state from 1861 to 1869.

The next morning he hid Jenny's sandwiches inside his coat, and at the barn he picked up a few eggs from the nests up in the loft. He dug an apple out of the straw in the apple cave; no one would question that—a boy needed something to munch on in midmorning. He would like to have taken some coffee beans—a man lying out in the woods all night needed a hot drink; but that item was one he would not take. Not for Eb, not even for Bill or Shad, would he have taken his mother's coffee. He knew where there were good sassafras roots in the woods; maybe he would burn some brush in the fencerows and heat a little water for sassafras tea. He filched an old kettle and two lumps of sugar, just in case.

Eb was feeling a little better that morning. The quilts Jethro had taken from Nancy's house had made the long night more comfortable; he had washed himself in the creek and looked refreshed.

"You've brung me a feast, Jeth," he said gratefully.

They sat together for a while and talked in low voices.

"I'll be gittin' out in a day or so, Jeth. I caint hev you takin' all this risk."

"If you could go back to the army, you would, wouldn't you, Eb?"

"You're askin' a man if he had a chancet to

live, would he take it. But I've told you, Jeth—a deserter caint go back. I'll be hunted the rest of my days—but the rest of my days ain't goin' to be too many."

Jethro said nothing, but as he plowed that morning he made up his mind to send the letter. It was a frightening thing to do, but if one did nothing—well, that was frightening too. He knew Eb was not really planning to leave— Eb was a lost and frightened boy, and there was nowhere else to go. For Jethro there was nothing to do but send the letter.

The plowshares needed sharpening, Jethro told his father that noon. Hadn't he better drive over to Hidalgo and get that work done? He'd pick up the mail, too, for themselves and for Ed Turner. Was that all right with his father?

Matt seldom questioned Jethro's decisions. The boy was doing a man's work; he was due the dignity accorded to a man. Matt assented to the trip readily, and Jethro, with the letter in his pocket, drove off down the road, his heart pounding with excitement.

In Hidalgo the old man who took care of the mail glanced sharply at Jethro when he noticed the inscription[7] on the envelope. But he was a silent man with problems of his own; as long as a letter was properly stamped and addressed it was no affair of his. Privately he thought that some people were allowing their young ones to become a little forward, but that was their concern. He threw Jethro's letter in a big bag that would be taken by wagon down to Olney that evening.

The long wait for an answer was interminable. Jethro tossed at night and wondered: Had he done an impudent thing, had he laid himself open to trouble, had he been a fool to think that a boy of his age might act without the advice of his elders? Sometimes he got up

7. **inscription:** writing; here, an address.

WORDS TO OWN

impudent (im′pyo͞o·dənt) *adj.:* too bold; disrespectful.

----

and walked about his narrow room, but that was bad, for Jenny would hear him. Once she came to his door, and she was crying.

"Jeth—Jeth, what is it? What's botherin' you? Ain't we good friends anymore, ain't you goin' to tell me?"

He had to be <u>curt</u> with her to forestall any more questions. After that she didn't come to his door again, but he knew that if he stirred or moaned under his burden of worry, both Jenny and Nancy would hear him and worry through a sleepless night.

Eb's often <u>reiterated</u>, "I'll be goin' on soon, Jeth; I won't be a burden to you much longer," became like the whippoorwill's cry—always the same and never ending. Jethro closed his ears to it, but the tensions within him mounted, and the necessity of providing for Eb's needs in strictest secrecy became a task that seemed to grow in magnitude as the days went by.

"If I could be sure I'm doin' the right thing," he would say to himself, as he watched the dark earth fall away from his plowshares. "If I could feel really set-up about doin' a fine thing, but I don't know. Maybe I'm doin' somethin' terrible wrong; maybe the next time they come, the Federal Registrars will take me."

★ ★ ★ ★

The letter came one noon when they were all seated at dinner. As so often happened, it was Ed Turner who brought the mail out from town. Jenny ran to the door, eager for a letter from Shadrach; Nancy's eyes pleaded for word from John.

But Ed held only one large envelope, and that was addressed to Jethro in a small, cramped handwriting done in very black ink. It was postmarked Washington, D.C.

Abraham Lincoln, 1862 photograph by Mathew Brady.

"Looks like purty important mail you're gittin', Jethro," Ed said quietly. His eyes were full of puzzled concern.

Jethro's head swam. This was the showdown; now, all the family, Ed Turner, and soon the neighborhood would know everything. In the few seconds that passed before he opened the envelope, he wished with all his heart that he had not meddled in the affairs of a country at war, that he had let Eb work out his own problems, that he, Jethro, were still a sheltered young boy who did the tasks his father set for him and shunned the idea that he dare think for himself. He looked at the faces around him, and they spun in a strange mist of color—black eyes and blue eyes, gray hair and gold and black, pink cheeks and pale ones and weather-beaten brown ones.

He read the letter through, word for word, and while he read, there wasn't a sound in the cabin beyond the slight rustle of the page in the shaking hand that held it. When he was through, he held the letter out to Jenny, with a long sigh.

"You can read it out loud, Jenny."

Jenny stared at him as if he were a stranger; then she shook her head.

"It's your letter, Jeth; you'd best do the readin'."

He didn't know whether he could or not—there was a great pounding in his ears and his breath was short—but he ran his hand across his eyes and swallowed hard. After the first words, his voice grew steady, and he read the letter through without faltering.

- -
WORDS TO OWN

curt (kʉrt) *adj.*: brief to the point of rudeness.
reiterated (rē·it′ə·rāt′id) *v.*: repeated.
- -

Executive Mansion
March 14, 1863

Master Jethro Creighton
Hidalgo, Illinois

Dear Jethro:

Mr. Hay has called my attention to your letter, knowing as he does the place in my affection for boys of your age and the interest I have in letters coming from my home state of Illinois.

The problem which you describe is one, among so many others, that has troubled both my waking thoughts and those that intrude upon my sleep. The gravity of that problem has become of far-reaching significance and is one in which the authority of military regulations, the decline of moral responsibility, and the question of ordinary human compassion are so involved as to present a situation in which a solution becomes agonizingly difficult.

I had, however, made a decision relative to this problem only a few days before receiving your letter. There will be much criticism of that decision, but you will understand when I say if it be a wrong one, I have then erred on the side of mercy.

The conditions of that decision are as follows: All soldiers improperly absent from their posts, who will report at certain points designated by local recruit offices by April 1, will be restored to their respective regiments without punishment except for forfeiture of pay and allowances for the period of their absence.

This information you may relay to the young man in question, and I pray that the remorse and despair which he has known since the time of his desertion will bring his better self to the cause for which so many of his young compatriots have laid down their lives.

May God bless you for the earnestness with which you have tried to seek out what is right; may He guide both of us in that search during the days ahead of us.

Yours, very sincerely and respectfully,
Abraham Lincoln

WORDS TO OWN

gravity (grav′i·tē) *n.:* seriousness.
remorse (ri·môrs′) *n.:* deep sense of guilt over something one has done.

MEET THE WRITER

Haunted by Words

When **Irene Hunt** (1907–   ) was seven, her father died. She and her mother went to live on her grandparents' nearby farm in Illinois. Out of that experience came her first novel, *Across Five Aprils*. Hunt's grandfather fascinated her with stories of his childhood during the Civil War, stories she lived with for fifty years before writing about them.

Hunt wrote six more award-winning novels, through she didn't begin writing until she ended a long teaching career in Illinois public schools.

As a teacher, Hunt learned that "teaching history through literature" really sparked her junior-high students, so she finally fulfilled her obsession to write:

66 Words have always held a fascination for me, causing me to be teased often as a child when I used them lavishly without having the slightest idea of their meaning. The wish to write pages full of words, to make them tell the stories that I dreamed about, haunted me from childhood on. 99

MAKING MEANINGS

First Thoughts

1. Do you think Jethro is a believable eleven-year-old boy? Why or why not?

Shaping Interpretations

2. What does Eb's appearance tell you about the way he's been living since his desertion?

3. Eb says on page 590 that he doesn't know why he deserted. How would you explain why he deserted? Does his experience change your ideas about deserters? (Check your Quickwrite.)

4. Eb wishes he had never deserted. Why can't he just go back to his regiment? What does he mean when he says: "A soldier don't have to feel ashamed"? (See page 592.)

5. Why does Jethro think Mr. Lincoln might help him?

6. What does Lincoln mean when he says in the letter that if he is wrong, he has erred on the side of mercy?

Reading Check

a. Why are the soldiers looking for Eb?

b. What does Jethro find when he follows the turkey call into the woods?

c. Name two things Jethro does for his cousin Eb.

d. What **internal conflict** does Jethro face?

e. How is this conflict resolved?

Connecting with the Text

7. Suppose that Jethro had not gotten an answer from Lincoln. What do you think he should have done about Eb in that case? Why?

8. What did the story add to your **prior knowledge** about the Civil War? Were you surprised about any details in the story?

9. Think about how events like those in the story could happen today in another part of the world. Who would be fighting whom? How would ordinary people suffer? How might they face a problem like the one that Jethro faces?

Challenging the Text

10. What do you think about writers using real **historical characters** in a work of **fiction**?

Writer's Notebook

1. Collecting Ideas for an Informative Report

After reading "The Drummer Boy of Shiloh" and "The Deserter," think of what you want to know about the Civil War. Maybe you want to find out more of the facts behind these two pieces of **historical fiction.** With your classmates, make a list of questions you might research. Then, choose one question, and begin your research on the Internet or in a library. What key words or topics will you look up?

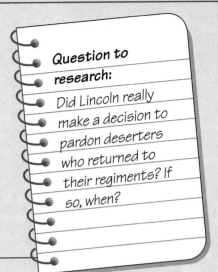

Question to research:
Did Lincoln really make a decision to pardon deserters who returned to their regiments? If so, when?

Creative Writing

2. Dear Diary

Imagine that it is the day after the story "The Drummer Boy of Shiloh" ends—that is, the actual day of the Battle of Shiloh. Write a diary entry from the point of view of Joby. Decide if you are writing in the morning, before the battle begins, or later, after it has ended.

Art

3. In My Mind's Eye

Find a passage in "The Drummer Boy of Shiloh" (or in "The Deserter") that creates a vivid image in your mind. Copy the passage at the bottom of a page. Use the rest of the page to draw the scene as you imagine it.

Creative Writing

4. Dear Mr. President

Irene Hunt shows us Lincoln's reply to Jethro, but she doesn't show us Jethro's original letter. Write that letter as if you were Jethro. You'll want to explain the situation, describe your conflicting feelings, and try to persuade President Lincoln to help Eb.

Supporting an Opinion

5. It's a Fake

The letter from Lincoln to Jethro was made up by Hunt for her novel. Yet the letter is written in a style that resembles Lincoln's. In your opinion, should writers of historical fiction make up letters like this?

In a paragraph, explain why or why not.

Performance

6. Try to See It My Way

With a partner, present an imaginary dialogue between two of the following characters from "The Drummer Boy of Shiloh" or "The Deserter":

- Joby and the general on the day of the Battle of Shiloh

- one of the Federal Registrar soldiers and Eb

- Jenny and Eb

- President Lincoln and his secretary, John Hay

GRAMMAR LINK MINI-LESSON

Capitalizing and Punctuating Titles

Language Handbook HELP

See Capital Letters, page 796; Underlining (Italics), page 804; Quotation Marks, page 807.

Technology HELP

See Language Workshop CD-ROM. *Key word entry: capitalization.*

Capitalize the first and last words and all important words in titles of books, periodicals, poems, stories, historical documents and speeches, movies, TV programs, works of art, and musical compositions. Words considered unimportant within a title include articles (*a, an, the*), prepositions of fewer than five letters (*of, to, for, from, with*), and coordinating conjunctions (*and, but, so, nor, yet, for*). NOTE: When one of these words is the first word in a title, it is capitalized.

EXAMPLES   *Journal of American History*
"Casey at the Bat"
"Too Soon a Woman"
The Autobiography of Miss Jane Pittman
"Follow the Drinking Gourd"

Titles of short creative works are enclosed in quotation marks; titles of other types of works are printed in italics (or underlined if typed or written by hand).

Try It Out

On a separate piece of paper, capitalize and punctuate each of the following titles correctly:

across five aprils (novel)
the devil and daniel webster (short story)
the gettysburg address (speech)
national geographic (magazine)
battle hymn of the republic (song)
gone with the wind (movie)

Quotation Marks	Italics (Underlining)
Magazine articles • short stories • essays • poems • songs • episodes of TV shows • chapters of books	Books • plays • movies • magazines • works of art • TV series • albums • long musical compositions

VOCABULARY HOW TO OWN A WORD

WORD BANK

benediction
resolute
tremor
grimace
preoccupation
impudent
curt
reiterated
gravity
remorse

Word Origin and Meaning Maps

Work with a partner to make a meaning map like the one below for each of the remaining words in the Word Bank. Use a dictionary to find the origin of the word. Then, think of at least two questions for each word. Compare maps with other teams.

When might you make a grimace?
- when you slam a door on your finger
- when you smell something bad

grimace

French < Old French < Frank *grima*, "a mask"

What feelings might a grimace show?
- pain
- disgust
- concentration

Before You Read

BARBARA FRIETCHIE

Make the Connection

Fighting the Current

Being a hero isn't easy. As the next poem shows, sometimes it means having the courage to be different from the crowd or to defend an unpopular view.

Quickwrite

With your class-mates, brainstorm examples of individuals (contemporary, historical, fictional, even yourself) who stood up for their beliefs. You might use a chart like this one:

Name	Belief	Action

Elements of Literature

Narrative Poem

"Barbara Frietchie" is a **narrative poem,** a story in verse. Like other stories, a narrative poem usually includes a plot, characters, and a setting. The events of the poem may be real, invented, or (as in this poem) some-where in between.

A **narrative poem** is a poem that tells a story.

For more on Narrative Poems, see the Handbook of Literary Terms.

Reading Skills and Strategies

Paraphrasing: Saying It Your Way

Paraphrasing means restating an author's ideas in your own words.

- A paraphrase differs from a **summary,** which retells only the most important points in a text.

- A paraphrase is usually longer than a summary.

Paraphrasing is a good way to check your understanding of a poem, especially one like "Barbara Frietchie," which includes some old-fashioned language.

Background

Literature and Social Studies

"Barbara Frietchie" is set during the Civil War. In 1862, after defeating Union forces at the second Battle of Bull Run, Confederate troops moved north from Virginia into Mary-land. Led by Generals Robert E. Lee and Stonewall Jackson, the troops marched into the town of Frederick on Septem-ber 6 singing "Maryland, My Maryland." Lee and his men were expecting a warm welcome, but the people of Frederick were actually loyal to the Union—though not all had the courage to display the U.S. flag as the Confederate forces advanced on the town. Whittier based "Barbara Frietchie" on these events.

go.hrw.com
LE0 8-7

Barbara Frietchie

John Greenleaf Whittier

Up from the meadows rich with corn,
Clear in the cool September morn,

The clustered spires of Frederick stand
Green-walled by the hills of Maryland.

5   Round about them orchards sweep,
Apple and peach tree fruited deep,

Fair as the garden of the Lord
To the eyes of the famished rebel horde,°

On that pleasant morn of the early fall
10 When Lee marched over the mountain wall;

Over the mountains winding down,
Horse and foot, into Frederick town.

Forty flags with their silver stars,
Forty flags with their crimson bars,

15 Flapped in the morning wind: the sun
Of noon looked down, and saw not one.

Up rose old Barbara Frietchie then,
Bowed with her fourscore years and ten;

Bravest of all in Frederick town,
20 She took up the flag the men hauled down

In her attic window the staff she set,
To show that one heart was loyal yet.

Up the street came the rebel tread,
Stonewall Jackson riding ahead.

25 Under his slouched hat left and right
He glanced; the old flag met his sight.

"Halt!"—the dust-brown ranks stood fast.
"Fire!"—out blazed the rifle blast.

It shivered the window, pane and sash;
30 It rent the banner with seam and gash.

Quick, as it fell, from the broken staff
Dame Barbara snatched the silken scarf.

8. horde (hôrd): moving crowd.

Barbara Frietchie (1876) (detail) by Dennis Malone Carter
(1827–1881). Oil on canvas ($36\frac{1}{4}$" × $46\frac{1}{4}$").

Kirby Collection of Historical Paintings, Lafayette College, Easton, Pennsylvania.
Photo by Thomas Kosa.

Stars and Stripes Forever

The U.S. flag hanging from Barbara Frietchie's window had only thirty-four stars. These stars stood for the thirty-four states that had been admitted to the Union by 1862. (Although the Southern states had seceded from the Union, President Abraham Lincoln refused to have their stars removed from the flag.)

Since 1960, the year after Hawaii became the fiftieth state, the U.S. flag has had fifty stars. Congress decided in 1818 that the number of stripes would be kept to thirteen, representing the thirteen original colonies. Known as the Stars and Stripes, the red, white, and blue flag has represented the United States at home, around the world, and even on the moon, where it was planted by astronauts in 1969.

She leaned far out on the windowsill,
And shook it forth with a royal will.

35   "Shoot, if you must, this old gray head,
But spare your country's flag," she said.

A shade of sadness, a blush of shame,
Over the face of the leader came;

The nobler nature within him stirred
40   To life at that woman's deed and word;

"Who touches a hair of yon gray head
Dies like a dog! March on!" he said.

All day long through Frederick street
Sounded the tread of marching feet:

45   All day long that free flag tossed
Over the heads of the rebel host.

Ever its torn folds rose and fell
On the loyal winds that loved it well;

And through the hill gaps sunset light
50 Shone over it with a warm good night.

Barbara Frietchie's work is o'er,
And the Rebel rides on his raids no more.

Honor to her! and let a tear
Fall, for her sake, on Stonewall's bier.°

55 Over Barbara Frietchie's grave,
Flag of Freedom and Union, wave!

Peace and order and beauty draw
Round thy symbol of light and law;

And ever the stars above look down
60 On thy stars below in Frederick town!

54. bier (bir): coffin and the platform on which it rests. Stonewall Jackson died in 1863 after being wounded in battle.

MEET THE WRITER

"Barbara Frietchie Was No Myth"

John Greenleaf Whittier (1807–1892) was born and raised on a farm in Haverhill, Massachusetts, where his Quaker family had lived since 1688. Whittier devoted most of his life to the antislavery movement, and his poems reflect his dedication to freedom and justice and his deep religious faith. Whittier was born in the same year as Henry Wadsworth Longfellow (whose poem "Paul Revere's Ride" appears on page 537) and was also a Fireside Poet. About "Barbara Frietchie" he wrote:

John Greenleaf Whittier (1833) by Robert Peckham. Oil on canvas.

66 This poem was written in strict conformity to the account of the incident as I had it from respectable and trustworthy sources. It has since been the subject of a good deal of conflicting testimony, and the story was probably incorrect in some of its details. It is admitted by all that Barbara Frietchie was no myth, but a worthy and highly esteemed gentlewoman, intensely loyal and a hater of the slavery rebellion, holding her Union flag sacred and keeping it with her Bible; that when the Confederates halted before her house and entered her dooryard, she denounced them in vigorous language, shook her cane in their faces, and drove them out; and when General Burnside's [a Union general] troops followed close upon Jackson's, she waved her flag and cheered them. It is stated that May Quantrell, a brave and loyal lady in another part of the city, did wave her flag in sight of the Confederates. It is possible that there has been a blending of the two incidents. 99

MAKING MEANINGS

- **First Thoughts**

  1. Would you have done what Barbara Frietchie did if you were in her place? Explain.

- **Shaping Interpretations**

  2. Is Barbara Frietchie a hero in this poem? Is Stonewall Jackson? Support your opinion with evidence from the text.

  3. Whittier's comment in Meet the Writer suggests that the incident described in this poem might not have occurred. Does this comment affect your feelings about the poem? Why or why not?

- **Extending the Text**

  4. Suppose Whittier were alive today. Who might make a good subject for his next **narrative poem**? (Go back to your Quickwrite, or look at one of your classmates' Quickwrites for ideas.)

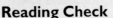

Reading Check

Paraphrase lines 26–42, which describe the most important actions in the poem. In your own words, describe the picture Whittier creates.

CHOICES: Building Your Portfolio

Writer's Notebook

1. Collecting Ideas for an Informative Report

Find and record facts about your state flag, including its history and symbolism.

WORK IN PROGRESS

Art/History

2. Flag of Freedom

Design a flag in honor of Barbara Frietchie (or another hero).

Performance

3. She Said

Perform a **dramatic reading** of "Barbara Frietchie." You could use pantomime, props, and sound effects. You might even set the poem to music. Watch punctuation at the ends of the lines. If there is no punctuation, read right on to the next line. If a comma, period, or other mark of punctuation is used, you must pause. Be sure to ask your audience for feed-

back. What was most effective about your performance?

Biographical Sketch

4. Courage Under Fire

Write a brief biographical sketch of Barbara Frietchie. Base your sketch in part on what you learned about her from the poem, from the illustration on page 602, and from Meet the Writer on page 604. You can do additional research on the Internet and in the library.

© Disney Enterprises, Inc.

Casey at the Bat

Ernest Lawrence Thayer

The outlook wasn't brilliant for the Mudville nine that day;
The score stood four to two, with but one inning more to play;
And so, when Cooney died at first, and Burrows did the same,
A sickly silence fell upon the patrons of the game.

5   A straggling few got up to go in deep despair. The rest
Clung to the hope which springs eternal in the human breast;
They thought, if only Casey could but get a whack, at that,
They'd put up even money now, with Casey at the bat.

But Flynn preceded Casey, as did also Jimmy Blake,
10   And the former was a pudding, and the latter was a fake;
So upon that stricken multitude grim melancholy sat,
For there seemed but little chance of Casey's getting to the bat.

But Flynn let drive a single, to the wonderment of all,
And Blake, the much-despised, tore the cover off the ball;
15 And when the dust had lifted, and they saw what had occurred,
There was Jimmy safe on second, and Flynn a-hugging third.

Then from the gladdened multitude went up a joyous yell;
It bounded from the mountaintop, and rattled in the dell;
It struck upon the hillside, and recoiled upon the flat;
20 For Casey, mighty Casey, was advancing to the bat.

There was ease in Casey's manner as he stepped into his place;
There was pride in Casey's bearing, and a smile on Casey's face;
And when, responding to the cheers, he lightly doffed his hat,
No stranger in the crowd could doubt 'twas Casey at the bat.

25 Ten thousand eyes were on him as he rubbed his hands with dirt;
Five thousand tongues applauded when he wiped them on his shirt;
Then while the writhing pitcher ground the ball into his hip,
Defiance gleamed in Casey's eye, a sneer curled Casey's lip.

And now the leather-covered sphere came hurtling through the air,
30 And Casey stood a-watching it in haughty grandeur there;
Close by the sturdy batsman the ball unheeded sped.
"That ain't my style," said Casey. "Strike one," the umpire said.

From the benches, black with people, there went up a muffled roar,
Like the beating of the storm waves on a stern and distant shore;
35 "Kill him! Kill the umpire!" shouted someone on the stand;
And it's likely they'd have killed him had not Casey raised his hand.

With a smile of Christian charity great Casey's visage shone;
He stilled the rising tumult; he bade the game go on;
He signaled to the pitcher, and once more the spheroid flew;
40 But Casey still ignored it, and the umpire said, "Strike two."

"Fraud!" cried the maddened thousands, and the echo answered, "Fraud!"
But a scornful look from Casey, and the audience was awed;
They saw his face grow stern and cold, they saw his muscles strain,
And they knew that Casey wouldn't let that ball go by again.

45 The sneer is gone from Casey's lips, his teeth are clenched in hate,
He pounds with cruel violence his bat upon the plate;
And now the pitcher holds the ball, and now he lets it go,
And now the air is shattered by the force of Casey's blow.

Oh! somewhere in this favored land the sun is shining bright;
50 The band is playing somewhere, and somewhere hearts are light;
And somewhere men are laughing, and somewhere children shout,
But there is no joy in Mudville—mighty Casey has struck out!

MEET THE WRITER

Shunning the Limelight

When the journalist **Ernest Lawrence Thayer** (1863–1940) submitted "Casey at the Bat" to the San Francisco *Examiner* in 1888, he had no idea it would become the most famous baseball poem ever written. In fact, he didn't even sign his own name to his work, choosing instead to use a nickname from his Harvard college days, "Phin."

Shortly after the poem appeared in the California newspaper, a copy was given to a vaudeville entertainer named William de Wolf Hopper, who was about to appear in a Baseball Night performance in New York. Hopper must have recognized a winner. After quickly memorizing the poem, he went onstage and recited it; the audience went wild. Hopper went on to make a successful career of touring the country reciting "Casey at the Bat."

Despite the poem's popularity, Thayer considered it badly written and for years would not admit authorship. Many people tried to take credit for writing the poem, and a number of baseball players claimed the dubious distinction of having been the model for Casey. When the author was finally identified, he refused to take money for the poem's many reprintings. "All I ask," he said, "is never to be reminded of it again."

Choosing Sides

Tim Meeker's hero has always been his brother Sam. Now Sam has joined the American Revolutionary Army to fight for independence—but their father remains loyal to the king of England. Tim must choose between the father and brother he loves in *My Brother Sam Is Dead* (Scholastic), by James Lincoln Collier and Christopher Collier.

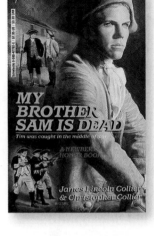

Pioneer Adventures

Girls in Wisconsin in 1864 are supposed to stay inside sewing and baking, but Caddie would rather hunt, plow, and get in and out of trouble. Carol Ryrie Brink based *Caddie Woodlawn* (Aladdin) on stories told to her as a child by her grandmother, the real Caddie.

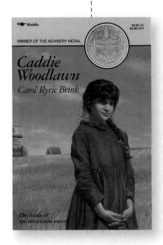

From Slavery to Freedom

What was it like *To Be a Slave* (Scholastic)? In this nonfiction book by Julius Lester, men and women who lived through slavery tell their stories in their own words. Lester's *Long Journey Home* (Scholastic), six true stories of freedom, is an uplifting sequel.

Other Picks

- Ann Rinaldi, *A Ride into Morning: The Story of Tempe Wick* (Gulliver). This historical novel is based on the legend of a New Jersey girl who hid her horse in her house to keep deserting Revolutionary Army soldiers from stealing him.

- Gary Paulsen, *Nightjohn* (Laurel-Leaf). This story is about a man who gives up his freedom to teach enslaved people to read, and a girl who will risk anything to learn.

- Elizabeth George Speare, *The Sign of the Beaver* (Dell). Twelve-year-old Matt has been left to survive alone in a cabin in the Maine wilderness. Then he is rescued by a Penobscot chief and his grandson. Will he join them and leave his lost family behind forever?

Speaking and Listening Workshop

INFORMATIVE COMMUNICATION

Speech to Teach

If you've ever explained a homework assignment to a classmate or helped your little sister with her foul shot, you've engaged in informative communication. With practice, standing in front of a group to share what you know can become just as easy and natural.

Choosing a Topic

1. Choose a topic that interests you and that you know well. Think about hobbies, skills, and family activities. What do you know or understand that your audience doesn't? (Do you speak a language most of your classmates don't, for example? You could teach them a song.)

2. Make sure your topic is specific enough to allow you to cover it effectively in the amount of time you plan to speak. A three-minute talk on how to hit a baseball will probably work; a three-minute talk on sports probably won't.

Setting Your Purpose

To make sure you have a purpose for speaking and not just a topic, complete the following sentence: "I want my audience to know or understand that . . ." The statement "I want my audience to know or understand that weight lifting" is not a complete sentence, so it can't be a statement of your purpose; weight lifting is just a topic. However, the statement "I want my audience to know or understand that creating resistance is the key to building muscles" does express a purpose.

Considering Your Audience

To make sure your listeners will be interested and involved, consider their needs as you prepare your speech. Ask yourself:

• What do my listeners already know about this topic? What background information do they need? How can I tailor my language so that they will understand me better?

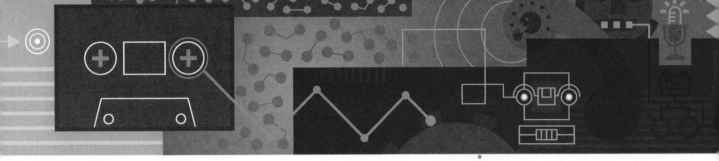

- What arrangement of ideas will be easiest for them to follow?
- Why should they care about what I have to say? How can I relate the information I'm presenting to their lives?

Giving Your Speech

- You may want to pause after each point or step to answer questions from your audience before you move on. (This is helpful whether you are speaking to one person or a group.)
- Don't write out your speech word for word. Instead, make a numbered note card for each main point or step. Referring to note cards, rather than reading a speech aloud word for word, will allow you to speak naturally and make eye contact with your audience.
- If possible, include **visual aids** such as props, drawings, or charts in your presentation. Your listeners will remember the information better if they can learn by seeing as well as hearing.
- Speak more loudly and slowly than you normally do. Your voice will probably sound strange to you, but it will sound just right to your audience.

Effective Listening

When you listen to an informative speech, ask yourself:

- Are the speaker's statements **facts** that can be verified, or is the speaker expressing **opinions**?
- Where did the speaker get this information? Is it reliable?
- How can I use this information?
- Does anything I'm hearing contradict my own experience?

If the speaker is explaining a process, make sure you understand each step and remember the order of the steps. Don't be afraid to ask the speaker to slow down, go over a point again, or explain something more fully.

HENRIETTA FAILS TO CONSIDER HER AUDIENCE... FOR THE LAST TIME.

© 1994 Dave Coverly/Creators Syndicate, Inc.

Try It Out

As you listen to your classmates' informative reports

- take notes
- listen for the main ideas and supporting details

When each speech is over, summarize in your own words the speaker's main ideas. Then, compare your summaries with those of two or three classmates.

Writer's Workshop

Technology HELP

See Writer's Workshop 1 CD-ROM. *Assignment: Report of Information.*

ASSIGNMENT

Research a historical topic and write a paper on it.

AIM

To inform.

AUDIENCE

Your teacher and classmates; other students in your school.

EXPOSITORY WRITING

INFORMATIVE REPORT

To write your **informative report,** you'll find, organize, and present information about someone or something from history.

Professional Model

Paul Revere rode into the hero's spotlight only in 1863, when Henry Wadsworth Longfellow wrote his famous poem about him, rescuing Revere from virtual obscurity. Historians say before the poem many Americans were not even familiar with Revere's name. In the early nineteenth century not a single editor included Revere in any compendium of American worthies, and Revere did not rate a mention in William Allen's comprehensive biographical dictionary, though there was room enough to list the accomplishments of seven thousand other people. After the poem's publication Revere's stock rose dramatically.

Writer clearly expresses a main idea about the subject.

Carefully chosen examples are used to elaborate the main idea.

Less than ten years later he made his way into Francis Samuel Drake's *Dictionary of American Biography*. Later J. P. Morgan reportedly offered to buy one of Revere's silver punch bowls for a hundred thousand dollars. By the end of the century Revere's reputation had improved so immensely that the Daughters of the American Revolution put a plaque on his home in Boston.

Writer speaks like an authority on the subject and shares information about it.

—Richard Shenkman, from *Legends, Lies & Cherished Myths of American History*

Prewriting

1. Choosing a Topic

Go back to your Writer's Notebook assignments for this collection. Would you like to write your report on any of the topics you worked with there? If not, ask your teacher to suggest other topics.

Make sure your topic is a manageable size. If you've decided to write about Abraham Lincoln, for example, consider narrowing your topic to several of his notable achievements. Before you start researching, think of your own list of questions about your topic—and look for answers.

2. Conducting Research

a. Finding Sources

You'll probably need at least three sources of information for your report. You can find print sources such as encyclopedias, books, magazines, and newspapers, as well as video

Communications Handbook
H E L P

See Research Strategies.

THE **INFORMATION BARN**
"EVERYTHING YOU WANT TO KNOW AT ROCK-BOTTOM PRICES"

DAY-OLD INFORMATION 2 lbs./$5

End-of-the-Season INFORMATION CLEARANCE 29¢ apiece

SLIGHTLY IRREGULAR INFORMATION

ARMY SURPLUS INFO 50¢ each

INFO OVERSTOCK ANY THREE ITEMS/$9.99

$2 bag

WRITER'S WORKSHOP 613

Paul Revere

I. Unknown before Longfellow's poem was published
   A. Not mentioned in books about famous Americans
   B. Not mentioned in Allen's biographical dictionary
II. Made famous by Longfellow
   A. Included in Drake's biographical dictionary
   B. J. P. Morgan offered $100,000 for Revere bowl
   C. D.A.R. put plaque on his Boston home

Framework for an Informative Report

Introduction: Hooks reader's interest; clearly identifies subject of report

Body: Discusses each main idea in one or more paragraphs; elaborates each main idea with facts, examples, quotations, etc.

Conclusion: Summarizes or restates main idea(s); draws conclusions

---

tapes, audiotapes, and microforms, at a library. You can access electronic sources on a computer, and you may be able to get historical information from museums, colleges, government offices, and experts in the field.

b. Taking Notes

- As you take notes, make a list of your sources, and give each a source number. Then, record each fact or idea on a separate note card or sheet of paper. Label every note with its source number and also the page number in the source where you found the information.

- Use abbreviations, short phrases, and lists of ideas. You don't need to write in complete sentences.

- Summarize ideas in your own words. If you do copy material word for word, be sure to put quotation marks around it in your notes. You'll need to give credit to the original source if you use the quotation in your report.

3. Organizing Your Report

You'll probably find it easier to draft your report if you first organize important information and ideas in an **outline.** (The example on the left is a formal outline, in which numbers and letters are used for headings and subheadings.) Sort your notes into several major categories; then, divide them further into subtopics. Decide how you will organize the information in your report—perhaps by order of importance or in chronological (time) order—and record your plan.

Be sure your report has an **introduction, body,** and **conclusion.** In your conclusion you should both **summarize** and **draw conclusions** from the information you gathered. (You may even pose additional unanswered questions.)

Drafting

1. Getting Started

Use your outline as a guide, but don't be afraid to make changes. As you write, you may decide to rearrange your ideas, take out information, or add new information. Keep referring to your notes, and go back to your sources if you need more information.

Write the report in your own words. If you do quote a source, be sure to give the writer credit. (Using a writer's words without crediting him or her is called **plagiarism.**) The Student Model is from a report about the Indian nationalist leader Mohandas K. Gandhi.

Gandhi was educated as a lawyer. Born in India, a country that was under British rule, he became the principal leader of the drive for India's independence from Britain. Gandhi was a deeply religious man who believed in eliminating the oppression of his people by the British without the use of force.

Introduces and describes subject: Gandhi.

States main idea: Gandhi's belief in nonviolence.

According to the *World Book Encyclopedia,* Gandhi was educated in London and spent over twenty years practicing law in South Africa. During this period in South Africa, he chose to claim his rights as a British subject, but since he was Indian, he was discriminated against by the government. As was the custom, Gandhi was married at age thirteen to a wife chosen for him by his family. He was assassinated in 1948 at the age of seventy-eight.

Mentions source for more facts about Gandhi's life.

The discrimination which Gandhi experienced during his life, and in particular the treatment he received while in South Africa, led him to believe that persons of all faiths, cultures, creeds, and beliefs should be able to live together equally. He used fasting to express this belief and once fasted for one week to get the Hindus and Muslims of India to stop fighting. As a result of that fast, the fighting stopped. Gandhi believed people could work out their disagreements through nonviolent confrontation, that is, without fighting.

Tells what caused his beliefs.

Describes his use of fasting with a specific example and its results.

Restates main idea: Gandhi's belief in nonviolence.

—Spencer Duncan,
   Topeka West High School, Topeka, Kansas

Strategies for Elaboration

As you elaborate each main idea, look through your notes to find relevant

- facts
- explanations
- specific examples
- quotations
- descriptions
- comparisons

Sentence Workshop
H E L P

Varying sentence structure: page 617.

Language/Grammar Link
H E L P

Using colons: page 554. Joining independent clauses: pages 572, 579. Capitalizing and punctuating titles: page 600.

2. Listing Sources

At the end of your report, include a list of your sources of information. The following examples use the style recommended by the Modern Language Association (MLA), but your teacher may ask you to use another style. Whatever style you use, follow its rules for capitalization, punctuation, and order of information exactly. (Notice that the author's last name comes first, followed by a comma and the author's first name.) List your sources in alphabetical order by the authors' last names. When there is no author, alphabetize by the first word of the title.

Works Cited

Chatterjee, Patricia. Gandhi. New York: S.A.R. Publications, 1996.

Gandhi, Mohandas. Gandhi: An Autobiography. Boston: Beacon Press, 1957.

"Gandhi, Mohandas Karamchand." The World Book Encyclopedia. 1998 ed.

MLA Guide for Listing Sources

To prepare your Works Cited list, follow the MLA style shown on pages 725–726 of the Communications Handbook, or another style your teacher specifies. The Communications Handbook gives detailed instructions and examples for the MLA style of citations for different kinds of electronic, print, and audiovisual sources.

Evaluating and Revising

Write the following questions on a sheet of paper:

1. What is the main thing you've learned from my paper?

2. What confused you? What do you want to know more about?

3. Do you have any other comments or suggestions?

Attach the sheet of paper to a copy of your draft, and give both to two classmates to read. (You will read and comment on their papers.) Use your readers' written responses to help you evaluate and revise your paper.

Sentence Workshop

VARYING SENTENCE STRUCTURE

We left home. We traveled for miles. We went across the prairie. The prairie was windy. We headed for the mountains.

If a story you were reading started this way, would you keep reading? The problem is a lack of variety in sentence structure, which can make even an interesting subject seem dull. If you look closely at the work of professional writers, you'll find a variety of sentence structures. Some are very simple; others are more complicated, like the structure of the sentence below:

"We left the home place behind, mile by slow mile, heading for the mountains, across the prairie where the wind blew forever."

—"Too Soon a Woman" (page 547)

If you divide this complicated-looking sentence into sections, you can see how it is put together:

We left the home place behind,/ mile by slow mile,/ heading for the mountains,/ across the prairie/ where the wind blew forever.

Working part by part, you can write a sentence of your own with a similar structure. For example:

I made the climb next,/ hold by precarious hold,/ aiming for the ledge,/ up the rock face/ where the rope swung down.

Try doing the same thing with other sentences written by professional writers. You'll get a sense of the variety of possible sentence structures and how they affect a writer's style.

Writer's Workshop Follow-up: Revising

Reread your informative report. If too many of your sentences seem to be put together the same way, try rewriting one or two.

Language Handbook
HELP

See Kinds of Sentences, pages 786–788.

Technology
HELP

See Language Workshop CD-ROM. *Key word entry: sentence structure.*

Try It Out

Write two sentences that are similar in structure to the sentences below:

"Along the Eastern Shore of Maryland,/ in Dorchester County,/ in Caroline County,/ the masters kept hearing whispers/ about the man named Moses,/ who was running off slaves."

—"Harriet Tubman" (page 558)

"In the April night,/more than once,/ blossoms fell from the orchard trees/ and lighted with rustling taps/on the drumhead."

—"The Drummer Boy of Shiloh" (page 581)

Now, go back to any selection you have read in this collection. Copy a sentence you like, and divide it into parts; then, write a sentence of your own with the same structure.

Reading for Life

Situation

This collection might have made you want to learn more about the Civil War. You can use these strategies to interpret any graphs and time lines you find in your research.

Strategies

Recognize time lines and different types of graphs.

- A **time line** lists events and their dates in **chronological order**—the order in which they took place. You'll find a time line on pages 344–345.

- A **bar graph** compares quantities at different times or in different situations.

- A **pie graph** (**circle graph**) shows proportions. The size of each "slice" represents its percentage of the total.

- A **line graph** shows changes in quantity over time.

Notice the parts of the graphic.

- Read the **title** of the graphic to determine its subject and purpose.

- Read the **labels** carefully.

- For bar or line graphs, identify the relationship between the **vertical**

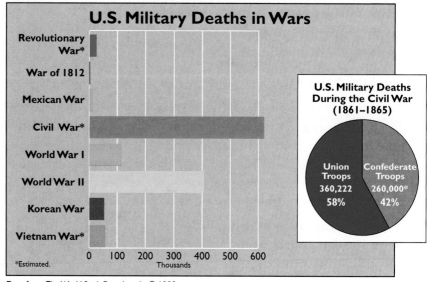

U.S. Military Deaths in Wars

Revolutionary War*
War of 1812
Mexican War
Civil War*
World War I
World War II
Korean War
Vietnam War*

0   100   200   300   400   500   600
Thousands

*Estimated.

U.S. Military Deaths During the Civil War (1861–1865)

Union Troops 360,222 58%

Confederate Troops 260,000* 42%

Data from *The World Book Encyclopedia* © 1998.

(up-and-down) **axis** and the **horizontal** (left-to-right) **axis.**

- Identify the **units of measurement** used (total number or percentage, for example).

- Check for a **key.** Note how colors, symbols, and abbreviations are used.

Interpret and evaluate the information.

- Note increases or decreases over time. Look for patterns.

- Draw conclusions from the information and from your own knowledge.

- Note the source of the data. Is it reliable? up-to-date?

Using the Strategies

1. What units of measurement does the bar graph above use?

2. Which war resulted in the most U.S. military deaths? in the fewest?

3. What is the source of the data in this bar graph?

4. Which side in the Civil War suffered more casualties? How many more casualties?

Extending the Strategies

Find a graph or time line in a book, magazine, or newspaper. Bring it to class, and interpret it for your classmates.

Learning for Life

Researching Modern Heroes

Problem

Have you ever heard the statement "Image is everything"? Many popular role models are people whose fame impresses us but whom we really know little about. How can we look past surface qualities and choose people who are truly admirable as our heroes?

Project

Research a contemporary hero, and publicize his or her accomplishments.

Preparation

You may already have an idea for a subject from one of the assignments in this collection. (See especially pages 536, 553, and 601.) If not, ask your teacher or family for ideas.

Procedure

Research and take notes on the person you have chosen. Possible sources:

Library (print) sources

- biographies

- entries in encyclopedias

- magazine and newspaper articles (ask your media specialist how to use periodicals indexes)

Electronic sources

- Most of the above sources can be researched on the Internet. Start your search using keywords.

- Many encyclopedias and reference works are available as databases and on CD-ROMs.

Interviews

- Talk with someone who knows about your subject.

Presentation

Present what you have learned in one of the following formats (or another that your teacher approves).

1. Trading Card

Create a trading card with a picture of your hero on the front and information about the person's notable accomplishments on the back. Make copies and present them to a class of younger students (with their teacher's permission).

2. Radio Commercial

Write a script for a sixty-second radio commercial promoting your hero. You may want to include sound effects or music. Tape-record your commercial, and play it for your class or over your school's public-address system.

3. Group Mural

Create a mural (wall painting) with a group of classmates, each person designing and painting a section showing his or her hero in action. (Do a sketch before you begin working on the mural.) If possible, display your mural in your school lobby or a hallway.

Processing

Write a brief reflection for your portfolio, using one of these starters:

- I chose to research this person because . . .

- If I could be like this person in one way, it would be . . .

Collection Eight

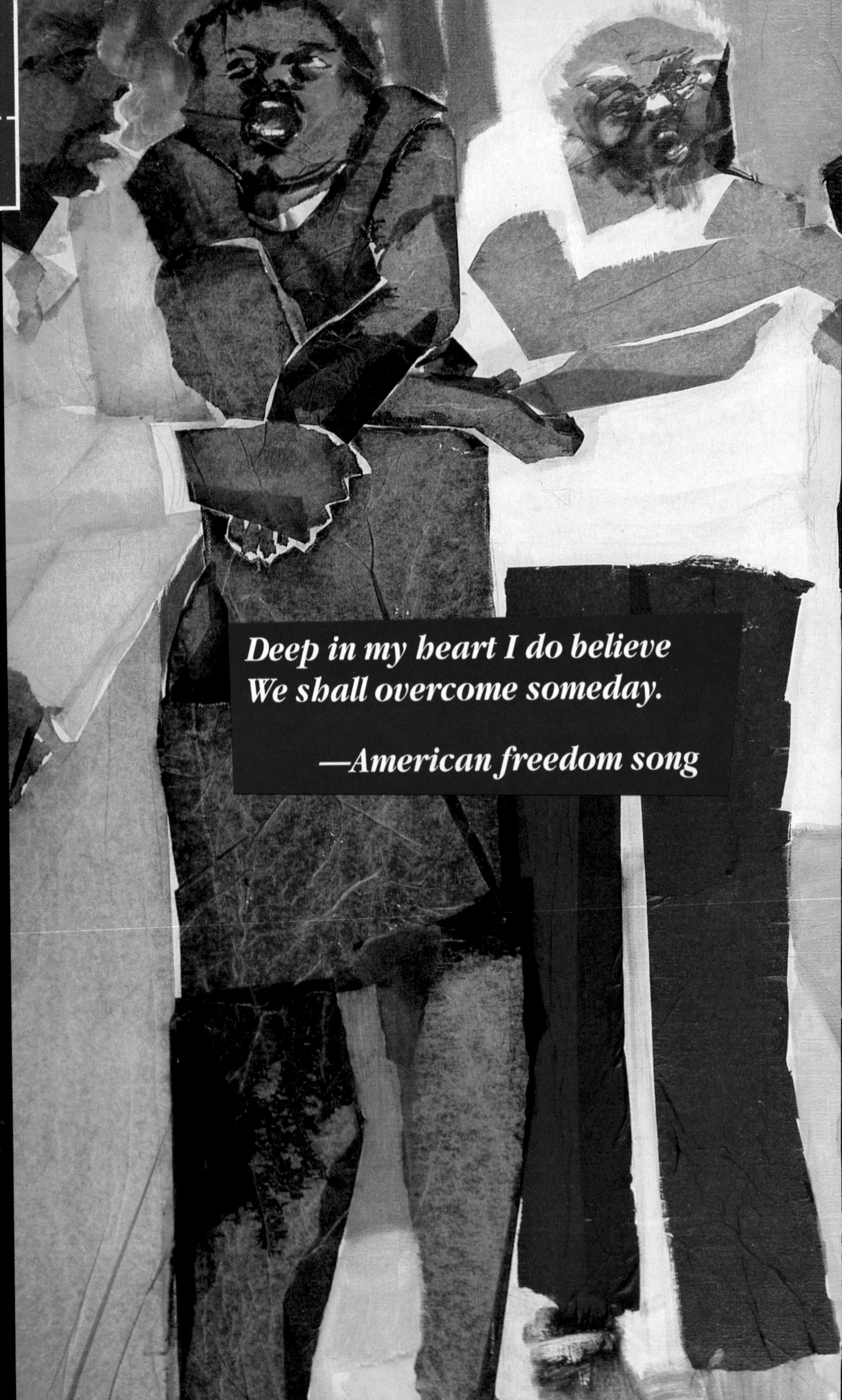

Deep in my heart I do believe
We shall overcome someday.

—American freedom song

***I Do Believe* (1988) by Phoebe Beasley. Collage.**

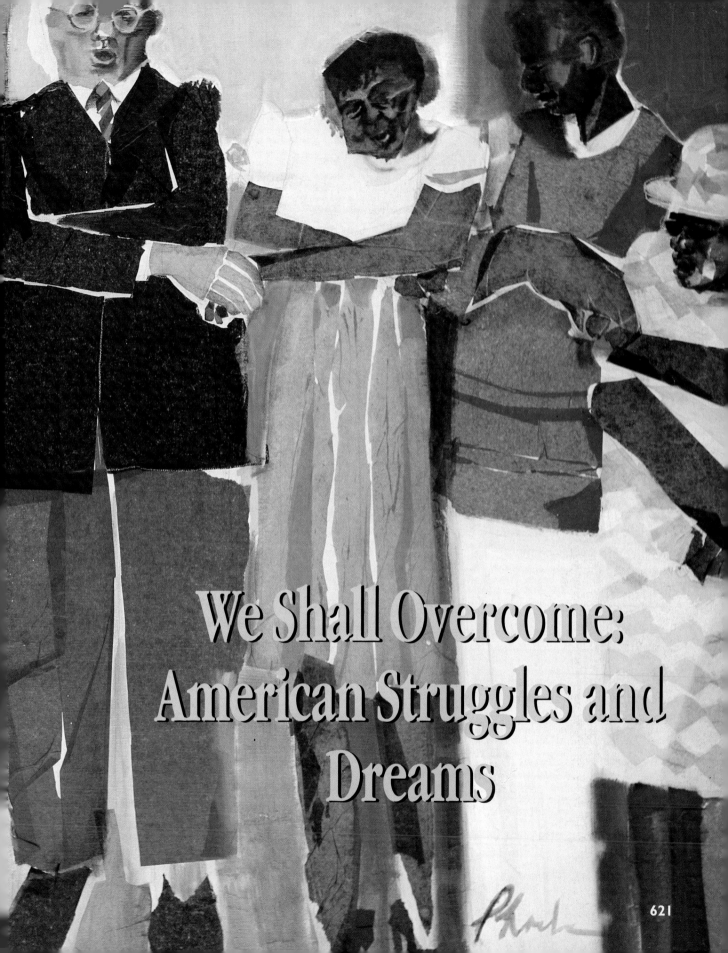

We Shall Overcome;
American Struggles and
Dreams

Before You Read

THE GETTYSBURG ADDRESS

Make the Connection

An American Quilt

Think about what America means to you. On an unlined sheet of paper, draw a symbol that represents your thoughts and feelings. Tape or staple your paper to your classmates' papers to create a class quilt, and explain the meaning of your symbol.

Elements of Literature

Refrain

Like poets, good speakers appeal to our sense of hearing. One way they do this is by using **refrains,** which create echoes in listeners' ears. Refrains are used to build rhythm and emphasize certain points. As you read the Gettysburg Address, look for the words and phrases that Lincoln has chosen to repeat.

> **A** **refrain** is a repeated sound, word, phrase, line, or group of lines.
>
> *For more on Refrain, see the Handbook of Literary Terms.*

Reading Skills and Strategies

Dialogue with the Text: Slow Down to Understand

Read the Gettysburg Address at least twice. Read slowly and carefully, just as you'd read any difficult text. Record any comments and questions suggested by your first reading in one color. Then, write down answers to your questions and additional thoughts in another color as you read the speech a second time. One student's notes on her first reading appear as an example.

Background

Literature and Social Studies

The Battle of Gettysburg, which took place in Pennsylvania in 1863, was a turning point of the Civil War. In that bloody three-day battle, Union forces prevented Confederate forces from moving north, thus confining the war mainly to the South. The battle left at least 48,000 soldiers dead, wounded, or missing.

On November 19, 1863, part of the battlefield was dedicated as a military cemetery. President Abraham Lincoln was asked to make some remarks at the dedication. Although very brief, Lincoln's Gettysburg Address is considered one of the greatest speeches by a U.S. political leader. It is noted especially for its vision of American democracy.

 go.hrw.com

LEO 8-8

The Gettysburg Address

Abraham Lincoln

November 19, 1863

Four score and seven years ago our fathers brought forth on this continent a new nation, conceived in liberty, and dedicated to the proposition that all men are created equal.

Now we are engaged in a great civil war, testing whether that nation, or any nation so conceived and so dedicated, can long endure. We are met on a great battlefield of that war. We have come to dedicate a portion of that field, as a final resting place for those who here gave their lives that that nation might live. It is altogether fitting and proper that we should do this.

But, in a larger sense, we cannot dedicate—we cannot consecrate—we cannot hallow°—this ground. The brave men, living and dead, who struggled here, have consecrated it, far above our poor power to add or detract. The world will little note nor long remember what we say here, but it can never forget what they did here. It is for us the living, rather, to be dedicated here to the unfinished work which they who fought here have thus far so nobly advanced. It is rather for us to be here dedicated to the great task remaining before us—that from these honored dead we take increased devotion to that cause for which they gave the last full measure of devotion—that we here highly resolve that these dead shall not have died in vain—that this nation, under God, shall have a new birth of freedom—and that government of the people, by the people, for the people, shall not perish from the earth.

° *Consecrate* and *hallow* are synonyms meaning "make or declare holy." Lincoln is using repetition to create rhythm and emphasize his point.

Dialogue with the Text

Four score . . . a score is twenty years, so . . . eighty-seven years ago . . . from what time?

Wait . . . so he's saying that the Civil War is a test of our country's Constitution.

I think the U.S. lost more lives in the Civil War than in all the wars we fought combined!

Many people were drafted. Bravery wasn't the only reason why they fought.

Lincoln didn't know that his speech would be famous.

What work is unfinished?

—Sabrina Braswell
Mansfield Middle School
Storrs, Connecticut

First draft of the Gettysburg Address, in Lincoln's handwriting.

Executive Mansion,

Washington, _____, 18C

Four score and seven years ago our fathers brought forth, upon this continent, a new nation, con in liberty, and dedicated to the proposition "all men are created equal"

Now we are engaged in a great civil war, whether that nation, or any nation so co and so dedicated, can long endure. We a on a great battle field of that war. We dedicate a portion of it, as a fine

The Battle of Gettysburg (1863) by John Frederick Rothermel. Oil on canvas.

MEET THE WRITER

Plain Speaking

Abraham Lincoln (1809–1865) was born in rural Kentucky. He spent his childhood there and in Indiana. At the age of twenty-one, he moved with his family to Illinois, where he taught himself law.

Lincoln soon became involved in politics, first at the state level and then at the national level. He was elected president in 1860, during a period of crisis that quickly erupted into war between the Northern and Southern states. In 1863, during the Civil War, he issued the Emancipation Proclamation. This proclamation led to the adoption of the Thirteenth Amendment to the Constitution, outlawing slavery.

Although Lincoln led the Union to victory, he did not live to see his country reunited. As he sat in a Washington theater, watching a play, Lincoln was shot by an assassin, John Wilkes Booth.

Lincoln believed in speaking and writing as clearly and simply as he could, so that people could understand exactly what he meant. He once explained:

    66 Among my earliest recollections I remember how, when a mere child, I used to get irritated when anybody talked to me in a way I could not understand. . . . I can remember going to my little bedroom, after hearing the neighbors talk of an evening with my father, and spending the night walking up and down and trying to make out what was the exact meaning of some of their, to me, dark sayings. I could not sleep when I got on such a hunt after an idea, until I had caught it; and when I thought I had got it, I was not satisfied until I had put it in language plain enough, as I thought, for any boy I knew to comprehend. This was a kind of passion with me, and it has stuck by me. **99**

*The American poet Walt Whitman wrote this poem after Abraham Lincoln's tragic death in April 1865. As you read, think about Whitman's **extended metaphor**. Who is the captain? What is the ship? Read the poem aloud to hear the effect of the **refrains**.*

O Captain! My Captain!

Walt Whitman

O Captain! my Captain! our fearful trip is done,
The ship has weathered every rack,° the prize we sought is won,
The port is near, the bells I hear, the people all exulting,°
While follow eyes the steady keel, the vessel grim and daring;
5   But O heart! heart! heart!
        O the bleeding drops of red,
          Where on the deck my Captain lies,
            Fallen cold and dead.

O Captain! my Captain! rise up and hear the bells;
10 Rise up—for you the flag is flung—for you the bugle trills,
For you bouquets and ribboned wreaths—for you the shores a-crowding,
For you they call, the swaying mass, their eager faces turning;
      Here Captain! dear father!
        The arm beneath your head!
15   It is some dream that on the deck,
           You've fallen cold and dead.

My Captain does not answer, his lips are pale and still,
My father does not feel my arm, he has no pulse nor will,
The ship is anchored safe and sound, its voyage closed and done,
20 From fearful trip the victor° ship comes in with object won:
      Exult O shores, and ring O bells!
        But I with mournful tread,
         Walk the deck my Captain lies,
           Fallen cold and dead.

2. **rack:** here, violent change or disorder, like that caused by a storm.
3. **exulting:** rejoicing.
20. **victor:** winner.

MAKING MEANINGS

• ## First Thoughts

1. What two American ideals seem most important to Abraham Lincoln? How do you know? Do you agree with him?

Shaping Interpretations

2. Why does Lincoln believe it is impossible for the battlefield to be made more sacred than it already is?

3. What challenge does Lincoln propose for the future? Why is honoring the dead connected to that challenge?

4. Find two examples of **refrains** in Lincoln's speech. What idea is he trying to emphasize in each case? Why are the two ideas important?

Extending the Text

5. What does Lincoln mean when he describes U.S. democracy as "government of the people, by the people, for the people"? What do you think people under voting age can do today to help make Lincoln's vision a reality?

6. Has the United States lived up to the ideals Lincoln describes in the Gettysburg Address? Give examples from history or current events to support your opinion.

7. In your opinion, what would a "new birth of freedom" in the United States today be like? (What changes would we see in our government? schools? communities?)

Challenging the Text

8. In Meet the Writer (page 625), Lincoln describes his efforts to express ideas in plain language. Do you think the Gettysburg Address is easy to understand? Support your opinion with examples from the text. Which passages, if any, gave you trouble? (Refer to the notes you made as you were reading.)

Reading Check

Divide a sheet of paper into three sections, and label them *Past, Present,* and *Future.* Fill in each section by answering the questions below.

a. What happened in the past—87 years before Lincoln's speech?

b. What is happening in the present (1863)? How is it related to the past, according to Lincoln?

c. What hopes does Lincoln express for the future?

CHOICES: Building Your Portfolio

Writer's Notebook

1. Collecting Ideas for a Problem Solution

With your classmates, make a list of obstacles to liberty or democracy for people in the United States or the world today. (You may want to look through recent newspapers and magazines for ideas.) Then, choose one item from the list, and answer the following questions about it.

- Why is it a problem?
- Whom does it affect?
- What are some possible solutions?

> Poor voter turnout:
> It's a problem
> because the people
> running the country
> should represent the
> majority—if most
> people don't vote, the
> people elected
> represent only a
> minority.

Journal Writing

2. On the Scene

Imagine that you are one of the twenty thousand people—many of whom were mourning friends and relatives recently killed in the Battle of Gettysburg—who stood outdoors for hours to watch the dedication of the new cemetery.

Write a **journal entry** describing the experience and your reactions to the president's speech. (You may want to do some research first on events that took place that day.)

Speaking and Listening

3. Sound and Sense

Prepare and present a **dramatic reading** of either the Gettysburg Address or "O Captain! My Captain!" (see *Connections* on page 626). Your delivery should be loud, slow, and clear. Emphasize the **rhythm** of the words, and pay special attention to **refrains.** Be sure to ask your audience to evaluate your reading. (For help, see the Speaking and Listening Workshop, pages 252–253.)

Research/ Social Studies

4. O Captain!

Using the Internet or the library, research a political leader who was assassinated, such as John F. Kennedy, Robert Kennedy, Martin Luther King, Jr., Malcolm X, or Mohandas K. Gandhi. Write a **poem,** a **letter,** or a **eulogy** (speech praising a person who has died) from the point of view of one of the person's followers.

Malcolm X

Mohandas K. Gandhi

Robert Kennedy

Reading Skills and Strategies

THINKING CRITICALLY: FACTS AND OPINIONS

Recognizing Facts and Opinions

> • A **fact** is something that can be proved true. It can be proved by direct observation or by checking a reliable reference source.
>
> • An **opinion** is a belief or an attitude. It cannot be proved true or false.

Which of the following sentences do you think are facts? Which do you think are opinions?

1. At six feet four, Abraham Lincoln still holds the record as the tallest president of the United States.

2. Lincoln was the best president the United States has ever had.

3. In 1860 Lincoln was elected despite winning only 40% of the popular vote.

4. Lincoln was intelligent and kind, but not very good-looking.

Sentences 1 and 3 are facts—they can be proved true by checking reliable sources. Sentences 2 and 4 are opinions—they express beliefs or attitudes. People have different opinions about who was the best president and who is good-looking.

Recognizing Valid Opinions

> • A **valid opinion** is an opinion that is supported by facts.

Sentences 2 and 4 are opinions, but they are not supported by facts. Therefore, they are not valid opinions. Sentences 5 and 6 below *are* valid opinions.

5. Lincoln was a great president because he freed the slaves and led our country through a bitter Civil War.

6. Very tall, thin, and angular, with what many considered a homely face, Lincoln was not particularly good-looking.

Reading Critically for Facts and Opinions

When you read a persuasive piece like "The First Americans," which follows, you must read critically to evaluate the writer's arguments. First, you must determine where the writer is presenting facts (could you look them up in a reference book?) and where the statements are merely opinions. Then, you must judge the validity of the opinions. Do they seem to be supported by facts or believable evidence? You must be the judge.

Although statements of opinion can't be proved, they *can* be supported with facts. Be a critical reader or listener whenever anyone is trying to persuade you.

Apply the strategy on the next page.

Before You Read

THE FIRST AMERICANS

Make the Connection

Stereotypes

Working with a group of class-mates, discuss the following questions, and write down your answers.

- What is a **stereotype**? (If people in your group disagree or aren't sure, check a dictionary.)

- What are some examples of stereotypes?

- Why are stereotypes a problem?

- Can a stereotype ever be useful? good? right?

Quickwrite

Freewrite for a few minutes about your own thoughts and feelings about stereotypes. (If you prefer, make a drawing about stereotypes instead.)

Reading Skills and Strategies

Distinguishing Fact from Opinion

As you read "The First Americans," look for **facts,** which can be proved, and **opinions,** which can't be proved. What evidence is given to support the opinions expressed? Do you find it persuasive?

Background

Literature and Social Studies

In 1927, an organization called the Grand Council Fire of American Indians sent a group of representatives from the Chippewa, Ottawa, Navajo, Sioux, and Winnebago peoples to address the mayor of Chicago. Their goal was to persuade him that the image of American Indians conveyed in textbooks and classrooms needed to be made more fair and accurate.

Mayor William Hale Thompson, who had been reelected just a month before the council met with him, had campaigned on the slogan "America First." (Thompson opposed U.S. involvement in world affairs and claimed that the British government influenced the U.S. government's policies.) "The First Americans" plays on this and other popular patriotic slogans of the time, such as "one hundred percent Americanism."

go.hrw.com
LEO 8-8

Teach children truth about the First Americans.

Sioux headdress (1910).

The First Americans

Pomo feathered basket (c. 1810).

The Grand Council Fire of American Indians
December 1, 1927

To the mayor of Chicago:
You tell all white men "America First." We believe in that. We are the only ones, truly, that are one hundred percent. We therefore ask you, while you are teaching schoolchildren about America First, teach them truth about the First Americans.

We do not know if school histories are pro-British, but we do know that they are unjust to the life of our people—the American Indian. They call all white victories battles and all Indian victories massacres. The battle with Custer[1] has been taught to schoolchildren as a fearful massacre on our part. We ask that this, as well as other incidents, be told fairly. If the Custer battle was a massacre, what was Wounded Knee?[2]

History books teach that Indians were murderers—is it murder to fight in self-defense? Indians

1. **battle with Custer:** the Battle of the Little Bighorn, which took place in 1876 in what is now Montana. General George A. Custer (1839–1876) led an attack on an Indian village and was killed along with all of his troops by Sioux and Cheyenne warriors.
2. **Wounded Knee:** Wounded Knee Creek, in South Dakota, was the site of a battle in 1890 between U.S. soldiers and Sioux whom they had captured. About two hundred Sioux men, women, and children were killed by the soldiers.

killed white men because white men took their lands, ruined their hunting grounds, burned their forests, destroyed their buffalo. White men penned our people on reservations, then took away the reservations. White men who rise to protect their property are called patriots—Indians who do the same are called murderers.

White men call Indians treacherous—but no mention is made of broken treaties on the part of the white man. White men say that Indians were always fighting. It was only our lack of skill in white man's warfare that led to our defeat. An Indian mother prayed that her boy be a great medicine man rather than a great warrior. It is true that we had our own small battles, but in the main we were peace loving and home loving.

White men called Indians thieves—and yet we lived in frail skin lodges and needed no locks or iron bars. White men call Indians savages. What is civilization? Its marks are a noble religion and philosophy, original arts, stirring music, rich story and legend. We had these. Then we were not savages, but a civilized race.

We made blankets that were beautiful, that the white man with all his machinery has never been able to duplicate. We made baskets that were beautiful. We wove in beads and colored quills designs that were not just decorative motifs but were the outward expression of our very thoughts. We made pottery—pottery that was useful, and beautiful as well. Why not make schoolchildren acquainted with the beautiful handicrafts in which we were skilled? Put in every school Indian blankets, baskets, pottery.

We sang songs that carried in their melodies all the sounds of nature—the running of waters, the sighing of winds, and the calls of the animals. Teach these to your children that they may come to love nature as we love it.

We had our statesmen—and their oratory has never been equaled. Teach the children some of these speeches of our people, remarkable for their brilliant oratory.

We played games—games that brought good health and sound bodies. Why not put these in your schools? We

Pueblo owl pottery (20th century).

Hopewell artifact.

WORDS TO OWN

penned (pend) v.: confined or enclosed. (A pen is a fenced area where animals are kept.)

treaties (trēt′ēz) n.: formal agreements between nations.

duplicate (do͞o′pli·kāt′) v.: make an exact copy; make or do again.

motifs (mō·tēfs′) n.: repeated figures in a design; themes.

oratory (ôr′ə·tôr′ē) n.: skill in public speaking; the art of public speaking.

---

told stories. Why not teach schoolchildren more of the wholesome proverbs and legends of our people? Tell them how we loved all that was beautiful. That we killed game only for food, not for fun. Indians think white men who kill for fun are murderers.

Tell your children of the friendly acts of Indians to the white people who first settled here. Tell them of our leaders and heroes and their deeds. Tell them of Indians such as Black Partridge, Shabbona, and others who many times saved the people of Chicago at great danger to themselves. Put in your history books the Indian's part in the World War. Tell how the Indian fought for a country of which he was not a citizen, for a flag to which he had no claim, and for a people that have treated him unjustly.

The Indian has long been hurt by these unfair books. We ask only that our story be told in fairness. We do not ask you to overlook what we did, but we do ask you to understand it. A true program of America First will give a generous place to the culture and history of the American Indian.

We ask this, Chief, to keep sacred the memory of our people.

Indians

Indians are native people
    here before the Pilgrims came
    here before Columbus came
    here before the Vikings came
5 Yet, we are treated
As though we don't belong here

Indians are native people
    here before the Pilgrims came
    here before Columbus came
10   here before the Vikings came
Yet, we are treated
As though we just got here.

—Ophelia Rivas
Santa Rosa Ranch Day School
Tucson, Arizona

MAKING MEANINGS

First Thoughts

1. What **stereotypes** are mentioned in "The First Americans"? How do you think the writers felt about those stereotypes? (You may want to refer to your Quickwrite notes.)

Shaping Interpretations

2. What **opinion** do the writers express at the beginning of the second paragraph? List three pieces of evidence they use to support this opinion.

3. **Paraphrase** (restate in your own words) what Ophelia Rivas is saying in her poem "Indians." How does her message relate to "The First Americans"?

Extending the Text

4. Do you think the popular image of American Indians has changed since 1927? What **stereotypes** of American Indians persist today? Use evidence from your own experience and from books, TV, and movies to support your response.

> **Reading Check**
>
> In a brief paragraph, **summarize** the **main points** in this speech, and cite the **details** the speakers use to support their main points.

CHOICES: Building Your Portfolio

Writer's Notebook

1. Collecting Ideas for a Problem Solution

If you could add a new subject to your school's curriculum, what would it be?

WORK IN PROGRESS

- Why do you believe this subject should be taught?
- How could it be fitted into the schedule?
- What problems do you foresee, and how could they be overcome?

Research/Social Studies

2. What Really Happened?

Using the Internet and the library, research and write a paragraph on one of these topics or another that your teacher approves:

- Pocahontas
- Tecumseh
- Chief Joseph
- Sacajawea
- the Trail of Tears
- events at Wounded Knee (in 1890 and 1973)

Visual Literacy

3. Beauty and Purpose

Look again at the illustrations for "The First Americans." React to whatever strikes you about the handicrafts shown—perhaps their colors, shapes, or designs. Think about how they might have been used. (Most Indian artwork has a specific purpose.) Then, write a **poem** or a **journal entry** in which you express your responses to the art.

GRAMMAR LINK   MINI-LESSON

Good or *Well*? *Bad* or *Badly*?

Language Handbook HELP

See Glossary of Usage, pages 817 and 818.

Technology HELP

See Language Workshop CD-ROM. Key word entry: usage.

1. Use *good* to modify (describe) a noun or a pronoun. Use *well* to modify a verb. *Good* should never be used to modify a verb.

STANDARD	Carla's essay is <u>good</u>. [*Good* modifies the noun *essay*.]
STANDARD	Carla writes <u>well</u>. [*Well* modifies the verb *writes*.]
NONSTANDARD	Carla does <u>good</u> in all her writing assignments.
STANDARD	Carla does <u>well</u> in all her writing assignments. [*Well* modifies the verb *does*.]

2. *Well* can be used as an adjective meaning "in good health" or "healthy."

STANDARD	She left school early because she didn't feel <u>well</u>. [*Well* modifies the pronoun *she*.]

3. *Bad* is an adjective. *Badly* is an adverb.

STANDARD	The fish was <u>bad</u>. [*Bad* modifies the noun *fish*.]
STANDARD	The man fished <u>badly</u>. [*Badly* modifies the verb *fished*.]

Try It Out

For each of the following sentences, choose the correct word from the underlined pair.

1. She planned <u>good/well</u> for our field trip.

2. We looked <u>good/well</u> in our waders.

3. Paul didn't feel <u>good/well</u> enough to go.

4. We didn't do <u>bad/badly</u> in practice.

5. I wonder if we'll do as <u>good/well</u> next time.

VOCABULARY   HOW TO OWN A WORD

WORD BANK

penned
treaties
duplicate
motifs
oratory

Words from the News

A. Find the Word Bank word that best completes each of these headlines.

1. **Dolly Exact _____ of Cloned Sheep!**
2. **Senator's Speech Shows Skills in _____**
3. **Judge Awards Indians Land Based on Old _____**
4. **Flamingos _____ at New Zoo Perish**
5. **Education and Economy Are Recurring _____ in President's Speech**

B. From newspaper or TV reports of today's current events, find five words you do not know. Look up their meanings, and use each word in a sentence of your own. Then, teach your words to a classmate.

Enter the Picture

THE GOLDEN DOOR: A NATION OF IMMIGRANTS

Make the Connection

Yearning to Breathe Free

Imagine this: The time is somewhere around 1900. You live on a farm in Italy that can no longer support your family, and you face a life of miserable poverty. Perhaps you are Jewish and you live in eastern Europe. Each day you fear that hostile mobs will kill you and destroy your village.

You pack your bags and set sail for America —across more than three thousand miles of ocean. You don't know what you will find there, but you hope—you hope with every fiber of your being. Will you be able to make a good life in this new world? Will you—and your children—come to call it home?

Reading Skills and Strategies

Visual Literacy: Reading a Photo Essay

"A picture is worth a thousand words." How many times have you heard that expression? The truth is that a picture *is* very different from words. The more strategies you have for viewing, or "reading," a picture, the more you will see.

As you read this photo essay, ask yourself:

- Who (or what) is pictured in each photograph?

- What can I learn about the people in the photos from their facial expressions, clothing, and settings?

- What **mood,** or feeling, do the photographs create?

- What **message** do you get from this photo essay? Does the essay present a **point of view** about its subject?

Background

Literature and Social Studies

The United States is a nation of immigrants. Even Native Americans, the first Americans, journeyed here from Siberia thousands of years ago. Since 1600, more than sixty million people have come here to start new lives.

From 1892 to 1954, Ellis Island served as the main port of entry to the United States— its "Golden Door." For many immigrants the passage in steerage across the Atlantic was a nightmare. This 1911 report from the U.S. Immigration Commission describes the conditions far below decks, in steerage:

The unattended vomit of the seasick, the odors of not too clean bodies, the reek of food, and the awful stench of the nearby toilet rooms make the atmosphere of the steerage such that it is a marvel that human flesh can endure it.

The Atlantic crossing could take anywhere from ten days to more than a month. No wonder, then, the utter joy of immigrants at their first sight of the Statue of Liberty, the symbol of America's freedom and promise.

After leaving Ellis Island, many immigrants settled in nearby northeastern cities, such as New York and Philadelphia, where they lived in cramped, squalid tenements. Many others went on long rail journeys across our vast country, often joining groups from their homelands to build a new life in America. Some of these immigrants might be your own ancestors.

 go.hrw.com
LEO 8-8

The Golden Door
A Nation of Immigrants

"The first time I saw the Statue of Liberty all the people were rushing to the side of the boat. 'Look at her, look at her,' and in all kind of tongues. 'There she is, there she is,' like it was somebody who was greeting them."

—Elizabeth Phillips, an Irish immigrant in 1920

The New Colossus

Emma Lazarus

Not like the brazen giant of Greek fame,°
With conquering limbs astride from land to land;
Here at our sea-washed, sunset gates shall stand
A mighty woman with a torch, whose flame
5   Is the imprisoned lightning, and her name
Mother of Exiles. From her beacon-hand
Glows world-wide welcome; her mild eyes command
The air-bridged harbor that twin cities frame.
"Keep, ancient lands, your storied pomp!"° cries she
10   With silent lips. "Give me your tired, your poor,
Your huddled masses yearning to breathe free,
The wretched refuse of your teeming° shore.
Send these, the homeless, tempest-tost° to me.
I lift my lamp beside the golden door!"

1. giant of Greek fame: The reference is to Colossus, a huge bronze (brazen) statue of the ancient Greek god Helios. It dominated the harbor of the Greek city of Rhodes from 280 to 225 B.C.
9. pomp: splendor; magnificence.
12. teeming: crowded.
13. tempest-tost: upset by storm. *Tempest* here refers to other hardships as well.

First Stop: Ellis Island

As they sailed into New York Harbor, immigrants spotted the Statue of Liberty in the distance and, nearby, Ellis Island. Ellis Island was their first stop in America. Here they were given medical examinations and officially permitted to enter the country. More than twelve million people arrived through this gateway between 1892 and 1954. The peak year was 1907—when more than one million newcomers entered through the "Golden Door."

"Well, I came to America because I heard the streets were paved with gold. When I got here, I found out three things: first, the streets weren't paved with gold; second, they weren't paved at all; and third, I was expected to pave them."

—*Old Italian Story*

(Inset) The faces of three immigrants.
(Top) View of Ellis Island in 1905.
(Bottom) Jewish war orphans arriving from eastern Europe in 1921.

"We naturally were in steerage. Everyone had smelly food, and the atmosphere was so thick and dense with smoke and bodily odors that your head itched, and when you went to scratch your head you got lice in your hands. We had six weeks of that."

—*Sophia Kreitzberg, a Russian Jewish immigrant in 1908*

"I can remember only the hustle and bustle of those last weeks in Pinsk, the farewells from the family, the embraces and the tears. Going to America then was almost like going to the moon."

—*Golda Meir, a Russian Jewish immigrant in 1906*

"Those who are loudest in their cry of 'America for Americans' do not have to look very far back to find an ancestor who was an immigrant."

—*New Immigrants' Protective League, 1906*

(**Top**) A Slovakian mother and daughter wait to be admitted to Ellis Island, about 1915.

(**Center**) Children's playground, Ellis Island roof garden.

(**Left**) Women from Guadeloupe, French West Indies, at Ellis Island on April 6, 1911.

By courtesy of the Ellis Island Immigration Museum.

After Ellis Island: A Triumph of the Human Spirit

How's this for an American dream:

It's 1874. You've just come off the boat from Poland. You speak no English. You're packed with your husband and four children in a tiny tenement apartment in New York's Lower East Side.

Then your husband disappears.

And your baby dies.

Nathalia Gumpertz survived all this, eking out a living for her three daughters by sewing dresses and trimming hats for eight dollars a week.

And now her life is a stunning history lesson featured in a most unusual museum, the Lower East Side Tenement Museum.

Everything here is real—a real tenement, restored with real objects owned by real people and animated with real stories of success and tragedy.

This building, 97 Orchard Street, was home to ten thousand people from twenty-five countries from 1863 until 1935, when it was closed and its residents evicted.

It was sealed up for fifty years—a time capsule awaiting the bulldozer.

But Ruth Abram and her partner found it first.

They had been searching the city for a tenement to house a museum that would, Abram says, "speak to the greatness of the human spirit."

A tenement museum, Abram believed, would help Americans appreciate where we've come from—and therefore be more tolerant of the newcomers now in our land.

That was ten years ago.

This year, Congress is poised to make the museum part of the National Park Service. And seventy-five thousand visitors will meet Nathalia Gumpertz and see how she lived.

They'll also meet the Baldizzi family, Catholics from Sicily, who lived in the building in the 1930s. And the Confino family, who came to America from Turkey in 1913.

Their lives have been re-created but not sanitized.

Visitors gather at 90 Orchard Street for guided tours of the tenement across the street. The hour-long tour begins in the cramped hallway of the six-story tenement, then leads up the creaking stairway. It's dark and scary.

As many as eighteen people lived in each apartment at the turn of the century, when Orchard Street was the most populated place on earth. Nearly half of the babies born in this building died.

Outside view of the Lower East Side Tenement Museum at 97 Orchard Street in New York City. The abandoned six-story tenement was turned into a museum in 1988.

Nathalia was successful enough to eventually move to the Upper East Side, where she died in 1894 at age fifty-eight.

Her story still touches Abram, the museum's president, as do the others.

"For everybody who emigrates, there is this potential for greatness, for great courage," she says. "These people are role models for all of us."

Abram still guides one tour through the tenement each week—and each time she is struck by the immigrants' self-sacrifice.

"Our story is the story of adults sacrificing their own dreams for their children's and grandchildren's dreams."

—from *The Palm Beach Post,* July 5, 1998

Tenement Life in New York

In 1900, New York City's Lower East Side was the most densely populated place on earth. Almost 75 percent of New Yorkers lived in crowded, dark, airless, and foul-smelling tenements like these. Disease was rampant.

> Here is a door. Listen! That short hacking cough, that tiny, helpless wail—what do they mean? . . . The child is dying with measles. . . . That dark bedroom killed it.
> —Jacob Riis, *How the Other Half Lives*

(Center) A family poses in their tenement apartment in New York City, about 1910. This photograph, by Jessie Tarbox Beals, is from the Jacob Riis Collection. Riis was famous for his dramatic pictures of slum life.

(Top right and bottom left) Restored apartments in the Lower East Side Tenement Museum. **(Top right)** Apartment of the Confino family, immigrants from Turkey. **(Bottom left)** Apartment of the Baldizzi family, immigrants from Italy.

Where Did They Settle?

This map shows the major areas where some of the largest immigrant groups settled.

Approximate Numbers of Immigrants Arriving in the United States

1892–1931 — Each figure equals 200,000 immigrants.

Italians	4,263,000
Jews	2,300,000
Poles	1,655,000
Irish	1,094,000
Greeks	775,000
Swedes	511,000
Hungarians	473,000
Norwegians	226,300
Czechs	206,600

... and Where They Went

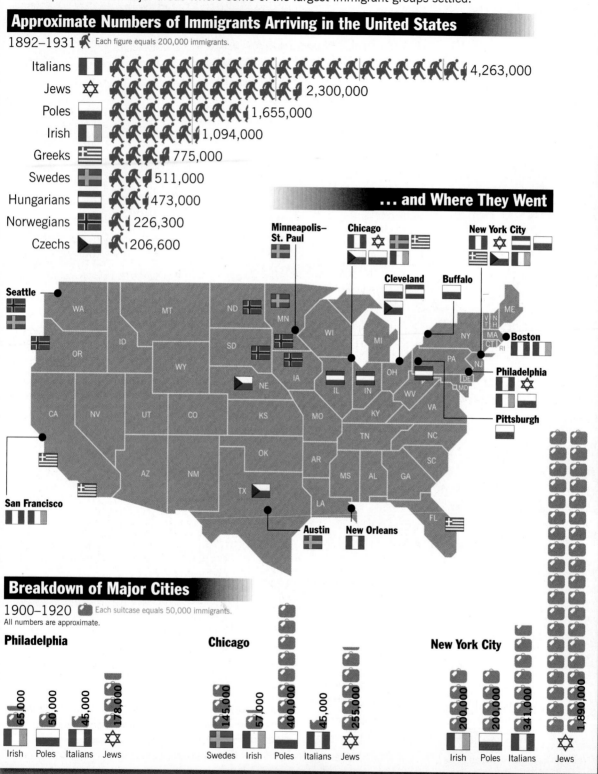

Minneapolis–St. Paul

Chicago

New York City

Cleveland

Buffalo

Seattle

Boston

Philadelphia

Pittsburgh

San Francisco

Austin

New Orleans

Breakdown of Major Cities

1900–1920 — Each suitcase equals 50,000 immigrants.
All numbers are approximate.

Philadelphia

Irish	Poles	Italians	Jews
65,000	50,000	45,000	178,000

Chicago

Swedes	Irish	Poles	Italians	Jews
145,000	57,000	400,000	45,000	255,000

New York City

Irish	Poles	Italians	Jews
200,000	200,000	341,000	1,890,000

Statistics based on data from *Harvard Encyclopedia of American Ethnic Groups*, 1980.

Infographic by Nigel Holmes.

Reflecting

Research/Graphic Organizer

1. Ancestors on Parade

Trace your family history back to your grandparents or great-grandparents (or even great-great-grandparents), and create a **family tree.** For each ancestor on your family tree, record the person's name and important dates and places in his or her life. You might share or display your family trees in class.

Visual Literacy

2. Talk to Me

Imagine that you are a TV talk show host in the early 1900s. (Imagine, first, that talk shows existed then!) You are interviewing the people in the photographs in this photo essay. What do you want to know about them? Write a list of questions that an interviewer might ask.

Visual Literacy/ Discussing an Evaluation

3. Talk Together

In a small group, discuss your evaluation of this photo essay. What did it teach you about immigration? What message does the essay seem to present? Do you think the editors show a biased or an objective point of view? If you had been the editor, what else would you have included? Assign a member of your group to summarize the main points of your discussion.

Interpreting Graphic Information/Performance

4. Tell Their Story

You and two partners can each choose three of the immigrant groups represented on the map and graphs on page 642. Then, prepare to tell the stories of your three groups as if you were a member of each group. Take notes on the following questions: How many of you came to the United States from 1892 to 1931? Where did you settle? Between 1900 and 1920, how many of you were living in Philadelphia, Chicago, and New York City? Exchange notes with your partners, and check to be sure that their information is accurate. Then, you might want to perform your "stories" for your class.

Oral Interpretation

5. "Send These . . . to Me"

With several classmates, prepare and perform an **oral interpretation** or a **choral reading** of "The New Colossus." (For help, see pages 252–253.) Your reading could serve as an introduction to a performance of the immigrants' stories (see activity 4, above).

By courtesy of the Ellis Island Immigration Museum.

Detail from *Family Supper* (1972) by Ralph Fasanella, displayed at the Ellis Island Immigration Museum. The son of Italian immigrants, Fasanella painted the teeming life and crowded spaces of New York City.

Before You Read

CAMP HARMONY

Make the Connection

Camp Harmony

What might a place called Camp Harmony be like? Why might people go there?

Quickwrite

Look at the paintings on pages 647, 648, and 650. Freewrite in response to one of them. You might use this starter:

- The first thing I noticed about this painting was . . .

Elements of Literature

Autobiography

Today, many Americans know little about the internment of Japanese Americans during World War II, but for Monica Sone and thousands of others, internment was a painful reality. "Camp Harmony," an excerpt from Sone's **autobiography,** *Nisei Daughter,* vividly describes the day her family arrived at a camp.

> **A**n **autobiography** is a writer's account of his or her own life.
>
> *For more on Autobiography, see pages 656–657 and the Handbook of Literary Terms.*

Reading Skills and Strategies

Making Generalizations: Putting It All Together

A **generalization** is a broad statement based on several particular situations. When you make a generalization, you combine evidence in a text with what you already know to make a broad, universal statement about some topic. For example, after you have read about Monica Sone's specific experiences, you might want to make a generalization about the treatment of Japanese Americans during World War II.

Background

Literature and Social Studies

In 1942, thousands of Japanese Americans living on the West Coast received notices requiring them to leave their homes and go to internment (prison) camps. They had committed no crime, but the United States had gone to war with Japan. Executive Order 9066 made it legal for the government to confine Americans of Japanese descent in these camps.

Many of those evacuated were nisei (nē′sā′), second-generation Japanese Americans. Although they were native-born U.S. citizens, the nisei were taken to the camps along with their immigrant parents, the issei (ē′sā′), who at the time were barred from citizenship by law. Ironically, many of the evacuated families had sons or brothers serving with the U.S. Army in the war overseas.

Most of the 110,000 Japanese Americans detained spent three years behind barbed wire. Released in 1945, at the end of World War II, they returned home to find their property stolen and their livelihoods gone. They had to wait more than forty years for an apology and compensation from the U.S. government.

go.hrw.com

LEO 8-8

Camp Harmony

from **Nisei Daughter**

What was I doing behind a fence, like a criminal?

Monica Sone

When our bus turned a corner and we no longer had to smile and wave, we settled back gravely in our seats. Everyone was quiet except for a chattering group of university students, who soon started singing college songs. A few people turned and glared at them, which only served to increase the volume of their singing. Then suddenly a baby's sharp cry rose indignantly above the hubbub. The singing stopped immediately, followed by a guilty silence. Three seats behind us, a young mother held a wailing red-faced infant in her arms, bouncing it up and down. Its angry little face emerged from multiple layers of kimonos, sweaters, and blankets, and it, too, wore the white pasteboard tag[1] pinned to its blanket. A

1. **white pasteboard tag:** All Japanese American families registering for evacuation were given numbered tags to wear and to attach to their luggage. Monica's family became family #10710.

young man stammered out an apology as the mother gave him a wrathful look. She hunted frantically for a bottle of milk in a shopping bag, and we all relaxed when she had found it.

We sped out of the city southward along beautiful stretches of farmland, with dark, newly turned soil. In the beginning we devoured every bit of scenery which flashed past our window and admired the massive-muscled workhorses plodding along the edge of the highway, the rich burnished copper color of a browsing herd of cattle, the vivid spring green of the pastures, but eventually the sameness of the country landscape <u>palled</u> on us. We tried to sleep to escape from the restless anxiety which kept bobbing up to the surface of our minds. I awoke with a start when the bus filled with excited buzzing. A small group of straw-hatted Japanese farmers stood by the highway, waving at us. I felt a sudden warmth toward them, then a twinge of pity. They would be joining us soon.

About noon we crept into a small town. Someone said, "Looks like Puyallup, all right." Parents of small children babbled excitedly, "Stand up quickly and look over there. See all the chick-chicks and fat little piggies?" One little city boy stared hard at the hogs and said <u>tersely</u>, "They're bachi—dirty!"

Our bus idled a moment at the traffic signal, and we noticed at the left of us an entire block filled with neat rows of low shacks, resembling chicken houses. Someone commented on it with awe, "Just look at those chicken houses. They sure go in for poultry in a big way here." Slowly the bus made a left turn, drove through a wire-fence gate, and to our dismay, we were inside the oversized chicken farm. The bus driver opened the door, the guard stepped out and stationed himself at the door again. Jim, the young man who had shepherded us into the buses, popped his head inside and sang out, "OK, folks, all off at Yokohama, Puyallup."

We stumbled out, stunned, dragging our bundles after us. It must have rained hard the night before in Puyallup, for we sank ankle deep into gray, <u>glutinous</u> mud. The receptionist, a white man, instructed us courteously, "Now, folks, please stay together as family units and line up. You'll be assigned your apartment."

We were standing in Area A, the mammoth parking lot of the state fairgrounds. There were three other separate areas, B, C, and D, all built on the fairgrounds proper, near the baseball field and the racetracks. This camp of army barracks was hopefully called Camp Harmony.

We were assigned to apartment 2-I-A, right across from the bachelor quarters. The apartments resembled <u>elongated</u>, low stables about two blocks long. Our home was one room, about eighteen by twenty feet, the size of a living room. There was one small window in the wall opposite the one door. It was bare except for a small, tinny wood-burning stove crouching in the center. The flooring consisted of two-by-fours laid directly on the earth, and dandelions were already pushing their way up through the cracks. Mother was delighted when she saw their shaggy yellow heads. "Don't anyone pick them. I'm going to cultivate them."

Father snorted, "Cultivate them! If we don't watch out, those things will be growing out of our hair."

Just then Henry stomped inside, bringing the rest of our baggage. "What's all the excitement about?"

Sumi replied <u>laconically</u>, "Dandelions."

WORDS TO OWN

palled (pôld) v.: became boring.
tersely (tʉrs′lē) adv.: briefly and clearly; without unnecessary words.
glutinous (glo͞ot′'n·əs) adj.: sticky; gluey.
elongated (ē·lôŋ′gāt′id) v. used as adj.: lengthened; extended.
laconically (lə·kän′ik·lē) adv.: with few words. *Laconically* and *tersely* are synonyms.

Topaz, August 1943 (1943) by Suiko Mikami. Watercolor.

Henry tore off a fistful. Mother scolded, "Arra! Arra! Stop that. They're the only beautiful things around here. We could have a garden right in here."

"Are you joking, Mama?"

I chided Henry, "Of course she's not. After all, she has to have some inspiration to write poems, you know, with all the 'nari keri's.'[2] I can think of a poem myself right now:

Oh, Dandelion, Dandelion,
Despised and uprooted by all,
Dance and bob your golden heads
For you've finally found your home
With your yellow fellows, nari keri, amen!"

Henry said, thrusting the dandelions in Mother's black hair, "I think you can do ten times better than that, Mama."

Sumi reclined on her sea bag[3] and fretted, "Where do we sleep? Not on the floor, I hope."

"Stop worrying," Henry replied disgustedly.

Mother and Father wandered out to see what the other folks were doing and they found people wandering in the mud, wondering what other folks were doing. Mother returned shortly, her face lit up in an ecstatic smile, "We're in luck. The latrine is right nearby. We won't have to walk blocks."

We laughed, marveling at Mother who could

2. **nari keri's:** *Nari keri* (nä·rē ke·rē) is a phrase used to end many Japanese poems. It is meant to convey wonder and awe.

3. **sea bag:** large canvas bag like the ones sailors use to carry their personal belongings. Each person was allowed to bring only one sea bag of bedding and two suitcases of clothing to the internment camps.

Progress After One Year, the Mess Hall Line (1943) by Kango Takamura. Watercolor.

be so poetic and yet so practical. Father came back, bent double like a woodcutter in a fairy tale, with stacks of scrap lumber over his shoulder. His coat and trouser pockets bulged with nails. Father dumped his loot in a corner and explained, "There was a pile of wood left by the carpenters and hundreds of nails scattered loose. Everybody was picking them up, and I hustled right in with them. Now maybe we can live in style, with tables and chairs."

The block leader knocked at our door and announced lunchtime. He instructed us to take our meal at the nearest mess hall. As I untied my sea bag to get out my pie plate, tin cup, spoon, and fork, I realized I was hungry. At the mess hall we found a long line of people. Chil-

dren darted in and out of the line, skiing in the slithery mud. The young stood impatiently on one foot, then the other, and scowled, "The food had better be good after all this wait." But the issei stood quietly, arms folded, saying very little. A light drizzle began to fall, coating bare black heads with tiny sparkling raindrops. The chow line inched forward.

Lunch consisted of two canned sausages, one lob of boiled potato, and a slab of bread. Our family had to split up, for the hall was too crowded for us to sit together. I wandered up and down the aisles, back and forth along the crowded tables and benches, looking for a few inches to squeeze into. A small issei woman finished her meal, stood up, and hoisted her legs modestly over the bench, leaving a space for one. Even as I thrust myself into the breach, the space had shrunk to two inches, but I worked myself into it. My dinner companion, hooked just inside my right elbow, was a bald-headed, gruff-looking issei man who seemed to resent nestling at mealtime. Under my left elbow was a tiny, mud-spattered girl. With busy, runny nose, she was belaboring her sausages, tearing them into shreds and mixing them into the potato gruel which she had made with water. I choked my food down.

We cheered loudly when trucks rolled by, distributing canvas army cots for the young and hardy, and steel cots for the older folks. Henry directed the arrangement of the cots. Father and Mother were to occupy the corner nearest the wood stove. In the other corner, Henry arranged two cots in an L shape and announced that this was the combination living room–bedroom area, to be occupied by Sumi and myself. He fixed a male den for himself in the corner nearest the door. If I had had my way, I would have arranged everyone's cots in one neat row, as in Father's hotel dormitory.

We felt fortunate to be assigned to a room at the end of the barracks, because we had just one neighbor to worry about. The partition wall separating the rooms was only seven feet high, with an opening of four feet at the top, so at night, Mrs. Funai next door could tell when Sumi was still sitting up in bed in the dark, putting her hair up. "Mah, Sumi-chan," Mrs. Funai would say through the plank wall, "are you curling your hair tonight, again? Do you put it up every night?" Sumi would put her hands on her hips and glare defiantly at the wall.

The block monitor, an impressive nisei who looked like a star tackle, with his crouching walk, came around the first night to tell us that we must all be inside our room by nine o'clock every night. At ten o'clock, he rapped at the door again, yelling, "Lights out!" and Mother rushed to turn the light off not a second later.

Throughout the barracks, there was a medley of creaking cots, whimpering infants, and explosive night coughs. Our attention was riveted on the intense little wood stove, which glowed so violently I feared it would melt right down to the floor. We soon learned that this condition lasted for only a short time, after which it suddenly turned into a deep freeze. Henry and Father took turns at the stove to produce the harrowing blast which all but singed our army blankets but did not penetrate through them. As it grew quieter in the barracks, I could hear the light patter of rain. Soon I felt the *splat! splat!* of raindrops digging holes into my face. The dampness on my pillow spread like a mortal bleeding, and I finally had to get out and haul my cot toward the center of the room. In a short while, Henry was up. "I've got multiple leaks, too. Have to complain to the landlord first thing in the morning."

All through the night I heard people getting up, dragging cots around. I stared at our little window, unable to sleep. I was glad Mother had put up a makeshift curtain on the window, for I noticed a powerful beam of light

> I stared at our little window, unable to sleep.

WORDS TO OWN

breach (brēch) *n.:* opening. *Breach* usually refers to a breakthrough in a wall or in a line of defense.
medley (med'lē) *n.:* jumble; mixture of dissimilar things.
riveted (riv'it·id) *v.:* fastened or held firmly, as if by rivets (metal bolts or pins).
harrowing (har'ō·iŋ) *v.* used as *adj.:* distressing.

Topaz Through the Door (1943) by Masao Mori. Watercolor.

sweeping across it every few seconds. The lights came from high towers placed around the camp, where guards with tommy guns kept a twenty-four-hour <u>vigil</u>. I remembered the wire fence encircling us, and a knot of anger tightened in my breast. What was I doing behind a fence, like a criminal? If there were accusations to be made, why hadn't I been given a fair trial? Maybe I wasn't considered an American anymore. My citizenship wasn't real, after all. Then what was I? I was certainly not a citizen of Japan, as my parents were. On second thought, even Father and Mother were more alien residents of the United States than Japanese nationals, for they had little tie with their mother country. In their twenty-five years in America, they had worked and paid their

taxes to their adopted government as any other citizen.

Of one thing I was sure. The wire fence was real. I no longer had the right to walk out of it. It was because I had Japanese ancestors. It was also because some people had little faith in the ideas and ideals of democracy. They said that after all these were but words and could not possibly ensure loyalty. New laws and camps were surer devices. I finally buried my face in my pillow to wipe out burning thoughts and snatch what sleep I could.

WORDS TO OWN
vigil (vij′əl) *n.*: watch; act of staying awake to keep watch.

MEET THE WRITER

"I Wanted to Tell Our Story"

Monica Sone (1919–   ) was born in Seattle, Washington. This is her explanation of how she came to write *Nisei Daughter:*

66 In the spring of 1942, shortly after Pearl Harbor [site of a U.S. naval base bombed by Japan], I was forced to leave my home in Seattle under U.S. Army orders. I was sent away to a prison camp built inside a state fairground in Puyallup, Washington. This camp, for some strange reason, was called Camp Harmony.

While incarcerated there, I wrote letters to my friend Betty McDonald [a well-known children's author], describing our living conditions, which were mind-boggling to me. I had gone from a fairly normal life to being herded into a camp with thousands of others, surrounded with barbed wire and armed guards. This occurred even though we were Americans and we had not been charged with any crime.

Betty had apparently preserved all of my letters. One day she showed the packet of letters to an editor from Little, Brown and Co. He immediately became interested in my camp experiences, especially since at that time no details had come out of camp to be reported in the media. The editor reacted to my letters, sensing in them a human-interest story as well as a major historical event in our country.

Monica Sone with her granddaughter.

The editor contacted me and inquired if I would be interested in expanding on my letters and writing a book. I was eager to do so. This was because after I eventually left camp and moved to the eastern part of the country, I discovered that the general public knew nothing about our evacuation and imprisonment of tens of thousands of Americans. I wanted to tell our story. 99

Like many native-born Americans of Japanese ancestry, Sone's future husband served in the U.S. Army during World War II. During the four and a half years he spent fighting overseas, his family was imprisoned in an internment camp in Poston, Arizona.

In Response to Executive Order 9066:

All Americans of Japanese Descent Must Report to Relocation Centers

Dwight Okita

Dear Sirs:
Of course I'll come. I've packed my galoshes
and three packets of tomato seeds. Denise calls them
"love apples." My father says where we're going
5 they won't grow.

I am a fourteen-year-old girl with bad spelling
and a messy room. If it helps any, I will tell you
I have always felt funny using chopsticks
and my favorite food is hot dogs.
10 My best friend is a white girl named Denise—
we look at boys together. She sat in front of me
all through grade school because of our names:
O'Connor, Ozawa. I know the back of Denise's head very well.
I tell her she's going bald. She tells me I copy on tests.
15 We're best friends.

I saw Denise today in Geography class.
She was sitting on the other side of the room.
"You're trying to start a war," she said, "giving secrets away
to the Enemy. Why can't you keep your big mouth shut?"
20 I didn't know what to say.
I gave her a packet of tomato seeds
and asked her to plant them for me, told her
when the first tomato ripened
she'd miss me.

MAKING MEANINGS

First Thoughts

1. Discuss your reactions to the autobiography and the poem (see *Connections* on page 652). If you like, use one or two of the starters below.

    - I realized . . .
    - I began to think of . . .
    - I felt . . .
    - If the writer were here, I would say/ask . . .

Shaping Interpretations

2. Sone says her camp "was hopefully called Camp Harmony" (see page 646). Do you think the name is appropriate? Support your opinion with evidence from the text.

3. Find several details that describe what conditions were like in Sone's camp. Using these details, make a **generalization** about the Japanese American internment camps.

4. Describe the attitudes of the people who were evacuated. Do you think you would respond the same way if you were in their situation? Why or why not?

5. The paintings shown on pages 647, 648, and 650 were made by Japanese Americans living in internment camps during World War II. Choose one and explain how it reminds you of, or seems different from, what you read in "Camp Harmony" or "In Response to Executive Order 9066" (see *Connections* on page 652). You may want to reread your Quickwrite before you respond.

Extending the Text

6. Find two details in Sone's description of Camp Harmony that would be unlikely to appear in an encyclopedia entry about the internment camps. What information might the encyclopedia include that Sone's **autobiography** doesn't?

Challenging the Text

7. Sone says that she was imprisoned "because some people had little faith in the ideas and ideals of democracy" (page 650). What does she mean? Is she stating a **fact** or an **opinion**? Do you agree or disagree with her statement? Explain.

Reading Check

Imagine that you are the editor who first reads "Camp Harmony" (see page 651). Write a one-paragraph **summary** for your boss, who doesn't have time to read every manuscript submitted. Be sure to include a sentence or two explaining why you think Monica Sone's autobiography should be published.

CHOICES: Building Your Portfolio

Writer's Notebook

1. Collecting Ideas for a Problem Solution

With a partner, list examples of conflicts or misunderstandings between different groups of people in your school or community. Then, brainstorm ways to help the people in the groups get to know each other better and create greater tolerance.

Set up a "buddy system"— have students with one kind of skill or talent (such as in sports, math, or art) tutor or coach other students. Everyone would be a teacher of one thing and a learner of something else.

Supporting an Opinion

2. Persuading FDR

Pretend you are Sone or the speaker of "In Response to Executive Order 9066" (see *Connections* on page 652). Write a letter to President Roosevelt to persuade him to cancel Executive Order 9066 and allow you and your family to go home. Use practical, moral, or legal arguments to make your case, supporting them with details from the text. (You may want to read the Fifth Amendment to the Constitution and refer to it in your argument.)

Critical Thinking/ Learning for Life

3. Time Capsule

You are a member of a present-day construction team working in Puyallup. One day your bulldozer uncovers a metal box with these words stenciled on it:

TIME CAPSULE
ASSEMBLED BY
THE TEENAGERS OF CAMP
HARMONY
1942

Write a **memo** to your supervisor, describing each item you find inside and explaining why you think it was included in the time capsule.

Art

4. Seeing the Setting

Create a **diorama** (three-dimensional model) of the family's room in the barracks or of the whole camp. If you can't find enough details in the text, you might invent some details or research the structure and living conditions of the internment camps.

GRAMMAR LINK

Avoiding Double Negatives

Language Handbook HELP

See Uses of Comparative and Superlative Forms, pages 767–768.

Technology HELP

See Language Workshop CD-ROM. Key word entry: double negative.

A **double negative** is the use of two negative words to express one negative idea. Avoid using double negatives in formal writing and speaking.

Listed below are some commonly used negative words.

barely	never	none	nothing
hardly	no	no one	nowhere
neither	nobody	not (-n't)	scarcely

NONSTANDARD	The family's room <u>didn't have no</u> furniture.
STANDARD	The family's room <u>had no</u> furniture.
STANDARD	The family's room <u>didn't have any</u> furniture.
NONSTANDARD	It was so crowded they <u>couldn't hardly</u> sit down.
STANDARD	It was so crowded they <u>could hardly</u> sit down.

Try It Out

Proofread the following paragraph, correcting any double negatives.

Monica and her family couldn't hardly believe dandelions were growing through their floor. Nobody didn't like it when the rain came through the roof. Scarcely no one in the family slept the first night. Nowhere else they had lived was like this.

VOCABULARY HOW TO OWN A WORD

Hink Pink

WORD BANK

palled
tersely
glutinous
elongated
laconically
breach
medley
riveted
harrowing
vigil

A **hink pink** is a riddle with a short, rhyming answer.

EXAMPLE   What do you call a transparent baseball? A clear sphere.

Match each hink pink with the best answer from the list on the right. What do you call

1. linoleum whose pattern has <u>palled</u> on you?
2. an answer that was made <u>tersely</u>?
3. a cartoon mouse eating <u>glutinous</u> jam?
4. an <u>elongated</u> strip of leather?
5. a robber who speaks <u>laconically</u>?
6. a <u>breach</u> in the paper on a birthday present?
7. a <u>medley</u> of twigs?
8. someone who's <u>riveted</u> by a tornado?
9. a <u>harrowing</u> Belgian pancake?
10. a bungled <u>vigil</u>?

sticky Mickey
awful waffle
short retort
wind pinned
wrap gap
long thong
brief thief
watch botch
sticks mix
boring flooring

Elements of Literature

NONFICTION: Just the Facts?

Fiction and Nonfiction: What's the Difference?

Would you find it odd if someone called a dog a non-cat? or vegetables nondessert? It may seem just as odd to call a kind of writing nonfiction. However, that's the only name we have for it right now!

Sometimes it's hard to see the difference between fiction and nonfiction. Fiction is supposed to be made up, and nonfiction is supposed to be based on fact. Yet, **historical fiction** deals with real, historical events. Many fiction writers show their made-up characters mixing with historical figures. Likewise, nonfiction writers use many of the elements of fiction: characterization, suspense, descriptions of thoughts and feelings. In fact, some of the nonfiction narratives in this book may seem just like short stories to you.

An Audience of One?

Most fiction is written for a wide audience, but nonfiction is often aimed at a much nar-

---

A Writer on Fiction and Nonfiction

"Like most writers, I intermingle fact and fiction. . . . I have occasionally used an incident that actually happened as the germ, the starting point, or the climax of a short story."

—Ann Petry, author of "Harriet Tubman" (page 557)

---

rower audience. Some nonfiction is written for an audience of only one. A **journal** (or **diary**), a daily record of the writer's experiences and thoughts, is often meant to be read only by the writer. **Letters** are usually addressed to one person. (**Letters to the editor** are an exception— they are published in newspapers or magazines.)

Diaries and historical letters are sometimes published and read by many people. An example is the diary kept by Anne Frank during her years in hiding from the Nazis.

Some nonfiction, such as articles in specialized magazines or journals, is written for a specific audience. The audience for nonfiction of this type can be extremely small. A paper written by an astronomer who studies a particular kind of star, for example, may be intended only for other astronomers studying the same kind of star. An article written for a magazine about fly-fishing would be geared to a specific audience that is into fly-fishing.

Nonfiction for Everyone

The nonfiction you're likely to see in a local bookstore or on a library shelf, on the other hand, is written so that most people can understand it. Writers of nonfiction for a general audience avoid **jargon** (special language used by people engaged in a particular activity or occupation) even when they write about specialized subjects such as psychology and medicine. Their goal is to make the information understandable and interesting to the average reader.

Getting Personal: Subjective Nonfiction

Writing that presents facts without revealing the writer's feelings and opinions is said to be **objective.** Journalists who report on current events for newspapers usually write in an objective style. Their readers want the facts; they do not want to hear how the events affected the reporter. In news-paper editorials and some feature articles, the writing is **subjective:** The writer uses a personal tone and deliberately reveals opinions and feelings.

A popular kind of subjective nonfiction is the **personal essay.** Personal essays are usually short reflections on something that interests the writer. Books of humorous personal essays are often on the best-seller lists. For exam-ple, Bill Cosby writes humor-ous personal essays about kids and family life. Today even doctors and scientists write personal essays, combining personal anecdotes with facts about topics like sports injuries and warts. Richard Feynman wrote many popular personal essays about his "adventures" in science.

Telling Lives: Biography and Autobiography

Among the most popular forms of nonfiction today are biography and autobiography. In a **biography** the writer tells the story of someone else's life. In an **autobiogra-phy** the writer tells the story of his or her own life. Writers of autobiographies have the advantage of being very famil-iar with their subjects. When we read an autobiography, we hear about the subject's experiences, thoughts, and feelings from the person who knows them best. Biographies have their own advantage, though: They should provide more objective accounts of their subjects' lives.

Oral histories combine elements of biography and autobiography. Writers of oral histories conduct interviews, which they record (usually on tape) and then put into written form.

In all its many forms, non-fiction has lately achieved a surprising position: It is now more popular than fiction!

Before You Read

THE CIRCUIT

Make the Connection

A Nation of Immigrants

The United States is often called a nation of immigrants because almost every family has roots in other parts of the world. Do you know any stories about the journey of an immigrant to the United States? If you like, share one of your stories with the class.

Quickwrite

Draw a line down the middle of a page in your notebook. On the left, list reasons why families come to the United States. On the right, list some of the difficulties you think they face.

Elements of Literature

Tone

As you read "The Circuit," think about the **tone** the narrator uses in describing his experiences. Is he sad? happy? angry? nostalgic? something else? What word would best describe his tone?

> **T**one is the attitude a narrator or writer takes toward the characters and events of a literary work or the work's audience.
>
> *For more on Tone, see the Handbook of Literary Terms.*

Reading Skills and Strategies

What's the Writer's Perspective?

Perspective is a long word that simply means "viewpoint" or "position on a topic." If you say "See the situation from my perspective," you mean "Try to see things from my point of view." As you read "The Circuit," think about the writer's perspective on his subject—migrant farm workers in California. The first thing to remember is that Jimenez has based this fictional story on his own experiences as a child.

(HRW) go.hrw.com
LEO 8-8

THE CIRCUIT
Cajas de cartón

Francisco Jiménez

I lay in bed thinking about how much I hated this move.

It was that time of year again. Ito, the strawberry share-cropper, did not smile. It was natural. The peak of the strawberry season was over, and the last few days the workers, most of them braceros,[1] were not picking as many boxes as they had during the months of June and July.

As the last days of August disappeared, so did the number of braceros. Sunday, only one—the best picker—came to work. I liked him. Sometimes we talked during our half-hour lunch break. That is how I found out he was from Jalisco,[2] the same state in Mexico my family was from. That Sunday was the last time I saw him.

When the sun had tired and sunk behind the mountains, Ito signaled us that it was time to go home. "Ya esora,"[3] he yelled in his broken Spanish. Those were the words I waited for twelve hours a day, every day, seven days a week, week after week. And the thought of not hearing them again saddened me.

As we drove home, Papá did not say a word. With both hands on the wheel, he stared at the dirt road. My older brother, Roberto, was also silent. He leaned his head back and closed his eyes. Once in a while he cleared from his throat the dust that blew in from outside.

1. **braceros** (brä·ser′ôs): Mexican farm laborers brought into the United States for limited periods to harvest crops. *Bracero* comes from the Spanish word *brazo,* meaning "arm."
2. **Jalisco** (hä·lēs′kô).
3. **Ya esora** (yä äs·ô′rä): *Ya es hora,* Spanish for "It's time."

Yes, it was that time of year. When I opened the front door to the shack, I stopped. Everything we owned was neatly packed in cardboard boxes. Suddenly I felt even more the weight of hours, days, weeks, and months of work. I sat down on a box. The thought of having to move to Fresno and knowing what was in store for me there brought tears to my eyes.

That night I could not sleep. I lay in bed thinking about how much I hated this move.

A little before five o'clock in the morning, Papá woke everyone up. A few minutes later, the yelling and screaming of my little brothers and sisters, for whom the move was a great adventure, broke the silence of dawn. Shortly, the barking of the dogs accompanied them.

While we packed the breakfast dishes, Papá went outside to start the "Carcanchita." That was the name Papá gave his old '38 black Plymouth. He bought it in a used-car lot in Santa Rosa in the winter of 1949. Papá was very proud of his little jalopy. He had a right to be proud of it. He spent a lot of time looking at other cars before buying this one. When he finally chose the Carcanchita, he checked it thoroughly before driving it out of the car lot. He examined every inch of the car. He listened to the motor, tilting his head from side to side like a parrot, trying to <u>detect</u> any noises that spelled car trouble. After being satisfied with the looks and sounds of the car, Papá then insisted on knowing who the original owner was. He never did find out from the car salesman, but he bought the car anyway. Papá figured the original owner must have been an important man, because behind the rear seat of the car he found a blue necktie.

Papá parked the car out in front and left the motor running. "Listo,"[4] he yelled. Without saying a word, Roberto and I began to carry the boxes out to the car. Roberto carried the two big boxes and I carried the two smaller ones.

Papá then threw the mattress on top of the car roof and tied it with ropes to the front and rear bumpers.

Everything was packed except Mamá's pot. It was an old, large galvanized pot she had picked up at an army surplus store in Santa María the year I was born. The pot had many dents and nicks, and the more dents and nicks it acquired the more Mamá liked it. "Mi olla,"[5] she used to say proudly.

I held the front door open as Mamá carefully carried out her pot by both handles, making sure not to spill the cooked beans. When she got to the car, Papá reached out to help her with it. Roberto opened the rear car door and Papá gently placed it on the floor behind the front seat. All of us then climbed in. Papá sighed, wiped the sweat off his forehead with his sleeve, and said wearily: "Es todo."[6]

As we drove away, I felt a lump in my throat. I turned around and looked at our little shack for the last time.

At sunset we drove into a labor camp near Fresno. Since Papá did not speak English, Mamá asked the camp foreman if he needed any more workers. "We don't need no more," said the foreman, scratching his head. "Check with Sullivan down the road. Can't miss him. He lives in a big white house with a fence around it."

When we got there, Mamá walked up to the house. She went through a white gate, past a row of rosebushes, up the stairs to the front door. She rang the doorbell. The porch light went on and a tall, husky man came out. They exchanged a few words. After the man went in, Mamá clasped her hands and hurried back to the car. "We have work! Mr. Sullivan said we

5. **Mi olla** (mē ô′yä): Spanish for "My pot."
6. **Es todo** (es tô′dô): Spanish for "That's all."

4. **Listo** (lēs′tô): Spanish for "Ready."

WORDS TO OWN
detect (dē·tekt′) v.: discover; perceive.

LITERATURE
AND
SOCIAL STUDIES

Cesar Chavez: Organizing Farm Workers

Thousands of migrant farm workers in California have experienced hardships like those described in "The Circuit." Among them was Cesar Chavez (1927–1993). Like Panchito, Chavez traveled with his family from region to region and worked long hours picking crops in the hot sun for very low wages. He was able to go to school only when the harvests allowed, and he had to quit after eighth grade.

Chavez believed that migrant farm workers needed a union to help them get fair wages and working conditions. In 1962, he organized the National Farm Workers Association (later called the United Farm Workers of America). The union's five-year strike against California grape growers drew support from around the country.

After some workers resorted to violence, Chavez went on a twenty-five-day fast to demonstrate his belief in nonviolent methods. "Our struggle is not easy," he once said. "But we have our bodies and spirits and the justice of our cause as weapons."

can stay there the whole season," she said, gasping and pointing to an old garage near the stables.

The garage was worn out by the years. It had no windows. The walls, eaten by termites, strained to support the roof, full of holes. The dirt floor, populated by earthworms, looked like a gray road map.

That night, by the light of a kerosene lamp, we unpacked and cleaned our new home. Roberto swept away the loose dirt, leaving the hard ground. Papá plugged the holes in the walls with old newspapers and tin can tops. Mamá fed my little brothers and sisters. Papá

and Roberto then brought in the mattress and placed it on the far corner of the garage. "Mamá, you and the little ones sleep on the mattress. Roberto, Panchito, and I will sleep outside under the trees," Papá said.

Early next morning Mr. Sullivan showed us where his crop was, and after breakfast, Papá, Roberto, and I headed for the vineyard to pick.

Around nine o'clock the temperature had risen to almost one hundred degrees. I was

---

WORDS TO OWN

populated (păp′yoo·lāt′id) *v.* used as *adj.*: inhabited; lived in or on.

---

completely soaked in sweat and my mouth felt as if I had been chewing on a handkerchief. I walked over to the end of the row, picked up the jug of water we had brought, and began drinking. "Don't drink too much; you'll get sick," Roberto shouted. No sooner had he said that than I felt sick to my stomach. I dropped to my knees and let the jug roll off my hands. I remained motionless with my eyes glued on the hot sandy ground. All I could hear was the drone of insects. Slowly I began to recover. I poured water over my face and neck and watched the dirty water run down my arms to the ground.

I still felt a little dizzy when we took a break to eat lunch. It was past two o'clock, and we sat underneath a large walnut tree that was on the side of the road. While we ate, Papá jotted down the number of boxes we had picked. Roberto drew designs on the ground with a stick. Suddenly I noticed Papá's face turn pale as he looked down the road. "Here comes the school bus," he whispered loudly in alarm. Instinctively, Roberto and I ran and hid in the vineyards. We did not want to get in trouble for not going to school. The neatly dressed boys about my age got off. They carried books under their arms. After they crossed the street, the bus drove away. Roberto and I came out from hiding and joined Papá. "Tienen que tener cuidado,"[7] he warned us.

After lunch we went back to work. The sun kept beating down. The buzzing insects, the wet sweat, and the hot, dry dust made the afternoon seem to last forever. Finally the mountains around the valley reached out and swallowed the sun. Within an hour it was too dark to continue picking. The vines blanketed the grapes, making it difficult to see the bunches. "Vámonos,"[8] said Papá, signaling to us that it was time to quit work. Papá then took out a pencil and began to figure out how much we had earned our first day. He wrote down numbers, crossed some out, wrote down some more. "Quince,"[9] he murmured.

When we arrived home, we took a cold shower underneath a water hose. We then sat down to eat dinner around some wooden crates that served as a table. Mamá had cooked a special meal for us. We had rice and tortillas with carne con chile, my favorite dish.

The next morning I could hardly move. My body ached all over. I felt little control over my arms and legs. This feeling went on every morning for days until my muscles finally got used to the work.

It was Monday, the first week of November. The grape season was over and I could now go to school. I woke up early that morning and lay in bed, looking at the stars and savoring the thought of not going to work and of starting sixth grade for the first time that year. Since I could not sleep, I decided to get up and join Papá and Roberto at breakfast. I sat at the table across from Roberto, but I kept my head down. I did not want to look up and face him. I knew he was sad. He was not going to school today.

He was not going tomorrow, or next week, or next month. He would not go until the cotton season was over, and that was sometime in February. I rubbed my hands together and watched the dry, acid-stained skin fall to the floor in little rolls.

When Papá and Roberto left for work, I felt relief. I walked to the top of a small grade[10]

---

7. **Tienen que tener cuidado** (tē·e′nen kā te·när′ kwē·dä′dô): Spanish for "You have to be careful."
8. **Vámonos** (vä′mô·nôs): Spanish for "Let's go."

9. **Quince** (kēn′sā): Spanish for "Fifteen."
10. **grade:** here, hill.

WORDS TO OWN

drone (drōn) *n.*: continuous buzzing or humming sound.
instinctively (in·stiŋk′tiv·lē) *adv.*: automatically; without thinking.

next to the shack and watched the Carcanchita disappear in the distance in a cloud of dust.

Two hours later, around eight o'clock, I stood by the side of the road waiting for school bus number twenty. When it arrived, I climbed in. Everyone was busy either talking or yelling. I sat in an empty seat in the back.

When the bus stopped in front of the school, I felt very nervous. I looked out the bus window and saw boys and girls carrying books under their arms. I put my hands in my pant pockets and walked to the principal's office. When I entered, I heard a woman's voice say: "May I help you?" I was startled. I had not heard English for months. For a few seconds I remained speechless. I looked at the lady, who waited for an answer. My first instinct was to answer her in Spanish, but I held back. Finally, after struggling for English words, I managed to tell her that I wanted to enroll in the sixth grade. After answering many questions, I was led to the classroom.

Mr. Lema, the sixth-grade teacher, greeted me and assigned me a desk. He then introduced me to the class. I was so nervous and scared at that moment when everyone's eyes were on me that I wished I were with Papá and Roberto picking cotton. After taking roll, Mr. Lema gave the class the assignment for the first hour. "The first thing we have to do this morning is finish reading the story we began yesterday," he said enthusiastically. He walked up to me, handed me an English book, and asked me to read. "We are on page 125," he said politely. When I heard this, I felt my blood rush to my head; I felt dizzy. "Would you like to read?" he asked hesitantly. I opened the book to page 125. My mouth was dry. My eyes began to water. I could not begin. "You can read later," Mr. Lema said understandingly.

For the rest of the reading period I kept getting angrier and angrier with myself. *I should have read,* I thought to myself.

During recess I went into the restroom and opened my English book to page 125. I began to read in a low voice, pretending I was in class. There were many words I did not know. I closed the book and headed back to the classroom.

Mr. Lema was sitting at his desk correcting papers. When I entered he looked up at me and smiled. I felt better. I walked up to him and asked if he could help me with the new words. "Gladly," he said.

The rest of the month I spent my lunch hours working on English with Mr. Lema, my best friend at school.

One Friday, during lunch hour, Mr. Lema asked me to take a walk with him to the music room. "Do you like music?" he asked me as we entered the building.

"Yes, I like corridos,"[11] I answered. He then picked up a trumpet, blew on it, and handed it to me. The sound gave me goose bumps. I knew that sound. I had heard it in many corridos. "How would you like to learn how to play it?" he asked. He must have read my face because before I could answer, he added: "I'll teach you how to play it during our lunch hours."

That day I could hardly wait to get home to tell Papá and Mamá the great news. As I got off the bus, my little brothers and sisters ran up to meet me. They were yelling and screaming. I thought they were happy to see me, but when I opened the door to our shack, I saw that everything we owned was neatly packed in cardboard boxes.

---

11. **corridos** (cō·rē′dôs): Mexican folk ballads.

MEET THE WRITER

"The Events Were Not Experienced in the English Language"

Francisco Jiménez (1943–   ) was born in San Pedro Tlaquepaque, Jalisco, Mexico, and came to the United States when he was four years old. At the age of six, he started working in the fields. The crop cycle took his family all over Southern California, where they picked strawberries, grapes, cotton, lettuce, and carrots. After many years, Jiménez acquired U.S. citizenship. Although he had great difficulty completing his public-school education (he failed first grade and was deported when he was in eighth grade), he went on to earn a PhD in Latin American literature.

Jiménez has won several awards for his short stories. About "The Circuit" he writes:

66 'The Circuit' is an autobiographical short story based on my experiences as a child growing up in a family of migrant farm workers. The setting is the San Joaquin Valley, a rich agricultural area in California, where my family made a living working in the fields.

The idea for the story goes back many years to the time when I was in Santa Maria High School. Miss Bell, my sophomore English teacher, encouraged the class to write detailed narrative accounts of personal experiences. Even though I had difficulty expressing myself in English, I enjoyed the assignments, and with much effort I wrote about what I knew best. Long after I left her class, I continued to reflect upon my life experiences and often thought of expressing them in writing.

I actually wrote the first version of the story in Spanish when I was a graduate student at Columbia University in 1972, and published it in a Spanish literary magazine in New York City. Later I expanded it and named it 'Cajas de cartón' ('Cardboard Boxes'), which I then translated into English under the title 'The Circuit.' I retitled 'Cajas de cartón' 'The Circuit' rather than 'Cardboard Boxes' because 'Cardboard Boxes' did not sound right to me. It did not convey the same meaning. 'The Circuit' seemed to me a more appropriate English title.

I wrote the original version of 'The Circuit' in Spanish because it was the language in which the events I describe occurred. In fact, I had difficulty finding the exact English words to translate the story because the events I describe in it were not experienced in the English language. This is why I kept some of the Spanish words in the translation. I write in both Spanish and English, but the language I write in is determined by what period in my life I write about. Since Spanish was the dominant language during my childhood, I generally write about those experiences in Spanish. 99

The Habit of Movement

Judith Ortiz Cofer

This speaker says she and her family were nomads—that is, people who were always moving around. Judith Ortiz Cofer came to Paterson, New Jersey, from Puerto Rico when she was four years old. Her father was a career Navy man, and whenever he went to sea, Judith, her mother, and her brother returned to Puerto Rico. When their father came back, they would return to New Jersey to be with him.

Nurtured in the lethargy of the tropics,°
the nomadic life did not suit us at first.
We felt like red balloons set adrift
over the wide sky of this new land.
5   Little by little we lost our will to connect
and stopped collecting anything heavier
to carry than a wish.
We took what we could from books borrowed
in Greek temples, or holes in the city walls,
10   returning them hardly handled.

We carried the idea of home on our backs
from house to house, never staying
long enough to learn the secret ways of wood
and stone, and always the blank stare
15   of undraped windows behind us
like the eyes of the unmourned dead.
In time we grew rich in dispossession°
and fat with experience.
As we approached but did not touch others,
20   our habit of movement kept us safe
like a train in motion—
nothing could touch us.

A farm laborer and his grandchild, 1949.

Russell Lee Photograph Collection, CN07202, Center for American History, University of Texas at Austin.

1. **lethargy of the tropics:** sleepiness; lack of energy caused by extreme heat.
17. **dispossession:** not owning property or possessions.

MAKING MEANINGS

First Thoughts

1. Work with a small group of classmates to illustrate the struggles and dreams of Panchito and his family. (Brainstorm first.)

Shaping Interpretations

2. Why does Papá become alarmed when he sees the school bus? How do you think he feels about the fact that his children do not go to school?

3. Draw a thought bubble like the one on the left, but larger. Fill it in with words and symbols showing what Panchito might be thinking and feeling at one of these points in the story:

   • when he watches the neatly dressed boys getting off the school bus

   • as he enters the school for the first time

   • when he comes home and sees the cardboard boxes again

4. Go back to your Quickwrite chart. Circle any items in either column that you think apply to the family in the story. Then, in a different-colored ink, add any new information that you learned from the story.

5. Think about Jiménez's **perspective,** or point of view, about migrant farm workers. Find two or three passages from the story that show how he feels about his childhood experiences.

Connecting with the Text

6. Imagine that Panchito is a new student at your school. What could you do to make him feel less nervous?

Challenging the Text

7. What does the **title** of the story mean to you? Do you agree with Jiménez's statement in Meet the Writer that "The Circuit" is a better title than "Cardboard Boxes"? Explain your response. (You may want to look up the word *circuit* in a dictionary.)

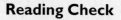

Reading Check

a. Explain why the family leaves the shack near Ito's farm.

b. Why does Panchito fall down in the field?

c. Why doesn't Panchito want to read in front of the class?

d. Why does Panchito consider Mr. Lema his best friend at school?

e. What happens at the end of the story? (What do the cardboard boxes indicate?)

CHOICES: Building Your Portfolio

Writer's Notebook

1. Collecting Ideas for a Problem Solution

Go back to the Quickwrite chart you made earlier. Choose one of the items from the right-hand side, and list as many solutions to the problem as you can. When you're finished, decide which solution you think is best, and label it #*1*. Label the second-best solution #*2*, and so on.

> Difficulty: not knowing local laws
>
> Possible solutions:
> —print a booklet in several languages explaining laws
> —people from the same country could volunteer to explain laws to new arrivals

Persuasive Writing

2. Urging Action

Imagine that you are one of Mr. Sullivan's workers. Write a **petition** (formal request) to persuade him to improve living and working conditions for you and the other workers. Draw on information in the story to describe current conditions. Be sure to explain exactly what you want Mr. Sullivan to do and why it would be in his best interests to agree. (Try to provide specific **facts** and **examples** to support your opinion.) What objections might he have? How can you overcome them?

Research/ Social Studies

3. The Circuit Today

"The Circuit" takes place during the 1950s. Find out if conditions have changed for migrant workers in California (and other parts of the country). Have wages and living quarters improved? What is life like for children? Have new problems arisen?

You should be able to find some information on the Internet or in a library. You may also want to try writing to or calling a farm workers' organization, such as the United Farm Workers of America, and government agencies like the Departments of Labor and Agriculture. Some information, such as the numbers of migrant workers or average wages, you may put in graphic form.

Comparing Texts

4. Families on the Move

In a paragraph compare Jiménez's story with Cofer's poem (see *Connections* on page 665). Before you write, collect your details in a chart like the one below. (Remember that **tone** is the writer's attitude toward what he or she is writing about. Tones can be sad, angry, resigned, forgiving, bitter, and so on.)

	Story	Poem
topic		
tone		
key details		

At the end of your paragraph, tell how you responded to each piece of writing.

LANGUAGE LINK   MINI-LESSON

- ## Style: Using Words from Other Languages

Francisco Jiménez and many other American writers occasionally include words and phrases from other languages in their work. They do so to bring characters to life, to convey meanings that would be lost in translation, and to make the writing—whether fiction or nonfiction—seem more "true."

If you want to use words in your writing that may be unfamiliar to some readers (whether they're foreign words, slang, regional expressions, or dialect), consider using one of the following methods to help your readers understand.

> **Try It Out**
>
> If you're working on a piece that you think would be improved by the inclusion of foreign words, try adding a few. A word of caution: Keep it light. A sprinkling of foreign terms adds color, but readers will have difficulty wading through many sentences with words in an unknown language.

1. **Translate or define the word or phrase right after you use it.**

   EXAMPLES   "Es todo," said Papá. "That's all."

   We ate carne con chile, the spicy dish of meat and peppers I liked better than any other dish.

2. **Give context clues.**

   EXAMPLE   "Mi olla," my mother said, looking proudly at her pot.

3. **Provide translations in footnotes or attach a glossary to the end of your piece.**

Words from languages that don't use the Latin alphabet (the one used in English), such as Hebrew, Chinese, and Russian, are often *transliterated* (written in the corresponding letters of the Latin alphabet).

VOCABULARY   HOW TO OWN A WORD

WORD BANK	Back to the Story
detect populated drone instinctively	1. If Papá were to <u>detect</u> noises in the car's engine, what could he do about it? 2. Do you think Mr. Sullivan's garage is fit to be <u>populated</u> by a family? Why or why not? 3. What would the <u>drone</u> of insects sound like? What other sounds could be described as drones? 4. On page 662, what does the word *instinctively* suggest about how often the boys have hidden from school buses?

Before You Read

Make the Connection

American Dreams

Imagine that one day a box arrives at your house. You open the card with your family and read it aloud:

This box contains anything you want it to. Your present can be as big as the sky or as small as a grain of sand. It can be exquisite, like a brilliant diamond, or exciting, like a brilliant idea. The one rule is that you can only choose once, and you must choose together as a family. Then, open and enjoy!

Quickwrite

Quickwrite for a few minutes about what you would want the present to be. Would your family agree easily, or would you all want different things? After you write, share your thoughts with your classmates.

Elements of Literature

Theme

Plot answers the question, "What happens?" **Theme** answers the question, "What does this story reveal about life?" Ask yourself that question as you read "Three Wise Guys."

go.hrw.com
LEO 8-8

The **theme** of a work of literature is the general idea or insight about life that the written work reveals.

For more on Theme, see page 264 and the Handbook of Literary Terms.

Reading Skills and Strategies

Discovering the Theme

To discover a theme, you'll have to read between the lines. A writer will rarely state the theme of a story directly.

Look for these clues that can help you determine the theme:

- the story's title
- changes the main characters experience
- discoveries the main characters make
- how conflicts or problems in the story are settled

Mexican Christmas ornaments illustrate the story.

Background

Literature and Culture

According to Christian tradition, the giving of Christmas gifts began with the Three Wise Men, who brought gold, frankincense, and myrrh to the stable where the Christ child was born. The visit of the Three Wise Men is celebrated on January 6, twelve days after Christmas. In many countries, people exchange gifts on January 6 rather than on Christmas. The Mexican Americans in this story give gifts on January 6, which they call Dia de los Reyes, the "Day of the Kings."

THREE WISE GUYS

UN CUENTO DE NAVIDAD
A CHRISTMAS STORY

Sandra Cisneros

WHAT COULD BE IN A BOX SO BIG?

The Three Kings: Los Tres Reyes Magos (1960) by Manuel Jiménez. Arrazola, Oaxaca, Mexico. Painted wood, figure on the left 9¼" high.

Girard Foundation Collection at the Museum of International Folk Art, a unit of the Museum of New Mexico, Santa Fe. Photo by Michel Monteaux.

The big box came marked DO NOT OPEN TILL XMAS, but the mama said not until the Day of the Three Kings. Not until Dia de los Reyes, the sixth of January, do you hear? That is what the mama said exactly, only she said it all in Spanish. Because in Mexico where she was raised, it is the custom for boys and girls to receive their presents on January sixth, and not Christmas, even though they were living on the Texas side of the river now. Not until the sixth of January.

Yesterday the mama had risen in the dark same as always to reheat the coffee in a tin saucepan and warm the breakfast tortillas. The papa had gotten up coughing and spitting up the night, complaining how the evening before the buzzing of the chicharras[1] had kept him from sleeping. By the time the mama had the house smelling of oatmeal and cinnamon, the papa would be gone to the fields, the sun al-

ready tangled in the trees and the urracas[2] screeching their rubber-screech cry. The boy Ruben and the girl Rosalinda would have to be shaken awake for school. The mama would give the baby Gilberto his bottle and then she would go back to sleep before getting up again to the chores that were always waiting. That is how the world had been.

But today the big box had arrived. When the boy Ruben and the girl Rosalinda came home from school, it was already sitting in the living room in front of the television set that no longer worked. Who had put it there? Where had it come from? A box covered with red paper with green Christmas trees and a card on top that said "Merry Christmas to the Gonzales Family. Frank, Earl, and Dwight Travis. P.S. DO NOT OPEN TILL XMAS." That's all.

Two times the mama was made to come into the living room, first to explain to the children

---

1. **chicharras** (chē·chä′räs): Spanish for "cicadas," insects that make a loud, high-pitched sound.

2. **urracas** ($\overline{oo}$·rä′käs): Spanish for "magpies," black-and-white birds known for their noisy chattering.

and later to their father how the brothers Travis had arrived in the blue pickup, and how it had taken all three of those big men to lift the box off the back of the truck and bring it inside, and how she had had to nod and say thank-you thank-you thank-you over and over because those were the only words she knew in English. Then the brothers Travis had nodded as well, the way they always did when they came and brought the boxes of clothes, or the turkey each November, or the canned ham on Easter, ever since the children had begun to earn high grades at the school where Dwight Travis was the principal.

But this year the Christmas box was bigger than usual. What could be in a box so big? The boy Ruben and the girl Rosalinda begged all afternoon to be allowed to open it, and that is when the mama had said the sixth of January, the Day of the Three Kings. Not a day sooner.

It seemed the weeks stretched themselves wider and wider since the arrival of the big box. The mama got used to sweeping around it because it was too heavy for her to push in a corner. But since the television no longer worked ever since the afternoon the children had poured iced tea through the little grates in the back, it really didn't matter if the box <u>obstructed</u> the view. Visitors that came inside the house were told and told again the story of how the box had arrived, and then each was made to guess what was inside.

It was the comadre[3] Elodia who suggested over coffee one afternoon that the big box held a portable washing machine that could be rolled away when not in use, the kind she had seen in her Sears Roebuck catalog. The mama said she hoped so because the wringer washer she had used for the last ten years had finally gotten tired and quit. These past few weeks she had had to boil all the clothes in the big pot she used for cooking the Christmas tamales. Yes. She hoped the big box was a portable washing machine. A washing machine, even a portable one, would be good.

But the neighbor man Cayetano said, What foolishness, comadre. Can't you see the box is too small to hold a washing machine, even a portable one. Most likely God has heard your prayers and sent a new color TV. With a good antenna you could catch all the Mexican soap operas, the neighbor man said. You could <u>distract</u> yourself with the complicated troubles of the rich and then give thanks to God for the blessed simplicity of your poverty. A new TV would surely be the end to all your miseries.

Each night when the papa came home from the fields, he would spread newspapers on the cot in the living room, where the boy Ruben and the girl Rosalinda slept, and sit facing the big box in the center of the room. Each night he imagined the box held something different. The day before yesterday he guessed a new record player. Yesterday an ice chest filled with beer. Today the papa sat with his bottle of beer, fanning himself with a magazine, and said in a voice as much a plea as a prophecy: air conditioner.

But the boy Ruben and the girl Rosalinda were sure the big box was filled with toys. They had even <u>punctured</u> it in one corner with a pencil when their mother was busy cooking, but they could see nothing inside but blackness.

Only the baby Gilberto remained uninterested in the contents of the big box and seemed each day more fascinated with the exterior of the box rather than the interior. One

---

3. **comadre** (kô·mä′dre): Spanish word referring to a woman relative or very close family friend. The word literally means "co-mother." It often refers to a godmother.

WORDS TO OWN
obstructed (əb·strukt′id) v.: blocked.
distract (di·strakt′) v.: draw the attention away in another direction.
punctured (puŋk′chərd) v.: made a hole in.

afternoon he tore off a fistful of paper, which he was chewing when his mother swooped him up with one arm, rushed him to the kitchen sink, and forced him to swallow handfuls of lukewarm water in case the red dye of the wrapping paper might be poisonous.

When Christmas Eve finally came, the family Gonzalez put on their good clothes and went to Midnight Mass. They came home to a house that smelled of tamales and atole,[4] and everyone was allowed to open one present before going to sleep. But the big box was to remain untouched until the sixth of January.

On New Year's Eve the little house was filled with people, some related, some not, coming in and out. The friends of the papa came with bottles, and the mama set out a bowl of grapes to count off the New Year. That night the children did not sleep in the living room cot as they usually did, because the living room was crowded with big-fannied ladies and fat-stomached men sashaying to the accordion music of the midget twins from McAllen. Instead the children fell asleep on a lump of handbags and crumpled suit jackets on top of the mama and the papa's bed, dreaming of the contents of the big box.

Finally, the fifth of January. And the boy Ruben and the girl Rosalinda could hardly sleep. All night they whispered last-minute wishes. The boy thought perhaps if the big box held a bicycle, he would be the first to ride it, since he was the oldest. This made his sister cry until the mama had to yell from her bedroom on the other side of the plastic curtains, Be quiet or I'm going to give you each the stick, which sounds worse in Spanish than it does in English. Then no one said anything. After a very long time, long after they heard the mama's wheezed breathing and the papa's

piped snoring, the children closed their eyes and remembered nothing.

The papa was already in the bathroom coughing up the night before from his throat when the urracas began their clownish chirping. The boy Ruben awoke and shook his sister. The mama, frying the potatoes and beans for breakfast, nodded permission for the box to be opened.

With a kitchen knife the boy Ruben cut a careful edge along the top. The girl Rosalinda tore the Christmas wrapping with her fingernails. The papa and the mama lifted the cardboard flaps and everyone peered inside to see what it was the brothers Travis had brought them on the Day of the Three Kings.

There were layers of balled newspaper packed on top. When these had been cleared the boy Ruben looked inside. The girl Rosalinda looked inside. The papa and the mama looked.

This is what they saw: the complete Britannica Junior Encyclopaedia, twenty-four volumes in red imitation leather with gold-embossed letters, beginning with Volume I, Aar-Bel and ending with Volume XXIV, Yel-Zyn. The girl Rosalinda let out a sad cry, as if her hair was going to be cut again. The boy Ruben pulled out Volume IV, Ded-Fem. There were many pictures and many words, but there were more words than pictures. The papa flipped through Volume XXII, but because he could not read English words, simply put the book back and grunted. What can we do with this? No one said anything, and shortly after, the screen door slammed.

Only the mama knew what to do with the contents of the big box. She withdrew Volumes VI, VII, and VIII, marched off to the dinette set in the kitchen, placed two on Rosalinda's chair so she could better reach the table, and put one underneath the plant stand that danced.

When the boy and the girl returned from

4. **atole** (ä·tō′lä): warm drink made with corn flour.

school that day they found the books stacked into squat pillars against one living room wall and a board placed on top. On this were arranged several plastic doilies and framed family photographs. The rest of the volumes the baby Gilberto was playing with, and he was already rubbing his sore gums along the corners of Volume XIV.

The girl Rosalinda also grew interested in the books. She took out her colored pencils and painted blue on the eyelids of all the illustrations of women and with a red pencil dipped in spit she painted their lips and fingernails red-red. After a couple of days, when all the pictures of women had been colored in this manner, she began to cut out some of the prettier pictures and paste them on looseleaf paper.

One volume suffered from being exposed to the rain when the papa <u>improvised</u> a hat during a sudden shower. He forgot it on the hood of the car when he drove off. When the children came home from school they set it on the porch to dry. But the pages puffed up and became so fat, the book was impossible to close.

Only the boy Ruben refused to touch the books. For several days he avoided the principal because he didn't know what to say in case Mr. Travis were to ask how they were enjoying the Christmas present.

On the Saturday after New Year's the mama and the papa went into town for groceries and left the boy in charge of watching his sister and baby brother. The girl Rosalinda was stacking books into spiral staircases and making her paper dolls descend them in a fancy manner.

Perhaps the boy Ruben would not have bothered to open the volume left on the kitchen table if he had not seen his mother wedge her name-day corsage in its pages. On the page where the mama's carnation lay pressed between two pieces of Kleenex was a picture of a dog in a space ship. FIRST DOG IN SPACE the caption said. The boy turned to another page and read where cashews came from. And then about the man who invented the guillotine. And then about Bengal tigers. And about clouds. All afternoon the boy read, even after the mama and the papa came home. Even after the sun set, until the mama said time to sleep and put the light out.

In their bed on the other side of the plastic curtain the mama and the papa slept. Across from them in the crib slept the baby Gilberto. The girl Rosalinda slept on her end of the cot. But the boy Ruben watched the night sky turn from violet. To blue. To gray. And then from gray. To blue. To violet once again.

WORDS TO OWN

improvised (im′prə·vīzd′) *v*.: made with whatever materials are available.

MEET THE WRITER

"I Just Love Words So Much"

Sandra Cisneros (1954–   ) grew up between two worlds as her family moved back and forth between Chicago and Mexico City.

What makes her stories and poems unique isn't just what she writes about, it's how Cisneros writes it. Critics have praised her distinctive style. She herself has said:

66 I just love words so much. I love seeing them on the sides of buildings or on menus or written on the floor. 99

For further details on Cisneros, see page 117.

MAKING MEANINGS

- **First Thoughts**

1. What do you think of the gift Ruben and his family received? How would you have liked it? (Check your Quickwrite notes.)

Shaping Interpretations

2. How do you interpret the last lines about Ruben watching the changing colors of the sky?

3. Toward the end of the story, Ruben emerges as the **main character.** How is he different from the others? (What has he discovered by the story's end?)

4. What do you think the **title** of the story means? (Who *are* the three wise guys?) What would be another good title for the story?

5. The subject of this story is gift-giving. What **theme,** or insight into our lives, do you think Cisneros is trying to convey through this story? What details in the story helped you figure out the theme?

Challenging the Text

6. Did Cisneros want you to guess what was in the box? Should she have given you more hints? Explain your responses.

Reading Check

a. Where did the box come from?

b. What does each person in the family imagine is in the box?

c. What actually is in the box?

d. How does each person in the house make use of the gift?

CHOICES: Building Your Portfolio

Writer's Notebook

1. Collecting Ideas for a Problem Solution

What do you think makes some children lose interest in learning? What could families, schools, or other people (television producers? video-game designers?) do to make learning more interesting? Brainstorm ideas.

Creative Writing

2. Dear "Guys"—Thanks

It is twenty years later. Because he loves to learn, Ruben has become a successful, well-known _____ (you decide). Now he wants to write to the Travis brothers to thank them for setting him on his way. Write his letter. (You could be Rosalinda instead; maybe she, too, read the encyclopedias.)

How-To Essay/Speech

3. Tamales, Too

Did you get hungry reading about the food in this story? Find a recipe for one of the Mexican dishes mentioned or for one of your own favorite foods. Then, write an essay/speech explaining how to make your dish. Be prepared to present your speech in class.

LANGUAGE LINK   MINI-LESSON

Style: Avoiding Clichés

How many times have you heard expressions like these?

as good as new	as solid as a rock
rise and shine	as stubborn as a mule
as straight as an arrow	as white as a sheet
as easy as pie	lay down the law
fallen on hard times	off the top of my head

At one time, they probably seemed fresh and vivid. Now, overuse has turned them into **clichés,** stale expressions that make writing sound tired and dull. Instead of turning to clichés, good writers come up with their own comparisons and turns of phrase, as Cisneros does in these expressions from "Three Wise Guys":

"She . . . put one underneath the plant stand that danced." (page 672)

"The girl Rosalinda let out a sad cry, as if her hair was going to be cut again." (page 672)

Try It Out

Using two or three of these starters, invent fresh expressions.

as good as . . .
as happy as . . .
as cool as . . .
as smart as . . .
as solid as . . .
as light as . . .
as straight as . . .
as tough as . . .

VOCABULARY   HOW TO OWN A WORD

WORD BANK

obstructed
distract
punctured
improvised

Latin Roots, Prefixes, and Suffixes

Learning the meaning of some Latin roots, prefixes, and suffixes can help you unlock the meaning of many English words. Work with a partner to make a **root chart** like the one below for the other three words in the Word Bank. See how many words you can list that have the same root. (You can look in a dictionary near each Word Bank word. You can also try to think of words that begin differently but contain the same root.)

obstructed
Meaning: "blocked"
Prefix: Latin *ob–*, "against"
Root: *struct,* from Latin *stuere,* "to pile up"
Words with the same root: obstruction, instruct, instruction, construction, construct, structure
Sentence: A foot of snow <u>obstructed</u> all traffic.

Before You Read

REFUGEE IN AMERICA / I HAVE A DREAM

Make the Connection

Idea Cluster

Form a group with two or three classmates. Pick one of the words below, and create a cluster map. Draw as many circles as you like on your map. When all the groups have finished, share your maps.

- freedom
- equality
- democracy
- liberty

Quickwrite

Freewrite briefly, using as a starter the sentence *I have a dream for America.*

Elements of Literature

Allusion

"I Have a Dream" draws much of its power from **allusions** to texts familiar to many Americans, such as this famous Bible passage from the Book of Isaiah (40:4–5).

Every valley shall be exalted, and every mountain and hill shall be made low: and the crooked shall be made straight, and the rough places plain:

And the glory of the Lord shall be revealed, and all flesh shall see it together: for the mouth of the Lord hath spoken it.

"Refugee in America" contains a less obvious allusion. As you read the poem, ask yourself in what contexts we usually come across the word *liberty*.

> **A**n **allusion** is a reference to someone or something from literature, religion, history, or another field or branch of culture.
>
> *For more on Allusion, see the Handbook of Literary Terms.*

Reading Skills and Strategies

Comparing and Contrasting Texts

When you **compare and contrast** texts, you look for ways in which they are alike and different. Both Hughes's moving poem "A Refugee in America" and King's stirring speech treat the subjects of freedom and equality. As you read, think about how the poem and speech are alike and different.

Background

Literature and Social Studies

On August 28, 1963, more than 200,000 Americans took part in a march in Washington, D.C. The marchers called on Congress to pass a civil rights bill proposed by President John F. Kennedy, and they demanded full equality for African Americans. People of all races, from almost every state in the Union, gathered in front of the Lincoln Memorial to sing and listen to speeches.

Late in the day, Dr. Martin Luther King, Jr., rose to speak. He began by describing how the promise of America had not yet been realized for African Americans. Then, setting aside his prepared speech, he improvised. His speech, which was heard by people across the country on TV and radio, deeply moved his listeners. King's concluding words, with their powerful rhythm and vivid images, are reprinted here as "I Have a Dream."

go.hrw.com

LEO 8-8

Refugee in America

Langston Hughes

There are words like *Freedom*
Sweet and wonderful to say.
On my heart-strings freedom sings
All day everyday.

There are words like *Liberty*
That almost make me cry.
If you had known what I knew
You would know why.

By the Gate (1953) by Ernest Crichlow. Oil on board.

Collection of Harmon and Harriet Kelley, San Antonio, Texas.

from
I Have a Dream

Martin Luther King, Jr.
August 28, 1963

Marchers gather in front of the Lincoln Memorial.

I say to you today, my friends, that in spite of the difficulties and frustrations of the moment I still have a dream. It is a dream deeply rooted in the American Dream.

I have a dream that one day this nation will rise up and live out the true meaning of its creed: "We hold these truths to be self-evident; that all men are created equal."

I have a dream that one day on the red hills of Georgia the sons of former slaves and the sons of former slaveowners will be able to sit down together at the table of brotherhood.

I have a dream that one day even the state of Mississippi, a desert state sweltering with the heat of injustice and oppression, will be transformed into an oasis of freedom and justice.

I have a dream that my four little children will one day live in a nation where they will not be judged by the color of their skin but by the content of their character.

I have a dream today.

I have a dream that one day every valley shall be exalted, every hill and mountain shall be made low, the rough places will be made plain, and the crooked places will be made straight, and the glory of the Lord shall be revealed, and all flesh shall see it together.

This is our hope. This is the faith with which I return to the South. With this faith we

WORDS TO OWN

creed (krēd) *n.*: statement of belief or principles.
oasis (ō·ā′sis) *n.*: place in a desert with plants and a supply of water; place or thing offering relief.
exalted (eg·zôlt′id) *v.*: raised; lifted up.

Martin Luther King, Jr., delivers his speech.

From every mountainside, let freedom ring.

will be able to hew out of the mountain of despair a stone of hope. With this faith we will be able to transform the jangling <u>discords</u> of our nation into a beautiful symphony of brotherhood. With this faith we will be able to work together, to pray together, to struggle together, to go to jail together, to stand up for freedom together, knowing that we will be free one day.

This will be the day when all of God's children will be able to sing with new meaning "My country 'tis of thee, sweet land of liberty, of thee I sing. Land where my fathers died, land of the pilgrim's pride, from every mountainside, let freedom ring."

And if America is to be a great nation, this must become true. So let freedom ring from the <u>prodigious</u> hilltops of New Hampshire. Let freedom ring from the mighty mountains of New York. Let freedom ring from the heightening Alleghenies of Pennsylvania!

Let freedom ring from the snowcapped Rockies of Colorado!

Let freedom ring from the curvaceous peaks of California!

But not only that; let freedom ring from Stone Mountain of Georgia!

Let freedom ring from Lookout Mountain of Tennessee!

Let freedom ring from every hill and molehill of Mississippi. From every mountainside, let freedom ring.

When we let freedom ring, when we let it ring from every village and every hamlet, from every state and every city, we will be able to speed up that day when all of God's children, black men and white men, Jews and Gentiles, Protestants and Catholics, will be able to join hands and sing in the words of the old Negro spiritual, "Free at last! Free at last! Thank God almighty, we are free at last!"

WORDS TO OWN

discords (dis′kôrdz′) *n.:* conflicts; disagreements.
prodigious (prō·dij′əs) *adj.:* huge; amazing.

MEET THE WRITERS

"Poems Are Like Rainbows"

Born in Joplin, Missouri, **Langston Hughes** (1902–1967) began writing poetry in his early teens. As a young man he traveled around the world and held many jobs. One day in 1926, he discovered that the famous poet Vachel Lindsay was staying at the Washington, D. C. hotel where Hughes was working as a busboy. Hughes left some of his poems beside Lindsay's dinner plate. That night, Lindsay read them aloud at a poetry reading, announcing that he had discovered a great new poet.

In his autobiography *The Big Sea* (1940), Hughes describes his writing process:

66 There are seldom many changes in my poems, once they're down. Generally, the first two or three lines come to me from something I'm thinking about, or looking at, or doing, and the rest of the poem (if there is to be a poem) flows from those first few lines, usually right away. If there is a chance to put the poem down then, I write it down. If not, I try to remember it until I get to a pencil and paper; for poems are like rainbows: They escape you quickly. 99

"Nonviolence Is the Answer"

Martin Luther King, Jr. (1929–1968), grew up in Atlanta, Georgia. He started college at the age of fifteen. After he graduated, he went on to Crozer Theological Seminary in Pennsylvania to become a Baptist minister, like his father and grandfather. King continued his studies in Boston, where he received his PhD. He then returned to the South to take a position as pastor of a church in Montgomery, Alabama. King was shocked by the intense racism and the strict segregation he saw in Montgomery. He helped organize the Montgomery bus boycott and went on to become a national leader in the civil rights movement, facing violence and risking arrest to spread his message of nonviolent resistance. In 1964, four years before he was assassinated, he accepted the Nobel Peace Prize with these words:

66 Nonviolence is the answer to the crucial political and moral questions of our time; the need for man to overcome oppression and violence without resorting to oppression and violence. 99

from **The Power of Nonviolence**

John Lewis, *interviewed by Joan Morrison and Robert K. Morrison*

When I was a boy, I would go downtown to the little town of Troy, and I'd see the signs saying "White" and "Colored" on the water fountains. There'd be a beautiful, shining water fountain in one corner of the store marked "White," and in another corner was just a little spigot marked "Colored." I saw the signs saying "White Men," "Colored Men," and "White Women," "Colored Women." And at the theater we had to go upstairs to go to a movie. You bought your ticket at the same window that the white people did, but they could sit downstairs, and you had to go upstairs.

Lunch counter segregation protest.

I wondered about that, because it was not in keeping with my religious faith, which taught me that we were all the same in the eyes of God. And I had been taught that all men are created equal.

It really hit me when I was fifteen years old, when I heard about Martin Luther King, Jr., and the Montgomery bus boycott. Black people were walking the streets for more than a year rather than riding segregated buses. To me it was like a great sense of hope, a light. Many of the teachers at the high school that I attended were from Montgomery, and they would tell us about what was happening there. That, more than any other event, was the turning point for me, I think. It gave me a way out. . . .

Lewis went on to college, where he attended workshops and studied the philosophy of nonviolence.

In February 1960, we planned the first mass lunch counter sit-in. About five hundred students, black and white, from various colleges showed up and participated in a nonviolent workshop the night before the sit-in. Some of them came from as far away as Pomona College in California and Beloit College in Wisconsin.

We made a list of what we called the "Rules of the Sit-in"—the do's and don't's—and we mimeographed it on an old machine and passed it out to all the students. I wish I had a copy of this list today. I remember it said things like, "Sit up straight. Don't talk back. Don't laugh. Don't strike back." And at the end it said, "Remember the teachings of Jesus, Gandhi, Thoreau, and Martin Luther King, Jr."

Lunch counter sit-in.

Then the next day it began. We wanted to make a good impression. The young men put on their coats and ties, and the young ladies their heels and stockings. We selected seven stores to go into, primarily the chain stores—Woolworth's, Kresge's, and the Walgreen drugstore—

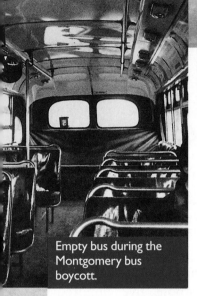

Empty bus during the Montgomery bus boycott.

and we had these well-dressed young people with their books going to the lunch counters. They would sit down in a very orderly, peaceful, nonviolent fashion and wait to be served. They would be reading a book or doing their homework or whatever while they were waiting.

I was a spokesperson for one of these groups. I would ask to be served, and we would be told that we wouldn't be served. The lunch counter would be closed, and they would put up a sign saying "Closed—not serving." Sometimes they would lock the door, leave us in there, and turn out all the lights, and we would continue to sit.

After we had been doing this for a month, it was beginning to bother the business community and other people in Nashville. We heard that the city had decided to allow the police officials to stand by and allow the hoodlum element to come in and attack us—and that the police would arrest us—to try to stop the sit-ins. We had a meeting after we heard that, to decide did we still want to go down on this particular day. And we said yes.

I was with the group that went into the Woolworth's there. The lunch counter was upstairs—just a long row of stools in front of a counter. My group went up to sit there, and after we had been there for half an hour or so, a group of young white men came in and began pulling people off the lunch-counter stools, putting lighted cigarettes out in our hair or faces or down our backs, pouring ketchup and hot sauce all over us, pushing us down to the floor and beating us. Then the police came in and started arresting *us*. They

didn't arrest a single person that beat us, but they arrested all of us and charged us with disorderly conduct.

That was the first mass arrest of students in the South for participating in a sit-in. Over one hundred of us were arrested that day. We were sentenced, all of us, to a fifty-dollar fine or thirty days in jail, and since we wouldn't pay the fine, we were put in jail. . . .

Lewis and his fellow students were jailed, but they continued their protests when they were released. In April 1960, the mayor of Nashville agreed that the lunch counters should be desegregated.

And so Nashville became the first major city in the South to desegregate its downtown lunch counters and restaurants. That was the power of nonviolence. . . .

I think one thing the movement did for all of us in the South, black and white alike, was to have a cleansing effect on our psyche. I think it brought up a great deal of the dirt and a great deal of the guilt from under the rug to the top, so that we could deal with it, so that we could see it in the light. And I think that in a real sense, we are a different people. We are better people. It freed even those of us who didn't participate—black people, white people alike—to be a little more human.

Civil rights activists march in Selma, Alabama.

MAKING MEANINGS

First Thoughts

1. Go back to the Quickwrite and the cluster map you made before you read the speech and the poem. Using a different-colored pen, add to the map any new feelings or ideas you have about the word. Then, look at your classmates' maps again, and do the same with theirs.

Shaping Interpretations

2. In your own words, describe some of the specifics of Martin Luther King, Jr.'s dream for America.

3. In his speech, King **alludes,** or refers, to the Declaration of Independence and to the patriotic hymn "My Country, 'Tis of Thee." Why would King want to remind his audience of these texts?

4. Find several examples of **refrain** (repeated words or sentences) in King's speech. What important ideas are being emphasized?

5. Describe in a sentence or two what you think the **theme,** or message, of "Refugee in America" is. How is it similar to King's message? How is it different?

6. The speaker of "Refugee in America" has different reactions to two words that mean nearly the same thing. Do you see any differences in meaning between the words *freedom* and *liberty*? Explain.

7. What is a refugee? (Look up the word in a dictionary if you're not sure of its meaning.) How can someone be a refugee in his or her own country?

Connecting with the Text

8. Choose either Hughes's poem or King's speech, and describe how it makes you feel about being an American. In what ways is its message still relevant today?

Extending the Theme

9. Do you agree with Lewis (see *Connections* on pages 681–682) that Americans are a different and better people since the days of the civil rights movement? How do you know? Use evidence from the text and current events to support your opinion.

> **Reading Check**
>
> Which of the following sentences best expresses the **main idea** of King's speech? Why?
>
> **a.** Freedom must ring from every mountaintop.
>
> **b.** People should love one another.
>
> **c.** Freedom and equality should be given to all Americans.

CHOICES: Building Your Portfolio

Writer's Notebook

1. Collecting Ideas for a Problem Solution

What would it take to make your dream for America a reality? Think of an improvement that you would like to see, and jot down your ideas on what could be done to make it happen. (Be specific.)

> Cleaner air:
> —invent electric-powered cars that don't pollute
> —persuade more Americans to quit smoking

Role-Play

2. Meeting of the Minds

Imagine a meeting taking place today between Langston Hughes and Martin Luther King, Jr. With a partner, role-play that meeting. What would they agree about? What would they disagree about? What might they say to each other about the state of affairs in the United States in their own times or today?

Before you start, try making a Venn diagram like the one below to **compare** the views expressed in "Refugee in America" and "I Have a Dream."

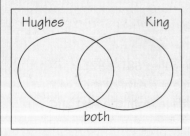

Creative Writing

3. You Are There, Too

Imagine that you are one of the thousands of marchers assembled in front of the Lincoln Memorial on that August afternoon in 1963. Write a **letter** or **diary entry** describing your reactions to the final speech of the day, by Martin Luther King, Jr. (If possible, first listen to a recording or watch a film of King delivering his speech.)

Art

4. A Vision of America

Create a work of art inspired by King's speech or Hughes's poem. You could make, for example, a mosaic, a collage, or a tapestry. Remember that you can use words in any of these art forms. Think of some way you can display your work in your community.

Speaking and Listening/Writing

5. Oral History

Working with a partner, interview an older person about his or her experiences and memories of the civil rights era. You can write up your oral history using only your subject's words, as did the authors of "The Power of Nonviolence" (see *Connections* on pages 681–682). If you prefer, you can use a question-and-answer format.

LANGUAGE LINK MINI-LESSON

• Style: Avoiding Wordiness

Language Handbook
H E L P

See Improving Sentence Style, pages 791-792.

Technology
H E L P

See Language Workshop CD-ROM. *Key word entry: wordiness.*

I believe that it is worth expressing to my listening audience on the present occasion the fact that in spite of the situation involving difficulties and feelings of frustration we are experiencing at the present time, I continue to maintain that there is a condition that I believe that we can achieve at a point in the future.

"I say to you today, my friends, that in spite of the difficulties and frustrations of the moment I still have a dream."

If Martin Luther King, Jr. had begun with the first of the sentences above instead of the second, would "I Have a Dream" be remembered today as a great speech—or at all? Using more words than you need doesn't make your writing better; it just gets in the way of your message.

When you revise your writing, weed out words that aren't needed to express your meaning. Whenever possible, replace groups of words with single words.

> **Try It Out**
> Count the words in a short piece you've written. Then, try to cut ten unnecessary words. (You may need to change some words, too.) Ask a friend to read the two versions and tell you which he or she prefers.

Wordy	Better
due to the fact that	because
despite the fact that	although
with great suddenness	suddenly
in an angry way	angrily
this book is a long one	this book is long
my brother, who is a great athlete	my brother, a great athlete
she is a person who	she

VOCABULARY HOW TO OWN A WORD

WORD BANK

creed
oasis
exalted
discords
prodigious

• Analogies

Complete each sentence below with the word that fits best from the Word Bank. Use each word only once. (You may want to review the explanation of analogies on page 76.)

1. *Suffering* is to *relief* as *desert* is to _____.
2. _____ is to *tiny* as *bright* is to *dim*.
3. *Arguments* is to _____ as *agreements* is to *harmonies*.
4. *Dream* is to *vision* as _____ is to *belief*.
5. *Raised* is to *sunken* as _____ is to *lowered*.

COMING TO

from **New Kids on the Block: Oral Histories of Immigrant Teens**
Janet Bode

AMITABH, AGE 15, FROM INDIA

It is really bad for us in the beginning. We were five in a two-room apartment. Every day my parents would get up and go out to look for jobs. They knew they had to start all the way at the bottom, that people here didn't count any experience from India. But my father had been a biologist. My mother was a chemistry professor at a university. In India they were both making good money.

Now, though, they would come home every evening and they wouldn't have found anything. They would be very, very sad. They didn't know the bus systems or the subway systems here. They'd get lost. They'd get to someplace and it would be too late. The job would be gone. They'd go to another place and the answer would be no. One day, my parents said,

go.hrw.com
LEO 8-8

I think Americans must be the same as us inside.

AMERICA

"This is a dead end. We can't find jobs. We don't have any more money. Nothing. We're going to have to jump into the river." I want to think that they were not being serious, but I still would feel so sad for them and so sad for us.

I couldn't always understand why we had come here. Why would they leave the country where they had been born, where their children had been born? Bhavnagar was a modern-ized city on the northwest side of India. It had a lot of factories, apartment houses, and pri-vate homes. Our home was three stories high, and we lived together with my uncle, my aunt, and my grandparents. My grandparents had an-other house in a small city called Mehsana. Every summer and during other vacations, we'd go there.

The weather was very warm. In the winters it would get cool enough to wear sweaters, but that was it. No snow. It also used to rain quite a bit. There was a dry and a rainy season, with monsoons[1] that occurred every year at a certain time. We had a good life there.

I know that people think that in India everybody is poor, that everything is backward. It's not that backward, and it's probably improved since I've been here. We had electricity and running water and traffic jams. I went to a good school. They taught the same subjects as over here, like art, general science, and math, and also some of the different languages of India. I think there are fifteen or sixteen languages. At home we spoke Gujarati, and I learned how to speak Hindi, too.

I knew the food. I loved cooked okra, the vegetable, and pouri, the bread. I had a favorite kind of curry. I knew my future. I knew that when I got married, I would bring my wife to live with my parents. The bride's family would provide a dowry, money and silverware and things like that.

My parents said, though, that we would move to America because us kids would have more opportunities for the future. This was a long time planning. I don't even remember the first time they told me. At first it went so slow. I did not know anything about America. Once, a friend of mine who was Christian took me to this place to get American hot dogs. At that time I had no idea what they were. I took a bite and I spit it out. It tasted disgusting!

But then sometimes I would get interested in coming here. I heard there were big buildings and fast cars. My older brother told me, "Over there in the United States you never see the sun. It's

Bombay, India.

always snowing. When the sun does shine, it's a holiday." I thought, Like WOW! About a month before we left, my parents said, "We're moving to America." That's how they told me. And I said, "Yes." I told my friends in school, and they said, "Yeah, sure, sure." I said, "Really. Watch."

After the first few months my parents found jobs, but the work was very tough on them. My father worked as a messenger, more a job for a boy than a man. He delivered letters and carried packages all over the city. Again, he would get lost the way he had when he was looking for work. He lasted about three or four months doing that until he found another job, and another job. All small jobs. Then he met an Indian man who owned a laboratory who hired him. Now he's sort of back in the area of biology, where he used to work.

My mother started working at a store. She had to fold clothes, mostly. Then she got a bet-

---

1. monsoons (män·sōōnz′): seasonal winds that bring heavy rains to India and other countries in southern Asia for several months of the year.

(Left) Indian neighborhood in Chicago.

ter job watching patients at a senior citizens' home. Eventually, she became the dietitian there. And now it's OK for me, too. Kids don't look at me strangely the way they did in the beginning. I had my first hamburger and said, "Forget it!" I threw it out. Eventually, though, I got used to it. Now I eat anything. I eat hot dogs, hamburgers, chicken, and french fries. I love pizza. In India I remember that once we had a fair and they had pizza, a small triangle, for eight rupees, about twenty-five cents. "It was better than the hot dog," I thought then.

Now we live in the suburbs in a big house with four bedrooms. I have my own bedroom, with military posters all over the place. My middle brother and I have a computer. We have more than six hundred games for it. He wants to work in computers. My older brother is in college, the University of Maryland. He wants to be a surgeon.

I'm in the tenth grade. ROTC is my favorite class. I'm planning to go into the military right after I finish high school. It should help me out a lot because ROTC trains us for the military. Since when I was in India, my ambition was to make the military a career. I remember every time my father would take us to a shop, I'd want to buy military-colored clothes. Just yesterday I was looking at some photographs taken at my aunt and uncle's wedding in India. There I was, just a kid, in a military uniform. I don't know why I'm into it so much.

I'm more Americanized than my parents. I still speak Gujarati at home, but now there's English mixed in a lot. I'm trying to get out of my accent as much as possible. And now I have what I guess you could call an American mouth: I have braces. I'd never seen braces in India. I hate wearing them!!! Just like American kids.

Xiaojun/"Debbie," age 13, from China

We had a relative, a second uncle, who lived in the United States. He sent us a tape. We all sat in the living room, put it on a tape recorder, and listened. He said we should come to the United States. He told us to bring "lots of clothes because it's really cold, but no cups or plates because they have them. And bring a blanket."

I didn't know any history of America, except someone had told me that everybody had a slave. I thought, great! I'd come here and get my very own slave. I would not have to carry water anymore!

I'm my parents' oldest daughter. I have a younger brother and a younger sister. We lived in a small village in a house made of brick. It had a big room in the middle, and all the way in the back we could go up a ladder to the two bedrooms. We shared the house with my uncle and his family, ten of us all together. Sometimes my parents and my uncle and aunt would talk about their early life. My father and mother came from the city. He was an architect and built houses. I don't know why they all moved to the country. They didn't talk about that.

We had no running water in the house, but we were lucky because we lived near the river. Every morning at 5:00 A.M. I would go and—pant, pant—get water. I used a big stick and carried the water in buckets balanced on it. The water we used for cooking and for bathing.

We slept on hard wooden beds with no mattresses. There was no telephone, no television, no VCR. There was no "I want my MTV." The most we could get was a radio. We had electricity in the house but used it only when my parents said we could. Usually we used candles.

There was a little houselike building with the cooking fire inside. We didn't have much wood, just sticks, so instead we used the stalks from the wheat. First we put them in the sun to dry or we boiled them with other things like carrots for feed for the pigs. We used every part of everything. Mostly my mother and I did the cooking. That was one of the duties of the oldest daughter. We ate mostly rice and vegetables, sometimes my favorite, bok choy. Only at New Year's would we have chicken and soup.

I had other chores. I had to clean the bathroom. Well, that is, it was a sort of bathroom. It was a bucket behind the bed or outside. (In big, big, big houses in the village, they have, like, latrines.) I had to change my brother's diapers. I had to help him take a bath and wash his hair. I had to take care of him and my sister after school. Sometimes I really got mad at them and yelled at them. In China the oldest starts cooking at five; you change diapers at six.

My mother—she was the oldest daughter in her family, too—had to feed the chickens, collect the eggs, and clean the coop. She and I helped tend the village's pigs. We had a garden; everybody did. And everybody worked on the village farm. Together we grew wheat and rice and other stuff; I forget what.

The weather and the crops were very important. If the weather got bad, oh, oh, we were in trouble. We worried and worried. When it was harvest time, we had to cut this and cut that. The adults were so busy they couldn't even stop to make lunch for the littlest kids.

We helped our families and we went to school. In China our parents were turning us over to the teachers to educate. They could use the same punishment as our parents. That meant the teachers were strict. If we were late, we had to stand outside the door for one hour. If the teachers didn't think we were paying attention, they took a stick and beat us. Or they took a ruler and smacked our hand until it turned red and black and blue. They pulled our ears like they were stretching them. When we talked, monitors wrote our name on the blackboard, or they made us sit without a chair, on an invisible chair. It was really painful when we didn't do good at school, and this was just elementary school!

After school, I would visit and play with my girlfriends. There weren't any games, no toys, no swings. We didn't have bicycles; only my father did. But we did have lots of homework, even for little kids. At my house we would all sit around the table and my mother would help us.

There was a nice thing about school, though. That's where the one TV was. Whole families would go together to watch television, like you might go to the movies together here.

If you want to move from China, it is very difficult. A lot of people sneak out. My father sneaked out using the ID card of my second uncle. First you take a plane. When those people ask you where you are going, you don't say America. You say Thailand, or something like that. Then you go to one place, change planes, and fly to either Mexico or Canada. If you go to Mexico, you have to climb through the mountains at the border, show the fake ID, and say you are just traveling. If you go to Canada, you just drive across. They don't check you a lot. If you're caught, you're in big trouble. They can even put you behind bars.

Xi'an, Shaanxi province, China.

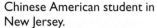

Middle school on a farm commune near Suzhou, Jiangsu province, China.

Chinese American student in New Jersey.

After my father got here, he began to work and to send money home. My mom used some of it to get fake ID cards for us. Then one day she was piercing my ears and using ginger and oil to help them heal. "Your father wrote a letter," she said. "He's earned enough money and he got an apartment for us."

It was real different in New York. It looked almost nothing like China. No foreigners ever came to my village. I had never seen a black person before. I'd never seen any Americans. My mother told me, "People kidnap and kill each other. You have to watch the window and the door all the time to make sure nobody comes in." I could hardly sleep.

The first night my parents prayed for good luck. They took strings and then put matches to them. And they prayed that I go to school and do well. I was very scared to go. The teacher said, "What's her name?" and my mom told him Xiaojun, my Chinese name. He said, "Does she have an English name? No? Well, what about Debbie?"

"Okay," said my mother and that's how I got my name.

Coming to America has changed my life. Now my parents work too much and too hard and I never see them. But we do have a TV, a radio, a microwave, and a washing machine. I still have things to do, like sweep and mop the floor, do the dishes, mop the table, clean the mirrors, wash the fans when they're dirty, wash the clothes in the washing machine, and take care of my brother. For this I get five dollars a week allowance.

I get up around 7:00 A.M. I leave for school between 7:30 and 8:00. School is over at 3:00. I have to go straight home every day after class. I can't go out at night. They know where I am right this minute. Once I'm home, I study for four hours. Before I eat dinner, my father gives me a little lecture. He says, "Work hard so when you grow up, it will be easier to get a good job and make money. If you don't get a good education and a scholarship, you might have to beg for money. You don't want that."

I think of being a doctor, help people get healthier and make their lives easier. I also think about being a model, like Christie Brinkley, or maybe an actress or a lawyer or a cop or a singer. My parents say, "Be a secretary." They tell me, too, "Stay involved with our Chinese community," and I do. But, of course, I'm not an ABC, an American-born Chinese. The ABCs sometimes curse at us and call me and my friends FOBs, "fresh off the boat." I don't like that. I turn my eyes away.

I cry at night sometimes. My father says, "What are you doing?"

I say, "Nothing. Nothing." I get real confused. In China my father went with me to the school to watch movies on television. We had time together. I used to tell him my problems. Now there is no time. Here I can watch TV anytime and I don't have to get the water or take care of the pigs. I guess I like it better in America.

MEET THE WRITER

"We Are a Nation of Immigrants"

"Coming to America" is from *New Kids on the Block: Oral Histories of Immigrant Teens* by **Janet Bode** (1943–   ), a nonfiction writer living in New York City. In addition to Amitabh's and Xiaojun's stories, the book includes interviews with teenagers from Afghanistan, El Salvador, Cuba, the Philippines, Mexico, South Korea, Greece, and Vietnam. In her introduction, Bode explains what led her to write her book:

66 We are a nation of immigrants with a national makeup that's forever shifting. We continue to be the American Dream, the land of opportunity. In the mid-1800s, when my German ancestors set sail for America, they were taking the same gamble that brings people here today. Then, nearly all immigrants were from northern and western Europe. Now only five percent come from that part of the world.

Then, if you wanted to come here, you came. But today immigration is more difficult. Over the last hundred-plus years, laws have been passed and extended and changed and amended. Now,

once again, Congress is debating the issue of who should be allowed in and who should be left out. And to this day, some of our residents—some of the children and grandchildren of yesterday's immigrants—want to close the borders to our future arrivals. Once inside, some people develop a kind of collective amnesia, forgetting their own immigrant roots. We forget that our country's power and beauty stem from the very fact that we are a collection of different cultures. 99

America

Neil Diamond

Far, we've been traveling far,
Without a home, but not without a star.
Free, only want to be free.
We huddle close, hang on to a dream.

On the boats and on the planes, they're coming to America.
Never looking back again, they're coming to America.

Home, don't it seem so far away.
Oh, we're traveling light today, in the eye of the storm,
In the eye of the storm.
Home to a new and a shiny place.
Make our bed, and we'll say our grace.
Freedom's light burning warm,
Freedom's light burning warm.

Everywhere around the world, they're coming to America.
Every time that flag's unfurled, they're coming to America.
Got a dream to take them there.
They're coming to America.
Got a dream they've come to share.
They're coming to America.
They're coming to America today.

My country 'tis of thee (today),
Sweet land of liberty (today),
Of thee I sing (today),
Of thee I sing today.

READ ON

Battle Cries

In 1861, the Union and Confederate armies met in their first great battle, at Manassas Junction, Virginia, near the stream known as Bull Run. In Paul Fleischman's novel *Bull Run* (HarperCollins), sixteen participants—Northern and Southern, male and female, black and white—tell of their dreams of glory and the grim reality of war.

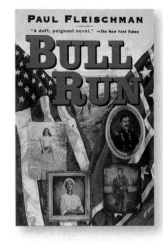

Punishment Without Crime

In 1942, seven-year-old Jeanne Wakatsuki and her family were sent to the Manzanar internment camp. Jeanne Wakatsuki Houston and James D. Houston's *Farewell to Manzanar* is the true story of a native-born American who grew up behind barbed wire in her own country. (This title is available in the HRW Library.)

Oh, Freedom

What was it like to walk through angry, violent mobs to integrate an all-white school? to be arrested for refusing to give up a seat at the front of a bus? to fight for freedom when other people your age were going to sports practice or attending their first dance? In *Freedom's Children* (G. P. Putnam's Sons), Ellen Levine presents thirty oral histories by African Americans who were involved as children or teenagers in the civil rights movement of the 1950s and 1960s.

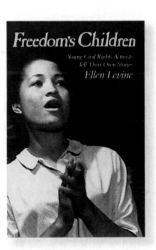

Other Picks

- Dee Brown, adapted by Amy Ehrlich, *Wounded Knee: An Indian History of the American West* (Henry Holt). This is Brown's classic history *Bury My Heart at Wounded Knee* adapted for young adult readers.

- Ossie Davis, *Just Like Martin* (Puffin). Fourteen-year-old Isaac wants to be just like his hero, Martin Luther King, Jr. Then, his church is bombed and two of his classmates are killed, and he must decide whether nonviolence is really the answer.

Technology HELP

See Writer's Workshop 1 CD-ROM. *Assignment: Problem Solution.*

ASSIGNMENT

Write an essay describing a problem and offering one or more solutions.

AIM

To persuade.

AUDIENCE

People who are affected by the problem, who are responsible for the problem, or who can act on your proposal.

Abraham Lincoln's Gettysburg Address appears on page 623.

PERSUASIVE WRITING

PROBLEM SOLUTION

In your **problem solution,** you'll define a problem and propose a solution for it. Your goal is to persuade your reader that the problem exists and is serious and that your proposed solution is a sensible, realistic one that should be put into practice.

Professional Model

> *In these notes, written several years before the Civil War, President Lincoln presents a persuasive argument against slavery.*
>
> If A can prove, however conclusively, that he may, of right, enslave B—why may not B snatch the same argument, and prove equally that he may enslave A?
>
> You say A is white, and B is black. It is color, then, the lighter having the right to enslave the darker? Take care. By this rule you are to be slave to the first man you meet with a fairer skin than your own.
>
> You do not mean color exactly? You mean the whites are intellectually the superior of the blacks and, therefore, have the right to enslave them? Take care again. By this rule, you are to be slave to the first man you meet with an intellect superior to your own.
>
> But, say you, it is a question of interest; and, if you can make it your interest, you have the right to enslave another. Very well. And if he can make it his interest, he has the right to enslave you.
>
> —Abraham Lincoln, 1854

Prewriting

1. Generating Ideas

The first step in writing a problem solution is finding a problem that you want to solve. Working with a group of classmates, list

The history
of the written
word is rich and
Page 1

as many problems as you can think of in a chart like the one below.

If you completed any of the Writer's Notebook assignments in this collection, begin by filling in the topics of those entries. (Even if you aren't interested in pursuing any of them further, another member of your group may get an idea from your topics.)

A problem is shown in each category as an example.

School	Local	National	World
student council doesn't accomplish much	unhealthy levels of lead in town's water supply	increase in teenage smokers	hunger

2. Exploring and Narrowing Topics

Look at your group's chart, and circle the three topics that interest you most. Make sure that the three topics are *not* all from the same column.

Next, write the three topics at the top of a chart like the one below, and fill it in with facts and opinions. (If you completed several of the Writer's Notebook assignments and you want to use one of the topics of those entries, you can skip this step and the next step.)

	Problem #1	Problem #2	Problem #3
Why it's a problem			
What and whom it affects			
Possible solutions			

3. Choosing a Topic

Look over the chart you just made, and choose one of the three
topics. You might consider these questions:

• Do any of these problems suggest a solution that seems
workable and practical?

• Do I care more (or know more or have a stronger desire to
learn) about one of them than about the others?

4. Targeting Your Audience

Whom do you want to persuade? Before you begin writing,
make sure you've identified the audience for your problem
solution. Your primary audience may be one or more of
these groups:

• people affected by the problem (These people may work with
you to solve the problem.)

• people responsible for causing the problem (These people
may change their ways when they read your essay.)

• people who can act on your proposed solutions (These are
the people you need to persuade that your solution is
workable.)

Your tone, word choice, and approach should be adapted to
your audience. What do they know about your topic? What are
their concerns about it? What arguments would they find
persuasive?

5. Organizing and Elaborating

The structure and organization of your paper can be very simple:

• Discuss the problem.

• Present your solution or solutions.

• Conclude by asking your readers to take a specific action.

Depending on your topic and approach, you could include some
or all of the elements listed below.

a. Problem

• clear statement of the problem

• evidence that the problem exists (such as anecdotes and
statistics)

• discussion of what caused the problem and why it
continues to exist

• prediction of what will happen if the problem is not solved

b. Solution

- clear statement of your proposed solution
- discussion of its practicality in terms of money, time, and difficulty
- description of the benefits of the solution
- acknowledgment of possible objections along with responses to them

Drafting

Consider opening your first draft with a letter-style salutation—for example, *To the members of the Orange County School Board* or *Dear Senator Castaneira*—as a way to remind yourself of your audience.

Student Model

Dear Councilman Duane:

More and more minors are smoking. When teens smoke, many problems arise. Something needs to be done to prove to minors that smoking is a bad thing. I am writing this letter to you in hopes that you will take steps to end this big problem.

States problem.

Many problems develop when teenagers smoke. When teens smoke, laws are broken. Merchants break laws by intentionally selling cigarettes to minors. Teenage smokers damage their bodies permanently by smoking. Cigarettes cause addictions; even when teens want to quit, they often find they can't. Smoking can even affect a teenager's schooling. When a teenager needs a cigarette badly, he or she may ditch school to get one.

Provides three reasons why it is a serious problem.

To help stop this problem, the city council could start a campaign against teenage smoking. You could make sure that schools with the sixth grade and older have a required class

States proposed solution.

(continued on next page)

Strategies for Elaboration

As you think about your solution, ask yourself these questions:

- How will it work? Give specific details: Who is involved? What will happen?
- Why is this solution better than other possible solutions? Give facts, examples, statistics.
- How much will it cost, and who will pay for it?

■ *Evaluation Criteria*

A good problem solution

1. *identifies the problem to be solved*
2. *offers convincing evidence that the problem exists and that it is serious*
3. *takes into account the point of view of the audience being addressed*
4. *acknowledges opposing opinions and addresses contradictory evidence*
5. *proposes one or more solutions to the problem*
6. *makes a convincing argument for the solution or solutions*

Sentence Workshop
H E L P

Parallel structure:
page 701.

Language/Grammar Link
H E L P

Good or well? Bad or
badly? page 635. Avoiding
double negatives: page
655. Using words from
other languages: page
668. Avoiding clichés:
page 675. Avoiding
wordiness: page 685.

Communications Handbook
H E L P

See Proofreaders' Marks.

Publishing Tips

- Mail your essay to the audience you've addressed.

- Present your essay as a speech to your intended audience.

- Send your essay as a letter to the editor of your school or local newspaper.

Student Model (continued)

about the hazards of smoking, especially before the legal age. You could sponsor contests in each school for the best "Don't Smoke" posters, poems, essays, and stories. You could put the winners' posters and writing up around New York City. An educational campaign aimed at young teenagers would definitely help solve the problem of smoking by minors.

Provides specific details.

Some teenagers think, "It's my body; I can do what I want with it." Most smoking teenagers haven't fully matured emotionally. That means that what they believe now can change drastically in the following three to ten years of their lives. Therefore, as adults they may seriously regret decisions they made as teenagers.

Answers objections.

Thank you for listening to my thoughts on this matter. I appreciate it and hope that you can do something to end the dilemma. Teenagers need to stop smoking, and you, as a person in power, can help them understand that it isn't all right to smoke.

Concludes with restatement of main idea.

—Hannah Fleury
St. Luke's School
New York City, New York

Evaluating and Revising

Exchange papers with a classmate, and read your partner's first draft. Then, on a separate sheet of paper, try to write at least two objections to the writer's proposed solution or to present at least two pieces of evidence casting doubt on the existence of the problem. Even if you don't really disagree with what your partner has written, you'll be helping him or her by pointing out objections other readers might have.

Exchange papers again, and read your partner's comments. In your second draft, make any changes you feel are necessary.

Sentence Workshop

PARALLEL STRUCTURE

Sentence elements that have the same function should have the same form. This use of grammatically equal structures to express equal ideas is called **parallel structure.**

NOT PARALLEL   Participating in the civil rights movement required <u>patience</u>, <u>courage</u>, and <u>having faith</u>. [two nouns and a phrase]

PARALLEL   Participating in the civil rights movement required <u>patience</u>, <u>courage</u>, and <u>faith</u>. [three nouns]

NOT PARALLEL   King hoped <u>to see an end to segregation</u> and <u>that he would live in a society free from racial prejudice</u>. [a phrase and a clause]

PARALLEL   King hoped <u>to see an end to segregation</u> and <u>to live in a society free from racial prejudice</u>. [two phrases]

Speakers often use parallel structure to create rhythm and emphasize certain ideas. Abraham Lincoln does this in the Gettysburg Address: "government of the people, by the people, for the people" (page 623). You can also find many examples of parallel structure in Martin Luther King, Jr.'s "I Have a Dream" (page 678), such as these lines taken from the Bible:

"... every valley shall be exalted,
and every hill and mountain shall be made low ..."

"... the rough places will be made plain,
and the crooked places will be made straight ..."

Writer's Workshop Follow-up: Proofreading

One place to look for parallel structure is in sentences where you have joined elements with *and, but,* or *or.* Remember the rule: same function, same form.

Try It Out

Revise each of the following sentences by expressing parallel ideas in the same grammatical form. (Each sentence can be rewritten correctly in more than one way.)

1. In 1955, Rosa Parks became famous for her refusal to give up her seat on a bus and being arrested.

2. Nine months before Parks was arrested and the beginning of the bus boycott, a Montgomery teenager was arrested for the same reason.

3. Fifteen-year-old Claudette Colvin said she shouldn't have to get up because it was her constitutional right as well as in moral terms.

4. Claudette Colvin deserves a place in history books for her determination and because she was brave.

Reading for Life

Situation

After reading about U.S. immigration, you might be curious about U.S. population figures. Here are strategies you can use in an Internet search for information.

Strategies

Search the Internet.

- Use one or more **search engines**.
- Decide what your **keywords** will be. (The page at the right was found by using the keywords "U.S. Immigration.")
- Check out the sites that seem most likely to have the facts you want.

Evaluate the sites.

- Evaluate a site's authority and reliability. Your first clue will be the site's URL (Uniform Resource Locator), or address, which on a Web site begins with http://www. At the end of the URL, look for abbreviations like these: *gov* (government), *edu* (education), *com* (commercial), *org* (organization). *Gov* and *edu* sites provide the most accurate,

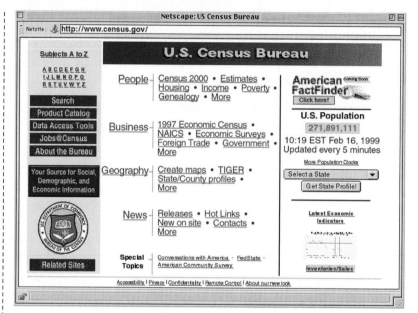

reliable data. In contrast, someone's personal home page is not reliable.

- Check for timeliness. Is the source recent? When was it last revised?
- Does the information seem objective? Does its author want, instead, to persuade you of a particular point of view?

Reading an electronic text.

- Many electronic texts contain "hot spots," called hyperlinks, which you can click on to get additional information. Hyperlinks often appear in colored type and are underlined.

Using the Strategies

Refer to the sample above.

1. What is the site's URL?
2. How reliable is this information? How do you know?
3. How frequently is the U.S. population total updated on this site?
4. Which hyperlink (underlined entry) would you click on to find information about the 2000 census?

Extending the Strategies

With your teacher's approval, use the Internet to research a topic that interests you. Keep a log telling how you searched.

Learning for Life

Using Community Resources to Solve Problems

Problem

The resources in our communities—whether they're people, books, or another source of information—can give us facts and ideas about community problems and show us how similar problems have been handled. How can we use these resources to solve problems?

Project

Find and use problem-solving resources in your school or community.

Preparation

With your classmates, think of an unresolved problem affecting your school, your community, the United States, or the world.

- You may want to go back to the charts you created for the Writer's Workshop to get ideas. If you didn't make them before, you can turn back to pages 696–697 and follow the directions.

- Another way to identify problems is to look at headlines and photographs in recent newspapers and magazines.

Procedure

Choose one of the suggested problems to investigate as a class. You can take a vote to decide.

Presentation

On your own or with a group of classmates, conduct one of the following activities. Then, share your results with your class.

1. Interviewing an Expert

Find someone in your school or community who knows a lot about either your specific problem or the general subject.

Present your problem to the expert you've chosen, and ask him or her for suggestions. Try to state the problem as clearly as possible and provide as much information as you can.

2. Conducting a Survey

Conduct a survey to get the opinions of a large section of your school or community. Ask yourself these questions:

- Will the survey call for spoken or written responses? (If you're asking for spoken responses, you'll need to record them.)

- How many questions will you ask? Will they be open-ended or multiple-choice?

The more questions you ask and the more open-ended they are, the more information you'll get from your survey. If your survey involves too much work, however, few people will be willing to participate.

3. Researching Precedents

A precedent is an act or decision that can be used as a guide for later acts or decisions. Ask your teacher, librarian, or media specialist to help you find out how problems similar to the one you're investigating have been handled in the past. What measures were taken? Did they work? Why or why not?

Processing

With your class, discuss the results of the investigations.

- What new solutions were proposed?

- Which solutions were the most popular?

- What did you learn from the investigations?

With your classmates, make a list of solutions. Then, vote for the one that seems like the best.

RESOURCE CENTER

HANDBOOK OF LITERARY TERMS

You will find more information about the entries in this Handbook on the pages cited at the end of the entries. To learn more about *Alliteration,* for example, turn to pages 290, 293, and 545 in this book.

Cross-references at the end of the entries refer to other entries in the Handbook that contain closely related information. For instance, at the end of *Autobiography* is a cross-reference to *Biography.*

ALLITERATION The repetition of consonant sounds in words that are close together. Alliteration occurs mostly in poetry, though prose writers use it from time to time. Although alliteration usually occurs at the beginning of words, it can also occur within or at the end of words. In the following stanza, notice the repeated *s, m,* and *b* sounds.

> The sun was shining on the sea,
>   Shining with all his might:
> He did his very best to make
>   The billows smooth and bright—
> And this was odd, because it was
>   The middle of the night.
>
>   —Lewis Carroll, from "The Walrus
>   and the Carpenter"

The repetition of vowel sounds in words that are close together is called **assonance.**

See pages 290, 293, 545.

ALLUSION A reference to a statement, a person, a place, or an event from literature, the arts, history, religion, mythology, politics, sports, or science. Allusions enrich the reading experience. Writers expect readers to recognize allusions and to think about the literary work and the allusions contained in it almost at the same time. Both "I Have a Dream" (page 678) and "America" (page 694) allude to the song "My Country, 'Tis of Thee." A reader who is not familiar with that song will miss some of the works' intended meaning.

See pages 676, 683.

ANALOGY A comparison made between two things to show how they are alike. Writers often make analogies to show how something unfamiliar is like something well known or widely experienced. Analogies are often used by scientific writers to explain difficult concepts.

See also *Metaphor, Simile.*

ANECDOTE A brief story told to illustrate a point. Anecdotes are frequently found in biographies and autobiographies. In "The Dogs Could Teach Me" (page 277), for example, Gary Paulsen uses two anecdotes about his huskies to illustrate their intelligence.

ASSONANCE See *Alliteration.*

ATMOSPHERE The overall mood or feeling of a work of literature. A work's atmosphere, or **mood,** can often be described in one or two adjectives, such as *scary, happy, sad,* or *nostalgic.* A writer produces atmosphere by creating images and using sounds that convey a particular feeling. "The Tell-Tale Heart" (page 202) is noted for its eerie atmosphere.

See pages 209, 210, 512, 520.

AUTHOR The writer of a literary work or document. Toni Cade Bambara is the author of "Raymond's Run" (page 3); Abraham Lincoln is the author of "The Gettysburg Address" (page 623).

AUTOBIOGRAPHY A person's account of his or her own life or of part of it. "Camp Harmony" (page 645) is an example of autobiographical writing.

See pages 19, 82–86, 288, 644, 653, 657.
See also *Biography.*

BALLAD A song or songlike poem that tells a story. Ballads usually tell stories of tragedy or adventure, using simple language and a great deal of repetition. They generally have regular rhythm and rhyme patterns that make them easy to memorize. "The Cremation of Sam McGee" (page 513) is a ballad.

See page 520.
See also *Narrative Poem*.

BIOGRAPHY An account of a person's life or of part of it, written or told by another person. The excerpt from *Harriet Tubman* (page 557) is part of a longer biography.

See page 657.

CHARACTER A person or an animal in a story, a play, or another literary work. Characters can be classified according to the changes they undergo. A **static character** does not change much in the course of a work. Johnny in "The Ransom of Red Chief" (page 482) is a static character. In contrast, a **dynamic character** changes as a result of a story's events. Squeaky in "Raymond's Run" (page 3) is a dynamic character.

A character's **motivation** is any force (such as love or fear or jealousy) that drives the character to behave in a particular way.

See pages 92, 103, 106–107, 119, 131, 254–258.
See also *Characterization, Motivation*.

CHARACTERIZATION The way a writer reveals the personality of a character. A writer may simply tell readers that a character is amusing or evil or dull or brave. This method is called **direct characterization**. Most often, though, writers use **indirect characterization**, revealing personality in one or more of the following ways:

1. through the words of the character
2. through description of the character's looks and clothing
3. through description of the character's thoughts and feelings

4. through comments made about the character by other characters in the story
5. through the character's behavior

When a writer uses indirect characterization, we must use our own judgment and the evidence the writer gives to infer the character's **traits.**

See pages 106–107.

CHRONOLOGICAL ORDER The arrangement of events in the order in which they occurred. Most stories are told in chronological order. Sometimes, however, a writer interrupts the chronological order to depict a past or future event. *The Diary of Anne Frank* (page 347), for example, begins in 1945, when Mr. Frank arrives at the hiding place. The main story, however, takes place from 1942 to 1944.

See pages 84, 214, 223, 331, 528.
See also *Flashback*.

CLIMAX The point in a story that creates the greatest suspense or interest. At the climax something happens that reveals how the conflict will turn out.

See pages 212, 340, 412.
See also *Drama, Plot, Short Story*.

COMEDY In general, a story that ends happily for its main characters. The hero or heroine usually overcomes a series of obstacles to get what he or she wants. (In contrast, the main character in a **tragedy** comes to an unhappy end.) The word *comedy* is not a synonym for *humor*. Some comedies are humorous; others are not.

See also *Tragedy*.

CONFLICT A struggle between opposing characters or opposing forces. In an **external conflict** a character struggles with an outside force, which may be another character, society as a whole, or a natural force. In contrast, an **internal conflict** takes place within a character's own mind. It is a struggle between opposing needs, desires, or emotions.

> See pages 2, 12, 15, 74, 89, 212, 340, 412, 552.
> See also *Plot*.

CONNOTATION **A meaning, association, or emotion suggested by a word, in addition to its dictionary definition, or denotation.** Words that have similar denotations may have different connotations. For example, suppose you wanted to describe someone who rarely changes plans in the face of opposition. You could use either *determined* or *pigheaded* to describe the person. The two words have similar denotations, but *determined* has positive connotations and *pigheaded* has negative connotations.

> See pages 151, 438.
> See also *Diction, Style, Tone*.

DENOTATION See *Connotation*.

DESCRIPTION **Writing intended to re-create a person, a place, a thing, an event, or an experience.** Description uses images that appeal to the senses of sight, smell, taste, hearing, or touch. It is often used to create a mood or emotion. Writers use description in all forms of fiction, nonfiction, and poetry. This description of the effect of extreme cold on a dog and its owner may make you feel cold, too:

> The frozen moisture of its breathing had settled on its fur in a fine powder of frost, and especially were its jowls, muzzle, and eyelashes whitened by its crystaled breath. The man's red beard and moustache were likewise frosted, but more solidly, the deposit taking the form of ice and increasing with every warm, moist breath he exhaled. Also, the man was chewing tobacco, and the muzzle of ice held his lips so rigidly that he was unable to clear his chin when he expelled the juice.

> The result was that a crystal beard of the color and solidity of amber was increasing its length on his chin. If he fell down, it would shatter itself, like glass, into brittle fragments.
>
> —Jack London, from "To Build a Fire"

> See pages 84, 104, 132, 286, 436, 526–530.
> See also *Imagery*.

DIALECT **A way of speaking that is characteristic of a certain geographical area or a certain group of people.** A dialect may have a distinct vocabulary, pronunciation system, and grammar. In a sense, we all speak dialects. One dialect usually becomes dominant in a country or culture, however, and is accepted as the standard way of speaking and writing. In the United States, for example, the formal language is known as **standard English.** (It's the kind of English taught in schools, used in national newspapers and magazines, and spoken by newscasters on television.)

Writers often reproduce regional dialects or speech to bring a character to life and to give a story color. For example, in "Brer Possum's Dilemma" (page 453), Brer Possum says, "I best git on outa here, 'cause ol' Brer Snake is mean and evil and low-down, and if I git to stayin' around 'im, he jist might git to bitin' me." In standard English, the same sentence might read, "I should leave because Brother Snake is mean, evil, and despicable, and if I stay near him, he might bite me." As you can see, the dialect version is much more entertaining and lifelike.

> See pages 452, 458, 510.

DIALOGUE **Conversation between two or more characters.** Most stage dramas consist entirely of dialogue together with stage directions. The dialogue in a drama must move the plot along and reveal character. Dialogue is also an important element in most stories and novels, as well as in some poems and nonfiction. By using dialogue, a writer can show what a character is like.

In the written form of a play, dialogue appears without quotation marks. In prose or poetry, however, dialogue is usually enclosed in quotation marks.

A **monologue,** or **soliloquy,** is a part of a drama in which one character who is alone on stage speaks aloud his or her thoughts and feelings.

See page 76.
See also *Drama.*

DICTION A writer's or speaker's choice of words. People use different types of words, depending on the audience they are addressing, the subject they are discussing, and the effect they are trying to produce. For example, slang words that would be suitable for a humorous piece like "The Ransom of Red Chief" (page 482) would not be appropriate for a serious essay like "A Tragedy Revealed: A Heroine's Last Days" (page 419). Diction is an essential element of a writer's style and has a major effect on the tone of a piece of writing.

See also *Connotation, Style, Tone.*

DRAMA A work of literature meant to be performed for an audience by actors. (A drama, or **play,** can also be enjoyed in its written form.) The actors work from the **playwright's** script, which includes dialogue and stage directions. The script of a drama written for the screen is called a **screenplay** (if it's for TV, it's a **teleplay**), and it also includes camera directions.

The action of a drama is usually driven by a character who wants something and takes steps to get it. The main stages of a drama are often described as **exposition, complications, climax,** and **resolution.** Most dramas are divided into **acts** and **scenes.**

See pages 340–341.

ESSAY A short piece of nonfiction prose that examines a single subject. Most essays can be categorized as either personal or formal.

The **personal essay** generally reveals a great deal about the writer's personality and tastes. Its tone is often conversational, sometimes even humorous, and there may be no attempt to be objective. In fact, in a personal essay the focus is the writer's feelings and response to an experience. Personal essays are also called **informal** or **familiar** essays.

The **formal essay** is usually serious, objective, and impersonal in tone. Its purpose is to inform readers about a topic or to persuade them to accept the writer's views. The statements in a formal essay should be supported by facts and logic.

See pages 656–657.
See also *Objective Writing.*

EXAGGERATION Overstating something, usually for the purpose of creating a comic effect. *He's so thin that if he turned sideways, he'd disappear* is an example of exaggeration. Much of the humor in "They Have Yarns" (page 496) comes from exaggeration.

See pages 480, 496, 499, 512, 520.
See also *Understatement.*

EXPOSITION The kind of writing that explains or gives information. You'll find exposition in newspaper and magazine articles, encyclopedias and dictionaries, and textbooks and other nonfiction books. In fact, what you're reading right now is exposition.

In fiction and drama, **exposition** refers to the part of a plot that gives information about the characters and their problems or conflicts.

See pages 254–258, 330–334, 612–616.
See also *Drama, Plot, Short Story.*

FABLE A brief story told in prose or poetry that contains a moral, a practical lesson about how to get along in life. The characters of most fables are animals that speak and behave like people. "Brer Possum's Dilemma" (page 453) is a traditional African American fable. Some of the most popular fables are those attributed to Aesop, who was supposedly a storyteller of ancient Greece. Often, as in the following fable by Aesop, the moral is stated at the end.

The Goose That Laid the Golden Eggs

A man and his wife had the good fortune to possess a goose which laid a golden egg every day. Lucky though they were, they soon began to think they were not getting rich fast enough, and, imagining the bird must be made of gold inside, they decided to kill it in order to secure the whole store of precious metal at once. But when they cut it open, they found it was just like any other goose. Thus, they neither got rich all at once, as they had hoped, nor enjoyed any longer the daily addition to their wealth.

Much wants more and loses all.

FICTION **A prose account that is made up rather than true.** The term *fiction* usually refers to **novels** and **short stories**. Fiction is often based on a writer's experiences or on historical events, but a writer may add or alter characters, events, and other details to create a desired effect. "The Inn of Lost Time" (page 227) is entirely made up. "The Medicine Bag" (page 120), on the other hand, is based to some extent on the writer's experiences.

See also *Historical Fiction, Nonfiction.*

FIGURE OF SPEECH **A word or phrase that describes one thing in terms of another and is not meant to be understood as literally true.** Figures of speech always involve some sort of imaginative comparison between seemingly unlike things.

The most common figures of speech are the **simile** (*The sun was shining like a new penny*), the **metaphor** (*The sun was a huge, unblinking eye*), and **personification** (*The sun smiled down on the bathers*).

See pages 28, 38, 41–42, 573, 580, 585.
See also *Metaphor, Personification, Simile.*

FLASHBACK **Interruption in the present action of a plot to show events that happened at an earlier time.** A flashback breaks the normal forward movement of a narrative. Although flashbacks often appear in the middle of a work, they can also be placed at the beginning. They usually give background information the audience needs in order to understand the present action. The first scene of *The Diary of Anne Frank* (page 347) takes place about one year after the main action of the play. Almost the entire play, then, is a flashback to an earlier time. Flashbacks are common in stories, novels, and movies and sometimes appear in stage plays and poems as well.

See pages 84, 343, 372.

FOLK TALE **A story that has no known author and was originally passed on from one generation to another by word of mouth.** Unlike myths, which are about gods and heroes, folk tales are usually about ordinary people—or animals that act like people, as in "Brer Rabbit and Brer Lion" (page 466). Folk tales tend to travel, and you'll often find the same **motifs**—elements such as characters, images, or story lines—in the tales of different cultures. Cinderella, for example, appears as Aschenputtel in Germany, Yeh-Shen in China, Cam in Vietnam, and Little Burnt Face among the Algonquin people of North America.

See pages 460–461.
See also *Fable, Legend, Myth, Tall Tale.*

FORESHADOWING **The use of clues or hints to suggest events that will occur later in the plot.** Foreshadowing is used to build suspense or anxiety in the reader or viewer. A gun found in a bureau drawer in Act One of a drama may foreshadow violence later in the play. In the early part of "The Landlady" (page 171), details that hint at mystery and danger suggest what later happens to the main character, Billy.

See pages 74, 170, 181, 209, 213, 493.
See also *Suspense.*

FREE VERSE **Poetry without a regular meter or rhyme scheme.** Poets writing in free verse try to capture the natural rhythms of ordinary conversation—or, as in this free-verse poem, a very unusual conversation:

Love in the Middle of the Air

CATCH ME!
   I love you, I trust you,
   I love you
CATCH ME!
   catch my left foot, my right
   foot, my hand!
   here I am hanging by my teeth
   300 feet up in the air and
CATCH ME!
   here I come, flying without wings,
   no parachute, doing a double triple
   super flip-flop somersault
   RIGHT UP HERE WITHOUT A
   SAFETY NET AND
CATCH ME!
   you caught me!
   I love you!

   now it's *your* turn

         —Lenore Kandel, from "Circus"

Poets writing in free verse may use **internal rhyme, repetition, alliteration, onomatopoeia,** and other sound effects. They also frequently use vivid imagery and striking metaphors and similes. "Legacy II" (page 109) and "Grandpa" (page 148) are other examples of poems written in free verse.

         See page 544.
See also *Meter, Poetry, Rhyme.*

HISTORICAL FICTION A novel, story, or play set during a real historical era. Historical events (such as battles that really happened) and historically accurate details give us an idea of what life was like during a particular period and in a specific setting. "The Deserter" (page 587) is an example of historical fiction. Its main characters are fictional, but it also includes historical characters, such as Abraham Lincoln.

         See also *Fiction.*

IDIOM An expression peculiar to a particular language that means something different from the literal meaning of the words. *Hold your tongue* (Don't speak) and *Bury your head in the sand* (Ignore a difficult situation) are idioms of American English.

         See pages 115, 118.

IMAGERY Language that appeals to the senses. Most images are visual—that is, they create pictures in the reader's mind by appealing to the sense of sight. In "Mrs. Flowers" (page 20), Maya Angelou uses words to paint a picture of a smile: "A slow widening of her thin black lips to show even, small white teeth, then the slow effortless closing."

Images can also appeal to the senses of hearing, touch, taste, and smell, or even to several senses at once.

         See pages 19, 26, 84, 134, 136.
See also *Description.*

INVERSION The reversal of the normal word order of a sentence. For example, a writer might change *Her hair was long* to *Long was her hair*, inverting the sentence to emphasize the word *long* or to fit a poem's rhyme scheme (*Long was her hair — she had plenty to spare*).

IRONY A contrast between expectation and reality. Irony can create powerful effects, ranging from humor to strong emotion. The following terms refer to three common types of irony.

1. **Verbal irony** involves a contrast between what is said or written and what is really meant. If you were to call a baseball player who has just struck out "slugger," you would be using verbal irony.
2. **Situational irony** occurs when what happens is very different from what we expected would happen. The situation that develops in "The Ransom of Red Chief" (page 482) is ironic—you would not expect a kidnapping victim to gain control over his kidnappers.
3. **Dramatic irony** occurs when the audience or the reader knows something a character

does not know. *The Diary of Anne Frank* (page 347) is filled with dramatic irony. We know about the tragic fate of the people in the Secret Annex, but they do not. Note the irony in the following words spoken by Mr. Frank to Mr. Van Daan. "Didn't you hear what Miep said? The invasion has come! We're going to be liberated! This is a time to celebrate!" (Act Two, Scene 3)

See pages 309, 341, 480, 481, 493, 494, 570.

LEGEND A story of extraordinary deeds that is handed down from one generation to the next. Legends are based to some extent on fact. For example, George Washington did exist, but he did not chop down his father's cherry tree when he was a boy.

See pages 460–461.
See also *Fable, Folk Tale, Myth, Tall Tale.*

LIMERICK A very short humorous or nonsensical poem. A limerick has five lines, a definite rhythm, and an *aabba* **rhyme scheme.** It tells a brief story. President Woodrow Wilson is said to have written this limerick:

> I sat next to the Duchess at tea;
> It was just as I feared it would be;
>   Her rumblings abdominal
>   Were truly phenomenal,
> And everyone thought it was me!

See also *Poetry, Rhyme.*

LYRIC POEM A poem that expresses the feelings or thoughts of a speaker rather than telling a story. Lyric poems can express a wide range of emotions, from deep admiration (as in "The Courage That My Mother Had," page 108) to amusement (as in "Point of View," page 288). Lyric poems are usually short and imply, rather than directly state, a single strong emotion.

See also *Narrative Poem.*

METAMORPHOSIS A miraculous change from one shape or form to another one. In myths and other stories, the change is usually from human or god to animal, from animal to human, or from human to plant. Greek and Roman myths contain many examples of metamorphosis. The myth of Narcissus, for example, tells how the vain youth Narcissus pines away for love of his own reflection and is finally changed into a flower.

METAPHOR An imaginative comparison between two unlike things in which one thing is said to be another thing. The metaphor is an important type of figure of speech. Metaphors are used in all forms of writing and are common in ordinary speech. When you say someone has a heart of stone, you do not mean that the person's heart is made of rock. You mean that the person is cold and uncaring.

Metaphors differ from **similes,** which use words such as *like, as, than,* and *resembles* to make comparisons. William Wordsworth's famous comparison "I wandered lonely as a cloud" is a simile because it uses *as.* If Wordsworth had written "I was a lonely, wandering cloud," he would have been using a metaphor.

Sometimes a writer hints at a connection instead of stating it directly. T. S. Eliot uses an **implied**

"I'm running a loose ship."

Drawing by Victoria Roberts; © 1992 The New Yorker Magazine, Inc.

metaphor in one of his poems when he describes fog as rubbing its back on windows, making a sudden leap, and curling around a house to fall asleep. By using words that we associate with a cat's behavior, Eliot implies a comparison without stating "The fog is a cat."

An **extended metaphor** is a metaphor that is extended, or developed, over several lines of writing or even throughout an entire work. "O Captain! My Captain!" (page 626) contains an extended metaphor in which the United States is compared to a ship and President Abraham Lincoln is compared to the captain of the ship.

> See pages 41, 626.
> See also *Figure of Speech, Simile.*

METER **A pattern of stressed and unstressed syllables in poetry.** It is common practice to show this pattern in writing by using two symbols. The symbol ´ indicates a stressed syllable. The symbol ˘ indicates an unstressed syllable. Indicating the metrical pattern of a poem in this way is called **scanning** the poem. The following lines by William Shakespeare have been scanned in part. (The lines make up the speech of the mischief-maker Puck, or Robin Goodfellow, at the end of the comedy *A Midsummer Night's Dream. Reprehend* means "criticize"; *serpent's tongue* means "hissing"; *Give me your hands* means "Clap.")

> If we shadows have offended,
> Think but this, and all is mended,
> That you have but slumbered here
> While these visions did appear,
> And this weak and idle theme,
> No more yielding but a dream,
> Gentles, do not reprehend.
> If you pardon, we will mend.
> And, as I am an honest Puck,
> If we have unearned luck
> Now to scape the serpent's tongue,
> We will make amends ere long,
> Else the Puck a liar call.
> So, good night unto you all.

> Give me your hands, if we be friends,
> And Robin shall restore amends.
>
> —William Shakespeare,
> from *A Midsummer Night's Dream*

> See page 544.
> See also *Poetry, Rhythm.*

MOOD See *Atmosphere.*

MOTIF See *Folk Tale.*

MOTIVATION **The reasons a character behaves in a certain way.** Among the many reasons for a person's behavior are feelings, experiences, and commands by others. It is often difficult to pinpoint a character's motivation.

> See pages 546, 552.
> See also *Character.*

MYTH **A story that explains something about the world and typically involves gods or other supernatural forces.** Myths reflect the traditions and beliefs of the culture that produced them. Almost every culture has **creation myths,** (like "Coyote Steals the Sun and Moon" on page 463), stories that explain how the world came to exist or how human beings were created. Other myths explain different aspects of life and the natural world. One of the ancient Greek myths, for instance, tells how Prometheus gave humans the gift of fire. Most myths are very old and were handed down orally before being put in written form. The exact origin of most myths is not known.

> See pages 460, 470.
> See also *Fable, Folk Tale, Legend, Tall Tale.*

NARRATION **The kind of writing that tells a story.** Narration is the main tool of writers of fiction. It is also used in any piece of nonfiction that relates a series of events in the order in which they happened (for example, in historical writing and science articles).

> See pages 82–86.
> See also *Exposition, Fiction, Nonfiction.*

NARRATIVE POEM **A poem that tells a story.** "Paul Revere's Ride" (page 537) and "Casey at the Bat" (page 606) are narrative poems.

See pages 601, 605.
See also *Lyric Poem.*

NONFICTION **Prose writing that deals with real people, things, events, and places.** Popular forms of nonfiction are the autobiography, the biography, and the essay. Other examples of nonfiction are newspaper stories, magazine articles, historical writing, science reports, and even diaries and letters.

See pages 656–657.
See also *Autobiography, Biography, Essay, Fiction.*

NOVEL **A long fictional story whose length is usually somewhere between one hundred and five hundred book pages.** A novel uses all the elements of storytelling—plot, character, setting, theme, and point of view. It usually has more characters, settings, and themes and a more complex plot than a short story.

See also *Plot, Short Story.*

OBJECTIVE WRITING **Writing that presents facts without revealing the writer's feelings and opinions.** Most news reports in newspapers are objective writing.

See page 657.
See also *Essay, Subjective Writing.*

ONOMATOPOEIA **The use of words whose sounds imitate or suggest their meaning.** *Buzz, rustle, boom, ticktock, tweet,* and *bark* are all onomatopoeic words. In the following lines the poet suggests the sound of sleigh bells in the cold night air by using onomatopoeia.

> Hear the sledges with the bells—
> Silver bells!

> What a world of merriment their melody
>   foretells!
> How they tinkle, tinkle, tinkle,
>   In the icy air of night!
> While the stars that oversprinkle
> All the Heavens, seem to twinkle
>   With a crystalline delight.

> —Edgar Allan Poe,
> from "The Bells"

See page 545.

PERSONIFICATION **A figure of speech in which an object or animal is spoken of as if it had human feelings, thoughts, or attitudes.** This poet writes about the moon as if it were a woman wearing silver shoes ("shoon"):

> Slowly, silently, now the moon
> Walks the night in her silver shoon;
> This way, and that, she peers and sees
> Silver fruit upon silver trees.

> —Walter de la Mare, from "Silver"

See pages 42, 214, 223.
See also *Figure of Speech.*

PERSUASION **A kind of writing intended to convince a reader to think or act in a certain way.** Examples of persuasive writing are found in newspaper editorials, in speeches, and in many essays and articles. The techniques of persuasion are widely used in advertising. Persuasion can use language that appeals to the emotions, or it can use logic to appeal to reason. When persuasive writing appeals to reason and not to the emotions, it is called **argument.** The Gettysburg Address (page 623) and "The First Americans" (page 631) are examples of persuasive writing.

See pages 104, 114, 150, 160–164, 286, 325, 437, 440–441, 654, 696–700.

PLAYWRIGHT The author of a play, or drama. Playwrights Frances Goodrich and Albert Hackett wrote *The Diary of Anne Frank* (page 347), which they based on Anne Frank's diary and life story.

See also *Author, Drama.*

PLOT The series of related events that make up a story. Plot is what happens in a short story, novel, play, or narrative poem. Most plots are built from these basic elements: An **introduction,** or **exposition,** tells us who the characters are and usually what their conflict is. **Complications** arise when the characters take steps to resolve the conflict. Eventually the plot reaches a **climax,** the most exciting moment in the story, when the outcome is decided one way or another. The final part of the story is the **resolution,** in which the conflict is resolved and the story is brought to a close.

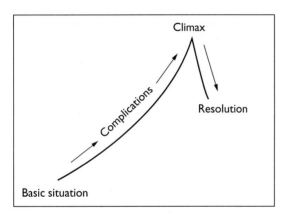

Not all works of fiction or drama have a traditional plot structure. Modern writers often experiment with plot. At times they eliminate some or almost all of the parts of a traditional plot in order to focus on other elements, such as character, point of view, or mood.

See pages 212, 472, 478.
See also *Climax, Drama, Exposition.*

POETRY A kind of rhythmic, compressed language that uses figures of speech and imagery designed to appeal to our emotions and imagination. Poetry is usually arranged in lines. It often has a regular pattern of rhythm and may have a regular rhyme scheme. **Free verse** is poetry that has no regular pattern of rhythm or rhyme, though it is generally arranged in lines. The major forms of poetry are the **lyric,** the **narrative,** the **epic,** and the **ballad.**

See also *Ballad, Figure of Speech, Free Verse, Imagery, Lyric Poem, Meter, Narrative Poem, Refrain, Rhyme, Rhythm, Speaker.*

POINT OF VIEW The vantage point from which a story is told. The most common points of view are the omniscient, the third-person limited, and the first person.

1. In the **omniscient** (all-knowing) **point of view,** the narrator knows everything about the characters and their problems. This all-knowing narrator can tell us about the past, the present, and the future of the characters. The narrator can also tell us what the characters are thinking and what is happening in several places at the same time. But the narrator does not take part in the story's action. Rather, the narrator stands above the action like a god. The omniscient is a familiar point of view; we have heard it in fairy tales since we were very young. "Coyote Steals the Sun and Moon" (page 463) is told from the omniscient point of view.

2. In the **third-person limited point of view,** the narrator focuses on the thoughts and feelings of only one character. From this point of view, we observe the action through the eyes of only one of the characters in the story. "The Treasure of Lemon Brown" (page 93) is told from the third-person limited point of view.

3. In the **first-person point of view,** one of the characters, using the personal pronoun *I,* tells the story. We become familiar with the narrator, but we can know only what this person knows and observe only what this person observes. All of our information about the story comes from this narrator, who may be unreliable. "The Moustache" (page 139) is told from the first-person point of view.

See pages 75, 224, 275, 285, 286, 288–289.

PROSE Any writing that is not poetry. Essays, short stories, novels, newspaper articles, and letters are all written in prose. Unlike poetry, prose is usually composed in paragraphs.

See also *Poetry*.

PROTAGONIST The main character in a work of literature. The protagonist is involved in the work's central conflict. If there is another character opposing the protagonist, that character is called the **antagonist.** In "Brer Possum's Dilemma" (page 453) Brer Possum is the protagonist and Brer Snake is the antagonist.

See also *Character*.

PUN A play on the multiple meanings of a word or on two words that sound alike but have different meanings. Most often puns are used for humor; they turn up in jokes all the time. *Where does an elephant put suitcases? Answer: In its trunk.* This pun is called a **homographic pun;** it is a play on a word (*trunk*) that has two meanings ("the proboscis of an elephant" and "a compartment in an automobile"). *Is Swiss cheese good for you? Answer: Yes, it is holesome.* This pun is called a **homophonic pun;** it is a play on words that sound alike but are spelled differently and have different meanings (*hole* and *whole*).

REFRAIN A repeated sound, word, phrase, line, or group of lines. Refrains are usually associated with songs and poems but are also used in speeches and other forms of literature. Refrains are most often used to build rhythm, but they may also provide emphasis or commentary, create suspense, or help hold a work together. Refrains may be repeated with small variations in a work to fit a particular context or to create a special effect. The phrase "coming to America" serves as a refrain in the song "America" (page 694).

See pages 622, 627, 683.

RHYME The repetition of accented vowel sounds and all sounds following them in words that are close together in a poem. *Mean* and *screen* are rhymes, as are *crumble* and *tumble*. The many purposes of rhyme in poetry include building rhythm, lending a songlike quality, emphasizing ideas, organizing poems (for instance, into stanzas or couplets), providing humor or pleasure for the reader, and aiding memory.

End rhymes are rhymes at the ends of lines. In the following poem, *ought* and *thought* form end rhymes, as do *afternoon* and *soon*.

> **Condition**
> I have to speak—I must—I should
>   —I ought . . .
> I'd tell you how I love you if I thought
> The world would end tomorrow afternoon.
> But short of that . . . well, it might be
>   too soon.
>
> —Vikram Seth

Internal rhymes are rhymes within lines. The following line has an internal rhyme (*turning/burning*):

> Back into the chamber turning, all my soul
>   within me burning
>
> —Edgar Allan Poe, from "The Raven"

Rhyming sounds need not be spelled the same way: *Gear/here,* for instance, is a rhyme. Rhymes can involve more than one syllable or more than one word; *poet/know it* is an example. Rhymes involving sounds that are similar but not exactly the same are called **approximate rhymes** (or **near rhymes** or **slant rhymes**). *Leave/live* is an example of an approximate rhyme. Poets writing in English often use this kind of rhyme because they believe it sounds less artificial and more like real speech than exact rhymes do. Also, it is difficult to come up with fresh, original exact rhymes. Poets interested in how a poem looks on the printed page sometimes use **eye rhymes,** or **visual rhymes**—"rhymes" involving words that are spelled similarly but pronounced differently. *Tough/cough* is an eye rhyme. (*Tough/rough* is a "real" rhyme.)

The pattern of end rhymes in a poem is called a **rhyme scheme.** To indicate the rhyme scheme of a poem, use a separate letter of the alphabet for each end rhyme. For example, the rhyme scheme of "A Time to Talk" (page 17) is *abcadbceed*.

See pages 16, 18, 114, 520, 544–545.
See also *Poetry, Free Verse.*

RHYTHM A musical quality produced by the repetition of stressed and unstressed syllables or by the repetition of certain other sound patterns. Rhythm occurs in all forms of language, both written and spoken, but is particularly important in poetry.

The most obvious kind of rhythm is the regular repetition of stressed and unstressed syllables found in some poetry. In the following lines, which describe a cavalry charge, the rhythm echoes the galloping of the attackers' horses.

> The Assyrian came down like the wolf on the fold,
> And his cohorts were gleaming in purple and gold;
> And the sheen of their spears was like stars on the sea,
> When the blue wave rolls nightly on deep Galilee.
>
> —George Gordon, Lord Byron, from "The Destruction of Sennacherib"

Writers also create rhythm by repeating words and phrases or even by repeating whole lines and sentences. The following passage by Walt Whitman is written in free verse and does not have a regular pattern of rhythm or rhyme. Yet the lines are rhythmical because of Whitman's use of repetition.

> I hear the sound I love, the sound of the human voice,
> I hear all sounds running together, combined, fused, or following,

> Sounds of the city and sounds out of the city, sounds of the day and night,
> Talkative young ones to those that like them, the loud laugh of work-people at their meals . . .
>
> —Walt Whitman, from "Song of Myself"

See pages 108, 111, 114, 536, 542, 628.
See also *Meter.*

SATIRE Writing that ridicules something, often in order to bring about change. Satire may poke fun at a person, a group of people, an attitude, a social institution, even all of humanity. Writers use satire to convince us of a point of view or to persuade us to follow a course of action.

SETTING The time and place of a story, play, or narrative poem. Most often the setting is described early in the story. For example, the story "Too Soon a Woman" (page 547) begins, "We left the home place behind, mile by slow mile, heading for the mountains, across the prairie where the wind blew forever." Setting often contributes to a work's emotional effect. It may also play an important role in the plot, especially in stories involving a conflict between a character and nature.

See pages 84, 520, 529.

SHORT STORY A short fictional prose narrative. The first short stories were written in the nineteenth century. Early short-story writers include Sir Walter Scott and Edgar Allan Poe. A short story's plot usually consists of these basic elements: the **introduction (basic situation** or **exposition); complications; climax;** and **resolution.** Short stories are more limited than novels. They usually have only one or two major characters and one important setting.

See pages 15, 212–213.
See also *Fiction, Novel, Plot.*

SIMILE **A comparison between two unlike things, using a word such as *like, as, than,* or *resembles*.** *Her face was as round as a pumpkin* and *This steak is tougher than an old shoe* are similes.

See page 41.
See also *Figure of Speech, Metaphor*.

SPEAKER **The voice talking to us in a poem.** The speaker is sometimes, but not always, the poet. It is best to think of the voice in the poem as belonging to a character the poet has created. The character may be a child, a woman, a man, an animal, or even an object.

STANZA **A group of consecutive lines in a poem that form a single unit.** A stanza in a poem is something like a paragraph in prose: It often expresses a unit of thought. A stanza may consist of any number of lines; it may even consist of a single line. The word *stanza* is an Italian word for "stopping place" or "place to rest." In some poems, each stanza has the same rhyme scheme.

STEREOTYPE **A fixed idea about the members of a particular group of people that does not allow for any individuality.** Stereotypes are often based on misconceptions about racial, social, religious, gender, or ethnic groups. Some common stereotypes are the ideas that all football players are stupid, that all New Yorkers are rude, and that all politicians are dishonest.

See pages 630, 634.

STYLE **The way a writer uses language.** Style results from **diction** (word choice), sentence structure, and tone. One writer may use many figures of speech, for example; another writer may prefer straightforward language with few figures of speech.

See pages 573, 578.
See also *Diction, Tone*.

SUBJECTIVE WRITING **Writing in which the feelings and opinions of the writer are revealed.** Editorials, personal essays, and autobiographies are examples of subjective writing.

See page 657.
See also *Objective Writing*.

SUSPENSE **The uncertainty or anxiety that a reader feels about what will happen next in a story, novel, or drama.** In "The Monkey's Paw" (page 186), the sergeant's tale of the fakir's spell hooks our curiosity early in the play. When Mr. White makes his first wish on the paw, the suspense is heightened. The suspense reaches a peak soon after the second wish, and we read on eagerly to find out who—or what—is knocking on the door.

See pages 185, 198, 212–213.
See also *Plot*.

SYMBOL **A person, a place, a thing, or an event that has meaning in itself and stands for something beyond itself as well.** Some symbols are so well-known that we sometimes forget they are symbols. The bald eagle, for example, is a symbol of the United States; the Star of David is a symbol of Judaism; and the cross is a symbol of Christianity. In literature, symbols are often personal and surprising. In "The Secret Heart" (page 112), for example, a father's hands cupped around a lit match symbolize the man's love for his son.

See pages 42, 112, 114.

TALL TALE **An exaggerated, far-fetched story that is obviously untrue but is told as though it should be believed.** Almost all tall tales, like "Davy Is Born" (page 521), are humorous.

See pages 460, 480, 496, 499, 509.
See also *Exaggeration, Folk Tale*.

THEME **The general idea or insight about life that a work of literature reveals.** A theme is not the same as a subject. The subject of a work can usually be expressed in a word or two: *love, childhood, death.* A theme is an idea or message that the writer wishes to convey *about* that subject. For example, one theme of "The Wise Old Woman" (page 152) might be stated as: *The elderly should be treated as valuable members of society.*

A work's themes (there may be more than one) are usually not stated directly. Most often the reader has to think about all the elements of the work and use them to make an **inference,** or educated guess, about what the themes are.

See pages 264, 272, 273, 669, 674.

"If you were to boil your book down to a few words, what would be its message?"

Drawing by Koren; © 1986 The New Yorker Magazine, Inc.

TONE **The attitude a writer takes toward his or her subject, characters, and audience.** For example, a writer's tone might be humorous, as in "Ode to a Toad" (page 292), or passionate and sincere, as in "I Have a Dream" (page 678). When people speak, their tone of voice gives added meaning to what they say. Writers use written language to create effects similar to those that people create with their voices.

See pages 658, 667.
See also *Connotation, Diction, Style.*

TRAGEDY **A play, novel, or other narrative in which the main character comes to an unhappy end.** A tragedy depicts serious and important events. Its hero achieves wisdom or self-knowledge but suffers a great deal—perhaps even dies. A tragic hero is usually dignified and courageous and often high ranking. The hero's downfall may be caused by a **tragic flaw** (a serious character weakness) or by external forces beyond his or her control. *The Diary of Anne Frank* and Shakespeare's *Hamlet* are tragedies.

See page 413.
See also *Drama, Comedy.*

UNDERSTATEMENT **A statement that says less than what is meant.** Understatement is the opposite of exaggeration. It is usually used for comic effect. If you were to say that the Grand Canyon is a nice little hole in the ground, you would be using understatement.

See page 480.
See also *Exaggeration.*

COMMUNICATIONS HANDBOOK ≡

PUTTING TOGETHER A MULTIMEDIA PRESENTATION

What Is a Multimedia Presentation?

When people talk about **media,** they mean both print and nonprint ways of communicating. Newspapers, magazines, advertisements, TV, radio, photographs, music videos, movies, and the World Wide Web are just a few of the many media.

The computer industry uses the word **multimedia** to refer to a combination of two or more of the following media:

- **text:** words and numbers

- **sound:** music; speeches; readings of stories, poems, and plays; sound effects, such as thunder

- **graphics:** drawings, paintings, photographs, charts, maps, cartoons, posters, patterns, color

- **film or video:** sections clipped from movies or from videos made with a camcorder

- **animation:** movement of objects and figures on screen

- **interactivity:** constant exchange of information between the computer and the user

People find new ways of working with media all the time. Don't worry if you don't have the latest equipment or software. You can learn a lot by working on both low-tech and high-tech multimedia projects. Follow these steps:

1. **Get together with others in a group.** When several students combine their talents and skills, they can often come up with a better product than a student working alone. You can learn a lot about yourself and other people by working with others. Besides, it's often more fun than working by yourself.

2. **Decide what you want to do.** Keep in mind
   - group members' interests and strengths
   - your equipment, tools, software, and hardware

3. **Design the project.** Use a word processing program to make a plan and a schedule. Keep a record of who is supposed to do what and of when each job has to be done.

High Tech 🖱

For a **high-tech presentation** including sound, you'll need a computer with a sound card and speakers. Find out if your school has the software you'll need to

- create and edit graphics, video, and sound
- combine all the media you want to include
- make your presentation interactive

Low Tech

Equipment for a **low-tech presentation** might include the following items:

- audio recorders
- musical instruments
- a copy machine
- an overhead projector
- cameras
- camcorders
- a VCR

---

4. **Create the content.** If you're doing skits based on American Indian myths, write a script, make costumes, and find props. If you're doing a computer multimedia presentation, create or find the text, graphics, and sounds you'll need. Check multimedia "galleries" (or graphics archives) of fine art on-line and on CD-ROMs to see if you can find American Indian works of art. You may be able to find a clip from a performance of Indian chanting or drumming to use as background music.

5. **Put it all together.** If you're doing a reading of American folk tales with background music, for example, you may need to hold several rehearsals. Try reading the folk tales in different sequences to see which you like best. Ask another group of students to give you feedback before you perform in front of the class. If your group would rather not perform live, you could videotape your work. With the right computer equipment, you can add some graphics and text to your video or use special software to make an interactive program.

Scanning, Clipping, and Creating

If you have access to a scanner, you can scan photos, artwork, and maps as well as handwritten and printed material from books, newspapers, and magazines. A scanner stores images in a digital format so that they can be used on a computer.

You can also find lots of material on the Internet and on CD-ROM disks. Multimedia programs give you access to graphics, video, and sound "galleries" from all over the world. If the program allows you to use as much material as you want, clip whatever you need.

It may be impossible for you to create certain kinds of material, such as pictures or video clips of historical events. Still, try to create your own text, graphics, sound, and video whenever you can. You can get CD-ROMs of actors reading stories, but why not do your own readings? You can find and download text about Langston Hughes, for example, but you'll learn more about his writing if you read two or three articles about him and write your own text.

Making an Interactive Program on the Computer

Multimedia or authoring software programs show you how to create interactive links. You can set up your presentation in either of these ways:

- The user moves from one screen to the next along a path you've laid out.

- The user has choices about how to move through the program.

To plan your presentation, try making a **flowchart,** a map showing what's on each screen. Draw a rectangle for each screen and arrows showing the paths the user can, or will, follow. The following example will give you an idea of how your flowchart might look.

Presenting Abraham Lincoln. Suppose your teacher has assigned the class to do a project on an American figure. Your group decides to do a computer multimedia presentation on Abraham Lincoln. The group chooses to include the information laid out in this flowchart, which shows the paths a user might follow.

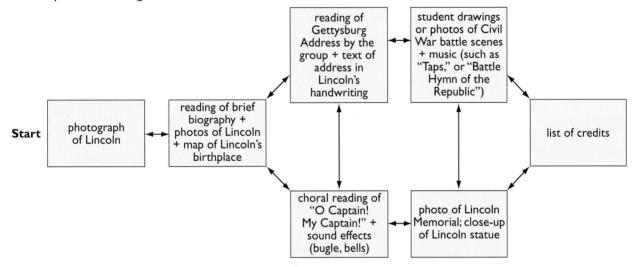

Word Processing

Use word processing programs to

- create schedules and assignment sheets for your project

- type original text, scripts, and programs

- correct errors and revise your writing

There's no substitute for peer editing. Spelling checkers and grammar checkers pick up only certain kinds of errors. Give everyone in the group a chance to edit your writing. Leave room for comments and questions by triple-spacing drafts, and make a copy for each group member. Have everyone put comments on his or her own copy or on screen. Make sure all the group members are in agreement before you create the final text.

Word processing programs offer many formatting options. You can choose from a number of type styles and sizes to create different effects. For example, you may want to use large type for headlines. If you have a drawing program, you can even design your own letters. Word processing programs also let you change the margins for parts of your text. For example, you may want to leave extra space around an important section. You can also use lines, boxes, and bullets, or dots, to separate items and make them easier to read.

Giving Credit Where It's Due

It's important to give credit to anyone who contributed in any way to your presentation. Even if the owner of the material gave it to you, you should credit the person who created it. Avoid **plagiarizing** (plā′jə·rīz′iŋ), or passing off others' work as your own.

You may want to create a separate page or screen of credits at the end of your presentation. See pages 725–726 for information on writing credits.

The Reference Section

Every library has materials you can use only in the library. Some examples are listed below. (Some reference works are available in both print and electronic form.)

Encyclopedias
Collier's Encyclopedia
The World Book Encyclopedia

General Biographical References
Current Biography Yearbook
The International Who's Who
Webster's New Biographical Dictionary

Special Biographical References
American Men & Women of Science
Biographical Dictionary of American Sports
Mexican American Biographies

Atlases
Atlas of World Cultures
National Geographic Atlas of the World

Almanacs
Information Please Almanac
The World Almanac and Book of Facts

Books of Quotations
Bartlett's *Familiar Quotations*

Books of Synonyms
Roget's International Thesaurus
Webster's New Dictionary of Synonyms

Using a Media Center or Library

To find a book, audiotape, film, or video in the library, start by looking in the **catalog.** Most libraries use an **on-line,** or computer, **catalog.**

On-line catalogs vary from library to library. With some you begin searching for resources by **title, author,** or **subject.** With others you simply enter **keywords** for the subject you're researching. With either system, you enter information into the computer and a new screen will show you a list of materials or subject headings relating to your request. When you find an item you want, write down the title, author, and **call number,** the code of numbers and letters that shows you where to find the item on the library's shelves.

Some libraries still use card catalogs. A **card catalog** is a collection of index cards arranged in alphabetical order by title and author. Nonfiction is also cataloged by subject.

Electronic Databases. **Electronic databases** are collections of information you can access by computer. You can use these databases to find such resources as encyclopedias, almanacs, and museum art collections.

There are two kinds of electronic databases. **On-line databases** are accessed at a computer terminal connected to a modem. The modem allows the computer to communicate with other computers over telephone lines. **Portable databases** are available on magnetic tape, diskette, or CD-ROM.

A **CD-ROM** (compact disc-read only memory) is played on a computer equipped with a CD-ROM player. If you were to look up *Maya Angelou* on a CD-ROM guide to literature, for example, you could see and hear her reading passages from her books and also read critical analyses of her work.

Periodicals. Most libraries have a collection of magazines and newspapers. To find up-to-date magazine or newspaper articles on a topic, use a computerized index, such as *InfoTrac* or *EBSCO.* Some of these indices provide a summary of each article. Others provide the entire text, which you can read on screen or print out. The *Readers' Guide to Periodical Literature* is a print index of articles that have appeared in hundreds of magazines.

Using the Internet

The **Internet** is a huge network of computers. Libraries, news services, government agencies, researchers, and organizations communicate and share information on the Net. The Net also lets you chat on-line with students around the world. For help in using the Internet to do research or to communicate with someone by computer, explore the following options.

The World Wide Web

The easiest way to do research on the Internet is on the World Wide Web. On the Web, information is stored in colorful, easy-to-access files called **Web pages.** Web pages usually have text, graphics, photographs, sound, and even video clips.

Using a Web Browser.   You look at Web pages with a **Web browser,** a program for accessing information on the Web. Every page on the Web has its own address, called a **URL,** or Uniform Resource Locator. If you know the address of a Web page you want to go to, just enter it in the location field on your browser.

Hundreds of millions of Web pages are connected by **hyperlinks,** which let you jump from one page to another. These links usually appear as underlined or colored words or images, or both, on your computer screen. With hundreds of millions of linked Web pages, how can you find the information you want?

Using a Web Directory.   If you're just beginning to look for a research topic, click on a **Web directory,** a list of topics and subtopics created by experts to help users find Web sites. Think of the directory as a giant index. Start by choosing a broad category, such as Literature. Then, work your way down through the subtopics, perhaps from Poetry to Poets. Under Poets, choose a Web page that looks interesting, perhaps one on Robert Frost.

Using a Search Engine.   If you already have a topic and need information about it, try using a **search engine,** a software tool that finds information on the Web. To use a search engine, just go to an on-line search form and enter a **search term,** or keyword. The search engine will return a list of Web pages containing your search term. The list will also show you

COMMON SEARCH OPERATORS AND WHAT THEY DO	
AND	Demands that both terms appear on the page; narrows search
+	Demands that both terms appear on the page; narrows search
OR	Yields pages that contain either term; widens search
NOT	Excludes a word from consideration; narrows search
–	Excludes a word from consideration; narrows search
NEAR	Demands that two words be close together; narrows search
ADJ	Demands that two words be close together; narrows search
" "	Demands an exact phrase; narrows search

Techno Tip

To evaluate a Web source, look at the top-level domain in the URL. Here is a sample URL with the top-level domain—a government agency—labeled.

top-level domain

http://www.loc.gov

the first few lines of each page. A search term such as *Frost* may produce thousands of results, or **hits,** including weather data on frost. If you're doing a search on the poet Robert Frost, most of these thousands of hits will be of no use. To find useful material, you have to narrow your search.

Refining a Keyword Search.   To focus your research, use **search operators,** such as the words AND or NOT, to create a string of keywords. If you're looking for material on Robert Frost and his life in Vermont, for example, you might enter the following:

Frost AND Vermont NOT weather

The more focused search term yields pages that contain both *Frost* and *Vermont* and nothing about weather. The chart on the left explains how several search operators work.

Evaluating Web Sources

Since anyone—you, for example—can publish a Web page, it's important to evaluate your sources. Use these criteria to evaluate a source.

Authority.   Who is the author? What is his or her knowledge or experience? Trust respected sources, such as the Smithsonian Institution, not a person's newsletter or home page.

Accuracy.   How trustworthy is the information? Does the author give his or her sources? Check information from one site against information from at least two other sites or print sources.

Objectivity.   What is the author's **perspective,** or point of view? Find out whether the information provider has a bias or hidden purpose.

COMMON TOP-LEVEL DOMAINS AND WHAT THEY STAND FOR	
.edu	Educational institution. Site may publish scholarly work or the work of elementary or high school students.
.gov	Government body. Information should be reliable.
.org	Usually a nonprofit organization. If the organization promotes culture (as a museum does), information is generally reliable; if it advocates a cause, information may be biased.
.com	Commercial enterprise. Information should be evaluated carefully.
.net	Organization offering Internet services.

Currency. Is the information up-to-date? For a print source, check the copyright date. For a Web source, look for the date on which the page was created or revised. (This date appears at the bottom of the site's home page.)

Coverage. How well does the source cover the topic? Could you find better information in a book? Compare the source with several others.

Listing Sources and Taking Notes

When you write a research paper, you must **document,** or identify, your sources so that readers will know where you found your material. You must avoid **plagiarism,** or presenting another writer's words or ideas as if they were your own.

Listing Sources

List each source, and give it a number. (You'll use these source numbers later, when you take notes.) Here's where to find the publication information (such as the name of the publisher and the copyright date) you'll need for different types of sources:

- **Print sources.** Look at the title and copyright pages of the book or periodical.

- **On-line sources.** Look at the beginning or end of the document or in a separate electronic file. For a Web page, look for a link containing the word *About.*

- **Portable electronic databases.** Look at the start-up screen, the packaging, or the disc itself.

There are several ways to list sources. The chart on page 726 shows the style created by the Modern Language Association.

Taking Notes

Here are some tips for taking notes.

- Put notes from different sources on separate index cards or sheets of paper or in separate computer files.

- At the top of each card, sheet of paper, or file, write a label that briefly gives the subject of the note.

- At the bottom, write the numbers of the pages on which you found the information.

- Use short phrases, and make lists of details and ideas. You don't have to write full sentences.

- Use your own words unless you find material you want to quote. If you quote an author's exact words, put quotation marks around them.

The sample note card at the right shows how to take notes.

Sample Source Card

3

Reuben, Paul P. "Chapter 4: Early Nineteenth Century—Emily Dickinson."

PAL: Perspectives in American Literature—A Research and Reference Guide.

<http://www.csustan.edu/english/reuben/pal/chap4/dickinson.html>.

Sample Note Card

3

Dickinson's definition of poetry
In letter to Thomas W. Higginson, editor *Atlantic Monthly*:
"If I read a book and it makes my whole body so cold no fire can ever warm me, I know that is poetry."

on-line source

Preparing a List of Sources

Use your source cards to make a **works cited** list at the end of your report. List your sources in alphabetical order, following the MLA guidelines for citing sources (see the chart below). Note the sample that follows.

Works Cited

Johnson, Thomas H., ed. Complete Poems of Emily Dickinson. Boston: Little, Brown, 1960.

Knapp, Bettina Liebowitz. Emily Dickinson. New York: Continuum, 1989.

Reuben, Paul P. "Chapter 4: Early Nineteenth Century—Emily Dickinson." PAL: Perspectives in American Literature—A Research and Reference Guide. 15 Dec. 1999. <http://www.csustan.edu/english/reuben/pal/chap4/dickinson.html>.

The chart below shows citations of print, audiovisual, and electronic sources.

MLA GUIDELINES FOR CITING SOURCES	
Books	Give the author, title, city of publication, publisher, and copyright year. Knapp, Bettina Liebowitz. Emily Dickinson. New York: Continuum Publishing Co., 1989.
Magazine and newspaper articles	Give the author, title of article, name of the magazine or newspaper, date, and page numbers. Markiewicz, B.S. "Poets and Friends." American History Nov./Dec. 1995: 42–47.
Encyclopedia articles	Give the author (if named), title of the article, name of the encyclopedia, and edition (year). "Dickinson, Emily." Collier's Encyclopedia. 1996 ed.
Interviews	Give the expert's name, the words *Personal interview* or *Telephone interview,* and the date. Randy Souther. Telephone interview. 2 Dec. 1999.
Films, videotapes, and audiotapes	Give the title, producer or director, medium, distributor, and year of release. Emily Dickinson. Directed by Veronica Young. Annenberg/CPB project, 1988.
CD-ROMs	In many cases, not all the information is available. Fill in what you can. Give the author, title of document or article; database title; publication medium (use the term CD-ROM); city of publication; publisher; date. "Dickinson, Emily." Microsoft Encarta 97 Encyclopedia Deluxe Edition. CD-ROM. Redmond, Washington: Microsoft Corporation, 1993–1996.
On-Line Sources	In many cases, not all the information is available. Fill in what you can. Give the author, title of document or article; title of complete work or database; name of editor; publication date or date last revised; name of sponsoring organization; date you accessed the site; the full URL in angle brackets. Reuben, Paul P. "Chapter 4: Early Nineteenth Century—Emily Dickinson." PAL: Perspectives in American Literature—A Research and Reference Guide. 15 Dec. 1999 <http://www.csustan.edu/english/reuben/pal/chap4/dickinson. html>.

READING STRATEGIES

Using Word Parts

Many English words can be divided into parts. If you know the meanings of various word parts, you can often determine the meanings of words.

A word part added to the beginning of a word or root is called a **prefix.** A word part added to the end of a word or root is called a **suffix.** Prefixes and suffixes can't stand alone. They must be added to words or other word parts. A **base word** can stand alone. Other word parts may be added to it to make new words.

Prefix	Base Word	Suffix	New Word
dis–	appear	–ance	disappearance
un–	manage	–able	unmanageable

Roots, like prefixes and suffixes, usually can't stand alone. Roots can combine with one or more word parts to form words.

Word Root	Meaning	Examples
–dem–, –demo–	people	democracy, epidemic
–dict–	to speak	diction, dictate
–geo–	earth	geography, geology
–luc–, –lum–	light	lucid, illuminate
–micro–	small	microscope, microbe
–ped–	foot	pedal, pedestrian
–vert–, –vers–	turn	revert, reversible

COMMONLY USED PREFIXES		
Prefix	Meaning	Examples of Prefix + Base Words
anti–	against, opposing	antiwar, antiwrinkle
extra–	beyond, outside	extraordinary, extracurricular
in–	not	incomplete, invisible
inter–	between, among	interstate, interweave
mal–	bad, wrongly	malfunction, malnourished
semi–	half, partly	semiannual, semifinal
trans–	across, beyond	transport, transcontinental

COMMONLY USED SUFFIXES		
Suffix	**Meaning**	**Examples of Base Words + Suffix**
–dom	state, condition	boredom, freedom
–ful	full of, characterized by	dreadful, thankful
–hood	condition, quality	childhood, motherhood
–ment	result, action	employment, investment
–ness	quality, state	happiness, carelessness
–ship	condition, state	friendship, leadership
–y	full of, characterized by, tending to	scratchy, sleepy

Summarizing, Paraphrasing, and Outlining

When you finish reading a text, check your understanding by writing a **summary,** a short restatement of the important ideas and details in a work. There are many ways to summarize; use the one that works best for the type of text you've read. For a short story, use a **story map** like the one shown at the left.

For a poem, try writing a **paraphrase.** In a paraphrase you express every idea, line by line, in your own words. Here is a paraphrase of Emily Dickinson's "I'm Nobody":

STORY MAP
Basic situation:
Setting:
Main character:
His or her problem:
Main events or complications:
Climax:
Resolution:

Poem	Paraphrase
I'm Nobody! I'm Nobody! Who are you? Are you Nobody too? Then there's a pair of us! Don't tell! they'd banish us, 　you know! How dreary to be Somebody! How public—like a Frog— To tell your name the 　livelong June To an admiring Bog!	The speaker says, "I'm Nobody? Who are you" in the first line. The speaker hopes the listener (reader?) is also nobody so the speaker will have an ally. If so, they must keep their secret. It's dreary to be somebody, to be famous. Then you must deal with the public and try to keep their admiration.

For a work of nonfiction, make an **outline** showing the **main ideas** and **supporting details:**

I. Main idea
  A. Supporting detail
    1. Supporting detail
      a. Supporting detail

Using a Dictionary

You can use a print or electronic dictionary to find the precise meanings and usage of words. The elements of a typical entry are explained below.

1. **Entry word.** The entry word shows how a word is spelled and how it is divided into syllables. It may also show capitalization and alternative spellings.

2. **Pronunciation.** Phonetic symbols and **diacritical marks** (symbols added to letters) show how to pronounce the entry word. A key to these symbols usually appears on every other page.

3. **Part-of-speech label.** This label shows how the entry word is used in a sentence. Some words may function as more than one part of speech. For words like these, a part-of-speech label is provided before each set of definitions.

4. **Other forms.** The spellings of plural forms of nouns, the principal parts of verbs, and the comparative and superlative forms of adjectives and adverbs are shown.

5. **Word origin.** A word's **derivation,** or **etymology** (et′ə·mäl′ə·jē), is its history. It tells how the word or its parts entered the English language. In the example shown at right, "OFr< L *largus*" means that *large* comes from Old French, and that the Old French term derives from the Latin word *largus*.

Sample Dictionary Entry

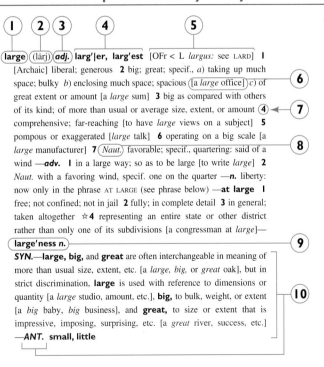

①②③ ④ ⑤

large (lärj) *adj.* **larg′|er, larg′est** [OFr < L *largus:* see LARD] **1** [Archaic] liberal; generous **2** big; great; specif., *a*) taking up much space; bulky *b*) enclosing much space; spacious (a *large* office) *c*) of great extent or amount [a *large* sum] **3** big as compared with others of its kind; of more than usual or average size, extent, or amount **4** comprehensive; far-reaching [to have *large* views on a subject] **5** pompous or exaggerated [*large* talk] **6** operating on a big scale [a *large* manufacturer] **7** (*Naut.*) favorable; specif., quartering: said of a wind —*adv.* **1** in a large way; so as to be large [to write *large*] **2** *Naut.* with a favoring wind, specif. one on the quarter —*n.* liberty: now only in the phrase AT LARGE (see phrase below) —**at large 1** free; not confined; not in jail **2** fully; in complete detail **3** in general; taken altogether ☆**4** representing an entire state or other district rather than only one of its subdivisions [a congressman at *large*]—

large′ness n. ⑨

SYN.—**large, big,** and **great** are often interchangeable in meaning of more than usual size, extent, etc. [a *large, big,* or *great* oak], but in strict discrimination, **large** is used with reference to dimensions or quantity [a *large* studio, amount, etc.], **big,** to bulk, weight, or extent [a *big* baby, *big* business], and **great,** to size or extent that is impressive, imposing, surprising, etc. [a *great* river, success, etc.] —*ANT.* small, little ⑩

⑥ ⑦ ⑧

©1994 *Webster's New World Dictionary of American English,* Third College Edition.

6. **Examples.** Phrases or sentences that show how the word is used.

7. **Definitions.** If a word has more than one meaning, the meanings are numbered or lettered.

8. **Special-usage labels.** These labels identify special meanings or special uses of the word.

9. **Related word forms.** These are other forms of the entry word, usually created by the addition of suffixes.

10. **Synonyms and antonyms.** Synonyms (words similar in meaning) and antonyms (words opposite in meaning) may appear at the end of an entry.

Using a Thesaurus

A **thesaurus** is a collection of synonyms. You use a thesaurus when you're looking for a word that expresses a specific meaning. There are two kinds of thesauruses.

One kind, developed by Peter Mark Roget, **groups words according to meaning.** Here's how to use it:

- In the index, look up the word that conveys your general meaning. Under the entry for **establish,** for example, you might find *begin, create, fix, make sure, originate,* and *prove.* Each of these subentries is followed by a number.

- Choose the subentry whose meaning is closest to what you have in mind. In this case, suppose you choose *begin.*

- In the body of the text, find the number that follows the subentry *begin* in the index. Then, look under this number to find synonyms for *establish* that have the meaning "begin."

The second kind of thesaurus **lists words in alphabetical order,** as in a dictionary. See the sample entry below.

Sample Thesaurus Entry

molten, *a.* heated, melted, fused, liquefied, running, fluid, seething; see also HOT 1.—*Ant.* COLD, cool solid.

©1990 *Webster's New World™ Thesaurus*

Reading Maps, Charts, and Graphs

Types of Maps

Physical maps show the natural landscape of an area. In these maps, shading is often used to show physical features such as mountains, hills, and valleys; colors are often used to show **elevation** (height above or below sea level). **Political maps** show political units, such as states and nations. They usually show borders and capitals. The map of Europe during World War II on page 343 is a political map. **Special-purpose maps** are used to present information that is related to geography, such as the route of the Underground Railroad (page 562).

How to Read a Map

1. **Identify the map's focus.** The map's title and labels tell you its focus—its subject and the geographical area it covers.

2. **Study the legend.** The **legend,** or **key,** explains the symbols, lines, colors, and shading used in the map. (The map on this page has a legend.)

3. **Check directions and distances.** Maps often include a **compass rose,** a diagram that shows north, south, east, and west. If you're looking at a map that doesn't have one, assume that north is at the top, west is to the left, and so on. Many maps also include a **scale** to help you relate distances on the map to actual distances. Note the compass rose and scale on the map on this page.

4. **Look at the larger context.** The **absolute location** of any place on earth is given by its **latitude** (the number of degrees north or south of the equator) and **longitude** (the number of degrees east or west of the **prime meridian,** or 0 degrees longitude). Some maps also include **locator maps,** which show the area depicted in relation to a larger area. Notice the locator map in the upper right corner of the map shown here.

Canada, the United States, and Mexico

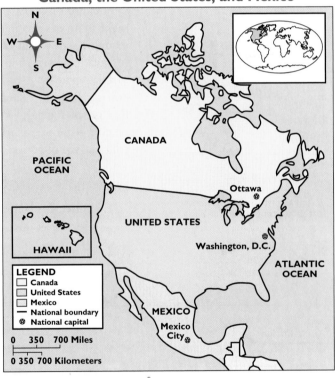

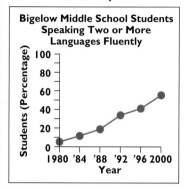

Bigelow Middle School Students Speaking Two or More Languages Fluently

Participation in After-School Sports in My Town

■ Girls
■ Boys

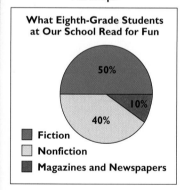

What Eighth-Grade Students at Our School Read for Fun

50%
10%
40%

■ Fiction
■ Nonfiction
■ Magazines and Newspapers

Types of Charts and Graphs

A **flowchart** shows a **sequence** of events or the steps in a process. Flow-charts are often used to show cause-and-effect relationships. The sequencing chart on page 721 is an example of a flowchart. A **time line** shows events in **chronological order** (the order in which they happen). (See the time line of Anne Frank's life on pages 344–345.)

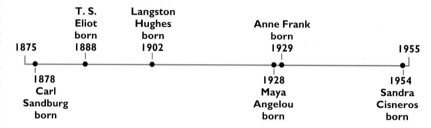

A **table** presents categorized facts arranged in rows and columns to make them easy to understand and compare. The table on page 762, for example, shows all of the personal pronouns categorized by number (singular or plural) and case (nominative, objective, or possessive).

Line graphs usually show changes in quantity over time. In line graphs, dots showing the quantity at different times are connected to create a line. **Bar graphs** generally compare quantities within categories. **Pie graphs,** or **circle graphs,** show proportions. A pie graph is a circle divided into different-sized sections, like slices of a pie.

How to Read a Chart or a Graph

1. **Read the title.** The title tells you the subject and purpose of the chart or graph.

2. **Read the labels.** The labels tell you what type of information is presented.

3. **Analyze the details.** Read numbers carefully. Note increases or decreases. Look for the direction or order of events and for trends and relationships.

STRATEGIES FOR TAKING TESTS

When you begin a test, **scan** it quickly and count the items. Then, decide how to spend your time. Here are some sample test questions and specific strategies for answering four kinds of test questions.

True/false questions ask you to determine whether a given statement is true or false. For example:

1. T F Anne Frank was born in France but moved to the Netherlands in 1933.

- Read the statement carefully. The whole statement is false if any part of it is false.
- Look for word clues, such as *always* and *never*. A statement is true only if it is always true.

Multiple-choice questions ask you to select a correct answer from several choices. For example:

1. Abolitionism was a movement against

A liquor   **C** voting rights for women

B slavery   **D** immigration

HOW TO ANSWER MULTIPLE-CHOICE QUESTIONS

- Read the question or statement carefully. Make sure you understand the key question or statement before you look at the choices.
- Look for words such as *not* and *always,* which may help you eliminate some choices.
- Read all the choices before selecting an answer. Eliminate choices that you know are incorrect.
- Think carefully about the remaining choices. Pick the one that makes the most sense.

Matching questions ask you to match the items in one list with the items in another list. For example:

Directions: Match each item in the left-hand column with its definition in the right-hand column.

_____ **1.** protagonist   **A** story of a person's life

_____ **2.** biography   **B** conversation between characters

_____ **3.** diction   **C** hero or main character

_____ **4.** dialogue   **D** word choice

HOW TO ANSWER MATCHING QUESTIONS

- Read the directions carefully. You may not use all the items in one column, and some items may be used more than once.
- Scan the columns. First, match items you are sure you know. Then, match items you think may be right.
- For the rest of the items, make the best guess you can.

Analogy questions ask you to figure out the relationship between two words and then identify another pair with a similar relationship. For example:

Directions: Select the pair of words that best completes the analogy.

STANZA : POEM : : _____

A metaphor : simile   **C** fiction : nonfiction
B chapter : book   **D** words : music

HOW TO ANSWER ANALOGY QUESTIONS
• Figure out the relationship between the words in the first pair. (In the example, a stanza is part of a poem.)
• Express the analogy in a statement or question. (In the example, a stanza is part of a poem. In what other pair is the first item part of the second item?)
• Select the pair of words with the same relationship as the first pair. (A chapter is part of a book.)

Essay questions in a test ask you to think critically about things you have learned and to express your understanding in a paragraph or more.

ESSAY QUESTIONS		
Key Verb	**Task**	**Sample Question**
analyze	Take something apart to see how it works.	Analyze the character of Squeaky in "Raymond's Run."
compare	Discuss likenesses. (Sometimes *compare* means "compare and contrast.")	Compare the themes in "Legacy II" and "Birdfoot's Grampa."
contrast	Discuss differences.	Contrast a legend about Davy Crockett with a historical account about him.
define	Give specific details that make something unique.	Define the term *meter* as it is used in poetry.
describe	Give a picture in words.	Describe the changes in Laurie's behavior after he begins kindergarten.
discuss	Examine in detail.	Discuss the use of humor in tall tales.
explain	Give reasons for something.	Explain why exaggeration creates humor.
identify	Discuss specific characteristics.	Identify the three types of irony and give an example of each.
list (*also* outline *or* trace)	Give all steps in order or certain details about a subject.	List the four main stages of a drama.
summarize	Briefly review the main points.	Summarize the plot of "The Monkey's Paw."

WRITING FOR LIFE

Writing Business Letters

To request information from someone who is far away or difficult to reach, write a business letter. Follow these guidelines:

1. **Write in formal English.** Avoid slang. The tone of your letter should be polite and respectful.

2. **Be clear.** Explain why you are writing. Include important information, and be as brief as possible.

3. **Make the letter look professional.** Type, print, or write your letter on unlined 8½- × 11-inch paper. Follow the **block form** (shown below).

Sample Business Letter

(1)
4597 West Thornhill Avenue
East Greenwich, RI 02818
August 3, 2000

(2)
Ms. Amy Kupla, Public Relations Director
Clear Ripple Water Bottling Company
3046 Medina Street
Ann Arbor, MI 48108

(3) Dear Ms. Kupla:

(4) I am researching the quality of the drinking water in my town. I would like to know how your company tests water to find out how clean it is.

Please send me any information that might help me with my research. I have enclosed a self-addressed, stamped envelope for your reply.

(5) Sincerely,

(6) *Emily Hanaford*

Emily Hanaford

---

(1) Heading
Your street address
Your city, state, and ZIP code
The date you write the letter

(2) Inside Address
The name and address of the person you are writing to. Use a title like *Mr., Ms.,* or *Mrs.* or a professional title, such as *Dr.* or *Professor,* before the person's name. Put the person's business title after the name.

(3) Salutation (greeting)
End the salutation with a colon.

(4) Body
Your message. If the body is more than one paragraph, leave an extra line between paragraphs.

(5) Closing
Use *Yours truly* or *Sincerely,* followed by a comma.

(6) Signature
Type or print your name, leaving space for your signature. Sign your name in ink below the closing.

Filling Out Forms

When you fill out a form, your purpose is to give clear, complete information. Follow these guidelines whenever you complete forms.

1. Look over the entire form before you begin.

2. Look for and follow special instructions (such as *Type or print* or *Use a pencil*).

3. Read each item carefully.

4. Supply all the information requested. If a question does not apply to you, write *does not apply,* or use a dash or the abbreviation N/A (meaning "not applicable"). Be sure to sign and date the form.

5. When you're finished, make sure nothing is left blank. Also, check for errors and correct them neatly.

6. Mail the form to the correct address or give it to the right person.

PROOFREADERS' MARKS

Symbol	Example	Meaning
≡	New mexico	Capitalize lowercase letter.
/	next Spring	Lowercase capital letter.
∧	a book quotations	Insert.
ℒ	a good good idea	Delete.
⌒	a grape fruit tree	Close up space.
∿	does nt	Change order (of letters or words).
¶	¶ "Who's there?" she asked.	Begin a new paragraph.
⊙	Please don't forget	Add a period.
∧	Maya did you call me?	Add a comma.
:	Dear Mrs. Mills	Add a colon.
;	Columbus, Ohio Dallas, Texas	Add a semicolon.
ᶺ ᶺ	Are you OK? he asked.	Add quotation marks.

1 THE PARTS OF SPEECH

THE NOUN

1a. A *noun* is a word used to name a person, a place, a thing, or an idea.

PERSONS	Maya Angelou, Dr. Strauss, children, team, baby sitter
PLACES	desert, neighborhood, outer space, New York City
THINGS	money, wind, animals, *Voyager 2*, Statue of Liberty
IDEAS	courage, love, freedom, equality, self-control

Compound Nouns

A *compound noun* is two or more words used together as a single noun. A compound noun may be written as one word, as separate words, or as a hyphenated word.

When you are not sure how to write a compound noun, look in a dictionary.

ONE WORD	seafood, footsteps, videocassette, daydream, Iceland
SEPARATE WORDS	compact disc, police officer, John F. Kennedy, "Flowers for Algernon"
HYPHENATED WORD	self-esteem, great-grandparents, fourteen-year-old, sister-in-law

Collective Nouns

A *collective noun* is a word that names a group.

EXAMPLES faculty   family   herd   team   crew

Common Nouns and Proper Nouns

A *common noun* is a general name for a person, a place, a thing, or an idea. A *proper noun* names a particular person, place, thing, or idea. Proper nouns always begin with a capital letter. Common nouns begin with a capital letter in titles and when they begin sentences.

COMMON NOUNS	PROPER NOUNS
poem	"Paul Revere's Ride," "Oranges"
nation	Mexico, United States of America
athlete	Michael Jordan, Zina Garrison-Jackson
river	Rio Grande, Congo River

QUICK CHECK I

Identify each noun in the following sentences. Classify each noun as *common* or *proper*.

EXAMPLE   **1.** Roald Dahl is the author of "The Landlady."
   1. *Roald Dahl—proper; author—common; "The Landlady"—proper*

1. Billy Weaver was going to The Bell and Dragon, an inn that was in Bath.
2. Was Billy wearing his brown suit and a navy-blue overcoat?
3. In his mind, briskness was a characteristic of businessmen.
4. "Big shots" in the company always seemed brisk to Billy.
5. How was the landlady like a jack-in-the-box?

Try It Out ✎

For the following paragraph about "Jack and the Beanstalk," replace the vague nouns with exact, specific nouns.

   [1] Have you read the story about the boy who traded an animal for seeds? [2] A huge vine grew from the seeds, and the boy climbed it. [3] At the top, he discovered a large man as well as a bird that laid golden eggs. [4] The boy stole the man's things. [5] The boy's parent forgave him for the foolish trade that he had made.

Using Specific Nouns

Whenever possible, use specific, exact nouns. Using specific nouns will make your writing more accurate and precise, as well as more interesting.

VAGUE   People crowded into the building.
PRECISE   **Men, women,** and **children** crowded into the **theater.**

VAGUE   Following the young person was a small dog.
PRECISE   Following the **child** was a **dachshund.**

THE PRONOUN

1b.   A *pronoun* is a word used in place of one or more nouns or pronouns.

EXAMPLES   After Bill fed the dog and cat, Bill let the dog and cat go outside.
   After Bill fed the dog and cat, **he** let **them** go outside.

The word that a pronoun stands for is called its ***antecedent.*** Sometimes the antecedent is not stated.

STATED ANTECEDENT   Mrs. Flowers opened the **book** and began reading **it.**
UNSTATED ANTECEDENT   **Who** wrote the book?

Personal Pronouns

A ***personal pronoun*** refers to the one speaking (*first person*), the one spoken to (*second person*), or the one spoken about (*third person*).

PERSONAL PRONOUNS		
	SINGULAR	**PLURAL**
First Person	I, me, my, mine	we, us, our, ours
Second Person	you, your, yours	you, your, yours
Third Person	he, him, his, she, her, hers, it, its	they, them, their, theirs

EXAMPLES   **He** and **his** friends caught several frogs and put **them** in a bag.

Did **you** say that **it** is too cold for **us** to go outside?

Reflexive and Intensive Pronouns

A *reflexive pronoun* refers to the subject and directs the action of the verb back to the subject. An *intensive pronoun* emphasizes a noun or another pronoun. Reflexive pronouns and intensive pronouns have the same form.

REFLEXIVE AND INTENSIVE PRONOUNS	
First Person	myself, ourselves
Second Person	yourself, yourselves
Third Person	himself, herself, itself, themselves

REFLEXIVE   Alfonso asked **himself** why he had taken off the chain.

INTENSIVE   Mrs. Flowers made the tea cookies **herself.**

Demonstrative Pronouns

A *demonstrative pronoun* (*this, that, these, those*) points out a person, a place, a thing, or an idea.

EXAMPLE   **This** is Ernie's bike.

Interrogative Pronouns

An *interrogative pronoun* (*what, which, who, whom, whose*) introduces a question.

EXAMPLE   **Who** is the author of "Flowers for Algernon"?

Relative Pronouns

A *relative pronoun* (*that, what, which, who, whom, whose*) introduces a subordinate clause.

EXAMPLE   Mr. White received the two hundred pounds **that** he had wished for.

NOTE The possessive pronouns *my, your, his, her, its, our,* and *their* are sometimes called *possessive adjectives.* Follow your teacher's instructions regarding these possessive forms.

NOTE If you are not sure whether a pronoun is reflexive or intensive, read the sentence aloud, omitting the pronoun. If the meaning stays the same, the pronoun is intensive. If the meaning changes, the pronoun is reflexive.

EXAMPLES   Rachel painted the fence **herself.** [Without *herself,* the meaning stays the same. The pronoun is intensive.]

They treated **themselves** to a picnic. [Without *themselves,* the sentence doesn't make sense. The pronoun is reflexive.]

☞ *This, that, these,* and *those* can also be used as adjectives. See page 741.

☞ For more about subordinate clauses, see pages 775–778.

Indefinite Pronouns

An *indefinite pronoun* refers to a person, a place, or a thing that is not specifically named.

Common Indefinite Pronouns				
all	both	everybody	none	several
any	each	few	no one	some
anyone	either	many	one	something

EXAMPLES   **All** of them wanted to hear the story of Urashima Taro.
The travelers saw **someone.**

 QUICK CHECK 2

Identify each of the pronouns in the following sentences as *personal, reflexive, intensive, demonstrative, interrogative, relative,* or *indefinite.*

EXAMPLE   **1.** That was a very strange person!
  1. *That—demonstrative*

1. Who were her previous tenants, and what happened to them?
2. That is the guest book that they signed.
3. Had they themselves or anyone else been suspicious of her?
4. The house, which was brightly lit, had a sign in its window.
5. She brought a pot of tea for him and herself.

THE ADJECTIVE

1c.   An *adjective* is a word used to modify a noun or a pronoun.

To *modify* a word means to describe the word or to make its meaning more definite. An adjective modifies a word by telling *what kind, which one, how much,* or *how many.*

WHAT KIND?	WHICH ONE?	HOW MUCH? *or* HOW MANY?
tall woman	*this* year	*less* time
steep mountain	*last* answer	*many* mistakes
exciting story	*middle* row	*few* marbles

An adjective may come before or after the word it modifies.

EXAMPLES   The **old** soldier told the **curious** couple that they could have **three** wishes.
The map, although **old** and **worn,** was **useful** to him.

Articles

The most frequently used adjectives are *a, an,* and *the.* The adjectives *a* and *an* are called **indefinite articles.** They indicate that the noun refers to someone or something in general. *A* is used before a word beginning with a consonant sound. *An* is used before a word beginning with a vowel sound.

EXAMPLE   He gave the salesclerk **a** nickel and **an** orange.

The adjective *the* is a **definite article.** It indicates that the noun refers to someone or something in particular.

EXAMPLE   Smiley went to **the** swamp to find **the** stranger a frog.

Proper Adjectives

A **proper adjective** is formed from a proper noun and begins with a capital letter.

PROPER NOUN	PROPER ADJECTIVE
Africa	**African** nations
Shakespeare	**Shakespearean** drama
Rio Grande	**Rio Grande** valley

Some proper nouns, such as *Rio Grande,* do not change spelling when they are used as adjectives.

Demonstrative Adjectives

This, that, these, and *those* can be used both as adjectives and as pronouns. When they modify a noun or a pronoun, these words are called **demonstrative adjectives**. When used alone, they are called **demonstrative pronouns**.

DEMONSTRATIVE ADJECTIVE   **This** poem was written by Amy Ling.
DEMONSTRATIVE PRONOUN   **This** is an example of personification.

☞ For more about demonstrative pronouns, see page 739.

 QUICK CHECK 3

In the following sentences, identify each adjective and the word that it modifies. Also, identify any articles, proper adjectives, or demonstrative adjectives.

EXAMPLE   **1.** Wasn't Christopher Mulholland a Cambridge under-graduate?
   1. *a (article)—undergraduate; Cambridge (proper)—under-graduate*

1. The houses were old and run-down but had once been grand.
2. This house looks like a nice, friendly place.
3. The room seems comfortable, with a large sofa and two pets.
4. The London train had been slow, and the weather was chilly.
5. What had happened to that Bristol man?

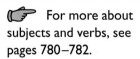 For more about subjects and verbs, see pages 780–782.

THE VERB

1d. A *verb* is a word used to express action or a state of being. The verb says something about the subject of a sentence.

EXAMPLES   Gary Soto **wrote** "Broken Chain."
"Oranges" **is** one of my favorite poems.

Action Verbs

1e. An *action verb* may express physical action or mental action.

PHYSICAL ACTION   jump, shout, search, carry, run
MENTAL ACTION   worry, think, believe, imagine, remember

Transitive and Intransitive Verbs

(1) A *transitive verb* is a verb that expresses an action directed toward a person or thing.

EXAMPLE   Alfonso **borrowed** Ernie's bike. [The action of *borrowed* is directed toward *bike*.]

With transitive verbs, the action passes from the doer—the subject—to the receiver of the action. Words that receive the action of a transitive verb are called **objects.**

EXAMPLE   Mr. White made three **wishes.** [*Wishes* is the object of the verb *made*.]

(2) An *intransitive verb* expresses action (or tells something about the subject) without passing the action to a receiver.

EXAMPLE   The broken chain **lay** beside the fence. [The action of *lay* is not directed toward a receiver.]

NOTE A verb may be transitive in one sentence and intransitive in another.

TRANSITIVE The teacher **read** "A Time to Talk."

INTRANSITIVE The teacher **read** aloud.

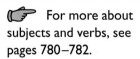 For more about objects, see pages 783–784.

Linking Verbs

1f. A *linking verb* links, or connects, the subject with a noun, a pronoun, or an adjective in the predicate.

EXAMPLES   The winner of the race **is** Squeaky. [winner = Squeaky]
Gretchen **is** one of her opponents. [Gretchen = one]
Squeaky's brother **looks** happy. [happy brother]

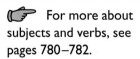 Linking verbs (*be, seem, feel,* etc.) never take direct objects. See pages 783–784 for more about linking verbs.

COMMON LINKING VERBS	
Forms of the Verb *Be*	am, are, be, been, being, is, was, were
Other Linking Verbs	appear, become, feel, grow, look, remain, seem, smell, sound, stay, taste, turn

All linking verbs except forms of *be* and *seem* may also be used as action verbs. Whether a verb is used to link words or to express action depends on its meaning in a sentence.

LINKING The tiger **looked** tame.

ACTION The tiger **looked** for something to eat.

Helping Verbs

1g. A *helping verb (auxiliary verb)* **helps the main verb to express an action or a state of being.**

EXAMPLES **should** be
might have won
will have been taken

A *verb phrase* consists of a main verb preceded by at least one helping verb.

EXAMPLE Dr. Strauss and Dr. Nemur **are studying** Charlie. [The main verb is *studying.*]

COMMONLY USED HELPING VERBS	
Forms of *Be*	am, are, be, been, being, is, was, were
Forms of *Do*	do, does, did
Forms of *Have*	have, has, had
Other Helping Verbs	can, could, may, might, must, shall, should, will, would

Sometimes the verb phrase is interrupted by other words.

EXAMPLES People **may** someday **communicate** with dolphins.
How much **do** you **know** about the writer Roald Dahl?
The narrator **could** not [*or* **couldn't**] **see** the old man's "vulture eye."

 QUICK CHECK 4

Identify each verb in the following sentences as either an *action verb* or a *linking verb*. Identify each action verb as either *transitive* or *intransitive*.

EXAMPLE **1.** A cold wind was blowing in Bath.

  1. *was blowing—action, intransitive*

1. The glow of a street lamp lit up the window.
2. The landlady did not look strange.
3. Billy looked past the green curtains.
4. She could have been the mother of a friend of his.
5. Have you ever read a story like this one?

THE ADVERB

1h. An *adverb* **is a word used to modify a verb, an adjective, or another adverb.**

An adverb tells *where, when, how,* or *to what extent* (*how much* or *how long*).

EXAMPLES   **Quite stealthily,** the narrator opens the door. [*Quite* modifies the adverb *stealthily,* telling *to what extent; stealthily* modifies the verb *opens,* telling *how.*]

He is **extremely** cautious. [*Extremely* modifies the adjective *cautious,* telling *to what extent.*]

He buries the body **there.** [*There* modifies the verb *buries,* telling *where.*]

Police officers arrive **soon.** [*Soon* modifies the verb *arrive,* telling *when.*]

The police officers do **not** hear the noise. [*Not* modifies the verb phrase *do hear,* telling *to what extent.*]

Note in the examples above that adverbs may come before, after, or between the words they modify.

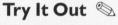

The word *not* is an adverb. When *not* is part of a contraction like *hadn't,* the *–n't* is an adverb.

For more about modifiers, see Part 5: Using Modifiers.

Avoiding the Overuse of Very

The adverb *very* is often overused. In your writing, try to replace *very* with more descriptive adverbs or to revise the sentence so that other words carry more of the descriptive meaning.

EXAMPLE   Poe's stories are very suspenseful.

REVISED   Poe's stories are **extremely** suspenseful.

or

Poe's suspenseful stories **shock, frighten, and entertain readers.**

 QUICK CHECK 5

Identify the adverbs in the following sentences. After each adverb, write the word or phrase that the adverb modifies.

EXAMPLE   1. The landlady seemed almost familiar.
1. *almost—familiar*

1. Suddenly, a woman appeared.
2. She spoke quite pleasantly to the young man.
3. Are eggs terribly expensive?
4. The young man had not taken his hat off.
5. No other hats or coats were there.

Try It Out ✎

For each of the following sentences, replace *very* with a more descriptive adverb, or rewrite the sentence to eliminate *very.*

1. The narrator in "The Tell-Tale Heart" is very deceitful.
2. At night, the old man's room is very dark.
3. This narrator seems very emotional.
4. Notice that Poe's use of italics is very effective.
5. When the heartbeat becomes very loud, the narrator confesses.

THE PREPOSITION

1i. A *preposition* is a word used to show the relationship of a noun or a pronoun to another word in the sentence.

Notice how a change in the preposition changes the relationship between the cat and the house in the following examples.

The dog chased the cat **under** the house.
The dog chased the cat **around** the house.
The dog chased the cat **through** the house.
The dog chased the cat **out of** the house.

Common Prepositions

about	because of	for	of
above	before	from	on
according to	behind	in	out of
across	beneath	in front of	over
after	beside	inside	through
against	between	into	to
around	by	like	under
at	during	near	with

The Prepositional Phrase

A preposition is generally followed by a noun or a pronoun, called the **object of the preposition.** All together, the preposition, its object, and any modifiers of the object are called a *prepositional phrase.*

EXAMPLE   The wagon train slowly traveled **across the dusty prairie.**

A preposition may have more than one object.

EXAMPLE   Ms. Larson told us to look closely **at the poem's rhyme and rhythm.**

 QUICK CHECK 6

Identify the prepositional phrase or phrases in each of the following sentences. Then, underline each preposition.

EXAMPLE   **1.** Edgar Allan Poe died at an early age.
              1. *at an early age*

1. Much sadness and pain had come into his life.
2. He was a superb critic of other writers' works.
3. His small text on composition is still a classic.
4. His talent for terror is appreciated by millions of people.
5. His stories are in many textbooks and anthologies.

 For more about prepositional phrases, see pages 768 and 769–771.

NOTE Be careful not to confuse a prepositional phrase that begins with *to* (*to town*) with a verb form that begins with *to* (*to run*).

THE CONJUNCTION

1j. A *conjunction* is a word used to join words or groups of words.

(1) *Coordinating conjunctions* connect words or groups of words used in the same way.

Coordinating Conjunctions						
and	but	or	nor	for	so	yet

EXAMPLES Gretchen **or** Squeaky [two nouns]
small **but** comfortable [two adjectives]
down the track **and** across the finish line [two prepositional phrases]
The stars seem motionless, **but** actually they are moving rapidly through space. [two independent clauses]

(2) *Correlative conjunctions* are pairs of conjunctions that connect words or groups of words used in the same way.

Correlative Conjunctions		
both . . . and	either . . . or	neither . . . nor
not only . . . but also	whether . . . or	

EXAMPLES **Neither** Alfonso **nor** Sandra has a bike to ride. [two nouns]
Either leave a message on my answering machine, **or** call me after 7:00 P.M. tomorrow. [two independent clauses]

THE INTERJECTION

1k. An *interjection* is a word used to express emotion. It has no grammatical relation to other words in the sentence. Usually an interjection is followed by an exclamation point. Sometimes an interjection is set off by a comma.

Common Interjections					
aha	aw	hey	oh	ouch	whew
alas	gosh	hooray	oops	well	wow

EXAMPLES **Wow!** What an exciting race that was!
Well, he did his best.

QUICK CHECK 7

Identify each *conjunction* and *interjection* in the following sentences.

EXAMPLE   **I.** Wow! Poe's rhythms are regular yet breathless.
            I. *Wow—interjection; yet—conjunction*

1. Notice the rich vocabulary and sentence structure in these stories by Edgar Allan Poe.
2. Oh, don't miss hearing a narration of "The Tell-Tale Heart."
3. Neither unfamiliar words nor long descriptive phrases should discourage you.
4. Skim them, but feel the speaker's emotions.
5. Let the sound and feeling of the poem fill you, and, pow, you will understand Poe.

DETERMINING PARTS OF SPEECH

The part of speech of a word is determined by the way that the word is used in a sentence. Many words can be used as more than one part of speech.

EXAMPLES   **Each** costs a dime. [pronoun]
            Each chocolate costs a dime. [adjective]

            He made a **wish.** [noun]
            For what did he **wish**? [verb]

            Mr. White makes his third wish, **for** he is afraid of what he may find behind the door. [conjunction]
            Mrs. Flowers had made the tea cookies **for** her. [preposition]

            The **well** has gone dry. [noun]
            Well, he seems to like Sandra. [interjection]
            He doesn't look **well** to me. [adjective]
            She writes **well.** [adverb]

 QUICK CHECK 8

Identify the part of speech of the italicized word in each sentence.

EXAMPLE   **I.** Each *beat* of the heart filled him with terror.
            I. *noun*

1. The heart *beat* on.
2. *That* was the heart of the old man.
3. Perhaps *that* terror was his own guilt.
4. Even *in* silence, he heard the sound.
5. The old man did not suspect the narrator *yet.*

2 AGREEMENT

NUMBER

Number is the form of a word that indicates whether the word is singular or plural.

2a. When a word refers to one person, place, thing, or idea, it is *singular*. When a word refers to more than one, it is *plural*.

SINGULAR	book	woman	one	I	he
PLURAL	books	women	many	we	they

Agreement of Subject and Verb

2b. A verb agrees with its subject in number.

(1) Singular subjects take singular verbs.

EXAMPLES   The **stranger shoots** the frog.
Johnny calls himself Red Chief.

(2) Plural subjects take plural verbs.

EXAMPLES   Six **girls compete** in the race.
Many **people laugh** at Charlie.

The first auxiliary (helping) verb in a verb phrase must agree with its subject.

EXAMPLES   **She is** helping Charlie.
They are helping Charlie.

Problems in Agreement

2c. The number of a subject is not changed by a prepositional phrase following the subject.

NONSTANDARD   The sparse furnishings on the stage creates a somber atmosphere.

STANDARD   The sparse **furnishings** on the stage **create** a somber atmosphere.

2d. The following indefinite pronouns are singular: *anybody, anyone, each, either, everybody, everyone, neither, nobody, no one, one, somebody, someone.*

EXAMPLE   **Each** of them **was sent** a bouquet.

2e. The following indefinite pronouns are plural: *both, few, many, several.*

EXAMPLE   **Both** of the stories **were written** by Shirley Jackson.

 For more about forming plurals, see pages 814–815.

TIPS FOR SPELLING

Generally, nouns ending in *s* are plural (*candles, ideas, neighbors, horses*), and verbs ending in *s* are singular (*sees, writes, speaks, carries*). However, verbs used with the singular pronouns *I* and *you* generally do not end in *s*.

EXAMPLE   **I walk** faster than **you do.**

2f. **The following indefinite pronouns may be either singular or plural: *all, any, most, none, some*.**

The number of *all, any, most, none,* or *some* is often determined by the number of the object in a prepositional phrase following the subject. If the subject refers to a singular object, the subject is singular. If the subject refers to a plural object, the subject is plural.

EXAMPLES   **All** of the **action occurs** on the top floor of a warehouse. [*All* refers to the singular object *action.*]

   All of the **events occur** on the top floor of a warehouse. [*All* refers to the plural object *events.*]

Using indefinite pronouns correctly can be tricky. To help yourself, you may want to create an indefinite pronoun guide. First, summarize the information in rules 2d–2f and 2o–2r. Then, choose several examples to illustrate the rules. Create a "Help" file in which to store this information. Call up the file whenever you run into difficulty using indefinite pronouns.

2g. **Subjects joined by *and* usually take a plural verb.**

EXAMPLE   **Sam** and **Bill kidnap** Johnny.

   A compound subject that names a single person or thing takes a singular verb. A compound noun used as a subject also takes a singular verb in most cases.

EXAMPLES   The **captain** and **quarterback** of the team **was** Lyle. [One person, Lyle, was both the captain and the quarterback.]

   Rock and roll is my favorite kind of music. [*Rock and roll* is a compound noun naming one kind of music.]

2h. **When subjects are joined by *or* or *nor*, the verb agrees with the subject nearer the verb.**

EXAMPLES   Neither the **director** nor the **players were** on time for rehearsal.

   Neither the **players** nor the **director was** on time for rehearsal.

QUICK CHECK I

For each of the following sentences, choose the correct form of the verb in parentheses.

EXAMPLE   **1.** Both of the girls (*love, loves*) running.
   1. *love*

1. My favorite story (*has, have*) always been "Raymond's Run."
2. Some of the story (*concern, concerns*) Squeaky's rival.
3. Neither Gretchen nor Mary Louise really (*smile, smiles*).
4. Squeaky's rival and schoolmate (*was, were*) Gretchen.
5. Insults and taunts directed at Raymond (*anger, angers*) his sister.

For more about contractions, see pages 808–809.

> **NOTE** When the subject of a sentence follows all or part of the verb, the word order is *inverted.* To find the subject of a sentence with inverted order, restate the sentence in normal word order.
>
> **INVERTED** **Did Robert Frost write** these poems?
> **NORMAL** **Robert Frost did write** these poems.
>
> **INVERTED** Into the clearing **stepped** a tiny **fawn**.
> **NORMAL** A tiny **fawn stepped** into the clearing.

2i. **Collective nouns (such as *crowd, family,* and *team*) may be either singular or plural.**

A collective noun takes a singular verb when the noun refers to the group as a unit. A collective noun takes a plural verb when the noun refers to the individual parts or members of the group.

EXAMPLES The Frank **family goes** into hiding. [The family as a unit goes into hiding.]

The Frank **family pack** their bags. [The individual members of the family pack bags.]

2j. **When the subject follows all or part of the verb, find the subject and make sure the verb agrees with it. The subject usually follows the verb in sentences beginning with *here* or *there* and in questions.**

EXAMPLES There **is** a **frog** on that lily pad.
Have any other **frogs jumped** on?

The contractions *here's, there's,* and *where's* contain the verb *is* and should be used only with singular subjects.

NONSTANDARD There's the books.
STANDARD There **are** the **books.**

2k. **Use the contraction *don't* with plural subjects and with the pronouns *I* and *you.* Use the contraction *doesn't* with other singular subjects.**

EXAMPLES The **police officers don't** hear the noise.
I don't like that song.
You don't have enough money to buy that.
The **frog doesn't** jump.

2l. **Words stating amounts are usually singular.**

A word or phrase stating a weight, a measurement, or an amount of money or time is usually considered one item. Such a word or phrase takes a singular verb.

EXAMPLE **Twenty-five months is** the amount of time Anne kept the diary.

2m. **The title of a creative work or the name of an organization or country, even when plural in form, usually takes a singular verb.**

EXAMPLE "Flowers for Algernon" **was made** into a movie.

2n. **A few nouns, though plural in form, are singular and take singular verbs.**

EXAMPLE **Mathematics is** my best subject.

QUICK CHECK 2

In the following sentences, choose the form of the verb in parentheses that agrees with the subject.

EXAMPLE   **1.** The people in her family (*work, works*) hard.
                1. *work*

1. *Hansel and Gretel* (*was, were*) the pageant that Squeaky was in.
2. Athletics (*has, have*) always interested Squeaky.
3. (*Don't, Doesn't*) she run well?
4. Fifty yards (*was, were*) the length of the run.
5. (*There's, There are*) not much dialogue in the story.

Agreement of Pronoun and Antecedent

A pronoun usually refers to a noun or another pronoun, called its *antecedent.*

2o.   **A pronoun agrees with its antecedent in number and gender.**

Some singular personal pronouns have forms that indicate gender. Masculine pronouns (*he, him, his*) refer to males. Feminine pronouns (*she, her, hers*) refer to females. Neuter pronouns (*it, its*) refer to things (neither male nor female) and sometimes to animals.

EXAMPLES   **Ernie** lent **his** bike to Alfonso.
                Squeaky protects **her** brother.
                The sergeant major took the **monkey's paw** and threw **it** into the fire.

Some antecedents may be either masculine or feminine. When referring to such antecedents, use both the masculine and the feminine forms.

EXAMPLE   **No one** on the committee gave **his or her** approval.

 Revising Awkward Pronoun Agreement

Sometimes, using both the masculine and the feminine forms to refer to an indefinite pronoun is awkward or confusing. To avoid such use, rephrase the sentence by using both a plural pronoun and a plural antecedent.

AWKWARD   **Everyone** except Fanny signed the petition because **he** or **she** did not like working with the "new" Charlie.

CLEAR   **All** of the workers except Fanny signed the petition because **they** did not like working with the "new" Charlie.

 For more about antecedents, see page 738.

NOTE   The antecedent of a personal pronoun can be another kind of pronoun, such as *all* or *one*. To determine the gender of a personal pronoun in such cases, look at the phrase that follows the antecedent.

EXAMPLE   **Each** of the **girls** took **her** place at the starting line.

Try It Out

Revise the following sentences to eliminate the awkward use of *his or her.*

1. Each of the characters had his or her own motives.
2. One of the stagehands had forgotten his or her tools.
3. Everyone in the play knew his or her lines.
4. Either Anna or Fred will drive his or her van.
5. Nobody forgot his or her costume.

Problems in Agreement

2p. A singular pronoun is used to refer to *anybody, anyone, each, either, everybody, everyone, neither, nobody, no one, one, someone,* or *somebody.*

EXAMPLE   **Everybody** will have an opportunity to express **his or her** opinion.

2q. A plural pronoun is used to refer to *both, few, many,* or *several.*

EXAMPLE   **Both** of the novels by Mark Twain were on **their** shelf in the library.

2r. Either a singular or a plural pronoun may be used to refer to *all, any, most, none,* or *some.*

The number of the pronoun *all, any, most, none,* or *some* is determined by the number of the object of the preposition in the prepositional phrase following the pronoun.

EXAMPLES   Only **some** of the paint spilled, but **it** made a big mess. [*Some* refers to *paint.*]

Some of the children are ready for **their** naps. [*Some* refers to *children.*]

2s. A plural pronoun is used to refer to two or more antecedents joined by *and.*

EXAMPLE   When **Bill and Sam** wrote the ransom note, **they** asked for fifteen hundred dollars.

2t. A singular pronoun is used to refer to two or more singular antecedents joined by *or* or *nor.*

EXAMPLE   **Julio or Van** will bring **his** football.

A singular and a plural antecedent joined by *or* or *nor* can create an awkward sentence. Revise such a sentence to avoid the problem.

AWKWARD   Either Mr. Reyes or the Wilsons will be bringing their volleyball net.

REVISED   Either **Mr. Reyes** will be bringing **his** volleyball net, or the **Wilsons** will be bringing **theirs.**

Sentences with singular antecedents joined by *or* or *nor* also can sound awkward if the antecedents are of different genders. If the sentence sounds awkward, revise it to avoid the problem.

AWKWARD   Either Lori or Tony will read her or his poem about the Holocaust.

REVISED   Either **Lori** will read **her** poem about the Holocaust, or **Tony** will read **his.**

✓ QUICK CHECK 3

For each blank in the following sentences, give a pronoun that will complete the meaning of the sentence.

EXAMPLE **1.** Both Alfonso and Ernie liked riding _____ bikes.
1. *their*

1. Alfonso took good care of _____ bike.
2. Each of the boys had _____ own problems.
3. Neither of the girls from the Halloween party had kept _____ promise to Ernie.
4. Perhaps both of them had _____ reasons for not meeting Ernie and Frostie at the corner.
5. Did Ernie or Frostie keep _____ word?

2u. **Either a singular or a plural pronoun may be used with a collective noun (such as *committee*, *flock*, and *jury*).**

EXAMPLES   The **committee** has prepared **its** recommendation. [The committee as a unit has prepared the recommendation.]

The **committee** are sharing **their** ideas for the new recycling campaign. [The separate members of the committee have various ideas.]

2v. **A few nouns, though plural in form, are singular and take singular pronouns.**

EXAMPLE   All of them had expected the **news** to be bad, but **it** wasn't.

2w. **Words stating amounts usually take singular pronouns.**

EXAMPLE   Although the landlady charged **five and sixpence** a night for a room, **it** was much less than he had expected to pay.

> **NOTE** The title of a creative work or the name of an organization or a country, even when plural in form, usually takes a singular pronoun.
>
> **EXAMPLE**   I enjoyed reading ***The Outsiders*** because **it** had interesting characters.

✓ QUICK CHECK 4

For each blank in the following sentences, give a pronoun that will complete the meaning of the sentence.

EXAMPLE **1.** Father's team was playing, but _____ lost.
1. *it*

1. The family were doing _____ chores.
2. "Oranges" is also by Gary Soto, and _____ is the next selection in the book.
3. He had only five cents, but _____ was enough for the candy.
4. Your checkers are all over the floor; please clean _____ up.
5. Checkers may be a good game, but I don't play _____ often.

3 USING VERBS

THE PRINCIPAL PARTS OF A VERB

The four basic forms of a verb are called the **principal parts** of a verb.

3a. The principal parts of a verb are the *base form,* the *present participle,* the *past,* and the *past participle.*

BASE FORM	PRESENT PARTICIPLE	PAST	PAST PARTICIPLE
return	(is) returning	returned	(have) returned
go	(is) going	went	(have) gone

Notice that the present participle and the past participle require helping verbs (forms of *be* and *have*).

Regular Verbs

3b. A *regular verb* forms its past and past participle by adding *–d* or *–ed* to the base form.

BASE FORM	PRESENT PARTICIPLE	PAST	PAST PARTICIPLE
use	(is) using	used	(have) used
attack	(is) attacking	attacked	(have) attacked
drown	(is) drowning	drowned	(have) drowned

> ☞ For information about how participles are used as modifiers, see page 771.

Avoid the following common errors when forming the past or past participle of regular verbs:

1. leaving off the *–d* or *–ed* ending

EXAMPLE The innkeeper used [*not* use] to be a samurai.

2. adding unnecessary letters

EXAMPLE Fortunately, no one in the boating accident drowned [*not* drownded].

 QUICK CHECK 1

For each of the following sentences, give the correct past or past participle form of the verb in parentheses.

EXAMPLE   **1.** Two families (*share*) the house in China.
              1. *shared*

> **TIPS FOR SPELLING**
>
> In general, double the final consonant before adding *–ed* or *–ing* if the verb
>
> (1) has only one syllable or has the accent on the last syllable
>
>   *and*
>
> (2) ends in a single consonant preceded by a single vowel.
>
> **EXAMPLES**   drop, dro**pped**, dro**pping**
>   refer, refe**rred**, refe**rring**
>
> See page 813 for exceptions.

1. A relative of theirs living in the United States (*record*) a message to them.
2. They had (*live*) close to a river.
3. Xiaojun has (*carry*) water in buckets.
4. The families (*cook*) with the water.
5. They have (*use*) wheat stalks instead of wood for a fire.

Irregular Verbs

3c. An *irregular verb* forms its past and past participle in some other way than by adding *–d* or *–ed* to the base form.

An irregular verb forms its past and past participle

- by changing vowels or consonants

BASE FORM	PAST	PAST PARTICIPLE
sing	sang	(have) sung
build	built	(have) built

- by changing vowels and consonants

BASE FORM	PAST	PAST PARTICIPLE
see	saw	(have) seen
write	wrote	(have) written

- by making no changes

BASE FORM	PAST	PAST PARTICIPLE
cut	cut	(have) cut
cost	cost	(have) cost

Avoid the following common errors when forming the past or past participle of irregular verbs:

1. using the past form with a helping verb

    NONSTANDARD   Coyote had stole the sun and the moon.
    STANDARD   Coyote had **stolen** the sun and the moon.

2. using the past participle form without a helping verb

    NONSTANDARD   They drunk the tea.
    STANDARD   They **have drunk** the tea.

3. adding *–d* or *–ed* to the base form

    NONSTANDARD   Brer Possum knowed not to trust Brer Snake.
    STANDARD   Brer Possum **knew** not to trust Brer Snake.

NOTE If you are not sure about the principal parts of a verb, look in a dictionary. Entries for irregular verbs give the principal parts of the verb.

COMMON IRREGULAR VERBS

GROUP I: Each of these irregular verbs has the same form for its past and past participle.

BASE FORM	PRESENT PARTICIPLE	PAST	PAST PARTICIPLE
bring	(is) bringing	brought	(have) brought
find	(is) finding	found	(have) found
get	(is) getting	got	(have) got *or* gotten
hold	(is) holding	held	(have) held
keep	(is) keeping	kept	(have) kept
lead	(is) leading	led	(have) led
lend	(is) lending	lent	(have) lent
make	(is) making	made	(have) made
spend	(is) spending	spent	(have) spent
teach	(is) teaching	taught	(have) taught

 QUICK CHECK 2

For each of the following sentences, give the correct past or past participle form of the verb in parentheses.

EXAMPLE   1. The family (*keep*) chickens and a garden.
     1. *kept*

1. Finally, Xiaojun's father had (*make*) enough money for the trip.
2. The letter said that he had (*find*) an apartment.
3. They (*bring*) suitcases out to the car.
4. A friend had (*lend*) them the car.
5. In China, the teachers (*teach*) according to strict rules.

COMMON IRREGULAR VERBS

GROUP II: Each of these irregular verbs has a different form for its past and past participle.

BASE FORM	PRESENT PARTICIPLE	PAST	PAST PARTICIPLE
begin	(is) beginning	began	(have) begun
break	(is) breaking	broke	(have) broken
choose	(is) choosing	chose	(have) chosen
drink	(is) drinking	drank	(have) drunk
eat	(is) eating	ate	(have) eaten
fly	(is) flying	flew	(have) flown
go	(is) going	went	(have) gone
know	(is) knowing	knew	(have) known
ring	(is) ringing	rang	(have) rung
take	(is) taking	took	(have) taken

QUICK CHECK 3

For each of the following sentences, give the correct past or past participle form of the verb in parentheses.

EXAMPLE **1.** Xiaojun and her family (*go*) to the United States.
1. *went*

1. They (*take*) boats, buses, and a train.
2. On the trip, she (*drink*) a soybean beverage.
3. They (*fly*) in an airplane from Hong Kong.
4. Their adventure had (*begin*).
5. She had not (*know*) about crayons and many other things.

COMMON IRREGULAR VERBS			
GROUP III: Each of these irregular verbs has the same form for its base form, past, and past participle.			
BASE FORM	**PRESENT PARTICIPLE**	**PAST**	**PAST PARTICIPLE**
burst	(is) bursting	burst	(have) burst
hit	(is) hitting	hit	(have) hit
hurt	(is) hurting	hurt	(have) hurt
let	(is) letting	let	(have) let
put	(is) putting	put	(have) put
read	(is) reading	read	(have) read
spread	(is) spreading	spread	(have) spread

 QUICK CHECK 4

For each of the following sentences, give the correct past or past participle form of the verb in italics.

EXAMPLE **1.** *read*   Xiaojun has _____ the encyclopedia.
1. *read*

1. *put*   They had _____ their hopes for the future into the trip.
2. *burst* When the match _____ into flames, they burned a string.
3. *hit*   In China, the teachers had _____ misbehaving students.
4. *hurt*   Discipline was strict, and penalties often _____.
5. *let*   Her mother has not _____ her go on dates yet.

VERB TENSE

3d. The *tense* of a verb indicates the time of the action or state of being expressed by the verb.

Every verb has six tenses. Listing all the forms of a verb in the six tenses is called *conjugating* a verb.

CONJUGATION OF THE VERB *GO*	
PRESENT TENSE	
SINGULAR	*PLURAL*
I go	we go
you go	you go
he, she, *or* it goes	they go
PAST TENSE	
SINGULAR	*PLURAL*
I went	we went
you went	you went
he, she, *or* it went	they went
FUTURE TENSE	
SINGULAR	*PLURAL*
I will go	we will go
you will go	you will go
he, she, *or* it will go	they will go
PRESENT PERFECT TENSE	
SINGULAR	*PLURAL*
I have gone	we have gone
you have gone	you have gone
he, she, *or* it has gone	they have gone
PAST PERFECT TENSE	
SINGULAR	*PLURAL*
I had gone	we had gone
you had gone	you had gone
he, she, *or* it had gone	they had gone
FUTURE PERFECT TENSE	
SINGULAR	*PLURAL*
I will have gone	we will have gone
you will have gone	you will have gone
he, she, *or* it will have gone	they will have gone

This time line shows how the six tenses are related to one another.

Past	*Present*	*Future*
existing or happening in the past	existing or happening now	existing or happening in the future

Past Perfect	*Present Perfect*	*Future Perfect*
existing or happening before a specific time in the past	existing or happening sometime before now, or starting in the past and continuing now	existing or happening before a specific time in the future

Consistency of Tense

3e. **Do not change needlessly from one tense to another.**

When writing about events that take place in the present, use verbs in the present tense. Similarly, when writing about events that occurred in the past, use verbs in the past tense.

INCONSISTENT   Billy pressed the doorbell, and immediately a woman opens the door. [*Pressed* is past tense, and *opens* is present tense.]

CONSISTENT   Billy **pressed** the doorbell, and immediately a woman **opened** the door. [Both *pressed* and *opened* are past tense.]

CONSISTENT   Billy **presses** the doorbell, and immediately a woman **opens** the door. [Both *presses* and *opens* are present tense.]

Sometimes, changing verb tenses is necessary to show the order of events that occur at different times.

EXAMPLES   Tomorrow I **will read** aloud the story I **wrote** last week. [The action of reading will take place in the future; the action of writing took place in the past.]

She **guessed** that he **had won** the spelling bee. [The action of winning was completed before the action of guessing.]

By the time he **returns,** they **will have finished** all their chores. [The action of finishing will be completed before the action of returning.]

 QUICK CHECK 5

Read the following paragraph, and decide whether it should be rewritten in the present or past tense. Then, change the verb forms to make the verb tense consistent.

EXAMPLE   [1] Many Japanese families went to Camp Harmony and staying there for the duration of the war.

   1. *Many Japanese families went to Camp Harmony and stayed there for the duration of the war.*

or

   1. *Many Japanese families go to Camp Harmony and stay there for the duration of the war.*

[1] Monica Sone's mother sees the best in things and admired the dandelions. [2] She planned for a garden of them and is grateful for any type of beauty. [3] She is even happy about the nearness of the latrine, though the others were not so thrilled. [4] Like her mother, Sone's father has been grateful for good things, however small. [5] He finds a pile of lumber and loose nails and envisioned these scraps as the family's furniture.

Voice

3f. *Voice* **is the form a verb takes to indicate whether the subject of the verb performs or receives the action.**

When the subject performs the action, the verb is in the *active voice* and has an object. When the subject receives the action, the verb is in the *passive voice* and does not have an object.

ACTIVE Saki **wrote** "The Open Window." [*"The Open Window"* is the direct object.]

PASSIVE "The Open Window" **was written** by Saki. [no object]

Avoiding Passive Voice

Whenever possible, avoid using the passive voice, because it is less direct and less forceful. In some cases, in fact, a passive voice construction sounds awkward.

AWKWARD The reason for the open window was explained to Framton by Vera. [passive voice]

IMPROVED Vera explained to Framton the reason for the open window. [active voice]

SPECIAL PROBLEMS WITH VERBS

Sit and Set

(1) The verb *sit* **means "rest in an upright, seated position."** *Sit* **seldom takes an object.**

(2) The verb *set* **means "put (something) in a place."** *Set* **usually takes an object.**

BASE FORM	PRESENT PARTICIPLE	PAST	PAST PARTICIPLE
sit (rest)	(is) sitting	sat	(have) sat
set (put)	(is) setting	set	(have) set

EXAMPLES Billy **sits** on the sofa. [no object]
Billy **sets** his suitcase in a chair. [Billy sets what? *Suitcase* is the object.]

Lie and Lay

(1) The verb *lie* **means "rest," "recline," or "be in a place."** *Lie* **never takes an object.**

(2) The verb *lay* **means "put (something) in a place."** *Lay* **usually takes an object.**

Try It Out 🖎

Revise each of the following sentences by changing verbs in the passive voice to active voice.

1. The Gettysburg Address was delivered by Abraham Lincoln.
2. It has been admired by writers and imitated by speakers for more than one hundred years.
3. Those who died in the Civil War are honored by this short, eloquent speech.
4. The living are reminded of their "great task" by the address.
5. Freedom must be embraced and guarded by people.

BASE FORM	PRESENT PARTICIPLE	PAST	PAST PARTICIPLE
lie (rest)	(is) lying	lay	(have) lain
lay (put)	(is) laying	laid	(have) laid

EXAMPLES Zenta and Tokubei thought they **had lain** asleep for fifty years. [no object]

The boy **had laid** a nickel and an orange on the counter. [The boy had laid what? *Nickel* and *orange* are the objects.]

Rise and Raise

(1) The verb *rise* means "go up" or "get up." *Rise* never takes an object.

(2) The verb *raise* means "lift up" or "cause (something) to rise." *Raise* usually takes an object.

BASE FORM	PRESENT PARTICIPLE	PAST	PAST PARTICIPLE
rise (go up)	(is) rising	rose	(have) risen
raise (lift up)	(is) raising	raised	(have) raised

EXAMPLES The full moon **rose** slowly through the clouds last night. [no object]

The cheering crowd **raised** banners and signs over their heads. [The crowd raised what? *Banners* and *signs* are the objects.]

 QUICK CHECK 6

For each of the following sentences, choose the correct verb in parentheses.

EXAMPLE **1.** As they (*set, sat*) in the car, Papa said nothing.
        1. *sat*

1. Cardboard boxes full of their belongings (*sat, set*) on the floor.
2. He couldn't fall asleep and (*laid, lay*) wide awake in bed.
3. Roberto (*rose, raised*) the big boxes and (*lay, laid*) them in the car.
4. They started working each morning when the sun (*rose, raised*).
5. The sun had (*raised, risen*) high, and sweat poured off the workers.

COMPUTER NOTE Most word processors can help you check your writing to be sure that you've used verbs correctly. For example, a spell-checker feature will highlight misspelled verb forms such as *drownded* or *costed*. Style-checking software can point out inconsistent verb tense or overuse of passive voice. Such software may also highlight questionable uses of problem verb pairs such as *lie/lay* or *rise/raise*. Remember, though, that the computer is just a tool to help you improve your writing. As a writer, you need to make style and content choices to suit what you are writing.

4 USING PRONOUNS

CASE

Case is the form that a noun or a pronoun takes to show its use in a sentence. There are three cases: *nominative, objective,* and *possessive.* Unlike nouns, most personal pronouns have different forms for all three cases.

PERSONAL PRONOUNS		
SINGULAR		
NOMINATIVE	**OBJECTIVE**	**POSSESSIVE**
I you he, she, it	me you him, her, it	my, mine your, yours his, her, hers, its
PLURAL		
NOMINATIVE	**OBJECTIVE**	**POSSESSIVE**
we you they	us you them	our, ours your, yours their, theirs

> **NOTE** Many possessive pronouns (such as *my, your, his, her, its, our,* and *their*) are also called adjectives. Follow your teacher's directions in labeling these possessive forms.

The Nominative Case

4a. A subject of a verb is in the nominative case.

EXAMPLES **I** enjoy Gary Soto's stories. [*I* is the subject of *enjoy.*]
He and **she** sold tickets. [*He* and *she* are the subjects of *sold.*]

To choose the correct pronoun in a compound subject, try each form of the pronoun separately.

EXAMPLE: (*He, Him*) and (*I, me*) read "Paul Revere's Ride" to the class.
He read "Paul Revere's Ride" to the class.
Him read "Paul Revere's Ride" to the class.
I read "Paul Revere's Ride" to the class.
Me read "Paul Revere's Ride" to the class.

ANSWER: **He** and **I** read "Paul Revere's Ride" to the class.

4b. A *predicate nominative* is in the nominative case.

EXAMPLES The last one to leave was **he.** [*He* identifies the subject *one.*]

Do you think it may have been **they**? [*They* identifies the subject *it.*]

> **NOTE** To choose the correct form of a pronoun used as a predicate nominative, remember that the pronoun could be used as the subject.
>
> **EXAMPLE** The fastest runners are **she** and **I.** [predicate nominatives]
> **She** and **I** are the fastest runners. [subjects]

> ☞ For more about predicate nominatives, see page 785.

The Objective Case

4c. A *direct object* is in the objective case.

EXAMPLES   Ernie surprised **him.** [*Him* tells *whom* Ernie surprised.]
She read some Norse myths and enjoyed **them.** [*Them* tells *what* she enjoyed.]

To choose the correct pronoun in a compound direct object, try each form of the pronoun separately.

EXAMPLE: Charlie met Joe and (*he, him*) at the factory.
Charlie met *he* at the factory.
Charlie met *him* at the factory.

ANSWER: Charlie met Joe and **him** at the factory.

☞ For more about direct objects, see pages 783–784.

4d. An *indirect object* is in the objective case.

EXAMPLES   Mrs. Flowers lent **her** a book of poems. [*Her* tells *to whom* Mrs. Flowers lent a book.]
Lana takes good care of her cockatiel and often feeds **it** fresh spinach. [*It* tells *to what* Lana feeds spinach.]

To choose the correct pronoun in a compound indirect object, try each form of the pronoun separately.

EXAMPLE: Ebenezer Dorset sent Bill and (*he, him*) a note.
Ebenezer Dorset sent *he* a note.
Ebenezer Dorset sent *him* a note.

ANSWER: Ebenezer Dorset sent Bill and **him** a note.

☞ For more about indirect objects, see page 784.

4e. An *object of a preposition* is in the objective case.

EXAMPLES   Johnny wanted to stay with **them.** [object of the preposition *with*]
Laurie talked about **him** almost every day. [object of the preposition *about*]

To choose the correct pronoun when the object of a preposition is compound, try each form of the pronoun separately in the sentence.

EXAMPLE: Anne stood behind (*he, him*) and (*she, her*).
Anne stood behind *he.*
Anne stood behind *him.*
Anne stood behind *she.*
Anne stood behind *her.*

ANSWER: Anne stood behind **him** and **her.**

☞ For a list of prepositions, see page 745. For more about prepositional phrases, see pages 768 and 769–770.

☑ QUICK CHECK 1

For each of the sentences on the following page, choose the correct pronoun in parentheses.

EXAMPLE 1. Mrs. Sappleton's niece would entertain (*he, him*).
1. *him*

1. (*She, Her*) told (*him, he*) a story about a tragedy.
2. A very nervous gentleman was (*he, him*).
3. The story about (*they, them*) upset Mr. Nuttel.
4. Saki's story surprised (*us, we*) and amused (*I, me*).
5. The story was an inspiration to (*them, they*) and (*her, she*).

SPECIAL PRONOUN PROBLEMS

Who and Whom

The pronoun *who* has different forms in the nominative and objective cases. *Who* is the nominative form; *whom* is the objective form. When deciding whether to use *who* or *whom* in a question, follow these steps:

STEP 1: Rephrase the question as a statement.

STEP 2: Decide how the pronoun is used in the statement—as subject, predicate nominative, object of the verb, or object of a preposition.

STEP 3: Determine the case of the pronoun.

STEP 4: Select the correct form of the pronoun.

EXAMPLE: (*Who, Whom*) is that girl with Alfonso?

STEP 1: The statement is *That girl with Alfonso is* (*who, whom*).

STEP 2: The subject is *girl,* the verb is *is,* and the pronoun is a predicate nominative.

STEP 3: A pronoun used as a predicate nominative should be in the nominative case.

STEP 4: The nominative form is *who.*

ANSWER: **Who** is that girl with Alfonso?

When you are choosing between *who* or *whom* in a subordinate clause, follow these steps:

STEP 1: Find the subordinate clause.

STEP 2: Decide how the pronoun is used in the clause—as subject, predicate nominative, object of the verb, or object of a preposition.

STEP 3: Determine the case of the pronoun.

STEP 4: Select the correct form of the pronoun.

EXAMPLE: Mark Twain, (*who, whom*) I admire, wrote funny stories.

STEP 1: The subordinate clause is (*who, whom*) I admire.

STEP 2: In this clause, the subject is *I,* and the verb is *admire.* The pronoun is the direct object of the verb.

For more about subordinate clauses, see pages 775–778.

STEP 3: A pronoun used as a direct object should be in the objective case.

STEP 4: The objective form is *whom.*

ANSWER: Mark Twain, **whom** I admire, wrote interesting books.

Pronouns with Appositives

To help you choose which pronoun to use before an appositive, omit the appositive and try each form of the pronoun separately.

EXAMPLE: (*We, Us*) students have memorized the Gettysburg Address. [*Students* is the appositive.]

We have memorized the Gettysburg Address.
Us have memorized the Gettysburg Address.

ANSWER: **We** students have memorized the Gettysburg Address.

☞ For more about appositives, see page 773.

Reflexive Pronouns

Reflexive pronouns (such as *myself, himself,* and *yourselves*) can be used as objects.

EXAMPLE Brer Possum found **himself** in a dilemma. [*Himself* is the direct object and tells *whom* Brer Possum found in a dilemma.]

Do not use the nonstandard forms *hisself* and *theirself* or *theirselves* in place of *himself* and *themselves.*

EXAMPLE Zenta figured out all by **himself** [*not* hisself] what was going on.

Do not use a reflexive pronoun where a personal pronoun is needed.

EXAMPLE Leon and **I** [*not* myself] prefer hiking to rock climbing.

☞ For more about reflexive pronouns, see page 739.

✓ QUICK CHECK 2

For each of the following sentences, choose the correct pronoun in parentheses.

EXAMPLE I. Mr. Nuttel need not wait by (*himself, hisself*).
I. *himself*

1. (*Who, Whom*) were they waiting for?
2. Mrs. Sappleton, (*who, whom*) was busy, would be down shortly.
3. (*We, Us*) girls wondered about the meanings of the characters' names.
4. Yes, they seemed meaningful to (*we, us*) boys, too.
5. Trish and (*myself, I*) will ask Ms. Reynolds about the names.

COMPUTER NOTE A computer can help you find pronoun problems in your writing. For example, a spelling checker will catch nonstandard forms such as *hisself* and *theirself.* To find other problems, you can use the "Search" command. If you sometimes use reflexive pronouns in place of personal pronouns, use the "Search" command to find each reflexive pronoun. Then, examine each pronoun to make certain that it is used correctly.

5 USING MODIFIERS

COMPARISON OF MODIFIERS

A *modifier* is a word, a phrase, or a clause that describes or limits the meaning of another word. Two kinds of modifiers—*adjectives* and *adverbs*—take different forms when they are used to compare things.

5a. The three degrees of comparison of modifiers are *positive, comparative,* and *superlative.*

POSITIVE	weak	proudly	likely
COMPARATIVE	weaker	more proudly	more likely
SUPERLATIVE	weakest	most proudly	most likely

Regular Comparison

(1) Most one-syllable modifiers form their comparative and superlative degrees by adding *–er* and *–est.*

POSITIVE	near	bright	brave
COMPARATIVE	nearer	brighter	braver
SUPERLATIVE	nearest	brightest	bravest

(2) Some two-syllable modifiers form their comparative and superlative degrees by adding *–er* and *–est.* Other two-syllable modifiers form their comparative and superlative degrees by using *more* and *most.*

POSITIVE	gentle	healthy	clearly
COMPARATIVE	gentler	healthier	more clearly
SUPERLATIVE	gentlest	healthiest	most clearly

(3) Modifiers that have three or more syllables form their comparative and superlative degrees by using *more* and *most.*

POSITIVE	important	happily	accurately
COMPARATIVE	more important	more happily	more accurately
SUPERLATIVE	most important	most happily	most accurately

Irregular Comparison

Some modifiers do not form their comparative and superlative degrees by using the regular methods.

POSITIVE	bad	good *or* well	many *or* much
COMPARATIVE	worse	better	more
SUPERLATIVE	worst	best	most

<aside>

NOTE To show decreasing comparisons, all modifiers form their comparative and superlative degrees with *less* and *least.*

POSITIVE
clear
neatly

COMPARATIVE
less clear
less neatly

SUPERLATIVE
least clear
least neatly

</aside>

QUICK CHECK I

Give the comparative and superlative forms for each of the following modifiers.

EXAMPLE **1.** happy
  1. *happier, happiest*

1. lightly **4.** silently **7.** easy **9.** furiously
2. luxurious **5.** many **8.** bad **10.** safe
3. well **6.** tall

Uses of Comparative and Superlative Forms

5b. Use the comparative degree when comparing two things. Use the superlative degree when comparing more than two things.

COMPARATIVE Squeaky is **faster** than Gretchen.
  Luisa can perform the gymnastic routine **more gracefully** than I.
SUPERLATIVE Mount Everest is the world's **highest** mountain.
  Of all the children in the class, Charles behaves the **most aggressively.**

Avoid the common mistake of using the superlative degree to compare two things.

EXAMPLE After reading both stories, I think "The Landlady" is the **more** [*not* most] interesting one.

5c. Include the word *other* or *else* when comparing a member of a group with the rest of the group.

NONSTANDARD Smiley's frog can jump farther than any frog in Calaveras County. [Smiley's frog is one of the frogs in Calaveras County and cannot jump farther than itself.]

STANDARD Smiley's frog can jump farther than any **other** frog in Calaveras County.

5d. Avoid using double comparisons and double negatives.

A **double comparison** is the use of both –er and *more* (*less*) or both –est and *most* (*least*) to form a comparison. A comparison should be formed in only one of these two ways, not both.

EXAMPLE Matsuzo is **younger** [*not* more younger] than Zenta.

A **double negative** is the use of two negative words to express one negative idea.

EXAMPLE I **can't** ever [*not* can't never] remember what the main character's name is.

Common Negative Words

barely	never	none	nothing
hardly	no	no one	nowhere
neither	nobody	not (–n't)	scarcely

 QUICK CHECK 2

For each of the following sentences, correct the error in comparison.

EXAMPLE   **I.** Brer Possum wasn't the most smartest critter.
          I. *Brer Possum wasn't the smartest critter.*

1. Apparently, Brer Snake was more smarter than Brer Possum.
2. Of the two, Brer Possum was the kindest.
3. Surely, Brer Snake was meaner than any critter in the woods.
4. He didn't seem to care about nobody.
5. He wasn't grateful, neither!

PLACEMENT OF MODIFIERS

5e. **Place modifying words, phrases, and clauses as close as possible to the words they modify.**

Prepositional Phrases

 For more about prepositions and prepositional phrases, see pages 745 and 769–771.

MISPLACED   I read a suspenseful story that Edgar Allan Poe wrote at lunch today..

    CLEAR   **At lunch today** I read a suspenseful story that Edgar Allan Poe wrote.

Avoid placing a prepositional phrase where it can modify more than one word. Place the phrase so that it clearly modifies only one word.

MISPLACED   Gabriela said **in the morning** she was going home.
           [Does the phrase modify *said* or *was going*?]

    CLEAR   Gabriela said she was going home **in the morning.**
           [The phrase modifies *was going*.]

    CLEAR   **In the morning** Gabriela said she was going home.
           [The phrase modifies *said*.]

Participial Phrases

 For more about participial phrases, see page 771.

MISPLACED   The narrator opened the door of the old man's room obsessed with the "vulture eye."

    CLEAR   **Obsessed with the "vulture eye,"** the narrator opened the door of the old man's room.

A participial phrase that does not modify any word in the sentence is a **dangling participial phrase.** To correct a dangling phrase, supply a word that the phrase can modify, or add a subject and verb to the phrase.

DANGLING	Wishing for the money, the monkey's paw twisted in his hands.
CLEAR	Wishing for the money, **he** felt the monkey's paw twist in his hands.
CLEAR	**When he wished** for the money, the monkey's paw twisted in his hands.

Clauses

MISPLACED	My brother saw a hawk circling as he looked up.
CLEAR	**As my brother looked up,** he saw a hawk circling.

✓ *QUICK CHECK 3*

Some of the following sentences contain a misplaced modifier or a dangling participial phrase. Correct each error. If a sentence is correct, write *C*.

EXAMPLE	I.	Brer Possum always helped others with kindness.
	I.	*With kindness, Brer Possum always helped others.*

1. The possum saw a snake walking in the woods.
2. The snake was lying at the bottom of a hole which was trapped.
3. Calling for help, Brer Possum went to rescue the snake.
4. Brer Possum was bitten by the snake when he tried to help.
5. Reading the folk tale, the possum learns a lesson.

6 PHRASES

6a. A *phrase* is a group of related words that is used as a single part of speech and does not contain a verb and its subject.

VERB PHRASE	should have been told [no subject]
PREPOSITIONAL PHRASE	for my sister and me [no subject or verb]

THE PREPOSITIONAL PHRASE

6b. A *prepositional phrase* includes a preposition, a noun or a pronoun called the *object of the preposition,* and any modifiers of that object.

EXAMPLES Robert Frost was born **in San Francisco.**
The note **from Johnny's father** surprised Sam and Bill.

A computer can help you find and correct problems with modifiers. A spelling checker can find nonstandard forms such as *baddest* and *carefuller.* However, you will need to examine phrase and clause modifiers yourself. If a phrase or a clause is misplaced, you can select it and move the whole phrase or clause closer to the word it modifies.

☞ For more about clauses, see Part 7: Clauses.

☞ For a list of commonly used prepositions, see page 745.

The Adjective Phrase

6c. An *adjective phrase* is a prepositional phrase that modifies a noun or a pronoun.

An adjective phrase tells *what kind* or *which one.*

EXAMPLES Wang Wei was a talented painter **of landscapes.** [What kind of painter?]

Mike is the one **with the moustache.** [Which one?]

An adjective phrase always follows the word it modifies. That word may be the object of another prepositional phrase.

EXAMPLE It is a poem **about a boy and a girl on their first date.** [The phrase *about a boy and a girl* modifies the noun *poem.* The phrase *on their first date* modifies the objects *boy* and *girl.*]

The Adverb Phrase

6d. An *adverb phrase* is a prepositional phrase that modifies a verb, an adjective, or an adverb.

An adverb phrase tells *how, when, where, why,* or *to what extent* (that is, *how long, how many,* or *how far*).

EXAMPLES She treated him **with respect.** [How?]

The painting hangs **over the fireplace.** [Where?]

They arrived early **in the morning.** [When?]

He had been a samurai **for a long time.** [How long?]

An adverb phrase may come before or after the word it modifies.

EXAMPLES The Sneve family lived in Iowa **for many years.**

For many years the Sneve family lived in Iowa.

An adverb phrase may be followed by an adjective phrase that modifies the object in the adverb phrase.

EXAMPLE **In her poems about the Southwest,** Leslie Marmon Silko uses images that appeal to the senses. [*In her poems* modifies the verb *uses. About the Southwest* modifies the noun *poems.*]

✓ QUICK CHECK I

Identify the prepositional phrase or phrases in each sentence in the following paragraph. Then, label each phrase as either an *adjective phrase* or an *adverb phrase.* Give the word (or words) the phrase modifies.

EXAMPLE [1] Who is the author of "Paul Revere's Ride"?

    I. *of "Paul Revere's Ride"—adjective phrase—author*

[1] One of the most famous American historical events is the ride by Paul Revere through Middlesex. [2] In his poem, Henry Wadsworth

---

 NOTE More than one adjective phrase may modify the same word.

EXAMPLE The box **of old magazines in the closet** is full. [The phrases *of old magazines* and *in the closet* modify the noun *box.*]

 NOTE More than one adverb phrase may modify the same word or words.

EXAMPLE Yoshiko Uchida was born **in Alameda, California, in 1921.** [Both *in Alameda, California,* and *in 1921* modify the verb phrase *was born.*]

Longfellow immortalizes this heroic ride. [3] Across the river, Revere had waited for the signal about the British. [4] When it came, he rode into the night and called to the people to warn them. [5] With his vivid description of sights and sounds, Longfellow almost brings Revere's ride to life.

VERBALS AND VERBAL PHRASES

A *verbal* is a form of a verb used as a noun, an adjective, or an adverb. There are three kinds of verbals: the *participle,* the *gerund,* and the *infinitive.*

The Participle

6e. A *participle* is a verb form that can be used as an adjective.

(1) *Present participles* end in *–ing.*

EXAMPLES   The **creaking** floorboard bothered Anne.
Miep's news was **encouraging.**

(2) Most *past participles* end in *–d* or *–ed.* Others are irregularly formed.

EXAMPLES   The **oiled** hinge works smoothly.
Charlie Parker, **known** as Bird, was a talented musician.

☞ For lists of irregular past participles, see pages 755–757.

The Participial Phrase

6f. A *participial phrase* consists of a participle and all of the words related to the participle. The entire phrase is used as an adjective.

A participle may be modified by an adverb and may also have a complement.

EXAMPLES   **Defending Jabez Stone,** Daniel Webster proved again that he was a persuasive speaker. [The participial phrase modifies *Daniel Webster.* The noun *Jabez Stone* is the direct object of the participle *defending.*]
Squeaky noticed him **running swiftly alongside the fence.** [The participial phrase modifies *him.* The adverb *swiftly* and the adverb phrase *alongside the fence* modify the participle *running.*]

☞ For more about placement of participial phrases, see pages 768–769.

The Gerund

6g. A *gerund* is a verb form ending in *–ing* that is used as a noun.

SUBJECT	**Skating** can be good exercise.
PREDICATE NOMINATIVE	My hobby is **collecting** baseball cards.
OBJECT OF PREPOSITION	Lock the door before **leaving.**
DIRECT OBJECT	Did they enjoy **singing**?

The Gerund Phrase

6h. A *gerund phrase* consists of a gerund and all the words related to the gerund.

A gerund may be modified by an adverb and may have a complement. Because a gerund functions as a noun, it may also be modified by an adjective.

EXAMPLES **Minding Raymond** is Squeaky's only responsibility. [The gerund phrase is the subject of the verb *is*. The noun *Raymond* is the direct object of the gerund *minding*.]

The murderer heard **the beating of the old man's heart.** [The gerund phrase is the direct object of the verb *heard*. The adjective *the* and the adjective phrase *of the old man's heart* modify the gerund *beating*.]

The Infinitive

6i. An *infinitive* is a verb form that can be used as a noun, an adjective, or an adverb. An infinitive usually begins with **to**.

NOUNS **To learn** is **to grow.** [*To learn* is the subject of *is; to grow* is the predicate nominative referring to *to learn*.]

Squeaky likes **to run.** [*To run* is the direct object of the verb *likes*.]

ADJECTIVES He always has time **to talk.** [*To talk* modifies the noun *time*.]

If you like mystery stories, "The Inn of Lost Time" is a terrific one **to read.** [*To read* modifies the pronoun *one*.]

ADVERBS The landlady was eager **to please.** [*To please* modifies the adjective *eager*.]

Tokubei and Zenta stopped at the inn **to rest.** [*To rest* modifies the verb *stopped*.]

The Infinitive Phrase

6j. An *infinitive phrase* consists of an infinitive and its modifiers and complements.

An infinitive may be modified by an adjective or an adverb and may also have a complement. The entire infinitive phrase may act as a noun, an adjective, or an adverb.

EXAMPLES **To escape without a trace** was impossible. [The infinitive phrase is a noun used as the subject of the verb *was*. The prepositional phrase *without a trace* modifies the infinitive.]

NOTE The word *to* followed by a noun or a pronoun (*to class, to them, to the dance*) is a prepositional phrase, not an infinitive. Be careful not to confuse infinitives with prepositional phrases beginning with *to*.

EXAMPLE Matthew wants **to talk** [infinitive] **to Kim** [prepositional phrase].

Singing to them was one way **to boost their spirits.**
[The infinitive phrase is an adjective modifying *way*.
The noun phrase *their spirits* is the direct object of
the infinitive *to boost*.]

The crowd grew quiet **to hear President Lincoln.**
[The infinitive phrase is an adverb modifying the
adjective *quiet*. The noun *President Lincoln* is the
direct object of the infinitive *to hear*.]

☞ For more on com-
plements, see Part 9:
Complements.

☑ QUICK CHECK 2

Each of the following sentences contains at least one verbal phrase.
Identify each verbal phrase as *participial, gerund,* or *infinitive.*

EXAMPLE   1. Do you know the story of the Israelites fleeing Egypt?
    1. *fleeing Egypt—participial phrase*

1. Who found baby Moses floating in the river?
2. Saved by the Pharaoh's daughter, Moses was taken to live at court.
3. Later, Moses went to the Pharaoh, warning him of the Lord's anger.
4. For decades, toiling for the Pharaoh had been the Israelites' fate.
5. To hear the song "Go Down, Moses" is to feel their sorrow.

APPOSITIVES AND APPOSITIVE PHRASES

6k.   An *appositive* is a noun or a pronoun placed beside
another noun or pronoun to identify or explain it.

EXAMPLES   The poet **Langston Hughes** wrote "Refugee in America."
[The noun *Langston Hughes* identifies the noun *poet*.]

The explorers saw a strange animal, **something** with
fur and a bill like a duck's. [The pronoun *something*
refers to the noun *animal*.]

Two or more nouns or pronouns may be used as a compound appositive.

EXAMPLE   John James Audubon, an **artist** and a **naturalist,** painted
pictures of birds in their habitats. [The nouns *artist* and
naturalist explain the noun *John James Audubon*.]

6l.   An *appositive phrase* consists of an appositive and its
modifiers.

EXAMPLES   Dana was always talking about Charles, **one of her
classmates.** [The adjective phrase *of her classmates*
modifies the appositive *one*.]

Black Hawk, **a famous chief of the Sauk,** fought hard
for the freedom of his people. [The article *a*, the adjective *famous,* and the adjective phrase *of the Sauk*
modify the appositive *chief*.]

Identify the appositives or appositive phrases in each of the following sentences. Give the word or words each appositive or appositive phrase identifies.

EXAMPLE   **1.** Read "Go Down, Moses," a favorite spiritual.

          1. *a favorite spiritual—"Go Down, Moses"*

1. Moses, Charlton Heston in the film, discovers his true identity.
2. He is really one of the Israelites, slaves to the Pharaoh's whims.
3. Moses decides to live with his true family, members of one tribe of the Israelites.
4. The Pharaoh, a father figure for Moses, rejects him.
5. Moses' name is removed from public record—all the monuments and scrolls—in Egypt.

Revising Choppy Sentences

Knowing how to use the different kinds of phrases can help you avoid writing short, choppy sentences. Simply turn at least one sentence into a phrase, and insert the phrase into another sentence.

CHOPPY	Roald Dahl was born in 1916. His birthplace was Wales.
PREPOSITIONAL PHRASE	Roald Dahl was born **in Wales** in 1916.
CHOPPY	Samuel Clemens wrote *Adventures of Huckleberry Finn*. Samuel Clemens is better known as Mark Twain.
PARTICIPIAL PHRASE	Samuel Clemens, **better known as Mark Twain,** wrote *Adventures of Huckleberry Finn*.
CHOPPY	Vera is Mrs. Sappleton's niece. She tells Mr. Nuttel a story.
APPOSITIVE PHRASE	Vera, **Mrs. Sappleton's niece,** tells Mr. Nuttel a story.

Try It Out

The following pairs of sentences are choppy. Revise each pair by turning one sentence into a phrase and inserting the phrase into the other sentence.

1. Casey was not at bat that day. Casey was known to all as an exceptionally strong player.
2. Jimmy Blake was up first. Blake was not a strong hitter.
3. He hit the ball hard. He ripped the hide from it.
4. The crowd roared. The crowd was in the bleachers.
5. Casey behaved arrogantly. He let two good balls go by.

7 CLAUSES

7a. A *clause* is a group of words that contains a verb and its subject and is used as a part of a sentence.

The two kinds of clauses are the *independent clause* and the *subordinate clause*.

THE INDEPENDENT CLAUSE

7b. An *independent* (or *main*) *clause* expresses a complete thought and can stand by itself as a sentence.

              S   V

EXAMPLES   Amy Ling moved to the United States.

                 S   V

              This poem is about her grandmother.

THE SUBORDINATE CLAUSE

7c. A *subordinate* (or *dependent*) *clause* does not express a complete thought and cannot stand alone as a sentence.

                S   V

EXAMPLES   when she was six years old

               S   V

            whom Ling visited in Taiwan

The meaning of a subordinate clause is complete only when the clause is attached to an independent clause.

EXAMPLE   Amy Ling moved to the United States **when she was six years old.**

☑ *QUICK CHECK 1*

Identify each of the following groups of words as an *independent clause* or a *subordinate clause*.

EXAMPLE   **1.** if you have read Amy Ling's poem "Grandma Ling"

              1. *subordinate clause*

1. answer these questions
2. as soon as she met her grandmother
3. before she traveled to Taiwan
4. because Ling could not speak her grandmother's language
5. her footsteps were soft

The Adjective Clause

7d. An *adjective clause* is a subordinate clause that modifies a noun or a pronoun.

         ADJECTIVE   an **intelligent** man
    ADJECTIVE PHRASE   a man **of intelligence**
    ADJECTIVE CLAUSE   a man **who is intelligent**

An adjective clause usually follows the word it modifies and tells *which one* or *what kind.*

EXAMPLES   Cheryl showed them the moccasins **that her grand-father had made.** [Which moccasins?]

Helen Keller was a remarkable woman **who could neither see nor hear.** [What kind of woman?]

An adjective clause is usually introduced by a ***relative pronoun,*** a word that relates an adjective clause to the word the clause modifies.

EXAMPLES   "The Tell-Tale Heart," **which tells the story of a murderer's guilt,** is great to read aloud. [The relative pronoun *which* begins the adjective clause and relates it to the compound noun *"The Tell-Tale Heart."*]

Everything **that could be done** was done. [*That* relates the adjective clause to the pronoun *everything.*]

One author **whose stories I enjoy** is Amy Ling. [*Whose* relates the adjective clause to the noun *author.*]

In addition to relating a subordinate clause to the rest of the sentence, a relative pronoun also has a function in the subordinate clause.

EXAMPLES   Is he the one **who wrote "The Moustache"**? [*Who* functions as subject of the verb *wrote.*]

She is a friend **on whom you can always depend.** [*Whom* functions as object of the preposition *on.*]

 QUICK CHECK 2

Identify the adjective clause in each of the following sentences. Underline the relative pronoun, and give the word or words the adjective clause refers to.

EXAMPLE   1. Davy Crockett, who is a legend, was born in Tennessee.

1. *who is a legend—Davy Crockett*

1. Irwin Shapiro's "Davy Is Born," which is in this book, is a tall tale.
2. Isn't it the story that is full of slang and dialect?
3. Mr. Shapiro, whose imagination is sizable, is an expert on dialect.
4. Was Davy Crockett one of the men who fought at the Alamo?
5. Crockett's father, whom Shapiro mentions, must have been proud.

The Adverb Clause

7e. An *adverb clause* is a subordinate clause that modifies a verb, an adjective, or an adverb.

ADVERB	You may sit **anywhere.**
ADVERB PHRASE	You may sit **in any chair.**
ADVERB CLAUSE	You may sit **wherever you wish.**

For a list of relative pronouns, see page 739. For information on when to set off adjective clauses with commas, see page 799.

NOTE The relative pronouns *who* and *whom* are used to refer to people only. The relative pronoun *that* is used to refer both to people and to things. The relative pronoun *which* is used to refer to things only.

NOTE An adjective clause may be introduced by a relative adverb such as *when* or *where.*

EXAMPLES He finally returned to the cabin **where he had left Mary in charge of his children.**
The time period **when dinosaurs ruled** lasted millions of years.

An adverb clause tells *where, when, how, why, to what extent,* or *under what condition.*

EXAMPLES   Put that package **wherever you can find room for it.**
[Where?]

Tokubei became furious **when he learned the truth.**
[When?]

My new friend and I talk **as if we've known each other for a long time.** [How?]

Because he dreads the cold grave, Sam McGee requests to be cremated. [Why?]

Johnny caused Sam and Bill more trouble **than they had expected.** [To what extent?]

If he sees two lanterns in the belfry, what will Paul Revere know? [Under what condition?]

Notice in these examples that an adverb clause does not always follow the word it modifies. When an adverb clause begins a sentence, the clause is followed by a comma.

An adverb clause is introduced by a ***subordinating conjunction***— a word that shows the relationship between the adverb clause and the word or words that the clause modifies.

☞ For more information about using commas with adverb clauses, see page 801.

Common Subordinating Conjunctions

after	as though	once	when
although	because	since	whenever
as	before	so that	where
as if	even if	than	wherever
as long as	how	though	whether
as much as	if	unless	while
as soon as	in order that	until	

 QUICK CHECK 3

Identify the adverb clause in each of the following sentences. In each adverb clause, circle the subordinating conjunction, and underline the subject once and the verb twice.

EXAMPLE   **1.** I laughed out loud when Uncle Roarious used a rake for a comb.

1. (when) Uncle Roarious <u>used</u> a rake for a comb

1. Although kerosene oil is toxic, Uncle Roarious drank it.
2. Shapiro's Davy Crockett could talk when he was still a baby.
3. They planted Davy so that the child would grow.
4. While he was in the earth, the wind blew on him.
5. Davy talked as though he were a grown man.

The Noun Clause

7f. A *noun clause* is a subordinate clause used as a noun.

A noun clause may be used as a subject, a complement (predicate nominative, direct object, indirect object), or an object of a preposition.

SUBJECT	**That Jabez Stone is unlucky** is evident.
PREDICATE NOMINATIVE	A three-year extension was **what the stranger offered Jabez.**
DIRECT OBJECT	The judges determined **who won.**
INDIRECT OBJECT	The sheriff gave **whoever volunteered to help in the search** a flashlight.
OBJECT OF A PREPOSITION	He did not agree to **what the kidnappers demanded.**

> ### Common Introductory Words for Noun Clauses
>
> | | | |
> |---|---|---|
> | that | which | whoever |
> | what | whichever | whom |
> | whatever | who | whomever |

In many cases, the word that introduces a noun clause has another function within the clause.

EXAMPLES   A trophy will be given to **whoever wins the race.**
[*Whoever* is the subject of the verb *wins*.]
Did anyone tell Alfonso **what he should do**? [*What* is the direct object of the verb *should do*.]
Their complaint was **that Charlie had changed.** [The word *that* introduces the noun clause but has no other function in the clause.]

QUICK CHECK 4

Identify the noun clause in each of the following sentences. Tell whether the noun clause is a *subject*, a *predicate nominative*, a *direct object*, an *indirect object*, or an *object of a preposition*.

EXAMPLE   **1.** Laurie could not accept that he had done something bad.
1. *that he had done something bad*—direct object

1. Whatever went wrong must be someone else's fault.
2. Laurie's mother does not know that he has been making up stories about Charles.
3. Charles certainly gives whomever he can find a hard time.
4. The whole family is quite amused by what Laurie said about Charles.
5. Charles's true identity was what they didn't know.

For guidelines on using *who* and *whom* correctly, see pages 764–765. The same guidelines apply to *whoever* and *whomever*.

THE SENTENCE

8a. A *sentence* is a group of words that has a subject and a verb and expresses a complete thought.

A sentence begins with a capital letter and ends with a period, a question mark, or an exclamation point.

EXAMPLES   He told a story about Urashima Taro**.**
He **Have** you read the novel *Shane***?**
He **What** a dangerous mission it must have been**!**

> ☞ For information about end marks, see pages 797–798.

Sentence or Sentence Fragment?

When a group of words either does not contain a subject and a verb or does not express a complete thought, it is a **sentence fragment.**

SENTENCE FRAGMENT	The protagonist of the story. [What about the protagonist of the story?]
SENTENCE	The protagonist of the story is unnamed.
SENTENCE FRAGMENT	After reading the poem. [Who read the poem? What happened afterward?]
SENTENCE	After reading the poem, we asked the teacher several questions.
SENTENCE FRAGMENT	While Smiley was in the swamp. [What happened while Smiley was in the swamp?]
SENTENCE	While Smiley was in the swamp, the stranger filled the frog with quail shot.

COMPUTER NOTE   Some style-checking programs can identify and highlight sentence fragments. Such programs are useful, but they aren't perfect. You still need to check each sentence yourself to be sure it has a subject and a verb and expresses a complete thought.

✓ *QUICK CHECK 1*

Tell whether each group of words is a *sentence* or a *sentence fragment.* If the word group is a sentence, correct it by adding a capital letter and end punctuation. If the word group is a sentence fragment, correct it by adding words, a capital letter, and end punctuation to make a complete sentence.

EXAMPLE   **1.** reading Robert Frost's poem "A Time to Talk"
1. *sentence fragment—I am reading Robert Frost's poem "A Time to Talk."*

1. a friend slowing down his horse on the road
2. he calls out
3. using a hoe for work on the hills near his home
4. to the walls made of stone comes the man
5. does he have time for a visit

THE SUBJECT AND THE PREDICATE

A sentence consists of two parts: a *subject* and a *predicate*.

8b. A *subject* **tells whom or what the sentence is about. The** *predicate* **tells something about the subject.**

Subject	Predicate

EXAMPLE   Laurie's mother / went to the meeting.

Finding the Subject

Usually, the subject comes before the predicate. Sometimes, however, the subject may appear elsewhere in the sentence. To find the subject of a sentence, ask *Who?* or *What?* before the predicate.

EXAMPLES   At the top of the tree, **a bird's nest** sat. [What sat? a bird's nest]

Lying beside the fence was **the broken chain.** [What was lying? the broken chain]

Does **Casey** strike out? [Who does strike out? Casey]

The Simple Subject

8c. A *simple subject* **is the main word or group of words in the complete subject.**

A ***complete subject*** consists of all the words that name and describe whom or what the sentence is about.

EXAMPLES   The long **trip** across the desert was finally over. [The complete subject is *the long trip across the desert.*]

One of my favorite poems is "The Cremation of Sam McGee." [The complete subject is *one of my favorite poems.*]

"The Cremation of Sam McGee" is a poem by Robert W. Service. [*"The Cremation of Sam McGee"* is both the simple subject and the complete subject.]

✓ QUICK CHECK 2

Identify the *complete subject* and the *simple subject* in each sentence of the following paragraph.

EXAMPLE   [1] Has your teacher read "Mrs. Flowers" yet?

   1. *complete subject—your teacher; simple subject—teacher*

[1] Maya Angelou's "Mrs. Flowers" characterizes a gentle woman. [2] Mrs. Flowers is a woman of great dignity and grace. [3] Out of kindness and genuine liking, she befriends young Marguerite. [4] A mutual love for literature links the two. [5] The warm respect of Mrs. Flowers' friendship gives Marguerite new self-esteem.

> **NOTE**   The subject of a sentence is *never* part of a prepositional phrase.
>
> **EXAMPLE**   The **tips** of the rabbit's ears were sticking up behind the large cabbage. [What were sticking up? *Tips* were sticking up.]

> **NOTE**   In this book, the term *subject* refers to the simple subject unless otherwise indicated.

The Simple Predicate, or Verb

8d. A *simple predicate, or verb,* is the main word or group of words in the complete predicate.

A **complete predicate** consists of a verb and all the words that describe the verb and complete its meaning.

EXAMPLES   The trees **sagged** beneath the weight of the ice. [The complete predicate is *sagged beneath the weight of the ice.*]

After the race, everyone **congratulated** Squeaky. [The complete predicate is *after the race . . . congratulated Squeaky.*]

In the roaring furnace **sat** Sam McGee. [The complete predicate is *in the roaring furnace sat.*]

The Verb Phrase

A simple predicate may be a one-word verb, or it may be a verb phrase. A **verb phrase** consists of a main verb and its helping verbs.

EXAMPLES   Our class **is reading** *The Diary of Anne Frank.*
Have you **done** your homework yet?

☞ For more about verb phrases, see page 743.

 **QUICK CHECK 3**

Identify the *complete predicate* and the *verb* in each of the following sentences. Keep in mind that parts of the complete predicate may come before and after the complete subject.

EXAMPLE   **1.** For no apparent reason, Mrs. Flowers asks Marguerite in.

1. *complete predicate—For no apparent reason . . . asks Marguerite in; verb—asks*

1. Surprisingly, she has made cookies especially for Marguerite.
2. Marguerite is delighted with the attention.
3. After their talk, Marguerite goes home.
4. She reads *A Tale of Two Cities* aloud.
5. How did the words of Charles Dickens help her?

The Compound Subject

8e. A *compound subject* consists of two or more connected subjects that have the same verb. The usual connecting word is *and, or,* or *nor.*

EXAMPLES   Traveling together were **Zenta** and **Matsuzo.**
Smoked **turkey,** baked **ham,** or roast **goose** will be the main course for Thanksgiving dinner.
Neither the **trousers** nor the **shoes** that I want are on sale yet.

The Compound Verb

8f. A *compound verb* consists of two or more verbs that have the same subject. A connecting word—usually *and, or,* or *but*—is used between the verbs.

EXAMPLES   Mr. Nuttel **sat** down and **waited** for Mrs. Sappleton.
              We **can go** forward, **go** back, or **stay** right here.

Both the subject and the verb of a sentence may be compound.

                 S   S   V   V
EXAMPLE   The **captain** and the **crew battled** the storm and **hoped** for better weather. [The captain battled and hoped, and the crew battled and hoped.]

 QUICK CHECK 4

Identify all *compound subjects* and *compound verbs* in the following sentences.

EXAMPLE   **1.** Mike and his sister had planned a visit to their grandmother.
              1. *compound subject—Mike, sister*

1. However, his sister wanted to go but fell ill.
2. Will his mother inspect his clothes or question him about his moustache?
3. Mike and his mother love and respect each other.
4. She does not like the moustache yet says little about it.
5. Mike's grandmother and the movie actress Ethel Barrymore look and sound alike.

Try It Out ✎

Use a compound subject or a compound verb to combine each of the following sets of short sentences.

1. Grandmother greets her grandson. She thinks he is someone else.
2. According to Grandmother, blue jays come to the bird feeder. Chickadees come there, too.
3. A nurse enters the room. She offers Grandmother some juice.
4. Orange juice does not interest her. Neither does cranberry juice or grape juice.
5. Mike should tell Grandmother the truth. He cannot.

Using Compound Subjects and Verbs to Combine Ideas

Sometimes a writer will repeat a simple subject or verb for special emphasis. Often, though, such repetition serves no purpose. Using compound subjects and verbs, you can combine ideas and reduce wordiness in your writing. Compare these examples.

WORDY   Roald Dahl wrote eerie short stories. Saki and W. W. Jacobs were two other authors who wrote eerie short stories, too.
REVISED   **Roald Dahl, Saki, and W. W. Jacobs** wrote eerie short stories.

WORDY   Toni Cade Bambara studied mime and took acting lessons. She also worked in a hospital.
REVISED   Toni Cade Bambara **studied** mime, **took** acting lessons, and **worked** in a hospital.

9 COMPLEMENTS

RECOGNIZING COMPLEMENTS

9a. A *complement* is a word or a group of words that completes the meaning of a verb.

INCOMPLETE	Mr. White held [*what?*]
COMPLETE	Mr. White held the **paw.**
INCOMPLETE	Marguerite thanked [*whom?*]
COMPLETE	Marguerite thanked **her.**
INCOMPLETE	Squeaky is [*what?*]
COMPLETE	Squeaky is **confident.**

As you can see, a complement may be a noun, a pronoun, or an adjective. A complement is never in a prepositional phrase.

OBJECT OF A PREPOSITION	Benjamin is studying for his math **test.**
COMPLEMENT	Benjamin is studying his math **notes.**

 **QUICK CHECK I**

Identify the *subject,* the *verb,* and the *complement* in each sentence in the following paragraph. [Remember: A complement is never in a prepositional phrase.]

EXAMPLE [1] Sandra Cisneros is a writer.
    1. *subject—Sandra Cisneros; verb—is; complement—writer*

[1] She wrote "A Smart Cookie." [2] In the story, the writer describes her mother. [3] Her mother is quite skillful. [4] Yet, the older woman seems sad about many events in her life. [5] Nevertheless, she gives Esperanza her best advice.

DIRECT OBJECTS

9b. A *direct object* is a noun or a pronoun that receives the action of the verb or that shows the result of the action. A direct object tells *what* or *whom* after a transitive verb.

EXAMPLE We watched a **performance** of *The Diary of Anne Frank.* [The noun *performance* receives the action of the transitive verb *watched* and tells *what* we watched.]

A direct object never follows a linking verb.

LINKING VERB William Wordsworth **became** poet laureate of England in 1843. [The verb *became* does not express action; therefore, it has no direct object.]

NOTE An adverb is never a complement.

ADVERB The frog is **outside.** [*Outside* modifies the verb by telling where the frog is.]

COMPLEMENT The frog is **heavy.** [The adjective *heavy* modifies the subject by describing the frog.]

☞ For more about transitive verbs, see page 742.

☞ For more about linking verbs, see pages 742–743.

For more about prepositional phrases, see pages 745 and 769–771.

NOTE Direct objects and indirect objects may be compound.

EXAMPLES Mrs. Flowers served **tea cookies** and **lemonade.**

The sergeant major showed **Mr. White** and his **family** the monkey's paw.

A direct object is never part of a prepositional phrase.

OBJECT OF A PREPOSITION They walked for **miles** in the Japanese countryside. [*Miles* is not the direct object of the verb *walked;* it is the object of the preposition *for.*]

INDIRECT OBJECTS

9c. An *indirect object* is a noun or a pronoun that comes between the verb and the direct object and tells *to what* or *to whom* or *for what* or *for whom* the action of the verb is done.

EXAMPLE Smiley gave the **stranger** a frog. [The noun *stranger* tells *to whom* Smiley gave a frog.]

Linking verbs do not have indirect objects. Also, an indirect object is never in a prepositional phrase.

LINKING VERB Her mother **was** a collector of rare books.

INDIRECT OBJECT She sent her **mother** a rare book.

OBJECT OF A PREPOSITION She sent a rare book to her **mother.**

 QUICK CHECK 2

Identify the *direct objects* and the *indirect objects* in the following sentences. [Note: Not every sentence has an indirect object.]

EXAMPLE **1.** Who gave Joe Iron Shell a ride?
1. *indirect object—Joe Iron Shell; direct object—ride*

1. Grandfather had given Cheryl moccasins.
2. Didn't he teach his grandson Sioux chants?
3. The grandchildren loved him for these gifts and more.
4. Yet, they did not show friends his picture.
5. Instead, they told the boys and girls exaggerated stories about him.

SUBJECT COMPLEMENTS

A subject complement completes the meaning of a linking verb and identifies or describes the subject.

Common Linking Verbs					
appear	become	grow	remain	smell	stay
be	feel	look	seem	sound	taste

 For more about linking verbs, see pages 742–743.

The two kinds of subject complements are the *predicate nominative* and the *predicate adjective.*

Predicate Nominatives

9d. A *predicate nominative* is a noun or a pronoun that follows a linking verb and identifies the subject or refers to it.

EXAMPLES Denise is a good **friend.** [*Friend* is a predicate nominative that identifies the subject *Denise.*]

Enrique is **one** of the best players. [*One* is a predicate nominative that refers to the subject *Enrique.*]

Predicate nominatives never appear in prepositional phrases.

EXAMPLE The prize was a **pair** of tickets to the movies. [*Pair* is a predicate nominative that identifies the subject *prize. Tickets* is the object of the preposition *of,* and *movies* is the object of the preposition *to.*]

Predicate Adjectives

9e. A *predicate adjective* is an adjective that follows a linking verb and describes the subject.

EXAMPLES The landlady is very **pleasant.** [*Pleasant* follows the linking verb *is* and describes the subject *landlady.*]

This ground looks **swampy.** [*Swampy* follows the linking verb *looks* and describes the subject *ground.*]

Some verbs, such as *look, grow,* and *feel,* may be used as either linking verbs or action verbs.

LINKING VERB The field worker **felt** tired. [*Felt* is a linking verb because it links the adjective *tired* to the subject *field worker.*]

ACTION VERB The field worker **felt** the hot wind. [*Felt* is an action verb because it is followed by the direct object *wind,* which tells what the field worker felt.]

✓ QUICK CHECK 3

Identify the *predicate nominatives* and *predicate adjectives* in the following sentences.

EXAMPLE 1. The old man did not seem tall enough or grand enough.
1. predicate adjectives—tall, grand

1. For him, home was the Rosebud Reservation in South Dakota.
2. Were his hands leathery and brown?
3. Joe Iron Shell was Mother's grandfather and Martin and Cheryl's great-grandfather.
4. His most precious possession was his medicine bag.
5. With age, his dark hair had become gray and stringy.

NOTE Expressions such as *It is I* and *That was he* may sound awkward because in conversation people more frequently say *It's me* and *That was him.* These nonstandard expressions may one day become acceptable in writing as well as in speech. For now, however, it is best to follow the rules of standard English in your writing.

NOTE A predicate nominative may be compound.

EXAMPLE Miss Kinnian was Charlie's **teacher** and **friend.**

NOTE A predicate adjective may be compound.

EXAMPLE A computer can be **entertaining** and **helpful,** but sometimes **frustrating.**

☞ For more about verbs that may be used as either linking verbs or action verbs, see page 743.

Try It Out

In each of the following sentences, change the *be* verb to an action verb. Then, revise the sentence to read smoothly.

1. Grandfather was all by himself on his journey.
2. He had never been so far from the reservation before.
3. His stories were about warriors and excitement.
4. Children were all around him each day.
5. Moccasins were on his feet.

NOTE A simple sentence may contain a compound subject, a compound verb, or both.

            S

EXAMPLE **Dr. Nemur**

      S   V

and **Dr. Strauss tested**

           V

Charlie and **monitored** his progress.

Avoiding the Overuse of *Be* Verbs

Overusing the linking verb *be* can make writing dull and lifeless. Wherever possible, replace a dull *be* verb with a verb that expresses action.

BE VERB Edgar Allan Poe **was** a writer of poems, literary criticism, and short stories.

ACTION VERB Edgar Allan Poe **wrote** poems, literary criticism, and short stories.

10 KINDS OF SENTENCES

SENTENCES CLASSIFIED BY STRUCTURE

Sentences may be classified according to **structure**—the kinds and the number of clauses they contain. The four kinds of sentences are *simple, compound, complex,* and *compound-complex.*

The Simple Sentence

10a. A *simple sentence* has one independent clause and no subordinate clauses.

EXAMPLE **Mr. Lema showed him the trumpet.**

The Compound Sentence

10b. A *compound sentence* has two or more independent clauses but no subordinate clauses.

The independent clauses are usually joined by a comma and a coordinating conjunction, such as *and, but, for, nor, or, so,* or *yet.* The clauses are sometimes joined by only a semicolon.

EXAMPLES **It was a large sum of money,** but **Tokubei was willing to pay it.**
Zenta looked at the woman's left hand; it had six fingers.

The Complex Sentence

10c. A *complex sentence* has one independent clause and at least one subordinate clause.

EXAMPLE   Mary ate some of the mushroom before she gave any of it to the children.

INDEPENDENT CLAUSE   **Mary ate** some of the mushroom

SUBORDINATE CLAUSE   before **she gave** any of it to the children

EXAMPLE   Some of the sailors who took part in the mutiny on the British ship *Bounty* settled Pitcairn Island.

INDEPENDENT CLAUSE   **some** of the sailors **settled** Pitcairn Island

SUBORDINATE CLAUSE   **who took** part in the mutiny on the British ship *Bounty*

The Compound-Complex Sentence

10d.   A *compound-complex sentence* has two or more independent clauses and at least one subordinate clause.

EXAMPLE   I have read several stories in which the main characters are animals, but the story that I like best is "Brer Possum's Dilemma."

INDEPENDENT CLAUSE   **I have read** several stories

INDEPENDENT CLAUSE   the **story is** "Brer Possum's Dilemma"

SUBORDINATE CLAUSE   in which the main **characters are** animals

SUBORDINATE CLAUSE   that **I like** best

Using a Variety of Sentence Structures

By varying the length and the structure of your sentences, you can make your writing more interesting to read. As a rule, simple sentences are best used to express single ideas. To describe more complicated ideas and to show relationships between them, you will usually need to use compound, complex, and compound-complex sentences.

SIMPLE SENTENCES   The cotton season began. He went to school. He met Mr. Lema.

COMPOUND-COMPLEX SENTENCE   When the cotton season began, he went to school, and there he met Mr. Lema.

 QUICK CHECK I

Label each of the following sentences as *simple, compound, complex,* or *compound-complex.* Then, identify each of the clauses in the sentence as *independent* or *subordinate.*

Try It Out ✎

Decide whether the information in each numbered item would be best expressed by a simple, compound, complex, or compound-complex sentence. Then, revise each item.

1. They took off their wings. There was not enough room on the ships.
2. The people had been able to fly. They had forgotten how.
3. The Master was a hard man. The Overseer was, too.
4. A slave collapsed in the heat. The Overseer whipped him.
5. She flew awkwardly at first. She soon soared freely. Everyone looked up to her.

EXAMPLE   1. Virginia Hamilton tells a story about people who could fly.

1. *complex: independent—Virginia Hamilton tells a story about people; subordinate—who could fly*

1. In the Africa of long ago, people flew.
2. Sarah's baby was crying, but she couldn't quiet the child.
3. Although the Overseer chased her, he could not catch her.
4. Before they knew it, she had flown over the trees and disappeared.
5. Toby told others the magic words, and they flew away while many slaves on the ground called for help.

SENTENCES CLASSIFIED BY PURPOSE

Sentences may be classified according to **purpose**. The four kinds of sentences are *declarative, interrogative, imperative,* and *exclamatory.*

10e.   A *declarative sentence* makes a statement. It is followed by a period.

EXAMPLE   According to Laurie, Charles was always causing trouble.

10f.   An *interrogative sentence* asks a question. It is followed by a question mark.

EXAMPLE   Did Daniel Webster defeat the devil?

10g.   An *imperative sentence* gives a command or makes a request. It is followed by a period. A strong command is followed by an exclamation point.

EXAMPLES   Look after the children while I'm gone. [mild command]
Father, tell us a story. [request]
Watch out! [strong command]

10h.   An *exclamatory sentence* shows excitement or expresses strong feeling. It is followed by an exclamation point.

EXAMPLE   What a sad day in Mudville that was!

✓ *QUICK CHECK 2*

Classify each of the following sentences according to its purpose: *declarative, interrogative, imperative,* or *exclamatory.*

EXAMPLE   1. For Monday, read "The People Could Fly."
1. *imperative*

1. Why did the people take off their wings?
2. Toby had not forgotten the magic words.
3. Listen to them.
4. Look up in the sky!
5. How the slaves must have imagined just such a scene!

NOTE The "understood" subject of an imperative sentence is always *you.*

EXAMPLES   Father, (you) tell us a story.
(You) Watch out!

For more about end marks of punctuation, see page 797.

11 WRITING EFFECTIVE SENTENCES

WRITING CLEAR SENTENCES

One of the easiest ways to make your writing clear is to use complete sentences. A **complete sentence** is a word group that has a subject, has a verb, and expresses a complete thought. Two of the stumbling blocks to the development of clear sentences are *sentence fragments* and *run-on sentences*. For information about sentence fragments, see page 779.

Run-on Sentences

11a. **Avoid using run-on sentences.**

If you run together two complete sentences as if they were one sentence, you get a **run-on sentence.**

RUN-ON	Margaret Bourke-White was a famous news photographer she worked for *Life* magazine during World War II.
CORRECT	Margaret Bourke-White was a famous news photographer. She worked for *Life* magazine during World War II.
RUN-ON	Bourke-White traveled all over the world, she even went underground to photograph miners in South Africa.
CORRECT	Bourke-White traveled all over the world. She even went underground to photograph miners in South Africa.

You can correct a run-on sentence

1. by making two sentences, as in the examples above

2. by using a comma and the coordinating conjunction *and, but,* or *or*

RUN-ON	Chinese people use kites in some religious ceremonies, they usually use them for sport.
CORRECT	Chinese people use kites in some religious ceremonies, **but** they usually use them for sport.

> **NOTE** To spot run-ons, try reading your writing aloud. A natural pause in your voice often marks the end of one thought and the beginning of another. If you pause at a place where you don't have any end punctuation, you may have found a run-on sentence.

COMBINING SENTENCES

11b. **Improve choppy sentences by combining them into longer, smoother sentences.**

You can combine sentences

1. by inserting words

ORIGINAL	Mrs. Flowers was an intelligent woman. She was generous, too.
COMBINED	Mrs. Flowers was an intelligent, **generous** woman.

2. by inserting phrases

ORIGINAL Henry David Thoreau lived at Walden Pond. He lived there for two years. He lived in a simple hut.

COMBINED **For two years** Henry David Thoreau lived **in a simple hut at Walden Pond.** [prepositional phrases]

ORIGINAL Harriet Tubman made the long journey to Philadelphia. She traveled at night.

COMBINED **Traveling at night,** Harriet Tubman made the long journey to Philadelphia. [participial phrase]

3. by using *and, but,* or *or*

ORIGINAL Eagle hunted for light. Coyote went with him.

COMBINED Eagle **and** Coyote hunted for light. [compound subject]

ORIGINAL The big box held the sun. The smaller box contained the moon.

COMBINED The big box held the sun, **and** the smaller box contained the moon. [compound sentence]

4. by using a subordinate clause

ORIGINAL Harriet Tubman did not believe that people should be slaves. She decided to escape.

COMBINED Harriet Tubman, **who believed no person should be a slave,** decided to escape. [adjective clause]

ORIGINAL Billy signed the guest book. He saw two other names.

COMBINED **When Billy signed the guest book,** he saw two other names. [adverb clause]

Try It Out ✎

Combine each of the following pairs of sentences. Make sure each revised sentence reads smoothly and shows the relationship you intend. If a pair of sentences should not be combined, write *C*.

1. Lemon Brown went to the window. Greg followed him.
2. The men were sitting down. They probably would not come back.
3. Greg asked about Lemon's injury. Lemon handed Greg the flashlight.
4. Lemon revealed his treasure. Greg stared at the strange package.
5. Greg was worried about Lemon. Lemon said that he would be fine.

Combining Related Sentences

When you combine sentences, you show the relationships between ideas. Different combinations show different relationships. When combining sentences, be sure that each sentence you create shows the relationship you intend.

ORIGINAL Jan practiced the piano. Leon did his homework.

COMBINED After Jan practiced the piano, Leon did his homework.

COMBINED While Jan practiced the piano, Leon did his homework.

ORIGINAL Kim told a story. I wrote a poem.

COMBINED Kim told a story, and I wrote a poem.

COMBINED Kim told a story about which I wrote a poem.

QUICK CHECK I

The following paragraph contains short, choppy sentences and run-on sentences. Use the methods you've learned in this section to make the sentences read smoothly.

EXAMPLE   [1] The building was dark. [2] It was scary.
        1. *The building was dark and scary.*

[1] The room was dark. [2] There was a table. [3] An old mattress was there, too. [4] Greg heard sounds. [5] The sounds were coming from the wall. [6] He could not see the man. [7] The man stepped into the light. [8] The man's name was Lemon Brown he had been a blues singer. [9] Now, the blues had left him. [10] He was left alone, he had only his treasure for comfort.

IMPROVING SENTENCE STYLE

11c. Improve *stringy* and *wordy* sentences by making them shorter and more precise.

Stringy sentences have too many independent clauses strung together with words like *and* or *but*.

STRINGY   Harriet Ross grew up as a slave in Maryland, and she worked on a plantation there, but in 1844, she married John Tubman, and he was a free man.

You can revise a stringy sentence

1. by breaking the sentence into two or more sentences

REVISED   Harriet Ross grew up as a slave in Maryland and worked on a plantation there. In 1844, she married John Tubman, a free man.

2. by turning some of the independent clauses into phrases or subordinate clauses

REVISED   Harriet Ross grew up as a slave in Maryland. She worked on a plantation there until, in 1844, she married John Tubman, who was a free man. [Notice that in addition to creating two separate sentences, this revision includes changing independent clauses into subordinate clauses.]

Wordy sentences tend to sound awkward and unnatural. You can revise a wordy sentence

1. by replacing a group of words with one word

WORDY   With great suddenness, the bicycle chain snapped.
REVISED   **Suddenly,** the bicycle chain snapped.

2. by replacing a clause with a phrase

WORDY   After the play had come to an end, we walked over to a restaurant and treated ourselves to pizza.

REVISED   **After the play,** we walked to a restaurant and treated ourselves to pizza.

3. by taking out a whole group of unnecessary words

WORDY   Daniel Webster was a persuasive orator whose speeches were very convincing.

REVISED   Daniel Webster was a persuasive orator.

✓ QUICK CHECK 2

The following paragraph is hard to read because it contains stringy and wordy sentences. Revise the paragraph to improve the sentence style.

EXAMPLE   [1] Then something happened that was frightening.
      1. *Then something frightening happened.*

[1] Some men called out and tromped around and called out again and wanted Lemon's treasure. [2] Lemon and Greg hid in the darkness and listened, and finally one man came upstairs, and Lemon went toward him. [3] With great fear, Greg heard the sounds of a fight. [4] Suddenly, the men ran away due to the fact that Greg had made a howling sound. [5] Then Greg asked Lemon about the treasure that he had.

12 CAPITAL LETTERS

12a.   **Capitalize the first word in every sentence.**

EXAMPLE   She has written a report on Harriet Tubman.

The first word of a sentence that is a direct quotation is capitalized even if the quotation begins within a sentence.

EXAMPLE   In her diary, Anne Frank wrote, "**In** spite of everything, I still believe that people are really good at heart."

12b.   **Capitalize the pronoun *I*.**

EXAMPLES   "What should **I** do?" **I** asked.

12c.   **Capitalize the interjection *O*.**

The interjection *O* is most often used on solemn or formal occasions. It is usually followed by a word in direct address.

EXAMPLES   Exult **O** shores! and ring **O** bells!
      —Walt Whitman, "O Captain! My Captain!"

NOTE   Traditionally, the first word in a line of poetry, including song lyrics, is capitalized. Some poets and songwriters do not follow this style. When you are quoting, follow the capitalization used in the source of the quotation.

EXAMPLE
Go down, Moses,
Way down in Egypt land
Tell old Pharaoh
To let my people go.
   —Traditional spiritual, "Go Down, Moses"

☞ For more about using capital letters in quotations, see page 805.

NOTE   The interjection *oh* requires a capital letter only at the beginning of a sentence.

EXAMPLES   **Oh,** that's all right.
I can't go, but, **oh,** I wish I could.

12d. **Capitalize proper nouns.**

A *common noun* is a general name for a person, a place, a thing, or an idea. A *proper noun* names a particular person, place, thing, or idea. A common noun is capitalized only when it begins a sentence or is part of a title. A proper noun is always capitalized. Some proper nouns consist of more than one word. In these names, short prepositions (those of fewer than five letters) and articles (*a, an, the*) are not capitalized.

COMMON NOUNS	holiday, man
PROPER NOUNS	Fourth of July, William the Conqueror

(1) Capitalize the names of persons and animals.

EXAMPLES Sandra Cisneros, Toni Cade Bambara, John McEnroe, Frank Van den Akker, Algernon, Kermit, Black Beauty

(2) Capitalize geographical names.

TYPE OF NAME	EXAMPLES	
Towns, Cities	Grover's Corners	St. Louis
Counties, States	Orange County	Georgia
Countries	Mexico	Japan
Islands	Long Island	Molokai
Bodies of Water	Crystal River	Dead Sea
Forests, Parks	Argonne Forest	Palmetto State Park
Streets, Highways	Euclid Avenue	Route 66
Mountains	Mount Everest	Pikes Peak
Continents	Europe	North America
Regions	the Middle East	New England

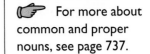

> For more about common and proper nouns, see page 737.

COMPUTER NOTE You may be able to use your spelling checker to help you capitalize people's names correctly. Make a list of the names you write most often. Then add this list to your computer's dictionary or spelling feature.

NOTE In a hyphenated street number, the second part of the number is not capitalized.

EXAMPLE
East Fifty-third Street

NOTE Words such as *north, east,* and *southwest* are not capitalized when they indicate direction.

EXAMPLES
traveling north
southwest of Austin

✓ *QUICK CHECK I*

For each of the following sentences, correct the word or words that have errors in capitalization.

EXAMPLE 1. Doesn't gary paulsen write about his dog columbia?
   1. *Gary Paulsen, Columbia*

1. Rose asked, "isn't the story set in the northwest territory?"
2. "no, i don't think so," will answered.
3. are you writing a poem about the dog obeah?
4. Yes, so far my best line is "o dog with heart for running sled."
5. Come to my house at 117 sixty-first street, and you can read it.

The word *earth* is not capitalized unless it is used along with names of other heavenly bodies. The words *sun* and *moon* are not capitalized.

EXAMPLES Water covers more than seventy percent of the surface of the earth.

Mercury and Venus are closer to the sun than Earth is.

The name of a season is not capitalized unless it is part of a proper name.

EXAMPLES
first day of spring,
Bluegrass Spring Festival

The word *god* is not capitalized when it refers to a god of mythology. The names of specific gods, however, are capitalized.

EXAMPLE The Egyptian sun god was Ra.

(3) Capitalize the names of planets, stars, and other heavenly bodies.

EXAMPLES Saturn, Canopus, Ursa Major

(4) Capitalize the names of teams, organizations, businesses, institutions, and government bodies.

TYPE OF NAME	EXAMPLES
Teams	Chicago Bulls Pittsburgh Pirates
Organizations	Future Farmers of America National Football League
Businesses	General Motors Corporation Kellogg Company
Institutions	Blake Memorial Hospital Lakeshore Junior High School
Government Bodies	Department of Education Governor's Council on Equal Opportunity

(5) Capitalize the names of historical events and periods, special events, and calendar items.

TYPE OF NAME	EXAMPLES	
Historical Events	Persian Gulf Conflict	the Crusades
Historical Periods	Paleozoic Era	Renaissance
Special Events	Kentucky State Fair	Olympic Games
Calendar Items	Monday	Memorial Day

(6) Capitalize the names of nationalities, races, and peoples.

EXAMPLES Italian, Japanese, African American, Caucasian, Hispanic

(7) Capitalize the names of religions and their followers, holy days, sacred writings, and specific deities.

TYPE OF NAME	EXAMPLES		
Religions and Followers	Christianity	Hindu	Judaism
Holy Days	Ramadan	Easter	Passover
Sacred Writings	Koran	Talmud	New Testament
Specific Deities	God	Allah	Vishnu

(8) Capitalize the names of buildings and other structures.

EXAMPLES Plaza Hotel   Eiffel Tower

(9) Capitalize the names of monuments and awards.

TYPE OF NAME	EXAMPLES
Monuments	**W**ashington **M**onument **V**ietnam **V**eterans **M**emorial
Awards	**N**ewbery **M**edal **P**ulitzer **P**rize

(10) Capitalize the names of trains, ships, aircraft, and spacecraft.

TYPE OF NAME	EXAMPLES	
Trains	*California **Z**ephyr*	*The **C**hief*
Ships	*Flying **C**loud*	*Santa **M**aria*
Aircraft	*Spirit of St. Louis*	*Air **F**orce **O**ne*
Spacecraft	*Voyager 2*	*Challenger*

(11) Capitalize the brand names of business products.

EXAMPLES   **R**eebok shoes, **F**ord station wagon, **B**ugle **B**oy jeans
[Notice that the names of the types of products are not capitalized.]

 QUICK CHECK 2

Correct each of the following expressions, using capital letters as needed. If an item is correct, write *C*.

EXAMPLE   **1.** the third reich
            1. *the Third Reich*

1. north star
2. a ship called the *skimmer*
3. battle of the little bighorn
4. beliefs of muslims
5. a 1930 black plymouth
6. oglala sioux
7. the purple heart
8. largest animal on earth
9. camp harmony
10. the meeting on monday

12e. **Capitalize proper adjectives.**

A **proper adjective** is formed from a proper noun and is almost always capitalized.

PROPER NOUN	PROPER ADJECTIVE
France	**F**rench cuisine
America	**A**merican heritage
William Shakespeare	**S**hakespearean actor

☞ For more about proper nouns and proper adjectives, see pages 737 and 741.

12f. Do not capitalize names of school subjects, except names of languages and of courses followed by a number.

EXAMPLES history, Spanish, Biology I

12g. Capitalize titles.

(1) Capitalize a title of a person when it comes before a name.

EXAMPLES They spoke to **G**overnor Adam and **D**r. Chang.

(2) Capitalize a title used alone or following a person's name only when you want to emphasize the position of someone holding a high office.

EXAMPLES Will the **S**ecretary of Labor hold a news conference? The **s**ecretary of our scout troop has the measles.

(3) Capitalize a word showing a family relationship when the word is used before or in place of a person's name.

EXAMPLES Did **M**om invite **A**unt Frances and **U**ncle Ralph?

(4) Capitalize the first and last words and all important words in titles of books, magazines, newspapers, poems, short stories, historical documents, movies, television programs, works of art, and musical compositions.

Unimportant words in titles include
- prepositions of fewer than five letters (such as *at, of, for, from, with*)
- coordinating conjunctions (*and, but, for, nor, or, so, yet*)
- articles (*a, an, the*)

TYPE OF NAME	EXAMPLES	
Books	*I Know Why the Caged Bird Sings* *Baseball in April*	
Magazines	*Latin American Literary Review* *Field and Stream*	
Newspapers	*Boston Herald*	*USA Today*
Poems	"A Time to Talk"	"Oranges"
Short Stories	"The Monkey's Paw" "The Inn of Lost Time"	
Historical Documents	Bill of Rights	Treaty of Ghent
Movies	*The Lion King*	*Star Wars*
Television Programs	*Full House*	*Murder, She Wrote*
Works of Art	*Mona Lisa*	*I and the Village*
Musical Compositions	*West Side Story*	*Rhapsody in Blue*

NOTE A title used alone in direct address is usually capitalized.

EXAMPLES Is everyone here, **R**everend? May I help you, **S**ir [*or* sir]?

NOTE Do not capitalize a word showing a family relationship when a possessive comes before the word.

EXAMPLES Barbara's **fa**ther and my **u**ncle Trent are the sponsors.

For information on what titles to italicize (underline), see page 804. For information on using quotation marks for titles, see page 807.

NOTE The article *the* before a title is not capitalized unless it is the first word of the title.

EXAMPLES Is that the late edition of the *Chicago Sun-Times*? I am reading "The Tell-Tale Heart."

QUICK CHECK 3

Correct each of the following expressions, adding or deleting capital letters as needed.

EXAMPLE   I. general George Armstrong Custer
              I. *General George Armstrong Custer*

1. parson walker
2. spanish class
3. the song "let me call you sweetheart"
4. st. bernard dogs
5. a hmong folk tale
6. the opera *pirates of penzance*
7. "Yes, captain."
8. a gift for my Uncle Ed
9. my Art Class
10. grandmother's dress

13 PUNCTUATION

END MARKS

An **end mark** is a mark of punctuation placed at the end of a sentence. The three kinds of end marks are the *period,* the *question mark,* and the *exclamation point.*

13a. **Use a period at the end of a statement.**

EXAMPLE   Jabez Stone sought the help of Daniel Webster**.**

13b. **Use a question mark at the end of a question.**

EXAMPLE   Did Paul Zindel write *Let Me Hear You Whisper***?**

13c. **Use an exclamation point at the end of an exclamation.**

EXAMPLE   What an exciting race that was**!**

13d. **Use a period or an exclamation point at the end of a request or a command.**

EXAMPLES   Kristi, please read the part of Miss Moray**.** [a request]
               Watch out**!** [a command]

13e. **Use a period after most abbreviations.**

TYPE OF ABBREVIATION	EXAMPLES			
Addresses	St**.**	Rd**.**	Blvd**.**	P**.**O**.** Box
Organizations and Companies	Co**.**	Inc**.**	Corp**.**	Assn**.**

(chart continued on next page)

Remember that correct capitalization of abbreviations is part of the proper spelling. Some abbreviations are capitalized.

EXAMPLES   Mrs.   CD   Ky.   FBI

However, some abbreviations, especially those for measurements, are not capitalized.

EXAMPLES   in.   yd   oz   cm   kg

Notice that abbreviations for most units of measurement are written without periods. (The abbreviation *in.* for *inch* needs a period so that it will not be confused with the word *in.*)

Consult a dictionary for the correct capitalization of an abbreviation.

For more about abbreviations, see the bottom of this page and page 798.

NOTE   A two-letter state abbreviation without periods is used only when it is followed by a ZIP Code.

EXAMPLE
Lodi, **CA** 95240

LANGUAGE HANDBOOK

For information about capitalizing abbreviations, see Tips for Spelling at the top of page 797.

TYPE OF ABBREVIATION	EXAMPLES			
Personal Names	O. Henry		W. W. Jacobs	
Titles Used with Names	Mr.	Mrs.	Jr.	Dr.
States	Ky.	Fla.	Tenn.	Calif.
Times	A.M.	P.M.	B.C.	A.D.

When an abbreviation with a period ends a sentence, another period is not needed. However, a question mark or an exclamation point is used as needed.

EXAMPLES   This is my friend J. R.
Have you met Nguyen, J. R.?

✓ QUICK CHECK I

For each of the following sentences, add periods, question marks, and exclamation points where they are needed.

EXAMPLE   **I.** What was your opinion of Dr Crocus
  I. *What was your opinion of Dr. Crocus?*

1. How that dolphin resisted them
2. The recipe on PBS called for 2 oz of milk
3. Hurry Call the fire department right now, C C
4. Contact him at P O Box 113, Fifth St, New York, NY
5. Was Robert W Service the poet laureate of Canada, T J

COMMAS

Items in a Series

13f. Use commas to separate items in a series.

Words, phrases, and clauses in a series are separated by commas to show the reader where one item in the series ends and the next item begins. Make sure there are three or more items in a series; two items often do not need a comma.

WORDS IN A SERIES   In late fall, the lake looked cold, gray, and calm.

PHRASES IN A SERIES   Tightening the spokes, checking the tire pressure, and oiling the gears, Carlos prepared his bike for the race.

CLAUSES IN A SERIES   I was late for school because my mother's car wouldn't start, my sister couldn't find her homework, and I forgot my lunch and had to go back to get it.

If all items in a series are joined by *and* or *or*, do not use commas to separate them.

EXAMPLE   Have you read *The Friends* **or** *Summer of My German Soldier* **or** *Bridge to Terabithia*?

13g. **Use a comma to separate two or more adjectives that come before a noun.**

EXAMPLE   Many ranchers depended on the small**,** tough**,** sure-footed mustang.

Sometimes the final adjective in a series is so closely linked to the noun that a comma is not used before the final adjective. If you aren't sure whether the final adjective and the noun are linked, use this test: Insert the word *and* between the adjectives. If *and* makes sense, use a comma.

EXAMPLE   Training a frisky colt to become a gentle, dependable **riding horse** takes great patience. [*And* doesn't make sense between *dependable* and *riding*.]

Compound Sentences

13h. **Use a comma before *and, but, or, nor, for, so*, or *yet* when it joins independent clauses.**

EXAMPLE   Outside, the wind was higher than ever**, and** the old man started nervously at the sound of a door banging upstairs.
—W. W. Jacobs, "The Monkey's Paw"

Interrupters

13i. **Use commas to set off an expression that interrupts a sentence.**

(1) **Use commas to set off a nonessential participial phrase or a nonessential subordinate clause.**

A *nonessential* (or *nonrestrictive*) phrase or clause adds information that can be omitted without changing the main idea of the sentence.

NONESSENTIAL PHRASE   The spider web**, shining in the early light,** looked like sparkling lace.

NONESSENTIAL CLAUSE   Edgar Allan Poe**, who wrote "The Tell-Tale Heart,"** is a master of the macabre.

Do not set off an *essential* (or *restrictive*) phrase or clause. Since such a phrase or clause tells *which one* or *which ones*, it cannot be omitted without changing the meaning of the sentence.

ESSENTIAL PHRASE   The discovery **made by Zenta** saved Tokubei fifty gold pieces. [Which discovery?]

ESSENTIAL CLAUSE   The book **that you recommended** is not in the library. [Which book?]

> **NOTE** A comma should never be used between an adjective and the noun immediately following it.
>
> **EXAMPLE**   Mary O'Hara wrote a tender, **suspenseful story** about a young boy and his colt.

> **NOTE** When the independent clauses are very short, the comma before *and, but,* or *or* may sometimes be omitted.
>
> **EXAMPLE**   They were hungry **and** they had nothing to eat.

> For more about compound sentences, see page 786.

> For more about participial phrases, see page 771. For more about subordinate clauses, see pages 775–778.

(2) Use commas to set off an appositive or an appositive phrase that is nonessential.

APPOSITIVE	Smiley's frog**, Dan'l Webster,** lost the contest.
APPOSITIVE PHRASE	Robert Frost**, my favorite poet,** won four Pulitzer Prizes.

(3) Use commas to set off words used in direct address.

EXAMPLE Do you know**, Elena,** who wrote "The Medicine Bag"?

(4) Use commas to set off a parenthetical expression.

A *parenthetical expression* is a side remark that adds information or relates ideas.

EXAMPLE Brer Possum should have known**, of course,** that Brer Snake would bite him.

Commonly Used Parenthetical Expressions

after all	for example	on the other hand
at any rate	for instance	I believe (hope, suppose, think)
by the way	generally speaking	in my opinion
in fact	of course	in the first place

Introductory Words, Phrases, and Clauses

13j. Use a comma after certain introductory elements.

(1) Use a comma after *yes, no,* or any mild exclamation such as *well* or *why* at the beginning of a sentence.

EXAMPLE Yes**,** I read "A Smart Cookie."

(2) Use a comma after an introductory prepositional phrase if the phrase is long or if two or more phrases appear together.

EXAMPLES **Underneath the moss-covered rock,** we found a shiny, fat earthworm.
By the end of the second day of the journey, they were exhausted.

(3) Use a comma after a participial phrase or an infinitive phrase that introduces a sentence.

PARTICIPIAL PHRASE	**Forced onto the sidelines by a sprained ankle,** Carlos was restless and unhappy.
INFINITIVE PHRASE	**To defend the honor of King Arthur's knights,** Sir Gawain accepted the Green Knight's challenge.

(4) Use a comma after an introductory adverb clause.

EXAMPLE   **As soon as he made the third wish,** the knocking stopped.

Conventional Situations

13k. Use commas in certain conventional situations.

(1) Use commas to separate items in dates and addresses.

EXAMPLES   The delegates to the Constitutional Convention signed the Constitution on Monday, September 17, 1787, in Philadelphia, Pennsylvania.
Her address is 6448 Higgins Road, Chicago, IL 60607.

(2) Use a comma after the salutation of a friendly letter and after the closing of any letter.

EXAMPLES   Dear Mrs. Flowers,   Sincerely yours,

 QUICK CHECK 2

For each of the following sentences, add commas where they are needed.

EXAMPLE   **1.** With hope in the future they packed got in the wagon and rode away.
1. *With hope in the future, they packed, got in the wagon, and rode away.*

1. They didn't ride in a big Conestoga wagon but of course they did have a wagon.
2. Well his pa two sisters and he set out for the mountains.
3. Pa a wary man didn't know who Mary was where she came from or much about her.
4. Stranded they could starve or eat their horse or find food.
5. That mushroom which could have been poisonous saved them.

SEMICOLONS

A *semicolon* separates complete thoughts as a period does and also separates items within a sentence as a comma does.

13l. Use a semicolon instead of a comma between closely related independent clauses when they are not joined by *and, but, or, nor, for, so,* or *yet.*

EXAMPLE   Motor activity is impaired; there is a general reduction of glandular activity; there is an accelerated loss of coordination.
—Daniel Keyes, "Flowers for Algernon"

For more about prepositional phrases, see pages 769–771. For more about verbal phrases, see pages 771–773. For more about adverb clauses, see pages 776–777.

Try It Out ✎

Read each of the following sentences, and revise any sentence that you think is too heavily punctuated.

1. Mary was just eighteen years old, but she had nerve and stood her ground; in the days to come, the family would have reason to be grateful to her.
2. She had run away, she bore scars, and she wouldn't say much about herself; because the family had no money, little food, and too much work for one man, Pa did not want to take her along with them, and, once he did, he did not even speak to her.
3. Life on the prairie broke the spirits of many people, such as those that the family met along the way; the people were glum and frightened, and many of them were past despair, yet they would give their help.
4. As you can well imagine, it must have been hard for the homesteaders to share their venison; food was difficult to come by, and they had little for themselves.
5. Mary prepared the mushroom, frying it in a pan; then, she ate some and sat up all night, waiting to see if death would come.

NOTE When a conjunctive adverb or a transitional expression *joins* clauses, it is preceded by a semicolon and followed by a comma. When it *interrupts* a clause, however, it is set off by commas.

EXAMPLES You are entitled to your opinion; **however,** you can't ignore the facts.
You are entitled to your opinion; you can't, **however,** ignore the facts.

Avoiding the Overuse of Semicolons

Semicolons are most effective when they are not overused. Sometimes it is better to separate a compound sentence or a heavily punctuated sentence into two sentences than to use a semicolon.

ACCEPTABLE In the tropical jungles of South America, it rains almost every day, sometimes all day; the vegetation there, some of which is found nowhere else in the world, is lush, dense, and fast-growing.

BETTER In the tropical jungles of South America, it rains almost every day, sometimes all day. The vegetation there, some of which is found nowhere else in the world, is lush, dense, and fast-growing.

13m. Use a semicolon between independent clauses joined by a *conjunctive adverb* or a *transitional expression.*

A *conjunctive adverb* or a *transitional expression* shows how the independent clauses that it joins are related.

EXAMPLES Mr. Scratch was formidable; **however,** he was no match for Daniel Webster.
Dorset decided not to pay the ransom; **in fact,** he demanded money from the two kidnappers.

Commonly Used Conjunctive Adverbs

accordingly	furthermore	instead	nevertheless
besides	however	meanwhile	otherwise
consequently	indeed	moreover	therefore

Commonly Used Transitional Expressions

as a result	for example	that is	for instance
in addition	in spite of	in fact	in conclusion

13n. Use a semicolon rather than a comma before a coordinating conjunction to join independent clauses that contain commas.

EXAMPLE We will practice Act I on Monday, Act II on Wednesday, and Act III on Friday; and on Saturday we will rehearse the entire play.

COLONS

13o. Use a colon before a list of items, especially after expressions like *as follows* or *the following*.

EXAMPLE Robert Frost wrote the following: "Nothing Gold Can Stay," "The Road Not Taken," and "A Time to Talk."

13p. Use a colon before a statement that explains or clarifies a preceding statement.

When a list of words, phrases, or subordinate clauses follows a colon, the first word of the list is lowercase. When an independent clause follows a colon, the first word of the clause begins with a capital letter.

EXAMPLES There are two kinds of people: cat lovers and dog lovers.

Our teacher asked us only one question: What had happened to the landlady's other boarders?

13q. Use a colon in certain conventional situations.

(1) Use a colon between the hour and the minute.

EXAMPLE 11:30 P.M.

(2) Use a colon after the salutation of a business letter.

EXAMPLES Dear Sir or Madam: Dear Sales Manager:

(3) Use a colon between chapter and verse in referring to passages from the Bible and between a title and a subtitle.

EXAMPLES John 3:16
"A Tragedy Revealed: A Heroine's Last Days"

 QUICK CHECK 3

For each of the following sentences, add commas, semicolons, and colons as needed.

EXAMPLE 1. There were no deer moreover all food was scarce.
1. *There were no deer; moreover, all food was scarce.*

1. Times were hard consequently some felt the emotions expressed in Psalm 22 1.
2. Daylight was precious by 7 00 A.M. travelers were on their way.
3. Their situation had become grave they had no food and the horse was worn out.
4. Mary a valiant woman found a mushroom a huge one and she cooked it.
5. The test tomorrow will cover the following setting theme and plot.

 NOTE Never use a colon directly after a verb or a preposition that comes before a list of items.

INCORRECT This marinara sauce is made of: tomatoes, bay leaves, onions, oregano, and garlic.

CORRECT This marinara sauce is made of tomatoes, bay leaves, onions, oregano, and garlic.

INCORRECT The main characters are: Sam, Bill, and Johnny.

CORRECT The main characters are Sam, Bill, and Johnny.

14 PUNCTUATION

UNDERLINING (ITALICS)

COMPUTER NOTE If you use a computer, you may be able to set words in italics yourself. Most word-processing software and many printers are capable of producing italic type.

Italics are printed letters that lean to the right, such as *the letters in these words*. In your handwritten or typewritten work, indicate italics by underlining.

EXAMPLE *Monica Sone wrote Nisei Daughter.*

If this sentence were printed, it would look like this:

Monica Sone wrote *Nisei Daughter.*

14a. Use underlining (italics) for titles of books, plays, periodicals, works of art, films, television programs, recordings, long musical compositions, ships, trains, aircraft, and spacecraft.

NOTE The article *the* before the title of a magazine or a newspaper is usually neither italicized nor capitalized when it is written within a sentence. Some periodicals do include *the* as part of their titles.

EXAMPLES My parents subscribe to **the** *Chicago Tribune*.
He wrote for ***The*** *New York Times*.

☞ For examples of titles that are not italicized but, instead, are enclosed in quotation marks, see page 807.

TYPE OF TITLE	EXAMPLES	
Books	*The Incredible Journey*	*Where the Red Fern Grows*
Plays	*Let Me Hear You Whisper*	*The Diary of Anne Frank*
Periodicals	*Newsweek*	*The Wall Street Journal*
Works of Art	*The Last Supper*	*Bird in Space*
Films	*The Wizard of Oz*	*Forrest Gump*
Television Programs	*Home Improvement*	*The X-Files*
Recordings	*Music Box*	*No Fences*
Long Musical Compositions	*A Sea Symphony*	*Peer Gynt Suite*
Ships	*Flying Cloud*	*Queen Elizabeth 2*
Trains	*Orient Express*	*Garden State Special*
Aircraft	*Spirit of St. Louis*	*Spruce Goose*
Spacecraft	USS *Enterprise*	*Voyager I*

14b. Use underlining (italics) for words, letters, and figures referred to as such.

EXAMPLES What is the difference between the words *emigrate* and *immigrate*?
Drop the final *e* before you add *-ing* to either of those words.
Is this number a *3* or an *8*?

✓ QUICK CHECK I

For each of the following sentences, add underlining wherever necessary.

EXAMPLE **I.** Who played Anne in The Diary of Anne Frank?
 I. *Who played Anne in <u>The Diary of Anne Frank</u>?*

1. Paleoworld is a great television show.
2. Be certain to distinguish between the words to, too, and two.
3. That handwritten d looks like an a.
4. In formal writing, write and rather than &.
5. How did the movie King of the Wind differ from the book?

QUOTATION MARKS

14c. **Use quotation marks to enclose a *direct quotation*—a person's exact words.**

DIRECT QUOTATION **"**Have you read *Let Me Hear You Whisper?***"** asked Ms. Estrada.

Do not use quotation marks for an ***indirect quotation***—a rewording of a direct quotation.

INDIRECT QUOTATION Ms. Estrada asked me whether I had read *Let Me Hear You Whisper*.

14d. **A direct quotation begins with a capital letter.**

EXAMPLE Abe Lincoln said, "**T**he ballot is stronger than the bullet."

When the expression identifying the speaker interrupts a quoted sentence, the second part of the quotation begins with a lowercase letter.

EXAMPLE "What are some of the things," asked Mrs. Perkins, "**t**hat the astronauts discovered on the moon?"

When the second part of a divided quotation is a sentence, it begins with a capital letter.

EXAMPLE "Sandra and Alfonso went bike riding," remarked Mrs. Perkins. "**T**hey left an hour ago." [Notice that a period, not a comma, follows the interrupting expression.]

14e. **A direct quotation is set off from the rest of the sentence by a comma, a question mark, or an exclamation point, but not by a period.**

Set off means "separated." If a quotation appears at the beginning of a sentence, a comma follows it. If a quotation falls at the end of a sentence, a comma comes before it. If a quoted sentence is interrupted, a comma follows the first part and comes before the second part.

NOTE When only part of a sentence is being quoted, the quotation generally begins with a lowercase letter.

EXAMPLE Abe Lincoln described the ballot as "**s**tronger than the bullet."

EXAMPLES   "I've just finished reading a book about Harriet
Tubman," Alison said.

Jaime said, "My favorite writer is Ray Bradbury."

"Did you know," asked Helen, "that O. Henry is the
pseudonym of William Sydney Porter?"

14f. **A period or a comma is always placed inside the closing
quotation marks.**

EXAMPLES   Mr. Aaron said, "The story is set in Fresno, California."

"Mrs. Flowers reminds me of my aunt," Ruth added.

14g. **A question mark or an exclamation point is placed inside
the closing quotation marks when the quotation itself is a
question or exclamation. Otherwise, the question mark
or exclamation point is placed outside.**

EXAMPLES   "Did Marjorie Kinnan Rawlings write *The Yearling*?"
asked Ken. [The quotation is a question.]

Sheila exclaimed, "I can't find my homework!" [The
quotation is an exclamation.]

What did the captain mean when he said "Hard aport"?
[The sentence, not the quotation, is a question.]

When both the sentence and the quotation at the end of the sentence
are questions (or exclamations), only one question mark (or exclamation
point) is used. It is placed inside the closing quotation marks.

EXAMPLE   Who wrote the poem that begins "How do I love thee?"

14h. **When you write dialogue (conversation), begin a new
paragraph each time you change speakers.**

EXAMPLE   "I'm listening," said the latter, grimly surveying the
board as he stretched out his hand. "Check."

"I should hardly think that he'd come tonight," said
his father, with his hand poised over the board.

"Mate," replied the son.

—W. W. Jacobs, "The Monkey's Paw"

14i. **When a quotation consists of several sentences, place
quotation marks at the beginning and at the end of the
whole quotation.**

EXAMPLE   "Oh, please come in. I'm so happy to see you. Let me
take your hat and coat," said Ms. Davis.

14j. **Use single quotation marks to enclose a quotation within
a quotation.**

EXAMPLE   "What Longfellow poem begins 'Listen, my children, and
you shall hear'?" Carol asked.

NOTE   When a quotation
ends with a ques-
tion mark or with an exclamation point, no comma is
needed.

EXAMPLES   "What were
the Whites' three
wishes?" asked Cynthia.
"What a surprise that
was!" exclaimed Meryl.

14k. Use quotation marks to enclose titles of short works such as short stories, poems, articles, songs, episodes of television programs, and chapters and other parts of books.

TYPE OF TITLE	EXAMPLES
Short Stories	"Raymond's Run" "Too Soon a Woman"
Poems	"O Captain! My Captain!" "Casey at the Bat"
Articles	"You and Your Computer" "The Best Word"
Songs	"Greensleeves" "The Streets of Laredo"
Episodes of Television Programs	"Tony Turns Fourteen" "An Englishman Abroad"
Chapters and Other Parts of Books	"Workers' Rights" "More Word Games"

 For examples of titles that are italicized (underlined), see page 804.

 QUICK CHECK 2

In the following dialogue, insert end marks, commas, and quotation marks. Correct any errors in capitalization, and begin new paragraphs as necessary.

EXAMPLE [1] Aren't you the one who said Who, me?

1. *Aren't you the one who said, "Who, me?"*

[1] Didn't you write music for the poem The Secret Heart Carl asked. [2] Yes, I had considered using music from the Beatles' song Yesterday Maria answered but it didn't work out. [3] I know what you mean, Carl replied. That reminds me of that poem To a Mouse. [4] Is that the one that says that plans don't always work? [5] Carl smiled and said yes, that's it!

Using Quotations in Interviews

If you are writing a report and want to use material from an interview, you need to quote information from the source material. In general, you should follow these two rules:

- When you use someone else's ideas, give him or her credit.
- When you use someone else's words, quote them accurately.

Try It Out ✎

You have conducted an interview with a famous writer named F. A. Moss. During the interview, Mr. Moss made the statements listed below. Write a paragraph or two based on Mr. Moss's quotations. Be sure to use at least three direct quotations.

1. "A poem can come at any time, so I always carry a small notebook."
2. "Some of my best ideas occur to me in the middle of the night."
3. "Poetry is the heart of literature."
4. "I once wrote a haiku while waiting for a traffic light to change."
5. "Anyone can write poetry if only he or she speaks the truth."

15 PUNCTUATION

APOSTROPHES

Possessive Case

15a. **The** *possessive case* **of a noun or a pronoun shows owner-ship or relationship.**

(1) **To form the possessive case of a singular noun, add an apostrophe and an** *s***.**

EXAMPLES   the boy's bike   Charles's father

(2) **To form the possessive case of a plural noun ending in** *s***, add only the apostrophe.**

EXAMPLES   students' records   citizens' committee

(3) **To form the possessive case of a plural noun that does not end in** *s***, add an apostrophe and an** *s***.**

EXAMPLES   mice's tracks   children's voices

(4) **To form the possessive case of most indefinite pronouns, add an apostrophe and an** *s***.**

EXAMPLES   everyone's opinion   somebody's umbrella

Contractions

15b. **To form a contraction, use an apostrophe to show where letters have been left out.**

A *contraction* is a shortened form of a word, a figure, or a group of words.

Common Contractions			
he is	he's	you will	you'll
1997	'97	of the clock	o'clock
let us	let's	they had	they'd
we are	we're	where is	where's

The word *not* can be shortened to *–n't* and added to a verb, usually without changing the spelling of the verb.

EXAMPLES	are not	aren't	have not	haven't
	does not	doesn't	had not	hadn't
	do not	don't	should not	shouldn't
	was not	wasn't	were not	weren't
EXCEPTIONS	will not	won't	cannot	can't

Do not confuse contractions with possessive pronouns.

CONTRACTIONS	POSSESSIVE PRONOUNS
It's raining. [*It is*]	**Its** wing is broken.
Who's there? [*Who is*]	**Whose** turn is it?
There's only one left. [*There is*]	This car is **theirs**.
You're a good student. [*You are*]	**Your** story is interesting.

Plurals

15c. **Use an apostrophe and an *s* to form the plurals of letters, numerals, and signs and of words referred to as words.**

EXAMPLES   The word has two *r*'s, not one.
My brother is learning to count by 5's.
Don't use &'s in place of *and*'s.

 **QUICK CHECK 1**

For each of the following sentences, insert apostrophes where they are needed.

EXAMPLE   **1.** Wont you please read "Paul Reveres Ride" aloud?
   1. *Won't, Revere's*

1. Arent these Tesss pliers?
2. I cant tell if theyre *f*s or *t*s.
3. The kitten was following its mothers example.
4. Dont you use Los Angeles public transportation?
5. Because its raining, the childrens picnic has been canceled.

 You may notice that an apostrophe is not always used in forming the four kinds of plurals covered by rule 15c. Many writers omit the apostrophe if the plural meaning is clear without it. However, to make sure that your writing is clear, it is best to use an apostrophe.

HYPHENS

15d. **Use a hyphen to divide a word at the end of a line.**

EXAMPLE   How long had the new bridge been under construction before it was opened?

When dividing a word at the end of a line, remember the following rules.

(1) Divide a word only between syllables.

INCORRECT   Charlene began her report with a series of four questions about Shakespeare.

CORRECT   Charlene began her report with a series of four questions about Shakespeare.

☞ If you are not sure how to divide a word into syllables, look up the word in a dictionary.

(2) Do not divide a word so that one letter stands alone.

INCORRECT	Tokubei and his bodyguard Zenta stayed o-vernight in an unusual inn.
CORRECT	Tokubei and his bodyguard Zenta stayed overnight in an unusual inn.

(3) Divide an already hyphenated word at a hyphen.

INCORRECT	We are going to see my brother and my sis-ter-in-law tomorrow.
CORRECT	We are going to see my brother and my sister-in-law tomorrow.

(4) Do not divide a one-syllable word.

INCORRECT	Mr. White held the paw while he wish-ed for two hundred pounds.
CORRECT	Mr. White held the paw while he wished for two hundred pounds.

15e. Use a hyphen with compound numbers from *twenty-one* to *ninety-nine* and with fractions used as adjectives.

EXAMPLES   **twenty-five** dollars   **one-half** cup of flour

PARENTHESES

15f. Use parentheses to enclose material that is added to a sentence but is not considered of major importance.

EXAMPLES   Robert P. Tristram Coffin **(**1892–1955**)** wrote "The Secret Heart."
On the Sabbath we eat braided bread called challah **(**pronounced khä′ lə**)**.

A short sentence in parentheses may stand by itself or be contained within another sentence.

EXAMPLES   Fill in the order form carefully. **(Do not use a pencil.)**
The old fort **(it was used during the Civil War)** has been rebuilt and is open to the public.

DASHES

15g. Use a dash to indicate an abrupt break in thought or speech.

EXAMPLES   Alfonso don't—I mean, doesn't—want to face Sandra.
The murderer is—but I don't want to give away the ending.

QUICK CHECK 2

For each of the following sentences, correct errors in the use of hyphens, and insert parentheses and dashes as needed.

EXAMPLE   1. Test answers should be at least twenty five words long.
   1. *Test answers should be at least twenty-five words long.*

1. The authors of all three stories that we've read excel in self-expression and in the use of imagery.
2. If I were in the same situation that you are, I would demand an apology from them.
3. Sixty five cents per pound is a good bargain.
4. Langston Hughes 1902–1967 is a major force in modern poetry.
5. The winner is oh, the envelope is empty!

16 SPELLING

USING WORD PARTS

Many English words are made up of two or more word parts. Some word parts have more than one form.

Roots

The **root** of a word is the part that carries the word's core meaning.

COMMONLY USED ROOTS		
WORD ROOT	**MEANING**	**EXAMPLES**
–port–	carry	portable, transport
–scrib–, –script–	write	describe, manuscript
–spec–	look	spectator, spectacles

Prefixes

A **prefix** is one or more letters or syllables added to the beginning of a word or word part to create a new word.

COMMONLY USED PREFIXES		
PREFIX	**MEANING**	**EXAMPLES**
dif–, dis–	away, off, opposing	differ, disagree
mis–	badly, not, wrongly	misbehave, misfortune
re–	back, again	rebuild, reclaim

Suffixes

A **suffix** is one or more letters or syllables added to the end of a word or word part to create a new word.

COMMONLY USED SUFFIXES		
SUFFIX	**MEANING**	**EXAMPLES**
–er, –or	doer, native of	actor, westerner
–ful	full of, characteristic of	joyful, truthful
–tion	action, condition	rotation, selection

SPELLING RULES

ie and ei

16a. Except after c, write ie when the sound is long e.

EXAMPLES	achieve	shield	chief	field	piece
	ceiling	conceit	deceit	deceive	receive
EXCEPTIONS	either	leisure	neither		
	protein	seize	weird		

16b. Write ei when the sound is not long e, especially when the sound is long a.

EXAMPLES	foreign	forfeit	height	heir	their
	freight	neighbor	reign	veil	weigh
EXCEPTIONS	ancient	conscience	pie	patient	
	friend	mischief	lie	efficient	

–cede, –ceed, and –sede

16c. The only English word ending in –sede is *supersede*. The only words ending in –ceed are *exceed, proceed,* and *succeed.* Most other words that end with this sound end in –cede.

EXAMPLES   concede   intercede   precede   recede   secede

Adding Prefixes

16d. When adding a prefix to a word, do not change the spelling of the word itself.

EXAMPLES   over + see = **over**see
in + exact = **in**exact
mis + spell = **mis**spell
il + legal = **il**legal

NOTE   This time-tested verse may help you remember the *ie* rule.

I before *e*
Except after *c*
Or when sounded like *a*,
As in *neighbor* and *weigh*.

The rhyme above and rules 16a and 16b apply only when the *i* and the *e* are in the same syllable.

COMPUTER NOTE   Keep in mind that software for checking spelling will identify only misspelled words, not misused words. For example, if you used *their* when you should have used *there*, a spelling checker won't catch the error.

Adding Suffixes

16e. When adding the suffix *–ly* or *–ness* to a word, do not change the spelling of the word itself.

EXAMPLES   usual + ly = usual**ly**   eager + ness = eager**ness**

EXCEPTIONS   For words that end in y and have more than one syllable, change the *y* to *i* before adding *-ly* or *-ness.*
happy + ly = happ**ily**   lazy + ness = laz**iness**

16f. Drop the final silent *e* before a suffix beginning with a vowel.

EXAMPLES   live + ing = liv**ing**   approve + al = approv**al**

EXCEPTIONS   Keep the final silent *e* in a word ending in *ce* or *ge* before a suffix beginning with *a* or *o.*
notice + able = notic**eable**
courage + ous = courag**eous**

16g. Keep the final silent *e* before a suffix beginning with a consonant.

EXAMPLES   hope + ful = hop**eful**   care + less = car**eless**

EXCEPTIONS   true + ly = tru**ly**   judge + ment = judg**ment**

16h. For words ending in y preceded by a consonant, change the *y* to *i* before any suffix that does not begin with *i.*

EXAMPLES   easy + ly = eas**ily**   cry + ing = cry**ing**

16i. For words ending in y preceded by a vowel, keep the *y* when adding a suffix.

EXAMPLES   obey + ed = obe**yed**   boy + hood = boy**hood**

EXCEPTIONS   day—da**ily**   lay—la**id**   pay—pa**id**   say—sa**id**

16j. Double the final consonant before a suffix beginning with a vowel if the word (1) has only one syllable or has the accent on the last syllable *and* (2) ends in a single consonant preceded by a single vowel.

EXAMPLES   occur + ed = occur**red**   forbid + en = forbi**dden**

EXCEPTIONS   Do not double the final consonant in words ending in *w* or *x.*
mow + ing = mo**wing**   wax + ed = wax**ed**

 NOTE   When adding *–ing* to words that end in *ie*, drop the e and change the *i* to y.

EXAMPLES
lie + ing = **lying**
die + ing = d**ying**

NOTE   In some cases, the final consonant either may or may not be doubled.

EXAMPLE   travel + er = trave**ler** *or* trave**ller**

✓ QUICK CHECK I

Each of the following sentences contains two misspelled words. Correct each misspelling.

EXAMPLE   **1.** Then he percieved the uniqueness of the expereince.
       1. *perceived, experience*

1. Many people beleive that biege creates a neutral background.
2. To sucede in business, you must not excede your funds.
3. Lonelyness saddly plagues many people, even in this crowded world.
4. My little brother is always taging along, manageing to ruin my fun.
5. The judgement went against him, causing arguements in the press.

Forming the Plurals of Nouns

16k. For most nouns, add –s.

SINGULAR	desk	idea	shoe	friend	camera	Wilson
PLURAL	desks	ideas	shoes	friends	cameras	Wilsons

16l. For nouns ending in s, x, z, ch, or sh, add –es.

SINGULAR	bus	fox	waltz	inch	dish	Suarez
PLURAL	buses	foxes	waltzes	inches	dishes	Suarezes

16m. For nouns ending in y preceded by a vowel, add –s.

SINGULAR	decoy	highway	alley	Riley
PLURAL	decoys	highways	alleys	Rileys

16n. For nouns ending in y preceded by a consonant, change the y to i and add –es.

SINGULAR	army	country	city	pony	ally	daisy
PLURAL	armies	countries	cities	ponies	allies	daisies
EXCEPTIONS	For proper nouns ending in *y,* just add -s.					

Brady—Bradys   Murphy—Murphys

16o. For some nouns ending in f or fe, add –s. For others, change the f or fe to v and add –es.

SINGULAR	belief	thief	sheriff	knife	giraffe
PLURAL	beliefs	thieves	sheriffs	knives	giraffes

16p. For nouns ending in o preceded by a vowel, add –s.

SINGULAR	radio	patio	stereo	igloo	Matteo
PLURAL	radios	patios	stereos	igloos	Matteos

16q. For nouns ending in o preceded by a consonant, add –es.

SINGULAR	tomato	potato	echo	hero
PLURAL	tomatoes	potatoes	echoes	heroes
EXCEPTIONS	For musical terms and proper nouns, add -s.			

alto—altos   Shapiro—Shapiros
solo—solos   Aquino—Aquinos

16r. The plural of a few nouns is formed in irregular ways.

SINGULAR	ox	goose	foot	tooth	woman	mouse
PLURAL	oxen	geese	feet	teeth	women	mice

16s. For most compound nouns, form the plural of the last word in the compound.

SINGULAR	bookshelf	push-up	sea gull	ten-year-old
PLURAL	bookshel**ves**	push-up**s**	sea gull**s**	ten-year-old**s**

16t. For compound nouns in which one of the words is modified by the other word or words, form the plural of the word modified.

SINGULAR	brother-in-law	maid of honor	eighth-grader
PLURAL	brother**s**-in-law	maid**s** of honor	eighth-grader**s**

16u. For some nouns the singular and the plural forms are the same.

SINGULAR	trout	sheep	Chinese	pliers
AND PLURAL	series	aircraft	Sioux	species

 QUICK CHECK 2

Write the plural of each of the following items.

EXAMPLE	**1.** Native American
	1. *Native Americans*

1. species
2. irony
3. cry
4. valley
5. peach
6. mosquito
7. child
8. sergeant-at-arms
9. shampoo
10. scarf

In some names, marks that show pronunciation are just as important as the letters themselves.

PEOPLE	Alemán Böll Ibáñez
	Khayyám Janáček Eugène
PLACES	Açores Bogotá Camagüey
	Gîza Köln Sainte-Thérèse

If you're not sure about the spelling of a name, ask the person whose name it is, or check in a reference source.

16v. For numbers, letters, symbols, and words used as words, add an apostrophe and –*s*.

EXAMPLES	four *2*'**s**	two *m*'**s**
	missing *$*'**s**	too many *so*'**s** and *and*'**s**

Using Apostrophes with Plurals

In your reading, you may notice that some writers do not use apostrophes to form the plurals of numbers, capital letters, symbols, and words used as words.

EXAMPLES   Laurence Yep grew up during the latter part of the 1900s.
Make sure that you put Xs or ✓s in all of the boxes on this form.

However, using an apostrophe is never wrong. Therefore, it is best always to use the apostrophe.

Try It Out ✎

For each of the following sentences, insert apostrophes where appropriate.

1. Do not use *its* to refer to people.
2. These *hers* should be written with *s*s.
3. As computer users know, *I*s are very important in computing.
4. In the 1200s, several great romances were created.
5. How many *0*s are in a billion?

Spelling Numbers

16w. Spell out a number that begins a sentence.

EXAMPLE   **Five hundred** people went to see the game.

16x. Within a sentence, spell out numbers that can be written in one or two words. Use numerals for other numbers.

EXAMPLES   In all, **fifty-two** people attended the family reunion.
More than **160** people were invited.

16y. Spell out numbers used to indicate order.

EXAMPLE   She came in **second** [*not* 2nd] in the race.

> ## ☑ QUICK CHECK 3
>
> The following sentences contain errors in spelling or the use of numbers. Correct each error.
>
> **EXAMPLE**   **1.** 1000's of ants rushed out.
> **1.** *Thousands of ants rushed out.*
>
> **1.** Why do these *t*s look like *f*s?
> **2.** Hey! I sold my batch of tickets for fifty cents apiece, but he got 75 cents for each one of his.
> **3.** In the 1st place, I don't know how to dance.
> **4.** The satellite that was launched yesterday will travel one million one hundred fifty thousand miles.
> **5.** 10 people showed up for the rehearsal.

> **NOTE**   If you use several numbers, some short and some long, it is better to write them all as numerals.
>
> **EXAMPLE**   He wrote **37** plays and **154** poems.

---

17 GLOSSARY OF USAGE

This Glossary of Usage is an alphabetical list of words and expressions that are commonly misused in English. Throughout this section some examples are labeled *standard* or *nonstandard*. **Standard English** is the most widely accepted form of English. It is used in *formal* situations, such as in speeches and writing for school, and in *informal* situations, such as in conversation and everyday writing. **Nonstandard English** is language that does not follow the rules and guidelines of standard English.

a, an   Use *a* before words beginning with consonant sounds. Use *an* before words beginning with vowel sounds. See page 741.

EXAMPLES   He did not consider himself **a** hero.
Market Avenue is **a** one-way street.
An oryx is a large antelope.
We waited in line for **an** hour.

accept, except   *Accept* is a verb that means "receive." *Except* may be either a verb or a preposition. As a verb, *except* means "leave out" or "exclude"; as a preposition, *except* means "other than" or "excluding."

EXAMPLES   Squeaky **accepts** the responsibility.
Some students will be **excepted** from this assignment.
No one **except** Diego had finished the assignment.

affect, effect   *Affect* is a verb meaning "influence." The noun *effect* means "the result of some action."

EXAMPLES   His score on this test will **affect** his final grade.
The **effect** of the medicine was immediate.

ain't   Avoid this word in speaking and writing; it is nonstandard English.

all ready, already   *All ready* means "completely prepared." *Already* means "before a certain point in time."

EXAMPLES   We were **all ready** for the quiz on "The Monkey's Paw."
I had **already** read "Flowers for Algernon."

a lot   *A lot* should always be written as two words.

EXAMPLE   I spent **a lot** of time making this poster.

all together, altogether   The expression *all together* means "everyone or everything in the same place." The adverb *altogether* means "entirely."

EXAMPLES   The director called us **all together** for one final rehearsal.
He is **altogether** pleased with his victory.

at   Do not use *at* after *where*.

EXAMPLE   Where does she live? [*not* Where does she live at?]

bad, badly   *Bad* is an adjective. *Badly* is an adverb.

EXAMPLES   The tea tastes **bad**. [*Bad* modifies the noun *tea*.]
The boy's wrist was sprained **badly**. [*Badly* modifies the verb phrase *was sprained*.]

between, among   Use *between* when referring to two things at a time, even though they may be part of a group containing more than two.

EXAMPLE   Alfonso avoided Sandra **between** classes.

Use *among* when referring to a group rather than to separate individuals.

EXAMPLE   The money was divided **among** the four of them.

bust, busted   Avoid using these words as verbs. Use a form of either *burst* or *break*.

EXAMPLES   The balloon **burst** [*not* busted].
Alfonso's bicycle chain **broke** [*not* busted].

NOTE   Many writers overuse *a lot*. Whenever you run across *a lot* as you revise your own writing, try to replace it with a more exact word or phrase.

☞ **among**   See **between, among.**
as   See **like, as.**
as if   See **like, as if, as though.**

☞ **because**   See **reason . . . because.**

choose, chose *Choose* is the present tense form of the verb *choose*. It rhymes with *whose* and means "select." *Chose* is the past tense form of *choose*. It rhymes with *grows* and means "selected."

EXAMPLES   What did you **choose** as your topic?
                Trish **chose** to do her report on Shel Silverstein.

could of Do not write *of* with the helping verb *could*. Write *could have*. Also avoid *ought to of, should of, would of, might of,* and *must of.*

EXAMPLE   Mr. White **could have** [*not* could of] heeded his old friend's advice.

    Of is also unnecessary with *had*.

EXAMPLE   If he **had** [*not* had of] seen it, he would have told me.

fewer, less *Fewer* is used with plural words. *Less* is used with singular words. *Fewer* tells "how many"; *less* tells "how much."

EXAMPLES   I have **fewer** errors to correct than I thought.
                The kidnappers asked for **less** money.

good, well *Good* is always an adjective. Never use *good* as an adverb. Instead, use *well*.

EXAMPLE   She works **well** [*not* good] with the others.

    Well may also be used as an adjective to mean "healthy."

EXAMPLE   Mary and the children didn't look **well;** they needed food.

had ought, hadn't ought *Ought* is not used with *had*.

EXAMPLE   He **ought** [*not* had ought] to proofread more carefully.

he, she, they Avoid using a pronoun along with its antecedent as the subject of a verb. This error is called the ***double subject.***

NONSTANDARD   Toni Cade Bambara she is a famous writer.
STANDARD   Toni Cade Bambara is a famous writer.

hisself *Hisself* is nonstandard English. Use *himself.*

EXAMPLE   Brer Possum finds **himself** [*not* hisself] in a dilemma.

how come In informal situations, *how come* is often used instead of *why*. In formal situations, *why* should always be used.

INFORMAL   I don't know how come he told me that story.
FORMAL   I don't know **why** he told me that story.

kind of, sort of In informal situations, *kind of* and *sort of* are often used to mean "somewhat" or "rather." In formal English, *somewhat* or *rather* is preferred.

INFORMAL   Alfonso was kind of shy.
FORMAL   Alfonso was **rather** shy.

☞ **doesn't, don't** See page 750.

☞ **except** See **accept, except.**

☞ **had of** See **could of.**

☞ **its, it's** See page 809.

learn, teach   *Learn* means "gain knowledge." *Teach* means "instruct" or "show how."

EXAMPLES   What did Brer Possum **learn** from Brer Snake?
What did Brer Snake **teach** Brer Possum?

like, as   In informal situations, the preposition *like* is often used instead of the conjunction *as* to introduce a clause. In formal situations, *as* is preferred.

EXAMPLE   Do you think Marguerite memorized a poem, **as** [*not* like] Mrs. Flowers had suggested?

like, as if, as though   In informal situations, the preposition *like* is often used for the compound conjunctions *as if* or *as though*. In formal situations, *as if* or *as though* is preferred.

EXAMPLE   Zenta acted **as if** [*not* like] he had never visited the inn.

 QUICK CHECK 1

Correct the errors in usage in each of the following sentences.

EXAMPLE   **1.** Anne Frank she lived for months in the Secret Annex.
1. *Anne Frank lived for months in the Secret Annex.*

1. It's hard to except the horrors of the concentration camps.
2. Alot of people reject the reality of these camps.
3. An visit to Majdanek learned Dara Horn about the camps.
4. Dara felt like the shoes in the huge pile there could of been hers.
5. Not surprisingly, Dara felt badly and claimed that a book doesn't teach as good as a visit to these camps.

of   Do not use *of* with other prepositions such as *inside, off,* and *outside.*

EXAMPLE   The sun is **inside** [*not* inside of] the larger box.

real   In informal situations, *real* is often used as an adverb meaning "very" or "extremely." In formal situations, *very* or *extremely* is preferred.

INFORMAL   Charlie became real intelligent.
FORMAL   Charlie became **extremely** intelligent.

reason . . . because   In informal situations, *reason . . . because* is often used instead of *reason . . . that.* In formal situations, use *reason . . . that,* or revise your sentence.

INFORMAL   The reason I like "Broken Chain" is because I identify with the protagonist, Alfonso.
FORMAL   The **reason** I like "Broken Chain" is **that** I identify with the protagonist, Alfonso.
or
I like "Broken Chain" **because** I identify with the protagonist, Alfonso.

 less   See **fewer, less.**

☞ **lie, lay**   See pages 760–761.

☞ **might of, must of**   See **could of.**

☞ **ought to of**   See **could of.**

☞ **rise, raise**   See page 761.

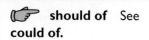

should of   See **could of.**

sit, set   See page 760.

sort of   See **kind of, sort of.**

teach   See **learn, teach.**

well   See **good, well.**

who's, whose   See page 809.

would of   See **could of.**

your, you're   See page 809.

some, somewhat   Do not use *some* for *somewhat* as an adverb.

EXAMPLE   The relationship between Squeaky and Gretchen improved **somewhat** [*not* some].

than, then   *Than* is a conjunction used in making comparisons. *Then* is an adverb that means "at that time."

EXAMPLES   Squeaky is a faster runner **than** Gretchen.

First we went to the store. **Then** we went to the library.

theirself, theirselves   *Theirself* and *theirselves* are nonstandard English. Use *themselves*.

EXAMPLE   They bought **themselves** [*not* theirself *or* theirselves] a telescope.

them   *Them* should not be used as an adjective. Use *those*.

EXAMPLE   Karen gave you **those** [*not* them] cassettes yesterday.

try and   In informal situations, *try and* is often used instead of *try to*. In formal situations, *try to* should be used.

INFORMAL   I will try and find you a picture of O. Henry.

FORMAL   I will **try to** find you a picture of O. Henry.

when, where   Do not use *when* or *where* incorrectly in stating a definition.

NONSTANDARD   A flashback is when a writer interrupts the action in a story to tell about something that happened earlier.

STANDARD   A flashback is an interruption of the action in a story to tell about something that happened earlier.

where   Do not use *where* for *that.*

EXAMPLE   I read **that** [*not* where] O. Henry spent time in prison.

✓ QUICK CHECK 2

Revise the following items according to the rules of formal English.

EXAMPLE   1. People did not have enough food for theirselves.
   1. *People did not have enough food for themselves.*

1. The reason they had to be quiet was because someone outside of their hiding place might hear them.
2. Wherever she was, Anne would try and help people with they're problems.
3. She was often more cheerful then the others.
4. Her sister Margot had become real sick and than died, as others had.
5. You're lucky not to have suffered them brutalities that so many had to bear.

GLOSSARY

The glossary below is an alphabetical list of words found in the selections in this book. Use this glossary just as you use a dictionary—to find out the meanings of unfamiliar words. (Some technical, foreign, and more obscure words in this book are not listed here but instead are defined for you in the footnotes that accompany many of the selections.)

Many words in the English language have more than one meaning. This glossary gives the meanings that apply to the words as they are used in the selections in this book. Words closely related in form and meaning are usually listed together in one entry (for instance, *compassion* and *compassionate*), and the definition is given for the first form.

The following abbreviations are used:

adj.	adjective	*n.*	noun
adv.	adverb	*v.*	verb

Each word's pronunciation is given in parentheses. A guide to the pronunciation symbols appears at the bottom of each right-hand glossary page.

For more information about the words in this glossary, or for information about words not listed here, consult a dictionary.

absurd (ab·sʉrd') *adj.*: laughably unreasonable; ridiculous.

accede (ak·sēd') *v.*: give in; consent.

acute (ə·kyo͞ot') *adj.*: sharp; sensitive.

aggressive (ə·gres'iv) *adj.*: bold and active; given to starting fights.

aghast (ə·gast') *adj.*: horrified.

agitator (aj'i·tāt'ər) *n.*: person who tries to stir up interest in and support for a social or political cause; often used in a negative sense.

alleviate (ə·lē'vē·āt') *v.*: relieve; reduce.

animation (an'i·mā'shən) *n.*: liveliness.

annihilation (ə·nī'ə·lā'shən) *n.*: destruction; killing.

apathy (ap'ə·thē) *n.*: lack of emotion or interest.

appall (ə·pôl') *v.*: horrify; shock.

append (ə·pend') *v.*: attach or add.

apprehensive (ap'rē·hen'siv) *adj.*: uneasy; fearful. —**apprehensively** *adv.*

aroma (ə·rō'mə) *n.*: pleasant smell.

arrogant (ar'ə·gənt) *adj.*: proud and haughty.

arsenal (är'sə·nəl) *n.*: collection or supply. *Arsenal* is often used to refer to a store of weapons.

attain (ə·tān') *v.*: accomplish or reach.

audacity (ô·das'ə·tē) *n.*: boldness.

avaricious (av'ə·rish'əs) *adj.*: greedy for money.

avert (ə·vʉrt') *v.*: 1. turn away. 2. prevent.

banish (ban'ish) *v.*: send away (from a country or community).

behold (bē·hōld') *v.*: look at.

benediction (ben'ə·dik'·shən) *n.*: blessing.

benign (bi·nīn') *adj.*: kind.

blemish (blem'ish) *n.*: imperfection or defect in appearance.

bluster (blus'tər) *v.*: speak or act in a bullying or noisy way.

breach (brēch) *n.*: opening. *Breach* usually refers to a breakthrough in a wall or a line of defense.

brittle (brit''l) *adj.*: 1. sharp and hard. 2. touchy or difficult to deal with.

cajole (kə·jōl') *v.*: coax.

cavort (kə·vôrt') *v.*: leap around happily; play.

cease (sēs) *v.*: stop.

chagrin (shə·grin') *n.*: embarrassment and annoyance caused by disappointment or failure.

channel (chan'əl) *v.*: send in a certain direction.

chide (chīd) *v.*: scold mildly.

chronic (krän'ik) *adj.*: lasting a long time; constant.

clamorous (klam'ər·əs) *adj.*: loud and confused; noisy.

clincher (klinch'ər) *n.*: fact or point that decides an argument.

collaborate (kə·lab'ə·rāt') *v.*: work together on some undertaking.

commence (kə·mens') *v.*: begin.

commend (kə·mend') *v.*: 1. recommend. 2. praise.

---

at, āte, cär; ten, ēve; is, īce; gō, hôrn, look, to͞ol; oil, out; up, fʉr; ə *for unstressed vowels, as* a *in* ago, u *in* focus; ' *as in* Latin (lat''n); chin; she; zh *as in* azure (azh'ər); thin, *the*; ŋ *as in* ring (riŋ)

---

communion (kə·myōōn′yən) *n.*: sharing of thoughts or feelings; a relationship of deep understanding.

compassion (kəm·pash′ən) *n.*: deep sympathy. —**compassionate** *adj.*

compel (kəm·pel′) *v.*: force. —**compulsion** *n.*

compliance (kəm·plī′əns) *n.*: act of giving in to a request, wish, or demand.

comprehension (käm′prē·hen′shən) *n.*: understanding.

compulsory (kəm·pul′sə·rē) *adj.*: required.

confines (kän′fīnz′) *n.*: borders; boundaries.

congenial (kən·jēn′yəl) *adj.*: agreeable; pleasant.

conjecture (kən·jek′chər) *v.*: guess; predict.

conspicuous (kən·spik′yōō·əs) *adj.*: obvious; noticeable.

conspiratorial (kən·spir′ə·tôr′ē·əl) *adj.*: suggesting a secret plot.

consult (kən·sult′) *v.*: 1. discuss things with. 2. ask for an opinion from.

contention (kən·ten′shən) *n.*: conflict; struggle.

couch (kouch) *v.*: put into words; express.

countenance (koun′tə·nəns) *n.*: face.

credulity (krə·dōō′lə·tē) *n.*: tendency to believe too readily.

creed (krēd) *n.*: statement of belief or principles.

crevice (krev′is) *n.*: crack.

culminate (kul′mə·nāt′) *v.*: bring to a climax.

cunning (kun′iŋ) *adj.*: clever; sly. —**cunningly** *adv.*

curt (kurt) *adj.*: brief to the point of rudeness.

cynical (sin′i·kəl) *adj.*: denying the sincerity of people's motives and actions. —**cynically** *adv.*

decree (dē·krē′) *n.*: official order or decision. —*v.*: order officially.

decrepit (dē·krep′it) *adj.*: broken down or worn out from old age or long use.

delusion (di·lōō′zhən) *n.*: false belief.

denunciation (dē·nun′sē·ā′shən) *n.*: harsh criticism; accusation.

deprive (dē·prīv′) *v.*: keep from having, using, or enjoying.

derision (di·rizh′ən) *n.*: contempt; ridicule.

desolate (des′ə·lit) *adj.*: lonely; miserable; deserted.

detect (dē·tekt′) *v.*: discover; perceive.

deterioration (dē·tir′ē·ə·rā′shən) *n.*: worsening; decline.

detract (dē·trakt′) *v.*: take away.

diatribe (dī′ə·trīb′) *n.*: condemnation; harsh, abusive criticism.

dilapidated (də·lap′ə·dāt′id) *adj.*: shabby; falling apart.

discipline (dis′ə·plin′) *n.*: system of rules; branch of knowledge.

disclose (dis·klōz′) *v.*: reveal.

discord (dis′kôrd′) *n.*: conflict or disagreement.

discordant (dis·kôrd′′nt) *adj.*: harsh; disagreeable sounding; not in harmony.

disgruntled (dis·grunt′′ld) *v.* used as *adj.*: displeased; annoyed.

disheveled (di·shev′əld) *adj.*: untidy; rumpled.

disorderly (dis·ôr′dər·lē) *adj.*: disturbing the public order and peace.

dispel (di·spel′) *v.*: scatter; drive away.

dispirit (di·spir′it) *v.*: make sad and discouraged.

dispute (di·spyōōt′) *n.*: argument or debate.

distract (di·strakt′) *v.*: draw the attention away in another direction.

divert (də·vurt′) *v.*: distract.

dogged (dôg′id) *adj.*: stubborn; not giving in easily. —**doggedly** *adv.*

drone (drōn) *n.*: continuous buzzing or humming sound.

duplicate (dōō′pli·kāt′) *v.*: make an exact copy of; make or do again.

ecstasy (ek′stə·sē) *n.*: great delight or joy. —**ecstatic** *adj.*

efficient (e·fish′ənt) *adj.*: producing a desired result with the least waste or expense. —**efficiency** *n.*

elapse (ē·laps′) *v.*: pass (said of time).

elongate (ē·lôŋ′gāt′) *v.*: lengthen; extend.

eloquence (el′ə·kwəns) *n.*: ability to write or speak gracefully and convincingly.

emaciate (ē·mā′shē·āt′) *v.*: make extremely thin, as from starvation or illness. —**emaciated** *v.* used as *adj.*

emanate (em′ə·nāt′) *v.*: come forth.

emerge (ē·murj′) *v.*: come into view.

endeavor (en·dev′ər) *v.*: try.

engulf (en·gulf′) *v.*: swallow up.

ensue (en·sōō′) *v.*: come afterward; follow immediately (said of events).

enterprising (ent′ər·prī′ziŋ) *adj.*: full of energy and ideas; willing to undertake new projects.

enunciate (ē·nun′sē·āt′) *v.*: pronounce clearly and distinctly. —**enunciation** *n.*

escort (es·kôrt′) *v.*: accompany to give protection. —**escort** (es′kôrt′) *n.*: one or more people accompanying others to give protection.

evoke (ē·vōk′) *v.*: call forth.

exalt (eg·zôlt′) *v.*: 1. raise or lift up. 2. praise or glorify.

exaltation (eg'zôl·tā'shən) *n.*: great joy.

expressly (eks·pres'lē) *adv.*: for the specific purpose; particularly.

extravagant (ek·strav'ə·gənt) *adj.*: **1.** showy **2.** excessive; unrestrained.

facade (fə·säd') *n.*: **1.** front of a building. **2.** false or artificial front or appearance.

fastidious (fas·tid'ē·əs) *adj.*: fussy; hard to please.

fatigue (fə·tēg') *n.*: exhaustion; tiredness.

finicky (fin'ik·ē) *adj.*: fussy; overly particular.

foreboding (fôr·bōd'iŋ) *n.*: feeling that something bad will happen.

forlorn (fôr·lôrn') *adj.*: abandoned and lonely.

fortify (fôrt'ə·fī') *v.*: strengthen.

fraudulent (frô'jə·lənt) *adj.*: based on deceit, trickery, or cheating.

frenzy (fren'zē) *n.*: wild outburst.

frivolous (friv'ə·ləs) *adj.*: not properly serious; silly.

fugitive (fyōō'ji·tiv) *n.*: person fleeing from danger.

functional (fuŋk'shə·nəl) *adj.*: designed mainly to be useful rather than to look good.

furtive (fur'tiv) *adj.*: done or acting in a secret manner; sneaky. —**furtively** *adv.*

garment (gär'mənt) *n.*: article of clothing.

garrulous (gar'ə·ləs) *adj.*: talking a great deal, especially about unimportant things.

gaunt (gônt) *adj.*: thin and bony; hollow-eyed.

gesticulation (jes·tik'yōō·lā'shən) *n.*: energetic gesture.

gingerly (jin'jər'lē) *adv.*: carefully; cautiously.

glower (glou'ər) *n.*: angry stare; scowl.

glutinous (glōōt''n·əs) *adj.*: sticky; gluey.

gravity (grav'i·tē) *n.*: seriousness.

grimace (grim'is) *n.*: twisting of the face expressing pain or disgust.

gritty (grit'ē) *adj.*: containing sand or dirt.

grueling (grōō'əl·iŋ) *adj.*: exhausting; extremely demanding.

gyration (jī·rā'shən) *n.*: circular motion.

habitation (hab'i·tā'shən) *n.*: act of living somewhere; occupancy.

haggard (hag'ərd) *adj.*: looking worn-out and exhausted.

harrowing (har'ō·iŋ) *v.* used as *adj.*: distressing; painful.

hasty (hās'tē) *adj.*: quick or hurried. —**hastily** *adv.*

hearth (härth) *n.*: fireplace.

hoax (hōks) *n.*: trick or fraud.

homely (hōm'lē) *adj.*: plain and everyday.

hubbub (hub'bub') *n.*: confused sound of many voices; uproar.

huddle (hud''l) *v.*: press close together, as for warmth.

humane (hyōō·mān') *adj.*: kind; merciful; sympathetic.

husky (hus'kē) *adj.*: **1.** sounding deep and hoarse; rough. **2.** big and strong.

hypothesis (hī·päth'ə·sis) *n.*: explanation or theory to be proved.

illiteracy (il·lit'ər·ə·sē) *n.*: inability to read or write.

illuminate (i·lōō'mə·nāt') *v.*: light up.

imminent (im'ə·nənt) *adj.*: likely to happen right away (said of danger, evil, misfortune).

impair (im·per') *v.*: damage.

implicit (im·plis'it) *adj.*: **1.** implied or suggested rather than expressed outright. **2.** without reservation or doubt; unquestioning. —**implicitly** *adv.*

impromptu (im·prämp'tōō') *adj.*: unplanned; made or done without preparation.

improvise (im'prə·vīz') *v.*: make or do with the materials at hand (usually to fill a need that was not foreseen).

impudent (im'pyōō·dənt) *adj.*: too bold; disrespectful.

inarticulate (in'är·tik'yōō·lit) *adj.*: **1.** unable to speak. **2.** unable to speak understandably or effectively.

inaudible (in·ôd'ə·bəl) *adj.*: incapable of being heard.

incentive (in·sent'iv) *n.*: reason to do something; motivation.

incessant (in·ses'ənt) *adj.*: constant; continual. —**incessantly** *adv.*

incomprehensible (in'käm'prē·hen'sə·bəl) *adj.*: impossible to understand.

incontinent (in·kän'tə·nənt) *adj.*: lacking self-control. —**incontinently** *adv.*

incredulous (in·krej'oo·ləs) *adj.*: unbelieving. —**incredulously** *adv.*

indignant (in·dig'nənt) *adj.*: expressing anger caused by something felt to be unjust. —**indignantly** *adv.*

---

at, āte, cär; ten, ēve, is, īce; gō, hôrn, look, tōōl; oil, out; up, fur; ə *for unstressed vowels, as* a *in* ago, u *in* focus; ' *as in* Latin (lat''n); chin; she; zh *as in* azure (azh'ər); thin, *the*; ŋ *as in* ring (riŋ)

---

indomitable (in·däm′i·tə·bəl) *adj.*: unconquerable.

industrious (in·dus′trē·əs) *adj.*: hard-working. **—industriously** *adv.*

ineffable (in·ef′ə·bəl) *adj.*: indescribable; too great to describe.

inexplicable (in·eks′pli·kə·bəl) *adj.*: incapable of being explained.

infamous (in′fə·məs) *adj.*: having a very bad reputation.

infuse (in·fyōōz′) *v.*: fill.

insatiable (in·sā′shə·bəl) *adj.*: incapable of being satisfied; always wanting more.

insolent (in′sə·lənt) *adj.*: boldly disrespectful. **—insolently** *adv.*

instill (in·stil′) *v.*: gradually put in (an idea or feeling). (*Stilla* is Latin for "drop"; *instill* literally means "put in drop by drop.")

instinctive (in·stiŋk′tiv) *adj.*: automatic; done without thinking. **—instinctively** *adv.*

insufferable (in·suf′ər·ə·bəl) *adj.*: unbearable.

intent (in·tent′) *adj.*: paying close attention. **—intently** *adv.*

interminable (in·tur′mi·nə·bəl) *adj.*: endless; seeming to last forever.

intersperse (in′tər·spurs′) *v.*: scatter or place here and there among other things or people.

intolerant (in·täl′ər·ənt) *adj.*: unwilling to put up with something.

introspective (in′trō·spek′tiv) *adj.*: looking inward; observing one's own thoughts and feelings.

invariable (in·ver′ē·ə·bəl) *adj.*: unchanging. **—invariably** *adv.*

jostle (jäs′əl) *v.*: bump or shove.

jubilation (jōō′bə·lā′shən) *n.*: happy celebration.

lackadaisical (lak′ə·dā′zi·kəl) *adj.*: showing lack of interest or spirit.

laconic (lə·kän′ik) *adj.*: using few words. **—laconically** *adv.*

legacy (leg′ə·sē) *n.*: **1.** money or property left to someone by a will. **2.** anything handed down, as from an ancestor.

lenient (lēn′yənt) *adj.*: forgiving; not harsh in punishing.

loathe (lōth) *v.*: hate.

lucid (lōō′sid) *adj.*: **1.** clearheaded. **2.** easily understood.

macabre (mə·käb′rə) *adj.*: gruesome; horrible.

mar (mär) *v.*: spoil or make imperfect.

medley (med′lē) *n.*: jumble; mixture of dissimilar things.

melancholy (mel′ən·käl′ē) *n.*: sadness; gloominess.

merge (murj) *v.*: mix; combine.

meticulous (mə·tik′yōō·ləs) *adj.*: extremely careful about details; fussy.

mislead (mis·lēd′) *v.*: deceive.

monotonous (mə·nät′'n·əs) *adj.*: unchanging in tone; boring because of lack of variety.

motif (mō·tēf′) *n.*: repeated figure in a design; theme.

multitude (mul′tə·tōōd′) *n.*: large number of people or things; crowd.

muster (mus′tər) *v.*: call forth; gather.

mutinous (myōōt′'n·əs) *adj.*: rebellious. *Mutiny* usually refers to a revolt of soldiers or sailors against their officers.

mystify (mis′tə·fī′) *v.*: puzzle.

nuance (nōō′äns′) *n.*: shade of meaning.

oasis (ō·ā′sis) *n.*: place in a desert with plants and a supply of water; place or thing offering relief.

oblivious (ə·bliv′ē·əs) *adj.*: unaware.

obscure (əb·skyoor′) *v.*: hide.

obstruct (əb·strukt′) *v.*: block.

officious (ə·fish′əs) *adj.*: bossy and interfering. **—officiously** *adv.*

omen (ō′mən) *n.*: thing believed to be a sign or warning of a future event.

ominous (äm′ə·nəs) *adj.*: threatening; seeming to indicate that something bad will happen.

onslaught (än′slôt′) *n.*: attack.

opportunist (äp′ər·tōōn′ist) *n.*: someone who acts only to further his or her own interests, without regard for basic principles.

oratory (ôr′ə·tôr′ē) *n.*: skill in public speaking; the art of public speaking.

ostentatious (äs′tən·tā′shəs) *adj.*: showy or exaggerated. **—ostentatiously** *adv.*

palatable (pal′ə·tə·bəl) *adj.*: fit to eat; acceptable.

pall (pôl) *v.*: become boring.

pallid (pal′id) *adj.*: pale.

pandemonium (pan′də·mō′nē·əm) *n.*: wild disorder, noise, and confusion.

paranoia (par′ə·noi′ə) *n.*: mental disorder that often causes people to believe they are being persecuted; false suspicions.

parasite (par′ə·sīt′) *n.*: person who lives at others' expense without making any contribution.

passive (pas′iv) *adj.*: inactive; offering no resistance.

pen (pen) *v.*: confine or enclose. (A pen is a fenced area where animals are kept.)

penance (pen′əns) *n.*: act of self-punishment done to express sorrow and regret for one's wrongdoing.

peremptory (pər·emp′tə·rē) *adj.*: commanding; allowing no debate or delay.

peril (per′əl) *n.*: danger.

pervade (pər·vād′) *v.*: exist throughout.

placid (plas′id) *adj.*: calm. **—placidly** *adv.*

plod (pläd) *v.*: move heavily or with great effort.

poignant (poin′yənt) *adj.*: causing sadness or pain; touching.

populate (päp′yoo·lāt′) *v.*: inhabit; live in or on.

portly (pôrt′lē) *adj.*: large and heavy in a dignified way.

postpone (pōst·pōn′) *v.*: put off until later. **—postponement** *n.*

precede (prē·sēd′) *v.*: be, come, or go before.

predecessor (pred′ə·ses′ər) *n.*: person who held a position before the person who currently holds it.

premonition (prēm′ə·nish′ən) *n.*: feeling that something, especially something bad, will happen.

preoccupation (prē·äk′yoo·pā′shən) *n.*: state of being absorbed in thought.

presumptuous (prē·zump′choo·əs) *adj.*: overly bold or confident; taking too much for granted.

proclivity (prō·kliv′ə·tē) *n.*: natural tendency.

prodigious (prō·dij′əs) *adj.*: huge; amazing.

prodigy (präd′ə·jē) *n.*: child with highly unusual talent or genius.

proffer (präf′ər) *v.*: offer.

proposition (präp′ə·zish′ən) *n.*: **1.** proposal; suggested plan. **2.** statement put forward for discussion or debate.

prosaic (prō·zā′ik) *adj.*: ordinary; unimaginative.

provisions (prō·vizh′ənz) *n.*: stock of food and other supplies.

psyche (sī′kē) *n.*: mind or soul.

punctual (puŋk′choo·əl) *adj.*: on time; prompt.

puncture (puŋk′chər) *v.*: make a hole in.

pursuit (pər·soot′) *n.*: chase.

qualm (kwäm) *n.*: sudden feeling of uneasiness or doubt.

quiver (kwiv′ər) *v.*: tremble.

rapacious (rə·pā′shəs) *adj.*: greedy.

rapt (rapt) *adj.*: completely absorbed.

raucous (rô′kəs) *adj.*: harsh sounding; loud.

ravenous (rav′ə·nəs) *adj.*: extremely hungry.

recede (ri·sēd′) *v.*: move back; become more distant.

reconciliation (rek′ən·sil′ē·ā′shən) *n.*: act of making up after an argument or disagreement.

reconnoiter (rek′ə·noit′ər) *v.*: survey a place to gather information.

refrain (ri·frān′) *v.*: hold back.

refuge (ref′yooj) *n.*: place of safety.

refute (ri·fyoot′) *v.*: prove wrong with evidence.

regal (rē′gəl) *adj.*: majestic; of or like a queen or king. **—regally** *adv.*

regression (ri·gresh′ən) *n.*: return to an earlier or less advanced condition.

reiterate (rē·it′ə·rāt′) *v.*: repeat.

relish (rel′ish) *n.*: pleasure; enjoyment.

reluctant (ri·luk′tənt) *adj.*: unwilling. **—reluctantly** *adv.*

reminiscence (rem′ə·nis′əns) *n.*: memory or retelling of past experiences.

remit (ri·mit′) *v.*: send as payment.

remorse (ri·môrs′) *n.*: deep feeling of guilt.

renegade (ren′ə·gād′) *n.*: traitor; person who abandons a cause and goes over to the other side.

renounce (ri·nouns′) *v.*: give up; abandon.

reprimand (rep′rə·mand′) *v.*: scold; correct sharply.

reproachful (ri·prōch′fəl) *adj.*: expressing blame or disapproval. **—reproachfully** *adv.*

requisition (rek′wə·zish′ən) *v.*: **1.** make a formal written order or request for. **2.** demand or take by authority.

resolute (rez′ə·loot′) *adj.*: purposeful; determined.

resound (ri·zound′) *v.*: echo.

reverberate (ri·vur′bə·rāt′) *v.*: echo.

revile (ri·vīl′) *v.*: speak abusively; call names.

rivet (riv′it) *v.*: fasten or hold firmly, as if by rivets (metal bolts or pins).

rove (rōv) *v.*: roam or wander.

---

at, āte, cär; ten, ēve; is, īce; gō, hôrn, look, tool; oil, out; up, fur; ə *for unstressed vowels, as* a *in* ago, u *in* focus; ′ *as in* Latin (lat′'n); chin; she; zh *as in* azure (azh′ər); thin, *the;* ŋ *as in* ring (riŋ)

---

rueful (rōō′fəl) *adj.*: feeling or expressing embarrassment and regret. —**ruefully** *adv.*

sagacity (sə·gas′ə·tē) *n.*: intelligence and good judgment.

savor (sā′vər) *v.*: enjoy and appreciate.

scoff (skäf) *v.*: mock or show scorn.

sedate (si·dāt′) *adj.*: calm and serious. —**sedately** *adv.*

serene (sə·rēn′) *adj.*: calm; peaceful. —**serenity** *n.*

simper (sim′pər) *n.*: silly or self-conscious smile.

simultaneous (sī′məl·tā′nē·əs) *adj.*: occurring, done, or existing at the same time. —**simultaneously** *adv.*

smirk (smʉrk) *v.*: smile in a conceited, knowing way.

somnolent (säm′nə·lənt) *adj.*: drowsy.

specter (spek′tər) *n.*: 1. ghost. 2. any object of fear or dread.

spendthrift (spend′thrift′) *n.*: person who spends money carelessly or wastefully.

stagger (stag′ər) *v.*: move unsteadily, as if about to collapse.

stalk (stôk) *v.*: walk in a stiff, grim, or proud way.

stately (stāt′lē) *adj.*: majestic; dignified; grand.

sterile (ster′əl) *adj.*: 1. free from germs. 2. unproductive.

stoop (stōōp) *v.*: bend forward from habit.

suavity (swäv′ə·tē) *n.*: smoothness; politeness.

sublime (sə·blīm′) *adj.*: majestic; grand.

succession (sək·sesh′ən) *n.*: a number of things or people coming one after another; series.

sufficient (sə·fish′ənt) *adj.*: enough.

sullen (sul′ən) *adj.*: sulky; resentful.

summon (sum′ən) *v.*: call for.

surplus (sʉr′plus′) *adj.*: extra.

surreptitious (sʉr′əp·tish′əs) *adj.*: done or acting in a secret or sneaky way. —**surreptitiously** *adv.*

swagger (swag′ər) *v.*: 1. walk in a bold or arrogant way. 2. boast loudly or show off.

tangible (tan′jə·bəl) *adj.*: capable of being felt, observed, or understood.

tantalizing (tan′tə·līz′iŋ) *adj.*: teasing by remaining unavailable or by withholding something desired by someone; tempting. (In Greek mythology, Tantalus was a king condemned after death to stand in water that moved away whenever he tried to drink it and to remain under branches of fruit that were just out of reach.)

taut (tôt) *adj.*: tightly stretched.

tentative (ten′tə·tiv) *adj.*: hesitant; uncertain. —**tentatively** *adv.*

termination (tʉr′mə·nā′shən) *n.*: ending.

terse (tʉrs) *adj.*: brief and clear; without unnecessary words. —**tersely** *adv.*

titanic (tī·tan′ik) *adj.*: of great size, strength, or power. (In Greek mythology the Titans were giant gods who were overthrown by their children, the Olympian gods.)

torrent (tôr′ənt) *n.*: flood.

tournament (tʉr′nə·mənt) *n.*: series of contests.

traumatic (trô·mat′ik) *adj.*: emotionally painful; causing shock.

treacherous (trech′ər·əs) *adj.*: 1. disloyal. 2. untrustworthy; giving a false appearance of safety. —**treachery** *n.*

treaty (trēt′ē) *n.*: formal agreement between nations.

tremor (trem′ər) *n.*: quiver; vibration; trembling movement.

tremulous (trem′yōō·ləs) *adj.*: 1. trembling. 2. fearful or timid.

tumult (tōō′mult′) *n.*: noisy commotion; uproar.

tyranny (tir′ə·nē) *n.*: cruel and unjust rule or use of power.

unabashed (un′ə·basht′) *adj.*: unembarrassed; unashamed.

unseemly (un·sēm′lē) *adj.*: not decent or proper.

vault (vôlt) *v.*: jump over.

vehement (vē′ə·mənt) *adj.*: forceful; passionate. —**vehemently** *adv.*

verify (ver′ə·fī′) *v.*: check or test for correctness; confirm.

vex (veks) *v.*: disturb; annoy.

vigil (vij′əl) *n.*: watch; act of staying awake to keep watch.

vile (vīl) *adj.*: disagreeable; disgusting.

visage (viz′ij) *n.*: face or facial expression.

vouch (vouch) *v.*: give a guarantee or assurance.

wary (wer′ē) *adj.*: cautious. —**warily** *adv.*

wrathful (rath′fəl) *adj.*: extremely angry.

writhe (rīth) *v.*: twist and turn.

wry (rī) *adj.*: twisted; grimly humorous. —**wryly** *adv.*

zeal (zēl) *n.*: great enthusiasm; devotion to a cause.

For permission to reprint copyrighted material, grateful acknowledgment is made to the following sources:

ABC/Kane Productions International, Inc.: From "Touched by a Dolphin," an ABC World of Discovery production by ABC/Kane Productions International, Inc., television transcript by Pamela Stacey. Copyright © 1997 by ABC/Kane Productions International, Inc.

Akwe:kon Press: From "Something to Be Proud of" by Virginia Driving Hawk Sneve from *Akwe:kon Journal,* vol. 10, no. 1, Spring 1993. Copyright © 1993 by Akwe:kon Press.

American Library Association: From "Starred Reviews: Books for Youth: *Parallel Journeys*" by Hazel Rochman from *Booklist,* vol. 91, no. 18, May 15, 1995. Copyright © 1995 by American Library Association. From "Of Life, Love, Death, Kids, and Inhalation Therapy: An Interview with Paul Zindel" by Audrey Eaglen from *Top of the News,* vol. 34, no. 2, Winter 1978. Copyright © 1978 by American Library Association.

The Bancroft Library: Text from "The Wise Old Woman" from *The Sea of Gold and Other Tales from Japan,* adapted by Yoshiko Uchida. Copyright © 1965 by Yoshiko Uchida.

Elizabeth Barnett, Literary Executor: "The Courage That My Mother Had" from *Collected Poems* by Edna St. Vincent Millay. Copyright © 1954, 1982 by Edna St. Vincent Millay and Norma Millay Ellis. Published by HarperCollins.

Susan Bergholz Literary Services, New York: Autobiographical comment by Sandra Cisneros. Copyright © 1987 by Sandra Cisneros. First published in *The Texas Observer,* September 1987. All rights reserved. "Bien águila" from *La casa en Mango Street* by Sandra Cisneros, translated by Elena Poniatowska. Copyright © 1984 by Sandra Cisneros; translation copyright © 1994 by Elena Poniatowska. Published by Vintage Español, a division of Random House, Inc. All rights reserved. "A Smart Cookie" from *The House on Mango Street,* by Sandra Cisneros. Copyright © 1984 by Sandra Cisneros. Published by Vintage Books, a division of Random House, Inc., and in hardcover by Alfred A. Knopf in 1994. All rights reserved. "Three Wise Guys" by Sandra Cisneros. Copyright © 1990 by Sandra Cisneros. First published by *Vista* magazine, December 23, 1990. All rights reserved.

Bilingual Press/Editorial Bilingüe, Arizona State University, Tempe, AZ: From "A Conversation with Leroy V. Quintana" by Douglas Benson from *The Bilingual Review/La Revista Bilingüe,* vol. 12, no. 3, September–December 1985. Copyright © 1985 by Bilingual Press/Editorial Bilingüe. "The Habit of Movement" from *Reaching the Mainland & Selected New Poems* by Judith Ortiz Cofer. Copyright © 1995 by Bilingual Press/Editorial Bilingüe.

The Boston Globe: "Reward They Get Is Just" by Omar Kelly from *The Boston Globe,* June 19, 1998, from "Boston Globe Online Archives," on-line. Available http://newslibrary.krmediastream.com.

Chronicle Books: "Oranges" from *New and Selected Poems* by Gary Soto. Copyright © 1995 by Gary Soto. Published by Chronicle Books, San Francisco.

Ruth Cohen for Lensey Namioka: Comment on "The Inn of Lost Time" by Lensey Namioka. Copyright © 1997 by Lensey Namioka. "The Inn of Lost Time" by Lensey Namioka from *Short Stories by Outstanding Writers for Young Adults,* edited by Donald R. Gallo. Copyright © 1989 by Lensey Namioka. All rights reserved.

Don Congdon Associates, Inc.: "The Drummer Boy of Shiloh" by Ray Bradbury. Copyright © 1960 by The Curtis Publishing Company; copyright renewed © 1988 by Ray Bradbury. From "Drunk, and in Charge of a Bicycle" from *The Stories of Ray Bradbury.* Copyright © 1980 by Ray Bradbury. "There Will Come Soft Rains" by Ray Bradbury. Copyright © 1950 by the Crowell-Collier Publishing Co.; copyright renewed © 1977 by Ray Bradbury. From "Ray Bradbury," an interview by Frank Filosa from *On Being a Writer,* edited by Bill Strickland. Copyright © 1967 by Frank Filosa.

The Continuum Publishing Company: From "Toni Cade Bambara" from *Black Women Writers at Work,* edited by Claudia Tate. Copyright © 1983 by Claudia Tate.

Alison Conway: From drafts of "Horsing Around" by Alison Conway. Copyright © 1997 by Alison Conway.

Robert Cormier: From "Robert Cormier" by Robert Cormier from *Speaking for Ourselves,* compiled and edited by Donald R. Gallo. Copyright © 1990 by Robert Cormier.

Jeannette Henry Costo: "Memorial and Recommendations of the Grand Council Fire of American Indians presented to the Hon. William Hale Thompson, mayor of Chicago, December 1, 1927" from "The Background" from *Textbooks and the American Indian* by the American Indian Historical Society, written by Jeannette Henry, edited by Rupert Costo. Copyright © 1970 by the Indian Historian Press, Inc.

The Literary Trustees of Walter de la Mare and the Society of Authors as their representative: From "Silver" from *The Complete Poems of Walter de la Mare.* Published in the United States in 1970.

Dial Books for Young Readers, a division of Penguin Putnam Inc.: Text and one illustration from "Brer Rabbit and Brer Lion" from *The Tales of Uncle Remus* by Julius Lester, illustrated by Jerry Pinkney. Text copyright © 1987 by Julius Lester. Illustrations copyright © 1987 by Jerry Pinkney.

Doubleday, a division of Random House, Inc.: From "Salvation Is the Issue" by Toni Cade Bambara from *Black Women Writers (1950–1980),* edited by Mari Evans. Copyright © 1984 by Mari Evans. From *Anne Frank: The Diary of a Young Girl* by Anne Frank. Copyright 1952 by Otto H. Frank.

Dramatists Play Service, Inc., and Paul Zindel: *Let Me Hear You Whisper* slightly adapted from *Let Me Hear You Whisper and The Ladies Should Be in Bed: Two Plays* by Paul Zindel. Copyright © 1973 by Paul Zindel. CAUTION: The reprinting of *Let Me Hear You Whisper* included in this volume is reprinted by permission of the author and Dramatists Play Service, Inc. The stock and amateur performance rights in this play are controlled exclusively by Dramatists Play Service, Inc., 440 Park Avenue South, New York, NY 10016. No stock or amateur production of the play may be given without obtaining in advance the written permission of the Dramatists Play Service, Inc., and paying the requisite fee. Inquiries regarding all other rights should be addressed to Gilbert Parker, William Morris Agency, Inc., 1325 Avenue of the Americas, New York, NY 10019.

Spencer Duncan: From "One Good Man" by Spencer Duncan from *Calliope,* vol. 5, 1992. Copyright © 1992 by Spencer Duncan. Published by Topeka West High School, Topeka, KS.

Mary Jennifer Ellison, Webb School of Knoxville, Knoxville, Tennessee: "Maiden-Savin' Sam (Ballad)" by Jenny Ellison from *Webb of Words,* 1992–93. Copyright © 1992 by Mary Jennifer Ellison. Published by the students of the Middle School of Webb School of Knoxville, TN.

Farrar, Straus & Giroux, Inc.: "Charles" from *The Lottery* by Shirley Jackson. Copyright © 1948, 1949 by Shirley Jackson; copyright renewed © 1976, 1977 by Laurence Hyman, Barry Hyman, Mrs. Sarah Webster, and Mrs. Joanne Schnurer.

Gale Research Company Inc.: From "Paul Zindel" from *Authors & Artists for Young Adults,* vol. 2, edited by Agnes Garrett and Helga P. McCue. Copyright © 1989 by Gale Research Company Inc. From "Ann Petry" from *Contemporary Authors: Autobiography Series,* vol. 6, edited by Adele Sarkissian. Copyright © 1988 by Gale Research

Company Inc. From "Yoshiko Uchida" from *Something About the Author: Autobiography Series,* vol. 1, edited by Adele Sarkissian. Copyright © 1986 by Gale Research Company Inc. From "Walter Dean Myers" from *Something About the Author,* vol. 41, edited by Anne Commire. Copyright © 1985 by Gale Research Company Inc. From "Gary Paulsen" from *Something About the Author,* vol. 54, edited by Anne Commire. Copyright © 1989 by Gale Research Company Inc.

Marcia Ann Gillespie: From "Maya Angelou," an interview by Marcia Ann Gillespie from *Essence,* December 1992. Copyright © 1992 by Marcia Ann Gillespie.

Grolier International, Inc.: From *New Kids on the Block: Oral Histories of Immigrant Teens* by Janet Bode. Copyright © 1989 by Janet Bode. Published by Franklin Watts.

Grove/Atlantic, Inc.: "Love in the Middle of the Air" from "Circus" from *Word Alchemy* by Lenore Kandel. Copyright © 1960, 1966, 1967 by Lenore Kandel.

Harcourt Brace & Company: "The Naming of Cats" and illustrations from *Old Possum's Book of Practical Cats* by T. S. Eliot, illustrated by Edward Gorey. Copyright 1939 by T. S. Eliot; copyright renewed © 1967 by Esme Valerie Eliot. Illustrations copyright © 1982 by Edward Gorey. From "Tentative (First Model) Definitions of Poetry" from *Good Morning, America* by Carl Sandburg. Copyright 1928 and renewed © 1956 by Carl Sandburg. From Poem No. 45 (retitled "They Have Yarns") from *The People, Yes* by Carl Sandburg. Copyright 1936 by Harcourt Brace & Company; copyright renewed © 1964 by Carl Sandburg. "Broken Chain" from *Baseball in April and Other Stories* by Gary Soto. Copyright © 1990 by Gary Soto.

HarperCollins Publishers: "Paul Bunyan" and "Point of View" from *Where the Sidewalk Ends* by Shel Silverstein. Copyright © 1974 by Evil Eye Music, Inc. "We Are All One" from *The Rainbow People* by Laurence Yep. Text copyright © 1989 by Laurence Yep. From *The Pigman and Me* by Paul Zindel. Copyright © 1991 by Paul Zindel.

Harvard University Press and the Trustees of Amherst College: From "Fame is a bee" from *The Poems of Emily Dickinson,* edited by Thomas H. Johnson. Copyright © 1951, 1955, 1979, 1983 by the President and Fellows of Harvard College. Published by The Belknap Press of Harvard University Press, Cambridge, Mass.

Hill and Wang, a division of Farrar, Straus & Giroux, Inc.: From "I've Known Rivers" from *The Big Sea* by Langston Hughes. Copyright © 1940 by Langston Hughes; copyright renewed © 1968 by Arna Bontemps and George Houston Bass.

Francisco Jiménez: Comment on "The Circuit" by Francisco Jiménez. Copyright © 1997 by Francisco Jiménez. "The Circuit" by Francisco Jiménez from *Cuentos Chicanos: A Short Story Anthology,* edited by Rodolfo A. Anaya and Antonio Marquez. Copyright © 1984 by the University of New Mexico Press. Published for *New America* by the University of New Mexico Press.

Daniel Keyes: "Flowers for Algernon" by Daniel Keyes from *The Magazine of Fantasy & Science Fiction.* Copyright © 1959, 1987 by Daniel Keyes. Quote by Daniel Keyes.

The Heirs to the Estate of Martin Luther King, Jr., c/o Writers House, Inc. as agent for the proprietor: "I Have a Dream" by Martin Luther King, Jr. Copyright © 1963 by Martin Luther King, Jr.; copyright renewed © 1991 by Coretta Scott King.

Alfred A. Knopf, Inc.: "The Landlady" from *Kiss, Kiss* by Roald Dahl. Copyright © 1959 by Roald Dahl. Originally appeared in *The New Yorker.* From "Lucky Break" from *The Wonderful Story of Henry Sugar and Six More* by Roald Dahl. Copyright © 1945, 1947, 1952, 1977 by Roald Dahl. "The People Could Fly" and excerpt from *The People Could Fly* by Virginia Hamilton. Text copyright © 1985 by Virginia Hamilton. "Refugee in America" from *Collected Poems* by Langston Hughes. Copyright © 1994 by the Estate of Langston Hughes. "Condition" from *All You Who Sleep Tonight* by Vikram Seth. Copyright © 1987, 1990 by Vikram Seth.

Barbara S. Kouts on behalf of Joseph Bruchac: "Birdfoot's Grampa" by Joseph Bruchac. Copyright © 1978 by Joseph Bruchac.

Amy Ling: "Grandma Ling" (and excerpts) by Amy Ling. Copyright © 1980 by Amy Ling. Originally published as "Grandma" in *Bridge: An Asian American Perspective,* vol. 7, no. 3, 1980. Photo caption by Amy Ling. Copyright © 1997 by Amy Ling.

Little, Brown and Company: Excerpt (retitled "Camp Harmony") from *Nisei Daughter* by Monica Sone. Copyright © 1953 and renewed © 1981 by Monica Sone.

Little Simon, an imprint of Simon & Schuster Children's Publishing Division: "The Old Grandfather and His Little Grandson" from *Twenty-two Russian Tales for Young Children* by Leo Tolstoy, translated by Miriam Morton. English translation copyright © 1969 by Miriam Morton.

Macmillan General Reference USA, a division of Ahsuog, Inc.: From *Webster's New World Dictionary,* Third College Edition. Copyright © 1988, 1991, 1994, 1996, 1997 by Simon & Schuster, Inc.

Macmillan Library Reference USA, a division of Ahsuog, Inc.: From "A Note on This Book" and "Strong but Quirky" (retitled "Davy Is Born") from *Yankee Thunder: The Legendary Life of Davy Crockett* by Irwin Shapiro. Copyright 1944 by Irwin Shapiro.

McIntosh and Otis, Inc.: "Too Soon a Woman" by Dorothy M. Johnson from *Cosmopolitan,* March 1953. Copyright © 1953 and renewed © 1981 by Dorothy M. Johnson.

Heather K. E. Melchert: "Freedom Walk" by Heather Melchert from *Ursa Major,* vol. III, Spring 1993. Copyright © 1993 by Heather Melchert. Published by Moscow Junior High School, Moscow, ID.

Merlyn's Pen: "Na Na" by Jaqueta Oliver from *Merlyn's Pen,* April/May 1991. Copyright © 1991 by Jaqueta Oliver. First appeared in *Merlyn's Pen: The National Magazines of Student Writing.* All rights reserved. "Ode to a Toad" by Anne-Marie Wulfsberg from *Merlyn's Pen,* April/May 1991. Copyright © 1991 by Anne-Marie Wulfsberg. First appeared in *Merlyn's Pen: The National Magazines of Student Writing.* All rights reserved. "She Is Watching Us" by Theresa Ireland from *Merlyn's Pen,* February/March 1993. Copyright © 1993 by Theresa Ireland. First appeared in *Merlyn's Pen: The National Magazines of Student Writing.* All rights reserved. "Walking with Living Feet" by Dara Horn from *Merlyn's Pen,* October/November 1993. Copyright © 1993 by Merlyn's Pen, Inc. First appeared in *Merlyn's Pen: The National Magazines of Student Writing.* All rights reserved. "The Cormorant in My Bathtub" by Brooke Rogers from *Merlyn's Pen,* vol. VIII, no. 5, Special Issue 1993. Copyright © 1993 by Merlyn's Pen. First appeared in *Merlyn's Pen: The National Magazines of Student Writing.* All rights reserved. "I Am Kwakkoli" by Bisco Hill from *Merlyn's Pen,* Middle School Edition, vol. X, no. 1, October/November 1994. Copyright © 1994 by Merlyn's Pen. First appeared in *Merlyn's Pen: The National Magazines of Student Writing.* All rights reserved.

Miami Herald: From "John Glenn Left Me Awed—Thank You" by Leonard Pitts, Jr., from *Miami Herald,* November 7, 1998. Copyright © 1998 by the Miami Herald.

Modern Curriculum Press, an imprint of Pearson Learning: Excerpt (retitled "The Deserter") from *Across Five Aprils* by Irene Hunt. Copyright © 1964 by Irene Hunt.

William Morrow & Company, Inc.: From "Founding Fathers" from *Legends, Lies & Cherished Myths of American History* by Richard Shenkman. Copyright © 1988 by Richard Shenkman.

Walter Dean Myers: "The Treasure of Lemon Brown" by Walter Dean Myers from *Face to Face: A Collection of Stories by Celebrated Soviet and American Writers,* edited by Thomas Pettepiece and Anatoly Aleksin. Copyright © 1990 by Walter Dean Myers. From "Walter Dean Myers" by Walter Dean Myers from *Speaking for Ourselves,* edited by Donald R. Gallo. Copyright © 1990 by Walter Dean Myers.

NEA Today: From "Making Intellect Cool," an interview with Walter Dean Myers by Nancy Needham, from *NEA Today,* December 1991. Published by the National Education Association.

Diana Nyad: From "Segment #10: Diana Nyad Discusses Iditarod Sled Dog Race" (retitled "The Last Great Race on Earth"), from *Morning Edition* on National Public Radio. Copyright © 1993 by Diana Nyad. Broadcast on March 18, 1993.

Dwight Okita: "In Response to Executive Order 9066" from *Crossing with the Light* by Dwight Okita. Copyright © 1992 by Dwight Okita. Published by Tia Chucha Press, Chicago.

The Palm Beach Post: "After Ellis Island: A Triumph of the Human Spirit" by Jan Tuckwood from *The Palm Beach Post*, July 5, 1998. Copyright © 1998 by The Palm Beach Post.

Pantheon Books, a division of Random House, Inc.: "The Moustache" from *Eight Plus One* by Robert Cormier. Copyright © 1975 by Robert Cormier. "Coyote Steals the Sun and Moon" and excerpts from *American Indian Myths and Legends* by Richard Erdoes and Alfonso Ortiz. Copyright © 1984 by Richard Erdoes and Alfonso Ortiz.

Shandin Pete: "Grandpa" (and excerpts) by Shandin Pete.

Philosophical Library, New York: From *What I Believe* by Albert Einstein. Copyright 1930 by Philosophical Library.

Leroy V. Quintana: "Legacy II" by Leroy V. Quintana from *The Face of Poetry*, edited by LaVerne Harrell Clark and Mary MacArthur. Copyright © 1979 by Leroy V. Quintana.

Random House, Inc.: Excerpts (retitled "Mrs. Flowers") from *I Know Why the Caged Bird Sings* by Maya Angelou. Copyright © 1969 and renewed © 1997 by Maya Angelou. "Raymond's Run" and "A Sort of Preface" from *Gorilla, My Love* by Toni Cade Bambara. Copyright © 1971, 1972 by Toni Cade Bambara. *The Diary of Anne Frank* by Albert Hackett, Frances Goodrich Hackett, and Otto Frank. Copyright © 1956 by Albert Hackett, Frances Goodrich Hackett, and Otto Frank. CAUTION: *The Diary of Anne Frank* is the sole property of the dramatists and is fully protected by copyright. It may not be acted by professionals or amateurs without written permission and the payment of a royalty. All rights, including professional, amateur, stock, radio broadcasting, television, motion picture, recitation, lecturing, public reading, and the rights of translation into foreign languages are reserved. All inquiries should be addressed to the dramatists' agent: Leah Salisbury, 234 West 44th Street, New York, N.Y.

Russell & Volkening as agents for Ann Petry: "Go On or Die" and "The Railroad Runs to Canada" from *Harriet Tubman: Conductor on the Underground Railroad* by Ann Petry. Copyright © 1955 and renewed © 1983 by Ann Petry.

Scholastic Inc.: From *A Fire in My Hands* by Gary Soto. Copyright © 1990 by Scholastic Inc.

Estate of Robert Service: From *Ploughman of the Moon* by Robert Service.

Simon & Schuster: "The Secret Heart" (and excerpt) from *The Collected Poems of Robert P. Tristram Coffin.* Copyright 1935 by Macmillan Publishing Company; copyright renewed © 1963 by Margaret Coffin Halvosa.

Simon & Schuster Books for Young Readers, an imprint of Simon & Schuster Children's Publishing Division: *Pecos Bill and the Mustang* by Harold W. Felton. Copyright © 1965 by Prentice Hall, Inc. Excerpt (retitled "The Dogs Could Teach Me") from *Woodsong* by Gary Paulsen. Copyright © 1990 by Gary Paulsen.

Virginia Driving Hawk Sneve: "The Medicine Bag" by Virginia Driving Hawk Sneve.

Monica Sone: Comment on "Camp Harmony" by Monica Sone. Copyright © 1997 by Monica Sone.

Gary Soto: Comment on "Broken Chain" by Gary Soto. Copyright © 1997 by Gary Soto.

Pamela Stacey: Comment on transcript for "Touched by a Dolphin." Copyright © 2000 by Pamela Stacey.

Stonebridge Music: Lyric to "America" by Neil Diamond. Copyright © 1980 Stonebridge Music.

Stone Soup, the magazine by children: From "Chinese New Year—Paying Respect" by Chris Hoe, 13 years old, from *Stone Soup, the magazine by children,* March/April 1991. Copyright © 1991 by the Children's Art Foundation.

Times Books, a division of Random House, Inc.: From "John Lewis: Hand in Hand Together" (retitled "The Power of Nonviolence") from *From Camelot to Kent State* by Joan Morrison and Robert K. Morrison. Copyright © 1987 by Joan Morrison and Robert K. Morrison.

Jackie Torrence: From "Brer Possum's Dilemma" by Jackie Torrence from *Homespun: Tales from America's Favorite Storytellers,* edited by Jimmy Neil Smith. Copyright © 1988 by Jackie Torrence.

United States Department of Interior, Bureau of Indian Affairs, Office of Public Affairs: From "Indians" by Ophelia Rivas. First published in *Arrow III,* 1971.

Viking Penguin, a division of Penguin Putnam Inc.: From "Robert Frost Interview" by George Plimpton, from *Writers at Work, Second Series,* edited by George A. Plimpton. Copyright © 1963 by The Paris Review.

Warner Bros. Publications U.S. Inc., Miami, FL 33014: From "Lean on Me" by Bill Withers. Copyright © 1972 by Interior Music (BMI). All rights reserved.

Weekly Reader Corporation: "Experiment 023681" by Peter Leary from *Writing!®,* vol. 15, no. 8, April 1993. Copyright © 1993 by Weekly Reader Corporation. All rights reserved.

Justina W. Gregory and Krishna Winston, literary executors, Estate of Richard and Clara Winston: "A Tragedy Revealed: A Heroine's Last Days" by Ernst Schnabel from *Life,* vol. 45, no. 7, August 18, 1958. Copyright © 1958 by Time, Inc.; copyright renewed © 1986 by Justina Winston Gregory and Krishna Winston.

Laurence Yep: From "Laurence Yep" by Laurence Yep from *Speaking for Ourselves,* compiled and edited by Donald R. Gallo. Copyright © 1990 by Laurence Yep.

SOURCES CITED

Quotes by Sandra Cisneros from *Interviews with Writers of the Post-Colonial World,* conducted and edited by Feroza Jussawalla and Reed Way Dasenbrock. Published by University Press of Mississippi, Jackson, MI, 1992.

Lyrics from "We Shall Overcome" (retitled "American Freedom Song") by Zilphia Horton, Frank Hamilton, Guy Carawan & Pete Seeger. Published by Ludlow Music, Inc., New York, NY, 1960.

Quote by Irene Hunt from *American Writers for Children Since 1960: Fiction,* edited by Glenn E. Estes. Published by Gale Research Company, Farmington Hills, MI, 1986.

From *My Life* by Golda Meir. Published by Dell Publishing Co., Inc., New York, NY, 1975.

Old Italian story quoted by Elly Shodell from *Particles of the Past: Sandmining on Long Island, 1870's–1980's* by Elly Shodell. Published by Port Washington Public Library, Port Washington, NY, 1985.

Quote by Shel Silverstein from "Shel Silverstein," an interview from *Publishers Weekly,* vol. 207, no. 8, February 24, 1975. Published by the R. R. Bowker Company, New York.

PICTURE CREDITS

The illustrations on the Contents pages are picked up from pages in the textbook. Credits for those illustrations can be found either on the textbook page on which they appear or in the listing below.

INDEX OF SKILLS

Literary Terms

The boldface page numbers indicate an extensive treatment of the topic.

Reading and Critical Thinking

Language (Grammar, Usage, and Mechanics)

Vocabulary and Spelling

Writing

Speaking, Listening, and Viewing

Research and Study

Crossing the Curriculum

INDEX OF ART

INDEX OF AUTHORS AND TITLES

Student Writers